First published in the U.S.A. in 1993 by
NEW YORK UNIVERSITY PRESS
Washington Square
New York NY 10003

Library of Congress Cataloging-in-Publication Data
Labor Law / edited by David L. Gregory.
p. cm. – (International library of essays in law and legal theory. Areas ; 22)
Includes bibliographical references.
ISBN 0-8147-3050-7
1. Labor laws and legislation. 2. Labor laws and legislation–United States. I. Gregory, David L. II. Series.
K1705.6.L33 1993
344'.01—dc20
[342.41] 93-27765
CIP

Contents

PART IV INTERNATIONAL AND COMPARATIVE LAW PERSPECTIVES

Acknowledgements

The editor and publishers wish to thank the following for permission to use copyright material.

Boston College Law Review for the essay: Marion Crain (1992), 'Images of Power in Labor Law: A Feminist Deconstruction', *Boston College Law Review*, **33**, pp. 481–537.

University of Chicago Law Review for the essays: Richard A. Epstein (1984), 'In Defense of the Contract at Will', *The University of Chicago Law Review*, **51**, pp. 947–82; Katherine Van Wezel Stone (1992), 'The Legacy of Industrial Pluralism: The Tension Between Individual Employment Rights and the New Deal Collective Bargaining System', *The University of Chicago Law Review*, **59**, pp. 575–644.

Chicago–Kent Law Review for the essay: Alan Hyde (1991), In Defense of Employee Ownership', *Chicago–Kent Law Review*, **67**, pp. 159–211.

William B. Gould IV (1989), 'Reflections on Workers' Participation, Influence and Power-sharing: The Future of Industrial Relations', *Cincinnati Law Review*, **58**, pp. 381–95. Copyright © William B. Gould IV.

Karl E. Klare (1988), 'Workplace Democracy & Market Reconstruction: An Agenda for Legal Reform', *Catholic University Law Review*, **38**, pp. 1–68. Copyright © 1989 by Karl E. Klare.

Mississippi College Law Review for the essay: David L. Gregory (1988), 'The Right to Unionize as a Fundamental Human and Civil Right', *Mississippi College Law Review*, **9**, pp. 135–54.

Theodore J. St. Antoine (1988), 'A Seed Germinates: Unjust Discharge Reform Heads Toward Full Flower', *Nebraska Law Review*, **67**, pp. 56–81.

Washington and Lee University for the essay: David L. Gregory (1988), 'Catholic Labor Theory and the Transformation of Work', *Washington and Lee Law Review*, **45**, pp. 119–57.

The Yale Law Journal and Fred Rothman & Company for the essay: Richard A. Epstein (1983), 'A Common Law for Labor Relations: A Critique of the New Deal Labor Legislation', *The Yale Law Journal*, **92**, pp. 1357–408. Reprinted by permission of The Yale Law Journal Company and Fred B Rothman & Company.

Every effort has been made to trace all copyright holders, but if any have been inadvertently overlooked the publishers will be pleased to make the necessary arrangements at the first opportunity.

Series Preface

The International Library of Law and Legal Theory is designed to provide important research materials in an accessible form. Each volume contains essays of central theoretical importance in its subject area. The series as a whole makes available an extensive range of valuable material which will be of considerable interest to those involved in the research, teaching and study of law.

The series has been divided into three sections. The Schools section is intended to represent the main distinctive approaches and topics of special concern to groups of scholars. The Areas section takes in the main branches of law with an emphasis on essays which present analytical and theoretical insights of broad application. The section on Legal Cultures makes available the distinctive legal theories of different legal traditions and takes up topics of general comparative and developmental concern.

I have been delighted and impressed by the way in which the editors of the individual volumes have set about the difficult task of selecting, ordering and presenting essays from the immense quantity of academic legal writing published in journals throughout the world. Editors were asked to pick out those essays from law, philosophy and social science journals which they consider to be fundamental for the understanding of law, as seen from the perspective of a particular approach or sphere of legal interest. This is not an easy task and many difficult decisions have had to be made in order to ensure that a representative sample of the best journal essays available takes account of the scope of each topic or school.

I should like to express my thanks to all the volume editors for their willing participation and scholarly judgement. The interest and enthusiasm which the project has generated is well illustrated by the fact that an original projection of 12 volumes drawn up in 1989 has now become a list of some 60 volumes. I must also acknowledge the vision, persistence and constant cheerfulness of John Irwin and the marvellous work done by Mrs Margaret O'Reilly and Sonia Hubbard.

TOM D. CAMPBELL
Series Editor
The Faculty of Law
The Australian National University

Introduction

The final two decades of this century represent a very exciting, interesting period in contemporary labor law during which a profound theoretical war is being waged for the intellectual heart, soul and future of labor law and its scholarship. Concomitantly, a comparable battle is underway throughout the world of work. The theoretical and practical influences of these conflicts are reciprocal, and their outcomes will dictate how the future world of work will be constituted, governed and enhanced. The present editorial assignment has been particularly challenging, given the obvious impossibility of selecting only a handful of salient theoretical essays from a tremendously impressive body of very sophisticated labor law scholarship.

If there is an overarching theme for contemporary labor law, it is one of destabilizing, seismic and rapid change. This change has been especially dramatic as labor law theory and practise move significantly away from national and federal statutory structures (such as the National Labor Relations Act in the US) and their corresponding conventional, adversarial union-management relations model. An overwhelming majority of employees in private sector workplaces today are not members of, or represented by, unions and are not protected by collective bargaining agreements or by individual employment contracts. The employment environment is increasingly, and perhaps inexorably and permanently, shifting from collective bargaining models and private sector workplaces of high union density to a private sector workforce that is increasingly individualized and even atomized, with workers left to their own individual devices in attempting to define a relationship with their employer.

These transmutations in the workplace are directly reflected in labor law theory, as scholars focus upon the loss of private sector collective labor relations and the decline in union membership, and also reexamine the fundamental theoretical premises of work.[1] Will statutory minimum terms and conditions of employment for all workers, together with continuing judicial and legislative modifications of the 'employment-at-will' doctrine in the US, continue to supplant labor unions and collective bargaining? The 50th 'golden' anniversary of the National Labor Relations Act was marked in 1985, in the midst of the Reagan regime's wholesale ideological assault upon workers' rights. This was achieved through the overtly political appointment of committed anti-labor ideologues to critical positions throughout the executive and administrative branches of the federal government, and was supported by the appointment of fellow hardliners to the federal judiciary.[2] From almost all quarters, therefore, the federal National Labor Relations Act and its labor-management collective bargaining structure and model were severely undermined and dismissed as no longer relevant, responsive or responsible to the world of work in the late 20th century. Many of the original and traditional advocates and champions of collective labor-management relations charge that the conventional model was utterly vitiated by President Reagan's free market ideologues on the National Labor Relations Board who, through a series of radical right-wing decisions throughout the 1980s, cynically overruled established labor law precedents. Indeed, the overtly pro-ownership labor law motif prevalent in the last two decades of this century was set by President Reagan's summary dismissal of 11,000 striking air-traffic controllers in the early fall of 1981, and by Prime Minister Thatcher's crushing of the strike by the miners' union in Great Britain a few years thereafter. The salient essays presented in this volume reflect these fundamental theoretical and political struggles in contemporary labor law.

The selections reprinted here reflect the deep-seated politics of both the modern workplace and of contemporary labor law scholarship, beginning with presentations advocating a resurgence of *laissez-faire* attitudes. Libertarian law and economics scholars of the ideological and political right thus dramatically urge the repudiation of all statutory law supporting unionization and collective bargaining.[3] Meanwhile, Critical Legal scholars of the left strongly deplore conventional collective labor-management relations as coopted and rendered ineffectual from their inception by the interests of ownership elites, thereby consistently frustrating workers' hopes and aspirations for dignity in the control of their working lives and destinies.[4] These incisive critiques from across the intellectual and political spectrum may yet lead to a truly transformed workplace, with enhanced worker self-determination, workplace democracy and employee ownership. As the collective highly-unionized workplace wanes, labor law scholars are scrutinizing alternative regulatory systems based on common law contract and public policy protection for individual workers.[5] Increasingly, labor law theoreticians are incorporating insights from comparative and international labor law.[6] This volume will also present some emerging interdisciplinary labor law scholarship which in turn examines the contributions of feminist theory[7] and practice in the workplace, as well as the potential for transformation that theologically grounded social justice analysis may offer to the world of work.[8]

Part I The Problematic Status of Conventional Labor Law

Concurrent with the first term of the administration of President Reagan and his dismissal *en masse* of the striking federal air-traffic controllers, prominent law and economics and libertarian legal scholars at the University of Chicago Law School directly questioned not only the justice and efficiency, but all of the fundamental premises of collective bargaining and labor-management relations inherent in the National Labor Relations Act of 1935. The NLRA originally became law during the first-term New Deal of President Franklin Roosevelt in the depths of the Great Depression and for almost 50 years it governed and regulated union labor-management relations in the private sector workplace. Professor Richard Epstein, an eminent scholar of Torts and Property law, wrote the foremost theoretical article for this reemergent deregulatory camp, resurrecting neoclassical economic themes originally asserted against the NLRA at the time of its enactment in 1935. In his highly controversial essay, reprinted as Chapter 1, Professor Epstein polemically and incisively questioned many of the fundamental premises upon which collective bargaining, labor-management relations and the NLRA itself were based.[9] From his libertarian and law and economics perspective, he attacked the national labor law as inefficient, unfair and unable to deliver justice in the private sector workplace. He instead advocated the repeal of the NLRA and the return of the legal regime to the common law models of contracts, property and torts to regulate employment relations. Ultimately, collective bargaining, endorsed and supported by the federal statutory and administrative law apparatus, was seen by Epstein and his fellow critics of collective labor-management relations as a socialist intrusion into fundamental constitutional and common law principles of freedom of contract and free alienability of property. These *laissez-faire* free-market champions urged the restoration of the prerogatives historically enjoyed by capitalist ownership elites prior to governmental intrusion and regulation of the workplace. They maintained that regulatory statutory devices, such as the National Labor Relations Act and related federal and state statutory instruments (including those governing minimum wages, hours, workplace safety, and prohibiting employment discrimination), should be repealed.[10] All employer-employee relationships should instead be governed by the common law hierarchy of so-called employment, or contract, 'at will'.

Prominent labor law scholars who reject the libertarian and law and economics ideologies of the political right have nevertheless had to account for the inexorable deregulatory shifts away from the union density and collective bargaining of the NLRA and towards local, state and federal statutes imposing minimum employment terms for many non-union workers. Some of these labor law scholars argue that the enactment of minimum employment terms be expanded to include everyone in private sector employment, since such types of protection are no longer widely achieved through collective bargaining and because the vast majority of workers are no longer represented by unions (see Chapter 3).[11] Increasingly, this has become a view shared by scholars from a wide range of the political and economic spectrum, advocating that health insurance, family care leave and most other prospective benefits in employment be provided in future by statutory governmental regulation applied to all employers, rather than through labor-management negotiation and collective bargaining which will protect comparatively few workers.

These scholars also advocate the extension of the alternative dispute-resolution model of universal arbitration throughout the private sector workplace.[12] More than 40 US states have modified the employment-at-will doctrine. Scholars are now advocating that a national act be devised to provide for statutory arbitration covering all discharges from employment, beyond the collectively bargained grievance-arbitration procedure.

Part II Workplace Democracy Initiatives

Other critics of conventional labor relations in private sector employment have urged the retention, reform and evolution of collective bargaining models as means still capable of achieving justice at work through increasing workplace democracy. Many of the intellectuals who adhere to this concept are diametrically opposed to the law and economics libertarians, identifying instead with the Critical Legal Studies movement of the theoretic and political left.[13] Thanks to Professor James Boyle's wonderfully comprehensive introduction to the volume entitled *Critical Legal Studies* in this series, no reiteration is required here regarding the complex and sophisticated offerings of that movement to legal academia and legal scholarship since the late 1970s. Critical Legal scholars working in labor law have focused their analyses upon the workplace, how it is structured and constituted, and how to democratize and transform it. In their investigations, they have unmasked and deconstructed many of the codes of behaviour and structures of collective bargaining that have yielded neither efficiency nor justice, but rather are perniciously disguised doctrinal instruments designed to perpetuate the subordination of workers and their unions in the service of capital owner elites.

Thus, rather than democratize the workplace or provide rough equilibrium in collective bargaining between workers and capital ownership elites (as was originally intended by the policy provisions of the NLRA), Critical Legal scholars have demonstrated that the conventional NLRA model was deliberately rendered inefficient and unjust, and not for the reasons set forth by the Chicago Law and Economics school. Rather, the ongoing subordination of rank-and-file employees was achieved by the federal judiciary vitiating the NLRA of its radical promise from the outset and thus depriving it of a meaningful role in the contemporary workplace.

The most prominent and one of the most eloquent of the Critical Legal scholars to scrutinize conventional labor relations models is Professor Karl Klare who, in 1978, published his now-landmark essay (reprinted as Chapter 5).[14] Klare posits that the Wagner Act, which was passed to stabilize and preserve the social order of American capitalism, did little to enhance the worker's role in helping to decide either the means of production or the organization of work. Liberal legalism – which supports the equal treatment of all citizens and the radical separation of morals, politics and personality from judicial action – collapsed. Ultimately, a hybrid school of thought called 'social conceptualism' emerged as a result of the Wagner Act. In essence, social conceptualism was a reemergence of the liberal legal order, continuing the subordination of labor to ownership elites in more subtle forms.

In the 15 years since his first essay appeared, Klare has produced a series of major articles, refining his original criticisms of the unfulfilled promises of the judicially deradicalized NLRA. By the late 1980s, Klare had not only responded forcefully to his critics, but had also devised a theoretical structure for significant democratization of the workplace through participatory initiatives to empower workers to have a full and effective voice in their working lives and in their workplace destinies. 'The preeminent role and guiding principle of labor law should be to expand and enhance democracy at every level of the experience and organization of work.'[15]

Klare's Critical Legal scholar colleague, Alan Hyde of Rutgers University Law School in Newark (New Jersey), has built upon this work (see Chapter 6).[16] In his most recent studies, Hyde has developed very sophisticated employee ownership models, especially those involving employee takeovers and purchases of businesses.[17] Employee ownership is a trend likely to continue and, with it, the potential to further democratize the workplace in a meaningful way.

Part III Interdisciplinary Feminist Theory and Theological Perspectives

Certainly one of the most innovative approaches to labor law scholarship has been the intersection and incorporation of feminist legal theory into labor law analysis. Professor Marion Crain of the University of Toledo College of Law has written a series of brilliant and comprehensive articles to demonstrate the tangible contributions that feminist theory[18] can potentially make to labor law (see Chapters 7 and 8).

Over time, unions have absorbed a patriarchal vision that is analogous to the hierarchical, authoritarian structure of most employers. One cure for current union woes is to restore solidarity by adopting a feminist approach. Unions need to organize the growing numbers of women and minorities at work, with a 'renewed commitment to communitarian values, participatory democracy, and consensus-style leadership. ...'[19] There are four common forms of patriarchal images of power: force, manipulation, persuasion and authority. Crain notes, however, that these patriarchal forms are characterized by a struggle for resources through overt conflict; 'consequently, the property of power is synonymous with the ability to coerce, dominate, or control others. ...'[20]

Unions did not always adopt these patriarchal power stances. At their inception, unions were democratic and radical. However, the rise of large corporations changed the workplace, whereupon unions changed as well. Thus, unions surrendered egalitarian values and grand visions of social reform, narrowing their goals to focus on tangible worker benefits and wage consciousness. Unions underwent isomorphism, becoming as bureaucratic as their employer organizations. 'The natural tendency of individuals within the hierarchy to strive to keep power reinforces the status quo once it is established.'[21] This had led to increased power at the top of the union and decreased power at rank-and-file levels, leaving union members isolated and powerless to affect the content of labor contracts.

A solution may be realized through feminist power – the ability, competence and capacity to influence others. Power is not property, but a function of relationships among people: power belongs to the group. Women tend to value intimacy and connection with others, while men value separation and autonomy. Men are transactional: formal authority is frequently used as a power source; goals are task oriented and subordinate performance is either rewarded or punished. Women are transformational: power stems from hard work, charisma and personal contacts; subordinates transform their interests into those of the group, with a win-win concept pursued under a long-run philosophy. Labor power in the feminist model occurs from the bottom up. Since today's workplace is heterogeneous, unions must build a community based on workers' commonality of interests. Workers must be able to empathize with each other. By doing this, solidarity can be achieved across race, sex and class boundaries. 'Transformed labor unions could capitalize on empathy as the source of labor solidarity. They could then utilize their heterogeneity as a strength – a force facilitating growth and change – rather than experiencing it as a weakness.'[22] The feminist approach may prove to be superior in organizing, bargaining and striking, with the best people self-empowered at the center, not at the top.

Professor Crain's scholarship examines workplaces which have significant voices and roles for women, many evolving from initial small group support systems and only later taking on aspects of more formal organizational and labor relations structures. Concomitantly, women with leadership positions in, and representing workforces not bound by, historically constricting gender-based stereotypes have the potential to transform workplaces. Professor Crain has focused upon several recent applied situations in higher education and university environments, for example, where innovative applications of employee support systems have been informed by feminist solidarity.

In my scholarship, I have advocated the incorporation of religious and theologically-based social justice considerations into labor relations and employment environments, focusing upon powerful social justice teachings which celebrate and reaffirm the rights and dignity of all workers (see Chapter 9).[23] The salient themes in the intersection of theology and religion with labor law theory reaffirm the ultimate dignity of all workers as autonomous subjects and stress the aspirational quality of furthering dignity through meaningful work for all persons, with the role of capital as a means in service of human ends. The salient emphasis is upon the primacy and importance of the worker as a human being, and the subordination of capital as a means, not as an end, in enhancing human existence. Work is valued both for its own sake and as a means of furthering human dignity.

Part IV International and Comparative Law Perspectives

Increasing consciousness of the imperative that labor law must take into account international law models and international developments has finally become more obvious in the contemporary post-cold war era.[24] Developments such as the Maastritch Treaty initiative in the European Community, the dramatic expansion of employment throughout Asia and Central and South America, and the North American Free Trade Agreement all demonstrate the need not only for increasing international cooperation, but also for comcomitant monitoring of capital ownership prerogatives and of workers' rights in an international legal regime. Since its inception in 1919 during the League of Nations period, the International Labor Organization has been the overarching mechanism for the furtherance of labor considerations in the international environment. ILO conventions have unequivocally supported the rights to free association and to collective bargaining. Labor law scholars are increasingly looking to comparative and international models to inform their theoretical and practical endeavors.

Conclusion

The salient theoretical essays included in this volume focus upon issues of workplace change; these are rapid, seismic and structurally deep, with profound implications for all observers of labor and of even more immediate concern to all those at work.

There will no doubt be a continuing role for labor unions to represent workers in collective bargaining with employers. But as recent international events increasingly demonstrate, there has occurred a dramatic decline in the numbers and power of union members from their status less than half a century ago, witness the UK coal miners. Meanwhile, however, other international examples (such as the Solidarity Movement in Poland, leading to Lech Walesa's election to head the Polish government, and the influence of Cyril Ramphosa, Secretary General of the ANC, who was originally a labor lawyer and a major leader of black unionized miners in South Africa) show that both an international labor model and an international labor consciousness, with prominent roles for organized labor unions, will also remain very much a part of labor realities in the years ahead. Within the US, however, it appears that for the foreseeable future labor unions will be relatively marginalized. But even if union membership is reduced to a level of 10 to 12 per cent in the US private sector (which most observers forecast by the year 2000), this will nevertheless represent approximately 12 to 18 million workers, with several million more being members of public sector labor unions.

In the private sector workplace model, in which more than 85 per cent of all workers now have non-union status, hours, wages, terms and conditions of employment are no longer regulated by union-management collective bargaining through the auspices of the National Labor Relations Act. Rather, minimum employment relationship terms are enacted through federal, state and local regulations, or through judicial or statutory modifications to the doctrine of employment-at-will. In this, the US experience increasingly reflects corresponding developments in the international community, trends which are likely to accelerate dramatically in the future. As US labor law theory and practise draw especially and increasingly from interdisciplinary scholarship and from international and comparative labor law, perhaps labor unions will even yet be revitalized, with workplaces of the future genuinely democratized and all workers empowered to actualize their full human and workplace dignity.

Notes

1 Several academic evaluations presented in major scholarly books have appeared during the last decade. See, for instance, S. Aronowitz (1984), *Working Class Hero: A New Strategy for American Labor*, New York: Pilgrim Press; J. Atleson (1983), *Values and Assumptions in American Labor Law*, Amherst, Massachusetts: University of Massachusetts Press; R. Epstein (1992), *Forbidden Grounds: The Case against Employment Discrimination Laws*, Cambridge: Harvard University Press; R. Freeman and J. Medoff (1984), *What Do Unions Do?*, New York: Basic Books; T. Geoghegan (1991), *Which Side Are You On?; Trying To Be for Labor When it is Flat on its Back*, New York: Farrar, Straus and Giroux; W. Gould (1984), *Japan's Reshaping of American Labor Law*, Cambridge: Massachusetts Institute of Technology Press; B. Hamper (1991), *Rivethead: Tales from the Assembly Line*, New York: Warner Press; M. Reynolds (1984), *Power and Privilege*, New York: Universe Books; P. Weiler (1991), *Governing the Workplace*, Cambridge: Harvard University Press.

2 W. Gould (1986), 'Some Reflections on Fifty Years of the NLRA: The Need for Labor Board and Labor Law Reform', *Stanford Law Review*, **38**, 937ff; D. Gregory and R. Mak (1985), 'Significant Decisions of the NLRB, 1984: The Reagan Board's Celebration of the Fiftieth Anniversary of the National Labor Relations Act', *Connecticut Law Review*, **18**, 7ff.

3 See Epstein, *supra* note 1; Epstein (1983), 'A Common Law for Labor Relations: A Critique of the New Deal Labor Legislation', *Yale Law Journal*, **92**, 1357ff; Epstein (1982), 'Historical Origins and Economic Structure of Workers' Compensation Law', *Georgia Law Review*, **16**, 775ff; Epstein (1984), 'In Defense of Contract at Will', *Chicago Law Review*, **51**, 945ff; Posner (1984), 'Some Economics of Labor Law', *Chicago Law Review*, **51**, 988ff; Posner (1987), 'The Efficiency and the Efficacy of Title VII', *Pennsylvania Law Review*, **136**, 513ff.

4 See Atleson, *supra* note 1. See also Hyde (1990), 'A Theory of Labor Legislation', *Buffalo Law Review*, **38**, 383ff; Hyde (1981), 'Economic Labor Law v. Political Labor Relations: Dilemmas for Liberal Legalism', *Texas Law Review*, **60**, 1ff; Hyde and Livingston (1989), 'Employee Takeovers', *Rutgers Law Review*, **41**, 1131ff; Hyde (1991), 'In Defense of Employee Ownership', *Chicago-Kent Law Review*, **67**, 159ff; Klare (1978), 'Judicial Deradicalization of the Wagner Act and the Origins of Modern Legal Consciousness, 1937–1941', *Minnesota Law Review*, **62**, 265ff; Klare (1981), 'Labor Law as Ideology: Toward a New Historiography of Collective Bargaining Law', *Pennsylvania Law Review*, **130**, 1358ff; Klare (1982), 'The Quest for Industrial Democracy and the Struggle against Racism: Perspectives from Labor Law and Civil Rights Law', *Oregon Law Review*, **61**, 157ff; Klare (1988), 'The Labor-Management Cooperation Debate: A Workplace Democracy Perspective', *Harvard Civil Rights – Civil Liberties Law Review*, **23**, 39ff; Klare (1985), 'Traditional Labor Law Scholarship and the Crisis of Collective Bargaining Law: A Reply to Professor Finkin', *Maryland Law Review*, **44**, 731ff; Klare (1988), 'Workplace Democracy and Market Reconstruction: An Agenda for Legal Reform', *Catholic University Law Review*, **38**, 1ff; Lynd (1979), 'Investment Decisions and the Quid Pro Quo Myth', *Case Western Reserve Law Review*, **29**, 396ff; Lynd (1987), 'Towards a not-for-Profit Economy: Public Development Authorities for Acquisition and Use of Industrial Property', *Harvard Civil Rights – Civil Liberties Law Review*, **22**, 13ff; Minda (1991), 'Rediscovering Progressive Labor Politics: The Labor Law Implications of F.T.C. v. Superior Court Trial Lawyers Association', *Vermont Law Review*, **16**, 71ff; Minda (1985), 'The Common Law of Employment-at-Will in New York: The Paralysis of Nineteenth Century Doctrine', *Syracuse Law Review*, **36**, 939ff; Minda (1989), 'Time for an Unjust

Dismissal Statute in New York', *Brooklyn Law Review*, **54**, 1137ff; Van Wezel Stone (1981), 'The Post-War Paradigm in American Labor Law', *Yale Law Journal*, **90**, 1509ff; Van Wezel Stone (1992), 'The Legacy of Industrial Pluralism: The Tension between Individual Employment Rights and the New Deal Collective Bargaining System', *Chicago Law Review*, **59**, 575ff.

5 See Epstein and Weiler, *supra* note 1; Klare and Van Wezel Stone, *supra* note 4; Summers (1984), 'The Contract of Employment and the Rights of Individual Employees: Fair Representation and Employment at Will', *Fordham Law Review*, **52**, 1082ff.

6 See Gould, *supra* note 1. See also Gould (1984), 'Union Involvement in Employer Decision-Making', *Tulane Law Review*, **58**, 1322ff; Summers (1987), 'An American Perspective of the German Model of Worker Participation', *Comparative Labor Law Journal*, **8**, 333ff; Summers (1984), 'Worker Participation in Sweden and the United States: Some Comparisons from an American Perspective', *Pennsylvania Law Review*, **133**, 175ff.

7 Crain (1991), 'Feminizing Unions: Challenging the Gendered Structure of Wage Labor', *Michigan Law Review*, **89**, 1155ff; Crain (1992), 'Feminism, Labor, and Power', *Southern California Law Review*, **65**, 1819ff; Crain (1992), 'Images of Power in Labor Law: A Feminist Deconstruction', *Boston College Law Review*, **33**, 481ff.

8 Gregory (1988), 'Catholic Labor Theory and the Transformation of Work', *Washington and Lee Law Review*, **45**, 119ff; Gregory (1988), 'The Right to Unionize as a Fundamental Human and Civil Right', *Mississippi College Law Review*, **9**, 135ff.

9 Epstein, *supra* note 3.

10 Epstein and Posner, *supra* note 3.

11 Van Wezel Stone, *supra* note 4.

12 Minda, *supra* note 4; Summers, *supra* note 5.

13 See *supra* note 4.

14 Klare, *supra* note 4.

15 Ibid.

16 Hyde, *supra* note 4.

17 Ibid.

18 Crain, *supra* note 7.

19 Ibid., at 1823.

20 Ibid., at 1869.

21 Ibid., 1835.

22 Ibid., at 1869.

23 Gregory, *supra* note 8.

24 See *supra* note 6.

Part I
The Problematic Status of Conventional Labor Law

[1]

The Yale Law Journal
Volume 92, Number 8, July 1983

A Common Law for Labor Relations: A Critique of the New Deal Labor Legislation

Richard A. Epstein†

During the nineteenth century, the area of labor relations was governed by a set of legal rules that spanned the law of property, contract, tort, and procedure. There was no special set of rules for labor cases as such. Since the advent of the New Deal, these common law principles have largely given way to a complex body of statutory and administrative law that treats labor law as a separate and self-contained subject. The central question in this paper is whether there is any warrant for the special treatment that labor law receives today. I shall concentrate upon the Norris-LaGuardia Act of 1932,[1] and the Wagner Act of 1935,[2] the latter a New Deal statute and the former nearly so. My conclusion is that this (for ease of expression) New Deal legislation is in large measure a mistake that, if possible, should be scrapped in favor of the adoption of a sensible common law regime relying heavily upon tort and contract law. The tort principles protect all individuals against the use or threat of force, and—of great relevance here—against the deliberate inducement of breach of contract. The contract principles allow individuals within this

† James Parker Hall Professor of Law, University of Chicago. I would like to thank Dennis Carlton, Frank Easterbrook, Bernard Meltzer, and Cass Sunstein for their valuable comments on an earlier draft of this Article. Ross Green provided valuable research assistance. I have also benefited from the comments made both at the Yale Law Journal Symposium in February, 1983, and at a faculty workshop at the University of Michigan in April, 1983.

1. 18 U.S.C. § 3692, 29 U.S.C. §§ 101-115 (1982).
2. 29 U.S.C. §§ 151-169 (1982).

social framework of entitlements to make whatever bargains they please with whomever they please.

At the outset it is important to note several important caveats about my analysis. In making these arguments I seek to analyze and evaluate labor law, not to construct a practical program or propose political reform. My operating premise is simple: No set of institutions should be exempt from serious criticism and review. The point is especially important in labor relations, where most modern legal scholarship is confined to the analysis of cases and practices within the current statutory framework. What is needed is an analysis of the statutory framework itself. Much of the critical writing on the subject dates from the 1930's and earlier,[3] before the recent advances both in general legal theory and in law and economics. The fiftieth anniversary of the New Deal is an appropriate occasion for renewed critical scrutiny, as well as for celebration.

The outline of this paper is as follows. In the first section, I argue that common law rules provide an appropriate benchmark against which to measure the modern statutory developments. In the second section, I show how a coherent theory of private law, with well developed principles of contract and tort, can govern labor relations. Section III shows the substantial convergence of libertarian and utilitarian principles as they apply to labor relations. In Section IV, I shall look at the way in which the New Deal reforms handled the tort and contract issues, particularly the soundness of a statutory list of "unfair labor practices" of employers and of its system of exclusive collective bargaining. Section V then examines and criticizes the broader justifications of industrial peace and industrial democracy used to justify the New Deal labor statutes. In dealing with the basic institutional structures, I shall look at both their inherent desirability and their dependence upon a large administrative apparatus. No constitutional questions are assayed. After the basic examination, I shall conclude with a brief discussion about the relationship between the New Deal legislation and the ends it seeks to advance.

I. The Common Law Benchmark

In conducting this investigation, one might ask, why look at common law rules? The answer is that traditional common law principles provide a benchmark, both theoretical and historical, against which the modern statutory schemes can be measured. The actual common law, however, is often highly unruly. Judges themselves often have profound disagreements

3. *See, e.g.*, F. FRANKFURTER & N. GREENE, THE LABOR INJUNCTION (1930); Magruder, *A Half Century of Legal Influence Upon the Development of Collective Bargaining*, 50 HARV. L. REV. 1071 (1937); Powell, *Collective Bargaining Before the Supreme Court*, 33 POL. SCI. Q. 396 (1918).

as to the first premises in the legal debate, and in any event the number of decisions is simply too great to allow harmony to reign here, just as it is (a fortiori) with administrative actions pursuant to complex legislative schemes. In speaking of "the" common law, therefore, I am referring to the best set of private-law rules that can be devised to handle the problems of labor relations. The rules themselves, however, cannot be judged sufficient simply because they give the ideal responses suitable to an ideal world. To the contrary, these rules, like all others, must be judged as well by the way in which they handle problems of uncertainty, error, and enforcement.

As a substantive matter, the defense of a common law system is not an assertion that the "market" can handle every social problem. The law of property and the law of torts are strictly required in order to establish the framework of original rights in which voluntary transactions can take place. Nonetheless, the reference to common law solutions throughout this article does reflect a basic intellectual orientation in favor of limited government and the maximization of private autonomy. This premise is not, of course, an endorsement of anarchy. It accepts—indeed insists—that the state is entitled to prevent the private use of force and violence and to enforce promises, except when those promises are induced by duress or misrepresentation, or made by persons of manifest incompetence such as infants and insane persons.[4]

One virtue of this basic set of rules is that it is capable of sustained application. The qualifications of the basic principle (misrepresentation, duress, and incompetence) are not, as has been suggested,[5] so infinitely expandable that they may be invoked almost as a matter of course to defeat every commercial or employment transaction, whenever either party has regrets after the fact. Misrepresentation may be expanded to cover cases of "a nod or a wink";[6] duress may include duress of goods;[7] and incompetence (or at least necessity) may reach bargains entered into by persons in imminent peril of their lives.[8] But taken together, only a tiny percentage of transactions will be caught by these escape clauses, even recognizing their central role in the theoretical structure of contract. In

4. *See* Epstein, *Unconscionability: A Critical Reappraisal*, 18 J.L. & ECON. 293 (1975), where I defend this basic position. Much of this paper is an extended application of that theory to labor relations.

5. Kennedy, *Distributive and Paternalist Motives in Contract and Tort Law, With Special Reference to Compulsory Terms and Unequal Bargaining Power*, 41 MD. L. REV. 563, 582 (1982).

6. Walters v. Morgan, 3 DeG. F. & J. 718, 724, 45 Eng. Rep. 1056, 1059 (Ch. App. 1861).

7. Duress of goods includes cases in which a party who has promised to supply goods at a given price will do so only if some higher price is paid. *See, e.g.*, Sistrom v. Anderson, 51 Cal. App. 2d 213, 124 P.2d 372 (1942). For discussions, see Dawson, *Economic Duress—An Essay in Perspective*, 45 MICH. L. REV. 253 (1947); Epstein, *supra* note 4.

8. *See, e.g.*, Post v. Jones, 60 U.S. (19 How.) 150 (1857).

any event, these grounds are generally inapposite in employment cases, a point tacitly conceded by the well-nigh universal insistence that such transactions should be set aside on a still broader ground—the "inequality of bargaining power." This principle, of course, is wholly incompatible with the liberal ideal that most contracts are for the mutual benefit of both sides, regardless of their original endowments of wealth.[9]

The strength of the common law's premises is also revealed by considering the alternatives. As a positive matter, Dean Verkuil is correct in noting that modern common law judges could develop rules for the contract of employment that are far worse than those created by the statute.[10] But the criticism is wide of the mark in this context, as the question is whether it is possible to develop a competing normative view of the subject. The program of "substantive justice" in contracting, although oft proposed, is as far from realization today as it has ever been.[11] Nor is that

9. Kennedy makes an effective critique of the usual arguments about standard form contracts, only to urge more fundamental measures to reshape the structure of American business institutions. *See* Kennedy, *supra* note 5, at 615-20.

More generally, one possible test of "inequality of bargaining power" asks us to imagine a perfect bilateral monopoly in which, for example, the issue was the division of $100 between A and B, where it was understood that neither party would get anything unless both agreed to the split. Inequality of bargaining power in this context refers to the situation in which one person is expected to receive more than $50. Yet even if this account is viable, it is very difficult to imagine what set of workable institutions could restore the even split without upsetting the balance in the other direction. In any event, the best way to handle the problem is to undermine the institutional structures that perpetuate these rigid bilateral monopolies, as by facilitating freedom of entry into various markets. *See infra* p. 1396. (discussion of bilateral monopolies).

10. *See* Verkuil, *Whose Common Law for Labor Relations?* 92 Yale L.J. 1409 (1983).

11. The work of Zweigert and Kotz is representative of the dominant tradition:

> We now realize that true freedom of contract cannot exist unless the parties to the contract are economically and socially equal.
>
> > Judge Pitney made this point brilliantly in *Coppage v. Kansas*, 236 U.S. 1, 17 (1915): "It is impossible to uphold the freedom of contract and the right of private property without at the same time recognizing as legitimate those inequalities of fortune that are the necessary result of the exercise of those rights . . . . Indeed, a little reflection will show that whenever the right of private property and the right of free contract co-exist, each party, when contracting, is inevitably more or less influenced by the question whether he has much property or little or none: for the contract is made to the very end that each may gain something he needs or desires more urgently than that which he proposes to give in exchange."
>
> Thus true freedom of contract could only operate in a Utopia, in a society in which businesses were independent, economically equal and fully automated, with neither labour nor management. If the parties are not socially and economically equal, only the stronger party is free to determine whether and how to form a contract. Such a society of equals does not exist anywhere, even in socialist countries, and probably never will, since it is a dream, freedom of contract in its pure form is itself a chimera, a fantasy and not in any way a reality. In the vast majority of the contracts which are concluded in modern society there is no freedom of contract, for the suppliers have fixed the conditions which the consumer can do nothing to alter. Freedom of contract exists only in contracts between large undertakings over atypical objects, and possibly in the area of labour law in the wage scale contracts produced by modern collective bargaining. Legal scholars must give up the habit of proclaiming that freedom of contract is a principle and then listing the exceptions to it. The main task is to discover criteria and procedures for the development of *contractual justice*, which the absence of freedom of contract makes it all the more necessary to promote.

program supplied by an insistence that the public interest or "public values"[12] forms an essential part of sound legal doctrine. Basically, this approach views regulation in all its aspects "to be not a matter of counting economic costs and benefits, or of defending private entitlements, but part of a continuing process of deciding what sort of a society we shall be."[13] One problem with this approach is that it defines the scope of public values residually: Public values cover only that ground not incorporated by theories of individual entitlement or social production. Yet this theory cannot, in and of itself, establish where matters of private right end and matters of public dominance begin; the things which can count as public values are so wide and varied that virtually any manifestation of the collective legislative power is in principle sufficient to displace private rights. This public-interest view of legal doctrine is very different from the view of government that regards protection of private rights—of rich and poor alike—as the chief justification for the use of force. Likewise the public-interest view is very different from a system that permits in some instances the taking of private property upon payment of just compensation. The eminent-domain vision of the world abandons any idea that an original set of property rights is immutable within the social order. But it still insists that these original property rights be respected even if they are abrogated to advance the social good, by making the state pay for what it takes by force.[14] By contrast, a public-interest view of the subject abandons any conception of private entitlements as its starting point, and thereby allows far greater latitude for government action.

To be sure, the common law theory developed here finds no place for the redistribution of wealth from rich to poor so characteristic of the modern state. Theories of redistribution are always difficult to construct: Welfare payments are never a matter of a legal entitlement of the recipients, but only an expression of collective benevolence by the transferors.[15] No

> The achievement of such contractual justice is no easy matter, and much further thought will have to be given to its answer.

2 K. ZWEIGERT & H. KOTZ, AN INTRODUCTION TO COMPARATIVE LAW: THE INSTITUTIONS OF PRIVATE LAW 8-9 (1977). The last sentence gives away the game. The entire passage is further flawed: It neglects the possibility that, even with economic inequality, the institution of contract still allows the weaker party to be left better off by the exchange.

12. Stewart & Sunstein, *Public Programs and Private Rights*, 95 HARV. L. REV. 1195, 1238 (1982).

13. *Id.*

14. For an elaboration, see Epstein, *Taxation, Regulation, Confiscation*, 20 OSGOODE HALL L.J. 433 (1982).

15. The point is often lost sight of in the modern terminological shifts in the welfare area. Originally welfare payments were called "handouts" or the "dole," which inescapably captured the precarious position of the transferee. The word "welfare" tends to obscure the nature of the legal relation and to emphasize the end for which the payments are made. The modern emphasis upon "human services" (as in the shift from the Department of Health, Education and Welfare to the (reconstituted) Department of Health and Human Services) makes it appear that the payments are obligatory on the

principle limits the power of a private party to choose who shall receive favors, and in what amounts; no private cause of action for want of benevolence forms the basis of the analogous public right, as does, for example, the law of nuisance for environmental protection. Private individuals find it difficult to identify who shall receive their bounty and to what extent. The problems are only compounded when these same matters are made the subject of collective decisions.

Nonetheless the indelible mark that the condition of the poor leaves on people of all political persuasions is enough to force any comprehensive theory of government to address the question.[16] That examination could still conclude that compulsory redistribution is out of bounds as a matter of principle; if it did, it would strengthen the argument here by showing that there is no additional feature of the basic situation that could require a reexamination of the positions taken thus far. The critique of current labor laws stands, however, even if redistribution from rich to poor is accepted: There is no solid moral case for treating union members, as such, as the favored class of wealth redistribution. To make union members wealthier is to make poorer not only employers (whose shareholders are often workers whose pension funds have been invested in the corporation) but also the nonunion workforce and the poorer members of the general population. Redistributions from rich to poor have far greater appeal than redistributions, for example, from a nonunionized worker to a unionized worker of initially comparable economic status. Desired redistributions (if any) are best accomplished by general tax measures. The possibility of factional or class legislation is thereby reduced, as is the likelihood that the process of redistribution itself will hamper the creation of wealth.[17]

transferor.

16. One commentator has asserted:

> My point is rather that this principle—that basic material needs be guaranteed by government to those who cannot meet them through their own efforts—has come to have an entrenched status as one of the fixed moral imperatives governing our political life . . . . No working American politician would, for instance, advocate the libertarian doctrine advanced in *Anarchy, State, and Utopia*, with its principled rejection of all income security programs. Our Reagans and Goldwaters argue that there is waste and fraud in our welfare programs, that people are receiving welfare who should support themselves, that benefit levels are too high. Those all are arguments within the terms of the principle of basic needs as I have stated it, and presuppose acceptance of the principle itself.

Grey, *Property and Need: The Welfare State and Theories of Distributive Justice*, 28 STAN. L. REV. 877, 901 (1976) [hereinafter cited as *Property and Need*]; *see also* Grey, *The First Virtue* (Book Review), 25 STAN. L. REV. 286, 323-25 (1973).

17. The difference between special labor legislation and general taxation best explain the constitutional response of the Supreme Court to various forms of social legislation in the period before the New Deal. The Court struck down, on constitutional grounds, both federal and state statutes prohibiting yellow dog contracts in employment. *See* Adair v. United States, 208 U.S. 161 (1908) (federal); Coppage v. Kansas, 236 U.S. 1 (1915) (state). Yet at the same time the Court allowed, without so much as a note of protest, forms of taxation which did have, and were intended to have, general

Common Law for Labor Relations

The weakness of overt redistributive arguments in the labor context is further revealed by the rhetoric used to justify both the Norris-LaGuardia and the Wagner Acts. While income redistribution to union employees from (amongst others) their employers was one apparent consequence of both these statutes, their passage was not overtly justified in these terms. Instead, it was said that the statutes were not designed to repudiate the market or to confiscate employer wealth. The statutes were said to be designed to cure the present system of its imperfections, if only to save capitalism from its own excesses. It seems therefore appropriate to put aside the question of income distribution as such, and to ask how any system of labor relations can be squared with a sound theory of individual entitlements and their social protection.

One further element is put aside in this analysis—the particular conditions of labor unrest both in the 1930's and before. It is often said that the massive social and economic dislocations of the Depression made it quite impossible to rest content with incremental adjustments to common law doctrine.[18] Many New Deal reforms perished during and after the Depression, however,[19] and there is no reason to hold modern labor law sacrosanct because it gained its maturity in the 1930's. Indeed, a sense of quiet desperation may well have led to the passage of labor statutes which in calmer times would have been rejected as destructive of both personal liberty and economic wealth for both society as a whole and most (but never all) individuals within it.

redistributive consequences. *See, e.g.*, Brushaber v. Union Pac. R.R., 240 U.S. 1 (1916) (rejecting challenges to a progressive income tax while upholding the 1913 federal income tax law); Knowlton v. Moore, 178 U.S. 41 (1900) (upholding the federal inheritance tax); Magoun v. Illinois Trust & Sav. Bank, 170 U.S. 283 (1898) (upholding the Illinois inheritance tax). *See generally* Blum & Kalven, *The Uneasy Case for Progressive Taxation*, 19 U. CHI. L. REV. 417, 424 n.21 (1952) ("The cases are not helpful on the merits of the principle of progression.").

18. For judicial expression of the sentiment, see Home Bldg. & Loan Ass'n v. Blaisdell, 290 U.S. 398, 442-48 (1934) (referring to emergency conditions that justified state mortgage moratoria against contract clause challenges).

The connection between social dislocations and labor law is a very different question, as no coherent theory links the common law of labor relations (unlike, for example, the management of the money supply) with bringing on the Depression, or shows that the legislation produced in the Depression contributed in any sensible way to economic recovery. There is certainly no explanation of why the common law of labor relations should be charged with the problems of the 1930's instead of being credited with the economic successes of earlier and better times.

19. *See, e.g.*, United States v. Butler, 297 U.S. 1 (1936) (striking down Agricultural Adjustment Act); Schechter Poultry Corp. v. United States, 295 U.S. 495 (1935) (striking down § 3 of National Industrial Recovery Act). Note too, that some programs have passed political muster, as with the deregulation of the airline industry, see Levine, *Revisionism Revised? Airline Deregulation and Public Interest*, 44 LAW & CONTEMP. PROBS. 179 (1981).

II. The Common Law of Labor Organization

In turning to our normative account of labor relations, it is proper to stress that common law rules in their ideal form make legal entitlements among strangers without reference to personal status. Legal rules do not refer to flesh-and-blood individuals, but to those lifeless abstractions, *A* and *B*, about whom nothing else is known or—more to the point—is relevant. It may well be that certain individuals will in the end assume certain well-specified roles, but if so there is no reason to have legal institutions either subsidize or penalize their efforts: Individuals should not have to sacrifice their rights against the rest of the world because they become an employer of *A* or an employee of *B*. Stating propositions in general form is, moreover, a powerful antidote to abuse and favoritism, even if standing alone it cannot guarantee a just set of rules or outcomes.[20] To use Rawls' popular phrase, generalizations place people behind the veil of ignorance, depriving them of the knowledge of whether their application will help or hurt themselves or their friends.[21] What, we ask, might these general rules look like in the context of labor organization?

We must begin with the original position: What are the rights and duties between strangers? We start first with the account offered under a theory of individual liberty, which can then be qualified by considerations of overall utility.[22] Here the common law (except for its unfortunate early flirtation with the law of criminal conspiracy)[23] took the sound position:[24] Every person owns his own person and can possess, use and dispose of his labor on whatever terms he sees fit.[25] To state otherwise is to say either

20. On the importance of generalization as protection against class intrigue, see Epstein, *The Social Consequences of Common Law Rules*, 95 HARV. L. REV. 1717 (1982).

21. *See* J. RAWLS, A THEORY OF JUSTICE 136-42 (1971).

22. For my own views on how these two areas might be reconciled, see Epstein, *Nuisance Law: Corrective Justice and its Utilitarian Constraints*, 8 J. LEGAL STUD. 49 (1979); Epstein, *Private Property and the Public Domain: The Case of Antitrust*, 24 NOMOS 48 (1982) [hereinafter cited as *Private Property and the Public Domain*].

23. *See, e.g.*, Commonwealth v. Pullis (Phila. Mayor's Ct. 1806) (the Philadelphia Cordwainer's case), *reprinted in* 3 J. COMMONS & E. GILMORE, A DOCUMENTARY HISTORY OF AMERICAN INDUSTRIAL SOCIETY 59-248 (1958). The turning point is often taken to be Shaw's opinion in Commonwealth v. Hunt, 45 Mass. (4 Met.) 111 (1842), but there were occasional strong anti-union sentiments thereafter. *See, e.g.*, State v. Donaldson, 32 N.J.L. 151 (Sup. Ct. 1867) (indictable conspiracy exists when several employees combine and notify their employer that unless he discharges certain enumerated persons, they will quit in a body).

24. *See* Witte, *Early American Labor Cases*, 35 YALE L.J. 825 (1926). Witte's central conclusion was as follows:

> It was never the law in the United States that labor unions are illegal per se, or that all strikes are unlawful. The unreported cases of the early nineteenth century did not turn upon the legality of the unions per se, but on the methods which they employed to gain their ends. Nor were the views expressed in these early cases as to the methods which might lawfully be employed less liberal than those now generally held by the courts.

Id. at 825-26.

25.

> Every person has a right under the law, as between him and his fellow subjects, to full

that the labor cannot be used or that someone else is entitled to direct its use. At the same time, the common law position also blocks off the institution of slavery—a constant theme in the debates over labor legislation[26]—at the outset.

Of the three rights in the original ownership bundle, ambiguity in the labor context attaches only to the right of disposition. In this context it could mean that a person has a right to dispose of his labor on his own terms, so that if I wished to dispose of my labor for $10 per hour, some other person would be required to acquire it at that price. Such a system of rights cannot be applied to all individuals, however,[27] for it would allow me to deny others the very liberties that I claim for myself: What could I say if someone wanted me to hire him for $1000 per hour? To be universal in application, the right of disposition must be understood to include only the right to offer one's services on whatever terms and conditions one sees fit. In good Hobbesian fashion, the appetite of every person determines the appropriate terms of exchange. The system can now specify the correlative obligations of the right to offer one's labor unhindered—without interference by force or fraud—which can be held simultaneously by all individuals.[28]

Over time, the original distribution of wealth is likely to change as labor is exchanged for labor or for capital. Within the liberty-based framework, no limitation is placed upon the voluntary recombination of entitle-

> freedom in disposing of his own labor or his own capital according to his own will. It follows that every other person is subject to the correlative duty arising therefrom, and is prohibited from any obstruction to the fullest exercise of this right which can be made compatible with the exercise of similar rights by others. Every act causing an obstruction to another in the exercise of the right comprised within this description—done, not in the exercise of the actor's own right, but for the purpose of obstruction—would, if damage should be caused thereby to the party obstructed, be a violation of this prohibition . . . .

W. ERLE, THE LAW RELATING TO TRADE UNIONS 12 (1869) (emphasis deleted). The passage is clearly correct when it notes that the articulation of the basic right is incomplete without the specification of the correlative duty. But it nowhere indicates why the "purpose of the obstruction" should be decisive instead of the means used to achieve it. And it hardly suffices to include a statement of the "actor's own right" in a description of the correlative duties.

26. The theme of the "wage slave" is evident enough in political theory. The provisions of the Clayton Act which stipulate that labor should not be regarded as an article of commerce also reflect that view. *See* Clayton Act, § 6, 15 U.S.C. § 17 (1982).

27. For an extended treatment of this theme, see Epstein, *Intentional Harms*, 4 J. LEGAL STUD. 391, 425-27 (1975).

28. The constraints upon a generalized system of entitlements reveal the intrinsic weakness of the view, advanced by Grey among many others, that all individuals are entitled to receive some minimum standard of support when they are unable to support themselves. *See Property and Need, supra* note 16, at 897-901. This standard must define the minimum level of support, and show how the system itself can generate sufficient wealth to meet its minimum obligations. It must also explain which individuals bear the correlative duties necessary to furnish the wealth in question. I am skeptical that these tasks can be discharged in a persuasive way, but for these purposes the central point is that this conception of entitlement is of no use in labor cases, where the redistributions will almost always be capricious, whatever its critical relevance to the question of welfare legislation.

ments by their holders, original or derivative.[29] Any set of moves is as good as another, so long as the moves themselves do not violate the rights of third parties and do not involve the use of prohibited means between competent parties. Becoming an employer or an employee is strictly a private act in which one person decides to offer his own capital in exchange for the services of another individual, or vice versa, on whatever terms the parties to the exchange see fit. The parties' decision to enter into a contractual agreement does not increase or decrease the sum of rights that they have against the rest of the world, or that the rest of the world has against them. The creation of voluntary arrangements is therefore never an occasion for increased state regulation of private transactions apart from the faithful enforcement of their agreement, be it in employment relations or anything else.

As the identities of the contracting parties and the terms on which they contract are of no special concern to the state, a contract between an employer and an employee is indistinguishable from one between two prospective employees. The protection of labor unions from doctrines of criminal conspiracy, therefore, should not depend upon any elaborate affirmative social justification for their use. If *A* could enter into a contract with a prospective employer, then there is no reason he cannot enter into a contract with his potential rival, *B*, to present a united front against the employer.[30] Similarly, the voluntary formation of labor unions need involve neither the use of force and fraud nor the inducement of breach of contract. There is therefore no need to appeal to special justification to account for the legality of labor unions, as it is already accounted for by a general theory of entitlements. To be sure, there are profound differences in the worth of the original set of endowments held by individuals (and by the firms or organizations that they create), but these have only descriptive significance in predicting what moves the parties will make within the rules. The refusal (or inability) to predict which arrangements will emerge in no way amounts to a defect of the theory. Prediction is within the province of economics and sociology. The function of a system of enti-

29. The position was well enunciated in the classical statement of libertarian principles in Coppage v. Kansas, 236 U.S. 1, 17 (1915). *Coppage* was, however, overruled sub silentio in Virginian Ry. v. System Fed'n No. 40, 300 U.S. 515 (1937), and expressly in Phelps Dodge Corp. v. NLRB, 313 U.S. 177, 187 (1941). The approach of *Coppage* has found modern philosophical support in R. NOZICK, ANARCHY, STATE, AND UTOPIA (1974).

30. The parallel between antitrust law and labor law is evident: There is no autonomy-based theory that accounts for antitrust law as applied to industry or for antitrust law as applied to labor law. I have explored this point in greater detail in *Private Property and the Public Domain*, *supra* note 22. The late nineteenth-century cases on economic harms show the close relationship between the two problems by treating both antitrust and labor cases within a single framework. *See, e.g.*, Mogul S.S. Co. v. McGregor Gow, & Co., [1889] 23 Q.B.D. 598, *aff'd*, 1892 A.C. 25; Allen v. Flood, 1898 A.C. 1; Quinn v. Leathem, 1901 A.C. 495; *see also* Mayor of Bradford v. Pickles, 1895 A.C. 587 (same analysis applied to nuisance cases).

tlements is only to determine after the fact whether the patterns that have emerged fall within the proper rules of the game. The law of contracts is no more designed to predict the terms contained in particular contracts than the rules of chess are designed to determine the soundness of the Ruy Lopez.

The strength of the theory is revealed by its treatment of three recurrent problems in the law of labor relations. The first problem is the role of "malice" and combination in labor disputes; the second concerns the place of the so-called "yellow dog" contract in employment relationships; and the last is the question of picketing.

A. *Malice and combination*

Malice and combination were at the heart of the great labor cases of the late nineteenth century in both England and the United States. One position, chiefly associated with the majority view in *Allen v. Flood*,[31] treated both malice and combination as wholly immaterial to the question of liability. When, therefore, one group of workers announced through their union leaders that they would not continue in the employ of a third party unless he dismissed the members of a rival union working under contracts at will, this conduct was held in *Allen* not to be tortious, even if actuated by malice.[32] The majority relied heavily on its earlier decision in *Mogul v. McGregor*,[33] which held that a combination of shippers could act to exclude rivals by predatory pricing even though their intention was to inflict economic harm in order to secure their own self-advancement.

Three years later, however, the House of Lords adopted a very different view of labor disputes in *Quinn v. Leathem*,[34] holding that a second-

31. For an interpretation of *Allen v. Flood* that stresses the factual argument that Allen was no more than a messenger for the iron-men in his union who did not induce the dismissal at all, see Petro, *Unions and the Southern Courts: Part III—The Conspiracy and Tort Foundations of the Labor Injunction*, 60 N.C.L. REV. 543, 558-67 (1982). Support for his view of the facts is found, for example, in the careful opinion of Lord Macnaghten, 1898 A.C. at 143-150. But Macnaghten also said: "Even if I am wrong in my view of the evidence and the verdict, if the verdict amounts to a finding that Allen's conduct was malicious in every sense of the word, and that he procured the dismissal of Flood and Taylor, that is, that it was his act and conduct alone which caused their dismissal, . . . I should still be of the opinion that judgment was wrongly entered for the respondents." *Id.* at 151. In addition, his view was sharply contested in other opinions, including that of Lord Morris, which found that Allen "proceeded to threaten the employers with the withdrawal of the boilermakers which would be most injurious to the employers, unless the plaintiffs were dismissed at once." *Id.* at 159. In any event, it is only on the point of principle—the rule of malice—that the case has any theoretical interest. It is quite incomprehensible why it should attract any attention if it turned on a simple question of fact. Note that Lord Herschell concluded his long opinion by saying "that I regard the decision under appeal as one absolutely novel, and which can only be supported by affirming propositions far-reaching in their consequences and in my opinion dangerous and unsound." *Id.* at 143.

32. 1898 A.C. at 1.

33. 23 Q.B.D. 598 (1889), *aff'd*, 1892 A.C. 25.

34. 1901 A.C. 495.

ary boycott by a labor union, which sought both to unionize the defendant's shop and to replace his current employees with union members, was actionable, given the conspiracy of the union members and their asserted malice toward the plaintiff. The decision has been rightly attacked as wholly inconsistent with the general principles of *Allen*, which itself could be transformed easily into a conspiracy case given that the defendant Allen represented a union, all of whose members were prepared to strike over the work issue.[35] In addition, *Quinn* seems difficult to reconcile with *Mogul* given that the union's actions were well calculated to serve the self-interest of its members, both by placing current members in high paying jobs and by choking off the powerful economic competition from nonunion shops.

The irreconcilable differences amongst these three English cases is warning enough of the difficulty of maintaining a harmonious set of common law rules. It should not be surprising therefore that these same doctrinal conflicts manifested themselves in the American cases, which in this particular instance rested very heavily upon the English decisions. *Plant v. Wood*,[36] strongly reminiscent of *Quinn*, held that liability turned on matters of intent when employees acted in concert—in this case, an effort to force nonunion workers to join a union shop.[37] The court in *Plant* took the general, if vague, position that workers who combined together to injure another engaged in wrongful conduct, whereas those who combined together to benefit themselves did not. The determination as to which ends were consonant with "legitimate" self-interest required courts to develop shadowy and unsatisfactory ways to distinguish between different brands of egoism: Should there be one response where the collective refusal to deal was intended to force other workers to join the striking union, and another where the goal was higher wages for union members? *Plant* and *Quinn* are clearly less consistent with a liberty-based theory than is *Allen*. That they impose greater restrictions upon labor unions is quite beside the point.

A closer analysis of the legal conception of malice helps clarify the proper rules of union liability. Malice in its pure form means more than an intention to inflict some temporal injury. All competition, and most economic activity, will do that. Instead it refers to actions done out of spite or ill will, whereby someone is prepared to impose costs upon himself solely to make someone else worse off. So defined, malice does not offer a viable route to either survival or advancement; indeed it is negated by the

35. *See* C. GREGORY, LABOR AND THE LAW 46-51 (2d ed. 1958).

36. 176 Mass. 492, 57 N.E. 1011 (1900).

37. *Id.* For a contrast to the majority view of *Plant*, see National Protective Ass'n v. Cumming, 170 N.Y. 315, 63 N.E. 369 (1902), which followed the argument of Holmes' classic dissent in *Plant*.

economic self-interest found in both *Quinn* and *Plant*. Any prohibition against malicious conduct, therefore, at most reaches only the fringes of individual and union behavior. *Allen* neatly avoids the problem of inquiring into motives for collective action entirely. But, by fastening exclusively on the means used, *Allen* did not reduce the law to conclusionary assertions about lawful and unlawful acts.

Under *Allen*, however, it is possible to supply an independent account of what constitutes unlawful means: force, fraud, and inducement of breach of contract. As long as workers, either alone or in combination, do no more than withhold or threaten to withhold labor that they are not bound by contract to supply, they have not trenched upon the rights of the rival workers, even if rival workers suffer as a consequence. The third-party employer could resist the demands of the defendants and continue to employ the plaintiffs, as did the employer in *Quinn*. Alternatively, the plaintiffs could agree to reduced wages or to different work in order to keep their previous positions. The targeted employer may even capitulate to the demands of the rival union. The autonomy-based theory does not predict outcome, but accepts whichever outcome emerges as the voluntary recombination of entitlements within the framework of the tort law.[38]

Unless, therefore, one wants to take the position that unions by their nature must engage in such illegal acts, they and a wide range of their activities remain protected under a strong theory of entitlements that contains not a whisper of special status or privilege. Labor unions should not be considered criminal conspiracies not because they do not operate in restraint of trade—many do—but because restraint of trade itself should not be illegal. The vacillation between *Allen* and *Quinn* has been attacked as a double standard of the private law—with harsher rules for labor than for business.[39] Whether this overall condemnation is justified is an open question. What is beyond dispute is the proposition that (at least in the libertarian view) legislation that secures the rules of *Allen* is appropriate, even if more massive labor legislation is not.

38. It remains true that if malice and combination are found in cases in which there is the threat or use of force, or an inducement of contractual breach, matters are worsened by the combination. Mobs are more dangerous than isolated individuals. But even here the important point is as before: The nature of the conduct must first be shown to be a violation of right before questions of motive and combination can be introduced by way of aggravation. The matter became quite cloudy in English law. *See, e.g.*, Crofter Hand Woven Harris Tweed Co. v. Veitch, 1942 A.C. 435; Sorrell v. Smith, 1925 A.C. 700. For discussion, see W. ROGERS, WINFIELD & JOLOWICZ ON TORT 461-67 (10th ed. 1975).

39. *See* C. GREGORY, *supra*, note 35, at 46-51. Note that the equivocation on the central point in both the American and the English cases makes it very difficult to draw any clear inferences of judicial bias from the legal decisions. If the judges had been so biased in the first instance, there would be no way to explain *Allen*.

B. *Yellow Dog Contracts*

The strong theories of individual entitlement applicable to labor unions apply with equal force to the "yellow dog" contract. In such contracts, a worker agrees as a condition of employment that he will not become a member of a labor organization. These contracts are today forbidden by explicit statutory command[40] and have been uniformly condemned by academic writers as being self-evidently unjust—even, as Calvert Magruder said, a "curse."[41] Their status as a matter of strict autonomy-based theory is, however, quite different: They should be accorded the same respect as any other voluntary agreement. Thus, in order to invalidate such an arrangement, one must show that it involves the use or the threat of force against a third party. To the extent that it requires only that a worker steer clear of unions in order to obtain or keep a job it does nothing of the sort.[42] To be sure, the yellow dog contract is improper if it requires an individual worker to breach a membership contract with his union. If the current statutory prohibition were directed only to that situation, it would be fully justified as a protection of vested rights. But no one thinks that the problem with yellow dog contracts is inducement of breach of intra-union contracts by employers. The opposition always takes the position that the yellow dog contract is against public policy in all its manifestations.[43] The support for the prohibition came from labor unions, its chief beneficiaries, who wanted to overcome any obstacles to unionization these contracts posed. Yet no attention was paid to the mode of that frustration, which by the general theory of entitlements is the one question that matters.[44]

In defense of the current prohibition of the yellow dog contract it is sometimes said that "[t]he Norris-LaGuardia Act introduced the only per-

40. National Labor Relations Act, 29 U.S.C. § 158(a)(3) (1982).

41. Magruder, *supra* note 3, at 1083. The relevant passage reads as follows:

> The *Adair* case was carried further in *Coppage v. Kansas*, where by a six-to-three vote the Supreme Court held invalid under the Fourteenth Amendment a state statute making it criminal for an employer to exact a yellow dog contract as a condition of employment. The curse has finally been taken from these cases by the recent decision upholding the National Labor Relations Act.

It seems an easy inference (especially from the tenor of the paper) to assume that *Adair* and *Coppage* were curses because the yellow dog contract was a curse. No argument is offered, however, to explain its social evil.

For similar sentiments, see A. COX, LAW AND THE NATIONAL LABOR POLICY (1960), where it is assumed that the errors in *Hitchman* are self-evident: "Decisions like the *Hitchman* case seemed to display either prejudice or a lack of elementary economics." Id. at 7. The only economic analysis offered here, however, consists of a theoretical and inaccurate assertion urging: "The *Hitchman* injunction thwarted the United Mine Workers but did not improve the lot of the coal miners." *Id.*

42. Justice Brandeis took the view that coercion should be very narrowly defined in labor cases. Hitchman Coal & Coke Co. v. Mitchell, 245 U.S. 229, 271-72 (1917) (Brandeis, J., dissenting).

43. F. FRANKFURTER & N. GREENE, *supra* note 3; A. COX, *supra* note 41.

44. A. COX, *supra* note 41, at 8.

iod of unqualified laissez faire in labor relations."[45] But the proposition is based upon a misapprehension of what laissez faire demands of government. To be sure, the Norris-LaGuardia Act (like the Wagner Act) did not involve government dictation of the terms and conditions of individual or collective agreements.[46] Yet the insistence, as revealed in the Norris-LaGuardia Act's exhortation, that workers obtain "acceptable terms and conditions of employment,"[47] hardly speaks to the process of contractual formation, much less to the glory of "the competitive struggle of life," that is central to the theory of laissez faire. To the contrary, the statute looks to the outcome of the process and demands a theory of just dessert that is incompatible with laissez faire principles.

Nor does the absence of any administrative structure convert the Norris-LaGuardia Act into a safeguard for laissez faire principles. For laissez faire, the ultimate question is *not* whether, given the established legal framework, the parties are entitled to bargain to whatever terms and conditions they see fit. It is whether the legal constraints within which the negotiation takes place are consistent with a rigorous theory of individual entitlements. Individuals can bargain with kidnappers without the benefit of state mediation on the amount of the ransom needed to secure release, but the prior question is, by what warrant must a person purchase the release of another individual when that individual ought already to be free as a matter of right? If we have learned anything from the law of the duress of goods,[48] it is that the existence of choice, without more, is not a sufficient condition for contractual freedom. The issue remains one of entitlements: Is the choice between something one owns and something one wants, or is it between two things one owns? In the former context we can speak of bargains worthy of respect. In the latter, by analogy to duress of goods, we can speak only of bargains under coercion.

These insights apply with undiminished force to the labor context. Why limit freedom of contract between employer and employee? It is often said that choices left to the worker under the common law are "illusory," in that without statutory protection the worker has no choice but to succumb

45. *Id.*

46. "The basic theory of the law [i.e., the Wagner Act] in its original form, as today, was that the arrangement of the substantive terms and conditions of employment is a private responsibility." *Id.* at 11. The position is endorsed in many judicial decisions. *See, e.g.*, H.K. Porter Co. v. NLRB, 397 U.S. 99 (1970). There is no question that the government is well advised to stay out of these matters. But it is quite a different proposition to treat massive structural interferences with voluntary transactions as though there were no interferences at all.

47. 29 U.S.C. § 102 (1982). The section also refers to the workers' right of "full freedom of association" as a justification for the limitation of the yellow dog contract, but does not address the question of how the statutory prohibition preserves the similar "full freedom of association" for both employers and workers who wish to sign yellow dog agreements.

48. *See supra* note 7.

to the employer's pressure. One factual objection to the theory is that it can neither account for the fact that the workers received positive wages for their employment before the adoption of the modern labor legislation, nor for the equally obvious fact that there were wage differentials between workers in different trades and with different skills. If inequality of bargaining power had any descriptive power as a model, then why did employers not use their power to reduce wages to the vanishing point, or refuse to accept unionization before the passage of either the Norris-LaGuardia or Wagner Acts? As a matter of principle, the liberal theory of contract draws a very powerful distinction between the duress which is imposed by the threat of force by one party against the other, and the duress, so-called, attributable to economic and personal pressures to which all parties are subjected by the inevitable considerations of scarcity. To adopt the modern language of "unconscionability,"[49] it is a meaningful choice to refuse employment altogether; no one would count it the loss of a meaningless choice if employers were given the right to conscript employees into service. To insist, therefore, that there be economic equality before there can be contract is to destroy the usefulness of contract by imposing a set of exacting conditions that can never be satisfied or even approached. To confuse economic inequality with duress is to say that no bargains are ever free from duress, and to swallow up freedom of contract by an unprincipled expansion of the principled limitations upon the basic rule. It is quite enough that the contracts leave the parties better off than they were before. It is too much to ask of any system of rules that it correct whatever asserted social imbalances exist before the contract formation.

The weakness of the arguments of economic duress can be demonstrated in yet another fashion. It is not coercive for a party to choose not to go into business at all, even though that exercise of rights reduces the options available to any prospective employee. It cannot therefore be an abuse to increase the options available to any person by giving him an opportunity to work that he cannot claim as of right and, in fact, would not have otherwise. A yellow dog agreement could be coercive only if prospective employees had a precontractual right to demand both union membership and employment. But it is unclear how any principled account of individual rights could generate that set of uneven entitlements. So long as the worker owns his labor, and the employer his capital, then the liberal theory of contract is neutral with respect both to the identity of contracting parties and to the terms of the agreement. No law prohibits two business partners from demanding exclusive loyalty from each other, nor

49. Williams v. Walker-Thomas Furniture Co., 350 F.2d 445, 449-50 (D.C. Cir. 1965).

is there any reason why such loyalty cannot be demanded of an employee by his employer, or of an employer by the employee (as in the promise not to hire nonunion labor). The Norris-LaGuardia Act can be regarded as compatible with laissez faire only if the sole permissible sequence of agreements dictates that agreements among workers precede those between workers in combination with employers. This is no more sensible than saying that sound industrial policy demands that cartelization amongst sellers should necessarily precede sales to customers.

In principle, there remains one other way to argue that public policy should prohibit the yellow dog contract. That is to show that the contracts themselves are of necessity entered into by processes (to wit, force and fraud) that themselves negate any true consent. There is a clear hint of this theme in the language of the Norris-LaGuardia Act, which states without elaboration that "the individual unorganized worker is commonly helpless to exercise actual liberty of contract and to protect his freedom of labor, and thereby to obtain acceptable terms and conditions of employment."[50] The source of the helplessness is left unspecified, but there is no indication that it is anything more than the difference between the two sides, command over resources, itself a factor immaterial to an entitlement theory of contract. And it is surely odd that a yellow dog contract should not count as an exercise in liberty of contract as much as a decision to cast one's lot with other workers.

The theory of laissez faire, then, is unambiguous in its support of the legality of the yellow dog contract. This was recognized by the believers in constitutionally based laissez faire when they struck down statutory prohibitions against the arrangements in *Adair v. United States.*[51] The strength of *Adair*'s conclusion is further supported by an examination of *Hitchman Coal & Coke Co. v. Mitchell,*[52] the key case upholding the legality of the yellow dog contract in the pre-New Deal era.

In *Hitchman*, the plaintiff coal mine had struggled through a protracted dispute with the United Mine Workers. On several occasions, management agreed to accept a closed union shop, but the arrangements always collapsed when up for renewal, producing a series of strikes that depleted the resources of both the firm and the union. During one of these strikes, several miners came to the employer offering to work on a nonunion basis for the prevailing union wages. It was agreed that the company would no longer recognize the United Mine Workers, and that no employee of the

50. 29 U.S.C. § 102 (1982).

51. 208 U.S. 161 (1908). Holmes' dissent, *id.* at 190, went not so much to the status of the agreement under the general common law theory, but to the separate and difficult question of the extent to which that theory has been incorporated into the Constitution. *Id.* at 191.

52. 245 U.S. 229 (1917).

firm could be a member of the union. These were contracts at will, so the workers were free to leave the employ of the company at any time and join the union. The agreement in question was accepted by all employees of the mine. Representatives of the United Mine Workers later attempted to secure workers' promises to go out on strike as members of the union when requested to do so. The organizers did not use force or misrepresentation against the employees to achieve their goals. The organizers did, however, request employees who agreed to join the union to remain on their jobs, fearing that the company could easily secure replacements if dissatisfied workers left on a gradual basis. When the company discovered the activities of the key union personnel, it sought to enjoin those activities on the ground that they constituted an inducement of breach of contract. In an analysis consistent with the general liberal theory of contract developed here, the Supreme Court held that the injunction was warranted, although overbroad in some of its particulars. There was no question that the contract of employment was valid as between the parties. As the arrangement was at will, the company could have dismissed individual workers on the spot if it discovered their affiliation with the union. More to the point, it could have argued that the employees were in breach of a material condition and therefore could have made a powerful claim to withhold (or perhaps recover) the wages paid to the workers during the period of their union affiliation. These conclusions could not be upset on the ground that the contract infringed the rights of third persons to be free, among other things, from force and fraud.

The only way to argue against an injunction was therefore to show that the tort of inducement of breach of contract did not apply to ordinary labor disputes. *Lumley v. Gye*,[53] the basic decision in the area, had granted the plaintiff impresario an injunction against a defendant who had knowingly induced a famous opera singer to breach her contract with the plaintiff. Thereafter, both the English and American courts extended *Lumley* to ordinary labor contracts, finding the use of the injunction uncontroversial.[54]

The application of *Lumley* to *Hitchman* is clear enough. So long as the current contract had any positive value to the promisee, the tort action is appropriate. As it was clear to all concerned that covert union membership (aside from being a fraud against the employer) weakened the employer's economic position against the employee, the common law tort applied to the case in a perfectly straightforward manner. The only question that remained was whether an injunction against the third party provided

53. 2 E. & B. 216, 118 Eng. Rep. 749 (1853).
54. *See* Walker v. Cronin, 107 Mass. 555 (1871); Bowen v. Hall, 6 Q.B.D. 333 (1881).

the proper remedy. Here the ongoing commission of the tort and the difficulty in estimating the damages that could flow from a sudden disruption of services brought about by a strike make such a remedy proper under the ordinary equitable principles governing injunctions.

In its own way, Brandeis's dissent is even more instructive than Pitney's admirable majority opinion. Brandeis utters not a single word against the common law conceptual framework that Justice Pitney used to analyze the case. The crux of Brandeis's argument follows:

> The contract created an employment at will: and the employee was free to leave at any time. The contract did not bind the employee *not* to join the union; and he was free to join it at any time. The contract merely bound him to withdraw from plaintiff's employ, if he joined the union. There is evidence of an attempt to induce plaintiff's employees to *agree* to join the union; but none whatever of any attempt to induce them to violate their contract. Until an employee actually joined the union he was not, under the contract, called upon to leave the plaintiff's employ. There consequently would be no breach of contract until the employee both joined the union *and* failed to withdraw from plaintiff's employ.[55]

At best this is an argument only of contract construction, and a very bad argument at that. As Pitney points out,[56] there is nothing of substance to distinguish joining the union from agreeing to join the union at some future time. The arrangement between the employer and the workers was that the workers' sole loyalty was to the employer. There is no question that dual and inconsistent loyalties are created even if a worker takes the neat precaution of not signing a membership card while remaining on the job at the behest of the union. If this had been a case in which one impresario had bid for the services of an opera star already under contract to a rival, a demonstration of the breach and its inducement would have been trivial matters. Pitney was clearly correct in observing that, as courts of equity had long looked "to the substance and essence of things and disregarded matters of form and technical nicety, it is sufficient to say that to induce men to *agree* to join is but a mode of inducing them to join. . . ."[57]

C. *Picketing*

It remains here only to consider the proper treatment of picketing within the libertarian framework. Here the point of departure is that the prohibition against the use of force reaches the threat of force. If killing is

55. 245 U.S. at 272.
56. *Id.* at 255 (italics in original).
57. *Id.*

illegal, then so too must be armed robbery, even if the gun is not fired. Wholly apart from the labor context, there has never been a difficulty in accepting the general proposition. But what are the limits of the rule? Blackstone's definition of assault was restrictive: It included an "attempt or offer to beat another, without touching him; as if one lifts up his cane, or his fist in a threatening manner at another."[58] Under this account the defendant must have both the capability and the immediate opportunity to inflict the harm in question, an overly restrictive view of liability, even for a common lawyer. Today the general view is that an action lies "when it is shown that one, in the absence of any privilege, intentionally subjects another to the mental suffering incident to serious threats to his physical well-being, whether or not the threats are made under such circumstances as to constitute a technical assault."[59] The creation of, as it were, an action on the case for an indirect assault lengthens the causal chain and complicates the manner of proof, but these difficulties do not preclude liability on theoretical grounds.

For our purposes the general rules of assault form the framework with which to analyze picketing. The first inquiry is whether "picketing" constitutes a threat of force against persons who cross the picket line. The question is difficult to answer because there are enormous variations in the form and style of "picketing." The presence of an isolated picketer etches in the mind of the observer the futility of the picketer's cause, while a group of angry men may well convey a different, if unmistakable, message. In principle, it is possible to wait until the damage manifests itself, allowing only individual actions of assault by aggrieved customers. That course of action, however, is tantamount to leaving a wrong wholly unredressed. Individual citizens at the picket line can cut their losses simply by not crossing the line. In any event, they will not be induced to maintain a cause of action that promises only small rewards after arduous litigation. The real victim is the proprietor deprived of customers. The only effective means of social control, therefore, is to grant an action to the proprietor of the picketed establishment. This action itself requires no innovation in principle, even if it may call for some novelty in application. The old schoolmaster's case[60] and *Tarleton v. McGawley*[61] both granted

58. 3 W. BLACKSTONE, COMMENTARIES 120 (1790).

59. State Rubbish Collectors Ass'n v. Siliznoff, 38 Cal.2d 330, 336, 240 P.2d 282, 284-85 (1952). *See* W. PROSSER, HANDBOOK OF THE LAW OF TORTS 59 (4th ed. 1971).

60. This case is referred to in Keeble v. Hickeringill, 11 East 574, 576, 103 Eng. Rep. 1127, 1128 (K.B. 1809): "But suppose Mr. Hickeringill should lie in the way with his guns, and fright the boys from going to school, and their parents would not let them go thither, sure that schoolmaster might have an action for the loss of his scholars."

61. 170 Eng. Rep. 153 (K.B. 1793).

actions for the (if it matters here, the deliberate) interference with prospective advantage by the threat or use of force.

To state the problem in this fashion is only to give some hint as to the problems that follow. Does picketing itself constitute a threat of force, or is it only an effort to convey information so that customers make an informed choice not to do business with the picketed establishment? In the celebrated case of *Vegelahn v. Guntner*,[62] the court was forced to confront this very question in passing on the scope of an injunction awarded against two trade unions and their members. In making his preliminary determination, Justice Holmes noted that the defendants had engaged in two separate types of activities, the first involving the use of "persuasion and social pressure," and the second "threats of personal injury or unlawful harm," that were often conveyed in a disguised manner.[63] The first of these he rightly treated as legal, and the second as illegal. The difficulty in the case was that the two patterns of behavior could be intertwined. Holmes tailored his original injunction to stop the second type of activity but to permit the first. In his dissent to the decision of the court, he justified his position by noting that if during the continuation of their picketing the defendants did use or threaten force, their conduct would fall under the injunction that he had granted so that the defendants would be "liable to summary punishment."[64] The court in turn ordered a broader injunction that forbade the defendants from interfering with the plaintiff's business "by any scheme . . . organized for the purpose of . . . preventing any person or persons who now are or may hereafter be . . . desirous of entering [the plaintiff's employment] from entering it."[65] The court's position is widely rejected today,[66] and is open to condemnation as an excessive use of the injunctive power. Nonetheless, the court's judgment is not subject to any categorical denunciation, even if wrong. Thus, the broader injunction can be defended by pointing to the weaknesses of the finely tuned injunction that Holmes had adopted. Leaving the pickets in place by the plaintiff's business invites, or at least increases the likelihood of, the threat or use of force, which will go unredressed because the summary remedies available in principle are imperfect in practice. Case-by-case determinations are expensive to make, and are subject to very high error rates, especially where disguised threats are a substantial possibility.

62. 167 Mass. 92, 44 N.E. 1077 (1896).

63. 167 Mass. at 95-96. The passage is not reproduced in 44 N.E.

64. *Id.* at 104, 44 N.E. at 1080 (Holmes, J., dissenting).

65. *Id.*

66. *See, e.g.*, Music Hall Theater v. Moving Picture Mach. Operators Local 165, 249 Ky. 639, 61 S.W.2d 283 (1933); People v. Nixson, 248 N.Y. 182, 161 N.E. 463 (1928). *Vegelahn* itself continued to enjoy some support. *See* Pierce v. Stablemen's Union, Local No. 8,760, 156 Cal. 70, 103 P. 324 (1909).

In some cases at least, the best solution may give too much protection instead of too little.

The case for the majority position in *Vegelahn* becomes more plausible in light of the very powerful regulation of police behavior done today on constitutional grounds. At its root, *Miranda v. Arizona*[67] rests upon the preference for broad over narrow injunctions, given that the simple appearance of a police officer can be so "inherently coercive" that constitutional rules of notice and right to counsel are necessary to help insure the "voluntariness" of a confession. The displaced rule—a case-by-case examination of the voluntariness of individual confessions—was rejected because it offered insufficient protection against official abuse. Picketing frequently constitutes an implicit threat of the use of force that may take the form of jostling or immediate contact. It may carry with it the implicit threat of the future infliction of harm: Who would not hesitate to cross a picket line if he saw a picketer filming persons crossing the line? To be sure, the picketers are not vested with the power of the state; but at the same time they are uncontrolled by any form of state power. The picketers can assert a weighty interest in freedom of speech,[68] but this is matched by the interests in freedom of property, contract, and association on the other side.

The question is in the end a close call. To be sure, there are some easy rules that dispose of some challenges to picketing: One cannot, for example, prohibit picketing solely because of the content of its message—a proposition which no one denies. But when the easy cases have been set to one side, a broad class of situations remain in which the sound discretion of the trial judge will be necessary to determine whether an injunction should issue, and if so on what terms. The factually dense nature of the question, moreover, makes this type of determination inescapable whether we deal with a judge guided only by the general principles of equity, by an administrative officer trying to enforce the provisions of a coherent picketing control statute, or by the Supreme Court trying to determine the appropriate limits of the First Amendment guarantees of freedom of speech. There is simply no general form of words that will determine the appropriateness of or proper terms for an injunction. In some cases, it might suffice to reduce the number of pickets, or to limit the places where they may go. In others, the threat of force may be more severe, and the correct response far greater.

With this said, the limits of the libertarian theory should be evident. It

67. 384 U.S. 436 (1966).

68. *See* Thornhill v. Alabama, 310 U.S. 88 (1940). The subsequent course of doctrine has not been smooth. *See, e.g.*, Hudgens v. NLRB, 424 U.S. 507 (1976); International Bhd. of Teamsters, Local 695 v. Vogt, Inc., 354 U.S. 284 (1957).

only goes so far as to establish two propositions: (i) to condemn the use of force, and (ii) to mandate that injunctions be tailored to minimize the sum of the errors of over- and under-inclusion. Matters of future uncertainty cannot be handled neatly by any normative theory—including those which rely on general legislation. The wide range of considerations identified here must be taken into account in the treatment of picketing under the first amendment or under the New Deal legislation. It is not my task here to reconcile the decided cases, nor to defend the record of the pre-New Deal courts in labor injunction cases.[69] Given the degrees of freedom and uncertainty, no final indisputable reconciliation is ever possible. The law of injunctions here is if anything more difficult than the analogous problem in the law of nuisances. The best one can demand is to understand the nature of the end—the restriction of the use or threat of force—and choose the means most likely to achieve it. The very meaning of the phrase "sound discretion" is that there is an irreducible class of cases in which honest disagreements over proper disposition cannot be resolved in a conceptually rigorous manner. The great strength of the libertarian theory is that it identifies why picketing is a problem. But unlike the treatment of conspiracy or yellow dog contracts, picketing is a problem to which neither it nor any other theory provides a clean conceptual answer.

III. Utilitarian Arguments

The questions of malice, combination, yellow dog contracts, and picketing have thus far been considered solely from the vantage point of a strong theory of entitlements that (with the possible exception of picketing) in no way depends upon explicit utilitarian concerns. While much can be said to support the view that this general theory dispenses with the need to develop any alternative framework of analysis, the soundness of the conclusions urged above does not stand or fall on this single set of premises. The rival tradition of utilitarian thought is very powerful in the Anglo-American philosophical and legal traditions.[70] It can be fairly asked whether its explicit consideration calls for any modification of the conclusions already advanced.

In making this inquiry, one should note at the outset that in historical terms the utilitarian issues arise more in the interpretation of statutes than in the development of common law principles. Combination in restraint of trade is often seen today to invite a utilitarian analysis, but the common

69. For such a defense, see Petro, *Injunctions and Labor Disputes: 1880-1932, Part I: What the Courts Actually Did—And Why*, 14 WAKE FOREST L. REV. 341 (1978).

70. For a recent defense of the wealth maximization variant of utilitarianism, see Posner, *Utilitarianism, Economics, and Legal Theory*, 8 J. LEGAL STUD. 103 (1979).

law cases that considered the legal status of unions never, either expressly or by implication, viewed the problem in a utilitarian light:[71] The social welfare function was not the idiom of common law judges. The central inquiry in the cases was the proper delineation of individual freedom and the proper account of the "coercion" directed against the immediate parties to the dispute, usually rival unions or employers caught in the middle of picketing or jurisdictional disputes. The concept of the private damage action as a rough surrogate for social losses[72] never surfaced in the cases.

The unwillingness of the common law to address the systemic economic issues meant that questions of social welfare were addressed, if at all, only in the great debate on whether labor unions should be subject to the sanctions of the Sherman Act, and later the Clayton Act, as combinations in restraint of trade.[73] On its face, the language of the Sherman Act applies to labor unions as it does to any other aggregation of individuals.[74] While the statutory construction and legislative history of the Sherman Act are complex,[75] for our purposes the critical question is again normative: How should utilitarian considerations, in particular the antitrust laws, apply to labor unions?

One point of considerable importance is that the liberal and utilitarian traditions of analysis differ only in unimportant respects in their treatment of the enforcement of contractual arrangements between the parties to them. Thus the libertarian account will stress that the content of the obligation is no business of the courts, and will decline to look further at the matter unless fraud or misrepresentation or incompetence is present. The utilitarian will generally assume that contracts move resources to more valued uses, so that both parties to the agreement are better off under the agreement than without it. Duress, misrepresentation, and undue influence become relevant to identify those conditions in which the general proposition may not hold because one party has been prevented by the other from soundly assessing the desirability of his agreement.

The key difference between the liberal and the utilitarian approaches

71. Petro, *supra* note 31; Petro, *supra* note 69, at 436-46.

72. *Cf.* Easterbrook, *Predatory Strategies and Counterstrategies*, 48 U. CHI. L. REV. 263 (1981) (suits by victims of predatory pricing protect consumers at large).

73. The statute reads:

> The labor of a human being is not a commodity or article of commerce. Nothing contained in the antitrust laws shall be construed to forbid the existence and operation of labor . . . organizations . . . or to forbid or restrain individual members of such organizations from lawfully carrying out the legitimate objects thereof; nor shall such organizations, or the members thereof, be held or construed to be illegal combinations or conspiracies in restraint of trade, under the antitrust laws.

15 U.S.C. § 17 (1982).

74. *See* Loewe v. Lawlor, 208 U.S. 274 (1908).

75. *See* Winter, *Collective Bargaining and Competition: The Application of Antitrust Standards to Union Activities*, 73 YALE L.J. 14 (1963).

lies in their evaluation of third-party effects. The liberal approach ignores shifts of wealth which are not preceded by a wrongful act such as the use of force or misrepresentation.[76] The utilitarian theory, in contrast, attempts to take these pure economic externalities into account in order to counter perceived economic dislocations that cannot be rectified by agreement because of high transaction costs. In principle, the utilitarian limits contractual freedom whenever the loss of utility to third parties exceeds the gains to the parties to the original transaction. The analysis is complicated, since the transfer of any resource from *A* to *B* will as a matter of course alter the prospects, and hence the utilities, of *C* through *Z*. In most situations, variations in the fortunes of third parties are regarded as random and offsetting, or as excessively costly to determine, and so they are rarely taken into account. The antitrust law—in particular the law of horizontal restraints of trade—is an effort to carve out a set of cases in which the systematic losses to society at large (measured by the failure to produce goods to the point where social marginal revenue equals social marginal cost) justify some restraint on freedom of contract.

It remains to see whether this general utilitarian approach requires us to revise the conclusions reached with respect to the four problems addressed above: malice, combination, yellow dog contracts, and picketing.

A. *Malice*

The structure of the utilitarian inquiry does not change the prior conclusion that malice is essentially an irrelevant factor in dealing with the legality of combinations of labor.[77] Malice could be regarded as a type of satisfaction, equal to other satisfactions. Malice in its unalloyed form, however, is not an important element in situations dominated by economic self-interest and thus deserves little consideration, given the high costs of its isolation and punishment. Ignoring malice per se is especially untroublesome since many cases of malice will be caught by the prohibitions against duress and misrepresentation.

B. *Combination*

The question of combination raises very different concerns. The legality of organizing across industries may allow unions to obtain a degree of market power that, in the absence of their antitrust exemption, would trigger the application of the antitrust laws. The matter becomes particularly pressing once it is recognized that prohibitions against horizontal

76. This is the doctrine of *damnum absque injuria*—harm without legal injury. *See generally* Epstein, *supra* note 27, at 432-33.

77. *See supra* pp. 367-69.

arrangements between firms will be less effective if unions remain free to capture monopoly profits in the form of higher wages. One can argue that entry from nonunion firms will discipline the behavior of the unions, but under antitrust law the absence of legal barriers to entry need not be regarded as any more decisive in labor than in ordinary product markets.[78] One could therefore extend the analysis quite naturally to argue that unions should be allowed to organize individual firms, but that no single union should be able to represent the workers of rival firms where a combination between those firms qua firms would represent impermissible market power. This compromise solution would permit unions to improve relationships between management and workers within the plant by handling personnel and public relation problems,[79] but it would blunt their monopoly power.[80] The effort to subject unions to antitrust laws therefore is supported by a coherent (if controversial) normative theory, even if the checkered history of the union exemption from antitrust laws itself defies rationalization.

C. *Yellow dog contracts*

The yellow dog contract is justifiable under the utilitarian as well as the libertarian analysis. Although it is commonly maintained that the yellow dog contract is unfair to the individual worker because of his weak economic position,[81] there is no reason why this should be so. Allowing employers to demand that their workers not join a union is very different from banning unions themselves. Any worker who accepts a yellow dog contract will demand some compensation for giving up the possibility of the gains of union membership. One has to assume an enormous degree of incompetence or ignorance by workers to ban the yellow dog contract on paternalistic grounds.[82]

The analysis here is borne out by looking again at the terms of the yellow dog contract sanctioned by the Supreme Court in *Hitchman.* The wages, it will be recalled, were set at union scale. Indeed, the agreement

78. *See supra* note 73.

79. For an account of unions that emphasizes this function, see Freeman & Medoff, *The Two Faces of Unionism*, THE PUBLIC INTEREST, Fall 1979, at 69.

80. Efforts to gain monopoly power are clearly central to unionization. A desire only to smooth relationships between the management and the worker would not require the elimination of competition from nonunion plants, be it by the device of coercion or by secondary boycotts. Yet these techniques were and remain commonplace in labor relations. See C. GREGORY, *supra* note 35, at 217 (by the 1920's all nationally affiliated unions were committed to closed shop in every industry).

81. *See* Powell, *supra* note 3, at 403-05.

82. Kennedy addresses the "distributive" and "paternalistic" justifications for the prohibition against yellow dog contracts in a discussion which seems to rest on the implicit assumption that the contract should be banned, apparently on the ground that such a ban enforces the solidarity among workers. *See* Kennedy, *supra* note 5, at 574-75. The question whether the interest of the workers in the plant should be equated with the social interest, however, is not addressed.

provided for a retroactive wage increase if union wages increased after the start of the agreement, but for unchanged wages if union wages fell.[83] "Union" wages implicitly understate the net wages to the nonunion workers, as union membership always imposes some obligations (dues, services) upon workers, wholly apart from the increased likelihood of substantial individual losses through strikes.

We must also take into account the duration of the contract, which was only at the will of both parties. The employer was not able to bind the workers for a fixed term, much less extract a promise from them not to join a union after they terminated their employment. This permitted workers who signed to keep the threat advantage of union membership without having to join one. They also gained an effective counterweight against any employer strategy of divide and conquer. By not signing a long-term employment contract, the workers preserved the option of joining a union at some subsequent time. Nor was the union precluded from organizing the workers while the yellow dog contracts were in effect. The ability retained by workers to quit and to join the union provided a valuable deterrent against the opportunistic behavior of the employer.[84] Had circumstances changed so as to make unionization more attractive, the workers would have been free to switch their allegiance. No worker who signs an employment contract today is disadvantaged in comparison to another employee who withholds his labor, for there is always an opportunity to reassess the basic situation. Indeed, a yellow dog contract does not even prevent the workers from quitting en masse and joining an existing union. The at-will feature of the yellow dog contract in *Hitchman* gave substantial protection to the workers, because the threat of unionization was always there.

The overall examination of the situation only confirms the general proposition that most contracts are in the mutual interest of the parties who sign them. The worker who signs a yellow dog contract may well be better off than one who does not. Certainly the terms of the arrangement in *Hitchman* cannot be explained by any theory under which an employer "dictates" terms to prospective workers. It is difficult to conclude therefore that these contracts, if reached, are necessarily the result of individual error and confusion, let alone desperation. The standard economic presumption of individual and rational self-interest better explains this case than theories of economic duress.

Our analysis of the yellow dog contract within the utilitarian framework is still not complete, however, because we have yet to take into ac-

83. 245 U.S. at 238.

84. On the problems of opportunism in contractual situations, see Muris, *Opportunistic Behavior and the Law of Contracts*, 65 MINN. L. REV. 521 (1981).

count the third-party effects of agreements. The complaint is that union members must bear all the costs of the increased wage structure while the nonunion workers capture the same, if not greater, benefits. This claim seems inconsistent with a concern for the supposed incompetence of nonunion workers, since now nonunion workers are viewed less as the victims of the employers and more as the coexploiters of their union rivals. Nonetheless, as a factual matter there is much truth to this account, though it fails to take into account the ability of unions, especially if unconstrained by a duty of "fair" representation, to exclude outsiders from the benefits of membership. In the extreme case, exclusion takes the form of a closed union shop. Indeed, if unions improved productivity, employers would be willing to forgo yellow dog contracts and share the gains of unionization under a collective bargaining agreement that left both sides better off. Similarly, if yellow dog contracts caused employee demoralization and a resulting drop in productivity, the yellow dog contract would be unattractive. There is therefore no reason for legislative fiat if unionized firms can outperform their nonunionized rivals. If, however, union firms are less efficient than their nonunion rivals, why protect them by imposing legal restrictions upon their competition?

It seems clear that unions have some ways in which they can respond to the efforts of nonunion workers to free ride on union activities. On the other hand, any private responses undertaken by unions will be more costly to them than a legislative ban on the yellow dog contract. But the critical point is that the relevant class of third-party effects embraces all the society at large, not just unions. Suppose a group of producers asked the legislature to prevent rival firms who refused to join their cartel from selling in the market place. The short response is that combination amongst producers is the very thing that the antitrust laws are designed to prevent, so that the nonjoiners are beneficial in undermining monopoly control. Under our principle of neutrality, the nonunion worker is entitled to a similar place of honor, for the yellow dog contract helps constrain the monopolistic practices of unions and thereby reduces the need for direct government control over the unions by the antitrust laws.

Yet it may be said that there is really no social concern with the yellow dog contract at all, at least in those industries with competitive product markets. The union, the argument will run, simply will not be able to extract a monopoly profit because none is to be found. At best, this argument makes the libertarian case in favor of allowing the yellow dog contract decisive. But even if taken on its own terms, the argument is wrong because it ignores the struggle over economic rents[85] that can coexist with

85. "The amount that a factor must earn in its present use to prevent it from transferring to

competitive market structures. To revert to *Hitchman*, all coal deposits are not of equal value, as some are more difficult to extract than others, while some are farther removed from their natural markets. In a competitive system, the low-cost coal will be developed first. But in virtually all markets the aggregate demand will be satisfied only if some more expensive coal is sold as well. The very need to market the expensive coal now is incorporated into the increased capital value of the better situated deposits as economic rents. When a union organizes a mine, it obtains wages or other concessions that appropriate to its membership some portion of the economic rents attributable to the coal without forcing the price of the coal above the competitive level. The firm will of course respond to the threat by taking steps to resist unionization. The struggles over economic rents between mineowners and workers thus follow the familiar pattern, as real resources are expended only to obtain transfer payments, thereby causing substantial efficiency losses even in fully competitive product markets. The yellow dog contract is one low cost device that helps reduce the level of expropriation of rents by hindering union organization. The struggle over rents depends upon the formation of a bilateral monopoly, which is countered whenever employers can adopt contracting strategies that help maintain competitive employment markets.[86] The great irony of *Hitchman*, then is that the location and immobility of the firm's key resource are the source of the economic rents that make the firm more vulnerable to individual exploitation than the individual workers.[87] Workers, to be sure, do not have perfect mobility. Moving away from their homes can disrupt family and personal ties; changing occupations requires them to write off large investments in human capital. But the mass migration of workers through the early part of this century shows that labor has greater mobility than coal buried in the ground.

another use is called its *transfer earnings*; any excess that it earns over this amount is called its *economic rent*." R. LIPSEY & P. STEINER, ECONOMICS 395 (2d ed. 1969).

86. *See* Klein, Crawford & Alchian, *Vertical Integration, Appropriable Rents, and the Competitive Contracting Process*, 21 J.L. & ECON. 297 (1978). The authors identify the quasi-rent value of an asset as "the excess of its value over its salvage value, that is, its value in its next best *use* to another renter." *Id.* at 298. They then note that these quasi-rents can occur in a competitive market, be it in situations in which efforts are made by opportunistic individuals to expropriate gains after two parties have entered into a long-term contract, or in the case closer to that in labor markets, where there is a contest for rents during the precontractual period. *Id.* at 300.

87. The fixed nature of the assets also explains why the firm cannot move to other locations where the labor markets are better, as in the case of the so-called "runaway" plants in textile and other industries. Note too that even where this mobility exists before a plant is opened, it is sharply reduced once a plant is placed in operation.

D. *Picketing*

Picketing is the last practice to be examined under the utilitarian perspective. The analysis is simple enough. To the utilitarian, the general libertarian prohibition against the use of force is granted on the belief that gainful output will be reduced to the inconvenience of all whenever the producer is forced to share his gain with a stranger.[88] Picketing that involves the use of force interferes with transactions that are otherwise beneficial, and it should thus be illegal. With the basic right established, the only question that remains is that of remedy. And here the utilitarian characterization of the problem is made explicit in the desire to reduce the sum of the errors of over- and under-enforcement. The two primary orientations thus yield the same outcome, with the same indeterminacies.

IV. Unfair Labor Practices

The theoretical discussion of the common law rules provides a useful backdrop against which to analyze the major provisions of the Wagner Act.[89] The basic protection to workers under the Act is contained in Section 7, which in its original form guaranteed that "[e]mployees shall have the right to self-organization, to form, join, or assist labor organizations, to bargain collectively through representatives of their own choosing, and to engage in concerted activities, for the purpose of collective bargaining or other mutual aid or protection."[90] Section 8 then sets out a group of five "unfair labor practices"—yet another instance of persuasive definition—that still lie at the heart of American labor legislation.[91] Section 9(a) sets forth the basic structure of labor dynamics as bargaining in "good faith" between the employer and a union, the exclusive representative of the relevant employees:

> Representatives designated or selected for the purposes of collective bargaining by the majority of the employees in a unit appropriate for such purposes, shall be the exclusive representatives of all the em-

88. *See* R. POSNER, ECONOMIC ANALYSIS OF LAW 121-22 (2d ed. 1977).

89. All citations here are to original act, *e.g.*, § 8(1). The modern form of citation, *e.g.*, § 8(a)(1), was introduced when the unfair labor practices by unions were added to the statute under § 8(b).

90. Wagner Act, ch. 372, § 7, 49 Stat. 449, 452 (1935) (codified as amended at 29 U.S.C. § 157 (1982)). The act was subsequently amended to provide that employees "shall also have the right to refrain from any or all of such activities except to the extent that such right may be affected by an agreement requiring membership in a labor organization as a condition of employment as authorized in section 8(a)(3)." Labor Management Relations Act, ch. 120, § 101, 61 Stat. 136, 140 (1947).

91. Ch. 372, § 8, 49 Stat. 449, 452-53 (1935) (codified as amended at 29 U.S.C. § 158 (1982)). Amendments under Taft-Hartley established a similar set of unfair labor practices for unions. Labor Management Relations Act, 61 Stat. 136 (1947), amended, 73 Stat. 519 (1959), 87 Stat. 314 (1973), 88 Stat. 395 (1974) (codified as amended at 29 U.S.C. § 158(a) (1982)). In my view the elaborate provisions of Taft-Hartley were in some measure a union victory, because they kept the original structure of the statute, making it more difficult to return to common law rules.

> ployees in such unit for the purposes of collective bargaining in respect to rates of pay, wages, hours of employment, or other conditions of employment: *Provided*, That any individual employee or a group of employees shall have the right at any time to present grievances to their employer . . . .[92]

It is not possible here to comment at any length on the enormous amount of litigation generated by the statute.[93] What is important, however, is to give some sense of how the structure of the statute has altered the dynamics and the outcomes of labor negotiations. Several questions help mold the general inquiry: (i) How does the statute answer to both the liberty-based and utility-based visions of the law?; (ii) Can any special justification for the statute be found in the necessities of labor relationships?; and (iii) What is the relationship between the substantive rules and the emergence of the modern administrative state?

A. *Section 8(1): Coercion, Interference and Restraint*

Section 8(1) of the original Wagner Act made it an unfair labor practice "to interfere with, restrain, or coerce employees in the exercise of the rights guaranteed in Section 7."[94] On its face, Section 8(1) does not appear to work much of a departure from the previous common law rules. There is no question that the use of force by employers to prevent unionization by workers was both tortious and criminal at common law, and suits for interference with prospective advantage should be available to a union on exactly the same terms and conditions as they are available to the employer. If the statute had confined its operation to the traditional categories, its chief effect would have been to shift jurisdiction of labor disputes from the courts to the National Labor Relations Board. Nonetheless, the Wagner Act was drafted not to enshrine common law principles in the statute, but to throw a larger mantle of protection over unions and union activities, so that as a matter of statutory construction "coercion, restraint and interference" all assumed the broader meaning implicit in

92. 29 U.S.C. § 159(a) (1982).

93. Much of it is collected in B. MELTZER, LABOR LAW: CASES, MATERIALS AND PROBLEMS (2d ed. 1977); R. SMITH, L. MERRIFIELD, & T. ST. ANTOINE, LABOR RELATIONS LAW (6th ed. 1979). For a hornbook treatment of the resulting law, see R. GORMAN, BASIC TEXT ON LABOR LAW, UNIONIZATION AND COLLECTIVE BARGAINING (1976).

94. Ch. 372, § 8, 49 Stat. 449, 452 (1935) (codified as amended at 29 U.S.C. § 158(a)(1) (1982)). This language tracks that of the Norris-LaGuardia Act, 29 U.S.C. § 102 (1982): "[I]t is necessary . . . that [the worker] shall be free from the interference, restraint, or coercion of employers of labor . . . " Norris-LaGuardia merely limits the scope of federal jurisdiction in injunction cases, however, while the Wagner Act creates substantive rights between the parties, *see supra* p. 1386. The constitutional doubts about the original Wagner Act were put to rest in Jones-Laughlin Steel Co. v. NLRB, 301 U.S. 1 (1937). The substantive challenges to the statute were never addressed, as *Adair* and *Coppage* were ignored, not refuted.

the parallel provisions of the Norris-LaGuardia Act.[95] The correlative duties imposed upon employers are therefore far more extensive than the common law, notwithstanding the section's ironic appeal to common law language.[96] In the context of 8(1) this broader construction has affected two types of behavior: attempts by the employer to keep his premises free both from organizational activities of the union and from employer speech.

At common law, the employer, like everyone else, was entitled to the exclusive possession and use of his own property. Persons who wanted to enter[97] or remain upon[98] property could do so only with the owner's consent and under the terms and conditions that he saw fit.

These rules could have been carried over to labor disputes. Nonetheless, in a manner consistent with the general philosophy of the Act, the cases have consistently held that any restriction or prohibition of union activity on company property constitutes an "interference" with Section 7 rights, which must therefore be justified by showing that some competing interest of the employer outweighs the rights of employees under Section 7 of the Act. Within this balancing framework the decisions exhibit a commendable logic. Thus the cases have generally curtailed union activity on the workshop floor during working hours, especially when it may be carried on elsewhere with little disruption, as in the employees' lunchrooms during mealtimes and work breaks.[99] Similarly, the cases have granted the employer a greater right to exclude outside organizers from his premises than to exclude workers already on the premises.[100] And, more questionably perhaps, the cases have given far greater rights to unions seeking economic advantage compared to those who want political influence.[101]

My concern here, however, is not with the reasonableness of the decisions under the statute, but with the soundness of the statute itself. The

95. *See also supra* note 94 (parallel provisions of Norris-La Guardia).

96. *See Hitchman*, 245 U.S. at 263 (Brandeis, J., dissenting).

97. The only exception to the rule was for the rare cases of personal necessity, which applied only to persons in imminent peril of life or limb, and then only on very restrictive terms: The passing of the necessity terminated the privilege, and compensation was required for any damage caused by the entrance. *See, e.g.*, Vincent v. Lake Erie Transp. Co., 109 Minn. 456, 124 N.W. 221 (1910); RESTATEMENT (SECOND) OF TORTS § 263 (1965). *See generally* Bohlen, *Incomplete Privilege to Inflict Intentional Invasions of Interests of Property and Personality*, 39 HARV. L. REV. 307 (1926).

98. *See* W. PROSSER, *supra* note 59, at 73-74: "The trespass may also be committed by remaining on the land after a right of entry has terminated. Thus it is a trespass to refuse to leave after a license to remain has been revoked, or to fail to remove property at the end of an agreed period."

99. Beth Israel Hosp. v. NLRB, 437 U.S. 483 (1978); Republic Aviation Corp. v. NLRB, 324 U.S. 793 (1945). The reach of *Republic Aviation* is shown by the Court's quick rejection of the argument that the anti-solicitation rule could not be an unfair labor practice because it was introduced long before the passage of the statute, 320 U.S. at 804-05, and applied to all solicitations, whether or not labor related, *id.* at 805. Both those points are relevant to the question of employer motive, which is in the balancing process displaced by considerations of the effect of the restriction upon activity.

100. NLRB v. Babcock & Wilcox Co., 351 U.S. 105 (1956).

101. See Hyde, *Economic Labor Law v. Political Labor Relations: Dilemmas for Liberal Legalism*, 60 TEX. L. REV. 1 (1981).

central mistake of the statute as construed is that it introduces any balancing test at all. Any balancing under the Act, however reasonable, quite clearly cuts back upon the absolute power to exclude that is the hallmark of any system of private property.[102] It is wholly incorrect to treat as coercive any action by an employer that works to the economic detriment of union members. The real question is whether a firm should be required to provide an in-kind subsidy to a union regarded as antithetical to its prosperity, and perhaps to its survival. Employers need not make cash contributions to unions; why must they make contributions in kind? If it is argued that access to the property may be critical to an organization drive, then the answer is that denial of access is equally critical to the employer. Here as elsewhere the relative needs of the parties do not in any sense determine the proper set of initial entitlements, but only the subsequent business question whether they will strike some bargain that works to their mutual advantage. There are many ways in which a union could use its own resources to advance its cause, *e.g.*, meetings, leaflets, or campaigns. There is no principled reason why a union should be able to impress a lien upon the property of the employer for its own advantage.

A similar analysis applies to the question of employer speech. In its early decisions, the Labor Board found that any speech by an employer designed to induce its employees to stay out of the union was coercive and improper.[103] In particular, special and vigorous condemnation was found for speeches in which the employer stated that he would bargain hard against the union, close his shop and move elsewhere, or eliminate some of the benefits to which his employees had grown accustomed. As a matter of principle, however, it is hard to imagine how suppression of truthful information could serve the interest of employees faced with deciding where to cast their lot. To be sure, one can understand why a prohibition against employer fraud might be required. But antifraud devices are notoriously difficult to apply to the bluffing that always goes on in hard contractual negotiations, where complex matters of fact are involved. Indeed, if any deviation from the common law rules were to be required, the rules against fraud might be relaxed; the likelihood of a prompt union response is a credible deterrent against fraud, which although imperfect suffers from none of the complexities of the common law action.

Nonetheless, the labor rules go quite beyond that limited objective of the prevention of fraud, attempting to assure something akin to employer

102. The constitutional status of the statute is not the concern here, since the tangled web of cases on the protection afforded possession under the eminent domain clause defies coherent exposition. *See, e.g.*, Loretto v. Teleprompter Manhattan CATV Corp., 458 U.S. 419 (1982); Pruneyard Shopping Center v. Robins, 447 U.S. 74 (1980); Kaiser Aetna v. United States, 444 U.S. 164 (1979).

103. *See* R. GORMAN, *supra* note 93, at 148-49.

neutrality on the question of unionization.[104] The point, however, is hardly one on which employers should be expected to be neutral, given their enormous self-interest in the question of firm organization. Putting to one side the serious constitutional questions, there is no independent account of coercion (or fraud) that can justify in principle the statutory restrictions of the rights of employers to bargain hard and to speak their piece. Speech itself is a proper subject for regulation when it threatens coercive action, but, as before, coercive action must be confined to reach only the threat or use of force or the breach of promise. Speech cannot be redefined as coercive simply by expanding through legislation the list of activities that are prohibited by law. As with the rules of company property, however, the statute appeals to traditional liberal fears of coercion and restraint, but uses them to justify the government control that any sound legal order should condemn.

Section 8(c) of the Taft-Hartley Act[105] reveals the extent to which the rules governing employer speech depart from those required by the principles of defamation and misrepresentation:

> The expressing of any views, argument, or opinion, or the dissemination thereof, whether in written, printed, graphic, or visual form, shall not constitute or be evidence of an unfair labor practice under any of the provisions of this Act, if such expression contains no threat of reprisal or force or promise of benefit.[106]

The section makes perfectly good sense—save for the final "if such expression" clause, which is in truth all that matters. The statute is clearly overbroad in its operation, for it does not ask whether there are less restrictive means to achieve the legitimate end of public control against truly coercive behavior. The "reprisal" language is also prey to all the criticisms of the statutory use of "interference, coercion and restraint" under Section 8(1). The far broader language of "promise of benefit" further compounds the original difficulty: The promise of a benefit is simply not the equal of the threat of force, even if it contains the implicit (but lawful) threat to withhold the benefit if the union is recognized. The current case

104. *See* NLRB v. Federbush Co., 121 F.2d 954, 957 (2d Cir. 1941) (Learned Hand, J.): Arguments by an employer directed to his employees have such an ambivalent character; they are legitimate enough as such, and pro tanto the privilege of "free speech" protects them; but, so far as they also disclose his wishes, as they generally do, they have a force independent of persuasion. The Board is vested with power to measure these two factors against each other, a power whose exercise does not trench upon the First Amendment . . . . What to an outsider will be no more than the vigorous presentation of a conviction, to an employee may be the manifestation of a determination which it is not safe to thwart. The Board must decide how far the second aspect obliterates the first.

105. 29 U.S.C. § 158 (1982).

106. *Id.* § 158(c).

law on the question recognizes that an employer is entitled to say something in opposition to a union. That case law insists, however, that under the statute "an employer is free only to tell 'what he reasonably believes will be the likely economic consequences of unionization that are outside his control'" and is not free to make "threats of economic reprisal to be taken solely on his own volition."[107] One can quarrel with this formulation on the ground that it reduces the law of employer speech to a discourse on grammar, style, and nuance that emphasizes the hidden virtues of the passive voice. But if in fact the basic structure of rights under the NLRA is correct, then this distinction, however murky, is about as serviceable as any that might be adopted. The structure of the NLRA is defective, however, and accordingly the decisive objection to the test is that it fails to explain why economic reprisals short of the use of force can be condemned. If the employer is entitled to close down his plant, or to hire non-union labor, then how can he be prevented from threatening what he has a right to do?[108]

B. *Section 8(2): Company unions*

Section 8(2) makes it illegal "to dominate or interfere with the formation or administration of any labor organization or contribute financial or other support to it."[109] There is little need to dwell at length on its oddities and difficulties. The prohibition against company support and contribution to a union was justified on the ground that company unions make a "sham" of the process of collective bargaining[110] by placing the employer on both sides of the bargaining table. This characterization misstates the nature of the bargaining process: The employers must still bargain with workers to hire and retain them. If the company union imposes costs upon the workers, then the employer will have to make appropriate adjustments elsewhere to maintain the quality of his workforce. Given a company union, the adversity of interest between the parties simply manifests itself before the worker joins the union instead of afterwards, while the protection against opportunism is provided by the at-will feature of the employment agreement. In any case, it is difficult to see why Congress should prohibit by law certain forms of labor organization. In a nation that treasures diversity, why is it so unreasonable for certain workers to decide that they wish to join a company-sponsored union? As with

107. NRLB v. Gissel Packing Co., 395 U.S. 575, 619 (1969) (citing NLRB v. River Togs, Inc., 382 F.2d 198, 202 (2d Cir. 1967)).

108. For an expression of the view that generally one ought to have a right to threaten to do that which one has a right to do, see Epstein, *Blackmail, Inc.*, 50 U. CHI. L. REV. 553 (1983).

109. 29 U.S.C. § 158(a)(2) (1982).

110. *See, e.g.*, 78 CONG. REC. 3443 (1934) (statement of Senator Wagner).

yellow dog contracts, workers will not surrender their rights to remain out of the company's orbit for nothing, and they may well gain substantial benefits from the internal procedures that prevent individual grievances from becoming the source of major employee discontent.

Making employer sponsorship of worker participation an unfair labor practice protects not the workers in the plant, but rather the unions that might want to organize the workers. Yet even here the irony is clear, for the prohibition against company "contributions" complicates negotiations for unions that have gained representation rights under the statute. Every union must obtain funds from its members, funds which typically come out of wages. The union and the employer may well wish to negotiate a direct payment from the firm to the union if that is agreeable to both.[111] As this is prohibited by the statute,[112] however, the union must collect the dues from its members. It is generally cheapest for the union to do so through a dues check-off system with the employer. This dues check-off is allowed under the statute, but cannot be imposed over the objection of the employer.[113] From the union point of view, however, a dues check-off is inferior to direct payment because it does not permit the charges to be levied against non-member workers within the bargaining unit. Here as before, the entire structure of the Act depends upon its perverse limitation of freedom of contract, which necessarily requires the substitution of a regime of complicated arrangements for simpler ones.

C. *Section 8(3): Dismissal Motivated by Union Affiliation*

Section 8(3) forbids the employer "by discrimination in regard to hire or tenure of employment or any term or condition of employment to encourage or discourage membership in any labor organization."[114] This language makes it an unfair labor practice for an employer to hire only workers who agree not to join any union. The limitations under Section 8(3) are far greater than the simple legislative prohibition of the yellow dog contract. No employer needs a yellow dog contract to fire workers who decide to organize or join a union. A contract at will is quite sufficient for that purpose; at common law, the explicit contractual provision

111. The employer might not want to provide a service which costs the union little and contributes materially to its strength. The real cost to the employer is the enhanced power conferred upon the union, not the tiny administrative expenses; yet to speak of them without sufficient justification is to invite charges of unfair labor practices under § 8(5) of the Act. Again, therefore, candor yields to a discussion of irrelevant points of detail. But then the sensible response is to allow the employer to refuse to provide either dues check-offs or direct payments unless he agrees to do so by contract.

112. 29 U.S.C. § 158(a)(2) (1982).

113. H. K. Porter Co. v. NLRB, 397 U.S. 99 (1970).

114. 29 U.S.C. § 158(a)(3) (1982).

was critical against third-party inducement, as in *Hitchman*.[115] The arguments against the anti-yellow dog provisions of Norris-LaGuardia apply a fortiori to the far more intrusive restrictions of the Wagner Act. The employer must continue to employ individuals whose loyalties are known to clash with their duties toward the employer, even though the success of the operation of the firm may well depend upon complete loyalty. Nor can it be said that the issue is a minor affair, though Holmes characterized it as such in his dissent in *Adair*. Membership in a union may be only one feature of a contract that contains a vast number of terms, but it is the one term that skews all the rest. Unions fought hard for Section 8(3) because they perceived it as critical to their success; one can easily imagine their response to its possible repeal.

It may be urged nonetheless that Section 8(3) is needed to protect workers not against the employer as such, but against foremen who engage in various capricious actions against the employee, including demands for favors and kickbacks.[116] The remedy for this ill, if it exists, is not the passage of Section 8(3) or any other labor statute. The problem is one of conflict of interest between principal and agent, often discussed under the heading of "agency costs."[117] Any abuse by the foreman diverts income from the employer and reduces the profitability of his operations, for while kickbacks may come out of the pockets of employees, the economic effect is indistinguishable from a direct payment of part of the workers' wages by the firm to the foreman. Since the workers care about their net salary, they will demand higher wages to compensate for the loss. The firm therefore has a strong financial incentive to monitor the behavior of its supervisory personnel wholly apart from Section 8(3).

The institutional structures established by Section 8(3) impose additional costs as well. The preferences of firms for non-union labor will not disappear with the passage of a statute. Indeed, since the statute increases the costs of unionization to the employer, unions will be less welcome after the Act than before it. As such, we should expect that employers will take elaborate measures to avoid unionization when they are barred from resorting to the simple contractual expedient. Efforts (often surreptitious) may be made to screen prospective employees for their past union affilia-

115. Adair v. United States, 208 U.S. 161, 191 (1908) (Holmes, J., dissenting). The definition of "employer" contained in § 2(3) was modified to exclude "any individual employer as a supervisor." On the origins of this important structural provision, see R. GORMAN, *supra* note 93, at 34-35. This definitional exception places a very powerful roadblock against union power, and the balance under the statute would be very different without it. It is one of the features that helps keep the balance of power under the Act.

116. *See* Winter, *supra* note 75, at 24-25.

117. *See generally* Jensen & Meckling, *Theory of the Firm: Managerial Behavior, Agency Costs and Ownership Structure*, 3 J. FIN. ECON. 305 (1976) (discussing conflicts of interests that pervade principal-agent relationships).

tions or present union sympathies. The organization, practices, and layout of a plant may be restructured to make it difficult for a union to know what workers do or where they live. These counterstrategies may constitute unfair labor practices under the statute, but the risk of their being identified as such will be treated in part as one of the costs that the firm is prepared to bear in order to escape the union. Whether the stratagems succeed or fail, it is quite clear that the statute channels resources into anti-unionization efforts—including the ubiquitous employer consultants. These same resources could be spent on the production of real goods and services if employers were allowed to use contractual measures to meet their objectives, which are, it must be stressed, legitimate under any normative overview of the question.

D. *Bargaining in "Good Faith"*

There is still a need to consider the last of the key unfair labor practices, that of an employer's refusal to bargain—judicially construed to mean bargaining in "good faith"—with the union, a mandate closely and necessarily linked to the exclusive representation provisions of Section 9. The question itself requires an examination of the relationships between the employer and the union and between the union and its members.

1. *Conflicts Between Employer and Union*

In order to understand the dramatic impact that the Wagner Act has had on employer-union relations, it is necessary to recall that the common law imposed no regulatory obstacles upon any collective bargaining agreement. Such agreements did occur before the passage of the Wagner Act, and their provisions were rightly held to bind employers as well as employees.[118] Yet here, as with individual contracts of employment, a court's sole function was to enforce agreements already made. It did not have to coerce the agreement itself; nor was it required to police the environment in which an agreement was being negotiated, beyond applying the usual rules of fraud and duress.

118. *See* Schlesinger v. Quinto, 201 A.D. 487, 498 (1922). There can of course be difficulties in enforcing these collective bargaining agreements. The union may be treated as an unincorporated association that has no legal status, *see, e.g.*, Karges Furniture Co. v. Amalgamated Woodworkers' Local Union No. 131, 165 Ind. 421, 75 N.E. 877 (1905); Pickett v. Walsh, 192 Mass. 572, 589, 78 N.E. 753, 760 (1906), which therefore could not sue or be sued in its own name. Other problems may stem from the fact that a collective bargaining agreement is not the same as an individual contract for employment, but only creates "a trade agreement" which forms the basis for individual employment contracts. *See* J.I. Case Co. v. NLRB, 321 U.S. 332, 335 (1944). These difficulties could have been resolved in ways that eliminate the obstacles against contractual freedom, however, rather than ways that override it. The judgment of Justice Jackson in *J.I. Case* contains the clearest possible acceptance (if not to say endorsement) of the principle that individual vested rights under a contract must yield to the collective good in order to implement the statutory scheme of the labor acts.

The passage of the Act, however, radically changed the nature of labor negotiations. In the previous situation, any refusal to make an agreement meant only that there was no agreement. Breaches of the duty to bargain in "good faith" were generally confined largely to matters of fraud in the inducement of contract. Otherwise the duty of good faith was confined to the infrequent cases in which there was some (non-negligent) precontractual "justifiable" reliance by the other party.[119] Limited in this way, the principle of "good faith" clearly has no bite in the area of labor relations, as employers easily can avoid the twin pitfalls of pre-contractual reliance and misrepresentation. One alternative is simply to refuse to negotiate with a union at all. Still another is explicitly to inform the union as a precondition to negotiation that it will have to bear its own costs in the event that some agreement is not reached.

The statute changes the legal environment, however, by imposing an affirmative duty to bargain. It demands therefore a theory of good faith consistent with the expanded duties that it imposes. Such a theory is not easy to develop. To be sure, one can begin to solve the problem by making the obvious point that the obligations require parties to comply with elaborate procedural requirements about the times and conditions of negotiations. Nonetheless one may also wish to honor the statute's ostensible support of freedom of contract by insisting (as did the Taft-Hartley provisions) that the obligation to bargain collectively in good faith "does not compel either party to agree to a proposal or require the making of a concession."[120] Yet there is an enormous gulf between a statute that rules out the obvious extremes and a workable rule for the many cases in which negotiations do not end in agreement. The case law on the question is an exercise in futility.[121]

The difficulties with the duty to bargain in good faith under the labor statute are perhaps clarified by a comparison with the issue of settlement in both the civil and the criminal law. In the civil case, litigation is settled

119. "[The law] has to provide for the restoration of the *status quo* by giving the injured party his negative interest or reliance damages. The careless promissor has only himself to blame when he has created for the other party the false appearance of a binding obligation. This is the meaning of *culpa in contrahendo.*" Kessler & Fine, Culpa in Contrahendo, *Bargaining in Good Faith, and Freedom of Contract: A Comparative Study*, 77 HARV. L. REV. 401, 402 (1964).

Kessler and Fine then give other instances in which the doctrine of *culpa in contrahendo* has been applied: incomplete agreements, informal agreements, silence, and want of an intention to contract. *Id.* at 412-20. None of these impose restrictions of any institutional importance for labor-management relations.

120. *See* National Labor Relations Act, § 8(d), 29 U.S.C. § 158(d) (1982), which was added to the Act in 1947.

121. For examples of the types of problems courts encounter in defining "good faith," *see, e.g.*, NLRB v. General Elec. Co., 418 F.2d 736 (2d Cir. 1969), *cert. denied* 397 U.S. 965 (1970); NLRB v. Katz, 369 U.S. 736 (1962); NLRB v. Insurance Agents' Int'l Union, 361 U.S. 477 (1960); NLRB v. Truitt Mfg. Co., 351 U.S. 149 (1956); NLRB v. American Nat'l Ins. Co., 343 U.S. 395 (1952).

with each party acting under the threat of coercion from the other side.[122] In contrast to most markets, neither party can go elsewhere if he does not like the offer received from the opposing side. The same is true about plea bargaining in the criminal context; the accused does not go free if he cannot strike a deal with the prosecutor.[123] With the duty to bargain in good faith, the labor situation is transformed from the market case to the litigation case. Protracted negotiations can take place to determine the ultimate outcome of what is, when all is said and done, a legally created bilateral monopoly. No nascent standard of good faith effectively constrains these negotiations, any more than it does for civil settlement or plea bargaining. The most that good faith can demand is that the parties not press claims or defenses known by them to be groundless. But this constraint is of virtually no relevance in the labor context, where the matters in dispute are economic demands, rather than the soundness of legal theories.

In civil litigation a bilateral monopoly results whenever voluntary transactions fail. Because there is no competition between borrowers in the collection market, resort to state-controlled coercion is indispensable. Likewise, the monopoly control of the state over criminal enforcement makes it quite impossible to avoid the bilateral monopoly problem under any system of criminal prosecution, with either public or private enforcement. Yet employment negotiations provide no comparable necessity for the creation of a complex institutional structure at contract formation. On matters of money and conditions of employment, the very notion of good faith has no internal intellectual coherence because there is no theory of the just contractual outcome to which it can be tied. All that can be done is to penalize individuals for candor (as with Boulwarism)[124] or inexperience, and to inject an element of public oversight that can only complicate any real negotiation.

Even without the passage of the Wagner Act, one can expect some very difficult negotiations between employers and workers over the division of the pie. Yet the statute, by making the union the exclusive bargaining representative, increases both the costs of negotiations and the likelihood that no effective agreement will be reached. The parties will play "non-cooperative" games with each other; their bluff and bluster will increase the chances of a strike, even if both sides would have been better off with

122. *See* Cook v. Wright, 1 B. & S. 559, 568-69, 121 Eng. Rep. 822, 826 (Q.B. 1861).

123. For a discussion of the difficult bilateral monopoly problems in plea bargaining, see Easterbrook, *Criminal Justice as a Market System*, 12 J. LEGAL STUD. 289, 291 (1983).

124. The practice involved the decision of the employer to make one "fair, firm offer" to the union which it treated as inflexible. The offer was also accompanied by a barrage of publicity designed to persuade the workers that the union demands were astronomical. *See* NLRB v. General Elec. Co., 418 F.2d 736, 756-62 (2d Cir. 1969) (practice violates § 8(a)(5)).

some agreement sparing them the extensive costs of strikes.[125] Matters only become more complicated when the response to unionization includes the possibility of industry-wide bargaining, or the concentration of economic pressure on some firms in the industry, perhaps after a quick settlement with others.[126] The increased frequency of impasse in turn gives greater scope to the Act's unfair labor provisions, which are sufficiently elastic to allow a colorable claim to be filed with the Board whether or not some agreement is reached. The creation of exclusive rights of representation coupled with duties to bargain shows the want of wisdom in replacing simple institutional arrangements with very complex ones.

The bargaining structure under the Act also increases third-party costs, as other individuals and firms are forced to reorganize their own affairs to respond to increased costs and lower reliability of the current labor structure.[127] Tracing the consequences through a chain of customers and suppliers raises administrative complexities sufficient to daunt the spirit of any common law court, which largely explains the common law's unwillingness to give much protection for interference with prospective advantage.[128] The preferred solution is to eliminate the structures that cause these dislocations. As political pressures have prevented the repeal of the Wagner Act, the response to the unfortunate status quo ante has been further government intervention to restore some balance to the system. The insistence upon "good faith" negotiations is one such effort. "Cooling off" periods and special congressional mandates to suspend or limit particular strikes are another;[129] federal limitations on secondary boycotts are yet a third;[130] and federal mediation services a fourth.[131] Yet since no one

125. The 1982 strike by the National Football League Players is a good example of such a situation. For an account of the strike, see *The NFL Players Run Out of Time*, BUS. WEEK, Nov. 29, 1982, at 35-36.

126. For the modern case law, see American Shipbuilding Co. v. NLRB, 380 U.S. 300 (1965); NLRB v. Brown, 380 U.S. 278 (1965).

127. These costs should obviously be taken into account under a utilitarian analysis. They must be considered under a libertarian perspective as well, for these dislocations are the product of improper statutory restrictions upon the freedom of the employer's right to negotiate at will with whomever he pleases.

128. *See, e.g.*, Robins Dry Dock & Repair Co. v. Flint, 275 U.S. 303, 308 (1927); Byrd v. English, 117 Ga. 191, 194, 43 S.E. 419, 420-21 (1903). *See generally* Rizzo, *The Theory of Economic Loss in the Law of Torts*, 11 J. LEGAL STUD. 281, 291-96 (1982) (limited recovery for loss of prospective advantage designed to "channel" suits through limited number of plaintiffs).

129. *See* Labor Management Relations Act, §§ 201, 206-210, 29 U.S.C. §§ 171, 176-180 (1982). Section 201 states the problems under the old order. Sections 206 to 210 address the mandatory powers of the President in emergency situations, and include the powers to enjoin both strikes and lockouts.

130. *See* National Labor Relations Act, §§ 8(b)(4) to 8(b)(7), 29 U.S.C. §§ 158(b)(4)-158(b)(7) (1982).

131. Section 202 of the Labor Management Relations Act, 29 U.S.C. § 172 (1982), creates the Federal Mediation and Conciliation Service, whose powers are defined in § 203 of the Act, 29 U.S.C. § 173 (1982).

can fine tune so complicated a mechanism, every effort at adjustment itself imposes additional tensions upon the system. The elimination of the basic structure is necessary, not the further embellishment of the regulatory pyramid.

2. *Conflicts Between Employees*

Sections 8(5) and 9(a) are also troublesome from the perspective of the employee as well as the employer. When the statute says that employers may not enter into direct negotiations with individual employees over the terms and conditions of employment, it imposes restrictions upon employees and employers alike. The justification offered for this exclusive right of negotiation is that without it the employer will skim off the best workers and discriminate against union supporters, thereby depriving the union of its strength. The discussion of this issue in connection with the yellow dog contract is sufficient to show that, while the factual assertion may be true, the asserted equation of the union with the social interest is not.

The problem here goes to the root of representative government. Under the older common law system, in the original position, each individual worker had a clear and well-defined set of rights good against the world. He was therefore entitled to bargain those rights away to either the union or the employer for whatever consideration he saw fit. The determination of rights under the system of collective bargaining creates far greater stress. Now no party derives its rights by agreement from a clear original position. Instead, a majority of the workers within an appropriate unit may choose the union as the bargaining representative of that unit. Thereafter the union represents both its supporters and its opponents within the unit, whether or not they are union members. The original entitlements are very much in doubt. The "union" interest itself is no unitary whole, but instead a complex amalgam of the individual interests of the many actors who play on the expanded stage. It is no accident that extensive administrative procedures are needed to determine the contours of an "appropriate bargaining unit" and to enforce fiduciary duties for the protection of minority interests.

In defining bargaining units, no vote can determine who is eligible to vote, nor can any simple principle, like territoriality or citizenship, serve that function. Voluntary arrangements are excluded by the very structure of the Act, for even if the union and the employer agree on the definition of the unit, and their determination is accepted by the Board, that determination is made in a legal environment where the employer is subject to statutory obligations that effectively limit his domain of choice. With negotiation from a set of original entitlements precluded, only a complex but formless weighing of "relevant factors" remains. Does one establish units by plant, by firm, or by craft? Is an agreement between the union and the company sufficient on the question? Or must the interests of anti-union workers or rival unions be taken into account? What about potential employees? The various shifts in preference between large trade unions and small craft unions reflect not only the powerful political divisions on the Board[132] but the utter impossibility of finding any neutral principle of coerced organization to replace the consensual formation of unions.[133] In addition, a host of tactical questions arise within a regulatory framework where an employer cannot simply walk away from a demand for unionization. Should the employer agree to a union for some fraction of its work force, hoping to stave off the unionization of its entire operation? Does a union have sufficient strength in certain core areas to risk seeking a plant-wide unit? What position, if any, should an employer take when it fears one of two rival unions more than another? Any system that allows unionization will have to bear some costs of organization. But at least the principle of selection in a voluntary system is clear enough. Those who agree to join are members, and none else. The statutory scheme imposes a much more complicated regime. Its costs are evident enough. Where are the benefits?

The problem of protecting the interests of a minority within a union is equally complex. One might allow the union to parcel out the benefits of unionization within the unit in any way it chooses, subject only to the constraint of continuing to command the support of a majority of the unit. This constraint is not as trivial as it sounds: If the union pushes too hard on some minority group within it, it risks the loss of that minority's support or even possible decertification if the minority was previously the block whose support allowed the union to command a majority. The possible gains from unionization can be distributed in countless ways without running afoul of these constraints. So too where the industry is in decline, although the distribution of losses in wages and benefits raises even more acute problems.

What additional legal constraints might limit the powers of unions to distribute the pie in whatever manner they see fit? There is the obvious fear that a union (or its dominant coalition) will discriminate on the basis of race, sex, religion, or national origin to benefit some members at the expense of others. Indeed, the duty of "fair representation," read into the

132. On the impact of politics on the composition of the Board, see F. McCulloch & T. Bornstein, The National Labor Relations Board 60-62, 107-09, 112-14 (1974).

133. For examples of the issues involved in certifying a bargaining unit under the NLRA, *see, e.g.*, Local 1325, Retail Clerks Int'l Ass'n v. NLRB, 414 F.2d 1194 (D.C. Cir. 1969); Mallinckrodt Chem. Works, 162 N.L.R.B. 387 (1966).

Wagner Act as a counterweight to union power, addressed these forms of discrimination even before the passage of the modern anti-discrimination laws.[134] This restraint, however, covers only a tiny fraction of the possible situations. Within a single unit, for example, the majority of unskilled workers may capture much of the surplus created by unionization for themselves by reducing the wage differentials between skilled and unskilled workers. The same problem may occur with the merger of separate seniority lists arising from the merger of separate plants or firms.[135] In the extreme case, individual workers may be required to give up benefits they secured under contract before the recognition of the union.[136] Yet even if some prohibition were placed upon tampering with vested rights, there is little to prevent the dominant coalition within the union from undercutting their value by reducing the future share of the common pool for the protected workers.[137]

As the problem itself arises from the unconstrained operation of majority will, the only bulwark against these abuses must depend upon some rule of "fairness" for the distribution of the surplus among all possible claimants. This theory of fairness cannot emerge from a consistent view of individual rights to liberty and property, for that theory flatly condemns the system of coerced collective bargaining on which labor law rests. The required vision of fairness therefore must come from a theory of forced exchanges. That theory, which lies at the root of a theory of eminent domain, in turn requires that those whose rights are taken receive in exchange rights that leave them at least as well off as before.[138] Unfortunately, difficulties block the application of this theory in the labor context.

First, the baseline against which the subsequent benefits should be measured must be determined. In principle this baseline could be the position that an individual worker would have achieved under the common law system; however, this is the one baseline which the labor law, with its insistence upon "full" freedom of contract, has rejected. The common law baseline could bar certain distributions reached under collective agreements, including any in which some workers receive less under collective

134. The first important case was Steele v. Louisville & Nashville R.R. 323 U.S. 192 (1944), which held that the Railway Labor Act imposed on a labor organization representing a craft or class of employees, the duty not to discriminate on the basis of race in the course of representation. Although *Steele* was decided under the Railway Labor Act, the same principles have been carried over to the National Labor Relations Act. Miranda Fuel Co., 140 N.L.R.B. 181 (1962) (employee right to fair and impartial treatment under the NLRA).

135. *See generally* Freed, Polsby & Spitzer, *Unions, Fairness, and the Conundrums of Collective Choice*, 56 S. CAL. L. REV. 462 (1982).

136. *See generally id.* at 484-87 (noting possibility of prospective wage adjustments).

137. *See* J.I. Case Co. v. NLRB, 321 U.S. 332, 338-39 (1944).

138. *See* Michelman, *Property, Utility, and Fairness: Comments on the Ethical Foundations of "Just Compensation" Law*, 80 HARV. L. REV. 1165 (1967).

bargaining than they did before unionization. These workers may not currently be willing to leave the union because their alternative sources of employment may be still less attractive: The restrictive practices of unions may make it difficult to find employment elsewhere within the industry and the aggrieved employees may be unable to transfer their acquired skills and contracts—their specific human capital—to a new line of work. It is difficult to guess the frequency with which this might happen, but as to the possibility there can be no doubt; the labor cases make it clear that the existing contract rights of workers do not survive the institution of collective bargaining.[139]

Let us suppose, however, that we can get over the baseline difficulty. There remains the problem of distributing the surplus. In the classical eminent domain situation, the surplus takes the form of a public good which by virtue of its non-exclusive nature is necessarily shared by the individuals taxed or otherwise charged with the cost of the taking. The subsequent distribution by the state is therefore unproblematic.[140] Unionization, by contrast, creates no nonappropriable public good, but only a complex network of institutions to distribute the cash or in-kind benefits to its members. As to the distribution of this surplus, the theory of eminent domain provides no clue.

The implications should be clear. Within the framework of individual rights, it is proper to accept Hobbes's injunction that the determinants of contractual fairness lie in the "appetites of the contracting parties." No one need undertake the impossible task of forming a theory of substantive justice in exchange, sufficient to cover all exchanges. The complex structures under the labor statute increase the need for a substantive theory but decrease the likelihood of finding it. State-protected unions mirror the problems of collective governance in the larger political context. While the political process is governed by an elaborate constitutional mechanism designed to curtail the excesses of majoritarianism with a finely honed catalogue of individual rights and limitations on state power, collective bargaining does not confront the parallel issues of public governance that it raises. To quarrel with how courts resolve individual cases is, again, to miss the central point. Their "deference" in these matters can be traced not only to a basic sympathy to the underlying Act, but also to the impossibility of developing a coherent theory of fairness for collective choice

139. *See supra* note 118.

140. The original insight that the regulation should leave those who are burdened by it better off in the long run than they were before dates from Michelman, *supra* note 138, at 1214–24. For my own reformulation of the position, see Epstein, *supra* note 14. For its application in the private law context, see Epstein, *Nuisance Law: Corrective Justice and its Utilitarian Constraints*, 8 J. LEGAL STUD. 49 (1979).

within the union context sufficiently powerful to override union determinations to the contrary.

The basic structure of the Wagner Act also precludes its effective justification on utilitarian grounds. As any surplus (or deficit) obtained by the union is not uniquely appropriated, the statute has in effect created a "common pool" of assets for members of the union, with the well-known attendant difficulties.[141] Resources are dissipated, if not by overfishing, then by political action undertaken to increase shares while simultaneously shrinking the total size. The battle will often be intense because a union protected by government order will be able to appropriate economic rents from firm-specific resources[142] and perhaps monopoly profits from industry-wide cartelization. Any worker who leaves the union will not be able to share in those profits. For this reason, the "exit" rights that are so important, for example, in disciplining capital markets, are far less reliable in the labor context, as workers are reluctant to shift jobs and abandon their share of the collective surplus. To avoid these problems, sensible legislation removes resources from common pools. The labor statutes place them there.

The conflicts brought on by the New Deal legislation also send out false signals to other product and labor markets. Thus where the union collapses the wage differential between skilled and unskilled workers, it reduces the incentives for individual workers to acquire those skills. Likewise, the presentation to the employer of a wage scale that does not accurately reflect the marginal levels of productivity will lead him at the margin to substitute, for example, capital improvements for high-priced unskilled workers.[143] The ultimate consequences of these distortions are beyond the power of lawyers (and perhaps economists) to measure, but there is no reason to believe that on balance they bring about an increase in levels of output, be it by worker or firm, industry or nation. The declining success of heavily unionized industries—steel, textiles, automobiles—is not some unfortunate coincidence unrelated to the central structures of American labor law. It is far more likely that it is the necessary outgrowth of a system that shrinks the pie for the benefit of those workers (typically those employees protected by seniority) and those offi-

141. *See generally* Sweeney, Tollison & Willett, *Market Failure, the Common-Pool Problem, and Ocean Resource Exploitation*, 17 J.L. & ECON. 179 (1974).

142. See the earlier discussion on the same point for yellow dog contracts, *supra* pp. 1370-75.

143. The distributional questions within unions are also relevant to one possible explanation of union behavior, which is that unions have to prevent outsiders from freeloading upon the wage scales that they develop at positive cost in their negotiations with employees. Assuming this concern to be valid, the union can control for the issue by trying to limit the circulation of the scale, which may in fact be very difficult to do. Nonetheless it is doubtful that any employer would want to rely upon the union differentials in setting his own standards because the internal union conflicts make it a very bad measuring rod for wage differentials in a nonunion setting where these problems are less acute.

cials who gain from the short-term maintenance of a supra-competitive wage structure.

V. The New Deal in Context

Having looked at its basic structure, we are now in a position to evaluate the Wagner Act in its relationship to the New Deal and the rise of the administrative state. The central theme concerns the relationship between substantive rules and the administrative structures that are necessary to enforce them. The simpler the rules, the easier it is to implement them by ordinary common law procedures; in part the simplicity of the common law rules, and their substance, are a reflection of the administrative limitations of courts. A collective rule that recognizes the individual right to exclude others from the property one owns, for example, transfers the balancing of interests to private parties, leaving the role of the state to enforce the private determinations so made. A rule that requires balancing of two types of rights—private property and rights of organization under Section 7, for example—demands a far greater level of public supervision. There is little need for the NLRB under a sensible version of common law rules, for the one thing that courts know well is the law of contract, property, and torts. And as we have seen, from these simple tools, one could fashion virtually all of the rules of labor relations. The labor statute, in contrast, breeds a need for administrative expertise. If ordinary judges cannot be expected to understand the intricacies of the tax code, how can they be expected to do better under the labor code? The need for administrative control is also critically shaped by the substantive rights and duties created under the statute. What court could determine the boundaries of a proper bargaining unit? And what court could supervise an election to see that it is not conducted in an "unfair" manner, as that term is defined by the statute? There are too many possibilities and too many parties to handle the question in ordinary litigation. Indeed, as there is no obvious plaintiff or defendant, adversary litigation will not do. We have no system of rights but an elaborate balancing of interests that invites and lends justification to the administrative process.

The same theme emerges from the structure of the unfair labor practices. As virtually every labor disagreement becomes the source of a possible legal dispute, it is very difficult to place upon the courts the enormous burden of sifting through these cases. An administrative board to relieve the stress gains an obvious sort of appeal, if only as a filter for unmeritorious claims. In the same vein, the remedial aspirations of the labor statutes are far greater than those of the common law. The common law spared itself massive complications when it enforced contracts at will. Within the administrative framework, damages and injunctions are only part of the picture. There are also elaborate rules for reinstatement of individual workers and complex rules for *post hoc* changes in union elections that go beyond the powers of courts of equity, which balked at any form of specific performance in labor contracts. The basic structure of the Wagner Act thus forges a powerful commitment to an administrative government to which courts will be required to give great deference.

Why should anyone want to adopt this structure? We are told that it is done in the name of industrial peace and industrial democracy. As regards the first we can assume the end is a good, but question whether the statute is the means to achieve it. Mandatory bargaining by exclusive representatives increases the likelihood of bilateral monopolies that reduce the likelihood of agreement.[144]

There remains the question of violence. In principle the response should be clear: Violence should be punished no matter who is responsible. But it is mistaken to ignore the heavy social costs that may be associated with its suppression, especially if there is widespread political support for those who have committed it. Here, therefore, it may be suggested that the purpose of the statute is to defuse violence that might otherwise occur by offering some improved chances of unionization. Yet support for the statute on this ground is itself fraught with peril. It is simply a pragmatic argument which says that sometimes it is better to surrender to the threat of illegal force than it is to resist it. What is lost is any prudential argument that these structures ought to be preserved as of right even in a world without violence. It therefore becomes a purely tactical question of whether the rest of society is better off with the adoption of the New Deal labor legislation or with the punishment of violence when it occurs.

Indeed, those prudential grounds could be used in ways inimical to the legitimate interests of unions. What, for example, could be said against those who support making unions illegal (as criminal conspiracies no less) on the ground that they are a breeding ground for violence which can only be controlled by powerful and draconian measures? One answer rests on the empirical assertion that these measures will be overbroad, but a complete answer must recognize that overbreadth exists only in relationship to some permitted end, which in turn rests upon some prior and independent conception of entitlement. That point in turn depends upon the further acceptance of the proposition (skirting the antitrust difficulty) that the voluntary combined activities of workers for their common good are themselves lawful if pursued by proper means. But it is this same independent sense of entitlement that supports the case of the employer to control the use and operation of his business by the same means, even when faced by

144. *See supra* p. 1396.

the threat of violence. To leap too quickly to the question of social costs is to ignore the question of entitlements altogether. To protect voluntary associations from violence from without, however, is itself a neutral principle that should be applied to both unions and employers.

An analogy to the issue of freedom of speech is appropriate. In certain cases it is said that speakers should not be allowed to air their views because others may respond with violence. Yet the general answer is that no one should (save in very extreme situations) be allowed to suppress the rights of another by committing or threatening a wrong. The speech should be protected and the violence punished or prevented if or when it occurs. If anticipatory measures are needed, they should be narrowly tailored to the evil at hand.[145]

Another analogy comes from the law of self-defense. There, a defendant who does not use excessive force may inflict harm upon a plaintiff that exceeds the harm which he expects to suffer—again on the principle that those in the right need not yield as a matter of course to those in the wrong. These same principles can be extended to labor disputes. If an employer wants to employ only non-union labor, his right (and it is a right) should be abridged only as a last resort when those opposed to his decision might take to the streets. There are, of course, problems in the administration of justice and in the control of the police, but initially these are best handled by direct reform of criminal and safety procedures and not by the introduction of an elaborate scheme of labor relations ill-tailored to the evil to be avoided.

It is also said that participation in democracy is essential to industrial stability. Here again the implicit analogy is to the general structure of government which in this country rightly takes democratic lines. The analogy is nonetheless flawed. The basic problem in general political theory is the question of political obligation: Why is it that any individual owes obedience to the commands of the state? Since Locke, the extensive efforts to account for the state have frequently appealed to notions of consent, however attenuated. The argument against this line is that the attenuated forms are often or wholly fictional, so that the obligation to the state in the end rests upon an uneasy mixture of consent and necessity: Given any vision of individual rights, some limited form of collective control is better than the anarchy that it replaces. By this version, democracy is required because voluntary transactions, however numerous and complex, fail to generate a single group of individuals vested with a monopoly of force within the jurisdiction.[146] Yet in the labor context, voluntary agree-

145. On picketing, see *supra* p. 1376-79.

146. Indeed, it is the inability by voluntary agreement for a single protective association to obtain a monopoly of force within a jurisdiction which explains why libertarian accounts of a state as a

ments by contract are a perfectly viable mechanism for social organization: The state with its monopoly of force is already in place. In the political context, we appeal to democracy because the building blocks of contract, property, and tort fail, singly and in combination, to account for any monopoly of force within the jurisdiction. Yet once the basic political order is assured, there is no reason to take the second-best alternative in labor relations when the best is still available. Those workers who want to form voluntary organizations should be allowed to do so. It is not part of a tradition of voluntarism or democracy to grant workers the power to conscript the employer and dissenting workers into the service of their cause.

It may be said that workers will be alienated from their jobs without the protection of the union. This argument cannot explain the fraction of workers who would rather deal with the employer directly. In no event can it justify the basic structural decision of the Wagner Act that forbids employers to negotiate contracts of employment directly with workers without union intercession, even with regard to their individual grievances under the collective agreement.[147] To repeat the central point, an argument against the Norris-LaGuardia Act and the Wagner Act is not an argument against unions as such. It is an argument against the special privileges and immunities that these statutes confer upon them. Where unions are necessary to foster communication, they can emerge in any voluntary situation, in a form less formal and less adversarial than it is today. The frequently cited goals of labor organization do not justify the essential features of the modern law.

Calvert Magruder wrote of the Wagner Act shortly after its passage:

> We seem to be moving slowly toward a more rational relationship between capital and labor. For the greater part of the past half century, the law tended, on the whole, to retard this consummation. In the latter years its influence, decisively, has been in the right direction. Such progress as we have made has been at needless cost of blood and tears, and economic wastage. If employers would accept with right good will the principles of the National Labor Relations Act, as the carriers generally have accepted its sister Act, it would mean: Away with yellow dogs, company unions, blacklists, deputy sheriffs in the pay of employers, barricades, tear gas, machine guns,

purely voluntary organization must fail. For an effort to overcome the difficulty by positing a set of "visible hand" explanations, see R. NOZICK, *supra* note 29, at 10-25. These explanations do not, however, eliminate the need to develop a good theory of forced exchanges.

147. *See* Vaca v. Sipes, 386 U.S. 171 (1967) (good faith judgment of a union not to take an individual claim to arbitration does not violate duty of fair representation); Feller, *A General Theory of the Collective Bargaining Agreement*, 61 CALIF. L. REV. 663 (1973); Summers, *The Individual Employee's Rights Under the Collective Agreement: What Constitutes Fair Representation*, 126 U. PA. L. REV. 251 (1977).

> vigilante outrages, espionage, and all that miserable brood of union-smashing detective agencies. Can anyone doubt the cordial response labor would make to such a gesture? The old ways will not work, could not work, really. It is time for an act of faith.[148]

No one can quarrel with the power of Magruder's prose. The strength of his arguments, both positive and normative, is quite another matter. In particular, there is no theory of behavior which can explain why labor will give a "cordial" response under the labor acts. While a theory of individual self-interest may not unlock all the secrets of family behavior or religious belief, it is by far the best predictor of behavior between strangers in an economic setting. That theory predicts that unions and their members (like employers) will press for their maximum advantage after the passage of the Act as well as before. There is a theory of "sunk benefits" as well as a theory of sunk costs. That theory of self-interest predicts that unions will never make voluntary concessions tomorrow because of an indefeasible benefit they have received today. On the normative level, too, Magruder's list of grievances against the old order is fatally flawed because of his willingness to condemn contractual practices such as the yellow dog contract and the company union in the same breath that he condemns the use of force in all its manifestations. And he never asks the hard question whether the use of force by employers was justified by the threats of violence by workers.[149]

The course of labor relations under the New Deal statutes has been far rockier and more complex than Magruder foresaw. Unions (except those in the public sector, where their monopoly power is greatest) have continued to lose ground notwithstanding their special legal advantages, a phenomenon best explained by the simple observation that they do not provide their membership with benefits that exceed their costs. It is also fair to say that the intellectual difficulties with the statutes have been far greater than Magruder realized, or could have realized. Increasing disenchantment with organized labor in this country is now a force to be reckoned with in the political arena. Much of that concern is with personalities and the subject matter of particular disputes. What is needed is a greater concern with the institutional structures in which these personali-

148. Magruder, *supra* note 3, at 117.

149. *Compare* F. FRANKFURTER & N. GREENE, *supra* note 3, at 132-33 *with* Petro, *supra* note 69, at 429, 434-35, 446-70. In my view Petro has much the better of the historical argument. The chief flaw of the Frankfurter and Greene study is, as Petro points out, that it never asks the question of whether the issuance of the labor injunction was a use or an abuse of power. Where there is the threat of force by workers, it is the failure to grant the injunction that is the abuse of discretion, not its issuance. Petro, *supra* note 69, at 436. And as Petro rightly points out, *id.* at 377-83, the application of the injunction to labor cases did not involve any departure from the well established equitable principle that injunctions are an appropriate response to threats of irreparable harm.

ties operate and these disputes take place. At present, there may be little prospect for the repeal of basic labor legislation, and there is none for its constitutional overthrow. The possibilities of incremental changes, however, are always present, and the opportunity for a major rehauling might even follow an intensive reexamination of the subject. The New Deal brought forth major labor law legislation, but as a normative and intellectual matter it did not conclude the debate on the nature and function of labor law.

[2]

In Defense of the Contract at Will

Richard A. Epstein†

The persistent tension between private ordering and government regulation exists in virtually every area known to the law, and in none has that tension been more pronounced than in the law of employer and employee relations. During the last fifty years, the balance of power has shifted heavily in favor of direct public regulation, which has been thought strictly necessary to redress the perceived imbalance between the individual and the firm. In particular the employment relationship has been the subject of at least two major statutory revolutions. The first, which culminated in the passage of the National Labor Relations Act in 1935,[1] set the basic structure for collective bargaining that persists to the current time. The second, which is embodied in Title VII of the Civil Rights Act of 1964,[2] offers extensive protection to all individuals against discrimination on the basis of race, sex, religion, or national origin. The effect of these two statutes is so pervasive that it is easy to forget that, even after their passage, large portions of the employment relation remain subject to the traditional common law rules, which when all was said and done set their face in support of freedom of contract and the system of voluntary exchange. One manifestation of that position was the prominent place that the common law, especially as it developed in the nineteenth century, gave to the contract at will. The basic position was well set out in an oft-quoted passage from *Payne v. Western & Atlantic Railroad:*

> [M]en must be left, without interference to buy and sell where they please, and to discharge or retain employees at will for good cause or for no cause, or even for bad cause without thereby being guilty of an unlawful act *per se*. It is a right which an employe may exercise in the same way, to the same

---

† James Parker Hall Professor of Law, University of Chicago.

[1] Act of July 5, 1935, ch. 372, 49 Stat. 449 (codified as amended at 29 U.S.C. §§ 151-169 (1982)).

[2] Pub. L. No. 88-352, 78 Stat. 253 (codified as amended at 42 U.S.C. §§ 2000e to 2000e-17 (1982)).

extent, for the same cause or want of cause as the employer.[3]

The survival of the contract at will, and the frequency of its use in private markets, might well be taken as a sign of its suitability for employment relations. But the contract at will has been in retreat even at common law, as the movement for public control of labor markets has now spilled over into the judicial arena. The judicial erosion of the older position has been spurred on by academic commentators, who have been almost unanimous in their condemnation of the at-will relationship, often treating it as an archaic relic that should be jettisoned along with other vestiges of nineteenth-century laissez-faire.[4] Thus it is commonly asserted

---

[3] Payne v. Western & Atl. R.R., 81 Tenn. 507, 518-19 (1884), *overruled on other grounds*, Hutton v. Watters, 132 Tenn. 527, 544, 179 S.W. 134, 138 (1915). The passage continues as follows:

> He may refuse to work for a man or company, that trades with any obnoxious person, or does other things which he dislikes. He may persuade his fellows and the employer may lose all his hands and be compelled to close his doors; or he may yield to the demand and withdraw his custom or cease his dealings, and the obnoxious person be thus injured or wrecked in business.

81 Tenn. at 519. It should be noted that *Payne* did not itself involve the discharge of an employee for a bad reason or no reason at all. As the last two quoted sentences indicate, the question of the status of the contract arose obliquely, in a defamation suit by a merchant against a railroad. The railroad's yard master had posted a sign that read: "Any employe of this company on Chattanooga pay-roll who trades with L. Payne from this date will be discharged. Notify all in your department." *Payne*, 81 Tenn. at 510.

The plaintiff Payne claimed that his business, which had been heavily dependent upon the trade of railroad workers, had thereby been ruined. The court held for the defendant on the grounds that (a) there was no defamation implicit in the announcement and (b) the employer's notice to its employees was within its rights because all the contracts with its workers were terminable at will. *Hutton* overruled *Payne*, not on the ground that contracts at will were against public policy, but on an abuse-of-rights theory according to which an employer cannot use his right to discharge employees for the sole purpose of harming third-party interests. The propriety of the *Hutton* theory is a difficult question, but my views tend toward those of the *Payne* court. *See* Epstein, *A Common Law for Labor Relations: A Critique of the New Deal Labor Legislation*, 92 YALE L.J. 1357, 1367-69, 1381 (1983).

[4] *E.g.*, Blackburn, *Restricted Employer Discharge Rights: A Changing Concept of Employment at Will*, 17 AM. BUS. L.J. 467, 491-92 (1980); Blades, *Employment at Will v. Individual Freedom: On Limiting the Abusive Exercise of Employer Power*, 67 COLUM. L. REV. 1404, 1405-06, 1413-14, 1435 (1967); Blumrosen, *Employer Discipline: United States Report*, 18 RUTGERS L. REV. 428, 428-34 (1964); Feinman, *The Development of the Employment at Will Rule*, 20 AM. J. LEGAL HIST. 118, 131-35 (1976); Murg & Scharman, *Employment at Will: Do the Exceptions Overwhelm the Rule?*, 23 B.C.L. REV. 329, 338-40, 383-84 (1982); Peck, *Unjust Discharges from Employment: A Necessary Change in the Law*, 40 OHIO ST. L.J. 1, 1-10 (1979); Summers, *Individual Protection Against Unjust Dismissal: Time for a Statute*, 62 VA. L. REV. 481, 484 (1976); Weynard, *Present Status of Individual Employee Rights*, PROC. N.Y.U. 22D ANN. CONF. ON LAB. 171, 214-16 (1970); Note, *Guidelines for a Public Policy Exception to the Employment at Will Rule*, 13 CONN. L. REV. 617, 641-42 (1980); Note, *Protecting Employees at Will Against Wrongful Discharge: The Public Policy Exception*, 96 HARV. L. REV. 1931, 1931-35 (1983); Note, *Protecting At Will Employees Against Wrongful Discharge: The Duty to Terminate Only in Good Faith*, 93

that, however congenial the contract at will might have been to the conditions of earlier times, major transformations in firm organization and industrial production have rendered it anachronistic today. One early and influential attack on the contract at will shows the importance of the issues that it raises:

> It is a widely accepted proposition that large corporations now pose a threat to individual freedom comparable to that which would be posed if governmental power were unchecked. The proposition need not, however, be limited to the mammoth business corporation, for the freedom of the individual is threatened whenever he becomes dependent upon a private entity possessing greater power than himself. Foremost among the relationships of which this generality is true is that of employer and employee.[5]

The contract at will is thus thought to be particularly unwise because it invites the exercise of arbitrary power by persons with a dominant economic position against individuals whose mobility is said to be limited by the structure of labor markets. The absence of viable alternative employment opportunities is thought to leave employees vulnerable to coercion and exploitation. In the extreme situation, employers (or their managers) are said to fire workers out of personal animosity; the animosity may stem from the worker's refusal to grant personal or sexual favors or from a simple and irrational dislike of the personal characteristics or habits of the employee.[6] Once the outcomes of these market imperfections are identified, the conclusion is said to follow swiftly: where discharges from employment are not made for sound economic reasons, or to advance the financial interest of the firm, the power of the law must be used to redress the perceived imbalance.

The courts have been heavily influenced by these arguments,

HARV. L. REV. 1816, 1824-28 (1980) [hereinafter cited as Note, *Wrongful Discharge*]; Note, *A Common Law Action for the Abusively Discharged Employee*, 26 HASTINGS L.J. 1435, 1443-46 (1975); Note, *Implied Contract Rights to Job Security*, 26 STAN. L. REV. 335, 337-40 (1974); Note, *California's Controls on Employer Abuse of Employee Political Rights*, 22 STAN. L. REV. 1015, 1015-20 (1970).

[5] Blades, *supra* note 4, at 1404 (footnotes omitted). Examples of the subsequent literature on the point are cited *supra* note 4.

[6] Such allegations were made in Alcorn v. Anbro Eng'g, Inc., 2 Cal. 3d 493, 496-97, 468 P.2d 216, 217, 86 Cal. Rptr. 88, 89 (1970) (employee dismissed due to employer's animosity toward employee on the basis of his race and his union activities); Monge v. Beebe Rubber Co., 114 N.H. 130, 131-32, 316 A.2d 549, 550-51 (1974) (employee dismissed due to refusal to date her foreman); Hutton v. Watters, 132 Tenn. 527, 529-30, 179 S.W. 134, 134-35 (1915) (employees dismissed for patronizing a boarding house whose owner was personally disliked by employer).

and the tempo of their intervention into market processes has increased rapidly in recent years.[7] The underlying rationale for the intervention is well captured by the conclusion of the New Hampshire Supreme Court in *Monge v. Beebe Rubber Co.*: "We hold that a termination by the employer of a contract of employment at will which is motivated by bad faith or malice or based on retaliation is not in the best interest of the economic system or the public good and constitutes a breach of the employment contract."[8] Once the wrongful discharge is established, damages can be awarded or reinstatement can be ordered. More recently, legislatures have begun to consider proposals that replace the contract at will with an action for wrongful discharge, so that all private contracts of employment would be terminable by the employer only upon a showing of

---

[7] There appear to be three theories under which courts have recognized a cause of action for wrongful discharge: (1) discharge violates public policy; (2) discharge violates an implied term of contract; and (3) discharge constitutes a tort of emotional harm.

The public-policy approach is the most widely accepted. *See, e.g.*, Tameny v. Atlantic Richfield Co., 27 Cal. 3d 167, 176-77, 610 P.2d 1330, 1336, 164 Cal. Rptr. 839, 844-45 (1980) (dismissal for refusal to participate in price-fixing scheme); Glenn v. Clearman's Golden Cock Inn, Inc., 192 Cal. App. 2d 793, 796-97, 13 Cal. Rptr. 769, 771 (1961) (employee dismissed for joining a union); Petermann v. Teamsters Local 396, 174 Cal. App. 2d 184, 188-89, 344 P.2d 25, 27-28 (1959) (employee dismissed for refusing to commit perjury); Kelsay v. Motorola, Inc., 74 Ill. 2d 172, 181-83, 384 N.E.2d 353, 358-59 (1978) (employee dismissed for filing workers' compensation claim); Frampton v. Central Ind. Gas Co., 260 Ind. 249, 252-53, 297 N.E.2d 425, 428 (1973) (same); Sventko v. Kroger Co., 69 Mich. App. 644, 648, 245 N.W.2d 151, 153 (1976) (same); O'Sullivan v. Mallon, 160 N.J. Super. 416, 417-18, 390 A.2d 149, 150 (Law Div. 1978) (medical technician fired for refusal to perform operation for which she was not licensed); Nees v. Hocks, 272 Or. 210, 218-19, 536 P.2d 512, 515-16 (1975) (employee dismissed for serving on a jury); Reuther v. Fowler & Williams, Inc., 255 Pa. Super. 28, 32, 386 A.2d 119, 120 (1978) (dismissal for serving on jury) (dictum); Harless v. First Nat'l Bank, 246 S.E.2d 270, 275-76 (W. Va. 1978) (employee dismissed for calling attention to employer's violation of law).

The contract theory has also been used by a number of courts. *See, e.g.*, McKinney v. National Dairy Council, 491 F. Supp. 1108, 1122 (D. Mass. 1980) (dismissal due to age); Cleary v. American Airlines, 111 Cal. App. 3d 443, 456, 168 Cal. Rptr. 722, 729 (1980) (dismissal without the investigation or hearing that was normally part of employer's procedure); Maddaloni v. Western Mass. Bus Lines, 386 Mass. 877, 878-80, 438 N.E.2d 351, 354-56 (1982) (discharge to avoid paying commissions due); Fortune v. National Cash Register Co., 373 Mass. 96, 101, 364 N.E.2d 1251, 1255-56 (1977) (same); Toussaint v. Blue Cross & Blue Shield, 408 Mich. 579, 598, 292 N.W.2d 880, 885 (1980) (implied term forbidding dismissal except for cause); Weiner v. McGraw-Hill, Inc., 57 N.Y.2d 458, 465-66, 443 N.E.2d 441, 445, 457 N.Y.S.2d 193, 197 (1982) (same).

Finally, courts have occasionally treated discharge as a tortious infliction of emotional harm. *See, e.g.*, Alcorn v. Anbro Eng'g, Inc., 2 Cal. 3d 493, 498, 468 P.2d 216, 218, 86 Cal. Rptr. 88, 90-91 (1970); Agis v. Howard Johnson Co., 371 Mass. 140, 144-45, 355 N.E.2d 315, 318-19 (1976).

[8] 114 N.H. 130, 133, 316 A.2d 549, 551 (1974). Note, however, that the New Hampshire Supreme Court has since retreated from this broad view. *See* Howard v. Dorr Woolen Co., 120 N.H. 295, 297, 414 A.2d 1273, 1274 (1980) (limiting the *Monge* approach to cases involving violations of specific public policies).

"just cause," which would often be determined by an elaborate structure of mediation, arbitration, and administrative action.[9]

There is thus today a widely held view that the contract at will has outlived its usefulness. But this view is mistaken. The contract at will is not ideal for every employment relation. No court or legislature should ever command its use. Nonetheless, there are two ways in which the contract at will should be respected: one deals with entitlements against regulation and the other with presumptions in the event of contractual silence.

First, the parties should be permitted as of right to adopt this form of contract if they so desire. The principle behind this conclusion is that freedom of contract tends both to advance individual autonomy and to promote the efficient operation of labor markets.

Second, the contract at will should be respected as a rule of construction in response to the perennial question of gaps in contract language: what term should be implied in the absence of explicit agreement on the question of duration or grounds for termination? The applicable standard asks two familiar questions: what rule tends to lend predictability to litigation and to advance the joint interests of the parties?[10] On both these points I hope to show that the contract at will represents in most contexts the efficient solution to the employment relation. To be sure, the stakes are lower where the outright prohibition is no longer in the offing. No rule of construction ever has the power of a rule of regulation, since the parties by negotiation can reverse what the law otherwise commands. Nonetheless, bad rules of contract construction have costs that should not be understated, here or elsewhere. The rule of construction is normally chosen because it reflects the dominant practice in a given class of cases and because that practice is itself regarded as making good sense for the standard transactions it governs. It is of course freely waivable by a joint expression of contrary intention. When the law introduces a just-cause requirement,

---

[9] Bills have been introduced in Michigan, California, Wisconsin, Ohio, Pennsylvania, and Massachusetts. Chicago Sun-Times, June 10, 1984, at 32, col. 1 (2-star ed.).

[10] The traditional rule has been codified under current California law: "An employment, having no specified term, may be terminated at the will of either party on notice to the other." CAL. LAB. CODE § 2922 (West 1971). Indeed, this should mean, as it now does, that where a contract speaks of "permanent" employment, the presumption should again be that the contract is terminable at will, for all that "permanent" connotes is the absence of any definite termination date. It does not imply one in which there is a lifetime engagement by either employer or employee, especially where none of the subsidiary terms for such a long-term relationship is identified by the parties. The proper rule of construction should be that the contract is terminable at will by either side.

it flies in the face of ordinary understandings and thus rests upon an assumption that just-cause arrangements are in the broad run of cases either more frequent or desirable than the contract at will, though neither is the case. Where this rule of construction is used, therefore, contracting-out will have to take place in the very large number of cases where the parties desire to conform to the norm by entering into a contract at will. Furthermore, it may be difficult to waive the for-cause requirement in fact, even if waiver is formally allowable as a matter of law, because of high standards for "informed" waiver that cannot be met after the fact. By degrees, the original presumption against the contract at will could so gain in strength that a requirement that is waivable in theory could easily become conclusive in fact.

These complications should all be avoided. The critics of the contract at will all point out imperfections in the current institutional arrangements, but they do not take into account the nonlegal means of preserving long-term employment relationships, and they ignore the greater imperfections that are created under alternative legal rules. Contracts at will are consistent with public policy and should be welcomed by it, not because they are perfect, but because in many contexts they respond to the manifold perils of employment contracts better than any rivals that courts or legislatures can devise.

In this area of private-contracting autonomy, there are some exceptions, arising out of the infrequent cases in which discharge of the contract at will is inconsistent with the performance of some public duty or with the protection of some public right. Just as a contract to commit murder should not be enforceable, neither should one to pollute illegally or to commit perjury.[11] But these

[11] This problem has arisen where employees at will have refused to perjure themselves on behalf of the employer, *e.g.*, Petermann v. Teamsters Local 396, 174 Cal. App. 2d 184, 188-89, 344 P.2d 25, 27-28 (1959) (discharge for refusal to commit perjury held wrongful), or where workers have been dismissed because they have filed workers' compensation claims, *e.g.*, Frampton v. Central Ind. Gas Co., 260 Ind. 249, 252-53, 297 N.E. 2d 425, 428 (1973) (discharge for filing claim held wrongful). It seems clear that any contract to commit perjury should simply be treated as illegal. The workers' compensation case is more difficult both because there is less justification for the coercive character of compensation, since no third-party interests are at stake, and because in all events the worker is entitled to file his claim and will do so if its value exceeds the gains he expects from the employment contract. A common law court cannot, however, attack the soundness of a statutory compensation system, so that this restraint on freedom of contract should be as valid as one imposed for the protection of strangers. At this point the central question concerns the proper remedy. Typically, reinstatement of the plaintiff is ordered, which has the disadvantage of requiring the court to supervise an ongoing relationship. It may well be that the employer should be able to fire the worker, but nonetheless be required to pay damages, preferably fixed by statute,

cases, however difficult in their own right, in no way require abandoning the basic common law presumption in favor of contracts at will. The recent efforts to undermine or abolish the contract at will should be evaluated not in terms of what they *hope* to achieve, whether stated in terms of worker participation, industrial harmony, fundamental fairness, or enlightened employment relations. Instead they should be evaluated for the generally harsh results that they actually produce. They introduce an enormous amount of undesirable complexity into the law of employment relations; they increase the frequency of civil litigation; and over the broad run of cases they work to the disadvantage of both the employers and the employees whose conduct they govern.

In the remainder of this paper, I examine the arguments that can be made for and against the contract at will. I hope to show that it is adopted not because it allows the employer to exploit the employee, but rather because over a very broad range of circumstances it works to the mutual benefit of both parties, where the benefits are measured, as ever, at the time of the contract's formation and not at the time of dispute. To justify this result, I examine the contract in light of the three dominant standards that have emerged as the test of the soundness of any legal doctrine: intrinsic fairness, effects upon utility or wealth, and distributional consequences. I conclude that the first two tests point strongly to the maintenance of the at-will rule, while the third, if it offers any guidance at all, points in the same direction.

I. The Fairness of the Contract at Will

The first way to argue for the contract at will is to insist upon the importance of freedom of contract as an end in itself. Freedom of contract is an aspect of individual liberty, every bit as much as freedom of speech, or freedom in the selection of marriage partners or in the adoption of religious beliefs or affiliations. Just as it is regarded as prima facie unjust to abridge these liberties, so too is it presumptively unjust to abridge the economic liberties of individuals. The desire to make one's own choices about employment may be as strong as it is with respect to marriage or participation in religious activities, and it is doubtless more pervasive than the desire to participate in political activity. Indeed for most people, their own health and comfort, and that of their families, depend

to the worker. On the clear public-policy exception to the validity of contracts at will, see generally Murg & Scharman, *supra* note 4, at 343-55.

critically upon their ability to earn a living by entering the employment market. If government regulation is inappropriate for personal, religious, or political activities, then what makes it intrinsically desirable for employment relations?

It is one thing to set aside the occasional transaction that reflects only the momentary aberrations of particular parties who are overwhelmed by major personal and social dislocations. It is quite another to announce that a rule to which vast numbers of individuals adhere is so fundamentally corrupt that it does not deserve the minimum respect of the law. With employment contracts we are not dealing with the widow who has sold her inheritance for a song to a man with a thin mustache. Instead we are dealing with the routine stuff of ordinary life; people who are competent enough to marry, vote, and pray are not unable to protect themselves in their day-to-day business transactions.

Courts and legislatures have intervened so often in private contractual relations that it may seem almost quixotic to insist that they bear a heavy burden of justification every time they wish to substitute their own judgment for that of the immediate parties to the transactions. Yet it is hardly likely that remote public bodies have better information about individual preferences than the parties who hold them. This basic principle of autonomy, moreover, is not limited to some areas of individual conduct and wholly inapplicable to others. It covers all these activities as a piece and admits no ad hoc exceptions, but only principled limitations.

This general proposition applies to the particular contract term in question. Any attack on the contract at will in the name of individual freedom is fundamentally misguided. As the Tennessee Supreme Court rightly stressed in *Payne*, the contract at will is sought by both persons.[12] Any limitation upon the freedom to enter into such contracts limits the power of workers as well as employers and must therefore be justified before it can be accepted. In this context the appeal is often to an image of employer coercion.[13] To be sure, freedom of contract is not an absolute in the employment context, any more than it is elsewhere. Thus the principle must be understood against a backdrop that prohibits the use of private contracts to trench upon third-party rights, including uses that interfere with some clear mandate of public policy, as

---

[12] Payne v. Western & Atl. R.R., 81 Tenn. 507, 518-19 (1884). *See supra* note 3 and accompanying text.

[13] *See supra* note 5 and accompanying text.

in cases of contracts to commit murder or perjury.[14]

In addition, the principle of freedom of contract also rules out the use of force or fraud in obtaining advantages during contractual negotiations; and it limits taking advantage of the young, the feeble-minded, and the insane.[15] But the recent wrongful discharge cases do not purport to deal with the delicate situations where contracts have been formed by improper means or where individual defects of capacity or will are involved. Fraud is not a frequent occurrence in employment contracts, especially where workers and employers engage in repeat transactions. Nor is there any reason to believe that such contracts are marred by misapprehensions, since employers and employees know the footing on which they have contracted: the phrase "at will" is two words long and has the convenient virtue of meaning just what it says, no more and no less.[16]

An employee who knows that he can quit at will understands what it means to be fired at will, even though he may not like it after the fact. So long as it is accepted that the employer is the full owner of his capital and the employee is the full owner of his labor, the two are free to exchange on whatever terms and conditions they see fit, within the limited constraints just noted. If the arrangement turns out to be disastrous to one side, that is his problem; and once cautioned, he probably will not make the same mistake a second time. More to the point, employers and employees are unlikely to make the same mistake once. It is hardly plausible that contracts at will could be so pervasive in all businesses and at all levels if they did not serve the interests of employees as well as employers. The argument from fairness then is very simple, but not for that reason unpersuasive.

II. The Utility of the Contract at Will

The strong fairness argument in favor of freedom of contract makes short work of the various for-cause and good-faith restrictions upon private contracts. Yet the argument is incomplete in several respects. In particular, it does not explain why the presumption in the case of silence should be in favor of the contract at

---

[14] *See supra* note 11.

[15] For my elaboration of this general point, see Epstein, *Unconscionability: A Critical Reappraisal*, 18 J.L. & Econ. 293 (1975).

[16] In the absence of force or fraud, any disclosure law would be regarded as only a nuisance by employers and employees alike, whatever the case for such laws in other contexts. *See, e.g.*, Kronman, *Mistake, Disclosure, Information, and the Law of Contracts*, 7 J. Legal Stud. 1, 11-18 (1978).

will. Nor does it give a descriptive account of *why* the contract at will is so commonly found in all trades and professions. Nor does the argument meet on their own terms the concerns voiced most frequently by the critics of the contract at will. Thus, the commonplace belief today (at least outside the actual world of business) is that the contract at will is so unfair and one-sided that it cannot be the outcome of a rational set of bargaining processes any more than, to take the extreme case, a contract for total slavery. While we may not, the criticism continues, be able to observe them, defects in capacity at contract formation nonetheless must be present: the ban upon the contract at will is an effective way to reach abuses that are pervasive but difficult to detect, so that modest government interference only strengthens the operation of market forces.[17]

In order to rebut this charge, it is necessary to do more than insist that individuals as a general matter know how to govern their own lives. It is also necessary to display the structural strengths of the contract at will that explain why rational people would enter into such a contract, if not all the time, then at least most of it. The implicit assumption in this argument is that contracts are typically for the mutual benefit of both parties. Yet it is hard to see what other assumption makes any sense in analyzing institutional arrangements (arguably in contradistinction to idiosyncratic, nonrepetitive transactions). To be sure, there are occasional cases of regret after the fact, especially after an infrequent, but costly, contingency comes to pass. There will be cases in which parties are naive, befuddled, or worse. Yet in framing either a rule of policy or a rule of construction, the focus cannot be on that biased set of cases in which the contract aborts and litigation ensues. Instead, attention must be directed to standard repetitive transactions, where the centralizing tendency powerfully promotes expected mutual gain. It is simply incredible to postulate that either employers or employees, motivated as they are by self-interest,

---

[17] Kronman, *Paternalism and the Law of Contracts*, 92 YALE L.J. 763, 777 (1983). The point is especially important in connection with the law of undue influence, where there is a long historical dispute over the relationship between the adequacy of consideration received and the procedural soundness of the underlying transaction. *See* Simpson, *The Horwitz Thesis and the History of Contracts*, 46 U. CHI. L. REV. 533, 561-80 (1979). Nonetheless, paternalistic explanations, whatever their force elsewhere, have little power in connection with employment relations. Indeed, if one thought it appropriate to restrict the powers of workers to make their own decisions during negotiations over the terms of employment, it might follow that restrictions on their right to participate in unions could be justified as well, for in both instances workers have proven that they often need to be protected against their own folly.

would enter routinely into a transaction that leaves them worse off than they were before, or even worse off than their next best alternative.

From this perspective, then, the task is to explain how and why the at-will contracting arrangement (in sharp contrast to slavery) typically works to the mutual advantage of the parties. Here, as is common in economic matters, it does not matter that the parties themselves often cannot articulate the reasons that render their judgment sound and breathe life into legal arrangements that are fragile in form but durable in practice.[18] The inquiry into mutual benefit in turn requires an examination of the full range of costs and benefits that arise from collaborative ventures. It is just at this point that the nineteenth-century view is superior to the emerging modern conception. The modern view tends to lay heavy emphasis on the need to control employer abuse. Yet, as the passage from *Payne* indicates,[19] the rights under the contract at will are fully bilateral, so that the employee can use the contract as a means to control the firm, just as the firm uses it to control the worker.

The issue for the parties, properly framed, is not how to minimize employer abuse, but rather how to maximize the gain from the relationship, which in part depends upon minimizing the sum of employer and employee abuse. Viewed in this way the private-contracting problem is far more complex. How does each party create incentives for the proper behavior of the other? How does each side insure against certain risks? How do both sides minimize the administrative costs of their contracting practices?

In order to show the interaction of all relevant factors, it is useful to analyze a case in which the problem of bilateral control exists, but where the overtones of inequality of bargaining power are absent. The treatment of partnership relations is therefore very instructive because partners are generally social and economic

---

[18] One striking example of the durability of at-will arrangements in other markets comes from an issue frequently litigated in the law of eminent domain: whether a tenant in possession under a lease is entitled to compensation for the simple expectation of renewal of the lease when the government condemns the fee or the leasehold itself. The legal conclusion is that the tenant should receive compensation equal to the market value of the leasehold that he could have received from a willing buyer, taking into account the expectation of renewal. *See* Almota Farmers Elevator & Warehouse Co. v. United States, 409 U.S. 470, 473-74 (1973). But the problem only arises because the value of the expectation to the tenant is high, which in turn suggests that the probability of renewal is great, and indeed often approaches one hundred percent.

[19] Payne v. Western & Atl. R.R., 81 Tenn. 507, 518-19 (1884). *See supra* note 3 and accompanying text.

equals between whom considerations of inequality of bargaining power, so evident in the debate over the contract at will, have no relevance. To be sure, the structural differences between partnership and employment contracts must be identified, but these will in the end explain why the at-will contract may make even greater sense in the employment context.

A. At-Will Arrangements in Partnerships

The economic motivation to form partnerships is easy enough to understand. Partnerships allow individuals to pool the capital necessary to undertake larger ventures, and they allow the parties to obtain the benefits of a division of labor within a single firm, where each partner retains some equity claim in the final output of the firm. By combining their separate resources and talents in a cooperative venture, the parties can produce more of value than they could by acting separately and then exchanging their outputs in discrete market transactions, such as sale or barter.

Nonetheless, the organization of the simplest firm, i.e., one with only two people, creates a set of problems that does not exist for the sole entrepreneur: the question of management. The efforts of the two individuals must be coordinated, and each person must be sure that some steps are taken to prevent the other party to the contract from acting to nullify or reduce the advantages that are promised at formation.

The first business question that confronts the partnership is the division of the proceeds. If these are to be evenly divided, then some steps, some costly steps, must be taken to ensure equal contributions. Thus, for example, the two parties may have different types of skills with different market values. Should some difference in the time allocated to the partnership be required? Should the less productive partner be required to commit some additional cash or property to the joint venture? Or should the equal division of partnership gains be abandoned in favor of some complex formula, with partners resorting to intricate capital structures complete with loans, preferred interests, and options to purchase? The matter is, moreover, not simply one of fairness when disputes occur, but also of the incentives created upon contract formation. The less effective the mechanics for controlling the contribution of resources and the distribution of gains, the less likely it will be that the venture will be formed, and the smaller will be the expected gains, both private and social.

A critical variable in partnership formation is the level of effort the parties will bring to the joint venture. One naive assumption is that the cooperative nature of the enterprise will not influence the effort and performance levels of the partners. Yet, as the economic literature on agency costs so tellingly demonstrates,[30] hidden conflicts of interest pervade all business organizations at birth, during life, and upon death. The obvious conflict of interest arises when the gains of one partner are the losses of the other, as with simple theft of partnership assets by a partner. A second form of conflict, less dramatic but more persistent, arises because each partner bears the full costs of his own individual action, while obtaining only some fraction of the partnership gain that that action produces. The wedge necessarily driven between private and social (i.e., firm) costs creates an incentive for each partner to produce only to the point where, at the margin, the total amount of private gain is some multiple (greater than one) of the additional unit of private cost.[31] That tendency can manifest itself in any number of ways. Each partner may not work as hard as he would were he in business alone. Each partner may divert firm business to his own private account, all at a sporting discount, if only the customer remains quiet about the special arrangement. If both partners engage in this opportunistic behavior, then the firm output will fall below the levels it would achieve if they both continued to labor until, at the margin, *partnership* gains matched *partnership* costs.

These potential conflicts of interest will not materialize in each and every case, but they do pose a persistent threat to the stability of the firm. Within this framework, therefore, the managerial task is to determine what devices increase the likelihood that both partners will produce to the ideal point. In part there are legal prohibitions. The diversion of partnership assets can be met

---

[30] *See* Jensen & Meckling, *Theory of the Firm: Managerial Behavior, Agency Costs and Ownership Structure*, 3 J. Fin. Econ. 305, 308-10, 312-13, 333-34 (1976). For a recent collection of materials on the subject, see The Agency Relationship (J. Pratt & R. Zeckhauser eds. forthcoming), which contains a paper I wrote dealing with many of the same issues discussed here: Epstein, *Agency Cost, Employment Contracts, and Labor Unions*.

[31] The conflict can be stated formally as follows: let C represent costs to the individual, and G represent gains to the firm. Then assume any division of gain, p, for each partner that is strictly less than one. The conflict then arises whenever tho following condition is established: $pG < C < G$. This inequality says that it is in the interest of the firm that the activity with cost C be undertaken, but that the individual actor will not undertake it because he is left worse off by the difference between C and pG. Good management rests in part upon the ability to narrow the gap between pG and G, or in the alternative to reduce the private costs to below pG. The challenge is to devise institutional arrangements that can overcome this fundamental conflict in discrete instances, and the problem in a sense is quite unending. If costs are reduced, then activities that were once unthinkable now become plausible, and with respect to some fraction of this new class, C will lie between pG and G.

with an action that recovers the proceeds for the benefit of the firm.[22] Yet litigation is always expensive and unpleasant. As a common sense matter an ounce of protection may be worth a pound of cure. With small partnerships one effective sanction is simply for each partner to watch the others: who comes to the office first, who leaves last; who does nonfirm work on firm time or with firm equipment; who receives the larger number of phone calls from customers; who generates the larger number of customer billings; whose services are in greater demand by outsiders.

The basic problem becomes only more complex as the size of the partnership increases—consider, for example, the division of profits in a large law firm, with its separate tiers of partners and, increasingly, permanent associates. A rough generalization is that as the size of the enterprise increases the demand for some internal organizational structure increases, perhaps exponentially, as well. Now the conflicts of interest become ever more acute as the gains from diversion increase because each partner receives a smaller fraction of firm profits.[23] Similarly, the informal social sanctions and affective ties among partners are attenuated by the sheer force of numbers. More formal procedures are required to control abuse, to protect, as it were, the well-intentioned partners from their fellows: personnel committees, formal audits, and managerial specialization quickly become standard parts of firm practice.

Partnership arrangements are difficult to police for yet another reason: all the partners are required to place all their eggs in

---

[22] The problem here is one of the misappropriation of either partnership or corporate opportunity, and has been recognized as an issue as early as Roman times:

> A partnership lasts as long as the parties remain of the same mind, but when one of them renounces the partnership, it is dissolved. But of course if one of the partners renounces for the purpose of profiting alone by some coming gain, for example, if my partner in a universal partnership [one embracing all assets, however acquired], having been left heir by somone, renounces the partnership in order to gain the inheritance for himself alone, he will be compelled to share this gain. If, however, he makes other gain which he has not sought for, this belongs to him alone. I, on the other hand, have the sole right to anything whatever that I acquire after his renunciation of the partnership.

GAIUS, INSTITUTES, III, 151 (F. De Zulueta trans. 1946). Note the at-will presumption coupled with rules to prevent diversions of opportunity from the partnership; these rules are skewed so that the party in breach is left worse off, since he must share his own private gains but has no share in the gains of the innocent party. The Roman rule is carefully crafted and in essence represents the modern law, though it is unlikely that the Romans had any understanding of the formal economic theory of agency.

[23] A more formal statement, using the symbols set out *supra* note 21, would begin by noting that as the size of the firm increases, p (the fraction of the gain that goes to each partner) decreases. Then, returning to the basic inequality ($pG < C < G$), we can see that as p decreases, the interval between pG and G increases, and with it the likelihood and severity of conflicts of interest.

a single basket. The principal contribution to most partnerships is the partner's labor. Labor, unlike money, is not easily divisible among multiple investment opportunities. Therefore, while partners obtain the many advantages of firm specialization, they must sacrifice the advantage of risk diversification that is normally available in capital markets.[24] Not only is it possible to diversify risk at low cost in capital markets, but it is also easy to redeploy assets across firms. The threat of such redeployment, in turn, may be the investor's most powerful means of protecting himself from abuse at the hands of the firm's managers, who are always wary of hostile tender offers.[25]

Labor markets differ from capital markets in both of these particulars. Labor cannot be diversified in the normal service partnership because a person cannot be in more than one or two separate ventures at any given time and hope to maintain productive activities. A mutual fund for jobs is quite unthinkable. In addition, entrance and exit in labor markets is highly complex, as is often stressed in the literature critical of the contract at will.[26] Thus, a party may be legally entitled to withdraw from a joint venture at will, but he cannot substitute someone else in his place without the consent of the remaining partners, given the delicate personal chemistry behind any joint venture.

The consequences of low diversification and impaired practical alienability are clear. Labor ventures are inherently more risky. The choice of partners is critical at the outset, as is the need to monitor their activities continually. Yet attending to these needs raises a powerful tension that pervades partnership relations. Long-term cooperative ventures require some permanent internal structure, while effective control against abuse often depends upon the ability to withdraw from the venture at any time, and without

[24] I have discussed some of these points in a similar vein in Epstein, *supra* note 20. For a convenient explanation of the principles of portfolio diversification, see Langbein & Posner, *Market Funds and Trust-Investment Law* (pt. 1), 1976 Am. B. Found. Research J. 1; *see also* Langbein & Posner, *Market Funds and Trust-Investment Law* (pt. 2), 1977 Am. B. Found. Research J. 1.

[25] Because the costs to shareholders of monitoring managerial decisions are high, they find it in their self-interest to remain passive and to avoid losses by simply selling their shares. *See* Easterbrook & Fischel, *The Proper Role of a Target's Management in Responding to a Tender Offer*, 94 Harv. L. Rev. 1161, 1170-71 (1981).

[26] *See, e.g.*, Blades, *supra* note 4, at 1405 ("Obviously, if every employee could go from job to job with complete ease, there would be little need to provide other means of escape from the improper exertion of employer pressure."). The effect of impaired mobility upon the desirability of the contract at will is discussed *infra* notes 45-46 and accompanying text.

cause, as most partnership agreements provide.[27]

The logic behind the right of withdrawal depends upon a delicate balance of advantage. In the simplest case, assume that the partnership originally calls for an even division of the gains between two partners. If partner *A* knows (or even has reason to believe) that partner *B* has misappropriated assets or opportunities belonging to the firm, his threat to withdraw will become instantly more credible because his losses from withdrawal must be measured against a (revised) baseline of less than half the partnership gains. *B*'s expected losses from dissolution will be correspondingly greater because he will lose the expected illicit gains obtained from improper behavior. *A*'s threat tends therefore to be made under those circumstances where it is most called for.

The at-will provision in partnership agreements by no means controls all abuse—nothing does that—because both sides will have to bear the costs of dissolution (including a costly partnership accounting) in the event that a break-up occurs. It is quite possible, for example, for *B* to engage in activities that net him more than his agreed-upon share of the assets if he knows that *A*'s costs of breaking up exceed his expected gains from dissolution. Nonetheless, the greater the wrongdoing by *B*, the more likely it is that dissolution will cost *A* less than continued abuse by *B*. The sanction of withdrawal remains imperfect, but it tends to become more credible as the abuses become greater. The provision for at-will dissolution of the partnership helps stabilize the arrangement after formation and thus tends to be in the interest of both parties at formation. To be sure, explicit legal remedies may be desired in cases of waste, but direct legal action always costs more than the simple act of separation, and any lawsuit is costly to bring and uncertain in its outcome. Thus, while resort to legal remedies is to be expected, it will not be frequent. Self-help by withdrawal may have a lower payoff, but its lower cost and greater predictability make it an effective sanction against misbehavior.

B. Employment at Will

When we move from partnerships to employment relations, we must determine how the differences in the relationships between

[27] *See* Hillman, *Misconduct as a Basis for Excluding or Expelling a Partner: Effecting Commercial Divorce and Securing Custody of the Business*, 78 Nw. U.L. Rev. 527, 531 (1983); Hillman, *The Dissatisfied Participant in the Solvent Business Venture: A Consideration of the Relative Permanence of Partnerships and Close Corporations*, 67 Minn. L. Rev. 1, 4 (1983).

the parties influence the mix of the formal and informal control devices available to the parties. The starting point of the analysis is the difference in the ways in which profit and loss are divided. The central feature of a partnership is that the residual gains and losses are shared by the partners under an internal formula that makes both parties equity claimants. In the employment-contracting situation, the employer is the sole residual claimant upon the earnings of the firm, while the employee receives a fixed wage.[28] But this important difference does not mean that the advantages of the at-will arrangement are of no importance to the employment relationship. On the contrary, it is possible to identify a number of reasons why the at-will contract usually works for the benefit of both sides in employment as well as partnership contexts.

1. *Monitoring Behavior.* The shift in the internal structure of the firm from a partnership to an employment relation eliminates neither bilateral opportunism nor the conflicts of interest between employer and employee. Begin for the moment with the fears of the firm, for it is the firm's right to maintain at-will power that is now being called into question. In all too many cases, the firm must contend with the recurrent problem of employee theft and with the related problems of unauthorized use of firm equipment and employee kickback arrangements.[29] As the analysis of partnerships shows, however, the proper concerns of the firm are not limited to obvious forms of criminal misconduct. The employee on a fixed wage can, at the margin, capture only a portion of the gain from his labor, and therefore has a tendency to reduce output.[30] The employee who receives a commission equal to half the

---

[28] Sometimes the employee's wage will be fixed, not in dollar terms, but as a function of his own productivity (for example, sales personnel who work on commission). But even if the employee's claim is a function of the firm's profit from particular transactions, he is in a different position than is an owner. An individual salesman can make a fortune while the firm loses money; a pure equity partner cannot.

[29] For example, in Perks v. Firestone Tire & Rubber Co., 611 F.2d 1363, 1364 (3d Cir. 1979), the plaintiff, a discharged employee, had allowed the representative of a supplier to procure prostitutes for him.

[30] By way of comparison, his position is like that of a lienholder who is quite happy so long as the value of the security remains above the level of the lien, even if the venture itself does not prosper. This is one reason why there is an enormous reluctance to allow the mortgagee to enter into possession before default, especially when the equity in the property is large. The risks, of course, change radically upon default, at which point a mortgagee will generally want to keep up the property because its value is less than that of his lien. Note too that the conflict of interest is of great importance to an equity investor in a limited partnership who, having relied upon the valuation of property prepared for the mortgage lender, discovers that the lender's assessor was less sensitive than he is to the positive po-

firm's profit attributable to his labor may work hard, but probably not quite as hard as he would if he received the entire profit from the completed sale, an arrangement that would solve the agency-cost problem only by undoing the firm.

The mismatch between benefits received and capital or labor contributed, then, can and does exist between employer and employee just as it does between partner and partner. The different ways in which firm proceeds are divided only determines where and how the conflicts will arise, not whether they will arise. Indeed, since the roles of employer and employee are radically asymmetrical, the potential source of conflict is, if anything, larger than it is in relations between copartners. The conflicts between employer and employee may sometimes call for the severance of the relationship, just as they do in the partnership context. But the rational response is to counteract the tendency for employee abuse only to the point where private gain equals private cost.[31] Agency costs are like other costs that must be minimized in order for production to proceed, and the persistence of firms shows that this can be done.

The problem of management then is to identify the forms of social control that are best able to minimize these agency costs. Here the choices are the same as they were in the partnership situation. One obvious form of control is the force of law. The state can be brought in to punish cases of embezzlement or fraud. But this mode of control requires extensive cooperation with public officials and may well be frustrated by the need to prove the criminal offense (including mens rea) beyond a reasonable doubt, so that vast amounts of abuse will go unchecked. Private litigation instituted by the firm may well be used in cases of major grievances, either to recover the property that has been misappropriated or to prevent the individual employee from further diverting firm busi-

---

tential of the project.

[31] There are analogies with corporate financial structures. Thus there is always a partial conflict of interest when a firm contains both debt and equity in its capital structure. The holders of the equity are, by virtue of the existence of the debt, induced to engage in riskier ventures than they would undertake without the debt. The explanation is clear enough. With the debt, the equity holders still obtain all the profits from the firm. But now the risk of bankruptcy is shared by others, thereby allowing the partial externalization of the costs of failure. *See* De Alessi, *Private Property and Dispersion of Ownership in Large Corporations*, 28 J. Fin. 839 (1973). The point does not condemn such debt structures, but it does invite the use of other control measures, such as limitations, contained in the original loan agreement, on the types of activities that the borrower may undertake. *See generally* Smith & Warner, *On Financial Contracting: An Analysis of Bond Covenants*, 7 J. Fin. Econ. 117 (1979).

ness to his own account. But private litigation, like public prosecution, is too blunt an instrument to counter employee shirking or the minor but persistent use of firm assets for private business.

As with the partnership, some alternative forms of control are needed. Internal auditors may help control some forms of abuse, and simple observation by coworkers may well monitor employee activities. (There are some very subtle tradeoffs to be considered when the firm decides whether to use partitions or separate offices for its employees.) Promotions, bonuses, and wages are also critical in shaping the level of employee performance.[32] But the carrot cannot be used to the exclusion of the stick. In order to maintain internal discipline, the firm may have to resort to sanctions against individual employees. It is far easier to use those powers that can be unilaterally exercised: to fire, to demote, to withhold wages, or to reprimand. These devices can visit very powerful losses upon individual employees without the need to resort to legal action, and they permit the firm to monitor employee performance continually in order to identify both strong and weak workers and to compensate them accordingly. The principles here are constant, whether we speak of senior officials or lowly subordinates, and it is for just this reason that the contract at will is found at all levels in private markets.

The parallels to the partnership situation are instructive, for the at-will arrangement is, if anything, even more effective between employers and employees. As with partnerships, the threat, be it of discharge or resignation, becomes more effective the greater the level of employee or employer abuse; it is thus an effective if informal means of encouraging self-restraint. In addition, within the employment context firing does not require a disruption of firm operations, much less an expensive division of its assets. It is instead a clean break with consequences that are immediately clear to both sides. The lower cost of both firing and quitting, therefore, helps account for the very widespread popularity of employment-at-will contracts. There is no need to resort to any theory of economic domination or inequality of bargaining power to explain at-will contracting, which appears with the same tenacity in relations

[32] *See, e.g.*, Malcomson, *Work Incentives, Hierarchy, and Internal Labor Markets*, 92 J. Pol. Econ. 486 (1984), for one effort to model the effectiveness of using internal promotions to improve workers' performance when monitoring is costly and hence imperfect. Malcomson's model does not address the question of whether the workers are under term contracts or contracts at will, but the structure of his argument is consistent with the at-will model of legal relations.

between economic equals and subordinates and is found in many complex commercial arrangements, including franchise agreements, except where limited by statutes.[33]

Thus far, the analysis generally has focused on the position of the employer. Yet for the contract at will to be adopted ex ante, it must work for the benefit of workers as well. And indeed it does, for the contract at will also contains powerful limitations on employers' abuses of power. To see the importance of the contract at will to the employee, it is useful to distinguish between two cases. In the first, the employer pays a fixed sum of money to the worker and is then free to demand of the employee whatever services he wants for some fixed period of time. In the second case, there is no fixed period of employment. The employer is free to demand whatever he wants of the employee, who in turn is free to withdraw for good reason, bad reason, or no reason at all.

The first arrangement invites abuse by the employer, who can now make enormous demands upon the worker without having to take into account either the worker's disutility during the period of service or the value of the worker's labor at contract termination. A fixed-period contract that leaves the worker's obligations unspecified thereby creates a sharp tension between the parties, since the employer receives all the marginal benefits and the employee bears all the marginal costs.[34]

Matters are very different where the employer makes increased demands under a contract at will. Now the worker can quit whenever the net value of the employment contract turns negative. As with the employer's power to fire or demote, the threat to quit

---

[33] As an example of a restriction upon the power of termination, automobile dealers may recover damages resulting from a manufacturer's failure to act in good faith in not renewing the dealer's franchise. 15 U.S.C. §§ 1221-1225 (1982). These provisions were conceived of as a supplement to the antitrust laws. Act of Aug. 8, 1956, Pub. L. No. 1026, 70 Stat. 1125 (codified at 15 U.S.C. §§ 1221-1225 (1982)) (statement of purpose).

[34] This makes it difficult to accept the argument that "[e]mployment at will is the ultimate guarantor of the capitalist's authority over the worker." Feinman, *supra* note 4, at 132-33. Yet, as Feinman notes, historically the employees who brought actions were generally those who earned high salaries. *Id.* at 118, 131-33. This is simply enough explained by noting that those would have been the only cases in which the amount in controversy exceeded the plaintiff's expected costs of suit. But the fact that employees could also quit at will makes it difficult to see in the at-will device the exploitation of the working class, especially since real wages were continually rising throughout the eighteenth and nineteenth centuries. *See* D. Diamond & J. Guiljoil, United States Economic History 277, 468 (1973); Herman E. Krooss, American Economic Development 395-98 (2d ed. 1966); S. Ratner, J. Soltow & R. Sylla, The Evolution of the American Economy 247, 308-09 (1979). Nor does a theory focusing on the employer's authority account for the right of the employee to *quit* at will.

(or at a lower level to come late or leave early) is one that can be exercised without resort to litigation. Furthermore, that threat turns out to be most effective when the employer's opportunistic behavior is the greatest because the situation is one in which the worker has least to lose. To be sure, the worker will not necessarily make a threat whenever the employer insists that the worker accept a less favorable set of contractual terms, for sometimes the changes may be accepted as an uneventful adjustment in the total compensation level attributable to a change in the market price of labor. This point counts, however, only as an additional strength of the contract at will, which allows for small adjustments *in both directions* in ongoing contractual arrangements with a minimum of bother and confusion.

The case for the contract at will is further strengthened by another feature common to contracts of this sort. The employer is often required either to give notice or to pay damages in lieu of notice; damages are traditionally equal to the wages that the employee would have earned during the notice period. These provisions for "severance pay" provide the worker with some protection against casual or hasty discharges, but they do not interfere with the powerful efficiency characteristics of the contract at will. First, lump-sum transfers do not require the introduction of any "for cause" requirement, which could be the source of expensive litigation. Second, because the sums are definite, they can be easily computed, so that administrative costs are minimized. Third, because the payments are unconditional, they do not create perverse incentives for the employee or heavy monitoring costs for the employer: the terminated employee will not be tempted to avoid gainful employment in order to run up his damages for wrongful discharge; the employer, for his part, will not have to monitor the post-termination behavior of the employee in order to guard against that very risk. Thus, provisions for severance pay can be used to give employees added protection against arbitrary discharge without sacrificing the advantages of a clean break between the parties.

2. *Reputational Losses.* Another reason why employees are often willing to enter into at-will employment contracts stems from the asymmetry of reputational losses. Any party who cheats may well obtain a bad reputation that will induce others to avoid dealing with him. The size of these losses tends to differ systematically between employers and employees—to the advantage of the employee. Thus in the usual situation there are many workers and a single employer. The disparity in number is apt to be greatest in

large industrial concerns, where the at-will contract is commonly, if mistakenly, thought to be most unsatisfactory because of the supposed inequality of bargaining power.[35] The employer who decides to act for bad reason or no reason at all may not face any legal liability under the classical common law rule. But he faces very powerful adverse economic consequences. If coworkers perceive the dismissal as arbitrary, they will take fresh stock of their own prospects, for they can no longer be certain that their faithful performance will ensure their security and advancement. The uncertain prospects created by arbitrary employer behavior is functionally indistinguishable from a reduction in wages unilaterally imposed by the employer. At the margin some workers will look elsewhere, and typically the best workers will have the greatest opportunities.[36] By the same token the large employer has more to gain if he dismisses undesirable employees, for this ordinarily acts as an implicit increase in wages to the other employees, who are no longer burdened with uncooperative or obtuse coworkers.

The existence of both positive and negative reputational effects is thus brought back to bear on the employer. The law may tolerate arbitrary behavior, but private pressures effectively limit its scope. Inferior employers will be at a perpetual competitive disadvantage with enlightened ones and will continue to lose in market share and hence in relative social importance. The lack of legal protection to the employees is therefore in part explained by the increased informal protections that they obtain by working in large concerns.[37]

3. *Risk Diversification and Imperfect Information.* The

---

[35] *See supra* note 5 and accompanying text. The possibility of the poor exploiting the rich is discussed in the context of the free-rider problem by Mancur Olson, who notes that it is often easy for a small property owner, for example, to free-ride off his larger neighbor's provision of certain common goods. MANCUR OLSON, THE LOGIC OF COLLECTIVE ACTION 27-29 (1965).

[36] To illustrate the problem, consider the firm that wants to reduce the size of its work force. If it makes a general promise of ample severance pay to whoever leaves the firm, it runs the very high risk that it will lose its most desirable employees, for it is just these workers who will find it easiest to recoup their income elsewhere. There are complications, however, since the skills of able employees may not be transferable, or at least may not be easily marketable. But the tendency is nonetheless clearly present.

[37] The point has a close analogue in the law of landlord and tenant. Landlords of large apartment complexes are often able to extract more favorable terms from tenants than the owner of a downstairs duplex can. But the large landlord has more to lose by capricious behavior, for he suffers from the same asymmetric reputational vulnerability as does the large employer. The greater legal power conferred on him by contract thus works to the benefit of both sides, as any tenant who has been relieved by the eviction of a noisy neighbor can easily attest.

contract at will also helps workers deal with the problem of risk diversification. In this regard the employee is in the same position as the partner. Ordinarily, employees cannot work more than one, or perhaps two, jobs at the same time. Thereafter the level of performance falls dramatically, so that diversification brings in its wake a low return on labor. The contract at will is designed in part to offset the concentration of individual investment in a single job by allowing diversification among employers *over time*. The employee is not locked into an unfortunate contract if he finds better opportunities elsewhere or if he detects some weakness in the internal structure of the firm. A similar analysis applies on the employer's side where he is a sole proprietor, though ordinary diversification is possible when ownership of the firm is widely held in publicly traded shares.

The contract at will is also a sensible private adaptation to the problem of imperfect information over time. In sharp contrast to the purchase of standard goods, an inspection of the job before acceptance is far less likely to guarantee its quality thereafter. The future is not clearly known. More important, employees, like employers, *know what they do not know*. They are not faced with a bolt from the blue, with an "unknown unknown." Rather they face a known unknown for which they can plan. The at-will contract is an essential part of that planning because it allows both sides to take a wait-and-see attitude to their relationship so that new and more accurate choices can be made on the strength of improved information. ("You can start Tuesday and we'll see how the job works out" is a highly intelligent response to uncertainty.) To be sure, employment relationships are more personal and hence often stormier than those that exist in financial markets, but that is no warrant for replacing the contract at will with a for-cause contract provision. The proper question is: will the shift in methods of control work a change for the benefit of both parties, or will it only make a difficult situation worse?[38]

---

[38] We should greet with skepticism any claim that takes the following form:

> The at will doctrine should be altered not because of "unequal bargaining power," but rather because it is inefficient. Courts must intervene, according to this view, in order to bring about the substantive outcome that the parties would have reached had transaction and information costs not precluded informed negotiation. When high costs of bargaining prevent negotiation between individual employees and employers, and inadequate access to information prevents parties from properly valuing the benefits of job security, judicial intervention is justified to ensure a more efficient result.

Note, *Wrongful Discharge*, *supra* note 4, at 1830. The author is right to dismiss inequality of bargaining power as a makeweight argument. But the discussion of imperfect information is nothing short of mystifying, for it simply assumes that universal arrangements are univer-

4. *Administrative Costs.* There is one last way in which the contract at will has an enormous advantage over its rivals. It is very cheap to administer. Any effort to use a for-cause rule will in principle allow all, or at least a substantial fraction of, dismissals to generate litigation. Because motive will be a critical element in these cases, the chances of either side obtaining summary judgment will be negligible. Similarly, the broad modern rules of discovery will allow exploration into every aspect of the employment relation. Indeed, a little imagination will allow the plaintiff's lawyer to delve into the general employment policies of the firm, the treatment of similar cases, and a review of the individual file. The employer for his part will be able to examine every aspect of the employee's performance and personal life in order to bolster the case for dismissal.

Nonetheless, it may be said that this inquiry is worth conducting because employers err in making decisions to fire and injustices will be done unless legal sanctions are imposed. But this analysis entirely ignores the fact that error costs always run in both directions. It has already been shown that there are powerful correctives against capricious discharge even under an at-will rule.[39] The chances of finding an innocent employee wronged by a firm vendetta are quite remote. By the same token, jury sympathy with aggrieved plaintiffs may result in a very large number of erroneous verdicts for employees. In principle it might be proper to tolerate the high error rate if the consequences of erroneous dismissal to the innocent employee were more severe than the consequences of erroneous reinstatement to the innocent employer. But quite the opposite is apt to be the case. Able employees are the very persons who have the greatest opportunity of obtaining alternate employment in the marketplace and who can therefore best mitigate their losses. Although their search for new work may be complicated because of the previous dismissal, the dismissed employee usually can get other persons, e.g., representatives of other companies with whom he has dealt, to help overcome the negative inference from the dismissal. Indeed there is less trouble in explaining away the dismissal if it is generally understood that contracts are terminable at will, since termination no longer implies employee misconduct.[40]

sally unsound, without recognizing any of their strengths or noting any of the defects in the alternative rules.

[39] *See supra* notes 36-37 and accompanying text.

[40] Other (imperfect) legal protections are available to the employee as well. If, for ex-

The results of this analysis are not upset in any way by the procession of cases that now reach the appellate courts.[41] First, these cases are never a random sample of all dismissals, but rather are selected because they promise the greatest chance of success under the applicable law. Yet the doctrines of wrongful discharge apply to all cases, including those in which superior results are reached by a simple application of the at-will rule. In addition, these cases frequently arise on a motion to dismiss, so that their assertions of improper motive may well be left unsubstantiated at trial. Finally, there is good reason for skepticism about the power of juries to divine motive and purpose from the evidence that is presented to them. A single case easily can be regarded either as employer oppression or employer benevolence, and there is every reason to expect that very different interpretations of similar fact patterns will proliferate under any version of the for-cause standard.[42]

---

ample, the previous employer deliberately gives false information in response to inquiries from prospective employers, his conduct may be actionable under the law of defamation, since the employer's bad faith would overcome any qualified privilege the employer might enjoy. If the employer volunteers the false information, the standard of liability may well be even stricter. *See, e.g.*, Clark v. Molyneux, 3 Q.B.D. 237, 243-44 (1877); R. Epstein, C. Gregory & H. Kalven, Cases and Materials on Torts 1154-57 (4th ed. 1984); *see also* W. Page Keeton, Prosser and Keeton on the Law of Torts § 115, at 832-34 (5th ed. 1984).

[41] *See* cases cited *supra* notes 6-8.

[42] Thus Monge v. Beebe Rubber Co., 114 N.H. 130, 316 A.2d 549 (1974), lends grist to the skeptic's mill. The facts of the case were summarized by another court as follows: "[f]emale employee wrongfully discharged for refusing to date foreman; court rejected employment-at-will defense as 'based on ancient feudal system.' " Novosel v. Nationwide Ins. Co., 721 F.2d 894, 897 n.5 (3d Cir. 1983). The reference to the feudal system is amusing since the contract at will by all accounts came to the fore in the last half of the nineteenth century, in part as a response to industrialization. *See* Feinman, *supra* note 4, at 125-29.

The summary of the facts found in the dissent to *Monge* itself, however, throws a very different light on the case:

> In my view, reasonable men could not find for the plaintiff on the evidence in this case even under the new rule of law which the court has fashioned today. The substance of the plaintiff's claim is that she was discharged because she did not accept an invitation of her foreman to go out with him. Although it was denied by the foreman, the jury could find on plaintiff's testimony alone that the invitation was extended. It was a single instance, however, and there is no claim that it was repeated or further pursued. It is not findable that this single refusal was the reason for the termination of plaintiff's employment. There was evidence, and none to the contrary, that it was a shortage of work and her lowest seniority that caused her press machine to be shut down and her loss of overtime. When her machine was shut down, she was given work on a degreasing machine at a higher rate of pay than when she started. When she told the foreman she "needed the money" from the overtime, he offered what from the uncontradicted evidence was the only work available to help her out until her overtime was restored. The only so-called harassment and ridicule claimed amounts to no more than once saying "How do you like my floor boy?" and "My wife wouldn't do that." It is uncontradicted that when she was having trouble with annoying phone calls and needed help, the per-

The difficulties are even greater once it becomes established that dismissals cannot be made at will. Now the employer will have to reconsider every aspect of personnel relations. If it is improper to dismiss at will, then it becomes improper to demote or to transfer at will, for an employee will be able to assert with perfect propriety that the employer had made work so unattractive to him that his conduct should amount to a "constructive dismissal" for which either damages or reinstatement is appropriate. Thus a rule that starts with modest ambitions will in the end regulate each and every aspect of the employment relationship. Professor Clyde Summers, for example, in his own proposal for the creation of a statutory cause of action for unjust dismissal recognizes that "[t]he statute [on unjust dismissal] must reach all forms of disciplinary action related to an employee's job, including demotion, reduction in pay, reduction in seniority, assignment to undesirable work, and forced resignation."[43] But he does not explain why the necessity for fashioning comprehensive regulation counts as a virtue instead of a vice, in light of the deleterious effects of increased regulation upon expected hiring patterns of employers. Where an employer might have been more willing to take risky employees under an at-will rule, he will now be less willing to do so under the for-cause rule because any subsequent demotion or dismissal will be an open invitation to a lawsuit by an aggrieved employee. Furthermore, in most at-will situations the dismissed employee is replaced by another, so it is hard to see how employees *as a class* benefit from a rule that can only hamper general mobility in labor markets.

These difficulties arise, moreover, no matter what the form of the rule. Thus, the rule could be stated as one that prohibits dismissals (or transfers) without cause, or it could be phrased only to prohibit a dismissal that is made in bad faith or with malice. The differences in formal expression will undoubtedly be significant in

---

sonnel manager personally went to the police and then to her home to talk with her and her husband; that when she could not pick up her Christmas turkey, the foreman personally delivered two instead of one to her home; and that he also at her request gave her husband, a mechanic, work on his automobile.

Her final termination was in accordance with established company rules and she neither contested the termination nor pursued the grievance procedures under the union contract. She was denied unemployment compensation on the ground that she was a "voluntary quit" and did not appeal that finding.

A finding that this company discharged the plaintiff because she refused her foreman a date eight months before could not reasonably be made and should not be permitted to stand.

Monge, 114 N.H. at 134-35, 316 A.2d at 552-53 (dissenting opinion).

[43] Summers, *supra* note 4, at 526-27.

the litigation of individual cases, as the for-cause standard should impose more stringent restrictions on employer freedom than the bad-faith standard. But from the institutional point of view the differences between the types of regulatory schemes would have only minor impact because *all* of them place costly and inconvenient restraints upon contractual freedom. So long as the cases align themselves in any continuous array, a large number of dismissals will be fair game for litigation no matter what the applicable legal standard. The administrative and error-cost considerations therefore reinforce the basic conclusion: there is no warrant for legal interference with the contract at will.

5. *Bilateral Monopoly and Inequality of Bargaining Power.* The account thus far given of the contract at will in no way depends upon any notion of an inherent inequality of bargaining power that pervades all employment contracts. Indeed if such an inequality did govern the employment relationship, we should expect to see conditions that exist in no labor market. Wages should be driven to zero, for no matter what their previous level, the employer could use his (inexhaustible) bargaining power to reduce them further, until the zero level was reached.[44] Similarly, inequality of bargaining power implies that the employee will be bound for a term while the employer (who can pay the peppercorn consideration) retains the power to terminate at will. Yet in practice we observe both positive wages and employees with the right to quit at will.

The reason why these contracts at will are effective is precisely that the employer must always pay an implicit price when he exercises his right to fire. He no longer has the right to compel the employee's service, as the employee can enter the market to find another job. The costs of the employer's decision therefore are borne in large measure by the employer himself, creating an implicit system of coinsurance between employer and employee against employer abuse. Nor, it must be stressed, are the costs to the employer light. It is true that employees who work within a firm acquire specific knowledge about its operation and upon dismissal can transfer only a portion of that knowledge to the new

[44] Note that the same arguments could be made in the consumer market as well, leading to the prediction that these same workers with a zero wage will pay infinite prices for the necessities of life. The only coherent models are those that assume that total wages and other income supply a budget constraint for purchases, so that both markets are in equilibrium simultaneously. Abstracting one market from another is a ploy that makes inequality of bargaining power seem more plausible than it is.

job.[48] Nonetheless, the problem is roughly symmetrical, as the employer must find, select, and train a replacement worker who may not turn out to be better than the first employee. Workers are not fungible, and sorting them out may be difficult: resumes can be misleading, if not fraudulent; references may be only too eager to unload an unsuitable employee; training is expensive; and the new worker may not like the job or may be forced to move out of town. In any case, firms must bear the costs of voluntary turnover by workers who quit, which gives them a frequent reminder of the need to avoid self-inflicted losses. The institutional stability of employment contracts at will can now be explained in part by their legal fragility. The right to fire is exercised only infrequently because the threat of firing is effective.

Thus far the account of inequality of bargaining power has been wholly negative. But the description of the employment relationship does suggest one way in which inequality can arise, even within the framework of generally competitive markets. In the course of an ongoing relationship between employee and employer, each side gains from the contract more than it could obtain by returning to the open market. The surplus that is created must be divided between the parties. In principle, either the worker or the employer could receive the entire surplus without inducing the other party, who still receives a competitive return, to sever the relationship. A fortiori any solution that divides the surplus between the parties should be stable as well. The contract at will thus creates a bilateral monopoly, but only to the extent of the surplus.

The question of inequality of bargaining power can now be helpfully restated: which side will appropriate most of the surplus in any negotiations between them? Unlike the typical formulations of the problem, this leaves the set of possible solutions strictly bounded because the employee cannot be driven below the competitive wage and the employer cannot be driven to a wage above the sum of the competitive wage plus the full amount of the surplus. An employer can therefore be said to possess an inequality of bargaining power when he is able to appropriate more than half the surplus, while the employee can be said to possess inequality of bargaining power if *he* can appropriate more than half the surplus.

[48] In some cases it is all too transferable, as with customer lists or trade secrets. When such information is transferred, an employer may look for redress to the elaborate body of law that regulates the transmission of trade secrets. *See* Kitch, *The Law and Economics of Rights in Valuable Information*, 9 J. LEGAL STUD. 683, 689-701 (1980).

To take an example, assume the employer is prepared to pay 20, while the worker is willing to work for 10. The agreed wage therefore could fall anywhere between those two numbers. If the employer is systematically able to appropriate more than 5 of this surplus, by keeping the wage level below 15, then he has unequal bargaining power, though still within the framework of overall competitive markets.

The existence of some surplus should be pervasive in all labor markets, given that labor is not perfectly fungible. In practice, the size of the surplus on average should be relatively small at the time of contract formation. Because the parties have not built up much specific capital in the relationship, quitting or firing will cause relatively small dislocations. As time passes, however, the gains to both sides from continuing the employment relationship are apt to increase, so that both sides have more to lose from separation. The bilateral monopoly problem now assumes greater significance. The increased size of the surplus can easily make wages somewhat indeterminate (which is why workers are commonly nervous about asking for a raise, and employers are nervous about refusing it). As the stakes become larger, the amount of resources spent in obtaining a larger portion of the surplus should increase. A contractual breakdown should nonetheless be an infrequent occurrence, as both sides have strong incentives to keep the relationship viable. The costs of negotiation tend to be reduced because each side is familiar with the other. The scope for bluffing is somewhat limited by each party's knowledge of the preferences of the other side. Finally, there are strong reasons for each side to avoid squeezing the last drop out of a relationship: miscalculation of the reserve price of the other party (i.e., the minimum he will accept or the maximum he will pay) could lead to a severance of the relationship and thus to a loss of the entire surplus.

It still remains to be determined which side is likely to appropriate most of this contract-specific surplus. One might guess that the employer will be able to achieve this objective, perhaps because his experience in repeat transactions with many workers fosters greater skills in negotiation. In addition, the employer may know in general the market wages available to beginning workers, as these typically will be public knowledge. Yet a number of considerations suggest the opposite conclusion. First, the employer often bargains through subordinate managers and thus faces an agency-cost problem avoided by the worker who bargains on his own account. Second, the worker's opportunity cost for his time will often be lower than the employer's, so that the increased time he can spend on the transaction may offset the employer's greater skill, if any, per unit of time. Third, the worker may be able to learn something about the employer's reservation price (i.e., the maximum wage he would be willing to pay) because the employer must reveal some information about his willingness to pay in negotiations with other long-term workers. Finally, it is not clear that the employer gains any real advantage because of his greater relative wealth, if any. To be sure, the wealthy employer can hold out for a larger share of the surplus because he has less, proportionally, to lose. Yet by the same token the employer's resolve may be weaker because he has less to gain by holding out.

This modest catalogue of considerations shows how difficult it is to determine the exact division of the surplus, although my suspicion is that in the broad run of cases it will tend to be evenly divided. But even if this guess is wrong, there is no reason for the law to interfere in the bargaining process. The whole question of inequality of bargaining power arises in the bounded context of how much of a *supra*competitive wage the worker will obtain. At the very worst, the worker will get the amount that is offered in some alternate employment where he has built up no specific capital. To try to formulate and administer a set of legal rules that will allow some trier of fact to measure the size of the surplus embedded in the ongoing transaction, and to allocate half (or more) of it to the worker, cannot be done at any social cost that is less than the expected size of the surplus itself, if it can be done at all. The entire exercise is fraught with the possibility of real error, as real resources would have to be expended solely to make transfer payments that can in no way enhance productive efforts. The existence of this transactional surplus does not negate the fact that markets are still competitive before prospective employers and employees enter into any transaction at all.

The size of the surplus, and thus the scope of any inequality problem, can be reduced more effectively by adopting legal rules that remove or minimize legal impediments to labor mobility. The contract at will, by allowing either side to sever relationships without legal impediment, tends to reduce rigidities in markets and thus to act as a counterweight to the bilateral monopoly problem that emerges even in voluntary markets. The complex rules that give workers "property" rights in their jobs tend to increase the size of any possible surplus and exacerbate the basic problem. The identification of a transaction-specific surplus, then, adds to our understanding of long-term employment relationships, but it affords no warrant for upsetting the contract at will on supposed grounds of public policy.

III. Distributional Concerns

Enough has been said to show that there is no principled reason of fairness or utility to disturb the common law's longstanding presumption in favor of the contract at will. It remains to be asked whether there are some hitherto unmentioned distributional consequences sufficient to throw that conclusion into doubt. One clear sign that there are not is that the advocates of the wrongful-discharge action themselves have not cast the argument in this form. Professor Lawrence Blades, for example, makes clear from the title of his own paper—*Employment at Will v. Individual Freedom*[46]—that he thinks abrogation of the contract at will helps advance the cause of individual liberty. While I believe that he is wrong in that conclusion, I think that he chose the correct ground on which to fight, for a moment's reflection makes it clear that distributional considerations enter at best only obliquely into the employment context.

The proposed reforms in the at-will doctrine cannot hope to transfer wealth systematically from rich to poor on the model of comprehensive systems of taxation or welfare benefits.[47] Indeed it is very difficult to identify in advance any deserving group of recipients that stands to gain unambiguously from the universal abrogation of the at-will contract. The proposed rules cover the whole range from senior executives to manual labor. At every wage level, there is presumably some differential in workers' output. Those who tend to slack off seem on balance to be most vulnerable to dismissal under the at-will rule; yet it is very hard to imagine why some special concession should be made in their favor at the expense of their more diligent fellow workers.

The distributional issues, moreover, become further clouded once it is recognized that any individual employee will have interests on both sides of the employment relation. Individual workers participate heavily in pension plans, where the value of the holdings depends in part upon the efficiency of the legal rules that govern the companies in which they own shares. If the regulation of the contract at will diminishes the overall level of wealth, the losses are apt to be spread far and wide, which makes it doubtful that there are any gains to the worst off in society that justify

[46] Blades, *supra* note 4.

[47] I have addressed these issues in detail in Epstein, *supra* note 3.

somewhat greater losses to those who are better off. The usual concern with maldistribution gives us situations in which one person has one hundred while each of one hundred has one and asks us to compare that distribution with an even distribution of, say, two per person. But the stark form of the numerical example does not explain how the skewed distribution is tied to the concrete choice between different rules governing employment relations. Set in this concrete context, the choices about the proposed new regulation of the employment contract do not set the one against the many but set the many against each other, all in the context of a shrinking overall pie. The possible gains from redistribution, even on the most favorable of assumptions about the diminishing marginal utility of money, are simply not present.

If this is the case, one puzzle still remains: who should be in favor of the proposed legislation? One possibility is that support for the change in common law rules rests largely on ideological and political grounds, so that the legislation has the public support of persons who may well be hurt by it in their private capacities.[48] Another possible explanation could identify the hand of interest-group politics in some subtle form. For example, the lawyers and government officials called upon to administer the new legislation may expect to obtain increased income and power, although this explanation seems insufficient to account for the current pressure. A more uncertain line of inquiry could ask whether labor unions stand to benefit from the creation of a cause of action for wrongful discharge. Unions, after all, have some skill in working with for-cause contracts under the labor statutes that prohibit firing for union activities, and they might be able to promote their own growth by selling their services to the presently nonunionized sector. In addition, the for-cause rule might give employers one less reason to resist unionization, since they would be unable to retain the absolute power to hire and fire in any event. Yet, by the same token, it is possible that workers would be less inclined to pay the costs of union membership if they received some purported benefit by the force of law without unionization. The ultimate weight of these considerations is an empirical question to which no easy answers appear.[49] What is clear, however, is that even if one could show that the shift in the rule either benefits or hurts unions and

---

[48] That this may be irrational does not imply that it is impossible. *See* Stigler, *Wealth, and Possibly Liberty*, 7 J. LEGAL STUD. 213 (1978).

[49] It has been reported that union leaders do not favor these reforms. Chicago Sun-Times, June 10, 1984, at 32, col. 1 (2-star ed.).

their members, the answer would not justify the rule, for it would not explain why the legal system should try to skew the balance one way or the other. The bottom line therefore remains unchanged. The case for a legal requirement that renders employment contracts terminable only for cause is as weak after distributional considerations are taken into account as before.

IV. Exceptions to the Contract at Will

An examination of the contracting objectives of parties explains why contracts at will are common. The same set of considerations, however, also helps explain why contracts at will are *not* found in all employment contexts, but are instead sometimes displaced by more elaborate contractual mechanisms. The central point is that the contract at will works only where performance on both sides takes place in lockstep progression. This condition will be satisfied where neither side has performed or where the worker's past performance has been matched by appropriate payment from the employer. In these cases the contract at will provides both employer and employee with a simple, informal "bond" against the future misfeasance of the other side: fire or quit. Where the sequence of performance requires one side to perform in full before the other side begins performance, this bonding mechanism will break down because there are no longer two unperformed promises of roughly equal value to stand as security for each other. That is why an employee will have to resort to legal action if the employer simply refuses to pay wages for work that has already been done. It is also why a contract at will cannot handle the question of compensation for job-related personal injuries, for after injury the value of the right to quit no longer balances off the right to fire.[80]

The same problem of imperfect bonding under the contract at will also arises where the nature of the employment requires work for extended periods of time. Thus, in the traditional apprenticeship contracts explicit provision had to be made to ensure that the indentured servant would not go elsewhere and likewise that the master would not abuse him during the period of service.[81] Simi-

---

[80] For an account of the elaborate consensual arrangements that grew up to handle this problem, see Epstein, *The Historical Origins and Economic Structure of Workers' Compensation Law*, 16 GA. L. REV. 775, 789-94, 798-803 (1982).

[81] The power of the common law's presumption in favor of at-will contracts is shown, however, by the courts' refusal to infer such terms. *See* 6 C.B. LABATT, COMMENTARIES ON THE LAW OF MASTER AND SERVANT § 2198 (2d ed. 1913). At various times, legislatures regu-

larly in earlier times, contracts for agricultural workers were understood to be for the year or for the growing season.[52] These arrangements accordingly contained extensive risk-sharing features. The worker received some interim compensation, typically in the form of room and board, that functioned as progress payments for services already rendered. Yet the contract often called for the payment of a large cash sum at the end of the harvest because the power of the employer to withhold some of the wages until that time was necessary to counteract the possibility that a worker, who had pocketed wages in advance, might abandon the employer in order to obtain high wages for day-work at harvest time when labor was at a premium.[53]

The same problems can exist with modern employment contracts. Suppose that a worker has put in the effort to obtain for the firm a large contract on which he is to be paid a commission. If the firm dismisses him under an at-will contract before the sale is consummated and the commission is formally due, most courts will (rightly) imply a term of good faith that gives the employee the commission for the work done, unless the agreement explicitly provides otherwise. Thus in *Coleman v. Graybar Electric Co.*,[54] the plaintiff's claim for compensation rested in part upon commissions that were paid annually based upon the sales record in the previous period. The court construed the contract to preclude the at-will norm: "We conclude that in this case the contract did not authorize the forfeiture of additional compensation provided in the plan of compensation if the services of the employee were terminated arbitrarily and without just cause."[55]

As the size of possible commissions increases, moreover, the

---

lated the duration of indentures. *See id.* § 2113.

[52] *See* Feinman, *supra* note 4, at 120. There is, however, no need to presume exploitation to account for this form of contract. *See infra* text following note 52.

[53] Usually the courts refused to allow the worker to recover on a quantum meruit count for the value of the services rendered when he quit before term. *See, e.g.*, Britton v. Turner, 6 N.H. 481, 486 (1834) (allowing the action but recognizing its deviation from the clear weight of authority); *see also* F. Kessler & G. Gilmore, Contracts, Cases and Materials 878 (2d ed. 1970). The majority result tends to be sound even though it requires the worker to continue the work in order to claim the deferred benefits and thus could result in some windfall to the employer. Where the worker quits before the end of the term, he can often obtain higher short-term wages in the market to offset the loss of the final payment. A rule that awarded some fraction of the deferred payment could give the worker both, which would provide him with the wrong incentives. Moreover, even when the employee loses on the wage claim, he has still obtained board and lodging, the value of which the employer would never recover by suit against the worker in breach, be it for legal or practical reasons.

[54] 195 F.2d 374 (5th Cir. 1952).

[55] *Id.* at 378.

potential gains from post-contractual exploitation will increase as well. But it does not follow that the parties are helpless to protect themselves against exploitation. Rather, when the stakes are high, it becomes worthwhile for the parties to fashion explicit allocations of the commission in the event of an employee dismissal.[56] Thus in *Fortune v. National Cash Register Co.*,[57] the commission contract in question was for the sale of a large cash register system. Under this contract, a salesman received seventy-five percent of the commission derived from a sale if the sales territory had been assigned to him at the date of the order; he received twenty-five percent of the commission if the territory had been assigned to him at the date of delivery; and he got the full commission if the territory had been assigned to him at both times.[58] The plaintiff in the action was a salesman who had been fired after the original deal had been struck but before it had been completed.[59] The seventy-five percent commission earned under the agreement had been paid, while the remaining twenty-five percent commission was paid by the firm to another employee, according to the express terms of the contract.[60] The court held that these express provisions were not dispositive and read into the agreement a covenant of good faith and fair dealing, on which it held that the plaintiff was entitled to a jury trial.[61]

The decision seems wrong in principle. The contractual provisions concerning commissions represent a rough effort to match payment with performance where the labor of more than one individual was necessary to close the sale. The case is not simply one where a strategically timed firing allowed the company to deprive a dismissed employee of the benefits due him upon completion of performance. Indeed, the firm kept none of the commission at all, so that when the case went to the jury, the only issue was whether the company should be called upon to pay the same commission twice. The court in *Fortune* did not try to understand the commis-

---

[56] The same problem commonly arises in brokerage cases where the owner tries to dismiss the broker after the buyer is located but before the agreement is concluded. A covenant of good faith is normally appropriate here to prevent the expropriation of labor by the owner-seller, and these provisions are now commonplace in brokerage agreements, which also typically provide that the brokers obtain no commission for buyers whom the seller independently locates after the brokerage period. For a collection of cases, see F. Kessler & G. Gilmore, *supra* note 53, at 337.

[57] 373 Mass. 96, 364 N.E.2d 1251 (1977).

[58] *Id.* at 97-98, 364 N.E.2d at 1253.

[59] *Id.* at 100, 364 N.E.2d at 1254.

[60] *Id.* at 99, 364 N.E.2d at 1254.

[61] *Id.* at 101-04, 364 N.E.2d at 1255-57.

sion structure that it was prepared to condemn; instead, it made the chronic mistake of thinking that what it intuited to be an unfortunate business outcome invalidated the entire contractual structure. In its enthusiastic meddling in private contracts, the court nowhere suggested an alternative commission structure that would have better served the joint interests of the parties at the time of contract formation. Here, as in so many cases, an unquestioning adherence to the principle of freedom of contract would have yielded results both simpler and superior to those generated after an extensive but flawed judicial examination of the basic terms.

Conclusion

The recent trend toward expanding the legal remedies for wrongful discharge has been greeted with wide approval in judicial, academic, and popular circles. In this paper, I have argued that the modern trend rests in large measure upon a misunderstanding of the contractual processes and the ends served by the contract at will. No system of regulation can hope to match the benefits that the contract at will affords in employment relations. The flexibility afforded by the contract at will permits the ceaseless marginal adjustments that are necessary in any ongoing productive activity conducted, as all activities are, in conditions of technological and business change. The strength of the contract at will should not be judged by the occasional cases in which it is said to produce unfortunate results, but rather by the vast run of cases where it provides a sensible private response to the many and varied problems in labor contracting. All too often the case for a wrongful discharge doctrine rests upon the identification of possible employer abuses, as if they were all that mattered. But the proper goal is to find the set of comprehensive arrangements that will minimize the frequency and severity of abuses by employers and employees alike. Any effort to drive employer abuses to zero can only increase the difficulties inherent in the employment relation. Here, a full analysis of the relevant costs and benefits shows why the constant minor imperfections of the market, far from being a reason to oust private agreements, offer the most powerful reason for respecting them. The doctrine of wrongful discharge is the problem and not the solution. This is one of the many situations in which courts and legislatures should leave well enough alone.

[3]

ARTICLES

The Legacy of Industrial Pluralism: The Tension Between Individual Employment Rights and the New Deal Collective Bargaining System

Katherine Van Wezel Stone†

As labor unions are declining,[1] so too is the legal framework that has governed labor relations in the United States since the New Deal. In the past decade, the New Deal labor laws,[2] which were intended to create collective rights for workers and to empower organized labor, have been undermined through a series of judicial and administrative decisions.[3] The underlying premises

---

† Professor of Law, Cornell Law School; and Professor, Cornell School of Industrial and Labor Relations. The author would like to thank participants in workshops at The University of Chicago, Cornell University, New York University, the University of Southern California, the State University of New York (Buffalo), and the University of Toronto Law Schools, as well as participants in workshops at the Cornell School of Industrial and Labor Relations, the Political Science Department of Yale University, and the Graduate Center of the City University of New York. She would also like to extend particular thanks to Cass Sunstein, Steve Shiffrin, Anne-Marie Burley, Nick Salvatore, Jim Atleson, Stewart Schwab, Roy Adams, Greg Alexander, Bob Hillman, and Gerd Korman for insightful suggestions, and to Philip Douglass, Daniel Shacknai, and Suzanne Woodland for exceptional research assistance. Finally, the author thanks the Fund for Labor Relations Research, which provided partial funding for this project.

[1] Union membership has declined from approximately 25 percent of the nonagricultural workforce in 1980 to 16.3 percent in 1990. See notes 6-7 and accompanying text (Table I).

[2] The most important federal labor laws enacted in the New Deal period were the National Labor Relations Act, Pub L No 49 Stat 449 (1935), codified at 29 USC §§ 151 et seq (1988) (the "NLRA"), and the Norris-La Guardia Act, Pub L No 47 Stat 70 (1932), codified at 29 USC §§ 101 et seq (1988).

[3] See generally Lee Modjeska, *The Reagan NLRB, Phase I*, 46 Ohio St L J 95, 130-31 (1985) ("In my view . . . the [Reagan Era] Board reversals are of major import and pro-

and assumptions of the labor relations system have also been the subject of intense scholarly attack.[4] Overall, it appears that the era of collective bargaining that was born in the New Deal and that blossomed in the post-war decades is coming to an end.

With the old system of collective bargaining fading away, something new is emerging to take its place. In the past decade, state legislatures and courts have created a plethora of new employment rights for individual workers—rights not to be fired abusively, rights for privacy on the job, rights to be free of drug testing, rights to be free of sexual harassment, rights for whistleblowers, and so forth. Paradoxically, these new individual employee rights are emerging just as labor's collective rights are waning. Do these new individual rights signify a fundamental change in the system of legal regulation of employment in this country? Or are they merely an accretion to, or embellishment of, the New Deal system of collective bargaining? This question is important if we want to understand what is happening to the law governing labor relations and influence its future course. If the New Deal system of collective bargaining is collapsing, and if a new system is emerging, it is important to recognize that fact, and initiate a public debate about the strengths and weaknesses of the new system, the old system, and others that might be imagined.

There is a plausible argument that the newly emerging individual employment rights are an evolution of the pre-existing system of collective bargaining. After all, the new individual employment rights seem perfectly compatible with the system of

foundly alter the preexisting balance of labor management relations . . . ."); James B. Atleson, *Reflections on Labor, Power, and Society*, 44 Md L Rev 841, 871 (1985) (arguing that recent Board and Supreme Court decisions have weakened union power, and that these decisions reflect, and further, the growing imbalance of power between unions and corporate structures); William B. Gould IV, *Some Reflections on Fifty Years of the National Labor Relations Act: The Need for Labor Board and Labor Law Reform*, 38 Stan L Rev 937, 939 (1986) (arguing that the Reagan Board has exhibited a "pronounced hostility to unions and collective bargaining"). See also Katherine Van Wezel Stone, *Labor and the Corporate Structure: Chcnging Conceptions and Emerging Possibilities*, 55 U Chi L Rev 73 (1988) (detailing recent legal decisions that have restricted the power of unions to influence strategic corporate decisionmaking).

[4] See, for example, Richard A. Epstein, *A Common Law for Labor Relations: A Critique of the New Deal Labor Legislation*, 92 Yale L J 1357 (1983); Charles Fried, *Individual and Collective Rights in Work Relations: Reflections on the Current State of Labor Law and Its Prospects*, 51 U Chi L Rev 1012 (1984); Katherine Van Wezel Stone, *The Post-War Paradigm in American Labor Law*, 90 Yale L J 1509 (1981); Karl E. Klare, *Judicial Deradicalization of the Wagner Act and the Origins of Modern Legal Consciousness, 1937-1941*, 62 Minn L Rev 265 (1978). See also James B. Atleson, *Values and Assumptions in American Labor Law* (Massachusetts, 1983).

collective bargaining. Indeed, they might enhance labor's strength in the workplace by setting a floor above which unions negotiate. They might also strengthen unions by removing the more general issues from the bargaining table, thus permitting unions to focus on those issues of particular concern to each workplace. This more finely-tuned form of bargaining could strengthen loyalty at the local level and thereby create stronger labor organizations. Greater individual employment rights might also remove sources of conflict within unions. Externally imposed employment terms represent tradeoffs made by a legislature or court, rather than by unions—tradeoffs between the young and the old, the black and the white, and so forth. Thus they spare unions the potentially divisive effects of making such decisions themselves.

However, despite the variety of ways in which external employment rights could be benign or even beneficial to organized labor, the rise of individual employment rights has not had that effect. Rather, there is a tension between the new individual employment rights and the New Deal system of collective bargaining, a tension that means, concretely, that organized workers do not share in the benefits of the new employment rights. Examining why this is so will enable us to see that the newly emerging system is a distinct and separate form of legal regulation. And recognizing that reality will enable us to confront the normative issue: What system of legal rules is best suited for regulating employment relations?

I begin in Section I with a description of union decline and a discussion of several theories that have been offered to explain it. In Section II, I summarize the developments of the past decade in labor and employment law in order to illustrate in more detail what I described above: that the National Labor Relations Board (the "NLRB") and the courts in recent years have diminished the ability of unions to provide job security for their members while, at the same time, state legislatures have begun providing some modicum of job security for individual employees.

In Section III, I ask: What has the rise of individual rights meant for unionized workers? The answer lies in the labor law doctrine of § 301 preemption. Section 301 of the Labor Management Relations Act grants federal jurisdiction over suits for violations of collective bargaining agreements. Under § 301, courts determine whether the collective bargaining agreement preempts claims an employee brings under external statutory or common law rights. I show that by means of a broad § 301 preemption doctrine, courts have erected a rigid barrier between collectively bargained rights and individual employment rights. As a result, unionized workers now have, in many respects, fewer employment rights than do their nonunion brothers and sisters.

In Section IV, I argue that the reason the courts have adopted such a broad § 301 preemption doctrine is the conception of collective bargaining that has dominated judicial and scholarly thinking about collective bargaining in the post-war era. That particular conception of labor relations, which I call "industrial pluralism,"[5] is based on private bargaining and private contractual rights. Its reasoning and rhetoric resists the injection of statutory or judicially-created employment rights into the workplace, promoting instead a vision of the workplace as a self-sufficient realm.

Finally, in Section V, I discuss three normative and policy questions that the analysis raises: First, is the emerging system of individual employment rights preferable to the New Deal system of collective bargaining? Second, are there forms of collective bargaining that do not insulate the unionized workplace from external sources of rights? And third, does the § 301 preemption analysis and legal incompatibility between individual and collective rights play a role in union decline? I then conclude by arguing that the individual rights model of employment relations does not provide an adequate substitute for collective bargaining, and that a new model of collective workplace rights is necessary if we are to promote workplace justice and protect workers' standards of living.

I. Union Decline

No discussion of modern labor relations can ignore the fact of union decline. Between 1980 and 1990, union membership declined from almost twenty-five percent of the nonagricultural work force to less than seventeen percent. The following table traces union decline both in absolute numbers and as a percentage of the nonagricultural workforce:

[5] Stone, 90 Yale L J at 1514-17 (cited in note 4); Katherine Van Wezel Stone, *Re-envisioning Labor Law: A Response to Professor Finkin*, 45 Md L Rev 978, 978-80 (1986).

TABLE I
DECLINING UNION MEMBERSHIP[6]

	Absolute Number of Workers in Unions		Union Members as Percentage of Non-Agricultural Workforce	
Year	Total	% Change	%	% Change
1950	14,267	———	31.5%	———
1960	17,049	19.5%	31.4%	(0.3%)
1970	19,381	13.7%	27.3%	(13.1%)
1980	22,366	15.4%	24.7%	(9.5%)
1990	16,740	(25.2%)	16.1%	(34.8%)

Note that the decade of the 1980s saw a marked hastening of the rate of decline.[7] Indeed, the declining rate in the 1980s is even more dramatic for *private* sector unionism. Between 1983 and 1989, union membership declined from 16.8 percent of the private, nonagricultural workforce to 12.4 percent[8] — an overall decline of more than twenty-five percent.

There are many theories to explain union decline. One theory, the employer-opposition theory, posits that unions have declined as a consequence of intensified union avoidance strategies by employers. This theory has several variations. One variation stresses the fact that, in the 1970s, the difference between union and non-

---

[6] 1950-70 data from Michael Goldfield, *The Decline of Organized Labor in the United States* 10 Table I (Chicago, 1987); 1980 data from id at 11 Table II; 1990 data from 38 Employment & Earnings 228-29, Tables 57 & 58 (Jan 1991).

[7] "During the 1980s, . . . private sector unions experienced one of their most severe drops in membership in United States history . . . ." Leo Troy, *Will a More Interventionist NLRA Revive Organized Labor?*, 13 Harv J L & Pub Pol 583, 607 (1990).

Professor Michael Goldfield, in his impressive book, *The Decline of Organized Labor* (cited in note 6), argues that union decline is nothing new: There has been a steady and constant decline in the percentage of the workforce unionized from the mid-1950s until 1980. Professor Goldfield attributes this trend primarily to class forces, growing management resistance, union passivity, and pro-employer public policy choices. Id at 180-217. Thus he discounts explanations that are based on phenomena such as short-term changes in the demographics of the workforce or employer attitudes. However, while Goldfield does demonstrate a long-term, slow union decline, he does not address the precipitous, almost free-fall decline that occurred in the 1980s. Most of his data predate the 1980s, and his data for the years 1980-85 suggest a new, steeper phase of union decline. Id at 16 (Table 3). To understand the dramatic decline of the past decade, we need a theory that at least partially disentangles it from the longer-run steady decline that Goldfield documents.

[8] *Statistical Abstract of the United States: 1991* 42 (Table 697) (GPO, 1991). See also Troy, 13 Harv J L & Pub Pol at 592-94 (cited in note 7).

union wages was at an all-time high. Therefore employers had powerful financial incentives to resist unions where they did not exist and to eliminate them where they did.[9] In other words, unions effectively priced themselves out of the market.

Another variation of the employer-opposition theory suggests that the Reagan Administration's treatment of the air traffic controllers' strike and similar actions encouraged employers to resist their unions.[10] In this view, employers have always been anti-union, and the shift in official attitudes in the past decade emboldened them to act on their predilections.

In yet another variation of the employer-opposition school of thought, some scholars attribute union decline to an increase in unlawful employer behavior during election campaigns and the inability of the NLRB effectively to police and remedy employers' unfair labor practices.[11] The most prominent spokesman of this viewpoint is Professor Paul Weiler of the Harvard Law School.[12]

Another group of scholars has attempted to explain union decline with a union-complacency theory. According to this theory,

---

[9] See, for example, Robert J. Flanagan, *NLRA Litigation and Union Representation*, 38 Stan L Rev 957, 984-85 (1986).

[10] See, for example, Charles McDonald, *U.S. Union Membership in Future Decades: A Trade Unionist's Perspective*, 31 Indus Rel 13, 15 (1992) (attributing the precipitous drop in union membership in the 1980s to President Reagan's actions); Michael J. Goldberg, *Cleaning Labor's House: Institutional Reform Litigation in the Labor Movement*, 1989 Duke L J 903, 1002 (hypothesizing the adverse effect of improper governmental intervention on the labor movement); David L. Gregory, *Book Review*, 53 Geo Wash L Rev 680, 681-83 (1985) (arguing that the Administration's treatment of the PATCO strike and its reshaping of the NLRB have combined with recent Supreme Court decisions to create an atmosphere hostile to unions). See generally Bernard D. Meltzer and Cass R. Sunstein, *Public Employee Strikes, Executive Discretion, and the Air Traffic Controllers*, 50 U Chi L Rev 731 (1983) (analyzing air traffic controllers' strike and its legal consequences).

[11] See, for example, Modjeska, 46 Ohio St L J at 131 (cited in note 3) (recent NLRB decisions reflect a "substantial deregulation of employer conduct with a concomitant, potential disenfranchisement of employee rights and interests"); Paul Alan Levy, *The Unidimensional Perspective of the Reagan Labor Board*, 16 Rutgers L J 269, 269-70 (1985) ("[I]n the three years since President Reagan's appointees began to join the Board, there has been an unprecedented assault on this country's labor laws . . . led by . . . Board members who are wholly unsympathetic to the [NLRA's] purposes.").

[12] Paul Weiler, *Promises to Keep: Securing Workers' Rights to Self-Organization Under the NRLA*, 96 Harv L Rev 1769 (1983) (arguing that the failure of the NLRB to police and remedy violations of § 8(a)(3) of the NLRA is a major factor in union decline). However, some scholars have disputed Weiler's data and conclusions. See Robert J. LaLonde and Bernard D. Meltzer, *Hard Times for Unions: Another Look at the Significance of Employer Illegalities*, 58 U Chi L Rev 953, 954-55 (1991), to which Professor Weiler responded powerfully in *Hard Times for Unions: Challenging Times for Scholars*, 58 U Chi L Rev 1015 (1991). See also Leo Troy, *Market Forces and Union Decline: A Response to Paul Weiler*, 59 U Chi L Rev 681 (1992). For a critique of employer-opposition explanations for union decline generally, see Troy, 13 Harv J L & Pub Pol at 590-95 (cited in note 7).

union decline is a result of the failure of unions to adjust to a changing economy. Some theorists of this school emphasize the failure of unions to aggressively organize new members.[13] Some also cite shifts in the composition of the workforce from white males to minorities and women—groups to which unions have not traditionally appealed.[14] Still others of this school stress the shift in the economy away from blue collar manufacturing jobs, which had been heavily unionized, toward white collar and service jobs, where unions traditionally have been weak.[15]

No doubt, the employer-opposition and the union-complacency theories each tell part of the story, but neither can fully account for the phenemonon. For example, while increased employer opposition to unions is undoubtedly a factor in union decline, it does not satisfactorily explain why unorganized workers have not made more efforts to unionize in the face of the declining real earnings of the 1980s.[16] Similarily, union complacency may explain why unions in the older manufacturing sectors are declining, but it does not explain why employees in the new sectors do not unionize.[17] Furthermore, to attribute union decline to the failure of unions to organize new types of workers in new types of industries is to ignore the facts. To the extent that unions have made gains in recent years, the gains have been among women and minorities, in the service and white collar sectors. Unions have been growing

---

[13] See, for example, Gregory, 53 Geo Wash L Rev at 681 (cited in note 10).

[14] See, for example, Marion Crain, *Feminizing Unions: Challenging the Gendered Structure of Wage Labor*, 89 Mich L Rev 1155, 1172 (1991) ("the influx of women into the workforce has been cited as a major barrier to union growth"); Theodore J. St. Antoine, *Federal Regulation of the Workplace in the Next Half Century*, 61 Chi Kent L Rev 631, 645 (1985) (attributing union decline, in part, to the failure of unions to appeal to the young, women, minorities, and white collar workers); Charles B. Craver, *The Vitality of the American Labor Movement in the Twenty-First Century*, 1983 U Ill L Rev 633, 648-49 (observing the traditional under representation of minorities and women in unions, and emphasizing the need to include these groups); Michael J. Goldberg, *Affirmative Action in Union Government: The Landrum-Griffin Act Implications*, 44 Ohio St L J 649, 652-66 (1983) (discussing the history of discrimination in the labor movement and proposing the use of affirmative action to increase the representation of minorities and women in union leadership).

[15] See, for example, Gould, 38 Stan L Rev at 942-43 (cited in note 3) (stressing unions' inability to organize in "high tech" and developing industries); Troy, 13 Harv J L & Pub Pol at 612-25 (cited in note 7) (describing shifts from manufacturing to producer services).

[16] Despite the unprecedented boom years of the 1980s in the financial and real estate markets, the real wages for production workers in the manufacturing industries declined over 11% between 1978 and 1988. *Statistical Abstract of the United States: 1990* 407, Table 668 (GPO, 1990).

[17] Professor Troy points to such structural factors to explain union decline, but does not explain why white collar service workers, or workers in the growing high-tech sector, do not unionize. Troy, 13 Harv J L & Pub Pol at 612-25 (cited in note 7).

among public sector employees, hospital workers, retail clerks, and other pink and white collar types of workers.[18] Thus it is just not true that unions have made no efforts toward those types of workers, nor is it true that unions have had no appeal.

In a recent article, Professor Henry Farber of Princeton University gave a new perspective on union decline. Professor Farber analyzed several studies of worker attitudes toward unions that were conducted between 1977 and 1984.[19] He concluded that workers were not unionizing for two reasons. First, there was an increase in job satisfaction among unorganized workers, which Farber attributed not to improvements in their pay or job security, but to their declining expectations.[20] Second, the number of nonunion workers who perceived that unions were effective in improving wages and working conditions had dropped significantly.[21] Pro-

---

[18] Between 1983 and 1991, the percentage of union members who are women, blacks, Hispanics, and managerial and professional employees has grown significantly. This can be seen in the following tables, which show that in these categories, union membership has either grown or declined only slightly, while overall union membership has declined substantially. This has resulted in a net percentage increase of total union membership among these groups.

TABLE II
Total Union Membership in Absolute Numbers

	Total Union	Women	Blacks	Hispanic	Managerial
1983	17,717	5,908	2,440	1,042	3,354
1991	16,568	6,138	2,425	1,275	3,802

TABLE III
Composition of Union Membership

	Total Union	Women	Blacks	Hispanic	Managerial
1983	100%	33.34%	13.77%	5.88%	18.93%
1991	100%	37.05%	14.63%	7.69%	22.94%

1983 data from 32 Employment & Earnings 208-09, Tables 52 & 53 (Jan 1985); 1991 data from 39 Employment & Earnings 228-29, Tables 57 & 58 (Jan 1992).

These data suggest that to the extent unions have effectively recruited during the 1980s, it has been among these groups. See also Weiler, 58 U Chi L Rev at 1017 (cited in note 12) ("[S]ince the '50s, unions have also lost major ground within their manufacturing and construction bases while simultaneously achieving major breakthroughs in the public sector, in such quintessentially 'female' service occupations as teaching, nursing, and government clerical work.").

[19] Henry S. Farber, *The Recent Decline of Unionization in the United States*, 238 Science 915 (Nov 13, 1987).

[20] Id at 917-19.

[21] Id. One of the studies Farber used was conducted by the Harris Survey in 1984. It concluded that nonunion employees saw unions as "an irrelevant way to solve their work problems." Troy, 13 Harv J L & Pub Pol at 600 (cited in note 7). Professory Troy also uses this data to argue that employee opposition is, quantitatively, a more significant factor in

fessor Farber called this a decline in the perception of "union instrumentality."[22] On the basis of a statistical model, Professor Farber concluded that "all of the decline in demand among nonunion workers can be accounted for by the increase in nonunion workers' satisfaction and decrease in perceptions of union instrumentality."[23]

In short, Farber attributes union decline in large part to declining employee confidence in the power of unions to better wages, job security, and other working conditions. If he is right, the problem of explaining union decline then becomes the problem of determining why the public perception of union effectiveness has changed in recent years.

Many factors, including cultural and economic factors exogenous to the labor relations system, shape public perceptions of union effectiveness. But undoubtedly one of these factors is a decline in *actual* union effectiveness. The decline in actual union effectiveness cannot summarily be dismissed as simply the natural result of the inherent weakness of unions. Actual union effectiveness is, to a large extent, a product of the legal rules that determine what unions can and cannot do.[24]

For example, some legal rules prevent unions from influencing corporate decisions of importance to their members, such as the rules prohibiting bargaining for work acquisition or bargaining to stop double-breasting.[25] Other legal rules influence union economic power, by prohibiting secondary boycotts or permitting employers to hire permanent replacements during strikes.[26] In short, because legal rules define union power and effectiveness, changes in the le-

---

the decline of private-sector unionism than *employer* opposition. Id at 599-600. See also Troy, 59 U Chi L Rev at 687-88 (cited in note 12).

[22] Farber, 238 Science at 918 (cited in note 19).

[23] Id at 919.

[24] See Stone, 55 U Chi L Rev at 85 & n 43 (cited in note 3) (discussing labor law rules that regulate labor's and management's power). See also Katherine Van Wezel Stone, *Legal Regulation of Economic Weapons: A Comparative Perspective*, in Bruno Stein, ed, *Proceedings of New York University 43d Annual National Conference on Labor* 79, 82-87 (Little, Brown, 1990) (discussing how the legal rules defining labor's right to strike and employers' right to hire replacements shapes each side's economic power). See generally Robert L. Hale, *Bargaining, Duress, and Economic Liberty*, 43 Colum L Rev 603, 625-28 (1943) (arguing that market power of employees and employers is a function of the compulsion they are legally permitted to bring against the other).

[25] See Stone, 55 U Chi L Rev at 114-17 (cited in note 3).

[26] See Paul C. Weiler, *Governing the Workplace* 264-73 (Harvard, 1991) (criticizing strike replacement rule and ban on union boycotts of struck product for unduly restricting union bargaining power); Atleson, *Values and Assumptions* at 19-34 (cited in note 4) (criticizing strike replacement rule on same grounds).

gal rules governing labor-management relations might partially explain the decline of union effectiveness. Accordingly, to understand union decline, we must examine the content of the labor laws.[27]

The Farber analysis suggests that changes in legal rules may be a factor in union decline. However, the causal arrows go both ways. Legal rules not only determine power, but are also a result of power. When labor is weak, the labor laws are weakened.[28] The decline of unions and the weakening of the labor laws are mutually reinforcing features of the labor relations landscape.

Part of my task here is to describe some of the legal rules that have compromised union effectiveness in the past decade. My thesis is that to the extent that unions are currently perceived as ineffective, this perception is not fanciful, but rather reflects a reasonably correct understanding of how present labor law doctrine inhibits the power of unions to improve the wages and working conditions of their members.

II. Recent Developments in American Labor and Employment Law

The past decade has witnessed a shift from a legal system that protects collective employee rights to one that protects individual employment rights. In this shift, labor relations have been deregulated and then reregulated in an individualized and decentralized fashion. Through a series of judicial and administrative decisions, federal judges and government officials have rewritten the legal rules of collective bargaining—rules that had once protected collective, as opposed to individual, bargaining between employers and employees—so as to strip them of their regulatory bite. At the same time, state legislatures and courts have reregulated labor relations by recognizing new individual employment rights.

---

[27] Professor Weiler has also suggested that the decline of unions can be explained by developments in the labor law. See Weiler, 96 Harv L Rev at 1774-81 (cited in note 12), in which he blames the law governing union organizing campaigns. Specifically, he argues that the dramatic increase in discriminatory discharges during representation campaigns, and the NLRB's ineffectiveness in preventing or remedying such unlawful employer conduct, plays a significant role in union decline. Id. See also Weiler, 58 U Chi L Rev 1015 (cited in note 12) (responding to LaLonde and Meltzer, 58 U Chi L Rev 953 (cited in note 12)). While I find the Weiler thesis compelling, my argument relies less on the law of employee organizing, and more on the law governing the exercise of union power at the bargaining table and in the economic arena.

[28] James B. Atleson, *The Prospects for Labor Law Reform*, 18 Pol Studies J 364, 371 (1989-90) (unions only achieve favorable legislation when they are "perceived to be vital and troublesome economic actors.").

A. Federal Deregulation of Collective Labor Rights

Since the 1930s, the National Labor Relations Act has empowered collective labor action by protecting the right to organize and to strike, and by requiring employers to bargain with their workers' collective representative.[29] However, in the past decade, the National Labor Relations Board ("NLRB") and the federal courts have reinterpreted the statute so as to dismantle its collective, group-empowering features.

For example, the NLRB has diluted severely the statutory protection of union organizing.[30] Whereas the NLRB once restricted when an employer could make knowingly false and prejudicial statements about a union during an organizing campaign, it now permits such statements.[31] Similarily, whereas previously an employer was prohibited from polling employees during union campaigns unless there were strict safeguards to guard against coercion, polls are now generally permitted.[32] These changes are part of the general trend toward deregulation of union election campaigns.[33]

An even more important aspect of the deregulation of labor relations has occurred in the area of union input into employer strategic-level decisionmaking.[34] In the past decade, such corporate

---

[29] NLRA §§ 7, 8(a), codified at 29 USC §§ 157, 158(a) (1988). See Stone, 55 U Chi L Rev at 83-84 & n 41 (cited in note 3) (arguing that NLRA § 8(a) furthers the collectivist aims of the statute).

[30] See Weiler, 96 Harv L Rev at 1788 (cited in note 12) ("[The NLRA's] remedial philosophy as it has evolved . . . is heavily oriented toward the repair of harm inflicted on individual victims of antiunion activity," instead of toward protecting the employees' collective rights.). See generally Levy, 16 Rutgers L Rev 269 (cited in note 11).

[31] *Midland National Life Insurance Co.*, 263 NLRB 127, 133 (1982), overruling *General Knit of California, Inc.*, 239 NLRB 619 (1978), and *Hollywood Ceramics Co., Inc.*, 140 NLRB 221 (1962).

[32] *Rossmore House*, 269 NLRB 1176, 1177-78 (1984) (overruling the per se prohibition of employer polling in favor of evaluating the poll in light of the totality of the circumstances), enforced as *Hotel Employees & Restaurant Union v NLRB*, 760 F2d 1006 (9th Cir 1985).

[33] See *Lechmere, Inc. v NLRB*, 112 S Ct 841 (1992) (permitting employer to prohibit solicitation by non-employee union organizers at employer's parking lot and overturning NLRB's balancing approach to union access cases). See also Weiler, 96 Harv L Rev at 1774-81 (cited in note 12) (discussing deregulation of election campaigns); Dan C. Heldman, James T. Bennett, and Manuel H. Johnson, *Deregulating Labor Relations* 49-76 (Fisher Institute, 1981) (calling for the deregulation of union representation elections).

[34] The notion of strategic-level corporate decisions is adopted from Thomas A. Kochan, Harry C. Katz, and Robert B. McKersie, *The Transformation of American Industrial Relations* 15-18 (Basic, 1986), in which they describe a three-tier framework of management decisions. Strategic-level decisions are about "what businesses to invest in, where to locate worksites, whether to make or buy various components, and the organizational arrangements used to carry out basic strategies . . . ." Id at 18.

decisions to engage in mergers, takeovers, or other restructurings have cost union members tens of thousands of jobs.[35] Despite this impact, the rules of collective bargaining have made it considerably more difficult for unions to protect their membership. The NLRB has exempted employers from the obligation to bargain about most such decisions, adopting instead a policy of deference to the employer's business judgment and business rationality.[36] In addition, under established doctrine, when a company sells its assets, the purchaser has no obligation to retain the former workforce or to honor labor agreements inherited from the seller.[37] And if a union negotiates a contractual provision that prevents an employer from

[35] The AFL-CIO estimates that in the 1980s its members lost over 80,000 jobs due to takeovers alone, and overall more than 500,000 jobs. Hostile Takeovers, Hearings Before the Senate Committee on Banking, Housing, and Urban Affairs, 100th Cong, 1st Sess 261, 262 (Apr 8, 1987) (statement of Thomas R. Donahue, Secretary-Treasurer, AFL-CIO).

Whether or not takeovers and other corporate restructurings have in fact harmed employees is a subject of debate. There is significant anecdotal evidence, in addition to Mr. Donahue's statement above, that employees have been harmed by corporate takeovers. See, for example, Andrei Shleifer and Lawrence H. Summers, *Breach of Trust in Hostile Takeovers*, in Alan J. Auerbach, ed, *Corporate Takeovers: Causes and Consequences* 33, 49-50 (Chicago, 1988) (in the TWA takeover, employee wage reductions amounted to one and one-half times the takeover premium stockholders received). There is also some empirical evidence that employment levels decrease after management buyouts. See, for example, Steven Kaplan, *The Effects of Management Buyouts on Operating Performance and Value*, 24 J Fin Econ 217, 241, Table 9 (1989) (finding that firms experiencing a management buyout between 1980 and 1986 had employment decreases of between 6% and 12%, when data adjusted according to industry); Krishna G. Palepu, *Consequences of Leveraged Buyouts*, 27 J Fin Econ 247, 252-53 (1990) ("[B]uyout firms offer lower growth in employment opportunities than other firms in their industries.").

On the other hand, some studies about the impact of takeovers on employees do not support the claim that takeovers cause job loss. See Frank R. Lichtenberg and Donald Siegel, *The Effect of Ownership Changes on the Employment and Wages of Central Office and Other Personnel*, 33 J L & Econ 383, 401-02 (1990) (showing that the disparity in employment levels between companies that changed owners and those that did not actually lessened after the change); Charles Brown and James L. Medoff, *The Impact of Firm Acquisitions on Labor*, in Auerbach, ed, *Corporate Takeovers* 9, 23 (finding that employment in firms involved in acquisitions declined approximately 5% after sales of assets, but that employment increased by 9% after simple sales and by 2% after simple mergers); Joshua G. Rosett, *Do Union Wealth Concessions Explain Takeover Premiums?*, 27 J Fin Econ 263, 279-80 (1990) (finding that firms that experienced hostile takeovers between 1976 and 1987 had a modest wage gain).

[36] See Stone, 55 U Chi L Rev at 86-96 (cited in note 3).

[37] *NLRB v Burns International Security Services*, 406 US 272, 281-91 (1972) (successor employer not bound by substantive provisions of predecessor's collective bargaining agreement); *Howard Johnson Co. v Detroit Local Joint Executive Board*, 417 US 249, 260-65 (1974) (same). In the event of a merger, unlike a sale of assets, an employer may have some obligations under the prior collective bargaining agreement. See *John Wiley & Sons, Inc. v Livingston*, 376 US 543, 548 (1964) ("[I]n appropriate circumstances, present here, the successor employer may be required to arbitrate with the union under the [predecessor's] agreement.").

transferring unionized work to a non-union subsidiary, it runs a risk of violating the secondary boycott restrictions.[38] As a result, employer decisions about plant location, introduction of new technology, closing part of an operation, or restructuring of the firm have become practically immune from challenge by unions.[39]

Of these new restrictions on union effectiveness, I will discuss only one—the diminishing scope of the employer's obligation to bargain with its employees, located in § 8(a)(5) of the NLRA.[40] It has long been accepted that the statutory duty to bargain only applies to certain areas, called "mandatory subjects of collective bargaining."[41] If a subject is a mandatory subject of bargaining, neither employer nor union can make a unilateral alteration until it has bargained with the other to the point of impasse.[42] And after impasse is reached, only a mandatory subject can be the subject of a protected strike.[43]

There has been a longstanding debate about the scope of mandatory bargaining, particularly as to whether it obligates an employer to bargain over strategic-level decisions that affect jobs—decisions such as plant relocation, partial shut-downs, automation, subcontracting, and so forth.[44] Some scholars and labor

---

[38] See, for example, *D'Amico v Painters District Council 51*, 120 Labor Rel Ref Man (BNA) 3473, 3474-80 (D Md 1985) (applying a two-part test to determine whether a "work preservation agreement" is invalid as secondary union activity).

[39] See Stone, 55 U Chi L Rev at 86-120 (cited in note 3).

[40] 29 USC § 158(a)(5) ("It shall be an unfair labor practice for an employer to refuse to bargain collectively with the representatives of his employees . . . .").

[41] *NLRB v Wooster Division of Borg-Warner Corp.*, 356 US 342, 348 (1958).

[42] *NLRB v Katz*, 369 US 736, 743 (1962); *Milwaukee Spring Division of Illinois Coil Spring Co.*, 268 NLRB 601, 602 (1984), enforced as *International Union, UAW v NLRB*, 765 F2d 175 (DC Cir 1985).

[43] *Borg-Warner*, 356 US at 349 (neither company nor union can insist to impasse on a nonmandatory bargaining subject). See Michael C. Harper, *Leveling the Road from* Borg-Warner *to* First National Maintenance*: The Scope of Mandatory Bargaining*, 68 Va L Rev 1447, 1447 (1982) ("After *Borg-Warner*, employers and unions [can] not resort to economic pressure to obtain agreement unless the proposal concerns 'wages, hours, [or] other terms and conditions of employment.' "). See also Julius G. Getman, *Labor Relations* 177 (Foundation, 1978) ("When no collective agreement is in force, the use of economic pressure by an incumbent union in support of its bargaining demands is protected if the subject matter of the demand constitutes a mandatory subject of bargaining.").

[44] See William B. Gould IV, *The Burger Court and Labor Law: The Beat Goes On*—Marcato, 24 San Diego L Rev 51, 64 (1987) (advocating broad scope for mandatory bargaining for decisions affecting job security); Comment, *Unfair Labor Practice and Contract Aspects of an Employer's Desire to Close, Partially Close, or Relocate Bargaining Unit Work*, 24 Duquesne L Rev 285, 306-08 (1985) (approving trend toward limiting bargaining obligations in the interest of facilitating free flow of capital essential to economic growth); James B. Atleson, *Management Prerogatives, Plant Closings, and the NLRA*, 11 NYU Rev L & Soc Change 83, 104-05 (1982-83) (advocating broad scope for mandatory bargaining over employer capital decisions); Note, *Partial Closings: The Scope of an Em-*

union activists have argued that, if there is no obligation for management to bargain over those decisions most important to workers, then collective bargaining is not true joint decisionmaking.[45]

Until 1981, it was generally believed that the bargaining obligation was broad, and that the realm of joint decisionmaking was expanding.[46] Then in 1981, the Supreme Court declared that the scope of bargaining was quite limited, and did not extend to most employer investment decisions. In *First National Maintenance Corp. v NLRB*, the Supreme Court held that an employer was not required to bargain about a decision to close part of its operation.[47] In setting forth its reasons, the Court introduced a balancing test for determining the scope of mandatory bargaining: When making decisions that have a direct impact on employment security, management is required to bargain "only if the benefit, for labor management relations and the collective-bargaining process, outweighs the burden placed on the conduct of the business."[48]

There has been considerable disagreement about what the *First National Maintenance* balancing test means.[49] However, the

---

ployer's Duty to Bargain, 61 BU L Rev 735, 763-72 (1981) (advocating broad duty to bargain in partial closing situations); Robert J. Rabin, Fibreboard *and the Termination of Bargaining Unit Work: The Search for Standards in Defining the Scope of the Duty to Bargain*, 71 Colum L Rev 803, 827-36 (1971) (suggesting guidelines for restricting duty to bargain about capital decisions); Thomas J. Schwarz, *Plant Relocation or Partial Termination—The Duty to Decision-Bargain*, 39 Fordham L Rev 81, 100-02 (1970) (advocating limiting bargaining obligation in relocation and partial closing cases to situations where employer proposes to substitute unit workers with non-unit workers); Note, *Labor Law Problems in Plant Relocation*, 77 Harv L Rev 1100, 1103-06 (1964) (proposing restricting duty to bargain about relocation decisions). See also Michael L. Wachter and George M. Cohen, *The Law and Economics of Collective Bargaining: An Introduction and Application to the Problems of Subcontracting, Partial Closure, and Relocation*, 136 U Pa L Rev 1349, 1352 (1988) (proposing efficiency criteria for evaluating capital mobility decisions).

[45] See Atleson, 11 NYU Rev L & Soc Change at 107-08 (cited in note 44); Gould, 24 San Diego L Rev at 61-64 (cited in note 44). See also Atleson, 44 Md L Rev at 845-47 (cited in note 3); Stone, 90 Yale L J at 1558-59 (cited in note 4).

[46] *Borg-Warner*, 356 US at 358 (Harlan concurring) ("Provisions which two decades ago might have been thought to be the exclusive concern of labor or management are today commonplace in such agreements."). See also Stone, 55 U Chi L Rev at 88 & nn 51-53 (cited in note 3) (referring to pre-1980 belief in the infinite expandability of bargaining topics).

[47] 452 US 666, 686 (1981). Much earlier the Supreme Court made it clear that an employer had no obligation to bargain about a decision to go out of business altogether. *Textile Workers Union v Darlington Mfg. Co.*, 380 US 263, 273-74 (1965).

[48] *First National Maintenance*, 452 US at 679.

[49] The NLRB attempted to interpret the test in *Otis Elevator Co.*, 269 NLRB 891 (1984). Rather than achieving clarity, however, the NRLB split three ways. The plurality said that *First National Maintenance* meant that an employer had to bargain when its decision turned on labor costs rather than on a change in the scope and direction of the enterprise. Id at 893. A concurring opinion said that an employer was obligated to bargain when the decision turned on labor costs *and* the potential benefit from bargaining out-

NLRB and the courts have agreed that an employer has no obligation to bargain about a decision that would fundamentally change the scope or direction of the enterprise.[60] Similarily, they agree that decisions made out of a concern for economic factors are exempt from the bargaining obligation.[61] Decisions concerning takeovers, mergers, or other transformations in the corporate identity fall into these excluded categories. Thus, for most strategic-level corporate decisions that threaten jobs, there is no legal bargaining obligation that might enable unions to protect employees at the time such decisions are made.[62] The recent reformulation of the

---

weighed the costs to the employer of engaging in bargaining. Id at 897. A dissenting opinion said that an employer should be required to bargain for any decision that turned on overall costs, because in that case labor costs would be a part of the employer's overall equation. Id at 900-01. Recently the NLRB reinterpreted the *First National Maintenance* test in *Dubuque Packing Co.*, 137 Labor Rel Ref Man (BNA) 1185, 1991 NLRB LEXIS 750, in which the NLRB repudiated all three of the tests in *Otis Elevator*, and announced yet another interpretation of *First National Maintenance*. 1991 NLRB LEXIS at *19-*20 & n 8. See note 51.

[60] *Dubuque Packing Co.*, 1991 NLRB LEXIS at *27; *Arrow Automotive Industries v NLRB*, 853 F2d 223, 225-27 (4th Cir 1988).

[61] In *Dubuque Packing*, the NLRB announced a new two-part test to determine the scope of mandatory bargaining in cases concerning a plant relocation: "Initially, the burden is on the General Counsel to establish that the employer's decision involved a relocation . . . unaccompanied by a basic change in the nature of the employer's operation. If the General Counsel successfully carries his burden in this regard, he will have established prima facie that the employer's relocation decision is a mandatory subject of bargaining." 1991 NLRB LEXIS at *27. Then the employer can attempt to rebut the prima facie case by showing that the work at the new location is significantly different from that at the former location, or that all work at the former location was to be discontinued. Id. Alternatively, the employer may show, in defense, that labor costs were not a factor in the decision to relocate, or that, even if labor costs were a factor, "the union could not have offered labor cost concessions that could have changed the employer's decision to relocate." Id at *27-*28.

This new test for determining the scope of bargaining, like the *Otis Elevator* test and the *First National Maintenance* test itself, retains the notion that an employer's market-based decisions are shielded from a bargaining obligation. However, *Dubuque Packing* shifts the burden of proof on the issue of the employer's motivation.

[62] When the labor law does not impose an obligation on an employer to bargain about a particular decision, it still imposes an obligation to bargain about the *effects* of the decision on the workforce. *First National Maintenance*, 452 US at 677-78 n 15. However, there is disagreement among scholars as to the actual scope of the requirement to bargain about effects. Compare Thomas C. Kohler, *Distinctions Without Differences: Effects Bargaining in Light of* First National Maintenance, 5 Indus Rel L J 402, 415 (1983) (courts have interpreted effects bargaining obligation broadly), with Wilbur Daniels and Seth Kupferberg, *Sale of Assets, Mergers, and Acquisitions: A Union View*, in Samuel Estreicher and Daniel G. Collins, eds, *Labor Law and Business Change: Theoretical and Transactional Perspectives* 185, 190-91 (Quorum, 1988) (courts and NLRB have been reluctant to require broad effects bargaining).

Effects bargaining usually takes place within a short time after the employer has made and implemented a decision, when the union no longer has leverage to protect its members. If an employer is found to have violated its obligation to engage in effects bargaining, the courts and the NLRB remedy the violation by requiring the employer to give limited back

scope of the bargaining obligation effectively insulates decisions based on overall profitability, efficiency, or other such market-based factors from the bargaining obligation.

The doctrinal development in the law of mandatory bargaining reflects the trend toward deregulation of labor relations in the 1980s. Deregulation does not merely mean the repeal of regulation; it also means the reinterpretation of regulation in such a way that it loses its regulatory bite.[53] While Congress has not repealed the NLRA, the federal courts and the NLRB have reduced the regime of regulation to a proxy for the market. In those areas in which regulation imposes no other obligations on employers than those imposed by the market, the law has rendered unions superfluous.[54]

---

pay. The standard formula is back pay for the period from five days after the date of the court or Board order until the time the parties reach either agreement or impasse, not to exceed the time the employee was actually out of work and not to be less than two weeks. *Transmarine Navigation Corp.*, 170 NLRB 389, 390 (1968). In practice, this means that when a violation is found, the employer quickly bargains to impasse and is liable for back pay for merely two weeks. See, for example, *Yorke v NLRB*, 709 F2d 1138, 1144-46 (7th Cir 1983) (imposing penalty of two weeks back pay under *Transmarine* formula).

[53] The development in the law of mandatory bargaining has been repeated in other areas. For example, in the area of employer discrimination against union members, what had been a blanket prohibition has now been muted by the addition of a business justification defense. See, for example, *Handy Andy Associates, Inc.*, 277 NLRB 208, 215-17 (1985) (no § 8(a)(3) violation for subcontracting decision made when employees refused to abandon union). See generally Stone, 55 U Chi L Rev at 96-102 (cited in note 3) (business justification defense is diluting § 8(a)(3) protections).

[54] Professors George Cohen and Michael Wachter have argued that the availability of market rationality as an employer defense is not a retreat from regulation but rather a better understanding of the function of labor regulation. They argue that the law should permit employers to make unfettered business decisions, and that it should only constrain an employer when he is acting opportunistically by trying to appropriate transaction-specific investments from his employees. Wachter and Cohen, 136 U Pa L Rev at 1415-17 (cited in note 44). See also George M. Cohen and Michael L. Wachter, *Replacing Striking Workers: The Law and Economics Approach*, in *43d Annual National Conference on Labor* 109 (cited in note 24).

This argument ascribes to unions, or to the labor law, the limited role of protecting workers against opportunistic employer behavior. However, it is both conceptually and practically difficult to draw the line between profit-maximizing behavior, which Professors Cohen and Wachter would protect, and opportunistic behavior, which they would constrain. Further, it is worth noting that the Cohen/Wachter argument does not distinguish between preventing employer opportunism by legal rules that empower unions and preventing employer opportunism by direct, legislatively-imposed employee safeguards. Under the logic of the Cohen/Wachter argument, unions limit employer opportunism only to the extent that there are no other generally available legal sanctions against unjust dismissal. If so, then legal protection against unjust dismissal would render unions even more superfluous. A more general form of this argument is discussed at notes 243-54 and accompanying text.

B. State Protection of Individual Employee Rights

At the same time that the federal courts and the NLRB have undermined the rights of collective labor in the past ten years, state courts and legislatures have initiated a renaissance of rights for individual employees. Until recently, the protections for individual employment rights in the United States have been minimal compared to the extensive protections in Western Europe.[55] They have been aimed at the margins of economic life, setting only minimum standards for the wage contract, and not otherwise interfering with its terms. For example, until the late 1970s and 1980s, nonunion employers could hire and fire at will, unrestrained by unjust dismissal laws of any sort. In addition, the United States government provides only minimal insurance against unemployment, retirement, or disability, and no universal health insurance at all. Health insurance, when it exists, is provided privately, usually by collective bargaining agreements between individual unions. Compared to the extensive income and job security protections that workers enjoy in most of Europe, American workers exist in an unmediated, unregulated labor market.[56]

In the wake of federal cutbacks in measures such as workplace health and safety regulations and affirmative action programs under the Reagan and Bush administrations, state courts and legislatures have become the protectors of the individual employee. This trend is most visible in the area of unjust dismissal. Beginning in the mid-1970s, some state courts began to hold that certain types of dismissals were unlawful, either as offending a public policy or as a breach of an implicit term of an employment contract.[57] In the 1980s, these isolated decisions became a nationwide trend: Courts in some thirty-nine states adopted some form of common law employee protection against unjust dismissal.[58] According to Professor Clyde Summers, as of 1988,

---

[55] See Michael Emerson, *Regulation or Deregulation of the Labour Market*, 32 Eur Econ Rev 775, 786-800 (1988) (discussing regulation of dismissals, layoffs, temporary employment, and part-time work in Europe).

[56] Id at 776.

[57] State courts have used various tort and contract theories. See, for example, *Monge v Beebe Rubber Co.*, 114 NH 130, 316 A2d 549 (1974) (employer breached at-will employment contract by firing employee for refusing to date her supervisor); *Frampton v Central Indiana Gas Co.*, 260 Ind 249, 297 NE2d 425 (1973) (employer committed tort by firing employee for filing workers' compensation claim); *Nees v Hocks*, 272 Or 210, 536 P2d 512 (1975) (employer committed tort by firing employee for serving on jury).

[58] Clyde W. Summers, *Labor Law as the Century Turns: A Changing of the Guard*, 67 Neb L Rev 7, 13-14 (1988).

> courts in thirty-two states ha[d] adopted public policy exceptions [to the at-will rule], eleven states ha[d] applied the covenant of good faith and fair dealing, and twenty-nine states ha[d] used employee handbooks to find contractual limitations on terminations.[59]

In addition, many states have enacted legislation to protect workers against dismissal in a variety of circumstances. For example, twenty-two states make it unlawful to dismiss an employee in retaliation for filing a workers' compensation claim.[60] Thirty-four states have given legislative protection for whistle-blowers, and forty-two states regulate the administration of employment-related lie detector tests.[61] The state of Montana has adopted a Comprehensive Unjust Dismissal law that gives workers protection against wrongful dismissal.[62]

The trend of state protection of individual employment rights is evident in other areas as well. Many states have protected the privacy of workers by restricting the use of drug testing in the workplace.[63] Some states have adopted more stringent protection for the employment rights of minorities than has the federal government,[64] and some have used their criminal laws to police industrial health and safety violations that the federal authorities have been unwilling to remedy.[65] In addition, some states have enacted statutes to protect employees in the event of corporate takeovers.[66]

---

[59] Id (citing *Individual Employment Rights Manual*, 9A Lab Rel Rptr (BNA) 505: 51-52 (Jan 1988)).

[60] Compiled from *Individual Employment Rights Manual*, 9A Lab Rel Rptr (BNA) 540-92 (1991).

[61] Id. Of these, statutes in nine states give protection only to public employees.

[62] Mont Code Ann §§ 39-2-901 to 39-2-914 (1991).

[63] Scott S. Cairns and Carolyn V. Grady, *Drug Testing in the Workplace: A Reasoned Approach for Private Employers*, 12 Geo Mason U L Rev 491, 520-30 (1990); Judith M. Janssen, *Substance Abuse Testing and the Workplace: A Private Employer's Perspective*, 12 Geo Mason U L Rev 611, 636-39 (1990). See generally, 9A Lab Rel Rptr (BNA) at 540-92 (cited in note 60).

[64] See Charles C. Heckscher, *The New Unionism: Employee Involvement in the Changing Corporation* 160 (Basic, 1988).

[65] See, for example, Comment, *State Prosecutions for Safety-Related Crimes in the Workplace: Can D.A.'s Succeed Where OSHA Failed?*, 79 Ky L J 139, 140 (1990-91); Comment, *State Criminal Prosecutions: Putting Teeth in the Occupational Safety and Health Act*, 12 Geo Mason U L Rev 737, 738-39 (1990); Rebecca S. Webber, *The OSH Act and State Criminal Law: A Prosecutor's Brief*, 25 Crim L Bulletin 234 (1989).

[66] In the 1980s, more than half of the states enacted statutes that permitted corporate directors to consider the effect of takeovers or mergers on employees. For a list of these stakeholder statutes, see *Appendix*, 21 Stetson L Rev 279 (1991). See generally Steven M.H. Wallman, *The Proper Interpretation of Corporate Constituency Statutes and Formulation of Director Duties*, 21 Stetson L Rev 163, 163-65 (1991) (describing statutes); Katherine

The increased state protection for individual workers in the past decade seems paradoxical in light of the deterioration of the federal protection for collective labor rights. However, the paradox disappears if we see that the emerging regime of individual employee rights represents not a complement to or an embellishment of the regime of collective rights, but rather its replacement. Viewed in this light, the emerging individual rights constitute a new system for organizing labor relations, one that is distinct from and opposed to the New Deal system of collective bargaining.

III. The Section 301 Preemption Doctrine

The New Deal system of collective bargaining, as it has been interpreted, is a distinctively privatized system. The aim of the NLRA is to provide a framework within which labor and management can negotiate the terms of their mutual dealings, free from outside interference; it is not to interfere with the substantive outcomes of the bargaining process.[67] This privatized form of collective bargaining has rendered collective bargaining legally incompatible with the emerging system of individual employment rights. In order to see this dynamic, it is necessary to examine the labor law doctrine of § 301 preemption.

Federal preemption of state statutory and common law is, of course, a fundamental aspect of our federal system. The Supremacy Clause of the U.S. Constitution states that when a federal law and a state law conflict, federal law prevails.[68] In the labor

---

Van Wezel Stone, *Employees as Stakeholders Under State Nonshareholder Constituency Statutes*, 21 Stetson L Rev 45, 45-47 (1991) (same); David Millon, *Redefining Corporate Law*, 24 Ind L Rev 223, 240-46 (1991) (noting the proliferation of state statutes permitting directors to pursue non-shareholder interests). The Connecticut stakeholder statute goes further than the others by requiring directors to consider employees' interests. See Conn Gen Stat Ann § 33-313(e) (West, 1991) ("For purposes of [making decisions with respect to mergers, consolidations, sales of assets, and business combinations with interested shareholders], a director of a corporation . . . shall consider . . . the interests of the corporation's employees . . . .").

In addition, two states have enacted statutes that require a corporate purchaser to honor its predecessor's collective bargaining agreement. See 19 Del Code Ann § 706 (1990); Mass Gen Laws Ann ch 149, § 20E (West, 1991).

[67] According to Dean Harry Shulman, the NLRA established a "bare legal framework [that] is hardly an encroachment on the premise that wages and other conditions of employment be left to autonomous determination by employers and labor." Harry Shulman, *Reason, Contract, and Law in Labor Relations*, 68 Harv L Rev 999, 1000 (1955). See also *NLRB v American National Insurance Co.*, 343 US 395, 402 (1952) ("The [NLRA] does not compel any agreement whatsoever between employees and employers. Nor does the Act regulate the substantive terms governing wages, hours and working conditions which are incorporated in an agreement.").

[68] The Supremacy Clause provides:

field, the potential for preemption is particularly vast. Federal labor laws touch on many aspects of labor-management relations and thus potentially preempt many types of state regulations, including state trespass, antitrust, defamation, and property laws.[69]

Section 301 of the Labor Management Relations Act makes collective bargaining agreements enforceable in a federal court.[70] Because many state employment rights duplicate, parallel, or implicate aspects of collective bargaining agreements, a § 301 preemption question is presented whenever a unionized employee attempts to vindicate a state-created employment right in a judicial forum.[71]

When a claim is preempted under § 301, there are two practical consequences. First, the Supreme Court has held that any and all claims for breach of a collective bargaining agreement that are even arguably subject to an arbitration clause must be decided in

---

> This Constitution, and the Laws of the United States which shall be made in Pursuance thereof; and all Treaties made, or which shall be made, under the Authority of the United States, shall be the supreme Law of the Land; and the Judges in every State shall be bound thereby, any Thing in the Constitution or Laws of any State to the Contrary notwithstanding.

US Const, Art VI.

[69] See, for example, *Teamsters Union v Oliver*, 358 US 283, 295-97 (1959) (NLRA preempts Ohio antitrust law that would wholly defeat the congressional purposes behind the NLRA). Compare *Farmer v United Brotherhood of Carpenters & Joiners*, 430 US 290, 301-02 (1977) (NLRA does not preempt tort action in state court by a union member against his union for damages from intentional infliction of emotional distress); *Sears, Roebuck & Co. v San Diego County Dist. Council of Carpenters*, 436 US 180, 199-207 (1978) (NLRA does not preempt state jurisdiction over an employer's action to enforce state trespass laws against union picketing).

[70] Section 301 says, in part:

> Suits for violation of contracts between an employer and a labor organization representing employees in an industry affecting commerce . . . may be brought in any district court of the United States having jurisdiction of the parties, without respect to the amount in controversy or without regard to the citizenship of the parties.

29 USC § 185(a) (1988).

[71] There are many other preemption issues that arise in the course of applying the NLRA in the face of various state laws that affect employment relations. See, for example, *San Diego Building Trades Council v Garmon*, 359 US 236, 245 (1959) (state court jurisdiction preempted if an activity was arguably prohibited or arguably protected by federal law); *Lodge 76, International Ass'n of Machinists v Wisconsin Employment Relations Comm'n*, 427 US 132, 149-51 (1976) (state regulation preempted when it interferes with the balance of economic weapons established by Congress, even though federal labor law did not prohibit the regulation). See William B. Gould IV, et al, *When State and Federal Laws Collide: Preemption—Nightmare or Opportunity?*, 9 Indus Rel L J 4, 5-6 (1987).

Here I am only focusing on one type of preemption—preemption of state laws by § 301 of the Labor Management Relations Act. More so than other types of labor law preemption, § 301 preemption most directly controls the interaction between the emerging state individual employment rights and the federal system of collective bargaining.

arbitration, rather than by a court.[72] It has also adopted an extremely narrow standard for judicial review of the arbitration decisions.[73] In practice, this means that once a claim is preempted under § 301, the employee's only recourse is private arbitration. As a result, unionized workers find that, by virtue of the combination of Section 301 preemption rules and their collective bargaining agreements, they do not have access to any court to assert their state law claims.

Second, and perhaps more significantly, when a claim is preempted under § 301, the state law rights are extinguished. In arbitration, the arbitrator applies the law of the collective agreement, not the external state law which the employee initially sought to invoke.[74] Thus the unionized employee whose state law claim is

---

[72] *United Steelworkers of America v American Mfg. Co.*, 363 US 564, 567-58 (1960) (on motion to compel arbitration, judicial role limited to determining whether the plaintiff has asserted "a claim which on its face is governed by the contract"); *United Steelworkers of America v Warrior & Gulf Navigation Co.*, 363 US 574, 582-83 (1960) (announcing presumption of arbitrability).

[73] *United Paperworkers Int'l Union v Misco, Inc.*, 484 US 29, 36 (1987) ("[C]ourts are not authorized to reconsider the merits of an [arbitral] award even though the parties may allege that the award rests on errors of fact or on misinterpretation of the contract."); *United Steelworkers of America v Enterprise Wheel & Car Corp.*, 363 US 593, 597 (1960) (upholding arbitral award "so long as it draws its essence from the collective bargaining agreement").

In addition, employees are required to exhaust their arbitration remedies under the agreement before coming to court. *Republic Steel Corp. v Maddox*, 379 US 650, 652-53 (1965). And, unless the complaint includes an allegation that the union breached its duty of fair representation, finality clauses in a collective agreement preclude judicial consideration of a breach of contract claim once arbitration is completed. *Hines v Anchor Motor Freight, Inc.*, 424 US 554, 567 (1976). Even in the absence of an express finality clause, courts defer to the decision of the arbitrator. *Enterprise Wheel*, 363 US at 596.

[74] *Warrior & Gulf*, 363 US at 582. Most commentators agree that when a contract does not mention external law, an arbitrator may not base his decisions upon his understanding of the requirements of external law. The role of the arbitrator is to interpret the collective agreement, not to apply external law. See, for example, Theodore J. St. Antoine, *Judicial Review of Labor Arbitration Awards: A Second Look at* Enterprise Wheel *and Its Progeny*, 75 Mich L Rev 1137, 1140-43 (1977); Harry T. Edwards, *Labor Arbitration at the Crossroads: The 'Common Law of the Shop' vs. External Law*, 32 Arb J 65, 90-91 (1977); David E. Feller, *The Coming End of Arbitration's Golden Age*, in Barbara D. Dennis and Gerald G. Somers, eds. *Proceedings of the 29th Annual Meeting of the National Academy of Arbitrators* 97, 110-11 (BNA, 1976); Bernard D. Meltzer, *Ruminations About Ideology, Law, and Labor Arbitration*, 34 U Chi L Rev 545, 557 (1967).

To the contrary, some commentators have argued that every collective bargaining agreement should be presumed to include all applicable law, and thus the arbitrator must consider external law in order to interpret the contract. See, for example, Robert G. Howlett, *The Arbitrator, the NLRB, and the Courts*, in Dallas L. Jones, ed, *Proceedings of the 20th Annual Meeting of the National Academy of Arbitrators* 67, 83 (BNA, 1967); Dennis O. Lynch, *Deferral, Waiver, and Arbitration Under the NLRA: From Status to Contract and Back Again*, 44 U Miami L Rev 237, 270-71 (1989). This position has not prevailed.

preempted receives neither the benefit of a judicial forum nor the benefit of the substantive provisions of the state employment right.

In the sections that follow, I demonstrate that the federal courts have adopted a very broad § 301 preemption doctrine.

A. The Evolution of the Section 301 Preemption Doctrine in the Supreme Court

1. The "peculiar" need for uniformity.

a) Lucas Flour *(1962)*. Since the early 1960s, the Supreme Court has given § 301 a broad preemptive scope. This trend began in 1962, in a case called *Local 174 Teamsters v Lucas Flour Co.*[75] There the Supreme Court held that when state courts decide cases involving collective bargaining agreements, they must apply the federal law of § 301 rather than state contract law.[76] The Court justified this broad approach to preemption on grounds that "the subject matter of § 301(a) 'is peculiarly one that calls for uniform law.' "[77] In particular,

> [t]he possibility that individual contract terms might have different meanings under state and federal law would inevitably exert a disruptive influence upon both the negotiation and administration of collective agreements. . . . [T]he process of negotiating an agreement would be made immeasurably more difficult by the necessity of trying to formulate contract provisions in such a way as to contain the same meaning under two or more systems of law which might someday be invoked in enforcing the contract. Once the collective bargain was made, the possibility of conflicting substantive interpretation under competing legal systems would tend to stimulate and prolong disputes as to its interpretation.[78]

---

[75] 369 US 95 (1962).

[76] Id at 103.

[77] Id (quoting *Penna. R. Co. v Public Service Comm'n*, 250 US 566, 569 (1919)). A few years earlier, in *Ass'n of Westinghouse Salaried Employees v Westinghouse Electric Corp.*, 348 US 437 (1955), the Supreme Court had remanded a § 301 case to the state court on the ground that the employees had valid state law claims, and that § 301 was not intended to permit a union to sue to enforce the rights of individuals that could be enforced elsewhere. Id at 460-61. The Court so decided in order to avoid ruling on the constitutionality of § 301. Id at 459-60. The Court did not address the preemption issue explicitly, but by holding as it did, the Court ruled, *sub silentio*, that the state law actions were not preempted.

[78] *Lucas Flour*, 369 US at 103-04.

b) Avco *(1968)*. Six years later, in *Avco Corp. v Aero Lodge No. 735*,[79] the Supreme Court had to determine whether § 301 preemption could provide the basis for removal jurisdiction under 28 USC § 1441.[80] In that case, an employer sued a union in state court for breach of a no-strike clause. The employer won, and obtained an injunction against the strike. The union tried to remove the action to a federal court in order to take advantage of the Norris-LaGuardia Act, a federal anti-injunction statute. The union argued that under *Lucas Flour*, § 301 preempted state breach-of-contract actions, and that the federal courts therefore had removal jurisdiction.[81]

The Supreme Court agreed, granted removal, and affirmed an order dissolving the injunction that the state court had issued.[82] In doing so, it overcame its usual refusal to find removal jurisdiction in cases in which the only federal issue is raised in defense.[83]

---

[79] 390 US 557 (1968).

[80] Section 1441(a) only permits removal in cases over which a federal court has *original* jurisdiction. 28 USC § 1441(a) (1988).

[81] *Avco*, 390 US at 558-60.

[82] Id at 560.

[83] Recall that § 1441(a) only permits removal when a federal court has original jurisdiction. In turn, § 1331 grants original federal jurisdiction over claims that raise a federal question. 28 USC § 1331 (1988). The scope of federal question jurisdiction is determined by the well-pleaded complaint rule. See *Franchise Tax Board v Construction Laborers Vacation Trust*, 463 US 1, 9-12 (1983). When the complaint presents no federal issue on its face, courts have disagreed as to what the well-pleaded complaint rule requires. Some hold that the rule limits the courts to a scrutiny of the complaint itself to determine the existence *vel non* of a federal question. Others hold that the rule requires a court to pierce the complaint and examine the underlying cause of action. See Comment, *Federal Preemption, Removal Jurisdiction, and the Well-Pleaded Complaint Rule*, 51 U Chi L Rev 634, 655-66 (1984). Under either approach, a federal defense is not, by itself, sufficient grounds for original federal jurisdiction or removal jurisdiction. *Gully v First National Bank*, 299 US 109, 112-13 (1936). Jurisdiction only exists if the plaintiff's case-in-chief involves federal law. A. Mark Segreti, Jr., *The Federal Preemption Question—A Federal Question? An Analysis of Federal Jurisdiction Over Supremacy Clause Issues*, 33 Cleve St L Rev 653, 666-67 (1984-85). Compare Donald L. Doernberg, *There's No Reason For It; It's Just Our Policy: Why the Well-Pleaded Complaint Rule Sabotages the Purposes of Federal Question Jurisdiction*, 38 Hastings L J 597, 621-26 (until 1894 federal courts found removal jurisdiction on the basis of a federal defense).

However, the issue of preemption poses a special problem for removal jurisdiction and the well-pleaded complaint rule. Preemption is normally pleaded as a defense. But when established, preemption renders the cause of action federal. See Comment, 51 U Chi L Rev at 657-58; Comment, *Artful Pleading and Removal Jurisdiction: Ferreting Out the True Nature of a Claim*, 35 UCLA L Rev 315, 330-31 (1987). The Supreme Court addressed this problem in *Franchise Tax Board*, 463 US at 13-22, noting that, in general, the defense of preemption does not confer federal jurisdiction.

2. Complete vs. partial preemption.

a) Franchise Tax Board *(1983)*. Later, in a non-labor case called *Franchise Tax Board v Construction Laborers Vacation Trust*,[84] the Supreme Court reaffirmed the broad preemptive scope of § 301 announced in *Lucas Flour* and *Avco*. In particular, the Court explained its *Avco* decision:

> The necessary ground of decision was that the pre-emptive force of § 301 is so powerful as to displace entirely any state cause of action "for violation of contracts between an employer and a labor organization." Any such suit is purely a creature of federal law, notwithstanding the fact that state law would provide a cause of action in the absence of § 301.[85]

Thus *Avco*, as interpreted in *Franchise Tax Board*, said that some claims of preemption would give rise to removal jurisdiction, while others would not. Jurisdiction is appropriate when the federal interest is so powerful as to completely eclipse the state law claim. Section 301, the Court said, involved one such powerful federal interest.

The Court in *Franchise Tax Board* called this the "complete preemption" doctrine, "an independent corollary of the well pleaded complaint rule."[86] Under this corollary, a claim involving interpretation or enforcement of a collective bargaining agreement is so completely a federal claim that it is converted into a § 301 claim from its inception, even if alternative causes of action are pleaded in the complaint.[87] The complete preemption corollary to the well-pleaded complaint rule has been applied primarily, if not exclusively, in cases raising claims preempted by § 301.[88] Thus the

---

[84] 463 US 1 (1983) (refusing to find removal jurisdiction in a state attachment action where preemption was raised in defense).

[85] Id at 23 (footnotes omitted).

[86] Id at 22.

[87] Id at 23-24 (citing *Avco* for the proposition that "if a federal cause of action completely pre-empts a state cause of action any complaint that comes within the scope of the federal cause of action necessarily 'arises under' federal law"). See *Caterpillar, Inc. v Williams*, 482 US 386, 393-94 (1987) (discussing the application of complete preemption to § 301); *Metropolitan Life Ins. Co. v Taylor*, 481 US 58, 65 (1987) (noting that § 301 has "extraordinary pre-emptive power"). See also Comment, 51 U Chi L Rev at 661 (cited in note 83) ("After *Franchise Tax Board*, however, where federal law has 'completely preempted' the state law cause of action, it is proper to recharacterize the action as one that actually arises under federal law, despite the plaintiff's usual mastery over his complaint.").

[88] *Metropolitan*, 481 US at 63-64 ("One corollary of the well-pleaded complaint rule . . . is that Congress may so completely pre-empt a particular area that any civil complaint raising this select group of claims is necessarily federal in character. *For 20 years, this Court*

complete preemption doctrine has extended even further the preemptive reach of § 301.

b) Allis-Chalmers *(1985).* In recent years, the Supreme Court has continued to give § 301 a broad preemptive scope. In 1985, in *Allis-Chalmers Corp. v Lueck*,[89] an employee had suffered a nonoccupational injury that qualified him for disability benefits under the terms of his collective bargaining agreement. However, the employer had harassed the employee about his insurance claim and had instructed the insurer to terminate the disability payments. The employee sued the employer under a Wisconsin law that made it a tort to handle an insurance claim wrongfully and in bad faith. The lower state court found that the claim was preempted by § 301.[90] The Wisconsin Supreme Court disagreed. It said that the suit was not preempted by § 301 because it raised a tort claim of bad faith, not a contract claim, so that the collective bargaining agreement was irrelevant.[91] The defendants sought Supreme Court review.

The Supreme Court reversed, holding that the tort claim was preempted under § 301. First, the Court reviewed the history of § 301 preemption and reaffirmed the *Lucas Flour* principle: Because of the need for uniformity and predictability in the interpretation of collective bargaining agreements, § 301 must be given a broad preemptive scope.[92] The Court then said:

> [W]hen resolution of a state-law claim is substantially dependent upon analysis of the terms of an agreement made between the parties in a labor contract, that claim must either be treated as a § 301 claim, . . . or dismissed as pre-empted by federal labor-contract law.[93]

The Court also said that § 301 would preempt such a state law claim whether it was pleaded in contract or in tort:

---

has singled out claims preempted by § 301 of the LMRA for such special treatment." (emphasis added)). See also *Adkins v General Motors Corp.*, 946 F2d 1201, 1207 (6th Cir 1991), cert denied, 60 USLW 3537 (May 18, 1992). ("The complete preemption corollary . . . is applied primarily in cases raising claims preempted by LMRA § 301.") petition for cert filed, 60 USLW 3537 (Jan 13, 1992).

[89] 471 US 202 (1985).

[90] Id at 203-06. The Wisconsin appeals court also found the claim preempted by other provisions of the federal labor law, id at 206 & n 3, but the Wisconsin Supreme Court disagreed. Id at 207. This issue was not presented for review by the Supreme Court. Id at 208.

[91] Id at 207.

[92] Id at 209-11.

[93] Id at 220 (citation omitted).

> [Q]uestions relating to what the parties to a labor agreement agreed, and what legal consequences were intended to flow from breaches of that agreement, must be resolved by reference to uniform federal law, whether such questions arise in the context of a suit for breach of contract or in a suit alleging liability in tort. Any other result would elevate form over substance and allow parties to evade the requirements of § 301 by relabeling their contract claims as claims for tortious breach of contract.[94]

Applying this doctrine to the facts before it, the Court reasoned that the collective agreement could contain implied terms defining the employer's duty to pay insurance benefits. It concluded that "[t]he duties imposed and rights established through the state tort thus derive[d] from the rights and obligations established by the contract."[95]

In addition, the Court found that the state tort alleged was "derived from the implied covenant of good faith and fair dealing found in every contract."[96] Because the state law right that the plaintiff asserted "not only derive[d] from the contract, but [wa]s defined by the contractual obligation of good faith, any attempt to assess liability here inevitably [would] involve contract interpretation."[97] Thus the Court held that the claim should have been dismissed, either for failure to exhaust the contractual arbitration procedure (if the plaintiff's complaint were interpreted, or amended, to assert a claim under § 301), or as preempted under § 301 (if the plaintiff had forgone his federal claim).[98]

c) Caterpillar *(1987).* Two years later, however, in *Caterpillar Inc. v Williams*, the Supreme Court held that an employee's claim for breach of an individual employment contract was *not* completely preempted by § 301.[99] In that case, employees claimed that their employer had breached a contract they had signed before they were in the bargaining unit or covered by the collective

---

[94] Id at 211.

[95] Id at 217.

[96] Id.

[97] Id at 218.

[98] Id at 220-21 (citing *Maddox*, 379 US at 652). On the disposition of cases in which a state court finds federal preemption, see Comment, 35 UCLA L Rev at 353 & n 181 (cited in note 83).

[99] 482 US 386, 396-97 (1987). The Court said, in dicta, that the defendant could raise, as a defense in state court, that plaintiff's action was preempted by other provisions of the NLRA. Id at 397-98.

bargaining agreement. They brought their claims in state court. The employer attempted to create a federal issue by arguing in defense that the collective bargaining agreement included a waiver of any pre-existing individual contractual rights.[100] On this basis, the employer removed the action to federal court and moved to have it dismissed, as a § 301 action, for failure to exhaust contractual remedies.

The federal district court found removal jurisdiction and dismissed. The Ninth Circuit, however, reversed, finding that the complaint did not arise under § 301, so that the federal courts did not have removal jurisdiction.[101] The Supreme Court affirmed. While acknowledging the broad preemptive scope of § 301, the Court refused to find preemption because the employees' complaint had not relied upon the collective bargaining agreement. Further, the Court found that the individual contractual rights upon which they had relied did not depend on an interpretation of the collective agreement.[102] The Court also rejected the employer's effort to "inject[] a federal question into an action that asserts what is plainly a state-law claim, transform the action into one arising under federal law, [and] thereby select[] the forum in which the claim shall be litigated."[103]

Unfortunately, the Court did not explain why the employer's argument in *Caterpillar* that the collective agreement limited the employer's obligation to the plaintiff was a mere defense, while in *Allis-Chalmers*, the employer's argument that the collective agreement limited or qualified its obligation to pay medical insurance preempted the plaintiff's claim. The opinions in *Allis-Chalmers* and *Caterpillar* thus created uncertainty as to whether § 301 preempted state law claims by employees to which the employer argued in defense that the case was dependent upon an implied term or waiver in a collective bargaining agreement. This type of preemption issue regularly arises when a unionized employee brings a state law wrongful discharge claim.

Some judges attempted to reconcile *Caterpillar* and *Allis-Chalmers* by interpreting *Caterpillar* as addressing only a question of § 1441 removal jurisdiction, not the substantive issue of preemp-

---

[100] Id at 388-90.
[101] Id at 390-91.
[102] Id at 395.
[103] Id.

tion under § 301.[104] That is, they reasoned that the complete preemption doctrine does not mean that all cases that are preempted under § 301 give rise to removal jurisdiction. Under this view, *Caterpillar* does not alter the standard for determining when an employer's defense creates removal jurisdiction, but it does mean that there is a stricter standard for asserting removal jurisdiction under § 1441 than for finding substantive preemption under § 301. Thus one court spoke of "the possibility that the *Caterpillar* plaintiffs' claims were *partially* preempted."[105]

The partial preemption theory has a serious flaw: How could a federal court *not* have removal jurisdiction over a claim that is completely preempted by § 301? If complete preemption means what it says—that § 301 displaces all state causes of action and converts an otherwise ordinary state law action into a § 301 action *from its inception*[106]—then the claim must involve a federal question, and removal jurisdiction must exist.

Most courts and commentators have rejected the partial preemption interpretation of *Caterpillar*. Instead, they view *Caterpillar* as limiting both substantive preemption under § 301 and removal jurisdiction under § 1441 in cases in which the employer raises a defense based on the collective bargaining agreement.[107] Indeed, the only circuit that has specifically embraced the partial preemption interpretation of *Caterpillar*—the Sixth Circuit in *Adkins*—noted that the claims which were preempted, but did not give rise to removal jurisdiction, were preempted by other provisions of the labor law, not by § 301.[108]

In other words, the tension between *Allis-Chalmers*'s broader § 301 preemption and *Caterpillar*'s narrower approach cannot so easily be resolved. However, the Court subsequently has indicated

---

[104] See, for example, *Adkins*, 946 F2d at 1207-08 (interpreting *Caterpillar* as a case of partial exemption); *Schacht v Caterpillar, Inc.*, 213 Ill App 3d 169, 571 NE2d 1215, 1217 (1991) (noting that "the issue in [*Caterpillar*] was removal jurisdiction, not the substantive merits of a pre-emption defense."), cert denied, 112 S Ct 1306 (1992). See also Richard E. Schwartz and James E. Parrot, *A New Look at Federal Labor Law Preemption: Unionized Employees' Claims in State Court*, 7 St Louis U Pub L Rev 297, 305 (1988) (noting the difficulty in reconciling *Allis-Chalmers* and *Caterpillar*).

[105] *Adkins*, 946 F2d at 1208.

[106] *Caterpillar*, 482 US at 393.

[107] See, for example, *McCormick v AT&T Technologies, Inc.*, 934 F2d 531, 534 (4th Cir 1991) (en banc), cert denied, 112 S Ct 912 (1992) (standard for § 301 preemption same as standard for removal jurisdiction). Accord *Berda v CBS, Inc.*, 881 F2d 20, 23-24, 26 (3d Cir 1989). See also Schwartz and Parrot, 7 St Louis U Pub L Rev at 305 (cited in note 104) ("[*Caterpillar*] made it clear that defensive federalization of a claim is no longer permitted.").

[108] *Adkins*, 946 F2d at 1208.

that it favors the broader preemptive scope that *Allis-Chalmers* exemplified.

3. Recent decisions broadening the scope of preemption.

a) Hechler *(1987)*. In 1987, the Supreme Court decided a case that posed the question of whether an employee's tort claim against her union was preempted under § 301. In *International Brotherhood of Electrical Workers v Hechler*, an injured employee sued her union in state court for breaching its implied duty to ensure its members a safe workplace.[109] The Supreme Court found the claim preempted because it was not "sufficiently independent of the collective-bargaining agreement to withstand the pre-emptive force of § 301."[110] The Court reasoned that, under Florida law, a union had no independent duty to provide a safe workplace; the union only could have assumed such a duty under a collective bargaining agreement. Thus to decide liability, the court would have to interpret the collective agreement to determine whether the union undertook such a duty.[111] In short, this decision, like *Allis-Chalmers*, affirmed the broad preemptive scope of § 301.

b) Lingle *(1988)*. In 1988, the Supreme Court again addressed the question of the scope of § 301 preemption. In *Lingle v Norge Division of Magic Chef*, an employee had brought a state law tort claim against her employer, alleging that she had been fired in retaliation for filing a workers' compensation claim.[112] The lower court had found that the claim was preempted, because the employee had been covered by a collective bargaining agreement, and because the facts underlying the tort of retaliatory discharge would have been the same as for a grievance under the just cause provision of the collective bargaining agreement.[113]

The Supreme Court reversed. It rejected the argument that factual parallelism between a state claim and a grievance automatically renders the state law claim preempted. Rather, "as long as the state-law claim can be resolved without interpreting the agreement itself, the claim is 'independent' of the agreement for § 301

[109] 481 US 851, 853 (1987).

[110] Id at 859.

[111] Id at 859-62.

[112] 486 US 399, 401 (1988).

[113] By the time the Seventh Circuit decided the case, Lingle had successfully arbitrated her claim and received reinstatement with back pay. *Lingle v Norge Division of Magic Chef, Inc.*, 823 F2d 1031, 1034 (7th Cir 1987).

pre-emption purposes."[114] The Court concluded: "[A]n application of state law is pre-empted by § 301 . . . only if such application requires the interpretation of a collective bargaining agreement."[115] The Court held that the state court could resolve the retaliation claim without reference to the collective agreement, so there was no § 301 preemption.

While the Court in *Lingle* did not preempt the claim of retaliatory discharge, the case did not directly address the question of whether § 301 would preempt a state law claim to which an employer interposed a contractual defense. However, one commentator has noted that the language of *Lingle* is a subtle but important departure from *Allis-Chalmers*, which said that only claims that were "substantially dependent" on the collective agreement were preempted.[116] She argues that the above-quoted language of *Lingle* suggests that if a court must interpret a collective agreement to resolve *any* aspect of a case—the plaintiff's case-in-chief or the defense—then the plaintiff's claim is preempted.[117] Indeed, she suggests that, after *Lingle*, employers need only assert a colorable contractual defense in order to supplant the state court's jurisdiction.[118] If she is right, then the *Lingle* test will result in more preemption than did either *Allis-Chalmers* or *Caterpillar*.[119]

---

[114] *Lingle*, 486 US at 410.

[115] Id at 413.

[116] Note, *The Need for a New Approach to Federal Preemption of Union Members' State Law Claims*, 99 Yale L J 209 (1989). The Eighth Circuit adopted this interpretation of *Lingle* in *Hanks v General Motors Corp.*, 859 F2d 67, 70 (8th Cir 1988):

> *Lingle* makes plain . . . that the defenses as well as the claims, must be considered in determining whether resolution of the state law claims requires construing the collective bargaining agreement. The factual background of the entire case must be examined against an analysis of the state tort claim and a determination made whether the provisions of the collective bargaining agreement come into play.

But see *Newberry v Pacific Racing Ass'n*, 854 F2d 1142, 1146-47 (9th Cir 1988) (finding no distinction between the *Lingle* and the *Allis-Chalmers* tests).

[117] Note, 99 Yale L J at 210 (cited in note 116). Footnote 12 in *Lingle* said that not every claim "tangentially involving a provision of a collective-bargaining agreement is preempted." 486 US at 413 n 12 (quoting *Allis-Chalmers*, 471 US at 211). The Court gave as a hypothetical example a state law claim that necessitated a look at the collective agreement to determine the back pay to which the claimant was entitled. Id. The Court said that the need to consult the agreement to determine back pay would not, standing alone, preempt the claim. Id. The extreme narrowness of this exception lends support to the argument that *Lingle* gave a broader scope to § 301 preemption than did *Allis-Chalmers*.

[118] Note, 99 Yale L J at 209-11 (cited in note 116).

[119] Id at 209. See also *Labor Arbitration and the Law of Collective Bargaining*, 7 Labor Law 747, 755-61 (1991) (during 1990, after *Lingle*, the trend was toward more preemption under § 301). But see Note, *Labor Law Preemption Under Section 301: New Rules for an Old Game*, 40 Syracuse L Rev 1279, 1291-93 (1989) (arguing that the *Lingle* test limited the preemptive scope of the *Allis-Chalmers* test). See also Note, *Federal Labor Law Preemp-*

B. A Topology of the Section 301 Doctrine in the Lower Federal Courts

Whether or not *Lingle* has brought about more instances of § 301 preemption, it certainly has not simplified the preemption doctrine. Just last year, the Ninth Circuit termed § 301 preemption a "thicket," a "tangled and confusing interplay between federal and state law,"[120] and "one of the most confused areas of federal court litigation."[121] However, despite this apparent confusion, lower federal courts have shown a strong tendency, both before and after *Lingle*, to find unionized workers' state law claims preempted.[122]

There are two distinct methods of reasoning that courts employ in deciding § 301 preemption cases, both of which are heavily tilted in favor of preemption. One method is to find preemption on the basis of a contract-interpretation issue raised by the employer in defense. Often such defenses are based on general contract provisions to which the employer urges an expansive interpretation. For example, one court has found a contractual provision granting an employer the right to make "reasonable rules and regulations from time to time" sufficient to preempt an employee's right to be free of drug testing under state law.[123] Other courts have found

---

tion of State Wrongful Discharge Claims, 58 U Cin L Rev 491, 526-27 (1989) (arguing that *Lingle* opened the door to union workers' state law suits).

[120] *Galvez v Kuhn*, 933 F2d 773, 774 (9th Cir 1991).

[121] Id at 776 (quoting Note, 99 Yale L J at 209 (cited in note 116)). See also *Singh v Lunalilo*, 6 IER Cases (BNA) 1682, 1684 (D Hawaii 1991) (on difficulty of reconciling the "dozens, if not hundreds, of federal cases addressing the issue of the scope of section 301 pre-emption on [sic] state law claims.").

[122] See notes 128-35 and accompanying text. See also Note, 58 U Cin L Rev at 555 (cited in note 119) (arguing that all wrongful discharge claims of unionized workers are preempted by § 301). But see Jane Byeff Korn, *Collective Rights and Individual Remedies: Rebalancing the Balance After* Lingle, 41 Hastings L J 1149, 1167 (1990) (arguing that, after *Lingle*, most employee claims based on state tort laws are not preempted).

Professor Korn concludes that *Lingle* opened the door for unionized employees to bypass their grievance procedures and bring a host of lawsuits in the state courts. 41 Hastings L J at 1165. My research reaches the opposite conclusion. Indeed, I believe that her research does too. Of the twenty-six cases cited by Korn in notes 53, 85, and 108 as the basis for her claim, twelve were cases involving retaliation for filing of workers' compensation claims, the precise issue decided by the Supreme Court in *Lingle*. In those cases, it is not at all surprising that the lower courts followed the Supreme Court's ruling in *Lingle*. Of the remaining fourteen cases Professor Korn cites, twelve were cases in which the state law claims were preempted by federal law, so that the unionized worker could not maintain the state court action. Thus, if one exempts the *Lingle* fact-pattern, only two of Professor Korn's twenty-six cases cited were cases in which the unionized worker was permitted to sue in state court.

[123] *Jackson v Liquid Carbonic Corp.*, 863 F2d 111, 113-15 (1st Cir 1988) (employee's claim preempted by the collective bargaining agreement, which contained a standard management rights clause giving the company the "right to post reasonable rules and regulations

preemption on the basis of implied contract clauses or novel readings of explicit ones.[124]

The other method is to find preemption by interpretation of state law. By this method, a court first looks to see whether an asserted state law employment right is waivable under state law.[125] If it is, then *theoretically* the court should look to see if the employee *in fact* waived the right in a clause of the collective bargaining agreement. However, this exercise requires the court to interpret the collective agreement, something which courts are extremely reluctant to do.[126] Instead they preempt the claim because to decide whether the state law claim was actually waived, the court would have to interpret the collective bargaining agreement. Hence, by this method, a state employment right that is waivable is automatically preempted.[127]

A survey of recent preemption cases reveals a very broad tendency for courts to preempt unionized workers' state law claims. Indeed, with very few exceptions, courts always preempt unionized workers' attempts to assert state law employment rights. The

---

from time to time"). See also *Utility Workers of America v Southern California Edison Co.*, 852 F2d 1083, 1086 (9th Cir 1988) (constitutional claims preempted by contractual language that granted the company the right to manage the plant, direct the work force, and implement safety rules); *Schlacter-Jones v General Telephone*, 936 F2d 435, 439 (9th Cir 1991) (employee's claims preempted because they were "inextricably intertwined" with analysis of the collective bargaining agreement, which governed working conditions at the company).

[124] See, for example, *McCormick*, 934 F2d at 536 (holding that plaintiff's claim against an employer involved "implied rights and duties" in the collective bargaining agreement, and thus the claims required interpretation of the agreement and were preempted); *Jones v General Motors Corp.*, 939 F2d 380, 383 (6th Cir 1991) (§ 301 preemption not limited to cases where the precise meaning of words in the collective bargaining agreement is the crux of the state-based claim); *Laws v Calmat*, 852 F2d 430 (9th Cir 1988) (drug testing claims preempted on the basis of implied terms).

[125] For example, in *Lingle*, the Supreme Court found that the Illinois state-law right not to be fired for filing a workers' compensation claim was not waivable. 486 US at 409 & n 9. Thus it found that the collective bargaining agreement could not have modified the state law right. Id. See also *Local No. 57, United Ass'n of Journeymen & Apprentices of Plumbing v Bechtel Power Corp.*, 834 F2d 884, 889-90 (10th Cir 1987) (no preemption because anti-blacklisting provisions of Utah Constitution not waivable); *Tellez v Pacific Gas and Electric*, 817 F2d 536, 538 (9th Cir 1987) (no preemption because state right not negotiable).

[126] See *Warrior & Gulf*, 363 US at 582 (arbitrators, not courts, should interpret collective bargaining agreements).

[127] See, for example, *Hyles v Mensing*, 849 F2d 1213, 1216-17 (9th Cir 1988) (preempting claims of emotional distress and defamation because they did not involve nonnegotiable state right); *Laws*, 852 F2d at 433 & n 4; *Utility Workers*, 852 F2d at 1086 (right to be free of drug testing, located in California's state constitution's privacy guarantee, can be waived). See also Angel Gomez III, *Preemption and Preclusion of Employee Common Law Rights by Federal and State Statutes*, 11 Indus Rel L J 45, 51 n 42 (1989) (discussing the waiver issue in *Utility Workers* and *Laws*).

broad trend, as well as the narrow exceptions, are apparent when we break the cases down into categories.

1. Claims that usually are preempted.

A great many of the developments in state employment law have been in the area of wrongful discharge. Unionized workers have been particularly disadvantaged in this area by the preemption rules.[128] In general, the following types of claims by employees against employers are almost always preempted:

1. unjust dismissal claims alleging breach of an implied covenant of good faith and fair dealing;[129]
2. unjust dismissal claims alleging a tort of wrongful discharge;[130]
3. unlawful drug testing claims;[131]
4. claims that the employer breached a promise to an employee who was a member of a bargaining unit;[132]

---

[128] Anthony Herman, *Wrongful Discharge Actions after* Leuck *and* Metropolitan Life Insurance*: The Erosion of Individual Rights and Collective Strength?*, 9 Indus Rel L J 596, 639-40 (1987). See also Daniel N. Kosanovich, *Inching Through the Maze: Recent Developments in Preemption Under the NLRA and the Impact of* Caterpillar, Hechler, *and Others*, 4 Labor Law 225, 253-54 (1988) (claims involving tort of wrongful discharge or contract breach routinely preempted).

[129] See, for example, *Bloom v Universal City Studios*, 734 F Supp 1553, 1560 (C D Cal 1990), aff'd without opinion, 933 F2d 1013 (9th Cir 1991); *Fox v Parker Hannifin Corp.*, 914 F2d 795, 801 (6th Cir 1990); *Cook v Lindsay Olive Growers*, 911 F2d 233, 238-39 (9th Cir 1990); *Newberry v Pacific Racing Ass'n*, 854 F2d 1142, 1147 (9th Cir 1988); *Paige v Henry J. Kaiser Co.*, 826 F2d 857, 866 (9th Cir 1987); *Harper v San Diego Transit Corp.*, 764 F2d 663, 668-69 (9th Cir 1985); *Taylor v St. Regis Paper Co.*, 560 F Supp 546, 549 (C D Cal 1983).

[130] See, for example, *Singh*, 6 IER Cases (BNA) at 1682, 1686-87; *Cook*, 911 F2d at 237-38; *Hanks v General Motors Corp.*, 859 F2d 67, 69 (8th Cir 1988); *Kirby v Allegheny Beverage Corp.*, 811 F2d 253, 256 (4th Cir 1987); *Desoto v Yellow Freight Systems, Inc.*, 811 F2d 1333, 1135-36 (9th Cir 1987); *Durrette v UGI Corp.*, 674 F Supp 1139, 1143 (M D Pa 1987); *Crocker v Synpol, Inc.*, 732 SW2d 429, 432-33 (Tex App 1987); *Nelson v Owens-Corning Fiberglas Corp.*, 648 F Supp 44, 47 (D Mont 1986); *Hohn v Kaiser Cement Corp.*, 624 F Supp 549, 551-52 (D Mont 1986); *Evangelista v Inlandboatmen's Union of the Pacific*, 777 F2d 1390, 1400-01 (9th Cir 1985); *Mitchell v Pepsi-Cola Bottlers Inc.*, 772 F2d 342, 344-45 (7th Cir 1985); *Faust v RCA Corp.*, 612 F Supp 540, 542 (M D Pa 1985); *Taylor*, 560 F Supp at 549.

[131] See, for example, *Schlacter-Jones*, 936 F2d at 440-42; *Jackson*, 863 F2d at 118-20; *Utility Workers*, 852 F2d at 1086-87; *Laws*, 852 F2d at 432-33; *Strachan v Union Oil Co.*, 768 F2d 703, 705 (5th Cir 1985).

[132] The claims are preempted whether the plaintiff pleads the breach of promise as a breach of contract, misrepresentation, promissory fraud, or promissory estoppel. See, for example, *Dougherty v AT&T*, 902 F2d 201, 204 (2d Cir 1990) (promise of job security); *Fox*, 914 F2d at 801-02 (promise to investigate harassment by co-workers); *Ulrich v Goodyear Tire and Rubber Co.*, 884 F2d 936, 938 (6th Cir 1989) (promise of right to reenter bargaining unit after transferring to supervisory position); *Terwilleger v Greyhound Lines, Inc.*, 882

5. claims of defamation for an employer's derogatory remarks about an employee made to co-workers;[133]

6. claims that an employer conducted an unlawful search of a person or automobile;[134]

7. claims concerning the mishandling of health insurance, medical leave, or other medical obligations.[135]

2. Claims that usually are not preempted.

On the other hand, there are a few types of claims by employees against employers which the courts almost never preempt:

1. claims of retaliatory discharge for filing a workers' compensation claim;[136]

F2d 1033, 1037-38 (6th Cir 1989) (promise of job security); *Bache v AT&T*, 840 F2d 283, 285-86 & n 1 (5th Cir 1988) (promise of job security at new position if employee agreed to transfer from bargaining unit); *Maushund v Earl C. Smith, Inc.*, 795 F2d 589, 589-90 (6th Cir 1986) (promise of job security), *Mason v Continental Group, Inc.*, 763 F2d 1219, 1222-24 (11th Cir 1985) (promise to keep plant open); *Eitmann v New Orleans Public Service, Inc.*, 730 F2d 359, 362-63 (5th Cir 1984) (promise of full compensation during period of disability). See also *Schacht*, 571 NE2d at 1218 (individual written apprenticeship contracts). But see *Wells v General Motors*, 881 F2d 166, 172-75 (5th Cir 1989) (no preemption of fraud and misrepresentation claims regarding promise that laid-off employees would be eligible for reemployment).

[133] See, for example, *Strachan*, 768 F2d at 706 (state law defamation claims are preempted unless plaintiff shows malice); *Mitchell*, 772 F2d at 348 & n 20. But see *Meier v Hamilton Standard Electronic Systems, Inc.*, 748 F Supp 296, 299-300 (E D Pa 1990) (defamatory statements not preempted if made to individuals outside the scope of the agreement); *Tellez*, 817 F2d at 538 (holding that the agreement does not govern defamatory statements), in which the courts refused to preempt defamation claims.

[134] See, for example, *Romero v Hilton Hotels Corp.*, 137 Labor Rel Ref Man (BNA) 2647, 2649-50 (D Hawaii 1991) (search of person); *Stikes v Chevron USA, Inc.*, 914 F2d 1265, 1269-70 (9th Cir 1990), cert denied, 111 S Ct 2015 (1991) (search of automobile); *Kirby*, 811 F2d at 256 (search of person and automobile).

[135] See, for example, *Perugini v Safeway Stores*, 935 F2d 1083, 1088 (9th Cir 1991) (preempting claims growing out of employer's refusal to give employee light duty during pregnancy and instead forcing her to take medical leave); *Terwilliger*, 882 F2d at 1037-38 (preempting right to reemployment after medical disqualification because created by contract, not state law); *Brinkman v State*, 224 Mont 238, 729 P2d 1301, 1308-09 (1989) (preempting wrongful discharge claim arising from termination for failing to provide proper request for medical leave).

[136] Since *Lingle*, courts have uniformly refused to preempt claims alleging retaliation for filing workers' compensation claims. See, for example, *Krashna v Oliver Realty, Inc.*, 895 F2d 111, 115 (3d Cir 1990) (distinguishing plaintiff's termination from ordinary wrongful discharge claim because the complaint involved a course of illegal conduct that preceded the discharge and because the plaintiff expressly alleged wrongs separate from the collective bargaining agreement); *McEwen v Delta Air Lines, Inc.*, 919 F2d 58, 59 (7th Cir 1990) (not discussing preemption, but applying Illinois law); *Eldridge v Felec Services, Inc.*, 920 F2d 1434, 1438-39 (9th Cir 1990) (holding that state law requires only a determination whether the workers' compensation claim was the primary cause of discharge, an injury that requires

2. claims that the employer breached a promise made to an employee *before* the employee entered the bargaining unit;[137]

3. claims of discrimination on the basis of race, age, gender, or some other protected classification.[138]

What is interesting about these three categories of non-preempted claims is that they all parallel specific Supreme Court deci-

---

no interpretation of the collective-bargaining agreement); *Smolarek v Chrysler Corp.*, 858 F2d 1165, 1168-69 (6th Cir 1988) (same). But see *Magerer v John Sexton & Co.*, 912 F2d 525, 529-30 (1st Cir 1990) (preempting workers' compensation retaliation claim because state statute exempts workers covered by collective bargaining agreements).

Prior to *Lingle*, the courts were divided on this issue. For retaliation claims that were not preempted, see, for example, *Baldracchi v Pratt & Whitney Aircraft Division*, 814 F2d 102, 105 (2d Cir 1987) (retaliation claim independent of agreement); *Bonner v Fleming Companies, Inc.*, 734 SW2d 764, 766 (Tex App 1987) (same); *Sutton v Southwest Forest Industries, Inc.*, 628 F Supp 1034, 1036 (D Kan 1985) (state policy of protecting workers from retaliatory discharge for filing workers' compensation claims does not conflict with the federal interest in protecting the collective-bargaining process); *Midgett v Sackett-Chicago, Inc.*, 105 Ill 2d 143, 473 NE2d 1280, 1283 (1984) ("[I]n order to provide a complete remedy it is necessary that the victim of a retaliatory discharge be given a remedy in tort, independent of any contract remedy the employee may have based in the collective-bargaining agreement."). For retaliation claims that were preempted, see, for example, *Richard v Portland General Electric*, 83 Or App 59, 730 P2d 578, 579 (1986)(citing state and federal policy of exclusivity of collective bargaining remedies); *Johnson v Hussmann Corp.*, 610 F Supp 757, 759 (E D Mo 1985) (because the state tort law directly affects the agreement, it is preempted); *Schuyler v Metropolitan Transit Co.*, 374 NW2d 453, 455-56 (Minn App 1985) (failure to exhaust grievances under federal law precluded suit for retaliatory discharge under state law); *Mouser v Granite City Steel Division of National Steel Corp.*, 121 Ill App 3d 834, 460 NE2d 115, 118 (5th Dist 1984) (employee cannot sue in tort separate from collective bargaining agreement).

[137] See, for example, *Berda v CBS, Inc.*, 881 F2d 20, 25-27 (3d Cir 1989) (pre-hire promise of job security); *Anderson v Ford Motor Co.*, 803 F2d 953, 958 & n 7 (8th Cir 1986) (promise that newly-hired employees would not be bumped by employees on preferential hiring list); *Varnum v Nu-Car Carriers, Inc.*, 804 F2d 638, 640 (11th Cir 1986) (pre-hire promises about potential income and job assignments). But see *Bales v General Telephone Co.*, 795 F2d 775, 779-80 (9th Cir 1986) (preempting suit to enforce pre-hire promises about future benefits and job security). Angel Gomez has stated that the circuits are split over whether to preempt claims involving pre-hire contracts. However, he refers only to *Bales* as a case of preemption. Gomez, 11 Indus Rel L J at 52 & n 48 (cited in note 127).

[138] See, for example, *Cook*, 911 F2d at 238 (religious discrimination); *Smolarek*, 879 F2d at 1332-33 (handicap discrimination); *Ackerman v Western Electric Co.*, 860 F2d 1514, 1517-18 (9th Cir 1988) (handicap discrimination); *Nelson*, 648 F Supp at 47 (sex discrimination); *Austin v New England Telephone*, 644 F Supp 763, 767 (D Mass 1986) (handicap discrimination); *Scott v New United Motor Mfg., Inc.*, 632 F Supp 891, 894-95 (N D Cal 1986) (race discrimination); *Peoples v Pennsylvania Power and Light Co.*, 638 F Supp 402, 408 (M D Pa 1985) (race discrimination). See also *Carrington v RCA Global Communications*, 762 F Supp 632, 641 (D NJ 1991) ("Following *Lingle*, courts have uniformly held that state anti-discrimination laws are not preempted by § 301 of the LMRA . . . even where the labor contract itself prohibits discrimination."). But see *Laczay v Ross Adhesives*, 855 F2d 351, 352 (6th Cir 1988) (describing district court action preempting allegation of violation of Michigan Age Discrimination statute and denying right to appeal).

sions. For example, claims for workers' compensation retaliation involve the same issue as did *Lingle*, in which the Court did not preempt the claim. Similarily, the claims for breach of pre-employment promises replicate the fact pattern in *Caterpillar*, which also found no preemption. And the discrimination claims pose a similar issue to that in *Alexander v Gardner-Denver Co.*, another case in which the Court did not defer to the contractual arbitration machinery.[139] Indeed, the Supreme Court in *Lingle* expressly endorsed an exception to § 301 preemption for claims under state anti-discrimination laws.[140] Thus all three categories are narrow exceptions to an otherwise broad preemption doctrine.[141]

There is one additional category of claims that are not preempted: claims not cognizable under a union's grievance procedure. Thus, for example, claims against persons who are not parties to a collective agreement, or who are not subject to the grievance and arbitration procedures, are rarely preempted.[142] Similarily, cases brought by persons who do not have access to the grievance procedure rarely are preempted.[143] In addition, claims

---

[139] 415 US 36 (1974). There the Supreme Court held that an employee can maintain a race discrimination action under the civil rights acts, even if she had previously arbitrated the same issue. That is, the federal courts need not *defer* to the decision of the arbitrator in matters involving discrimination. Id at 59-60. Deferral questions are similar but not identical to § 301 preemption questions. Section 301 preemption resolves the tension between collectively-bargained rights and *state*-created individual employment rights. Deferral resolves the tension between collectively-bargained rights and *federally*-created individual employment rights. Section 301 preemption is derived from the Supremacy Clause and thus is constitutionally compelled. Deferral is derived from the federal courts' authority to reconcile and harmonize two conflicting federal statutes; it may reflect prudent judicial policy, but it is not constitutionally compelled.

When an individual maintains a claim under *state* fair employment laws, the issue is preemption rather than deferral, but the courts reach the same conclusion as in *Gardner-Denver*. That is, a union's grievance procedure does not preempt a claim for discrimination based on state law. Id at 51-52. One commentator has suggested that courts should use the reasoning of *Gardner-Denver* to decide all issues of § 301 preemption, not merely those involving discrimination. Herman, 9 Indus Rel L J at 615-16 (cited in note 128).

[140] 486 US at 412-13.

[141] See *Singh*, 6 IER Cases (BNA) at 1686 (noting exceptions to § 301 preemption for claims alleging workers' compensation retaliation and employment discrimination).

[142] See, for example, *Meier*, 748 F Supp at 300-01 (defamatory statements made by employer to persons not employed by company and not involved in investigation of employee); *Dougherty v Parsec, Inc.*, 872 F2d 766, 770-71 (6th Cir 1989) (tortious interference claim against client of plaintiff's employer who allegedly requested plaintiff's dismissal in retaliation for filing an OSHA complaint, even though the employee attempted to use the grievance procedure to protest the firing).

[143] See, for example, *White v National Steel Corp.*, 938 F2d 474, 484 (4th Cir 1991) (no preemption because plaintiffs were not represented by union and had no access to grievance procedure); *Scott v New United Motor Manufacturing, Inc.*, 632 F Supp 891, 893-94 (N D Cal 1986) (no preemption of fraud and IIED claims because plaintiff was a probationary

arising after the expiration of the collective bargaining agreement are not preempted.[144] There, too, courts reason that if no grievance and arbitration procedure is available to remedy the issue, they should not preempt.

This last exception to the otherwise broad tendency to preempt indicates the central role that union grievance and arbitration procedures play in the courts' determination of whether or not to preempt.[145] Ostensibly this factor should be irrelevant because, under *Allis-Chalmers* and *Lingle*, it is the relationship between the state law claim and the collective bargaining agreement that should decide the preemption question, not the relationship between the state law claim and the *means to enforce* the collective agreement. In Section IV below, I explore the logic that links the contractual enforcement procedure and the decision by a court to preempt.

3. Claims that sometimes are preempted and sometimes are not.

There are also a few categories of § 301 preemption claims that go both ways:

---

employee and, under the applicable collective agreement, was not entitled to file a grievance). See also *Caterpillar*, 482 US at 395 & n 9 (no preemption for claims of employees not covered by collective bargaining agreement). But see *Young v Anthony's Fish Grottos, Inc.*, 830 F2d 993, 1000 & n 3 (9th Cir 1987) (preempting probationary employee's claim of wrongful discharge even though employee was not covered by the job security terms of the collective agreement, because the employee had access to the grievance procedure).

Professor William Gould IV critizes the *Scott* decision as inconsistent with *The Steelworkers Trilogy* (see note 200) and the "virtues of industrial self-government." Gould, 9 Indus Rel L J at 11-12 (cited in note 71).

[144] See, for example, *Overby v Chevron, USA*, 132 Labor Rel Ref Man (BNA) 2334, 2337 (9th Cir 1989) (for § 301 purposes, the agreement ceases to exist when it expires, so there can be no preemption).

[145] *National Steel*, 938 F2d at 481 (The driving force behind the Supreme Court's decision in *Lueck* was "not only the need for uniformity of interpretation that was identified in *Lucas Flour*, but the need to preserve the central role of arbitration established in collective bargaining contracts."); *McCormick*, 934 F2d at 538 ("There are few workplace quarrels that could not be framed as some form of tortious conduct. Our holding that [the plaintiff's] state law claims are preempted by § 301 protects the continued vitality of grievance procedures as a fair and efficient means for the resolution of labor disputes, and it also furthers the uniformity concerns underlying § 301."); *Beatrice Foods*, 921 F2d at 1020 ("[T]he holdings in *Allis-Chalmers* and *Bechtel Power* are consistent with the 'Steelworkers Trilogy" [in which the Supreme Court] stated a broad policy favoring arbitration under collective bargaining agreements."); *Marine Transport Lines v Int'l Organization of Masters*, 609 F Supp 282, 287 (S D NY 1985) ("It was precisely the need to maintain the effectiveness of arbitration that prompted the Court in *Lueck* to find that a derivative tort claim was preempted by federal law under Section 301 where the collective bargaining agreement imposed the same rights and obligations as would the derivative tort.").

1. claims concerning issues that were not addressed by the collective agreement, and thus cannot be brought in arbitration;[146]

2. claims for intentional infliction of emotional distress ("IIED"), due to outrageous conduct by the employer;[147]

---

[146] Cases not preempting these claims include *Meier v Hamilton Standard Electronic Systems, Inc.*, 748 F Supp 296 (E D Pa 1990), in which a plaintiff alleged that his employer falsely accused him of drug trafficking, and fired him. The plaintiff prevailed in arbitration and was reinstated. Id at 298 n 1. Thereafter, he sued for defamation, intentional infliction of emotional distress, invasion of privacy, and various other torts. The district court refused to preempt the defamation, intentional infliction of emotional distress ("IIED"), and privacy claims because the grievance procedure under the union contract could not redress such wrongs. Id at 300. See also *Fox*, 914 F2d at 802 (no preemption for claims of emotional distress because unrelated to collective bargaining agreement); *Wells*, 881 F2d at 174-75 (no preemption for claim of fraud because collective agreement did not address issue); *Tellez*, 817 F2d at 538 (no preemption for claim of defamation because collective agreement did not envision it); *Bloom*, 734 F Supp at 1558 n 2 (noting exception to preemption for "claims that concern jobs not covered by a collective bargaining agreement").

Courts preempting them include *Young*, 830 F2d at 997; and *Truex v Garnett Freightlines, Inc.*, 784 F2d 1347, 1351 (9th Cir 1985).

Professor Gomez refers to these as claims involving conduct outside the collective bargaining agreement. Gomez, 11 Indus Rel L J at 53-54 (cited in note 127), and notes that this is a "highly limited" exception to preemption. Id at 53. His evidence supports mine: that claims involving conduct outside the collective bargaining agreement sometimes are preempted, and sometimes are not.

[147] See *McCormick*, 934 F2d at 546 n 4 (Phillips dissenting) (noting that IIED claims are sometimes preempted, and sometimes not); *Beatrice Foods*, 921 F2d at 1021 (noting that circuits have reached "varying results" on the question of whether to preempt IIED claims).

Courts preempting such claims include *McCormick*, 934 F2d at 537; *Romero v Hilton Hotels*, 137 Labor Rel Ref Man (BNA) at 2650; *Singh*, 6 IER Cases (BNA) at 1686; *Beatrice Foods*, 921 F2d at 1021-22; *Cook*, 911 F2d at 239-40; *Douglas v American Information Technologies Corp.*, 877 F2d 565, 572-73 (7th Cir 1989); *Newberry*, 854 F2d at 1149-50; *Hyles*, 849 F2d at 1216-17; *Willis v Reynolds Metals Co.*, 840 F2d 254, 255 (4th Cir 1988); *DeTomaso v Pan American World Airways*, 733 P2d 614, 620-21 (Cal 1987); *Truex v Garnett Freightlines, Inc.*, 784 F2d at 1347, 1350-51 (9th Cir 1985). See also *McCormick*, 934 F2d at 536 (preempting IIED claim for actions taken by employer after terminating employee).

Courts not preempting them include *Perugini*, 935 F2d at 1089 (no preemption of claim based on discriminatory remarks because agreement set no standards to determine outrageous conduct in that regard); *Hanks*, 906 F2d at 345 (no preemption of outrageous conduct and IIED claims because collective agreement provided no remedy); *Sauls v Union Oil Co. of California*, 750 F Supp 783, 786-87 (E D Tex 1990) (agreement provided no remedy for defendant's dealings with non-union management employees); *Meier*, 748 F Supp at 300 (E D Pa 1990) (no preemption of IIED claim because grievance procedure under the union contract could not redress such wrongs); *Hanks*, 859 F2d at 69-70; *Tellez*, 817 F2d at 539 (no preemption of IIED claim because the collective agreement was vague on disciplinary procedures and gave no guidance regarding the plaintiff's claim); *Zaks v American Broadcasting Companies, Inc.*, 626 F Supp 695, 698 (C D Cal 1985) (no preemption because the emotional distress was linked to clearly unpreempted claims).

3. whistleblower claims, in which the employer fires an employee in retaliation for reporting the employer's violation of a state or federal law, and the employee sues for wrongful discharge.[148]

The IIED cases are particularly hard to distinguish from each other.[149] One dimension upon which many of the IIED decisions can be distinguished is the *degree* of outrageousness of the alleged harassment. Some courts preempt when they find that the conduct alleged is not very outrageous.[150] On the other hand, some courts refuse to preempt when the conduct alleged is extremely outrageous.[151]

---

[148] See notes 162-64 and accompanying text. Courts that have preempted whistleblower claims include *Masters v Daniel Int'l Corp.*, 917 F2d 455, 457 (10th Cir 1990) (employee fired for reporting safety violations at nuclear power plant); *Vincent v Trend Western Technical Corp.*, 828 F2d 563, 566 (9th Cir 1987) (employee fired for reporting employer's violation of terms of government contract); *DeSoto v Yellow Freight Systems*, 811 F2d 1333, 1336 (9th Cir 1987) (employee fired for refusing to drive trailer whose registration and vehicle tag had expired); *Snow v Bechtel Construction*, 647 F Supp 1514, 1520 (C D Cal 1986) (employee fired for reporting safety violations to Nuclear Regulatory Commission).

Courts that have not preempted them include *Dougherty v Parsec*, 872 F2d at 771 (employee fired for filing complaint under Occupational Safety and Health Act); *Miller v Fairchild Industries*, 668 F Supp 461, 467 (D Md 1987) (employee fired for reporting violations of state environmental law); *Brevik v Kite Painting, Inc.*, 416 NW2d 714, 718 (Minn 1987) (employee fired for filing complaint under state occupational safety and health act); *Garibaldi v Lucky Food Stores*, 726 F2d 1367, 1375-76 (9th Cir 1984) (employee fired for reporting violation of state health law).

[149] For example, in *Truex*, 784 F2d at 1344, plaintiffs claimed that their supervisors had harassed them with warning letters, and then had suspended one of them. The Ninth Circuit preempted their IIED claims because they involved administration of discipline, which was a matter covered by the collective agreement. Id at 1350. In response to the plaintiffs' argument that under the collective agreement, warning letters were not grievable, the court held that plaintiffs were bound by contractual provisions as to when grievances may be raised as well as by contractual limitations on the available remedies. Id at 1353.

In contrast, in *Sauls v Union Oil Co. of California*, 750 F Supp 783 (E D Tex 1990) a worker claimed he had been harassed by his supervisor and co-workers and then fired. He filed a grievance, prevailed at arbitration, was reinstated, and then sued for IIED. The Texas District Court refused to preempt because the record indicated that the plaintiff had been subjected to a great deal of malicious and outrageous conduct, and that such conduct was not addressed in the collective bargaining agreement. Id at 788.

[150] In *Truex*, for example, the district court specifically noted that the allegations were not outrageous enough to withstand preemption. 784 F2d at 1352. See also *Romero*, 137 Labor Rel Ref Man (BNA) at 2649 (defendants' conduct was not sufficiently outrageous to save plaintiffs' claim from preemption).

[151] In *Zaks*, 626 F Supp at 698, for example, the California district court declared that "[t]he tortious conduct alleged here is so outrageous that no national labor policy would be served by preempting these claims; no federal interest would be harmed by enforcement of the state-created rights here." See also *Fox*, 914 F2d at 802 ("claims premised upon abusive behavior above and beyond the routine exercise of [collective bargaining] rights are not preempted"); *Perugini*, 935 F2d at 1089 (harassment claim not preempted where collective bargaining agreement did not establish standard for outrageous conduct).

It is unclear why the degree of outrageousness should be a factor in § 301 preemption analysis. Some courts, when using a degree-of-outrageousness factor to determine whether to preempt, cite *Farmer v United Brotherhood of Carpenters and Joiners*[152] as authority for that distinction.[153] In *Farmer*, the Supreme Court held that the NLRA did not preempt a claim for extremely outrageous tortious conduct, because policing such conduct was so vital to local concerns that the state's interest overrode the federal interest in uniform application of the labor laws.[154] However, *Farmer* preemption was under the NLRA, not under § 301 of the Labor Relations Management Act. The Supreme Court has not ruled on whether *Farmer* applies to § 301 preemption. The Tenth Circuit, however, has refused to rely on *Farmer* in a § 301 preemption case, ruling that "*Allis-Chalmers* and *Lingle*, not *Farmer* control § 301 preemption."[155] Thus *Farmer*'s relevance to § 301 preemption remains unclear.

Recently, the Seventh Circuit developed an approach to § 301 preemption of IIED claims which, if adopted by other circuits, could lead to preemption of most IIED claims in the future. In *Douglas v American Information Technologies Corp.*, an employee had been injured on her job.[156] When she returned to work, she refused to work overtime or to accept certain high-stress job assignments. She claimed that, as a result of these refusals, the company engaged in a series of acts with the intent of inflicting emotional distress upon her, including denying her "stress relief days," giving her a final warning, and excessively scrutinizing her work.[157]

The Seventh Circuit began its analysis by enumerating the three elements necessary to establish the tort of intentional infliction of emotional distress: (1) extreme and outrageous conduct; (2) that the perpetrator intends to cause severe emotional distress; and (3) that the perpetrator does in fact cause severe emotional distress.[158] It then said that to decide whether the conduct alleged is extreme and outrageous involves determining whether it was au-

---

[152] 430 US 290 (1977).

[153] Cases that cite *Farmer* include *Truex*, 784 F2d at 1350-51; *Romero*, 137 Labor Rel Ref Man (BNA) at 2649.

[154] 430 US at 302-04. Specifically, *Farmer* allowed a limited exception to NLRA preemption for IIED claims where the conduct complained of is "so outrageous that 'no reasonable man . . . should be expected to endure it.'" and where the claim does not allege discriminatory hiring hall practices. Id at 302-03 & n 11 (citation omitted).

[155] *Beatrice Foods*, 921 F2d at 1021.

[156] 877 F2d 565 (7th Cir 1989).

[157] Id at 567-68.

[158] Id at 570.

thorized by an express or implied term in the collective bargaining agreement[159]:

> Because [the plaintiff's claim] consists of allegedly wrongful acts directly related to the terms and conditions of her employment, resolution of her claim will be substantially dependent on an analysis of the terms of the collective bargaining agreement under which she is employed. A court will be required to determine whether her employer's conduct was authorized by the explicit or implicit terms of the agreement.[160]

Thus the Seventh Circuit found the claim preempted.

This analysis suggests that any IIED claim that alleges wrongful acts relating to the terms and conditions of employment should be preempted under § 301 on the grounds that the court could not assess the outrageousness of the conduct without determining whether the express *or implied* terms of the collective agreement authorize the conduct. This approach obviously would expand the number of IIED claims that are preempted.[161]

"Whistleblower cases" are another area where the decisions are mixed. These are cases in which an employer fires an employee in retaliation for reporting the employer's violation of a state or federal law, and the employee sues for wrongful discharge. Whistleblower cases differ from other wrongful discharge cases in that the employee bases her argument on a definite, independent public policy embodied in the law alleged to have been violated.

Some of the whistleblower cases can be distinguished on the basis of whether the violation reported is of a state or federal law. Most of the preempted claims allege retaliation for reporting a violation of a *federal* law. In those cases, the courts frequently preempt the claims on the basis of both § 301 *and* the federal statute involved, under what might be called a "§ 301-plus" preemption analysis.[162]

On the other hand, most of the whistleblower cases that allege retaliation for reporting violations of state law have not been pre-

---

[159] Id at 571-72.

[160] Id at 573.

[161] For a critique of the *Douglas* opinion, see Note, 99 Yale L J at 222 n 77 (cited in note 116).

[162] See, for example, *Snow*, 647 F Supp at 1517-20 (preemption based both on § 301 and the Atomic Energy Act); *Olguin v Inspiration Consol. Copper Co.*, 740 F2d 1468, 1475 (9th Cir 1984) (preemption based in part on federal statute governing mine safety).

empted.[163] These state-law whistleblower cases can be seen as applications of *Lingle*. Recall that the Supreme Court in *Lingle* refused to preempt a claim that an employee had been discharged for asserting rights under a state workers' compensation law. So too, the state whistleblower cases involve alleged retaliation for asserting rights under other state laws.[164]

C. The Future of the Section 301 Preemption Doctrine

As we have seen, in most of the areas in which states have been expanding the rights of individual employees, unionized employees who have tried to assert such rights have found their claims preempted. The only consistent exceptions are for claims that follow the fact patterns of particular Supreme Court decisions, or for issues for which the grievance procedure is not available.

In the past two years, some courts have recognized that the scope of § 301 preemption is expanding to new frontiers.[165] For example, in *Jones v General Motors Corp.*, a plaintiff sued for breach of an agreement between his union and his employer to settle a former grievance.[166] The Sixth Circuit found the claim preempted, even though the claim implicated no term of the collective bargaining agreement. The court reasoned that resolution of the claim would not entail the interpretation of the collective bargaining agreement, but rather, would "require a court to address relationships that have been created through the collective bargaining

---

[163] See, for example, *Fairchild Industries*, 668 F Supp at 467 (no preemption of claim that employee was fired for reporting violations of state environmental law); *Brevik*, 416 NW2d at 718 (no preemption of claim that employee was fired for filing complaint under state occupational safety and health act); *Garibaldi*, 726 F2d at 1375-76 (no preemption of claim that employee was fired for reporting violation of state health law).

[164] In *Gonzalez v Prestress Engineering Corp.*, 115 Ill 2d 1, 503 NE2d 308 (1986), a pre-*Lingle* workers' compensation retaliation case, the Illinois Supreme Court suggested another reason why state-law whistleblower cases should not be preempted. The Court refused to preempt because to do otherwise would mean that the existence of the tort claim depended upon the interpretation of the "just cause" provision in the labor agreement. If this were the case, "the public policy of this State would become a mere bargaining chip, capable of being waived or altered by the private parties to a collective bargain." Id at 312. See also Schwartz and Parrot, 7 St Louis U Pub L Rev at 308-09 (cited in note 104) (applying same reasoning to state whistleblower cases in general).

[165] See generally Committee on Labor Arbitration and the Law of Collective Bargaining Agreements, *Labor Arbitration and the Law of Collective Bargaining Agreements*, 7 Labor Law 747, 755-61 (1991) (noting trend toward more § 301 preemption in 1990).

[166] 939 F2d 380 (6th Cir 1991).

process . . . ."[167] The court candidly admitted that this reasoning was an extension of the *Allis Chalmers* and *Lingle* tests, but said:

> We have not applied a cramped and narrow construction of the dictates of *Lingle* and *Allis-Chalmers* in reaching our decisions, nor have we limited § 301 preemption to cases where the precise meaning of precise words in the [collective bargaining agreement] is the crux of the state-based claim. Rather, we have found many state-based claims pre-empted because they have implicated the federal policies underlying federal labor law.[168]

The court then enumerated four types of claims it had preempted which did not require the interpretation of a collective bargaining agreement: (1) when "employment relationships which are subject to a collective bargaining agreement" are implicated; (2) when "the rights to be vindicated and the relationship between the parties are created not by state law, but by the collective agreement itself"; (3) "when a state-based claim requires examining the practices and customs of a workplace whose conditions are governed by a [collective bargaining agreement]"; and (4) when employees covered by a collective bargaining agreement "rely upon the existence of a separate, individual employment contract giving rise to state law claims."[169]

In a similar vein, in *Schlacter-Jones v General Telephone of California*, the Ninth Circuit recently preempted a claim of unlawful drug testing.[170] The court reasoned that drug testing was a working condition, and the working conditions of the plaintiff's employment were generally governed by a collective bargaining agreement.[171] In fact, the court said it would have preempted the claim "whether or not [drug testing] is specifically discussed in the [collective bargaining agreement]."[172]

Furthermore, in *Schlacter-Jones*, the Ninth Circuit proposed a principle of § 301 preemption that would extend it beyond what any court has yet done. In dicta, the court stated that, in a union-

---

[167] Id at 382. See also *DeSherlia v Alpha Beta Co.*, 1988 US App LEXIS 9378 (9th Cir) (unpublished disposition) (preempting an employee's claim that her employer breached a settlement agreement).

[168] *Jones*, 939 F2d at 383.

[169] Id (citations omitted).

[170] 936 F2d 435, 439 (9th Cir 1991).

[171] Id at 440.

[172] Id (quoting *Laws*, 852 F2d at 433). The court also said, in a footnote, that "it is immaterial . . . that no provision of the CBA explicitly deals with drug testing or gives [the company] the right to adopt drug and alcohol policies." Id at 439 n 2.

ized workplace, claims about any working conditions that were within the scope of collective bargaining would be preempted.[173] This suggestion, if accepted, would effectively seal off all unionized workplaces from state employment regulation.

In the past year, two federal judges have written powerful dissenting opinions which criticized these trends in § 301 preemption. In *McCormick v AT&T Technologies*,[174] Judge Phillips of the Fourth Circuit undertook a careful and detailed discussion of the relevant Supreme Court decisions and concluded that the cases consistently held that § 301 only preempts "state-law claims [that] formally alleg[e] violations of labor contracts [or] state-law claims that can be determined to be claims for violation of laborcontracts [sic] in substance though not in form . . . ."[175] Accordingly, Judge Phillips argued that the Supreme Court consistently has insisted that preemption analysis focus on the "nature of the claim advanced rather than any defense put forward," and that the employers' "defensive positions are irrelevant."[176] Judge Phillips concluded that many federal courts had "gotten off the track,"[177] and accused those courts of adopting a mistakenly expansive approach to § 301 preemption, one that was rewriting the act of Congress.[178]

Judge Alex Kozinski of the Ninth Circuit also has delivered a dissenting opinion that challenges the broad § 301 preemption doctrine. In *Livadas v Aubry*,[179] Judge Kozinski not only critized the origin of the expansive approach, but also decried its ultimate consequences. In that case, a state labor commissioner declined to prosecute the plaintiff's claim against her employer for three days

---

[173] *Schlacter-Jones*, 936 F2d at 441. See also *Douglas*, 877 F2d at 573 (preempting IIED claim because the alleged harassment related to the terms and conditions of employment).

[174] 934 F2d 531 (4th Cir 1991).

[175] Id at 543. Judge Phillips further noted:

> Where, though advanced as a tort or otherwise "independent claim," it has been apparent that the duty allegedly violated could *only* have been created by the labor contract, preemption has resulted, *Lueck* (employer's contractual duty to process insurance claims); *Hechler* (union's contractual duty to provide safe workplace); *Rawson* (union's contractual duty to make safety inspections); where the duty allegedly violated has plausibly been located "independently" of any labor contract, in general tort law or elsewhere, preemption has not resulted, *Caterpillar* (employer's duty under individual employee contracts); *Lingle* (employer's general statutory duty not to discharge retaliatorily).

Id (emphasis in original).

[176] Id at 543-44.

[177] Id at 544.

[178] Id at 547-48.

[179] 943 F2d 1140 (9th Cir 1991).

pay, on the grounds that she was covered by a collective bargaining agreement. The commissioner had done so out of an honest but mistaken belief that the plaintiff's claim was preempted under § 301. The plaintiff sued in federal district court under 42 USC § 1983, alleging that the commissioner had interfered with her right under the NLRA to bargain collectively. The district court granted summary judgment to the plaintiff, and the commissioner appealed.[180]

The Court of Appeals reversed, noting that to hold otherwise "would require us to hold that she is entitled under the NLRA to a correct interpretation of California law regarding enforcement of [state employment law] claims."[181] It then added:

> Given the primacy of the federal scheme for handling labor disputes, we believe that Congress would not want state officials erring on the side of adjudicating state law disputes whenever it is a close call as to whether a claim is preempted.[182]

Judge Kozinski wrote a powerful dissent, in which he decried what he called "a novel doctrine of quasi-preemption."[183] He accused his colleagues of "divining some preemptive corona surrounding the federal labor laws."[184] He argued that this approach was contrary to Supreme Court precedent as well as inconsistent with a proper judicial role. In a footnote, Judge Kozinski further argued that the quasi-preemption approach was potentially detrimental to collective bargaining:

> It is not inconceivable that an employer could point to this discrepancy [between rights for unionized workers and rights for unorganized workers] as an argument against an effort to unionize: "Look here, if you vote for the union, the first thing that happens is that the state Labor Commissioner abandons you." In a closely fought election, this type of argument might make a difference.[185]

In sum, § 301 preemption is very broad and, notwithstanding the protests of Judges Phillips and Kozinski, threatens to become even broader in the future. As a result of this expansive approach

---

[180] Id at 1141-42.

[181] Id at 1146.

[182] Id at 1147.

[183] Id at 1148 (Kozinski dissenting).

[184] Id at 1149.

[185] Id at 1150 n 2.

to § 301 preemption, unionized workers have not gotten the benefit of the explosion of individual employee rights in the past decade.[186]

IV. Explaining the Section 301 Preemption Doctrine: The Industrial Pluralist Conception of Collective Bargaining

Why have the courts adopted such a broad § 301 preemption doctrine? The explanation cannot lie in general principles of federal preemption of state law. For, as I demonstrate in Section IV.A. below, § 301 preemption is much broader than preemption in other areas of federal law. Hence we must look for an explanation unique to labor law. Toward this end, in Section IV.B., I argue that the broad § 301 preemption doctrine is attributable to the industrial pluralist approach to collective bargaining that has predominated in the post-war era. Put simply, industrial pluralism conceives of labor relations as industrial self-government, in which management and labor act like political parties in a representative democracy. By this view, the workplace is an autonomous realm, resistant to the intrusion of externally-defined rights and obligations. It is this vision of labor relations that motivates the broad § 301 preemption doctrine.

Finally, in Section IV.C., I consider whether § 301 preemption is simply part of a larger modern trend toward private arbitration to resolve all kinds of disputes, labor and otherwise. I conclude that labor arbitration is different from other kinds of arbitration, for it *extinguishes* the statutory right in question. By contrast, other kinds of arbitration *enforce* statutory rights. In short, § 301 preemption is a unique phenomenon, which can only be explained by the industrial pluralist metaphor of labor relations.

A. The Unusual Breadth of Section 301 Preemption

In many other areas, the federal courts have cut back on the scope of federal preemption. Two recent Supreme Court cases in particular express a deliberate intention to curtail federal preemption. In 1985, in *Hillsborough County v Automated Medical Laboratories*, the Court stated that, when states regulate health and safety, there is a presumption *against* federal preemption.[187] And

---

[186] Note, 99 Yale L J at 229 (cited in note 116); Herman, 9 Indus Rel L J at 638-39 (cited in note 128) (arguing that unionized workers should have the same state employment rights as do nonunion workers).

[187] 471 US 707, 715 (1985).

in 1991, in *Gregory v Ashcroft*, the Court articulated a "clear statement" rule of preemption, which says that state regulation is only preempted when the federal legislation clearly states it was intended to have preemptive effect.[188] Both of these cases indicate a trend away from federal preemption of state legislation. Even in areas of labor law preemption other than § 301, the trend has been toward less preemption.[189]

In contrast to this trend, the courts in § 301 cases routinely find state claims to be preempted even when there is only the slightest shred of a federal issue involved. If ever there were a statute that lacked a clear statement of intent to preempt related state regulation, it is § 301. With its bare fifty words, § 301 has no ostensive content whatsoever.[190] Indeed, soon after its enactment, many scholars, as well as a majority of the Supreme Court, opined that the provision was unconstitutional because it created federal jurisdiction without providing any substantive law which could be the basis of a federal question.[191] In order to save the constitutionality of the statute, Justice Douglas in *Textile Workers v Lincoln Mills* held that it authorized federal courts to develop a federal common law of collective bargaining to provide the substance.[192] In other words, any federal issue that exists in an employee's state law employment claim comes not from an explicit congressional command, but rather from a vague and elusive federal common law that originated as a controversial judicial gloss on § 301.[193]

Moreover, the courts adopted a broad interpretation of § 301 preemption in the face of several narrower alternatives which were available within existing legal doctrines. For example, courts could have stayed with the well-pleaded complaint rule, and confined the preemption inquiry to the substance of the plaintiff's allegations. Such an approach would have permitted plaintiffs to vindicate

---

[188] 111 S Ct 2395, 2400 (1991) (applying clear statement rule to find no preemption of state law by Age Discrimination in Employment Act). See also *Will v Michigan Department of State Police*, 491 US 58, 65 (1989) ("Congress should make its intention 'clear and manifest' if it intends to pre-empt the historic powers of the states.") (quoting *Rice v Santa Fe Elevator Corp.*, 331 US 218, 230 (1947)).

[189] Kosanovich, 4 Labor Law at 250-56 (cited in note 128). But see Eileen Silverstein, *Against Preemption in Labor Law*, 24 Conn L Rev 1, 33-52 (1991) (criticizing courts' unusually broad standard of preemption under the NLRA).

[190] See note 70.

[191] See, for example, *Ass'n of Westinghouse Salaried Employees v Westinghouse Electric Corp.*, 348 US 437, 447-51 (1955) (questioning whether § 301 was constitutional).

[192] 353 US 448, 450-51 (1957).

[193] See id at 460-61 (Frankfurter dissenting) (accusing the Court of avoiding the "difficult problems raised by § 301 . . . by attributing to the section an occult content").

state law rights by choosing *not* to sue on their collective bargaining agreements. Instead, as we have seen, most courts permit the defendant to federalize a case by invoking the collective bargaining agreement in defense, notwithstanding *Caterpillar*.

Alternatively, courts could have ruled that when a claim is based upon state law, the fact that the claim requires some interpretation of a collective bargaining agreement does not deprive the state court of jurisdiction, or render it a § 301 claim. The Supreme Court took a parallel approach in *NLRB v C & C Plywood Corp.*, holding that the NLRB had jurisdiction to interpret a collective bargaining agreement when necessary to ruling on an unfair labor practice charge.[194] The Court could similarily have held that, when the graveman of an action involves a state law issue, the state court has jurisdiction to decide ancillary issues, even if the court must interpret a collective bargaining agreement.[195]

Either of these approaches would have made state law employment rights cumulative with collectively bargained rights, and would have permitted unionized employees to enjoy the state law employment rights available to nonunion employees. Instead of adopting either of these approaches, however, the courts have adopted a predisposition, if not a presumption, to preempt.

B. Industrial Pluralism

In order to understand why the courts have chosen to adopt such a broad § 301 preemption doctrine, it is necessary to see how the issue of preemption is linked with the industrial pluralist conception of collective bargaining. Industrial pluralism is a set of beliefs, doctrines, and institutions that together have dominated the interpretation of the NLRA in the post-war period.[196]

Industrial pluralism is based on a simple metaphor: that collective bargaining is industrial self-government. Management and labor are like political parties in a representative democracy—each represents its own constituency and, as in a legislature, engages in debate and compromise. Thus, management and labor together determine wages and working conditions through a legislative-type process. These rules are embodied in the collective bargaining agreement, which the industrial pluralist metaphor calls a statute or a constitution.

---

[194] 385 US 421, 428 (1967).

[195] The dissent in *McCormick*, 934 F2d at 538-39, urges this approach.

[196] See Stone, 90 Yale L J 1509 (cited in note 4); Stone, 44 Md L Rev 978 (cited in note 5), where I have developed this theme in more detail.

Industrial pluralism is a descriptive and prescriptive vision of the workplace as a microcosmic constitutional democracy, a mini-democracy in the private sphere. One central aspect of the industrial pluralist metaphor is that the workplace, as a mini-democracy, has a separation of powers, and checks and balances, akin to those found in the greater political democracy. Thus, in addition to the workplace legislature—collective bargaining negotiations—and the workplace executive—management—there is a workplace judiciary—private arbitration. The role of private arbitration is to decide disputes concerning application and interpretation of the collective bargaining agreement. And, like the independent judiciary in our political system, private arbitration is supposed to provide a neutral vantage point for enforcing the rules, divorced from the power contests that went into the making of the rules in the first place. With this separation of powers, industrial pluralism portrays the workplace as a democratic institution, rather than the enclave of private power that many social critics have claimed it to be.[197]

The industrial pluralist vision is not merely a neutral description of the workplace. It is a description with a normative message about how collective bargaining should be structured. The picture of the workplace as an autonomous, self-sufficient, democratic realm suggests that conditions inside the workplace are fair and just. The normative message is that all is well, and that outsiders, such as legislatures, should not intervene. In addition, the picture suggests that for the autonomous mini-democracy to function it must replicate the political democracy. Thus private arbitration, rather than the outside judiciary, should be the exclusive tribunal for resolving disputes. These two programmatic consequences of the industrial pluralist conception have had a profound impact on

[197] In the 1950s and 1960s, some democratic theorists were concerned that American society was not truly democratic because, despite the existence of democratic political institutions, most people experienced authoritarian control over one of the most important aspects of their lives—their workplace. See, for example, Robert A. Dahl and Charles E. Lindblom, *Politics, Economics, and Welfare: Planning and Politico-Economic Systems Resolved into Basic Social Processes* 482-83 (Chicago, 2d ed 1976) (describing the power of business managers as highly discretionary and antidemocratic); Grant McConnell, *Private Power and American Democracy* 251-55 (Knopf, 1966) (noting the power of the corporation and discussing the problem of its illegitimacy); Seymour Martin Lipset, *Political Man: The Social Bases of Politics* 273 (Johns Hopkins, exp ed 1981) (discussing the lack of "integrative participation" by American workers). See also Leon H. Keyserling, *Why the Wagner Act?*, in Louis G. Silverberg, ed, *The Wagner Act: After Ten Years* 13 (BNA, 1945) (the American institution of collective bargaining, by introducing self-government into industry, preserves our democratic way of life) (quoting Senator Robert F. Wagner, address at National Democratic Club Forum, May 8, 1937).

the development of the law of collective bargaining in the postwar era.

One result of industrial pluralist rhetoric is that the Supreme Court has elevated private arbitration to an exalted status within labor law doctrine.[198] In a series of benchmark decisions in the late 1950s and early 1960s, the Supreme Court adopted the pluralist rationale of defending the mini-democracy from external, particularly judicial, intervention.[199] It announced a national labor policy of promoting private arbitration and adopted a policy of extreme deference to the arbitral process.[200] In fact, it decreed an amount of judicial deference to labor arbitration which was much greater than the deference paid to arbitration in any other field.[201] Accordingly, the Court erected a structure in which rulings by labor arbitrators were placed effectively beyond the reach of judicial review.[202]

The industrial pluralist interpretation of the labor laws thus had the effect of reprivatizing labor relations. It also established a rigid barrier between the workplace and external sources of law. As a result, the collective bargaining system has not been able to accommodate the proliferating individual employment rights of the 1980s.

1. Explaining the broad Section 301 preemption doctrine.

Understanding the industrial pluralist belief in the sanctity of the mini-democracy can illuminate the predisposition of judges to

---

[198] *News America Publications v Newark Typographical Union*, 918 F2d 21, 24 (3d Cir 1990) (on "exalted status" of arbitration). See also *United Paperworkers v Misco, Inc.*, 484 US 29, 37-38 (1987) (discussing need to "insulat[e] arbitral decisions from judicial review").

[199] See Stone, 90 Yale L J at 1526-31 (cited in note 4).

[200] *Lincoln Mills*, 353 US at 456 (§ 301 represents a national policy to enforce arbitration agreements); *United Steelworkers of America v American Manufacturing Company*, 363 US 564, 567-68 (1960) (courts should enforce agreements to arbitrate regardless of the merits of the specific grievance); *United Steelworkers of America v Warrior & Gulf Navigation Co.*, 363 US 574, 585 (1960) (strong presumption of arbitrability); and *United Steelworkers of America v Enterprise Wheel & Car Corp.*, 363 US 593, 597-98 (1960) (Court will enforce arbitrator's judgment, even if arbitrator's opinion is ambiguous, so long as it "draws its essence from the collective bargaining agreement.").

[201] See notes 73-74, 221 and accompanying text.

[202] *United Paperworkers*, 484 US at 37-38. See also note 73 (on *Enterprise Wheel* test). At the same time, the Court constricted the jurisdiction of the NLRB so as to make arbitration the primary, and final, adjudicator of the statutory as well as contractual rights of organized workers. See *Carey v Westinghouse*, 375 US 261, 270-71 (1964) ("If by the time the dispute reaches the Board, arbitration has already taken place, the Board shows deference to the arbitral award, provided the procedure was a fair one and the results were not repugnant to the [NLRA].").

find state employment rights preempted by § 301. Under the industrial pluralist view, the terms of the bargain that the parties to the mini-democracy reach, and the enforcement mechanism that the parties establish, are superior to any state-imposed employment terms. Thus it would only do harm to interfere.

To the extent that courts believe the rhetoric of industrial pluralism, they want to keep judicial scrutiny as well as external law out of the workplace as much as possible. Accordingly, they have insisted upon insulating collective bargaining from external sources of employment rights. Section 301 preemption provides them with a means to do so.[203] By expanding the scope of § 301 preemption, courts keep state employment law out of the unionized workplace. Thus, the unstated belief in the superiority of the mini-democracy is the driving force behind the judicial predisposition to preempt.[204]

---

[203] When a *federal* law regulates conduct within a unionized workplace, the issue is deferral, not preemption. In that area, the Supreme Court has permitted more penetration by external law. Recall that in *Gardner-Denver*, the Supreme Court held that an individual may bring a Title VII claim of discrimination, even though an arbitration procedure had heard and decided the same dispute. 415 US at 59-60. See note 139. The Court similarily has held that an individual may bring claims under the Fair Labor Standards Act and under § 1983 in federal court, notwithstanding a prior arbitration. *Barrantine v Arkansas-Best Freight System*, 450 US 728 (1981) (FLSA); *McDonald v City of West Branch*, 466 US 284 (1984) (§ 1983). Many management labor lawyers have found these doctrines unduly restrictive of their ability to use arbitration in lieu of litigation for employee statutory claims. See, for example, Jay W. Waks and Louis Ginsberg, *Arbitrating Executive and Other Employment Disputes: Let's Put a Pin in* Gardner-Denver! in *43d Annual National Conference on Labor* 245, 303-05 (cited in note 24) (urging that *Gardner-Denver* be overturned).

In 1991, the Supreme Court decided a case that arguably cuts back on the scope of deferral to employees' federal statutory claims. *Gilmer v Interstate/Johnson Lane Corp.*, 111 S Ct 1647 (1991), held that an individual who agreed to arbitrate all disputes concerning his employment was required to arbitrate his statutory claim under the Age Discrimination in Employment Act. Some labor lawyers and scholars are predicting that, after *Gilmer*, the Supreme Court will reverse *Gardner-Denver*. Stephen A. Mazurak, *The Status of the Employment Relationship: The 1990-91 Supreme Court Term*, 7 Labor Law 849, 865-66 (1991); Robert L. Duston, Gilmer v Interstate/Johnson Lane Corp.: *A Major Step Forward for Alternative Dispute Resolution, or a Meaningless Decision?*, 7 Labor Law 823, 834 (1991).

[204] See, for example, *McCormick*, 934 F2d at 538 ("Our holding that McCormick's state law claims are preempted by § 301 protects the continued vitality of grievance procedures as a fair and efficient means for the resolution of labor disputes . . . ."); *White*, 938 F2d at 481 ("Driving the Court's decision in [*Allis-Chalmers* was] the need to preserve the central role of arbitration established in collective bargaining contracts."). On the close relationship between § 301 preemption and the grievance and arbitration system, see also *Beatrice Foods*, 921 F2d at 1020 (*Allis-Chalmers* consistent with broad policy favoring arbitration that the Supreme Court stated in *The Steelworkers Trilogy*). See also Clyde W. Summers, *Labor Law as the Century Turns: A Changing of the Guard*, 67 Nebr L Rev 7, 20 (1988) (decisions like *Allis-Chalmers* "cast a cloud" over possibility of unionized workers using state courts to remedy wrongful dismissals, thereby preserving "central role of arbitration in interpreting the [labor] contract").

An example will illustrate this point. In *Jackson v Liquid Carbonic Corp.*, an employee had been terminated after he had tested positive in an employer-instituted drug testing program.[205] Although he was covered by a collective bargaining agreement, he elected to sue in state court on the basis of a state privacy statute and the state constitutional right to privacy. The employer argued that the claim was preempted, removed to federal court, and moved to dismiss.[206]

In analyzing the preemption issue, the court had to interpret the state law. At the time, the state law was new, so it had not yet been interpreted by the state courts. The First Circuit interpreted the state law not as imposing an absolute prohibition on drug testing, but rather as calling for a balancing test—between the employee's right to privacy and the employer's legitimate interest in conducting the test.[207] Thus it said that the statute prohibited "only unreasonable interferences with a person's privacy."[208] The court concluded that to perform the balance and to decide what was reasonable required the court to interpret the collective bargaining agreement.[209] More specifically, what was reasonable regarding drug testing had to be

> assessed in light of the practices and exigencies of the industry, factors which are routinely considered when interpreting a collective bargaining agreement. [Therefore plaintiff's privacy claim is] inseparable from an interpretation of what is or is not 'reasonable' under the labor contract. . . . [It is] both negotiable and bound up in the interstices of the Agreement . . . .[210]

The collective bargaining agreement contained a clause that gave management a right "to post reasonable rules and regulations

[205] 863 F2d 111, 112-13 (1st Cir 1988).

[206] Id at 113.

[207] Id at 115-16.

[208] Id at 116 (quoting *Bratt v International Business Machines Corp.*, 392 Mass 508, 467 NE2d 126, 135 (1984)).

[209] Significantly, the court admitted that the state courts had not yet addressed the issue of employee drug testing. But it surmised that the state courts "would view the collective bargaining process as an appropriate datum in constructing the needed balance between the worker's privacy rights and the legitimate concerns of management." Id at 117. "A right subject to a balance involving the needs and interests of the parties is, almost of necessity, defined by the parties themselves." Id.

[210] Id at 119. Later the court reiterated that, in determining reasonableness under the state privacy statute, it did "not see how, under state law, the Agreement can be omitted from the equation." Id at 121.

from time to time."[211] This, the court said, established a sufficient nexus between the drug testing and the collective agreement to preempt the employee's claim.[212] Embellishing upon this reasoning, the First Circuit went on to note the central role of arbitration in the system of industrial self-government, and ultimately concluded that to permit this plaintiff to sue on a state law claim "would surely undermine the structure of industrial self-government."[213]

There are three problems with the First Circuit's analysis. First, the court found that the state right required balancing. However, the state right might not have required balancing at all—it might have been an absolute prohibition of employer drug testing. In that event, there would be no room for the collective bargaining agreement to limit, define, or waive the state law right. The court could have certified this question to the state court rather than interpreting the state law in the first instance.[214]

Second, the court did not give a convincing account as to why the employer's right to make reasonable rules had any bearing on the plaintiff's privacy claim. The dissent argued that the management rights clause in the collective agreement was far too general and vague to support preemption of this particular claim,[215] evidently interpreting the clause giving management the right to make "reasonable rules and regulations" as boilerplate. In the face of explicit rules imposed from without, the dissent said, the employer-made rules should yield. The dissent concluded that, even if the state statute required balancing, the balancing inquiry was not necessarily bound up with the collective agreement.[216]

The third and most significant problem with the First Circuit's reasoning was that it did not explain why the contractual provision giving the employer the right to make "reasonable rules and regulations from time to time" trumped state law. That is, even if the state law did call for balancing, the court assumed that, in the balance, the employer's rules outweighed the legislature's rules. In essence, the court was saying that the rules made within

---

[211] Id at 113.

[212] Id at 119.

[213] Id at 121-22.

[214] See Note, 40 Syracuse L Rev at 1296 (cited in note 119) (suggesting that the *Jackson* court should have taken this approach).

[215] 863 F2d at 122 (Bownes dissenting) ("In the instant case, there [was] nothing in the collective-bargaining agreement which even remotely deal[t] with the subject of drug testing or privacy rights.").

[216] Id at 124.

the mini-democracy were superior to those of external law. Presumably the court believed that because parties had bargained to give management the right to make reasonable rules, the rules imposed by the state legislature should yield. The court could have assumed, to the contrary, that the employer's contractual right to make rules must be exercised consistently with state law.

In short, the relationship between the bargained-for right of management to make "reasonable rules" and the specific requirements of state law depends upon assumptions about the superiority *vel non* of the mini-democracy. The *Jackson* case exemplifies a favorable view of the industrial pluralist mini-democracy. In that view, the rules of the autonomous world of the unionized workplace are superior to external law. If those rules vest management with discretion in a particular area, then management is free to exercise that discretion, despite restrictions imposed by a state legislature.

Even in the absence of an explicit contractual provision giving management the right to make "reasonable rules," many courts have said that such a provision might be implied.[217] It is increasingly common for courts to recognize the possibility that a collective agreement contains implied terms, particularly terms that grant discretion to management.[218] Such an implied term, under the *Jackson* court's reasoning, would preempt a state law right, even in the absence of *any* contractual language on the subject.

The industrial pluralist assumption about the superiority of the mini-democracy explains not only the courts' expansive approach to § 301 preemption, but also the exceptions to § 301 preemption that were described above. As we saw, courts find that most claims by unionized workers invoking state employment rights are preempted. There are exceptions for the cases presenting the precise fact patterns which the Supreme Court has already addressed, and for claims not cognizable under the grievance procedure. The industrial pluralist assumption that the mini-democracy is superior to external law explains this latter exception. When a plaintiff cannot bring a claim within the internal judiciary of the workplace, there is no reason to preempt.

---

[217] See, for example, *Douglas*, 877 F2d at 572-73.

[218] See, for example, *Consolidated Rail Corp. v Railway Labor Executives' Ass'n*, 109 S Ct 2477, 2485 (1989) ("*Conrail*"). See also Katherine Van Wezel Stone, *Labor Relations on the Airlines; the Railway Labor Act in the Era of Deregulation*, 42 Stan L Rev 1485, 1513-22 (1990); Harry Shulman, *Reason, Contract, and Law in Labor Relations*, 68 Harv L Rev 999, 1010-16 (1955).

2. Limitations of the mini-democracy.

The industrial pluralist conception of collective bargaining forces workers to choose between contractual rights which they can obtain in a union setting, or statutory rights, which they can obtain in a nonunion setting. Because workers often can achieve superior substantive rights in the collective bargaining context than they have under external law, one could argue that the loss of statutory rights is more than compensated by the gain in contractual rights. This argument would be true *if* unions in fact achieve superior rights in collective bargaining, and *if* unions can effectively enforce those rights in the grievance and arbitration system. The latter precondition is problematic.

Despite its rhetoric of providing workplace democracy, the arbitration system has not provided a satisfactory means for workers to enforce collectively bargained employment rights.[219] Arbitration is ineffective partly because it does not provide the due process protections available in a public tribunal, be it a court or an administrative agency. As Justice Brennan has said,

> Arbitral factfinding is not generally equivalent to judicial factfinding. . . . "[T]he record of the arbitration proceedings is not as complete; the usual rules of evidence do not apply; and rights and procedures common to civil trials, such as discovery, compulsory process, cross-examination, and testimony under oath, are often severely limited or unavailable."[220]

In addition, there is no effective right of appeal.[221]

Furthermore, remedies in arbitration are not as effective or as generous as remedies in a judicial forum. For example, most arbitrators believe that they do not have the power to award damages for intangible harms, or to award punitive or consequential dam-

---

[219] See Stone, 90 Yale L J at 1529-30 (cited in note 4); Atleson, 11 NYU Rev L & Soc Change at 95 (cited in note 44).

[220] *McDonald v West Branch*, 466 US 284, 291 (1984) (quoting *Gardner-Denver*, 415 US at 57-58).

[221] The Supreme Court has propounded an extremely narrow standard of review for labor arbitration. In *Enterprise Wheel*, the Court said that an arbitral award should be overturned only if it failed to derive its essence from the agreement. 363 US at 597. It also said that mere ambiguity about the essential foundation of the award would not be grounds for overturning the award. Id at 598. The "essence test" combined with the "presumption of arbitral regularity" have rendered judicial review of arbitrator rulings practically unobtainable. See Peter Feuille and Michael LeRoy, *Grievance Arbitration Appeals in the Federal Courts: Facts and Figures*, 45 Arb J 35, 40-45 (Mar 1990) (since the *Steelworkers Trilogy* in 1960, less than 1% of all arbitral awards have been challenged in court, and of those challenged, almost three-quarters have been upheld).

ages.[222] In addition, arbitrators almost never grant interest on back pay awards, even when they are issued months or years after an unjust dismissal.[223] It is common practice for an arbitrator to award reinstatement but no back pay at all to a worker fired without just cause.[224] In contrast, prevailing parties in unjust dismissal litigation receive jury awards in the mid to high six figures.[225] Furthermore, most arbitrators believe that they do not have the power to order provisional relief.[226] Thus many contract violations, such as improper job assignments or safety matters, can neither be prevented nor remedied after the fact. In addition, arbitrators do not provide the accountability of a public forum. They are not bound by precedent, their awards are rarely published, the hearings are not held in open court, and arbitrators are not public officials accountable to public pressures and sworn to uphold public policies.[227]

Thus the legacy of industrial pluralism has been to weaken the employment rights of unionized workers within the mini-democracy by not providing adequate means for their enforcement. At

---

[222] Frank Elkouri and Edna Asper Elkouri, *How Arbitration Works* 401-06 (BNA, 4th ed 1985); Otis H. King, *How Whole is Whole?: Remedies in Labor Arbitration*, 3 J Contemp Legal Issues 167, 169-73 (1989-90) (on reluctance of arbitrators to award consequential damages); E. Allan Farnsworth, *Punitive Damages in Arbitration*, 20 Stetson L Rev 395, 400-01 (1991) (speculating about why arbitrators might be reluctant to award punitive damages). See also Note, *Protecting Intangible Expectations Under Collective Bargaining Agreements—Overcoming the Proscription of Arbitral Penalties*, 61 Minn L Rev 127, 128 (1976) (urging arbitrators to use penalties to protect employees' intangible interests in their labor contracts).

[223] See, for example, *Intermountain Operators League*, 26 Labor Arb (BNA) 149, 154 (1956) (Kadish, Arbitrator) ("[I]t is not customary in arbitrations for the arbitrator to grant interest on claims which he finds owing.").

[224] King, 3 J Contemp Legal Issues at 171 (cited in note 222); Howard Lesnick, *Response*, 11 NYU J L & Soc Change 142, 145 (1982-83).

[225] A study of 121 awards in wrongful discharge litigation in California between 1980 and 1986 found that prevailing plaintiffs won, on average, $650,000 in the initial jury award, of which about 40% was for punitive damages. It also found that the median award was $177,000. James Dertouzos, Elaine Holland, and Patricia Ebener, *The Legal Consequences of Wrongful Termination* vii (Rand Institute for Civil Justice, 1988). This figure may somewhat overstate the comparison because many of the prevailing plaintiffs in the Rand study were middle-level managerial employees, whose salary, and hence back pay, is higher than that of most union members. See also Cliff Palefsky, *Wrongful Termination Litigation: "Dagwood" and Goliath*, 62 Mich Bar J 776 (1983) (discussing a 1982 study finding that 90% of California discharge cases that went to trial resulted in verdicts for plaintiff, and that the average award on these verdicts was $450,000).

[226] Elkouri and Elkouri, *How Arbitration Works* at 401-02 (cited in note 222).

[227] Stone, 90 Yale L J at 1529-30 (cited in note 4). See also Owen M. Fiss, *Against Settlement*, 93 Yale L J 1073, 1085-87 (1984) (criticizing alternative dispute resolution because its aim is to provide peace rather than justice, thereby sacrificing important public values).

the same time, the industrial pluralist ideology has fueled the trend toward expansive § 301 preemption. It has both hindered unionized workers' ability to implement their contractual rights and deprived them of employment rights under external law.

3. The historical development of industrial pluralism.

These limitations of collective bargaining were not apparent until the 1970s and 1980s, when unorganized workers began to receive legislative and judicial assistance in the form of the explosion of individual employee rights. Until then, whatever rights were available to unionized workers through the bargaining and arbitration system were the only rights workers had, so there was no standard by which to measure such rights. But now, the proliferation of state employment rights, together with the current § 301 preemption doctrine, means that collectively bargained rights are not always better.

One might ask, how could this system of collective bargaining have flourished for so long if it is indeed destructive of union strength? Here some historical perspective is helpful.

Industrial pluralism developed in the postwar years, at a time when an expanding economy and United States dominance in the world led to a rising standard of living for most Americans and a general feeling of optimism about the future. Part of this optimism included the view that employers would come to accept unionism, that the scope of bargaining between management and labor would continually expand, and that unions would come to play greater and greater roles in corporate decisionmaking.[228] In an environment of economic expansion, stable markets and thriving companies, job security was not a particularly pressing concern. Collective bargaining about such items as wages, seniority, pensions, and so forth was sufficient to protect workers' interests. In the first decades after World War II, unions successfully negotiated regular wage increases, established health and pension benefit programs, and protected employees against arbitrary treatment.[229] For a workforce that recently had experienced the Great Depression and the wage freezes of World War II, these were enormous accom-

[228] See Kochan, Katz, and McKersie, *Transformation of American Industrial Relations* at 45-46 (cited in note 34) (describing optimism of the postwar period).

[229] See Neil W. Chamberlain, *The Union Challenge to Management Control* 74-88 (Harper, 1948) (describing union penetration of traditional managerial areas such as wages, hours, advancement policies, health and safety, disciplinary control, hiring practices, and layoffs).

plishments. Thus industrial pluralism was helpful to unions because it forced employers to deal with them about issues of importance to their members.[230]

At the same time, the analogy of the workplace to a mini-democracy gave the labor movement a mantle of respectability in the public mind—a mantle that it never before had, and since has lost. This mantle paid off in real terms: In strike situations, the public was loathe to cross picket lines and the unemployed were loathe to accept jobs as replacements. Thus the high public esteem of organized labor played a role in strengthening the labor movement.

Labor's demise in the public mind paralleled the demise of union strength. Throughout the 1950s and 1960s, well-publicized stories of labor corruption and scandal turned public opinion away from labor.[231] Other social causes like the civil rights movement and the anti-war movement captured the hearts and minds of the liberal intelligentsia. At the same time, industrial pluralism's emphasis on the mini-democracy led unions to focus their attention on plant-specific or company-specific gains, and to refrain from developing strategies or coalitions with other groups to achieve broader legislative goals.

The decade of the 1980s was a watershed for American workers in several respects. First, in that decade there was a distinctly sharper rate of membership decline, a decline so pronounced that some scholars predicted the end of organized labor as a significant force on the American scene.[232] At the same time, the dramatic corporate transformations of the decade produced correspondingly dramatic employee dislocations.[233] This led to a public climate which was receptive to, if not insistent upon, some protection for

---

[230] Kochan, Katz, and McKersie, *Transformation of American Industrial Relations* at 45-46 (cited in note 34) (New Deal System of labor relations worked well until the 1970s).

[231] For an account of the declining esteem of organized labor amongst the public at large from the 1940s through the 1960s, see Derek Curtis Bok and John Thomas Dunlop, *Labor and the American Community* 15-19 (Simon & Schuster, 1970).

[232] See note 8 and accompanying text. Paul Weiler has given data suggesting that, by the year 2000, unions would represent less than 10% of the American private sector workforce. Weiler, *Governing the Workplace* at 10 (cited in note 27). See also Troy, 59 U Chi L Rev at 683 (cited in note 12) (estimating 7%). But see McDonald, 31 Indus Rel at 15 (cited in note 10) (Assistant to the Secretary-Treasurer of the AFL-CIO) (disputing Weiler's projection and arguing that unions probably would not decline as sharply in 1990s as in 1980s).

[233] There is considerable disagreement about whether takeovers and corporate restructurings actually cause net job loss. See Stone, 21 Stetson L Rev at 45 n 4 (cited in note 66) (summarizing debate). Whether the case can be made or not, however, the AFL-CIO *believes* that takeovers cause massive job loss. See note 35 and accompanying text. Large sectors of the American public share that belief.

the job security of individual employees. The legislative and judicial protections that have resulted, while minimal, have begun to rival the protection offered by unions.

Under a different system of collective bargaining, the new legislation and judicial protections for employees might have been cumulative with collective bargaining.[234] But under the industrial pluralist system, there was no place for state-created rights.

C. Industrial Pluralism and the Trend Toward Private Arbitration

One could argue that expansive § 301 preemption, while unfortunate for labor, derives not from a particular view of collective bargaining, but rather from a larger trend toward alternative dispute resolution in the legal system generally. For example, one could argue that the § 301 preemption trends are no different from recent developments in the areas of securities, antitrust, and age discrimination, where the Supreme Court has been expanding the role of private arbitration.

In a series of decisions in the 1980s, the Supreme Court held that many types of judicially cognizable claims are subject to arbitration under the Federal Arbitration Act (the "FAA").[235] In 1983, in *Moses H. Cone Memorial Hospital v Mercury Construction Corp.*, the Supreme Court found that a state law claim for breach of contract was subject to arbitration by virtue of an arbitration clause in the parties' agreement.[236] In language reminiscent of *The Steelworkers' Trilogy*, the Court said that

> [t]he Arbitration Act establishes that, as a matter of federal law, any doubts concerning the scope of arbitral issues should be resolved in favor of arbitration, whether the problem at

[234] For example, in western Europe, the welfare state measures enacted in the postwar era were compatible with collective bargaining. See, for example, Charles S. Maier, *"Fictitious bonds . . . of wealth and law": on the theory and practice of interest representation*, in Suzanne Berger, ed, *Organizing Interests in Western Europe: Pluralism, Corporation, and the Transformation of Politics* 27, 54-55 (Cambridge, 1981) (*"Fictitious Bonds"*).

[235] See, for example, *Mitsubishi Motors v Soler Chrysler-Plymouth*, 473 US 614, 640 (1985) (Sherman Act claims); *Shearson/American Express v McMahon*, 482 US 220, 238, 242 (1987) (claims under § 10(b) of the Securities Exchange Act of 1934 and RICO); *Rodriguez de Quijas v Shearson/American Express*, 490 US 477, 480 (1987) (claims under the Securities Act of 1933); *Gilmer v Interstate/Johnson Lane Corp.*, 111 S Ct 1647, 1657 (1991) (ADEA claim).

[236] 460 US 1, 24-25 (1983).

hand is the construction of the contract language itself or an allegation of waiver, delay, or a like defense to arbitrability.[237]

In 1985, the Supreme Court found claims arising under the federal antitrust laws to be subject to mandatory arbitration under the FAA. In *Mitsubishi Motors v Soler Chrysler-Plymouth*, the Court invoked the presumption of arbitrability and ordered the parties to arbitrate claims arising under the Sherman Antitrust Act, even though their arbitration agreement did not explicitly apply to statutory claims.[238] The Court said that, so long as the parties even arguably had agreed to arbitrate the statutory issue, and so long as Congress had not intentionally removed the statutory issue from arbitration, the parties were required by the FAA to submit to arbitration.[239] Since then, the Supreme Court has ordered arbitration of other federal statutory claims, including claims for securities act violations, civil RICO claims, and age discrimination claims.[240]

The rise of arbitration in non-labor areas thus seems to parallel the rise of arbitration in the labor area twenty-five years earlier. Indeed, in *Mitsubishi*, the Court drew support from labor law cases for the presumption of arbitrability it applied to the Federal Arbitration Act.[241] However, there is a crucial difference between the new wave of arbitration under the FAA and labor arbitration under § 301. When the FAA compels arbitration of a statutory issue in a non-labor context, the issue for the arbitrator to decide is the statutory right in dispute. For example, in *Mitsubishi*, the issue to be arbitrated was the application of the Sherman Antitrust Act to the respondent's alleged behavior. The arbitration clause only functioned to indicate the parties' choice between an arbitral or judicial forum. As the Supreme Court said in *Mitsubishi*, "[b]y agreeing to arbitrate a statutory claim, a party does not forgo the substantive rights afforded by the statute . . . ."[242] In keeping with the FAA arbitrator's responsibility to enforce the parties' substan-

---

[237] Id.

[238] 473 US 614, 624-26, 640 (1985).

[239] Id at 626-28.

[240] *McMahon*, 482 US at 238 (Securities Exchange Act of 1934 and civil RICO); *Rodriguez de Quijas*, 490 US at 480 (Securities Act of 1933); *Gilmer*, 111 S Ct at 1657 (ADEA).

[241] See *Mitsubishi*, 473 US at 626, citing *Warrior & Gulf*, 363 US at 582-83.

[242] 473 US at 628. See also *Volt Information Sciences v Board of Trustees*, 109 S Ct 1248, 1255 (1989).

tive rights under the statute at issue, courts vacate awards when the arbitrator has shown "manifest disregard of the law."[243]

In contrast, an arbitration requirement under § 301 does not involve merely a change in the forum for resolving a statutory dispute. Rather, labor arbitrators are required to decide cases by interpreting the collective bargaining agreement, not by interpreting external law.[244] Thus, despite the superficial similarity between § 301 and FAA arbitration, the two types of arbitration are entirely different. Arbitration under the FAA enforces statutory claims; arbitration under § 301 extinguishes statutory claims. Section 301 preemption cannot be understood as part of the general tendency by the courts to move statutory issues into arbitral tribunals. Rather, it must be understood as part of the unique and uneasy relationship between the labor law system and external law.

V. Evaluating the New System of Labor Regulation

So far I have shown that the current system of labor relations in the United States creates a tension between collective bargaining and individual employment rights. As collective labor rights have declined, and as states have sought to compensate by strengthening individual employee rights, the broad § 301 preemption doctrine has placed union workers at a disadvantage relative to nonunion workers, by denying the former the benefit of the state law employment rights. I have also shown that § 301 preemption cannot be explained as part of the general trend of the past decade to refer statutory claims to arbitration. Rather, I have argued that the broad § 301 preemption doctrine must be understood as an aspect of the industrial pluralist interpretation of the labor laws, an interpretation that relies on a sharp distinction between contractual rights and statutory rights, between collective bargaining and external law. By so embracing industrial pluralist forms of collective bargaining, the current system of labor relations in the United States sets up a dichotomy between collective bargaining and individual employment rights.

---

[243] See, for example, *McMahon*, 482 US at 232 (judicial review of FAA arbitration "is sufficient to ensure that arbitrators comply with the requirements of the statute"). See C. Evan Stewart, *Securities Arbitration Appeal: An Oxymoron No Longer?*, 79 Ky L J 347, 351-55 (1990-91) (history of the "manifest disregard of the law" standard); Comment, *Overcoming the Presumption of Arbitrability of ADEA Claims: The Triumph of Substantive over Procedural Values in* Nicholson v. CPC International, Inc., 138 U Pa L Rev 1817, 1824 (1990).

[244] See note 74 on arbitrators' use of external law.

We are thus left with several normative questions: First, are workers better off dispensing with collective bargaining and instead seeking workplace justice under the emerging regime of individual rights? Second, can we conceive of alternative legal regimes in which collective and individual employment rights are compatible and mutually reinforcing? Third, do the developments in Section 301 preemption and the legal incompatibility between unionism and individual rights play a role in union decline? I will address each of these questions below.

A. The Minimal Terms/Individual Rights Model of Labor Relations

The growth of individual employment rights and the reduction in protection for collective bargaining suggest that the emerging system of labor regulation is one in which there are legislatively and judicially imposed minimal terms of employment, without collective bargaining. I call this the individual rights/minimal terms model of labor relations.

If the emerging system of individual employment rights does in fact provide universal employment rights, then it is plausible that most workers would benefit by dispensing with collective bargaining altogether. That is, perhaps individual workers have regained legislatively what they have lost in collective bargaining, so that on balance they have not been harmed by the broad § 301 preemption doctrine and the decline of unions.

Professor Charles Fried has been a spokesman for this point of view. Professor Fried has advocated that we move "toward direct imposition of specific minimal terms and standards where problems in the workplace have been perceived [and] away from governmentally sheltered monopoly status for labor unions."[245] Unemployment insurance, workplace safety regulations, anti-discrimination protection, and protection against unjust dismissal are laudatory examples of such minimal terms.[246] He argues that, without collective bargaining, the law could achieve the larger goals of ensuring free association, a social minimum level of resources, job security, industrial democracy, dignity on the job, allocative efficiency and industrial peace.[247]

---

[245] Fried, 51 U Chi L Rev at 1040 (cited in note 4).
[246] Id at 1036-37.
[247] Id at 1020-21.

While Professor Fried's approach seems to describe the trends we have seen in the law, there are several problems with his normative conclusions: First, providing individual employment rights without a union does not allow employees to participate in corporate decisionmaking. To the extent that we value not only minimal employment standards but also the opportunity for employees to have a say about workplace issues that concern them, the nonunion rights model is not an adequate substitute.[248]

Second, there is some evidence that productivity improves when employees have an avenue for expressing discontent with voice rather than exit.[249] Some nonunion firms have established internal grievance mechanisms to gain the benefits of a voice mechanism without incurring the costs and disadvantages of having a union.[250] However, some have argued that such mechanisms, when not truly independent, ultimately breed distrust, cynicism, and low morale.[251]

Third, minimal terms are too uniform and rigid to address the preferences of employees at all workplaces; they cannot accommodate local differences. Therefore they are not a particularily efficient way to improve wages and working conditions.[252] They can provide basic minima, but above a very low level they cannot provide meaningful improvements.[253]

Fourth, minimal terms often are not effective. For example, the Occupational Safety and Health Act of 1970 directed the Labor Department and the National Institute of Safety and Health to set standards for all potentially hazardous industrial substances in use, to apply to all workplaces.[254] Such a project is so vast, and the interests affected so varied, that today, twenty years after the enactment of the legislation, standards have only been set for a small number of the tens of thousands of industrial chemicals in com-

---

[248] Summers, 67 Nebr L Rev at 26 (cited in note 204).

[249] Richard B. Freeman and James L. Medoff, *What Do Unions Do?* 162-80 (Basic, 1984).

[250] Sanford M. Jacoby, *Employing Bureaucracy: Managers, Unions, and the Transformation of Work in American Industry, 1900-45* 257 (Columbia, 1985).

[251] See Mike Parker and Jane Slaughter, *Choosing Sides: Unions and the Team Concept* 222-23 (South End, 1988).

[252] See Steven L. Willborn, *Individual Employment Rights and the Standard Economic Objection: Theory and Empiricism*, 67 Nebr L Rev 101, 109-27 (1988).

[253] See Susan Rose-Ackerman, *Progressive Law and Economics—And the New Administrative Law*, 98 Yale L J 341, 364-66 (1988) ("In more general cases regulation is likely to reduce employment levels and the real value of take-home pay . . . .").

[254] Pub L No 91-596, 84 Stat 1590, codified at 29 USC §§ 651 et seq (1988).

mon use.[255] As a result, the effort to establish minimal terms at the national level has left most workplaces without any terms at all.[256]

The fifth and final flaw in the individual rights/minimal terms model is that it is inherently unstable. Any improvements in protections for individual employees that occur without the presence of a strong union movement are vulnerable and transitory. This is because employees who are not in unions are not organized into a political constituency that can protect the minimal terms in the future. Without an organized constituency, any minimal terms enacted can always be repealed or negated through judicial interpretation.

Within a democratic polity, if there is no organized constituency that can articulate and advocate the interests of a segment of the population, those interests almost certainly will be ignored. This is true whether the polity is conceived to be a pluralistic competition of interest groups or a republican search for a common public good. As the labor movement continues to decline, there may soon be no organized pressure group that is capable of defending or improving individual employment rights in the future. Thus the individual rights/minimal terms model of labor relations contains a built-in self-destruct dynamic. It functions to disorganize labor, to prevent the very group-formation that is necessary to retain or improve the minimal terms. For that reason, the individual rights and minimal terms in this model have an inherent tendency to disappear.[257]

B. Alternative Nonpluralist Forms of Collective Bargaining

If the minimal terms/individual rights model of labor regulation is not a reliable means of providing workplace justice, then we must ask whether there exist forms of labor regulation based upon collective rights that do not reinstate the failures of industrial pluralism. Elsewhere I have described two such models—one actual and one imagined—and I briefly summarize them below. The actual one is that of the Railway Labor Act, as it existed from 1926

---

[255] See John M. Mendelhoff, *The Dilemma of Toxic Substance Regulation: How Overregulation Causes Underregulation at OSHA* 74-78 (MIT, 1988).

[256] Id at 74-102. See also Cass Sunstein, *After the Rights Revolution* 82 (Harvard, 1990) (OSHA ineffective).

[257] Professor Richard Epstein has advocated a "no rights" form of labor regulation, in which workers have neither protection for collective bargaining nor individual employment rights. He justifies this as furthering economic efficiency. See Richard Epstein, *In Defense of Contract-at-Will*, 51 U Chi L Rev 947 (1984); Richard Epstein, *A Common Law of Labor Relations: A Critique of the New Deal Labor Legislation*, 92 Yale L J 1357 (1983).

until recent judicial attempts to dismantle it.[258] The imagined one is an expanded bargaining model, based on a nexus-of-contracts view of the firm.

1. The Railway Labor Act model.

The Railway Labor Act (the "RLA"),[259] which governs labor relations in the airline and railroad industries, establishes a form of employee representation and collective bargaining that does not treat the workplace as an insulated realm. Rather, the RLA calls upon courts to play an active role in ensuring that management and labor jointly determine working conditions. The RLA presumes that all existing conditions and practices are the product of agreements between management and labor. Moreover, it presumes that all existing conditions and practices will continue indefinitely unless and until either management or labor wants to make a change.[260] Management and labor must negotiate any such change before it can be implemented.

The procedure for making a change is specified in Section 6 of the RLA: A party seeking to make a change must serve on the other a Notice of Intent to Change Existing Conditions (a "Section 6 Notice").[261] The service of the Notice triggers an obligation for both parties to meet and discuss the proposed change; it also forbids either one to alter the status quo while the conferences go on.[262] Thirty days after the end of the conferences, however, both parties can take unilateral action. The union can strike and the employer can change a working condition.

Courts enforce the status quo requirement with injunctive remedies. The status quo period is, in the words of the Supreme Court, "purposely long and drawn out," so that the pressure of the passage of time helps resolve the dispute.[263] The party who wants to make a change, faced with the possibility of substantial delay,

---

[258] See Stone, 42 Stan L Rev at 1513-37 (cited in note 218) (describing judicial attempts to dismantle RLA).

[259] 45 USC §§ 151 et seq (1982 & Supp 1987).

[260] See Stone, 42 Stan L Rev at 1496-98 (cited in note 218) (describing RLA bargaining and impasse procedures).

[261] 45 USC § 156.

[262] If no agreement is reached, then a mediator is assigned and the conferences continue. If and when the mediator concludes that further meetings would be futile, he declares an impasse and offers the parties final and binding arbitration. If either party declines, then the mediator terminates his efforts and a 30-day count-down period begins. Id.

[263] *Detroit & Toledo Shore Line R.R. Co. v United Transportion Union*, 396 US 142, 149 (1969).

has an incentive to compromise or give the other side something it wants in return.[264]

Congress inserted this system of settling disputes into the Railway Labor Act in 1926. It was designed to compel collective decisionmaking and to reduce the incentives to strike. The power to compel the other side to maintain the status quo was seen as a substitute for the power to strike.[265]

The RLA has proven to be particularily helpful to unions in their efforts to influence strategic-level corporate decisions, such as decisions to introduce new technology or to transform the corporate enterprise. With time and the pressure of the status quo on their side, unions have often negotiated for outcomes that either altered the employer's initial decision or cushioned its impact on union members. In numerous cases—for instance, when carriers have sought to close part of their operations, to automate and displace existing job categories, or to transfer work to a nonunion affiliate—courts have imposed bargaining obligations and a judicially enforceable status quo.[266]

Under the RLA, either side can invoke judicial power to enforce the status quo obligations. In defining the status quo, a court must determine whether there were past practices, implied contract provisions, or implied waivers of discretion that support either side's claim as to what constitutes the status quo. Thus the structure of the RLA calls for substantial judicial intrusion into the details of company policy and industrial life.[267] In the course of

---

[264] Id at 150.

[265] See Stone, 42 Stan L Rev at 1498-99 (cited in note 218) (history of the Section 6 procedures and the status quo requirement).

[266] See, for example, *Order of Railroad Telegraphers v Chicago & North Western R. Co.*, 362 US 330, 341-42 (1960) (holding that railroad's decision to close obsolete and unprofitable stations and to lay off some agents and telegraphers was subject to bargaining and status quo obligation); *Southern Ry. Co. v Brotherhood of Locomotive Firemen*, 337 F2d 127, 132-33 (DC Cir 1964) (enjoining effort by railroad to eliminate firemen on trains and to cease hiring new firemen); *Ruby v TACA International Airlines*, 439 F2d 1359, 1362-64 (5th Cir 1971) (enjoining airlines' attempt to transfer pilot base from New Orleans to El Salvador); *United Industrial Workers v Board of Trustees of Galveston Wharves*, 351 F2d 183, 189-92 (5th Cir 1965) (enjoining carrier's effort to lease its facility to another company and permamently lay off all its employees).

[267] For example, in *Air Line Pilots v Wien Air Alaska*, 120 Labor Rel Ref Man (BNA) 3388 (D Alaska 1984), a district court ruled that a carrier could not close down its operation and furlough its pilots for administrative reasons because such an action was not within its agreed-upon past practices. Id at 3391. In contrast, in *Conrail*, the Supreme Court ruled that a railroad could unilaterally institute random drug screening of employees because the union had permitted the company to institute other forms of medical testing in the past. 109 S Ct at 2485-89. See Stone, 42 Stan L Rev at 1518-22 (cited in note 218) (discussing *Conrail*).

this intrusion, courts can and do inject public employment values and policies into the unionized workplace. Thus, while the RLA does not eliminate the tension between collective bargaining and individual employment rights, it does make it possible for those rights to inform the resolution of disputes.

2. Expanded bargaining within a nexus of contracts.

There is another model of collective bargaining which does not share the assumptions of industrial pluralism. I call it an expanded bargaining model. In this model, labor is one stakeholder in the firm among others, free to contend and bargain with the others for a role in decisionmaking. This model eliminates the barrier between collective bargaining and external law.

Traditional theories of the firm assume that shareholders are the only group with a stake in major corporate decisions. Under this view, labor contracts with the firm, but is not a part *of* the firm.[268] Further, labor's contracts with the firm are not quite the same as those of other groups who do business with the firm. Labor's contracts take the form of collective bargaining agreements and are governed by a special body of law, the NLRA, which determines what subjects can be included in those contracts and the rules by which they are negotiated.

However, there are new theories of the corporation that give a much more rich and complex picture of the interests of corporate actors, and which advocate a broader view of corporate governance. In a pathbreaking 1976 article in corporate law theory, Jensen and Meckling proposed that a corporation consists of nothing more than a bundle of contractual arrangements among a variety of parties—customers, suppliers, lenders, investors, managers, and workers.[269] With this insight, the black box view of the corporation collapsed, and the "nexus of contracts" view was born.

Under the nexus of contracts view, no group has an *a priori* privileged relation to the entity as a whole. All use their input and their leverage to strike the best bargain they can. Thus labor stands on an equal footing with all other contenders for power

---

[268] See Victor Brudney, *The Independent Director—Heavenly City or Potemkin Village?*, 95 Harv L Rev 597, 602-03 (1982); Masahiko Aoki, *The Co-operative Game Theory of the Firm* 8-9 (Clarendon, 1984).

[269] Michael C. Jensen and William H. Meckling, *Theory of the Firm: Managerial Behavior, Agency Costs and Ownership Structure*, 3 J Fin Econ 305, 311 (1976). See also R. H. Coase, *The Nature of the Firm*, in R. H. Coase, *The Firm, the Market, and the Law* 33 (Chicago, 1988) (reprinted from 4 Economica (Nov 1937)) (arguing that the firm is a substitute for a series of discrete market contractual arrangements).

within the concern. Under this conception of the firm, for example, we can imagine collective bargaining transposed to the boardroom, where unions can then contend with not only management, but all the other constituent groups that comprise the firm. This expanded bargaining is already occurring in the United States in Chapter 11 bankruptcy reorganization proceedings, where unions sit on creditor committees and negotiate with all the different classes of creditors about the fate of the enterprise. Similar forms of expanded bargaining are occurring in troubled industries.[270] Collective bargaining is beginning to overspill its borders and claim new roles in corporate life.

This model of expanded collective bargaining is fundamentally different from industrial pluralist views of collective bargaining. It does not envision labor-management relations as an insulated mini-democracy. Rather, it permits, even requires, labor to bring to the bargaining table whatever legal rights, powers and immunities it has under external sources of law.

For example, creditors have all sorts of liens, collection procedures, and priorities under state and federal laws. These rights form the background against which creditors make their bargains with other groups within the firm. So too, under the "nexus of contracts" model, if employees have rights under external law, they may use them to exert leverage in their bargaining with the other groups.

Under this conception of collective bargaining, unions would take externally imposed employment rights as the starting point from which to negotiate, the background against which bargaining would take place. Workers would not have to choose between individual employment rights and collective bargaining; the two systems of rights would be compatible and mutually reinforcing.[271] This regime would help move American labor law in the direction of European labor law, where individual rights and collective bar-

---

[270] See Stone, 55 U Chi L Rev at 76-77 (cited in note 3) (giving examples).

[271] Of course, such a model requires careful consideration of the rules governing economic weapons. In this model, unions only have clout in negotiations with other constituents of the firm to the extent that unions can bring a credible threat of withholding their investment and thereby harming the others. The ability to withhold investments and the consequence to others—the "negative market power" of unions—is determined by the legal rules governing strikes, secondary boycotts, picketing, and so forth. Thus this model is incomplete without specifying the rules of economic warfare.

gaining are mutually reinforcing aspects of the social welfare state.[272]

C. Section 301 Preemption, Industrial Pluralism, and Union Decline

If we are to imagine any alternative regime of collective labor rights, we must again consider the issue of union decline. If unions are declining to the vanishing point, then any legal regime based on collective employment rights is outdated before it begins. In Part I, I presented several theories of union decline, and argued in favor of the view which attributed union decline to a decline in the actual and perceived effectiveness of unions. One of the most important factors in explaining union effectiveness is the legal rules which define the legitimate scope of union activity. In Part II, I showed that, over the past decade, there have been many changes in legal rules which have restricted the power of unions to affect strategic-level corporate decisions. These changes no doubt diminish union effectiveness in actuality and in the public mind. We can see now that Section 301 preemption might also play a role in union decline.

To the extent that unionized workers have fewer rights than nonunion workers, § 301 preemption has created significant disincentives for workers to unionize. While most workers, like most judges and law professors, are not familiar with the intricacies of § 301 preemption doctrine, it is entirely plausible than many workers have a general sense that state employment law offers as many or more benefits than do unions. Furthermore, employers frequently inform their employees during organizing drives that they will lose various state law rights if they form a union. Under existing preemption rules, these claims are true. Thus if workers believe such employer claims, and if the claims influence workers'

---

[272] See Maier, *Fictitious bonds* at 54-55 (cited in note 234). Labor relations scholarship in this country has not adequately addressed the problem of harmonizing individual employee rights with collective employee rights. Instead, most scholars in the field have staked out a position in favor of one type of right and against the other. However, legal scholars writing in another contexts have suggested ways to reconceive both types of rights as complementary. See, for example, Ronald R. Garet, *Communality and Existence: The Rights of Groups*, 56 S Cal L Rev 1001 (1983) (suggesting ways that group rights and individual rights can be conceived as complementary); Gregory S. Alexander, *Dilemmas of Group Autonomy: Residential Associations and Community*, 75 Cornell L Rev 1 (1989) (suggesting that both individual and group rights must be understood as limited by a shared commitment to certain external norms).

decisions about whether or not to unionize, then the broad § 301 doctrine is a significant factor in union decline.

Conclusion

To conclude, the labor relations system in the United States is undergoing a fundamental change. At the present time, the system of collective worker empowerment established during the New Deal stands in opposition to an emerging system based on individual worker rights, due in large part to an unnecessarily broad § 301 preemption doctrine. As a result, unions have declined in numbers and in political power, endangering collective as well as individual employment rights. I have attempted to show the fault lines in the New Deal system of collective regulation that enabled this new structure to emerge. I have also offered two alternative nonpluralist legal regimes of collective bargaining in order to demonstrate that it is possible to harmonize individual and collective rights. Either would be a form of regulation that could promote a revitalized labor movement into the next century. Without some program, we risk a future with a workforce that is disorganized, disempowered, and disenfranchised.

[4]

Theodore J. St. Antoine*

A Seed Germinates: Unjust Discharge Reform Heads Toward Full Flower

TABLE OF CONTENTS

I. INTRODUCTION

"Seminal" is one of the most overworked words in the legal lexi-

---

* James E. & Sarah A. Degan Professor of Law, University of Michigan. A.B., Fordham College, 1951; J.D., University of Michigan, 1954. The author has recently been selected by the Commissioners on Uniform State Laws to serve as reporter to a committee drafting a model statute on employment termination. This article had been planned long before that appointment. The opinions expressed herein are solely the author's. At this writing the Commissioners have not begun their formal deliberations.

con. But if ever two pieces of writing deserved that appellation, they are the 1967 article by Professor Lawrence Blades[1] advocating judicial development of the tort of "abusive discharge" as a limitation on the doctrine of employment at will, and the 1976 article by Professor Clyde Summers[2] advocating legislation to protect individual employees against unjust dismissal. At the time Blades wrote there was virtually no precedent directly supporting his position, and he may have been unaware of what little did exist.[3] After concluding that the rigidities the consideration requirement would prevent resort to contract theory, Blades argued for the extension of tort law.[4] He relied principally on the notion that even the exercise of a right may be actionable if ulterior purposes or wrongful motives intrude, citing as an analogy the abuse of legal process.[5] Within a dozen or so years following Blades's piece, the highest courts of such influential states as California,[6] Illinois,[7] Massachusetts,[8] Michigan,[9] and New York[10] had drawn upon a variety of both tort and contract doctrines to engraft qualifications on the conventional employment-at-will principle. By now a total of about forty jurisdictions have recognized some modification of the traditional rule.[11] Unlike Blades, who viewed the prospects for legislative reform as "dim" because of the absence of any strong lobby favoring it,[12] Summers considered statutory protection against unjust dismissal a necessity, on the grounds the courts had demonstrated "an unwillingness to break through their self-created crust of legal doctrine."[13] As it has turned out, we have profited from the differing insights of both men. Blades was right that the legislatures would be slow to move, and that a modest extension and adaptation of well-established common law principles would enable the courts to provide at least some measure of relief. Summers was right, as I shall indicate shortly, that accepted legal doctrines permit only a limited and inade-

1. Blades, *Employment at Will vs. Individual Freedom: On Limiting the Abusive Exercise of Employer Power*, 67 COLUM. L. REV. 1404 (1967).
2. Summers, *Individual Protection Against Unjust Dismissal: Time for a Statute*, 62 VA. L. REV. 481 (1976).
3. *E.g.*, Petermann v. Local 396, Int'l Bhd. of Teamsters, 174 Cal. App. 2d 184, 344 P.2d 25 (1959) (public policy prevents employer from firing employee for refusing to perjure himself on behalf of employer).
4. Blades, *supra* note 1, at 1420-23.
5. *Id.* at 1423-24.
6. Tameny v. Atlantic Richfield Co., 27 Cal. 2d 167, 610 P.2d 1330, 164 Cal. Rptr. 839 (1980).
7. Palmateer v. International Harvester Co., 85 Ill. 2d 124, 421 N.E.2d 876 (1981).
8. Fortune v. National Cash Register Co., 373 Mass. 96, 364 N.E.2d 1251 (1977).
9. Toussaint v. Blue Cross & Blue Shield, 408 Mich. 579, 292 N.W.2d 880 (1980).
10. Weiner v. McGraw-Hill, Inc., 57 N.Y.2d 458, 443 N.E.2d 441 (1982).
11. [IERM] 9A Lab. Rel. Rep. (BNA) 505:51 (1987).
12. Blades, *supra* note 1, at 1434.
13. Summers, *supra* note 2, at 521.

quate response to employees' legitimate claims. Legislation will ultimately be needed.

There are signs the idea is taking root. Bills forbidding wrongful discharge have been introduced in a dozen or more legislatures.[14] A special committee of the Labor and Employment Law Section of the State Bar of California has recommended statutory regulation of unjust dismissal.[15] The individual rights committee of the ABA Section on Labor and Employment Law has drafted a questionnaire regarding the critical issues to be considered in any proposed legislation.[16] The AFL-CIO's Executive Council has discarded organized labor's longstanding ambivalence about the subject by endorsing the concept of wrongful discharge legislation.[17] The Commissioners on Uniform State Laws have decided to draft a model statute.[18] And finally, just twenty years after Blades's trail-blazing article, Montana became the first state to enact a comprehensive law protecting employees against unjust discharge.[19]

In this paper, I shall briefly review the nature and limitations of the theories most frequently invoked by the courts in dealing with wrongful dismissal. I shall then examine the major arguments for and against a general overhaul of the doctrine of employment at will. Lastly, I shall discuss some of the particular questions that will have to be addressed in fashioning a statutory solution.

II. JUDICIAL THEORIES OF UNJUST DISCHARGE

During the past decade or so American courts have employed three main theories to soften the worst rigors of what was once the well-nigh universal rule that employers "may dismiss their employees at will . . . for good cause, for no cause or even for cause morally wrong."[20] Those three doctrines include tort—violations of public policy, or "abusive" or "retaliatory" discharge; breach of an express or implied contract; and breach of the covenant of good faith and fair dealing. In addition to the claim of wrongful discharge, employees suing their former employers often add more traditional claims, such as

14. California, Colorado, Connecticut, Massachusetts, Michigan, Montana, New Jersey, Ohio, Pennsylvania, Virgin Islands, Washington, Wisconsin, and the U.S. Congress. *See, e.g.*, Ann Arbor, [Mich.] News, June 10, 1984, at C5, col. 1; Daily Lab. Rep. (BNA), Sept. 3, 1987, at A-8.

15. Labor and Employment Law News (State Bar of Cal. Lab. & Emp. L. Sec.), Feb. 8, 1984, at 1-46.

16. 1 LAB. LAW. 784 (1985).

17. [IER cases] 1 Lab. Rel. Rep. (BNA), Mar. 3, 1987, at 1.

18. Conversation on September 11, 1987 between the author and Professor William J. Pierce, Excecutive Director of the Commissioners on Uniform State Laws.

19. Daily Lab. Rep. (BNA), Sept. 3, 1987, at A-8.

20. Payne v. Western & A.R.R., 81 Tenn. 507, 519-20 (1884). *See also* H. WOOD, LAW OF MASTER AND SERVANT 272-73 (1877).

intentional infliction of emotional distress; defamation and injury to business reputation; fraud and misrepresentation; invasion of privacy; negligence; and tortious interference with contractual relations. I shall not deal with these miscellaneous causes of action.

A. Tort Theories

1. Discharges Contrary to "Public Policy"

The first cracks in the inhospitable "crust" of judicial doctrine that formerly precluded relief against wrongful dismissal came, as one might have expected, in some cases that were simply too malodorous for the courts to tolerate. Typical was *Petermann v. Local 396, International Brotherhood of Teamsters,*[21] where an employee was fired for refusing to perjure himself at the behest of his employer. Not to recognize a cause of action in such circumstances would effectively condone a grave violation of a basic public policy. The public policy exception to the at-will principle spans a spectrum of situations. *Petermann* is at one extreme; the employee was actually discharged for declining to commit a crime. I should like to think that today no court would be so enmeshed in outworn theory that it would hesitate to remedy a dismissal based on an employee's refusal to engage in a clearcut instance of unlawful conduct. Next along the spectrum are cases where employees are fired for performing a public duty, such as serving on a jury[22] or "blowing the whistle" on wrongdoing within a company.[23] Finally, there are situations where the discharge results from the exercise of a legal right or privilege. An employee may have filed a workers' compensation claim,[24] for example, or spoken out against his company's stand on pending legislation.[25]

Surely the crassest (and easiest) of these public policy cases — where criminal conduct has been importuned — will be few and far between. As one moves across the spectrum toward more common situations, the issues become more difficult for the courts. What is the reach of "public policy"? It may be one thing if the "whistleblower"

21. 174 Cal. App. 2d 184, 344 P.2d 25 (1959). *See also* Tameny v. Atlantic Richfield Co., 27 Cal. 3d 167, 610 P.2d 1330 (1980) (refusal to join price-fixing conspiracy).
22. Nees v. Hocks, 272 Or. 210, 536 P.2d 512 (1975).
23. Causes of action were recognized in Sheets v. Teddy's Frosted Foods, Inc., 179 Conn. 471, 427 A.2d 385 (1980), and Palmateer v. International Harvester Co., 85 Ill. 2d 124, 421 N.E.2d 876 (1981), but rejected in Geary v. United States Steel Corp., 456 Pa. 171, 319 A.2d 174 (1974), and Murphy v. American Home Prod. Corp., 58 N.Y.2d 293, 448 N.E.2d 86 (1983). Some of these seemingly contrary decisions are reconcilable on their facts.
24. Causes of action were recognized in Kelsay v. Motorola, Inc., 74 Ill. 2d 172, 384 N.E.2d 353 (1978), and Firestone Textile Co. v. Meadows, 666 S.W.2d 730 (Ky. 1983), but rejected in Martin v. Tapley, 360 So. 2d 708 (Ala. 1978), and Segal v. Arrow Indus. Corp., 364 So. 2d 89 (Fla. Dist. Ct. App. 1978).
25. Novosel v. Nationwide Ins. Co., 721 F.2d 894 (3d Cir. 1983).

has been subpoenaed to appear at an official inquiry. It may be quite another if he has taken it upon himself to share his good-faith (but erroneous and damaging) suspicions with the media. What inference does one draw if the legislature has not expressly prohibited employer reprisals against employees filing workers' compensation or unemployment insurance claims?[26] One court may be so bold as to draw upon the United States Constitution's First Amendment as a source of public policy protecting employees' speech even against private employers.[27] Other courts may find controlling the traditional view that constitutional rights can ordinarily be asserted only against governmental action.[28] Still other courts have treated the whole concept of public policy as unsuited for judicial application in this context, and instead have declared it a matter to be left to the legislature.[29] Except perhaps in the most egregious circumstances, therefore, common-law principles of public policy provide no guaranteed recourse for the wronged worker.

2. *"Abusive" or "Retaliatory" Discharges*

Beyond the more standard public policy exceptions, some courts have recognized a cause of action when an employer has sought to exploit his position for personal advantage. One celebrated decision sustained a suit by a female worker who was fired for refusing to date her foreman.[30] Other courts, however, have declined to remedy such personal abuse or similar retaliatory conduct.[31] They apparently believe that the public policy exception should not be stretched to cover what essentially are disputes between individuals. Despite commentators' arguments that all unjust dismissals subvert the community's interest in industrial stability and productivity,[32] there is a growing tendency to require that the public policy relied upon be "clearly articulated" and "well accepted,"[33] or even that it be "evidenced by a constitutional

26. *See supra* note 24.

27. Novosel v. Nationwide Ins. Co., 721 F.2d 894 (3d Cir. 1983).

28. Allen v. Safeway Stores, Inc., 699 P.2d 277 (Wyo. 1985); Barr v. Kelso-Burnett Co., 106 Ill. 2d 520, 478 N.E.2d 1354 (1985).

29. Murphy v. American Home Prod. Corp., 58 N.Y.2d 293, 488 N.E.2d 86 (1983); *see also* Kelly v. Mississippi Valley Gas Co., 397 So. 2d 874 (Miss. 1981).

30. Monge v. Beebe Rubber Co., 114 N.H. 130, 316 A.2d 549 (1974). *But cf.* Howard v. Dorr Woolen Co., 120 N.H. 295, 296-97, 414 A.2d 1273, 1274 (1980).

31. *E.g.*, Fawcett v. G.C. Murphy & Co., 46 Ohio St. 2d 245, 348 N.E.2d 144 (1976); Givens v. Hixson, 275 Ark. 370, 631 S.W.2d 263 (1982).

32. Note, *Protecting Employees At Will Against Wrongful Discharge: The Public Policy Exception*, 96 HARV. L. REV. 1931, 1948 (1983).

33. Clifford v. Cactus Drilling Corp., 419 Mich. 356, 367, 353 N.W.2d 469, 474 (1984) (Williams, C.J., dissenting); *see also* Wagenseller v. Scottsdale Memorial Hosp., 147 Ariz. 370, 710 P.2d 1025, 1034 (1985).

or statutory provision."[34] That is not going to help many workers subjected to arbitrary or capricious treatment or personally motivated abuse.

B. Contract Theories

In the past, not even an employer's assurance of "permanent" employment would change the arrangement from that of an at-will contract.[35] In the early 1980s, however, a number of courts began taking employers at their word. Statements of policy set forth in personnel manuals or employee handbooks, or oral commitments to employees at the time of hiring, were found to constitute, either separately or in combination, an express or implied contract that the employee would not be discharged except for "just cause." Leading decisions included *Pugh v. See's Candies, Inc.*,[36] in California, *Toussaint v. Blue Cross & Blue Shield*,[37] in Michigan, and *Weiner v. McGraw-Hill, Inc.*,[38] in New York. But many courts continued to regard such employer declarations as merely nonbinding expressions of present intent.[39]

Even in states whose courts accept the new contractual qualification on employment at will, an employer with a careful lawyer should have little trouble in avoiding liability. Unequivocal language in a job application that any resulting employment will be only at will,[40] or a clear and prominent disclaimer in an employee handbook that any policy statements are not legally binding,[41] will generally foreclose employee claims.

A greater problem is the employer's unilateral deletion of a job

34. Brockmeyer v. Dun & Bradstreet, 113 Wis. 2d 561, 573, 335 N.W.2d 834, 840 (1983); *see also* Adler v. American Standard Corp., 290 Md. 615, 432 A.2d 464 (1981).
35. *See, e.g.*, Edwards v. Kentucky Utils. Co., 286 Ky. 341, 150 S.W.2d 916 (1941); Note, *Employee Handbooks and Employment At-Will Contracts*, 1985 DUKE L.J. 196, 200-04.
36. 116 Cal. App. 3d 311, 171 Cal. Rptr. 917 (1981). *Accord* Cleary v. American Air Lines, Inc., 111 Cal. App. 3d 443 (1980); Pine River State Bank v. Mettille, 333 N.W.2d 622 (Minn. 1983); Shah v. American Synthetic Rubber Corp., 655 S.W.2d 489 (Ky. 1983).
37. 408 Mich. 579, 292 N.W.2d 880 (1980).
38. 57 N.Y.2d 458, 443 N.E.2d 441 (1982).
39. Mau v. Oklahoma Nat'l Bank, 207 Neb. 308, 299 N.W.2d 147 (1980); Heideck v. Kent Gen. Hosp., 446 A.2d 1095 (Del. 1982); White v. Chelsea Indus., 425 So. 2d 1090 (Ala. 1983).
40. Reid v. Sears, Roebuck & Co., 790 F.2d 453 (6th Cir. 1986); French v. Dillard Dep't Stores, Inc., 285 Ark. 332, 686 S.W.2d 435 (1985). *But cf.* Tirano v. Sears, Roebuck & Co., 99 A.D.2d 675, 472 N.Y.S.2d 49 (1984).
41. Woolley v. Hoffman-LaRoche, Inc., 99 N.J. 284, 289-91, 491 A.2d 1257, 1260, *modified on other grounds*, 101 N.J. 10, 499 A.2d 515 (1985); Thompson v. St. Regis Paper Co., 102 Wash. 2d 219, 685 P.2d 1081 (1984). *But cf.* Wagenseller v. Scottsdale Memorial Hosp., 147 Ariz. 370, 710 P.2d 1025 (1985) (unclear); Schipani v. Ford Motor Co., 102 Mich. App. 606, 302 N.W.2d 307 (1981) (subsequent assurance); Ferraro v. Koelsch, 124 Wis. 2d 154, 368 N.W.2d 666 (1985) (same).

security guarantee previously contained in an employee handbook or other policy statement. As to subsequently hired employees, of course, there should be no doubts about the efficacy of the revocation.[42] The bothersome question concerns incumbent employees, who have operated under the protective provision for some period of time. If the employer has retained the power, either expressly[43] or impliedly,[44] to change working terms and personnel policies unilaterally, that would seem to be dispositive. If such a reservation of power cannot be found, the question becomes even stickier. Where is the consideration for the employee's surrender of an existing right? Yet an employer can fairly argue that *all* the terms of employment are inherently variable, and that consideration can be found in the employer's continuation of (or, better, increase in) pay and other benefits.[45] Such an approach would not seem at odds with the proposition that an employer could not fire at his whim a particular individual while he still has in effect a "just cause" guarantee as part of his overall personnel policy. Naturally, if a given employee could demonstrate that she had specifically and detrimentally relied on her employer's assurances of job security, for example, by declining alternative work opportunities, that might immunize her against a later withdrawal of the safeguard.[46]

Apart from the employer's capacity to eliminate or restrict contractual rights, another deficiency in the contract approach is that policy declarations are likely to be confined to the more enlightened business firms, and that oral assurances or other individualized guarantees are likely to be confined to middle-level or higher ranking management

42. *See supra* notes 40 & 41 and accompanying text.

43. *See* Toussaint v. Blue Cross & Blue Shield, 408 Mich. 579, 619, 292 N.W.2d 880, 894-95 (1980).

44. *See* Bullock v. Automobile Club, 146 Mich. App. 711, 720-21, 381 N.W.2d 793, 797 (1985), on appeal as Dkt. No. 78027, Mich. Sup. Ct.

45. *Cf.* Enis v. Continental Ill. Nat'l Bank & Trust Co., 795 F.2d 39, 41 (7th Cir. 1986). This position would appear analogous to the view of a number of courts that consideration for the employer's promise of job security lies in the employee's continued rendition of services. *See, e.g.*, Woolley v. Hoffman-La Roche, Inc., 99 N.J. 284, 301-03, 491 A.2d 1257, 1267, *modified on other grounds*, 101 N.J. 10, 499 A.2d 515 (1985); Watson v. Idaho Falls Consol. Hosps., 720 P.2d 632 (Idaho 1986); Cook v. Heck's, Inc., 342 S.E.2d 453, 459 (W. Va. 1986). For the view that a job protection provision *cannot* be rescinded without "independent" consideration, see Stack v. Allstate Ins. Co., 606 F. Supp. 472, 477-78 (S.D. Ind. 1985). In Bankey v. Storer Broadcasting Co., Dkt. No. 84-1296, the U.S. Court of Appeals for the Sixth Circuit certified to the Michigan Supreme Court, Dkt. No. 78200, the question whether an employer who has created a "just cause" employment contract can later unilaterally alter the employment relationship as to existing employees to permit discharge at will.

46. RESTATEMENT (SECOND) OF CONTRACTS § 90 (1979); *cf.* Scott v. Lane, 409 So. 2d 791, 794 (Ala. 1982); Mers v. Dispatch Printing Co., 19 Ohio St. 3d 100, 105, 483 N.E.2d 150, 155 (1985).

personnel. That leaves the rank-and-file worker in the small, marginal plant or shop — the very person who probably needs protection the most — bereft of contract rights.

C. Good Faith and Fair Dealing

Potentially the most expansive judicial qualification of the employment-at-will doctrine is based on the covenant of good faith and fair dealing.[47] The principle was first elaborated as to employment contracts in the leading Massachusetts case of *Fortune v. National Cash Register Co.*[48] The facts, as a jury was permitted to find them, were appalling. A veteran salesman of twenty-five years had been working for some time on a five million dollar order. Just after the sale was consummated, he was fired. By special verdict a jury determined that the employer had acted in "bad faith." The Supreme Judicial Court of Massachusetts concluded the jury could properly have found that the employer's reason for terminating the salesman was to deprive him of a portion of the full commission due him. Such action was deemed a breach of the covenant of "good faith and fair dealing" imposed by law on the parties to any contract.

Fortune plainly suggests a substantial extension of the traditional contract doctrine of good faith and fair dealing. Ordinarily it has not been seen as a catch-all safeguard against any arbitrary conduct on the part of a contracting party, such as an unjust dismissal, but rather as a fairly specific duty imposed by law that neither party do anything which will interfere with the other's performance of its contractual obligations or which will interfere with the right of the other to receive the benefits of the agreement.[49] The doctrine has not been concerned with the right to terminate a contract as such. Furthermore, resort to a novel articulation of the good faith concept was hardly necessary in *Fortune*. Good faith could have been invoked concerning the nonpayment only, without regard to the discharge itself. Or the classic principle that full or substantial performance entitles a contracting party to the agreed price would have served quite adequately.[50]

At least one California court has indicated that the covenant of

---

47. Arguing for a broad reading of the covenant that could well eviscerate the whole at-will doctrine is Note, *Protecting At-Will Employees Against Wrongful Discharge: The Duty to Terminate Only in Good Faith*, 93 HARV. L. REV. 1816 (1980). Coming close to this view is Crenshaw v. Bozeman Deaconess Hosp., 693 P.2d 487 (Mont. 1984); *see also* Gates v. Life of Montana Ins. Co., 196 Mont. 178, 638 P.2d 1063 (1982); Dare v. Montana Petroleum Mktg. Co., 687 P.2d 1015 (Mont. 1984).

48. 373 Mass. 96, 364 N.E.2d 1251 (1977). *See also* Maddaloni v. Western Mass. Bus Lines, Inc., 386 Mass. 877, 438 N.E.2d 351 (1982); Buysse v. Paine, Webber, Jackson & Curtiss, 623 F.2d 1244 (8th Cir. 1980) (Minnesota law).

49. *See, e.g.*, RESTATEMENT (SECOND) OF CONTRACTS § 205 (1981); 3 A. CORBIN, CORBIN ON CONTRACTS §§ 570-71 (1960).

50. 3A A. CORBIN, CORBIN ON CONTRACTS § 700 (1960).

good faith and fair dealing does protect at least a long-service employee from discharge without just cause. In *Cleary v. American Airlines, Inc.*,[51] the employer had established an internal grievance procedure for resolving employee disputes, and the employee in question was an eighteen-year veteran at the time of his discharge. The California Court of Appeals seemed to concentrate at one point only on the latter factor when it stated: "Termination of employment without legal cause after such a period of time offends the implied-in-law covenant of good faith and fair dealing contained in all contracts including employment contracts."[52] *Cleary* also held that a breach of the covenant of good faith and fair dealing sounds in tort as well as contract, thereby allowing punitive in addition to compensatory damages.[53]

Several courts have expressly rejected a broad application of the implied covenant of good faith. In *Murphy v. American Home Products Corp.*,[54] the New York Court of Appeals reasoned that any implied covenant would have to be "in aid and furtherance of other terms of the agreement of the parties." The court then went on to observe that the plaintiff's employment in this instance was at will, leaving the employer "an unfettered right to terminate."[55] The court concluded: "In the context of such an employment it would be incongruous to say that an inference may be drawn that the employer impliedly agreed to a provision which would be destructive of his right of termination."[56] This logic seems sufficiently compelling that the good-faith covenant appears unlikely to become a universally accepted

51. 111 Cal. App. 3d 443, 168 Cal. Rptr. 722 (1980). Later California decisions have differed over the significance of an employee's longevity in good-faith covenant cases. *Compare* Wheeler v. Hershey Chocolate Co., No. 196250 (Cal. App. Aug. 18, 1985) (longevity alone not sufficient) *with* Gray v. Superior Court, 181 Cal. App. 3d 813, 821, 226 Cal. Rptr. 570, 573 (longevity helpful but not essential). *Cf.* Foley v. Interactive Data Corp., 184 Cal. App. 3d 241, 219 Cal. Rptr. 866 (1985), *cert. granted*, 222 Cal. Rptr. 740, (1986) (seven years longevity not enough).

52. Cleary v. American Airlines, 111 Cal. App. 3d 443, 455, 168 Cal. Rptr. 772, 729 (1980).

53. Although *Fortune* and other decisions have treated breaches of the covenant as sounding in contract, the notion that there may be a tortious breach in certain circumstances (thus opening the door for punitive damages) has been followed in Wallis v. Superior Court, 160 Cal. App. 3d 1109, 207 Cal. Rptr. 123 (1984); Eller v. Houston's Restaurants, Inc., 117 L.R.R.M. (BNA) 2651, 2653-54 (D.D.C. 1984).

54. 58 N.Y.2d 293, 448 N.E.2d 86, 461 N.Y.S.2d 232 (1983). *Accord* Walker v. Modern Realty, 675 F.2d 1002 (8th Cir. 1982); Martin v. Federal Life Ins. Co., 109 Ill. App. 3d 596, 440 N.E.2d 998 (1982); Gordon v. Matthew Bender & Co., 562 F. Supp. 1286 (N.D. Ill. 1983); Brockmeyer v. Dun & Bradstreet, 113 Wis. 2d 561, 335 N.W.2d 834 (1983); Wagenseller v. Scottsdale Memorial Hosp., 147 Ariz. 370, 710 P.2d 1025 (1985); Hinson v. Cameron, 742 P.2d 549 (Okla. 1987).

55. Murphy v. American Home Prod. Corp., 58 N.Y.2d 293, 304, 448 N.E.2d 86, 91, 461 N.Y.S.2d 232, 237 (1983).

56. *Id.* at 304-05, 448 N.E.2d at 91, 461 N.Y.S.2d at 237.

panacea for wrongfully discharged employees.[57]

III. THE PROS AND CONS OF AT-WILL EMPLOYMENT

In my judgment the courts of the more progressive states, like California, Massachusetts, and Michigan, have gone about as far with unjust discharge actions as they are going to go. They will entertain suits alleging serious violations of accepted public policy. They will hold employers to their unretracted word not to fire except for good reason. But ordinarily they will not impose an affirmative obligation on employers to prove just cause to support a discharge. And even where a contractual protection is found, the trial court may, as in a leading California case, instruct the jury that it cannot substitute its opinion for the employer's as to whether plaintiff's work performance was satisfactory, and that "just cause" for termination means a "fair and honest cause or reason, regulated by good faith on the part of the party exercising the power."[58] In short, the courts are unlikely to subject nonunion firms, as a matter of common law, to the same requirements exacted contractually of nearly every employer party to a collective bargaining agreement. The next move therefore seems up to the legislatures. That calls for a thorough appraisal of the theory and operation of employment at will.

Following the pioneering studies of Blades[59] and Summers,[60] a veritable tidal wave of scholarly condemnation has descended upon the at-will employment doctrine.[61] For most commentators, it is a matter

57. No more than a dozen states have accepted the good-faith covenant theory in holdings or dictum. [IERM] 9A Lab. Rel. Rep. (BNA) 505:51 (1988) (twelve states with Oklahoma now excluded); Lab. L. Rep. (CCH), Insight at 4 (May 1987) (five states with Oklahoma now excluded).

58. Pugh v. See's Candies, Inc., 116 Cal. App. 3d 311, 330, 171 Cal. Rptr. 917, 928 (1981) (on remand); *see also* Simpson v. Western Graphics Corp., 293 Or. 96, 100-01, 643 P.2d 1276, 1278-79 (1982). *But cf.* Toussaint v. Blue Cross and Blue Shield, 408 Mich. 579, 623-24, 292 N.W.2d 880, 896 (1980). There are differences of view whether a plaintiff employee should bear the ultimate burden of persuasion concerning the issue of employer breach, or whether, as in the usual labor arbitration proceeding, the burden is on the employer. *Compare* Pugh v. See's Candies, Inc., 116 Cal. App. 3d 311, 171 Cal. Rptr. 917 (1981) *and* Schmidly v. Perry Motor Freight, Inc., 735 F.2d 1086 (8th Cir. 1984) (Arkansas law) *with* Rasch v. City of East Jordan, 141 Mich. App. 336, 367 N.W.2d 856 (1985).

59. Blades, *supra* note 1.

60. Summers, *supra* note 2.

61. *See, e.g.*, Aaron, *Constitutional Protections Against Unjust Dismissals from Employment: Some Reflections*, in NEW TECHNIQUES IN LABOR DISPUTE RESOLUTION 13 (H. Anderson ed. 1976); Blackburn, *Restricted Employer Discharge Rights: A Changing Concept of Employment At Will*, 17 AM. BUS. L.J. 467 (1980); Blumrosen, *Strangers No More: All Workers Are Entitled to "Just Cause" Protection Under Title VII*, 2 IND. REL. L.J. 519 (1978); Peck, *Unjust Discharges from Employment*, 40 OHIO ST. L.J. 1 (1979); St. Antoine, *Protection Against Unjust Discipline: An Idea Whose Time Has Long Since Come*, in ARBITRATION ISSUES FOR

of simple justice. Conceptually, there appears little or nothing to be said in favor of an employer's right to treat its employees arbitrarily or unfairly. Moreover, it is not just a theoretical problem. One careful observer has estimated:

> Some 60 million U.S. employees are subject to the employment-at-will doctrine and about 2 million of them are discharged each year . . . . About 150,000 of these workers would have been found to have been discharged without just cause and reinstated to their former jobs if they had had the right to appeal to an impartial arbitrator as do almost all unionized workers.[62]

Probably the most vigorous and undaunted academic defender of the at-will principle is Professor Richard Epstein[63] of the University of Chicago. He launches a three-pronged counterattack. First, at-will contracts are fair because freedom of contract is an aspect of individual liberty; "the employee is the full owner of his labor," and he and the employer are generally "free to exchange on whatever terms and conditions they see fit."[64] Second, at-will contracts are mutually beneficial. They enable both parties to monitor the other's behavior; "the worker can quit whenever the net value of the employment contract turns negative."[65] Workers also benefit from the "asymmetry of reputational losses;" the single large employer has more to lose if his many good employees perceive the dismissal of a coworker as arbitrary.[66] In addition, workers are helped in dealing with "risk diversification" since the contract at will offsets "the concentration of individual investment in a single job."[67] Furthermore, the system is "very cheap to administer;" there aren't any litigation costs and personnel expenses are kept down.[68] Finally, no inequality of bargaining power can be demonstrated; if it did, "[w]ages should be driven to zero, for no matter what their previous level, the employer could use his (inexhaustible) bargaining power to reduce them further."[69] Profes-

---

THE 1980S — PROCEEDINGS OF THE THIRTY-FOURTH ANNUAL MEETING, NATIONAL ACADEMY OF ARBITRATORS 43 (J. Stern & B. Dennis eds. 1982); Stieber, *The Case for Protection of Unorganized Employees Against Unjust Discharge*, in PROCEEDINGS OF THE THIRTY-SECOND ANNUAL MEETING, INDUSTRIAL RELATIONS RESEARCH ASSOCIATION 155 (B. Dennis ed. 1980); Symposium, *Individual Rights in the Workplace: The Employment-at-Will Issue*, 16 U. MICH. J. REF. 199 (1983).

62. Stieber, *Recent Developments in Employment-at-Will*, 36 LAB. L.J. 557, 558 (1985).

63. Epstein, *In Defense of the Contract at Will*, 51 U. CHI. L. REV. 947 (1984); *see also* Heinsz, *The Assault on the Employment at Will Doctrine: Management Considerations*, 40 MO. L. REV. 855 (1982); Power, *A Defense of the Employment at Will Rule*, 27 ST. LOUIS U.L.J. 881 (1983); Note, *Limiting the Right to Terminate at Will—Have the Courts Forgotten the Employer?* 35 VAND. L. REV. 201 (1982).

64. Epstein, *supra* note 63, at 955.

65. *Id.* at 966.

66. *Id.* at 967-68.

67. *Id.* at 969.

68. *Id.* at 970.

69. *Id.* at 973. But even the overly pessimistic "iron law of wages" propounded by

sor Epstein's third principal point deals with distributional concerns. He contends that modifications in the at-will doctrine "cannot hope to transfer wealth systematically from rich to poor on the model of comprehensive systems of taxation or welfare benefits."[70]

A wondrous Oz-like air of unreality pervades much of the Epstein thesis. His analysis admits of no living, breathing human beings, who develop irrational antagonisms or exercise poor judgment, on the one hand, or who suffer the psychological as well as the economic devastation of losing a job, on the other. Numerous studies document the increases in cardiovascular deaths, suicides, mental breakdowns, alcoholism, ulcers, diabetes, spouse and child abuse, impaired social relationships, and various other diseases and abnormal conditions that develop even in the wake of impersonal permanent layoffs resulting from plant closures.[71] It seems reasonable to presume that such effects are at least as severe when a worker is singled out to be discharged for some alleged deficiency or misconduct. Even if Epstein is right in everything he has to say about employees collectively, it is this piercing hurt to individuals which justifies the call for reform of the at-will doctrine.

There is a logical nicety to the notion that abolition of at-will employment would jeopardize a worker's present "freedom to quit," capacity for "risk diversification," and so on. But that whole argument turns on an erroneous equation of an employee's right to leave with an employer's right to fire. In fact, there is probably no more discredited concept in modern contract law than the unqualified requirement of "mutuality of obligation."[72] Consideration on the part of the employee is the essential element, and for an increasing number of modern courts that is found in her actual rendition of services.[73] Even more important, in the real world of industrial relations, employees

---

Malthus, Marx, and others could only reduce workers' pay to the minimum subsistence level. *See, e.g.*, P. SAMUELSON, ECONOMICS 553 (6th ed. 1965). For a more realistic discussion of the disparity in employer and employee bargaining power, see L. REYNOLDS, S. MASTERS & C. MOSER, LABOR ECONOMICS AND LABOR RELATIONS 7-8 (9th ed. 1986) [hereinafter LABOR ECONOMICS].

70. Epstein, *supra* note 63, at 977.

71. *See, e.g.*, H. BRENNER, ESTIMATING THE SOCIAL COSTS OF NATIONAL ECONOMIC POLICY: IMPLICATIONS FOR MENTAL AND PHYSICAL HEALTH AND CLINICAL AGGRESSION (1976); B. BLUESTONE & B. HARRISON, THE DEINDUSTRIALIZATION OF AMERICA 63-66 (1982), and authorities cited; L. FERMAN & J. GORDUS, THE ECONOMY AND MENTAL HEALTH (1979); L. FERMAN, M. AIKEN & H. SHEPPARD, ECONOMIC FAILURE, ALIENATION, AND EXTREMISM (1968).

72. *See, e.g.*, 1A A. CORBIN, CORBIN ON CONTRACTS §§ 152, 163, 165-67 (1963); Eales v. Tanana Valley Medical-Surgical Group, Inc., 663 P.2d 958, 959-60 (Alaska 1983); Pugh v. See's Candies, Inc., 116 Cal. App. 3d 311, 325-26, 171 Cal. Rptr. 917, 924-25 (1981).

73. *See, e.g.*, 1A A. CORBIN, CORBIN ON CONTRACTS § 163 (1963); *see also* sources cited *supra* note 45.

seldom quit voluntarily.[74] It is they, not the employer, who most need protection. It is thus neither unfair nor contrary to contemporary contract theory to eliminate the employer's power to discharge arbitrarily without eliminating the employee's right to leave.

It is probably true that some costs would be associated with altering the at-will nature of employment contracts. One scholar has suggested a lower wage level would result because of both a decrease in the demand for labor and an increase in the supply.[75] In effect, the employees themselves would have paid at least partially for their greater job security. That is a time-honored tradeoff among unionized workers,[76] however, and should not be considered inappropriate here. It is hard to determine what, if any, would be the net increases in employers' costs in maintaining a for-cause discharge system. But there is evidence they would not be exorbitant. For example, in all the demands by unionized firms for "givebacks" or bargaining concessions during the early 1980s, practically never did employers seek the removal of "just cause" contract clauses, or the grievance and arbitration procedures supporting them.

American business would not lose out in "competitiveness" in international markets by elimination of at-will employment, even though it might lose some degree of flexibility in job arrangements. Protection against unfair discharge is now provided by statute in about sixty countries around the world, including all the Common Market, Sweden and Norway, Japan, Canada, and others in South America, Africa, and Asia.[77] The International Labor Organization recommended in 1963 and again in 1982 that workers not be terminated except for a valid reason.[78] The United States remains the last major industrial democracy that has not heeded the call for unjust dismissal

74. *See, e.g.*, LABOR ECONOMICS, *supra* note 69, at 9 ("most workers regard resort to the market — that is, a change of employers — as a disaster rather than as an opportunity"). *Cf.* Kerr, *The Balkanization of Labor Markets*, in LABOR MOBILITY AND ECONOMIC OPPORTUNITY (E. Bakke ed. 1954), reprinted in L. REYNOLDS ET AL., READINGS IN LABOR ECONOMICS AND LABOR RELATIONS 66, 68 (4th ed. 1986).

75. Harrison, *The "New" Terminable-at-Will Employment Contract: An Interest and Cost Incidence Analysis*, 69 IOWA L. REV. 327 (1984).

76. *See, e.g.*, R. FREEMAN & J. MEDOFF, WHAT DO UNIONS DO? 55-56 (1984); LABOR ECONOMICS, *supra* note 69, at 533.

77. Association of the Bar of the City of New York, Committee on Labor and Employment Law, *At-Will Employment and the Problem of Unjust Dismissal*, 36 THE RECORD 170, 175 (1981).

78. *Id.* at 179-80; *Convention Concerning Termination of Employment at the Initiative of the Employer* (No. 158) INTERNATIONAL LABOUR CONFERENCE AND RECOMMENDATIONS (Supp.) (Sixty-eighth session) (June 22, 1982). It must be noted, however, that foreign legislation is hardly everything that workers might desire. Reinstatement is rare; backpay is usually limited to a brief period; and sometimes a short notice (*e.g.*, 30 days) will suffice. *See, e.g.*, Estreicher, *Unjust Dismissal Laws: Some Cautionary Notes*, 33 AM. J. COMP. L. 310 (1985).

legislation. Furthermore, experience both here and abroad suggests that the prevention of arbitrary treatment of employees may be not only humane but also good business. Marked correlations have been observed between a secure work force and high productivity and quality output.[79]

Under a more rational, systematic method of dealing with improper terminations, many employers would be saved the crushing financial liability incurred by companies that have felt the wrath of aroused juries under our existing, capricious common-law regime. For example, an early study showed that plaintiffs in California won as many as 90 percent of the discharge cases that went to juries, with the average award being $450,000.[80] A more recent California survey by a management attorney revealed relatively little change. Juries returned verdicts for plaintiffs in 78 percent of the cases, averaging a total of $424,527 in general and punitive damages.[81] Single individuals have received jury awards covering actual and punitive damages as high as $20 million, $4.7 million, $3.25 million, $2.57 million, $2 million, $1.5 million, $1.19 million, and $1 million.[82] One could well imagine that eventually an informed employer lobby might conclude that comprehensive just cause legislation, which would exclude jury verdicts and punitive damages, was the preferable solution.

A critical factor in securing legislative relief may be the attitude of organized labor.[83] It is about the only nationwide interest group that might be willing to take the lead in promoting such a cause. A common assumption, however, is that many unions will not favor legislation protecting employees against arbitrary treatment by employers because it will eliminate or detract from one of the unions' prime selling points in their efforts to organize the unorganized. I cannot deny this possibility, but I think it would be as shortsighted as was organized labor's initial hostility toward the Fair Labor Standards Act.[84] First, and not insignificantly, organized labor could profit considerably from refurbishing its image as the champion of the disadvantaged. Second, and perhaps more practically, a universal rule against dismis-

79. Foulkes, *Large Nonunionized Employers*, in U.S. INDUSTRIAL RELATIONS 1950-1980: A CRITICAL ASSESSMENT 129, 134-36, 141-44, 155-56 (1981); R. PASCALE & A. ATHOS, THE ART OF JAPANESE MANAGEMENT 131-57 (1979). *Cf.* Special Task Force, U.S. Dep't of Health, Education & Welfare, WORK IN AMERICA 93-110, 188-201 (1973).

80. Palefsky, *Wrongful Termination Litigation: "Dagwood and Goliath,"* 62 MICH. B.J. 776 (1983).

81. *Discharge Verdicts Average $424,527 in California*, 9 Lab. Rel. Rep., 1 Individual Employment Rts. (BNA) No. 14, at 3 (Mar. 3, 1987).

82. K. Lopatka & J. Martin, *Developments in the Law of Wrongful Discharge*, in ABA NATIONAL INSTITUTE ON LITIGATING WRONGFUL DISCHARGE AND INVASION OF PRIVACY CLAIMS vii, 13-18 (1986).

83. *See supra* note 17 and accompanying text.

84. F. DULLES, LABOR IN AMERICA 283-85 (2d rev. 1960).

sal without cause should actually prove beneficial to unions in their organizing drives. Now, when a union sympathizer is fired in the middle of a campaign, it must be established by a preponderance of the evidence that a motivating factor in the discharge was the exercise of rights protected by the National Labor Relations Act.[85] This is frequently a burden too heavy to bear. With a just cause requirement generally applicable, it would be up to the employer to show that some positive, acceptable basis existed for the discharge. Finally, I believe there is a strong likelihood that just cause standards will act more as a spur than a hindrance to union organizing. The promise of fair treatment will be held out to employees; the promise may remain a tantalizing and unrealized dream, however, unless there is present the means to realize it. Constant, effective representation and advocacy is the surest way to ensure any right. That is a lesson public sector unions have already learned in representing employees in civil service proceedings.

In addition to the possible reservations of organized labor, some neutrals in industrial relations might oppose a statutory just cause requirement for fear that it would erode such worthy values as voluntarism, private initiative, and workplace creativity, and more particularly the collective bargaining process itself. I, too, treasure the unique American institution of union-employer bargaining, but when even so hardheaded an observer as John Dunlop can be found rhapsodizing on its "beauty,"[86] I think we should all be wary about being carried away by the mystique of the process. Collective bargaining, after all, is a means and not an end. The objective is the betterment of the individual working person. When only about a quarter to a third of the labor force is currently afforded protection against unjust discipline, I feel the needs of the great majority outweigh some theoretical risk to traditional bargaining processes. Even then, assuming history is any guide, we underrate the flexibility and resilience of collective bargaining if we believe it cannot adapt to, and indeed exploit, a new legal environment.[87]

IV. LEGISLATIVE PROPOSALS

If employees are to be fully and effectively protected against unjust discipline, new specialized legislation will ultimately be necessary.

85. Miller Elec. Mfg. v. NLRB, 265 F.2d 225 (7th Cir. 1959); NLRB v. West Point Mfg. Co., 245 F.2d 783 (5th Cir. 1957); *cf.* NLRB v. Transportation Management Corp., 462 U.S. 393 (1983).

86. Dunlop, *The Social Utility of Collective Bargaining*, in CHALLENGES TO COLLECTIVE BARGAINING 168, 173 (L. Ulman ed. 1967).

87. Traditionally, labor unions have used statutory minimum standards as a base on which to build greater employee protections. *See generally* Fillion & Trebilcock, *The Duty to Bargain Under ERISA*, 17 WM. & MARY L. REV. 251 (1975).

The judiciary, as we have seen, may be able to respond to extreme cases and to the atypical situations of middle-management personnel. But the courts have no capacity to construct an administrative apparatus for enforcement purposes, and their more formalized processes are not readily accessible to rank-and-file workers. Nor do I see much hope in either the Constitution or existing civil rights legislation. To me the former route seems barred by the courts' increasing reluctance to expand the "state action" concept,[88] and the latter by the need to accord some modicum of respect to the legislative intent to forbid job discrimination only on the specified bases of "race, sex, religion, national origin, age," and the like.[89] It comes down, then, to a matter of further legislation. A federal statute applying uniformly to employers in all sections of the country would probably be the best solution, but it seems unlikely in the near future. State legislation appears more promising, and it offers the compensating advantage of an opportunity for some healthy experimentation with alternative procedures. During the past few years bills have been drafted in such states as California,[90] Michigan,[91] and New Jersey[92] to provide "just cause" protection to unorganized workers. The first comprehensive statute has now been enacted in Montana.[93] In the remainder of this paper I shall consider some of the principal issues almost any statutory proposal will have to confront. Obviously, there will often be substantial values in competing approaches, and more than one choice could be supported. My own suggestions will try to take account of both the ideal and the politically feasible.

A. "Just Cause" Standard

The first question can be disposed of the easiest. The statute should articulate a standard for lawful discharge or discipline in terms of "just cause" or equivalent language, without further definition. Even in Western European countries having nothing like the body of American arbitral precedent interpreting "just cause" requirements, there has apparently been little difficulty in applying broadly phrased statutory criteria. Any effort at specification is bound to risk underinclusiveness. The decisionmakers can be counted on to flesh out "just cause" in the same way as have the arbitrators. Nonetheless, political

88. *See, e.g.*, Moose Lodge No. 107 v. Irvis, 407 U.S. 163 (1972).

89. Civil Rights Act of 1964, 78 Stat. 255 (1964) (codified as amended 42 U.S.C. § 2000e-2 (1982)); Age Discrimination in Employment Act of 1967, 81 Stat. 602 (1967) (codified as amended, 29 U.S.C. § 671 (1982)).

90. Cal. A. B. 3017 (1984); Cal. S. B. 1348 (1985); Cal. A. B. 1400 (1985).

91. Mich. H.B. 5155 (1983).

92. N.J.A.B. 1832 (1980).

93. Mont. H.B. 241 (now codified at MONT. CODE ANN. § 39-2-901 (1987)).

expediency might call for restricting statutory protection, at least as a first step, to an enumerated list of the most common abuses.

The statute should probably remain discreetly silent on such items as the burden and the quantum of proof. The differing standards that have been applied by public tribunals in job discrimination cases and by private arbitrators under collective bargaining agreements will tug in opposite directions. Concrete cases would appear to provide the best vehicle for dealing with such issues.

B. Protected Classes of Employees

It is hard to argue in principle that any employee should be subject to an unjust termination. Still, when one reaches the presidency of a Fortune 500 company, it does not seem wholly unfitting that one accepts the risk of being confronted one day by an announcement from the chairman of the board, "I'm getting rid of you because I don't like you." Beyond that, there are practical reasons for excluding certain classes of employees from the protection of a statute.

1. *Managers and Supervisors*

In the higher ranges of management, one official's evaluation of another's business judgment may become so intertwined with questions of fair personal treatment that the two cannot be separated. That does not reach down to the level of shop foremen and other supervisors, who are excluded from the organizational protections of the National Labor Relations Act because they are management's immediate representatives to rank-and-file employees and any union that may be bargaining for them. This concern about potential conflicts of interest plainly does not apply to "just cause" legislation, and supervisors as such should be covered. More troubling is the position of middle-management personnel, who are among the most exposed and vulnerable. Unfortunately, our lexicon of industrial relations usage does not contain a convenient term distinguishing middle management, who we should protect, from higher management, who we may wish to exclude. A sensible solution is to except persons entitled to a pension above a certain amount, or persons with a fixed-term contract of two years or more.

2. *Probationary Employees*

There is almost a presumption that an employer will not dismiss an employee unfairly in the early days of employment—otherwise, why hire? Moreover, the first few weeks or months of employment enable the employer to size up the new recruit and assess his or her performance on the job. At the same time, it is not until an employee has been part of an establishment for some measurable time that he can reasonably feel he possesses anything like an equity in his position. For all these reasons it is generally recognized in collective bargaining agreements and elsewhere that so-called "probationary" employees are not entitled to just cause protections. One expert would make the probation period one year;[94] Summers and the Michigan and New Jersey bills opt for six months.[95] The latter seems adequate to me. But this is an appropriate area of compromise, and the California bill specifies two years.[96]

3. *Small Employers*

Theoretically, job protections should not depend on the size of the employer. Indeed, arbitrariness and individual spite may well be more common on the part of an idiosyncratic sole entrepreneur than on the part of a large, structured corporation. Nonetheless, we feel uneasy about intruding too hastily into the sometimes intensely personal relationships of small, intimate establishments. There is also concern about dissipating our resources in an endless pursuit of minor culprits instead of concentrating on the major malefactors. A suitable dividing line, at least at the outset, would seem to be employers having between ten[97] and fifteen[98] or more employees.

4. *Public Employees*

Public employees generally have constitutional guarantees against the deprivation of their "vested" job interest without due process. Approximately half also have more specific civil service or tenure protections against unjust dismissal. At least the latter group, as the California and Michigan bills propose, could properly be excluded from any new statutory procedures. In addition, since American employment legislation has traditionally differentiated between the public and private sectors, it may be politically advantageous to maintain that distinction by limiting any new protections to private industry.

5. *Organized Employees*

Most of the arguments in favor of just cause requirements have been phrased in terms of protecting "unorganized" workers. The Michigan bill expressly excludes employees "protected" by a union

94. Howlett, *Due Process for Nonunionized Employees: A Practical Proposal*, in PROCEEDINGS OF THE THIRTY-SECOND ANNUAL MEETING, INDUSTRIAL RELATIONS RESEARCH ASSOCIATION 164, 167 (B. Dennis, ed. 1980).
95. Summers, *supra* note 2, at 525; Mich. H.B. 5155, § 2(c) (1983); N.J.A.B. 1832, § 1 (1980).
96. Cal. A.B. 3017, § 2880(b) (1984).
97. Summers, *supra* note 2, at 526; Mich. H.B. 5155, § 2(d) (1983).
98. Cal. A.B. 3017, § 2880(a) (1984).

contract.[99] The New Jersey bill more specifically limits protection to an employee "without the benefit of . . . a collective bargaining agreement that contains a grievance procedure covering these matters which terminates in binding arbitration."[100] The California bill takes the tack of requiring prior exhaustion of an employer's internal procedures that "have been devised with substantial employee involvement."[101] Montana's new law does not apply to employees covered by written collective bargaining agreements or written contracts for a set term.[102]

There is plainly the possibility of a federal preemption problem in covering unionized workers, as any state statute would necessarily affect collective bargaining and the enforcement of union contracts under the National Labor Relations Act and other federal labor laws. Arguably, there are several applicable strands of Supreme Court doctrine, pointing in somewhat different directions. First, state law claims are preempted if they are "substantially dependent" upon an analysis of the terms of a collective agreement.[103] On the other hand, "minimum state labor standards" may be imposed on union and nonunion employees alike.[104] Perhaps most pertinent, the Supreme Court has generally taken a liberal attitude toward state regulation in the areas of employment discrimination,[105] unemployment compenstaion,[106] and similar welfare matters of a compelling local concern.[107] The federal courts of appeals are divided. When an employee covered by a union contract is fired for exercising such a traditional state right as filing a workers' compensation claim, there is some tendency to find no preemption.[108] But claims of retaliatory discharges for filing safety and health complaints have led to divergent preemption rulings within the same federal circuit.[109]

---

99. Mich. H.B. 5155, § 2(c) (1983).
100. N.J.A.B. 1832, § 1 (1980).
101. Cal. A.B. 3017, § 2888(a) (1984).
102. Mont. H.B. 241, as enacted, § 7(2) (1987); MONT. CODE ANN. § 39-2-912(2) (1987).
103. Allis-Chalmers Corp. v. Lueck, 471 U.S. 202, 220 (1985); IBEW v. Heckler, 107 S. Ct. 2167, 2168 (1987).
104. Metropolitan Life Ins. Co. v. Massachusetts, 471 U.S. 724 (1985); *cf.* Fort Halifax Packing Co. v. Coyne, 107 S. Ct. 2211 (1987).
105. *E.g.*, Colorado Anti-Discrimination Comm'n v. Continental Air Lines, 372 U.S. 714 (1963).
106. New York Tel. Co. v. New York State Dept. of Labor, 440 U.S. 519 (1979).
107. *See, e.g.*, Teamsters Local 24 v. Oliver, 358 U.S. 283, 297 (1959).
108. *Compare* Peabody Galion v. A. V. Dollar, 666 F.2d 1309 (9th Cir. 1981), Herring v. Prince Macaroni, Inc., 799 F.2d 120 (3d Cir. 1986) *and* Baldracchi v. Pratt & Whitney Div., 814 F.2d 102 (2d Cir. 1987) (no preemption) *with* Johnson v. Hussman Corp., 805 F.2d 795 (8th Cir. 1986) *and* Lingle v. Norge Div. of Magic Chef, 2 I.E.R. (BNA) 354 (7th Cir. 1987) (preemption).
109. *Compare* Olguin v. Inspiration Consol. Copper Co., 740 F.2d 1468, 1475 (9th Cir. 1984) (preemption when employee filed complaint with Federal Mine Safety and Health Administration) *with* Garibaldi v. Lucky Food Stores, 726 F.2d 1367 (9th

At the very least I think a state would have sufficiently deep-rooted local interests to justify protecting employees within its borders from being importuned to commit a crime or violate some other basic public policy. Furthermore, by a modest expansion of either the "minimum labor standards" or "employment discrimination" exceptions to the preemption doctrine, it seems that a state might be able to prohibit all arbitrary, abusive, or unjust dismissals, except those based on union activity.[110] These lines are not all that easy to draw, however, and it is understandable that several bills and the new Montana law have opted not to cover employees subject to a collective agreement.[111]

Nevertheless, except for the possible conservation of limited administrative resources, I see no principled grounds for treating organized employees differently from the unorganized with respect to basic statutory protections. If we conclude that workers in general are entitled to invoke a just cause standard, the same public policy should apply to all, regardless of the existence of parallel protections in a collective bargaining agreement. There is federal precedent for such an approach in both the NLRA and civil rights legislation, which clearly extend to workers who are also covered by antidiscrimination guarantees in their union contracts.[112] Furthermore, one might ask why the state should shield nonunion workers gratis, and force unionized employees to expend bargaining chips to obtain the same safeguards.

For me the difficult question is the proper relationship of statutory and contractual rights and remedies, when both are available. Summers would give the contract priority to the extent of requiring a disciplined employee to exhaust the contractual grievance procedure, and

---

Cir. 1984), *cert. denied*, 471 U.S. 1099 (1985) (no preemption when employee notified local health officials about spoiled milk). *Cf.* De Soto v. Yellow Freight Systems, 811 F.2d 1333 (9th Cir. 1987) (preemption when employee refused to drive truck he mistakenly believed was not legally licensed or registered). *But cf.* Keehr v. Consolidated Freightways, 125 L.R.R.M. (BNA) 3235 (7th Cir. 1987) (no preemption of state tort claims of intentional infliction of emotional distress and invasion of privacy when supervisor adverted to supposed immoral sexual behavior of employee's wife). *See generally* Note, *NLRA Preemption of State Law Actions for Wrongful Discharge in Violation of Public Policy*, 19 U. MICH. J.L. REF. 441 (1986).

110. Viestenz v. Fleming Cos., 681 F.2d 699 (10th Cir. 1982), *cert. denied*, 459 U.S. 972 (1982). Of course, if a collective bargaining agreement is present containing a blanket prohibition of unjust discharge, there is not only the possibility of unfair labor practice preemption under the NLRA; there is also the possibility of federal contract law preemption under § 301 of the Labor Management Relations Act, 29 U.S.C. § 185 (1982). Teamsters Local No. 174 v. Lucas Flour Co., 369 U.S. 95 (1962).

111. *See supra* notes 99-102 and accompanying text.

112. General Am. Transp. Corp., 228 N.L.R.B. 808 (1977); Alexander v. Gardner-Denver Co., 415 U.S. 36 (1974).

would make any arbitral award that is obtained final and binding.[113] But he would not let the union enter a binding settlement with the employer, as it now may do under *Vaca v. Sipes*,[114] subject only to its duty of fair representation toward the employee. Instead, if the union declines to arbitrate under the contract, Summers would permit the employee to proceed on his or her own to the neutral tribunal provided by the state. He believes only "the most stubborn individual" would persist in the face of the union's settlement. From my experience with the United Automobile Workers' Public Review Board, I suspect there are more such "stubborn individuals" around than Summers imagines. My own inclination would be to put more trust in the flexibility of collective bargaining, and to leave some of these questions for future resolution amidst the counterpoint of particular facts, negotiated tradeoffs, dollar costs, and the union's overriding duty of fair representation. I see no reason here to engage in the same close scrutiny of union, employer, or arbitrator conduct that may be appropriate in dealing with such sensitive and divisive issues as race and sex discrimination.[115] Having said all that, I realize there may be much practical wisdom in the decision to finesse all these complications by excluding unionized workers from the new statutory protections.

C. Discipline Covered

Advocates of employee protection have usually talked about protection against discharge, the so-called economic "capital punishment" of industrial relations. That is dramatic. But an extended suspension, a demotion, a denied promotion, or an onerous job assignment, while not as blatant, can be almost as distressful. Such job actions should be regarded as the functional equivalent of discharge. The Michigan bill may be politically astute in the way it puts the matter, in effect creating a "constructive discharge," though it requires the employee to engage in a variation on Russian roulette: "Discharge includes a resignation or quit that results from an improper or unreasonable action or inaction of the employer."[116] The new Montana law explicitly reaches "constructive discharge," defined as a "voluntary termination of employment by an employee because of a situation created by an act or omission of the employer . . . so intolerable that voluntary termination is the only reasonable alternative."[117]

European experience indicates that protections against unjust discipline will inevitably force inquiries into an employer's handling of "redundancies," that is, layoffs or other employee reassignments to

113. Summers, *supra* note 2, at 528.
114. 386 U.S. 171 (1967).
115. General Am. Transp. Corp., 228 N.L.R.B. 808 (1977).
116. Mich. H.B. 5155, § 2(b) (1983).
117. Mont. H.B. 241, as enacted, § 3(1) (1987); MONT. CODE ANN. § 39-2-903(1) (1987).

meet economic downturns or reduced production demands. Otherwise, there is simply too much opportunity to disguise unfair treatment of an individual employee as part of an employer's overall reaction to business oscillations. This hardly imposes an oppressive burden on employers. All they need do is establish almost any sort of rational, verifiable criterion — seniority, skills, past productivity, etc. — as the basis for their job determinations, and they are practically impervious to challenge.

D. Adjudicators and Procedure

A new statute could pick and choose across a broad spectrum of possible enforcement devices. Most persons would probably rule out the courts as too formal, too costly, and already overloaded. Existing administrative agencies, either the labor relations boards or the civil rights commissions, are more likely candidates. Robert Howlett, the former chairman of the Michigan Employment Relations Commission, favors placing administration in the hands of state labor departments.[118] He feels the hearing officers of the conventional labor relations agencies are more attuned to organizational than to individual concerns. He also believes the whole proposal would face less political opposition if it were divorced from the usual union-employer regulatory context. My view is that a question like this is best answered by reference to the governmental structure and industrial relations climate of each state.

More significant, I think, than the locus of administration is whether we follow the hearing officer-agency model or the arbitration model. I hope I am not merely exhibiting crass professional bias when I join the overwhelming majority of my fellow arbitrators who have addressed the issue in concluding that arbitration is the superior procedure for "just cause" determinations. The California and Michigan bills provide for arbitration, and the Montana statute makes it a preferred option.[119] Adopting the arbitration format would immediately make available the vast body of arbitral precedent concerning substance and procedure that has been developed in countless decisions over the years. It would permit the use of an established nucleus of experienced arbitrators, and of the growing number of young, able aspirants who are caught in the vicious circle of being denied experience because they have no experience. It would facilitate maximum flexibility, at least until more is learned about future caseloads, because there would be no need to engage a large permanent staff at the outset. It would leave open the option, however, of utilizing a mix, as

118. Howlett, *supra* note 94, at 167.

119. Cal. A.B. 3017, § 2282 (1984); Mich. H.B. 5155, § 6 (1983); Mont. H.B. 241, as enacted, § 9 (1987); MONT. CODE ANN. § 39-2-914 (1987).

New York has done, of "staff" arbitrators and of free-lancers drawn from a panel for ad hoc assignments. The relative informality and speed of arbitration — though both those qualities are now often much eroded — should also appeal to rank-and-file employees. Finally, just cause rulings do not call for the minute technical expertise that may be essential in a permanent hearing officer specializing in unemployment compensation or Social Security claims.

Although arbitration is the customary capstone of collectively bargained grievance procedures, only a small percentage of the grievances that are filed reach arbitration. Arguably the whole system would collapse if all claims went to the final step. Most are settled or dropped along the way. It would seem highly desireable to have some comparable sieve in the statutory procedure. The most obvious would be a preliminary mediation stage of minimum duration, and in California and Michigan bills so provide.[120] Howlett would have an official in the administering agency make a "reasonable cause" determination before a case could go to arbitration.[121] I agree such a requirement makes sense, especially if the state is to bear the major share of the cost of the proceedings.

Another advantage of the arbitral model is that the award is final and binding, without the need for agency adoption or review as in the case of the hearing officer's report or decision. Ordinarily, of course, a private arbitration award will not be set aside by the courts unless the arbitrator exceeded his jurisdiction or the award was obtained by fraud, collusion, or similar means. That ought to be the standard here. Since a statutory arbitrator is imposed on the parties, however, there may be considerable pressure to adopt the stiffer "substantial evidence" standard. Moreover, some state constitutions require that rulings by public agencies and officials be supported by "competent, material, and substantial evidence on the record considered as a whole."[122] If "substantial evidence" is the standard, one way or another, it raises the grim prospect of verbatim transcripts, with all the attendant delays and added costs. Although some persons seem to eye a tape recorder in a hearing room the way certain people are said to view cameras — as if cameras were out to capture their souls — the sponsor of the Michigan bill was persuaded to accept this cheap, handy device as a sufficient means of documentation,[123] and I should hope others would follow suit.

120. Cal. A.B. 3017, § 2881(d) (1984); Mich. H.B. 5155, § 5 (1983).
121. Howlett, *supra* note 94, at 169.
122. *E.g.*, MICH. CONST. art. VI, § 28.
123. Mich. A.B. 5155, § 9(5) (1983).

E. Remedies

Arbitrators under labor contracts have demonstrated both ingenuity and common sense in devising a range of remedies to counter unjust discharge and other discipline. They have, for instance, evolved the cardinal principle that the punishment must fit not only the offense but also the offender. What is suitable for the short-term employee of spotty record is not right for the long-time veteran of irreproachable deportment. Presumably statutory arbitrators will temper their judgments accordingly.

More specifically, remedies for unjust discharge in the United States have traditionally included reinstatement with or without back pay. In Europe reinstatement is the exception. Apparently it is felt that the lone, unwanted employee can seldom regain a comfortable position in his old workplace, and it is better to award him severance pay and let him go. A number of American experts also seem to believe that reinstatement is unfeasible without the presence of a labor union to support the restored employee. I think awarding severance pay in lieu of reinstatement is an option the arbitrator should have. But I see no reason for precluding reinstatement out of an exaggerated regard for the employee's psychic well-being. American workers are probably more transient than their European counterparts, and they are used to handling unfamiliar job situations. A reinstatement order also gives them extra bargaining leverage in working out any future adjustment with the employer. I would grant reinstatement when it seemed appropriate, and let the employee decide what use to make of the award.

The California bill offers a rather elaborate set of alternative remedies for the arbitrator, including reinstatement, backpay with interest, income and related losses for two years if reinstatement is not appropriate, and attorneys' fees and costs to the prevailing party.[124] The Michigan bill is somewhat similar. It includes a "severance payment" but not attorneys' fees.[125] The new Montana legislation expressly preempts common law actions but, somewhat surprisingly, retains punitive damages for "actual" fraud or malice, in addition to the more common lost wages and benefits, with interest, here limited to a period of four years from the date of discharge.[126] Interim earnings are to be deducted. Reinstatement is not mentioned.

124. Cal. A.B. 3017, § 2884 (1984).

125. Mich. H.B. 5155, § 10(2) (1983). Future versions of the bill are expected to authorize attorneys' fees.

126. Mont. H.B. 241, as enacted, §§ 5, 8 (1987); MONT. CODE ANN. §§ 39-2-905, 39-2-913 (1987).

F. Costs

The arbitrator's fee and expenses under collectively bargained arrangements are normally shared, 50-50, by the parties, although occasionally the loser pays all. Each side bears its own representation costs, if any. Some years ago my former colleague, Judge Harry Edwards, calculated that the typical one-day hearing costs a union $2200;[127] that might be a prohibitive figure for many individual employees, especially those out of work. Clyde Summers declares that "in principle" under the statutory scheme the state should cover administrative costs and the arbitrator's fee, just as it bears the expense of courts and judges.[128] He would allow a nominal filing fee, perhaps $100, to discourage frivolous claims. Howlett would require such a fee at the point a case is referred to arbitration by a screening officer.[129]

In theory one cannot fault that approach. But there may be practical problems in implementing it. There is now a strong tradition in the collective bargaining sector that the parties shall pay the arbitrator. Although a few states, like Connecticut and Wisconsin,[130] provide arbitrators at public expense, the trend has been, in a kind of reversal of Gresham's Law, for privately paid arbitrators to replace publicly paid arbitrators. Thus, prior to the Taft-Hartley Act, the old United States Conciliation Service furnished free arbitration through staff personnel. Now, of course, the FMCS simply offers parties the names of private arbitrators. New York continued to provide a choice of staff arbitrators paid by the state and "panel" arbitrators whom the parties had to pay.[131] But Robben Fleming reported that "the amount of free service is declining by deliberate choice of the state agency."[132] The list of private arbitrators was publicized and the availability of staff personnel was not. Moreover, in a period of severe financial stringency for many state governments, the prospect of one more new and perhaps substantial expense is sure to generate even further oppostion to a proposal that is not going to elicit universal acclaim in any event. The California and Michigan bills heeded the counsel of prudence and provided that the employer and the employee shall bear "equally" the cost of the arbitrator.[133] Under the Montana law, a discharged employee who prevails in the arbitration is entitled to have the employer

---

127. Edwards, *Problems Facing Arbitration Process*, in Lab. Rel. Y.B. — 1977 (BNA) 206 (1978).

128. Summers, *supra* note 2, at 524.

129. Howlett, *supra* note 94, at 169. The California bill requires the employee and the employer each to file $500 with the state mediation service "for the costs of resolving the dispute." Cal. A.B. 3017, § 2881(c) (1984).

130. Summers, *supra* note 2, at 524; Mueller, *The Role of the Wisconsin Employment Board Arbitrator*, 1963 WIS. L. REV. 47, 49.

131. Summers, *supra* note 2, at 522.

132. R. FLEMING, THE LABOR ARBITRATION PROCESS 51 (1965).

133. Cal. A.B. 3017, § 2888(b)(3) (1984); Mich. H.B. 5155, § 7 (1983).

pay "the arbitrator's fees and all costs of arbitration."[134] Either party whose valid offer of arbitration is rejected will be awarded reasonable attorneys' fees if he prevails in the ensuing court action.[135]

If the state pays the bill, the state will almost certainly, like Connecticut, set the rate.[136] That may be fine for fledgling arbitrators, but it may not be adequate for obtaining the services of highly qualified, experienced professionals. In my opinion, it would probably be best for the statute to leave open the issue of amount, letting the parties themselves determine the level of quality for which they are willing to pay.

V. CONCLUSION

Unjust dismissal makes no sense ethically, little sense legally, and at best marginal sense in industrial relations and economic terms. Its elimination is fast becoming a moral and historical imperative. This is not "uncharted territory,"[137] as some timid courts have exclaimed. This is terrain that has been carefully mapped in thousands of arbitration decisions since the Second World War. That body of arbitral precedent and a large and potentially much larger body of arbitrators stand ready to be drawn upon in the forging of a new set of statutory guarantees.

The debates that remain over this detail or that detail of proposed legislation should not obscure one central fact. In this the twentieth anniversary year of Blades's truly seminal piece,[138] an academic consensus has blossomed, a judicial consensus has taken root, and the makings of a legislative consensus have been planted. Whether it will be in the coming decade or the following, we shall shortly see on the legal landscape only the decaying husk of the doctrine of employment at will. The far more wholesome theory of just cause will have taken its place.

134. Mont. H.B. 241, as enacted, § 9(5) (1987); MONT. CODE ANN. § 39-2-914(5) (1978).
135. MONT. H.B. 241, as enacted § 9(4) (1987); MONT. CODE ANN. § 39-2-914(4) (1987).
136. Summers, *supra* note 2, at 522.
137. Geary v. United States Steel Corp., 456 Pa. 171, 174, 319 A.2d 174, 175 (1974).
138. See *supra* note 1.

Part II
Workplace Democracy Initiatives

[5]

ARTICLES

WORKPLACE DEMOCRACY & MARKET RECONSTRUCTION: AN AGENDA FOR LEGAL REFORM*

*Karl E. Klare***

** Professor of Law, Northeastern University. This is a revised and annotated text of a paper presented to the centennial Symposium on "Cycles In Labor Law and Industrial Relations: Projections Into the Next Century," convened April 14 and 15, 1988, by The Columbus School of Law, The Catholic University of America. In this Article, I intend to continue a discussion commenced in my paper entitled: *The Labor-Management Cooperation Debate: A Workplace Democracy Perspective*, 23 HARV. C.R.-C.L. L. REV. 39 (1988). I am deeply grateful to Dean Ralph J. Rohner and his colleagues for the invitation to speculate about and present my views on the Symposium topic. I am grateful to Hugh Collins, Duncan Kennedy, and Michael J. Trebilcock for critically reviewing the manuscript, and to Roger C. Hartley for invaluable advice and encouragement.

Whether through an excess of caution or wishful thinking, it was still possible as recently as a few years ago to question whether American industrial relations and labor law had entered a period of profound transformation. Lingering skepticism has now receded in the face of dramatic changes in employer/employee relations, the siege of the unionized sector, and the crisis of labor law.

This is a time of great risks to our fragile institutions of workplace democracy. The economic, political, and legal climates seem distinctly inhospitable to the values and assumptions that have been embodied in labor law since the New Deal and that have informed the prevailing legal conception of industrial democracy. Yet it would be a mistake for friends of employee rights and of collective bargaining to dig in behind defensive barricades. The current period of transformation harbors dangers but also great potential for expanding and enriching workplace democracy. Employee rights advocates should defend and protect the enduring contributions of collective bargaining and of the labor movement's best traditions of egalitarianism and solidarity. Yet simultaneously we must be ready to rethink old assumptions and to confront our very real problems with new ideas and approaches. Above all, we need to enlarge our conceptions of workplace democracy. We must be ready to experiment and to take conceptual and practical risks to seize the opportunities and potential of the times. In considering this challenge, I have drawn inspiration from many colleagues in the labor law community and in the labor movement itself who are searching so imaginatively for new concepts and approaches. My hope here is to make some small contribution to advancing the discussion.

In a symposium subtitled "Projections Into the Next Century," one assumes contributors may take certain liberties in formulating their proposals; specifically, that they may look beyond the constraints of practical politics and sketch out a vision of desirable, if not necessarily presently enactable, paths of development. As will be obvious, I have fully availed myself of this prerogative. I have not attempted to predict what labor law *will* look like two or three decades hence. Rather, my question is, what *should* labor law look like twenty or thirty years from now? What should be its goals and mission over that time span?

What I am proposing is an agenda for a generation, not for next year's legislative session. I assumed it would be most useful here to attempt to generate reflection and debate, and consequently I have drawn my projection in broad strokes. Whether the exercise is valuable depends on how well it serves to clarify issues of principle and direction in legal and industrial relations theory, and whether such a general projection assists us in identifying good questions about institutional strategies worth pursuing in greater detail.

Part I of this Article proposes that expansion of democracy in work should be the guiding principle of our labor laws and social policy. I defend that view by reference both to the philosophical ideal of self-determination and to the pragmatic business considerations stemming from changes occurring in our economic and technological environment. Part II discusses the relationship between markets and planning in the employment context and provides the foundations for a "market reconstruction" approach to labor law reform. This section also anticipates and rebuts several likely objections to the approach, notably that expansive market reconstruction violates contractual liberty and is inefficient. Part III surveys several areas of labor law in urgent need of reform. It outlines a series of examples of reforms suggested by the market reconstruction approach, in light of the proposed democracy-enhancing imperative.

I. A Mission For Labor Law: Enhancing Workplace Democracy

A. *Basic Premises*

Several goals are customarily ascribed to labor law, chief among which is the maintenance of industrial peace. Equalizing bargaining power is also mentioned, and occasionally even the concept of industrial democracy is cited, usually in vague and general terms. My central thesis is this: as our vision projects into the twenty-first century, *the preeminent role and guiding principle of labor law should be to expand and enhance democracy at every level of the experience and organization of work.* This democratization should extend both to the upper tiers of the firm's governance and strategic decisionmaking processes, and to the mundane levels of the organization and structure of day-to-day operations and decisionmaking. Democratization is also needed with respect to the institutional and social mechanisms that control entry into and exit from paid employment. This "entry/exit" aspect of workplace democratization must be concerned with equalizing access to employment opportunities in the most desirable jobs, and with developing policies on long-term leave and day-to-day scheduling that will permit relatively equal labor force participation by employees who desire off-the-job training or who have parenting or other caretaking responsibilities.

In this Article, I sketch some future institutional and legal changes suggested by the democracy-enhancing perspective. One point seems fundamental. Collective bargaining plays a central role in my projected vision of a desirable labor law framework for the next generation. Regrettably, this is not equally obvious to all other observers, so I will briefly cite some of the primary reasons why an adherent of a democracy-enhancing perspective on labor law reform would consider collective bargaining to be an essential component.[1]

At least so long as massive inequalities of power in the workplace exist, employees will have a need for autonomous organization to aggregate their interests and voices, and to identify and articulate their collective needs independent of employer domination. Autonomous organization is needed to maximize employees' collective strength, and to allow pursuit of independent, concerted action to protect their interests. In addition, collective bargaining promotes employee autonomy and participation, and, hence, self-determination, because of its unique capacity, when functioning well, for flexible adaptation to local conditions and therefore for decentralized, participatory problem solving. Finally, unions, as institutions of working people, can contribute to civic and political democracy. This is particularly so in a political system like ours, which lacks an established social democratic tradition and major labor or social democratic parties. For these and other reasons, it is unfortunate that there is at present no consensus in the United States on the enduring value and potential of collective bargaining to democratic life.

Having said this, however, I believe that any program for labor law reform projecting into the next century must come to terms with the fact that the historic project of attaining industrial democracy has been at most only partially fulfilled. Without doubting the profound contributions of New Deal labor law, it is fair to say that the process of democratizing work remains uncompleted. That unionization covers a small and shrinking portion of the workforce is only one reason why the agenda remains unfinished. An equally fundamental problem is that all along our collective bargaining and labor standards law remained only partially and ambivalently committed to the democratization of work and of labor markets. The New Deal system that has framed industrial relations for much of the postwar era takes for granted management control over the strategic level of business decision-

1. A "critical" school of labor law scholarship has emerged in the past decade that has criticized numerous aspects of the prevailing system of collective bargaining law in the United States and called for greater democratization of labor law. To my knowledge, however, virtually every one of the authors associated with the critical school remains committed to the basic principles of collective bargaining and credits collective bargaining's contributions to workplace democracy. Many practice labor law on the union side or with the National Labor Relations Board (NLRB) or did so before entering law teaching. Many of the academic critics continue to assist organizing campaigns or other labor movement projects and to perform pro bono legal work for unions or in the area of union democracy.

making.[2] It accepts that work must be organized on a hierarchical and authoritarian basis.[3] It made a significant but inherently limited effort to reconstruct labor markets.[4]

In the next cycle of labor law reform, the agenda inaugurated by the Wagner Act[5] must be brought to completion. Henceforth, public policy should no longer remain indifferent to the hierarchical governance structures found in most firms. Nor should law be indifferent to, much less embrace, the hierarchical command structure of work operations, or occupational segregation along gender, race, and class lines. Nor should law retain its abstentionist posture toward the substantive results of collective bargaining. Labor law should be framed and administered with a commitment to democratizing decisionmaking in the workplace and to redistributing power in labor markets in favor of employees, both in the collective bargaining setting and in the unorganized sector. Law should steadily raise the social minimum wage and benefits package so as to mitigate the discriminatory effects of labor market segmentation.

My projection calls for large changes in the role and function of labor unions. I foresee a more politicized, more European style[6] labor policy and labor movement emerging in the "next cycle" of American industrial relations. Unions would likely experiment with new structures of industrial democracy and new forms of shopfloor organization. They would likely seek to accomplish relatively more of their goals in the political as distinct from the collective bargaining arena.[7] Unions would seek, more than ever before,

---

2. *See* T. KOCHAN, H. KATZ, & R. MCKERSIE, THE TRANSFORMATION OF AMERICAN INDUSTRIAL RELATIONS 27-28 (1986).

3. *See, e.g.*, Feller, *A General Theory of the Collective Bargaining Agreement*, 61 CALIF. L. REV. 663 (1973)[hereinafter Feller, *General Theory*]; *see id.* at 722 ("[t]he industrial enterprise is, and must be, bureaucratically organized")(note deleted); *see also id.* at 737 ("[i]mplicit in these [basic] rules [under collective bargaining agreements] is the essential characteristic of the industrial agreement: an acceptance of the authoritarian nature of the employment relationship").

4. *See infra* text accompanying notes 89-94.

5. National Labor Relations (Wagner) Act, ch. 372, 49 Stat. 449 (1935) (codified as amended at 29 U.S.C. §§ 151-69 (1982 & Supp. II 1984))[hereinafter NLRA].

6. In recently announcing that he would permit the Worker Adjustment & Retraining Notification Act, Pub. L. No. 100-379, 102 Stat. 890 (1988) (to be codified at 29 U.S.C. §§ 2101-2109), to become law without his signature, President Ronald Reagan attacked the bill as an unfortunate step "down the road of European labor policy." 24 WEEKLY COMP. PRES. DOCS. 990 (Aug. 2, 1988). Would that it were true.

7. This, and numerous other themes explored herein, *see e.g.*, *infra* text accompanying note 95, were discussed some years ago in a series of prescient articles by Alan Hyde, to whom I am very much indebted. *See* Hyde, *Beyond Collective Bargaining: The Politicization of Labor Relations Under Government Contract*, 1982 WIS. L. REV. 1; Hyde, *Economic Labor Law v. Political Labor Relations: Dilemmas For Liberal Legalism*, 60 TEX. L. REV. 1 (1981).

to champion the interests of nonunion employees and unpaid workers[8] by leading a society-wide political effort to raise the socially acceptable wage and benefit floor.

No doubt these new union roles and institutional structures would require alterations of or departures from established collective bargaining norms and practices. My proposals may appear to conflict with the old and venerable tenet of private ordering or the "autonomy" of collective bargaining. One of my goals here is to explore the theoretical foundations of the traditional commitment to the autonomy of collective bargaining and, I hope, to show that expansive legal intervention aimed at democratically reconstructing labor markets poses no threat to collective bargaining. Indeed, the proposed law reform agenda will ultimately enhance the virtues of collective bargaining.

In any case, organized labor has no choice but to achieve some such fundamental reorientation. Gallons of ink have been spilled demonstrating that the unique institutional structures of American labor relations and labor law follow from and synchronize with the equally unique features of American social history and political culture, particularly, the special traditions and aspirations of the American labor movement.[9] There is some force in these arguments, but times are changing. We now have an economy steadily more exposed to a highly integrated and competitive world market. Perhaps the powerful economic and political pressures that have eroded organized labor's strength in recent years will induce a new openness to ideas and methods that have not commanded support in the past. For collective bargaining to be revitalized, and for unions to recapture the initiative, the labor movement must reconceive its goals and purposes. To my mind, its best hope is to link the interests of organized, unorganized, and unpaid workers in a new vision of and program for democratizing and enhancing the quality of workplace life and the connections between employment and other central aspects of human experience. While I stake my case on the independent desirability of the changes proposed, I also believe that some form of major transformation in our conception of industrial democracy is essential to the future prospects of the labor movement. Whether it takes the form suggested here or

8. The working time of millions of Americans, predominantly women, is occupied with unwaged labor such as homemaking and caregiving.

9. In sharp contrast to the apologetic character of much of the American exceptionalism literature, Joel Rogers' account argues that the distinctive institutional structures of American industrial relations have "codified and furthered the weakness of American labor" by "institutionalizing a socially perverse set of incentives and rewards," a consequence of which is that "unions rationally adopt highly particularistic bargaining strategies." Rogers, *Divide and Conquer: Further Reflections On the Distinctive Character of American Labor Laws* (to be published in 1988 WIS. L. REV.).

another, without such a metamorphosis, collective bargaining may not survive into the next century as a significant institution in the American workplace and in political life.

Before elaborating and defending my thesis that all labor law should be democracy-enhancing, I should state the premises which underlie it. My elevation of workplace democracy over competing values is grounded in certain basic normative commitments. I view democracy-enhancing labor law as right because democracy is right. As I have argued elsewhere, however, advocates of employee rights can ill-afford to ignore questions of productivity and efficiency.[10] Efficiency is simply too important a matter to be left to management. My commitment to a democracy-enhancing perspective on labor law is therefore grounded secondarily in a certain understanding of America's economic woes and future. Democracy is not only desirable for its own sake. It also makes good business sense.

B. Values Informing the Workplace Democracy Approach

Fundamentally, my approach to labor law is grounded in a set of philosophical commitments. The motivating ideal is *self-determination* or *self-realization*, by which I mean the full and free development by each person of his or her own powers and abilities.[11] Of course, no one can develop all of their potential capacities in one lifetime. The thought is that we should each be free over the course of our lives to make meaningful self-developmental *choices*.

Self-realization stresses individual autonomy, but it is not an individualistic ideal. For reasons amply recounted both in classical and contemporary social theory, individual autonomy assumes, and can only meaningfully occur in, a context of community, that is, in the context of democratic relations with others. This is both an ontological and practically grounded premise. The individual is partially constituted by his or her relationships with others, and moreover, human fulfillment requires a developmentally oriented social context. Free development of the individual assumes that we are not only permitted to make choices but are so situated in terms of the basic necessities of life that our choices are meaningful. This requires a democratic and egalitarian social organization.

Implicit in the self-realization ideal is that the human species has the capacity and the vocation for self-determination. The aspiration of a demo-

10. *See* Klare, *The Labor-Management Cooperation Debate: A Workplace Democracy Perspective*, 23 HARV. C.R.-C.L. L. REV. 39, 47-50, 78-81 (1988).

11. *See* Elster, *Self-Realization in Work & Politics: The Marxist Conception of the Good Life*, 3 SOC. PHIL. & POLICY 97 (1986).

cratic culture should be to awaken and nurture in all people their capacities for self-realization and self-governance. The aspiration of such a culture should be to democratize the entire existential space of the world. It follows that all spheres of social life, and specifically for purposes of this Article, the paid workplace, ought to be organized so as to enhance human self-realization. To the extent possible, work itself, the processes for governing work, and avenues of access to paid employment opportunities should all be structured to provide opportunities for learning, self-discovery, growth, and expression. This should be in addition to the role of employment in providing means to achieve material benefits, security, respect, and immediate psychic gratifications. The workplace should provide opportunities to live adulthood as a continuous, developmental experience.[12]

From this perspective, work operations and workplace governance should be designed so that, at a minimum, all employees can participate directly and/or through representatives in selecting and implementing the strategic goals of the firm and in assessing and periodically revising its organizational structure. Participation in making the decisions that affect one's working life is a good in itself. Participatory decisionmaking is a fundamental component of democracy, even in the so-called "private" or nonpolitical sphere. However, democratic involvement in employment also contributes to civic democracy by enhancing peoples' inherent capacities to participate in politics. I refer here to politics in the best sense of the word: the making of principled, socially significant choices respectful of human need and individual rights, under circumstances of constraint due to resource, technological, and other limitations. Democratizing work and labor markets contributes to political democracy by breaking down the rigid divisions of labor that stunt and inhibit civic participation.[13]

If these ideals were simply personal views, I might hesitate to offer them as a foundation for future labor policy. In fact, however, they have a bit more momentum. Elsewhere I would be prepared to argue that the notion of democratizing the private sphere represents the logical completion of the best ideals in our intellectual and cultural heritage. For present purposes the more telling point is that in fact American workers increasingly desire and expect self-realization in and through paid employment. To be sure, the demand is not typically expressed in the words and phrases used here, but the essential concerns are the same. Employee concerns often focus more on

12. The concept of social organization facilitating a "developmental adulthood" derives from the work of Fred Block. *See, e.g.*, Block, *The New Left Grows Up*, WORKING PAPERS FOR A NEW SOC'Y, Sept.-Oct. 1978, at 41, 46.

13. *See generally* C. PATEMAN, PARTICIPATION & DEMOCRATIC THEORY 45-84 (1970); Green, *Considerations on the Democratic Division of Labor*, 12 POL. & SOC'Y 445 (1983).

day-to-day operations than on enterprise strategic decisionmaking, but the plea for democratic participation surfaces at that level as well, particularly in recent years in plant closing situations.

A profound change is undoubtedly occurring in the sensibilities, aspirations, and expectations of American workers. The civil rights and other social and political movements of the 1960s have contributed to this, but perhaps the central influence has been the values and social movements associated with modern feminism. Increasingly, work is understood not simply as a paycheck or a fate, but as one of the most important opportunities in life to grow and to experience personal autonomy, self-governance, and interpersonal connection. On the job, employees increasingly demand not only "job satisfaction," understood to mean more pleasant and interesting work under safer, less onerous and regimented working conditions, but self-realization in a deeper sense. This refers to work that has a meaning, work that presents opportunities for learning and expression, work that constantly challenges one to enhance operational and professional skills and interpersonal capacities.

Hitherto excluded groups, notably women and minorities, are demanding the right not just to break into paid employment, but to have good, well-paying, personally satisfying jobs. Parents are demanding job timetables structured to mesh with their family responsibilities, so that home life and work life can be mutually reinforcing rather than antagonistically conflicting developmental arenas. The massive entry of women into the paid labor force in recent decades, which is perhaps the single most significant change in the world of work during this time period, potentially represents a profoundly democratizing force in employment. This potential can only be realized, of course, if labor market segmentation, work scheduling practices, and other barriers to equal employment opportunity are successfully tackled.

As we project into the next century, there is every reason to assume that expectations about the content of work will continue to rise. Yet, because of problems of market failure and imperfection,[14] economic inequality, and shortcomings of collective bargaining law, rising employees' aspirations for greater participation, autonomy, and democratic input in work have thus far been regularly frustrated.

---

14. *See infra* text accompanying notes 77-88. *See generally* McPherson, *Efficiency and Liberty in the Productive Enterprise: Recent Work in the Economics of Work Organization*, 12 PHIL. & PUB. AFFAIRS 354, 362-63 (1983); Stone, *Labor and the Corporate Structure: Changing Conceptions and Emerging Possibilities*, 55 U. CHI. L. REV. 73, 152-61 (1988).

C. The Business Environment

I would support workplace democracy even if it had serious drawbacks from a business standpoint. Moreover, I do not deny that democratization may entail transaction costs, certainly in the short run. Nevertheless, I am confident in the belief that over the long run, democratization is the best, indeed the only, sensible strategy for confronting the considerable woes that beset the American economy. One bit of evidence of this is that nations abroad that have developed elaborate welfare-state infrastructures and that have experimented with various forms of employee participation are clobbering the United States in trade competition. In a phrase, workplace democracy is good for business.

A full and proper defense of this claim is beyond the scope of this paper. In any event, others are more competent than I to make the case.[15] Here I will briefly outline the contours of the argument.

Thoughtful observers claim that America's trade crisis is but a symptom of deeper transformations occurring in the economy. At one level, there is a growing realization that "Fordist" business strategies are outmoded. Fordism connotes the era of business strategy built around the mass manufacture of standardized goods with heavy fixed capital investment in "dedicated" (inflexible) machinery.[16] Labor relations in the Fordist era have been dominated by the model of "Taylorism," except insofar as that pattern was altered by the onset of collective bargaining. Taylorism refers to an industrial relations strategy that combines extremely fine subdivision of jobs into routinized and inflexible tasks; the separation of conception and execution; coordination of all work operations by management direction and command; and intensive monitoring, control, and discipline of employees.[17]

These observers claim that we are entering a new, "post-Fordist" era of "diversified quality production," in which further growth and competitive success for the advanced economies requires more flexible business and employee relations strategies. These strategies will include much more variable production of specialty or customized goods in smaller runs; less fixed in-

15. For background, *see generally* F. BLOCK, THE ECONOMIC SOCIOLOGY OF POSTINDUSTRIALISM (forthcoming: University of California Press 1989); L. HIRSCHHORN, BEYOND MECHANIZATION: WORK & TECHNOLOGY IN A POSTINDUSTRIAL AGE (1984); M. PIORE & C. SABEL, THE SECOND INDUSTRIAL DIVIDE (1984); R. REICH, THE NEXT AMERICAN FRONTIER (1983); C. SABEL, WORK & POLITICS: THE DIVISION OF LABOR AND INDUSTRY (1982).

16. As used here, the concept of "Fordism" derives from C. SABEL, *supra* note 15.

17. On "Taylorism," see generally H. BRAVERMAN, LABOR & MONOPOLY CAPITAL: THE DEGRADATION OF WORK IN THE TWENTIETH CENTURY 85-152 (1974); R. EDWARDS, CONTESTED TERRAIN: THE TRANSFORMATION OF THE WORKPLACE IN THE TWENTIETH CENTURY 111-29 (1979); Stone, *supra* note 14, at 140-44.

vestment in dedicated machinery and, conversely, an emphasis on development and deployment of "flexible," usually computer-driven, cybernetic technologies; and abandoning persisting Taylorist approaches in favor of more participatory, less hierarchical forms of work organization.

At a somewhat higher level of generality, the claim is not simply that a new business approach must supersede obsolete and failing competitive strategies, but that the technological and economic changes now occurring are absolutely fundamental, that we are entering a new era of history: the period of "postindustrial transition." Postindustrial transition connotes a complex of emergent and mutually reinforcing trends: the decline of labor inputs in manufacturing, despite continuing output growth; the shift to a service-based economy, so that even manufacturing increasingly resembles a service in its growing focus on design and development of custom products;[18] the emergence of electronic, feedback-based technologies that fundamentally alter the experience and organization of work; and workers' changing aspirations referred to above, particularly the rapidly changing roles of women in paid employment. The various social and technological changes linked in the concept of postindustrial transition create both pressures and opportunities for significant reorganization of the structure of work.

The pressure to find new business strategies in the context of these epochal changes is linked to the question of workplace democracy in numerous ways. The new technological and trade environments—emphasizing flexibility in and feedback from both markets and machines—create a demand for new skills and a new type of worker, and therefore for new, less hierarchical work structures.[19] In an historical reversal of the routinization and degradation of work characteristic of Taylorism, advanced firms now increasingly expect employees to be learners, investigators, and problem solvers. Employees are expected to be multiskilled and able to respond and adjust quickly. They are expected to be interpersonally as well as technically competent, so that they can perform as members of integrated production teams. In a phrase, the demand for labor, at least in the primary sector of the economy, is increasingly a demand for developmentally oriented workers. Satisfying this demand will require changes in both public and business policy, implicating in turn fundamental debates about the future of labor law.

Additionally, some analysts and managers are beginning to understand that the key to business success in the new environment is skillful organiza-

18. *See generally* Jaikumar, *Postindustrial Manufacturing*, HARV. BUS. REV., Nov.-Dec. 1986, at 69.

19. *See generally* L. HIRSCHHORN, *supra* note 15.

tion of the interplay between fixed capital and labor inputs, and particularly the skillful management of intellectual resources and workers' problem-solving capacities. It is increasingly apparent that horizontal coordination of work by highly trained, integrated, and relatively autonomous teams is much more productive than vertical (hierarchical) coordination of workers locked into finely subdivided tasks. Studies have shown, for example, that identical, state-of-the-art technology is many times more productive in Japanese industry, with its emphasis on integrated teamwork, than in the American setting still wedded to Taylorist conceptions of work organization.[20] Theoretical economists have frequently hailed the efficiency advantages of hierarchy,[21] but successful business people know better. They have begun to discover some of the transaction cost superiorities of horizontal (less hierarchical and more democratic) work organization. To be sure, even the most advanced management initiatives to flatten hierarchy or to organize work around integrated teams fall well short of my vision of workplace democracy. This is particularly so when, as is the norm, management retains unilateral control over strategic decisionmaking. Nonetheless, even these nascent and limited developments in employee involvement represent a significant acknowledgment of the productivity advantages of democratic work organization and of a developmental perspective on work.

For these and related reasons, progressive employers are coming to realize that the most productive asset in the economy, the asset most important to future economic growth and success, is employee skill, adaptability, creativity, and pride in work. Quite apart from the intrinsic appeal of democratization, in practical terms our future well-being depends upon adopting what some call a "human capital strategy" of economic growth by investing heavily in this asset through work reorganization and social welfare policy. Such an approach would aim to reduce hierarchy and encourage employee participation in workplace decisionmaking, so as to fully mobilize employees' learning and problem-solving capacities. Simultaneously, it would gear social policy to continuous enhancement of the skills and productive potential of American workers. Together, workplace and social policy should be designed so that industry can draw upon the talents of all who seek paid employment opportunities. A human capital strategy for economic growth must feature enormously expanded retraining and adult education opportunities, vastly expanded child care services, and a general rise in the social minimum wage and benefits package. It must have a "security dimension,"

20. *See generally* Jaikumar, *supra* note 18.

21. *See, e.g.*, Alchian & Demsetz, *Production, Information Costs, and Economic Organization*, 62 AM. ECON. REV. 777 (1972); Williamson, *The Organization of Work: A Comparative Institutional Assessment*, 1 J. ECON. BEHAVIOR & ORG. 5 (1980).

significantly improving protections against job loss, so that employees will more readily accept and accommodate economic restructuring rather than adamantly and, from their point of view, quite rationally, resisting it.

II. Market Reconstruction

A. *Introduction*

We could approach from several angles the formulation of an agenda for labor law reform in the service of workplace democracy. This Article focuses particularly on the relationship between markets and planning in determining the content and governance structures of the employment relationship. I will advocate systematic and vigorous law reform designed to enhance democracy in the employment relationship and in labor markets, an approach that might be called "expansive" or "democracy-enhancing market reconstruction." It is to be distinguished from the mainstream approach to collective bargaining, which I call "self-limiting market reconstruction."[22]

Expansive market reconstruction is, of course, opposed by supporters of the so-called free market approach to labor relations. And even though labor's supporters may endorse this or that particular proposal, the idea of radical, systematic market reconstruction is often thought to be in tension with the traditional collective bargaining philosophy that extols its "autonomy" from governmental or legal intervention. I will attempt to show that the standard, dichotomous contrast of free market and regulation is misleading. The distinction is grounded upon an outwardly plausible but ultimately incoherent notion that markets *can* be autonomous.

Over the years, and especially in the current atmosphere, the overdrawn market/regulation opposition has tended to set up an unjustifiable presumption in favor of the market and against law reform. It has even promoted unnecessarily restrained and limiting approaches among those who favor market reconstruction. Clarification of these issues opens the door to a more expansive law reform agenda. Of course, I realize that by undermining this one conceptual barrier to the expansive market reconstruction approach, I have not thereby established its overall desirability on the merits. In the end, the approach must justify itself in the normative and economic terms mentioned above. But as a step toward reaching and opening that terrain of debate, it will be useful first to clear away this constraining conceptual underbrush.

---

22. *See infra* text accompanying notes 89-94.

B. *A Spectrum of Views*

A useful place to begin is with how the content of the employment relationship is determined. Under content I include not only obvious matters, such as wages, hours, and working conditions, but also questions of access or entry to paid employment and issues of how the workplace is to be governed. In this latter aspect, the employment relationship also includes institutional arrangements for determining its future content.

The content of the employment relationship is partly determined by deeply embedded social patterns and structures, most notably the gender-based role differentiation underlying the sexual division of labor. These social forces particularly affect access opportunities. Regrettably, industrial relations and labor law theory have only recently begun to focus systematically on the sexual division of labor, racism, and other social-structural constraints.[23]

Beyond this, the employment relationship derives most of its structure and content from three processes: exchange or bargaining in light of "market forces"; planning internal to the firm; and planning external to the firm through the medium of public law. Thus, beyond social-structural constraints, the employment relationship is partly bargained and partly administered (the latter by both public and private actors).

Contemporary debate about the reform of industrial relations and labor law, echoing earlier views, may be organized as a spectrum of different conceptions of the proper relationship between bargaining and planning. It is conventional in American political and legal rhetoric to treat bargaining, described as "freedom of contract" or "private ordering," and administration through law, known as "governmental intervention" or "regulation," as dichotomous, polar opposites. In the customary view, where regulation begins, freedom of contract ends. The problem for public policy, then, lies in making the proper choices or in finding the proper balance between free contract and regulation, with a strong presumption in favor of the former.

For reasons to become clear, I prefer the notion of a spectrum of views rather than a dichotomous choice. Partly, I wish to emphasize that market exchange, internal planning, and public planning are interrelated modes of determining the content of the employment relationship. How these methods should be combined in any given setting depends both on the broader philosophical considerations guiding social and economic policy and specific contextual factors. An emphasis on one or another of these three linked

23. *See, e.g.*, Conaghan, *The Invisibility of Women In Labour Law: Gender-Neutrality in Model Building*, 14 INT'L. J. SOC. L. 377 (1986).

regulatory modes cannot be settled by presumption and must always be defended in social and ethical terms.

At one end of the spectrum of today's diverse views on these matters, advocates of the "free market" approach stress the general superiority of market exchange to planning.[24] In questioning nonmarket approaches, the free marketeers are usually challenging government planning through legal regulation. Their models tend to ignore planning internal to the firm and, thus, are quite out of touch with modern principles of personnel management. One of the central teachings of modern labor economics is that many of the most significant aspects of the employment relation are determined neither by market forces, nor by law, but by planning internal to the firm.[25] Free market advocates are commonly thought to urge that law play a minimal role in structuring the employment relationship ("deregulation"), but this is not quite their view. While Richard Epstein and others have advocated repeal of the National Labor Relations Act (NLRA),[26] the free market perspective does not, in fact, hold that wage bargaining should occur in an environment free from law. Rather the proposal is to substitute for the NLRA the aggressively pro-employer common law of the late nineteenth century,[27] which is seen as embodying the proper framework of public planning of the employment relationship.

Another perspective sees a broader role for law but rejects federal law's special solicitude for collective bargaining. There are many variants of this perspective. Former Solicitor General Charles Fried has offered a conservative version,[28] but the structure of his approach, if not the specifics, is occa-

24. For one of the leading statements of the position, see Epstein, *A Common Law For Labor Relations: A Critique of the New Deal Labor Legislation*, 92 YALE L. J. 1357 (1983)[hereinafter Epstein, *Common Law*]. For related arguments, see Epstein, *In Defense of the Contract at Will*, 51 U. CHI. L. REV. 947 (1984)[hereinafter Epstein, *Contract at Will*].

25. *See infra* text accompanying notes 78-85. *See generally* P. WEILER, THE LAW AT WORK [hereinafter P. WEILER, LAW AT WORK](unpublished manuscript).

26. *See* Epstein, *Common Law*, *supra* note 24.

27. *See* Cook, *Privileges of Labor Unions in the Struggle For Life*, 27 YALE L. J. 779 (1918); Hurvitz, *American Labor Law and the Doctrine of Entrepreneurial Property Rights: Boycotts, Courts, and the Juridical Reorientation of 1886-1895*, 8 INDUS. REL. L. J. 307 (1986); Kelman, *American Labor Law and Legal Formalism: How "Legal Logic" Shaped and Vitiated the Rights of American Workers*, 58 ST. JOHN'S L. REV. 1 (1983); *see also* C. TOMLINS, THE STATE AND THE UNIONS: LABOR RELATIONS, LAW, AND THE ORGANIZED LABOR MOVEMENT IN AMERICA, 1880-1960 32-95 (1985); Nockleby, *Tortious Interference With Contractual Relations in the Nineteenth Century: The Transformation of Property, Contract, and Tort*, 93 HARV. L. REV. 1510 (1980). [Editors' Note: In deference to the author, who believes that student writers should receive credit for their work, and in the spirit of the democracy-enhancing ideals reflected in this Article, student notes cited herein identify authors by name although this is a departure from conventional citation form.]

28. Fried, *Individual and Collective Rights in Work Relations: Reflections on the Current State of Labor Law and Its Prospects*, 51 U. CHI. L. REV. 1012 (1984); *see also* Sunstein,

sionally echoed by liberal advocates of employee rights who have grown disillusioned with collective bargaining. In this second view, public law is seen as playing an active and potentially quite expansive role in guaranteeing such minimal protections and entitlements as are necessary to assure the basic dignity, well-being, and associational liberties of employees. It is understood within this perspective that, due to excessive inequality or market failure, bargaining may not provide such basic guarantees and, therefore, legal "intervention" (meaning here, the revision or overriding of market outcomes) may be appropriate.

Thus, the free market perspective argues that law should leave the market in its "natural state." That is, this view holds that the law should once again structure markets as it did in the late nineteenth and early twentieth centuries, and workers should protect their rights through bargaining and contract. The second view holds that law should correct for market failure or extreme inequality on an ad hoc basis, but otherwise leave the content of the employment relationship to bargaining.

Advocates of collective bargaining, both in the past and today, assign a different role to law, which has been called "market reconstruction." The theory is that the results of private bargaining are socially unacceptable. Traditionally, advocates have stressed inequality of bargaining power in labor markets. This is still a frequently voiced concern, but contemporary theory adds another. Because many of the most significant aspects of the employment relationship are planned and administered within the firm, collective bargaining is favored not only for its contribution to bargaining equality but also for its contribution to democratizing firm governance by affording employees a voice in planning processes.[29]

All proponents of collective bargaining agree that public law should "reconstruct" the "free market" so as to remove obstacles to and encourage collective bargaining. Among the many other important ways in which the New Deal represents a watershed in American law, its validation of the concept of market reconstruction is one of its most significant contributions. The Wagner Act is generally understood to have sought to accomplish its basic goals by altering the background legal regime of bargaining processes

Rights, Minimal Terms, and Solidarity: A Comment, 51 U. CHI. L. REV. 1041 (1984) (Epstein's and Fried's views thoughtfully discussed and criticized).

29. For a classic version of this position, see Feller, *supra* note 3 ("governmental function" theory of collective bargaining). In the current literature, two of the most important statements of the position are R. FREEMAN & J. MEDOFF, WHAT DO UNIONS DO? (1984) and P. WEILER, LAW AT WORK, *supra* note 25. Freeman and Medoff derived the concept of "voice" as a determinant of social conditions from A. HIRSCHMAN, EXIT, VOICE, AND LOYALTY: RESPONSES TO DECLINE IN FIRMS, ORGANIZATIONS, AND STATES (1970).

in labor markets, rather than by mandating particular substantive results. The NLRA vindicated the legal and political thinkers who had for a generation argued that law is always involved in structuring markets and that a collective bargaining regime therefore represents not a choice for regulation over the free market, but rather a choice to regulate labor markets according to one, rather than another, set of assumptions.

As will be seen, however, the New Deal approach embodied distinct, built-in limitations on the extent of market reconstruction thought to be desirable. Therefore, completing the spectrum, this Article raises the possibility of an *expansive* market reconstruction approach.[30] In several European countries there is widespread agreement on the use of state power to alter labor markets and even to impose substantive employment terms.[31] The expansive market reconstruction approach has until now garnered little support in the United States. As argued above, however, it may be that present exigencies and future possibilities will increasingly incline reformers to reconsider the traditional commitment to self-limiting market reconstruction and to review more favorably the expansive approach advocated here.

C. Myths of the Free Market

In utilizing the spectrum metaphor to present the current array of views, I intend to reinforce the point that there is no question as to *whether* public power should be deployed to structure bargaining processes, since that is inevitable. There are only questions of *how* this should be done, consistent with prevailing ideals and goals of public policy (such as a commitment to employee autonomy and self-determination). To put it another way, all markets are based on and constituted by a structure of legal rules. Because such rules establish bargaining groundrules, they are intimately involved in shaping substantive outcomes, and therefore the distributive results of all bargaining processes. Thus, background legal rules always constitute a regulatory regime.

Regulation is not something separate from markets. There is no possibility of an "unregulated" or "free" market. The creation of the background

30. Theoretically, the far end of the spectrum would be occupied by an approach calling for "total" planning of the employment relationship and the complete disappearance of bargaining, contract, and markets in labor. This hardly seems an attractive possibility, if it is coherent at all. To my knowledge, no one in current labor law debates seriously advocates this position, so I will not pursue it further.

31. A dramatic example of the latter is the practice of "extension laws," by which terms agreed in collective bargaining are automatically extended to the nonunion sector. *See generally* Bok, *Reflections on the Distinctive Character of American Labor Laws*, 84 HARV. L. REV. 1394, 1436-39 (1971); Summers, *Worker Participation in the U.S. and West Germany: A Comparative Study from an American Perspective*, 28 AM. J. COMP. L. 367, 377-78 (1980).

legal regime partly establishes the parties' starting bargaining positions. When bargaining, private planning, and government planning are combined in an institutional system, regulation is not added to or superimposed upon markets. Regulatory choices are made at every step along the way in which markets come into being. Accordingly, the question for public policy is not whether we ought to regulate contracts and markets, but always to determine which regulatory regime will best serve our spiritual and material needs. In particular, because law partially constitutes both the structure of labor markets and the governance structures of firms, a sound and democratic public policy must explicitly define a posture toward these structures.

To many readers, all this will seem about as startling as last week's news. Nevertheless, a somewhat different way of talking about these issues apparently has great resiliency and appeal in American legal and political rhetoric. It is conventionally asserted that public policy faces not choices among regulatory regimes but a choice between regulation and bargaining, between governmental intervention and free contract or the free market. This overdichotomized way of framing the issues cannot withstand serious analytical scrutiny. Market and regulation are so inextricably linked that it is incoherent to talk of a choice *between them* as modes of social organization, as distinct from debate about what regulatory choices should be made in structuring various markets.

By the 1920s and 1930s, the Legal Realists had developed most of the essential points of the critique of the idea of the free market, thereby establishing the theoretical foundations of the market reconstruction perspective.[32] As is well known, their work provided important intellectual support for New Deal reformism in labor law and many other fields. Yet New Deal

32. Classics of the genre include: F. Cohen, *Transcendental Nonsense and the Functional Approach*, 35 COLUM. L. REV. 809 (1935); M. Cohen, *Property and Sovereignty*, 13 CORNELL L. Q. 8 (1927)[hereinafter Cohen, *Property*]; M. Cohen, *The Basis of Contract*, 46 HARV. L. REV. 553 (1933); Hale, *Bargaining, Duress, and Economic Liberty*, 43 COLUM. L. REV. 603 (1943)[hereinafter Hale, *Bargaining*]; Hale, *Coercion and Distribution in A Supposedly Non-Coercive State*, 38 POL. SCI. Q. 470 (1923)[hereinafter Hale, *Coercion*]; Kessler, *Contracts of Adhesion—Some Thoughts About Freedom of Contract*, 43 COLUM. L. REV. 629 (1943); Llewellyn, *Some Realism About Realism—Responding to Dean Pound*, 44 HARV. L. REV. 1222 (1931).

Of course, in a broader sense the intellectual foundations of the attack on the idea of the free market were laid in the classical texts of continental social theory, particularly in the works of Karl Marx and Max Weber.

Note that the form of the critique of the free market discussed here does not rest on the familiar ground that the free market "never really existed" because, as a matter of historical fact, government has regularly intervened in markets. The claim is of a different nature, namely that the very ideal of autonomous or self-regulating markets is incoherent. For the classic presentation of the historical form of the critique, see K. POLANYI, THE GREAT TRANSFORMATION (1957) (originally published 1944).

labor policy only ambivalently embraced the implications of the market reconstruction approach.[33] For reasons of political and intellectual history too complex to survey here, the notion of a choice between markets and regulation has had a curious and stubborn persistence in our legal culture. Contemporary free marketeers have launched what is in essence a pre-Realist attack on New Deal market reconstruction. It thus becomes necessary to relearn, update, and extend the Realists' half-century-old arguments.

Some members of the critical legal studies movement have taken up this project of extending and modernizing the insights of Legal Realism. The major contribution has been made by Duncan Kennedy, notably in his critique of the standard treatment of law in neoclassical microeconomic theory.[34] In a sense, the proposals offered here are but an application of the theoretical arguments developed within this intellectual tradition to contemporary labor law. In particular, I want to mobilize the tradition to advance one of my central claims: namely, that it is mistaken to think that the ideal of free collective bargaining requires law to be indifferent to hierarchy and domination in the internal governance structures of firms.[35]

Before proceeding to the implications of market reconstruction, I will enlarge on its theoretical bases and examine two common objections to expansive, democracy-seeking reforms of the type proposed. These objections are based, respectively, on the claim that such reforms are paternalistic and that they are inefficient.

1. Naturalism, Convention, and Indeterminacy

A market is a set of practices and institutional arrangements for regularized and voluntary exchange. It is a precondition of having a market that there exist—whether explicitly or implicitly, formally or informally—some rules, understandings, and/or practices that determine property entitlements (i.e., specify who owns what); that indicate how ownership can be transferred; and that define "voluntariness" (i.e., set groundrules for the bargaining process). In modern societies these understandings are usually embodied in legal rules. This is not essential. Such understandings can be embedded in customary or religious norms, as in some premodern or contemporary societies that lacked or lack an autonomous legal order. The distinction may

33. *See generally* Klare, *Traditional Labor Law Scholarship and the Crisis of Collective Bargaining Law: A Reply to Professor Finkin*, 44 MD. L. REV. 731 (1985)[hereinafter Klare, *Traditional Scholarship*]; Klare, *Judicial Deradicalization of the Wagner Act and the Origins of Modern Legal Consciousness, 1937-1941*, 62 MINN. L. REV. 265 (1978).

34. Kennedy, *The Role of Law in Economic Thought: Essays on the Fetishism of Commodities*, 34 AM. U. L. REV. 939 (1985).

35. *Cf. supra* note 3 and accompanying text.

be highly significant for some theoretical contexts, but it does not seem essential here. For ease of presentation, I will assume the typical modern case in which the background rules and understandings are embodied in what we call law (although law can and frequently does refer to custom). With that qualification, we can restate the central point as follows. At a minimum, the notion of a market assumes a law of property, contracts, and torts. Economists have always understood this, although economic theory pays scant attention to the knotty problems of how property and bargaining rules are actually defined.[36] Generally these issues are referred to the lawyers.

When economists and political philosophers assign questions of entitlement and groundrule definition to lawyers, it may appear to these theoreticians that only "technical" problems are involved. If the notions of ownership and voluntariness were self-defining, the nonchalance of economic theory toward law might be unproblematical. However, one of the Realists' most important contributions was to show that legal concepts are not and cannot be self-defining, nor can they be derived from any natural or transhistorical structure of the human personality or condition.[37] Legal rules are always *conventional*, that is, they are fashioned as the product of human choices within particular historical and normative contexts. Moreover, general concepts like property and free exchange are not self-defining, they are *indeterminate*. To be applied to legal problems they must be given ever more precise institutional content. To be sure, norms, traditions, and mental habits internal to legal discourse ordinarily guide the process of giving particularized content to general legal concepts, but the process always to some extent involves choices based on general ethical and political values. Legal formalists aspire to provide a deductive method of legal reasoning largely purged of extralegal value judgments, but no one has ever come close to achieving this.

The choices made in defining legal rules, even the very basic or background rules of property, contract, and tort, have important distributive implications. The incidents of property ownership (i.e., what you can do with it and what you can prevent others from doing with it) significantly affect the property's value. Likewise, all detailed, conventional definitions of "voluntary exchange" must specify permissible and impermissible (e.g., coercive or fraudulent) bargaining tactics. Such rules significantly affect the parties' bargaining strength in the market. This is actually quite an old lesson. Af-

36. For a casual but revealingly typical example of how the matter is presented to beginning students, see J. HIRSHLEIFER, PRICE THEORY AND APPLICATIONS 10-13 (3d ed. 1984).

37. For a contemporary statement of the critique of naturalism and objectivism in legal and social thought, see Unger, *The Critical Legal Studies Movement*, 96 HARV. L. REV. 561 (1983).

ter all, Oliver Wendell Holmes taught us a century ago that one can speak of "free bargaining" in both labor markets that treat peaceful picketing as a coercive invasion of the employer's rights and therefore as an enjoinable tort, as well as in those that do not. But there are likely to be very different bargaining outcomes depending on which rule is chosen to structure labor markets.[38]

One might try to escape the dilemma through a minimalist definition of impermissible tactics, for example, by defining coercion solely in terms of the use or threat of physical force. This approach, however, does not make indeterminacy problems go away. For example, a long and continuing debate has raged in American law as to whether peaceful picketing constitutes physical coercion or a threat thereof. For present purposes, the point is that even a minimalist definition of coercion is conventional, rather than "natural," because among other things, virtually every modern legal system has used a broader definition. Defining coercion solely in terms of force, and therefore permitting other forms of pressure (e.g., accelerated foreclosure on debts, "cut-throat" pricing, or undue influence over psychologically dependent individuals), will significantly affect who gets what in many transactions. Like all definitions of coercion, the minimalist one has distributive implications and therefore must be justified, if at all, in ethical and political terms. A minimalist approach to this and similar problems is as much a choice for a particular form of regulatory regime as would be advocacy of tripling the list of forbidden practices contained in the NLRA.

To sum up so far, there is no natural or "a-legal" form of bargaining or markets. All markets are structured by law. Legal concepts are malleable and not self-defining. The design and application of legal rules is always a product of historically contingent, value-laden human choices. Each set of the infinite variety of possible property and bargaining groundrules has distinct distributive consequences. Every market therefore rests on conventional legal foundations—a regulatory regime—which must in turn be understood as embracing a public policy commitment to particular distributive consequences.

Since the idea of a free market, a market autonomous from regulation, is incoherent, the case for free labor markets generally amounts to an argument for a minimalist regulatory regime, based on the common law as it is imagined to have stood in the years around the turn of the century.[39] Mini-

38. *See* Vegelahn v. Guntner, 167 Mass. 92, 104-09, 44 N.E. 1077, 1079-82 (1896) (Holmes, J., dissenting); *see also* Holmes, *Privilege, Malice, and Intent*, 8 HARV. L. REV. 1 (1894).

39. In fact, the common law rules relating to employment matters underwent rapid and systematic transformation during this period. Just how "unnatural" the emergent rules

malist arguments typically naturalize the common law and treat as determinate legal concepts that are extremely open-ended. They largely ignore rather than seek to vindicate the distributive consequences of the then-prevailing common law rules. But even those who grant a broader role for law in setting minimum conditions or establishing a collective bargaining process argue that, once these minima or processes are established, the role of law should be to await and enforce the parties' bargains. This view mistakenly assumes that law is uninvolved in and neutral regarding the bargains themselves, except to the extent that it invites a bargaining process in either a "free" or "reconstructed" market. Simple reference to the bargain of the parties to validate the morality of contract enforcement is circular reasoning. Directly or indirectly, law shapes the parties' bargains. Justifying enforcement of market outcomes requires law to accept some responsibility for the content of the bargains. That is, a theory of contractual justice in labor law must be explicit about its distributive premises.

Obviously, I am not asserting that because minimalism or "laissez faire," on the one hand, and elaborate statutory encouragement of collective bargaining, on the other, are both forms of regulation that no important differences between them exist. Nor am I asserting that no difference exists between regimes that leave wide scope for employee bargaining and regimes that rely heavily on central planning. To the extent that bargaining permits employees to participate directly and on a decentralized basis in determining the rules and conditions that affect their working lives, bargaining processes themselves are of social value and contribute to employee self-determination. This is a basic reason to support the institution of collective bargaining.[40]

Rather, the effort here is simply to get beyond the tired and unilluminating rhetoric of "free market versus regulation." My claim is that the superiority of a market orientation cannot be established on the ground that it is nonregulatory. The superiority of particular market institutions can only be established by describing in detail the precise content and effects of the market's background rules, and then justifying the complex of rules in terms of their contribution to advancing overarching social and philosophical goals.

This is as much an issue for supporters of collective bargaining as for the free marketeers. Supporters of collective bargaining often hesitate to advocate or resist proposals for extending industrial democracy on the ground

---

were—that is, how much they were a product of contingent human choices and judgments in response to particular historical and political problems—is painstakingly documented in Hurvitz, *supra* note 27.

40. Professor Weiler has spiritedly defended freedom of contract in these terms. *See* Weiler, *Striking A New Balance: Freedom of Contract and the Prospects for Union Representation*, 98 HARV. L. REV. 351, 419 (1984)[hereinafter Weiler, *Striking A New Balance*].

that such proposals will violate the "basic principles" of freedom of contract and the autonomy of collective bargaining from government regulation. These concepts are often invoked in vague and unreflective terms. As I have insisted, employee involvement in bargaining over working conditions can be a value of great significance to democratic theory, but by themselves the general notions of free contract and autonomous bargaining cannot tell us precisely how to structure labor markets. With respect to every problem and context, we need to ask: What degree of individual and group choice is provided by the existing or proposed market structure? Does or will the background legal regime enhance or stifle human self-realization in work and other basic democratic values? These questions cannot be answered in general terms, as legal reasoning often purports to do.[41] Such questions demand socially and historically contextualized inquiry and analysis.

Given this, there is simply no *a priori* reason why a vigorous and systematic program of egalitarian market reconstruction aimed at enhancing direct workplace participation and workers' self-realization opportunities is not fully compatible with the general ideals of liberty and autonomy, and specifically with the ideal of employee participation in setting the terms and conditions of employment through free collective bargaining. Because all labor markets are structured by law, there is no reason why they should not be restructured, so long as a particular proposed change reflects wise social policy. With respect to every workplace rule or practice, it is fair inquiry to ask

41. A classic instance is Justice Black's opinion in the leading case of H.K. Porter Co. v. NLRB, 397 U.S. 99 (1970), holding that the NLRB lacks the power to order employers to grant a particular union-sought contract provision as a remedy for bad faith bargaining. The core argument is contained in these well-known words:

> One of [the] fundamental policies [of the National Labor Relations Act] is freedom of contract. While the parties' freedom of contract is not absolute under the Act, allowing the Board to compel agreement when the parties themselves are unable to agree would violate the fundamental premise on which the Act is based—private bargaining under governmental supervision of the procedure alone, without any official compulsion over the actual terms of the contract.

Id. at 108.

As the dissent was quick to point out, Justice Black's conclusion does not inexorably follow from his premise, largely because the premise is stated in such general terms. *Id.* at 110 (Douglas, J., dissenting). One could easily argue, for example, that in the particular but recurring circumstance of egregious employer evasion of bargaining, allowing the proposed remedy would actually vindicate, not derogate, Congress's policy to encourage a collective bargaining process that sets employment terms largely by contract. To choose between the Court's position and the dissent's position requires a more focused inquiry into the structure of labor markets, and how, in the relevant contexts, the proposed remedy would serve or disserve the stated goal of governmental promotion of an employment bargaining system.

This type of error in reasoning is quite common in labor law discourse. A similar lapse appears, for example, in Finkin, *Revisionism In Labor Law*, 43 MD. L. REV. 23, 38-41 (1984), as I demonstrate in Klare, *Traditional Scholarship*, *supra* note 33, at 798-804.

whether it enhances or impedes employee self-determination, economic productivity, and other basic social values. There is no reason to favor market autonomy in the abstract. To put it another way, it is illogical to treat market autonomy, as such, as a "basic value" or fundamental premise, without showing that in particular circumstances regulatory restraint conduces to industrial democracy or some other value *besides* market autonomy.

2. Antipaternalism and Efficiency

The goal of my argument is to open space for debate about the impact of labor law rules on employee self-determination, with an eye toward advocating extensive democratizing reform. As a first step, I have attempted to show that this program cannot be attacked on the oft-invoked, general ground that it is "over-regulatory" and, for *that* reason, inconsistent with employee choice and autonomy. A critic might respond by conceding the point that all markets are structured by legal rules comprising a regulatory regime and yet still rebel at open-ended market reconstruction, with its inevitable appeal for vastly elevated minimum employment standards and bargaining groundrules designed to favor workers. That is, the critic might argue for the presumptive validity of free, minimally-regulated contract, on grounds other than a general preference for markets over regulation. Accordingly, before turning to a discussion of the reform agenda, it pays to review some typical claims of this kind.

So-called free contract could be defended in distributive terms. For example, one could argue that a high level of economic inequality, such as that which existed when labor markets were only minimally structured by late nineteenth century common law rules, provides the proper incentive structure and information flow needed to maximize productivity and social wellbeing. This type of argument is rarely heard, at least in contemporary labor law circles. More common are arguments framed in antipaternalist terms and arguments based on efficiency.

The antipaternalist theme is that minimal regulation of bargaining and agreements is faithful to the general precept that each individual is the best judge of his or her desires and interests. Therefore, law should ordinarily allow individuals to make whatever bargains with whomsoever they please.[42] Here again there is a problem of abstraction or indeterminacy. If the antipaternalist conception of liberty or autonomy simply means that people should be allowed to make what bargains they please, then the argument for

42. Professor Epstein's defense of a common law for labor relations, see Epstein, *Common Law*, *supra* note 24, is based in large part on a libertarian formulation of the antipaternalist perspective. *See id.* at 1359, 1364-78; *see also infra* note 45 and accompanying text.

a minimalist free contract regime is tautological.[43] If, on the other hand, this conception of contractual liberty is given a richer philosophical content, if it is linked to more elaborate conceptions of human fulfillment and self-determination, then there arise very complex and problematic empirical difficulties in showing that particular common law rules actually serve such ideals. This is a fundamental insight upon which the sociology of law is based. As Max Weber wrote long ago: "A legal order which contains ever so few mandatory and prohibitory norms and ever so many 'freedoms' and empowerments can nonetheless in its practical effects facilitate a quantitative and qualitative increase not only of coercion in general but quite specifically of authoritarian coercion."[44] We are back to the need for contextualized inquiry and political argument.

Another line of attack on expansive reform is to defend free contract in terms of the value of efficiency. This approach has enjoyed great currency in recent years, particularly among academic lawyers and in the policy analysis community.[45] A typical claim is that common law rules provide the optimal framework for structuring labor markets because these rules will lead to efficient outcomes.[46] At the very least, pre-NLRA common law rules are pre-

---

43. Professor Epstein simply equates "freedom of contract" as an institutional system with autonomy and freedom of choice. *See* Epstein, *Contract at Will, supra* note 24, at 953. This move permits him to avoid many of the hard questions raised by his argument.

44. Weber, *Freedom and Coercion*, in ON LAW IN ECONOMY & SOCIETY 191 (M. Rheinstein ed. 1954).

45. The approach is exemplified by Posner, *Some Economics of Labor Law*, 51 U. CHI. L. REV. 988 (1984)[hereinafter Posner, *Some Economics*]. *See also* R. POSNER, ECONOMIC ANALYSIS OF LAW 299-312 (3d. ed. 1986); Fischel, *Labor Markets and Labor Law Compared with Capital Markets and Corporate Law*, 51 U. CHI. L. REV. 1061 (1984). Professor Epstein's defense of free labor markets is based primarily on a libertarian, "autonomy-based" theory. *See* Epstein, *Common Law, supra* note 24, at 1364-79; *see also supra* notes 42-43 and accompanying text. However, he argues that there is a "substantial convergence of libertarian and utilitarian principles as they apply to labor relations." *Id.* at 1358. Epstein cites particularly the "wealth maximization variant of utilitarianism" championed by Posner. *Id.* at 1379 n.70. Elsewhere he argues that freedom of contract "tends both to advance individual autonomy and to promote the efficient operation of labor markets." Epstein, *Contract at Will, supra* note 24 at 951.

As might be expected, the efficiency perspective on labor law is not monolithic and contains many variations. Recently economic perspectives on labor law have emerged that are considerably more refined than the widely known but less sophisticated Epstein and Posner analyses that supply the basis of my portrayal of the efficiency arguments. *See, e.g.*, Campbell, *Labor Law and Economics*, 38 STAN. L. REV. 991 (1986); Leslie, *Labor Bargaining Units*, 70 VA. L. REV. 353 (1984); Schwab, *Collective Bargaining and the Coase Theorem*, 72 CORNELL L. REV. 245 (1987); Wachter & Cohen, *The Law and Economics of Collective Bargaining: An Introduction and Application to the Problems of Subcontracting, Partial Closure, and Relocation*, 136 U. PA. L. REV. 1349 (1988).

46. According to Epstein, the NLRA and other New Deal labor legislation is "in large measure a mistake that, if possible, should be scrapped in favor of the adoption of a sensible

sumptively efficient,[47] whereas expansive, or even limited, market reconstruction is presumptively inefficient and therefore socially retrograde.[48] Advocates of this view sometimes argue that there is a natural common law regime, and that it is efficient. Once the conventionality of legal rules becomes clear, however, the naturalistic underpinnings of free market efficiency claims cannot survive. The position is then transformed to the view that a particular ideal set of common law rules or the set of rules said to exist at a given time (e.g., 1890-1910) are relatively more efficient than alternative market structures, and that by comparison modern statutory reform necessarily entails efficiency costs.[49]

This argument cannot be sustained, at least not at the level of dismissive generality at which it is frequently offered. Neither the efficiency consequences of legal rules, nor the shape of a perfectly or presumptively efficient rule system can be determined *a priori*. How particular rules impact on efficiency concerns is something that can be known, at best, only on the basis and in the light of specific, ad hoc judgments about social and institutional contexts, peoples' actual and potential wants, and their adaptive potentialities. Highly general claims about the presumptive efficiency of free contract, private property, and minimalist regulation are wholly undemonstrable. This does not mean that efficiency concerns are unimportant or that inquiry regarding efficiency effects is useless. Rather, it means that efficiency inquiry must be conducted in a focused, contextualized manner and must incorporate a multitude of social and political judgments. Accordingly, the criterion of efficiency by itself cannot serve as the foundation of a general policy favoring minimally regulated labor markets. Nor can it supply the basis of a wholesale, *ex ante* condemnation of the program of democracy-enhancing reconstruction of the countless institutional contexts that make up the world of work.

---

common law regime relying heavily upon tort and contract law." Epstein, *Common Law*, *supra* note 24, at 1357; *see also* R. EPSTEIN, TAKINGS: PRIVATE PROPERTY & THE POWER OF EMINENT DOMAIN 279-82, 328 (1985) (questioning constitutionality of modern labor legislation). I should note, however, that Posner does not advocate repeal of the NLRA, although he argues that its primary function is to cartelize labor markets. *See* Posner, *Some Economics*, *supra* note 45, at 990, 999.

47. *See*, Posner, *Some Economics*, *supra* note 45, at 991-92 & n. 11.

48. Epstein's analysis is prescriptive. *See supra* note 46. On the other hand, Posner states that his "analysis is positive, not normative." Posner, *Some Economics*, *supra* note 45, at 990. This description of the status of his discussion is belied by his overt hostility to historical claims and academic evidence running contrary to his cartel theory of unionization. *See, e.g.*, *id.* at 991, 999-1009.

49. Epstein argues for an ideal set of common law rules, *see* Epstein, *Common Law*, *supra* note 24, at 1359, but his case is largely built on a discussion of the common law as Epstein believes it to have stood in the late nineteenth century.

"Efficiency" means the satisfaction of peoples' preferences under circumstances of constraint. The constraining conditions include the technological state of the art and the distribution of wealth, personal entitlements, and endowments. It is well-established that given *any* legal regime (so long as it contains neither direct prohibitions on making bargains nor compulsory or nonwaivable terms in permitted bargains), and given the absence of transaction or information costs that block or distort bargaining, there will be an efficient outcome. The outcome will be efficient in the sense that all desired exchanges will be effected, thereby yielding their accompanying gains. The proposition is true regardless of the initial allocation of entitlements. Similarly, if transaction or information costs exceed zero, *no* legal regime will generate a perfectly efficient outcome.[50]

It is possible by legal reform to move to a relatively more efficient outcome; that is, to increase consumer satisfaction, other things being equal. This will occur if the legal change (a) reduces or eliminates the adverse effects of transaction or information costs, without causing outweighing reductions in consumer satisfaction; and/or (b) permits the making of previously forbidden exchanges or eliminates compulsory terms, where the gains from these changes outweigh any collateral diminution in consumer satisfaction.

It should be obvious that whether a reversion to late nineteenth century common law rules would produce efficiency gains in labor markets cannot be answered without performing an empirical inquiry of staggering complexity.[51] I do not believe anyone has ever proposed a research design that would permit even a preliminary test of the efficiency superiority of the old common law rules, let alone has anyone actually undertaken to make the empirical case. The best existing quantitative studies suggest that legally mandated collective bargaining generates gains in efficiency.[52]

Conceding, or even invoking, the problem of empirical evidence, proponents of minimalist regulation on efficiency grounds typically repair to yet another line of argument. The claim becomes that while we may never know for sure the efficiency consequences of many legal rules, *some* important rules can be identified as inefficient *a priori* and therefore worthy of condemnation. The rules so designated are what might be termed "substantive" or "direct" restrictions on freedom of contract.

In considering this sort of claim, it will be helpful first to set out a rough

50. *See generally* Kennedy & Michelman, *Are Property and Contract Efficient?*, 8 HOFSTRA L. REV. 711 (1980).

51. *See generally* Kennedy, *supra* note 34, at 963 & n.43 and sources cited therein.

52. *See* R. FREEMAN & J. MEDOFF, *supra* note 29, at 3-25.

typology of the kinds of rules that make up a labor law regime. There are two main categories. The first, "Type I rules," covers a wide territory of rules that structure bargaining behavior. The second, "Type II rules," refers to substantive restrictions on freedom of contract, which operate directly on bargaining content.

With respect to Type I rules, a first subcategory, Type I(a), consists of rules that in effect determine what a person can do to others against their will, what powers he or she can exercise over them. Many such rules are general background rules that are not particularly designed for application to labor contexts. Such rules may seem so obvious and general that their implications for labor law are often invisible. It was one part of the Realists' contribution to expose the significance to labor law of these familiar rules.[53] I would include in subcategory I(a) such things as the law of trespass. It is fundamental that the employer can obtain state assistance in preventing employees from occupying and using the means of production for their own ends.[54] Trespass and property rules give the employer great power, namely the power to withhold access to productive resources and earning opportunities except on terms suitable to the employer. I would also include in subcategory I(a) rules forbidding battery, assault, and false imprisonment.

A second subcategory, Type I(b), includes background rules specifically devised or developed for the labor context. They may, however, apply in other settings as well. Examples of such rules include the common law rules regulating picketing, secondary boycotts, and interference with protected economic expectancies. These rules were crucial in the era of industrialization and still influence modern decisions, particularly regarding picketing. Since the New Deal, however, most Type I(b) rules have been statutory in origin. Examples include: the NLRA prohibitions against secondary boycotts[55] and industrial espionage;[56] the rules governing organizer access to the workplace;[57] and the rule requiring employers to provide relevant information to incumbent unions.[58]

---

53. *See generally* Hale, *Bargaining*, *supra* note 32; Hale, *Coercion*, *supra* note 32; and Cohen, *Property*, *supra* note 32.

54. Ordinarily the law of trespass is state law. In a landmark case, the Supreme Court held additionally that employee sitdown strikes and similar trespassory activity are unprotected under the NLRA. NLRB v. Fansteel Metallurgical Corp., 306 U.S. 240, 252-57 (1939).

55. NLRA § 8(b)(4)(B), 29 U.S.C. § 158(b)(4)(B) (1982).

56. NLRA § 8(a)(1), 29 U.S.C. § 158(a)(1) (1982) (forbidden conduct includes employer surveillance of union activity); *see* 1 THE DEVELOPING LABOR LAW 127 (C. Morris, 2d ed. 1983).

57. *See, e.g.*, NLRB v. Babcock & Wilcox Co., 351 U.S. 105, 112-14 (1956).

58. *See, e.g.*, NLRB v. Truitt Mfg. Co., 351 U.S. 149, 152-53 (1956) (discussing connection between information provision and good faith bargaining).

A third subcategory, Type I(c), consists of rules governing the construction of employment agreements and collective bargaining contracts. Again, some of these rules are so "obvious" as to appear "natural," and hardly to be rules of law at all. This is an illusion, of course, given the conventionality of all legal rules. An example is the basic doctrine that, in the absence of express contrary contractual language, it is an assumed aspect of the employment relationship that the employer owns and can dispose of the product. Another example of a Type I(c) rule is the now eroding common law principle, often mistakenly thought to be ancient but actually of quite recent origin, that employment is presumed to be at-will. A sophisticated example of a Type I(c) rule is the presumption of coterminous application of the no-strike and arbitration clauses.[59]

No doubt there are other subcategories as well. All of these Type I rules can affect the parties' bargaining positions, and therefore such rules can affect the substantive content of the employment relationship. But the essential characteristic of Type I rules is that they operate on substantive content indirectly, by structuring or facilitating bargaining processes.

By contrast, Type II rules, which place substantive restrictions on freedom of contract, operate directly on bargaining content. They require or prohibit certain parties from contracting, specify the identity of mandatory bargaining partners, or mandate or prohibit certain content in agreements. Rules of this type existed in the late nineteenth century, but were not as common as they are today. An historical example of a Type II rule is labor standards protection for women and children. Modern labor law contains quite a number and variety of Type II rules. Examples include:

— labor standards legislation regarding wages, hours, and safety requirements,[60] and equal employment opportunity laws that forbid invidious discrimination;[61]

— the duty to bargain, as under section 8(a)(5) of the NLRA[62] and parallel statutes, obliging employers to bargain collectively with the union and to refrain from negotiating individual contracts, even with willing employees, once an exclusive bargaining representative has been designated;[63]

59. Gateway Coal Co. v. United Mine Workers, 414 U.S. 368, 382 (1974).

60. *See, e.g.*, Fair Labor Standards Act (FLSA), 29 U.S.C. §§ 201-219 (1982 & Supp. IV 1986); Occupational Safety & Health Act of 1970, 29 U.S.C. §§ 651-678 (1982 & Supp. IV 1986).

61. *See, e.g.*, Civil Rights Act of 1964, 42 U.S.C. §§ 2000e - 2000e-17 (1982 & Supp. IV 1986) (forbidding employment discrimination on the basis of race, color, gender, religion, or national origin).

62. NLRA § 8(a)(5), 29 U.S.C. § 158(a)(5) (1982) (employer has duty to bargain with union designated by majority of employees).

63. *See* J. I. Case Co. v. NLRB, 321 U.S. 332, 337-339 (1944) (majority rule).

— the prohibition against company unions;[64]

— the Quebec statute forbidding the use of strike replacements;[65]

— the doctrine of "illegal" topics of bargaining, barring insertion of certain types of clauses in collective agreements;[66]

— section 8(e) of the NLRA, which prohibits "hot cargo" agreements (an example of a pro-management restriction on free contract);[67]

— antitrust[68] and Shipping Act[69] rules that proscribe certain anticompetitive labor agreements;

— the complex of rules regarding union security agreements, which flatly bar some forms of union security (e.g., the closed shop),[70] and yet

64. *See* NLRA § 8(a)(2), 29 U.S.C. § 158(a)(2) (1982) (forbidding employer domination of or interference with the formation of any labor organization).

65. Quebec Labour Code, §§ 109.1-.3, QUE. REV. STAT., ch. c-27, §§ 109.1-.3 (1979).

66. An "illegal clause" may not be included in a collective bargaining agreement and is unenforceable. Insistence on such a clause or use of strike or lockout to obtain an "illegal clause" violates the duty to bargain. The inclusion of certain illegal clauses is itself an unfair labor practice. Examples of illegal clauses include: provisions for a hiring hall that gives preference to union members; racially discriminatory clauses; clauses that involve the union in a breach of the duty of fair representation; clauses that impermissibly alter the bargaining unit; and clauses forbidding employees to solicit for rival unions on nonworking time. *See generally* 1 THE DEVELOPING LABOR LAW 863-69 (C. Morris 2d ed. 1983); R. GORMAN, BASIC TEXT ON LABOR LAW 529-31 (1976). Further examples are "hot cargo" clauses, see *infra* note 67 and accompanying text. For examples of anticompetitive agreements unprotected by a labor exemption, see *infra* notes 68-69 and accompanying text. For a discussion of invalid union security agreements, see *infra* note 70 and accompanying text.

67. *See* NLRA § 8(e), 29 U.S.C. § 158(e) (1982), which makes it an unfair labor practice to enter a "hot cargo" agreement and renders such agreements void and unenforceable. Hot cargo agreements bind the employer to cease and/or refrain from doing business with another employer with which the union has a dispute or which it seeks to organize. NLRA § 8(b)(4)(A), 29 U.S.C. § 158(b)(4)(A) (1982), makes it unlawful for a union to threaten or coerce an employer into agreeing to a hot cargo clause. The Labor Management Relations Act (LMRA), § 303, 29 U.S.C. § 187 (1982), creates a civil action in favor of any employer injured by a violation of § 8(b)(4). These sections reveal an irony in the free market approach. Hot cargo clauses generally advantage the union and are opposed by employers, who in most other contexts invoke free market rhetoric. Yet employers are not typically heard to call for the repeal of § 8(e). In this instance, employers seek statutory protection from the results of free bargaining. Of course, the anomaly is thought to be explained by the argument that, without legally encouraged collective bargaining, labor would never be in a position to press for hot cargo clauses in the first place. The argument is doubtful, since contracts of this type, or efforts to obtain them, predate the NLRA.

68. *See, e.g.*, United Mine Workers v. Pennington, 381 U.S. 657 (1965) (union agreement with one set of employers to impose a certain wage scale on other bargaining units is subject to attack under the Sherman Antitrust Act).

69. *See, e.g.*, 46 U.S.C. § 814 (1982); Federal Maritime Comm'n v. Pacific Maritime Ass'n, 435 U.S. 40 (1978) (collective bargaining agreement subject to Federal Maritime Commission scrutiny for anticompetitive restraints).

70. *See* NLRA § 8(a)(3), 29 U.S.C. § 158(a)(3) (1982)(barring agreements that make union membership a condition of employment on entry).

which authorize other forms (e.g., valid union shop agreements), thereby compelling unwilling third parties (nonunion or conscientiously objecting bargaining unit members) to contribute to defraying union costs;[71]

— the unenforceability of "yellow dog contracts" under section 3 of the Norris-LaGuardia Act;[72] and,

— nonwaivable protections against unjust dismissal of at-will employees.[73]

Type II provisions directly forbid the making of, or refuse enforcement to, certain kinds of contracts because of their substantive content, or they forbid willing parties to deal, or compel dealings between unwilling parties. As such, free marketeers argue that Type II rules not only violate the liberal presumption that respect for individual autonomy requires enforcement of willingly entered contracts, but also that rules of this type are inefficient by definition. Let us assume for the moment that efficiency is the preeminent social value; that is, let us temporarily set equity considerations aside.[74] It does not follow that Type II rules are automatically condemned. The problem with *a priori* condemnation of substantive restrictions is that it fails to deal with the wide variety of problems of market failure and third party effects. There are many recurrent reasons other than bad luck or miscalculation why a willingly entered contract may fail to benefit one (or both) of the parties or why parties may fail to enter utility-enhancing contracts.[75] Proscribing or refusing enforcement to such utility-impairing contracts or exerting legal pressure to bargain in certain situations may yield an outcome that

71. Under valid union security agreements, all bargaining unit employees may be compelled as a condition of employment (on or after the thirtieth day of employment) to contribute to the union amounts equal to the portion of union dues devoted to routine collective bargaining expenses. *See* NLRA § 8(a)(3), 29 U.S.C. § 158(a)(3) (1982); *see also* Communications Workers v. Beck, 108 S. Ct. 2641 (1988) (most recent Supreme Court interpretation of NLRA § 8(a)(3)).

72. Section three of the Norris-LaGuardia Act, 29 U.S.C. § 103 (1982), holds unenforceable in federal court promises by employees to refrain from joining a union while employed by the employer. Agreements of this kind are traditionally called "yellow dog contracts."

73. Many jurisdictions now provide relief for at-will employees discharged in violation of public policy. *See* Employment at Will: State Rulings Chart, 9A [IERM] Lab. Rel. Rep. (BNA) 505:51-52 (1988). A sound rule would be that rights created by the tort of retaliatory discharge are nonwaivable.

74. This is done solely for purposes of discussion and as a way of engaging the efficiency critique of law reform. In fact, equity and efficiency considerations are inextricably linked. *See infra* note 76.

75. *See* Kelman, *Choice and Utility*, 1979 WIS. L. REV. 769; Kennedy & Michelman, *supra* note 50; Sunstein, *Two Faces of Liberalism*, 41 U. MIAMI L. REV. 245 (1986); *see also* Hedlund, *An Economic Case for Mandatory Bargaining Over Partial Termination and Plant Relocation Decisions*, 95 YALE L. J. 949 (1986); Savarese, *Protecting At Will Employees Against Wrongful Discharge: The Duty to Terminate Only in Good Faith*, 93 HARV. L. REV. 1816 (1980).

is more efficient than the one that would occur under "free contract." In other words, there may be perfectly valid justifications *strictly from an efficiency standpoint* for substantive restrictions on freedom of contract. Once it is understood that efficiency concerns must be considered and worked through on a case-by-case basis, it is clear that efficiency in the abstract does not necessarily either favor or disfavor any particular form or modification of either Type I or Type II rules. Whether to conclude that a particular substantive restriction on freedom of contract undermines or actually serves efficiency will depend on ad hoc, historically and socially contextualized judgments about peoples' circumstances and wants. It is elementary that judgments of this kind are inevitably influenced by political values and assumptions, including one's vision of the meaning, possible forms, and significance of employee self-determination. In any case, the claim that Type II rules are *a priori* inefficient is false.[76]

As it happens, there is a wealth of scholarship suggesting that problems of market failure and third party effects are pervasive in labor markets, giving rise to cogent efficiency arguments for substantive restrictions such as mandated, majority-rule collective bargaining. Some of the most important recent work in labor economics focuses on these issues, and, in turn, this work has begun to have an exciting impact on labor law scholarship.[77] To give a sense of the literature, I will briefly recount some of the major arguments.[78]

Labor economists in recent decades have devoted considerable attention to how labor markets depart in practice from the idealized neoclassical

76. The way I have structured the discussion implicitly concedes that if transaction and information costs are zero and there are no externalities, third party effects, free rider problems, or similar market failure issues, then a substantive restriction on freedom of contract is definitionally inefficient. While I cannot develop the point in detail here, I want to insist that in conceding this much I do *not* concede that the fact that a legal reform is inefficient is by itself an ethical argument to forego enacting the reform. Whether or not we should proceed in the face of efficiency losses depends on whether they are outweighed by equity gains, a question which economic theory refers to social philosophy. It is incoherent to say that efficiency costs, by themselves, provide an ethical objection to a proposed change. If the reform effects desirable distributive consequences (accounting for the efficiency losses), then the inefficiency is ethically objectionable only if there is an alternative way to accomplish the redistribution that has lower efficiency costs. Similarly, just because a reform would yield an efficiency gain is not, by itself, a reason to enact the reform. We must examine the distributive consequences of the change and satisfy ourselves that there is a sufficient ethical basis to bring about those consequences (in light of the efficiency gains). On these points, see generally, Dworkin, *Is Wealth a Value?*, 9 J. LEG. STUDIES 191 (1980).

77. Professor Weiler's important manuscript, *see* P. WEILER, LAW AT WORK, *supra* note 25, draws on and contributes to this scholarship. *See also* Stone, *supra* note 14, at 152-61 (labor law theory and transaction cost economics).

78. The following discussion draws upon R. FREEMAN & J. MEDOFF, *supra* note 29; and P. WEILER, LAW AT WORK, *supra* note 25. For a brief, but illuminating summary, see L. THUROW, THE ZERO-SUM SOCIETY 54-61 (1980).

model. According to neoclassical theory, casual and fluid employee entry into and exit from the jobs offered by a multitude of competing employers conduces to frequent and flexible adjustments of wage/benefit packages to changing employee preferences, as well as to changes in demand and technology. The price of labor is adjusted in labor markets so as to correspond to the marginal productivity of the worker, and consequently, social resources are efficiently allocated. Contemporary scholarship shows this image of labor markets to be misleading in many if not most cases. Flexible adjustments, particularly downward adjustments, of wage/benefit packages may have serious adverse morale and productivity consequences. Therefore, compensation is "downwardly rigid," that is, compensation packages tend not to be reduced routinely. Moreover, because in many sectors skill acquisition takes place largely within the firm (i.e., there is no independent labor supply curve), employers attempt to use internal labor markets to induce employee continuity and cooperation in training fellow employees, so as to capture the rewards of their investment in human capital. "Internal labor markets" are institutional devices (job ladders, seniority systems, step increases, internal job bidding) designed to encourage promotion from within or career employment with the firm. The linkage of benefits to seniority and the importance of firm-specific skills exercise a powerful "lock-in" effect on employees (and sometimes firms). The consequence of these practices is to make long-term employment common, if not the norm in many leading sectors of the economy. This means that much of the content of the employment relationship is internally planned, and that in much of the economy the forces of supply and demand exercise only an indirect, often weak influence on employment terms. For employees, the lock-in effect of career employment with the firm makes exit or the threat of exit (employees' primary device for impacting labor markets) extremely costly and risky. This gives rise to a series of classic problems of market failure, including instances of "transaction-specific asset" problems.[79]

Legal regulation, including Type II rules, can correct for the adverse efficiency consequences stemming from the long-term lock-in effect and similar barriers to exit. I emphasize again that we are not talking here of equity arguments (e.g., long-term workers are at an unfair disadvantage in bargain-

79. Oliver Williamson has developed the notion of a "transaction-specific asset" — an asset that is significantly more valuable in its present use than in its next best use. Williamson, *Corporate Governance*, 93 YALE L. J. 1197, 1202-03 (1984); Williamson, *Transaction-Cost Economics: The Governance of Contractual Relations*, 22 J. L. & ECON. 233, 239-42 (1979). A long-term employee's investment in a job commonly has the attributes of a transaction-specific asset. *See also* Hedlund, *supra* note 75, at 955-57 (exploration of transaction-specific asset problems in labor markets); Stone, *supra* note 14, at 152-61.

ing with employers), but of claims of market failure, that is, arguments formulated entirely under the rubric of efficiency.[80] For example, Freeman and Medoff have made the case that, quite apart from any equity considerations, legally mandated, majority-rule collective bargaining overcomes a host of market failure problems.[81] These problems include: the unresponsiveness of labor markets to the preferences of inframarginal employees (with consequent dampening effects on productivity);[82] information cost and myopia problems; problems of "unrevealed preferences" (i.e., the inhibition of preference revelation by long-term employees caused by their perception of the risks and high costs of dismissal);[83] all sorts of free rider problems, particularly acute in the workplace setting where many important benefits resemble "public goods" (e.g., safety measures and pension plans);[84] and certain third party effects (e.g., young workers may fail to appreciate the need for fringe benefit protection for future dependents and for retirement).[85]

Other problems of market failure abound and may call out for mandated bargaining, nonwaivable terms, or other substantive restrictions on freedom of contract on efficiency grounds. There are a wide variety of third-party effects or externality problems. A particularly pressing example is the plant closing situation, where failure of the employment contract to protect against the social consequences of capital flight may have profoundly destructive effects on third parties including family members, small community businesses, and clients of municipal services. To overcome this problem it has been proposed that all employment contracts contain nonwaivable protections against plant closure.[86]

In a somewhat different vein, Professor Sunstein has highlighted the question of "adaptive preferences," which are preferences conditioned by the absence of alternatives.[87] This is analogous to a form of market failure, since efficiency analysis assumes the exogeneity of preferences. Where the absence of alternatives is due to the structure of law, the efficiency argument for the status quo necessarily involves an element of circularity. For example, it is sometimes claimed (quite incorrectly, I believe) that employees "do not

80. Of course, the boundary between efficiency arguments and equity arguments is often blurred. *See* Kennedy, *Distributive and Paternalist Motives in Contract and Tort Law, With Special Reference to Compulsory Terms and Unequal Bargaining Power*, 41 MD. L. REV. 563, 574-75 (1982).

81. *See* R. FREEMAN & J. MEDOFF, *supra* note 29, at 3-25.

82. *Id.* at 9-10.

83. *Id.*

84. *Id.* at 8-10.

85. *Id.* at 9-10, 61-77.

86. *See* Kennedy, *supra* note 80, at 629-31.

87. *See* Sunstein, *supra* note 75, at 248-49.

want" enhanced participation in workplace decisionmaking, and therefore legally mandating such participation is inefficient as well as illiberal. But if the legal system has historically been heavily biased in favor of hierarchy and against participation, the alleged employee preference for hierarchy may be "adaptive." If so, the efficiency attack on legal reform aimed to increase participation is circular reasoning. Legal reforms of the sort proposed here might enhance efficiency by removing the endogenous conditioning of employee preferences.[88]

My goal in this discussion is not to establish an efficiency case for any particular proposal. Rather, the point is that the value of efficiency does not *a priori* rule out, and may actually be served by, substantive restrictions on freedom of contract. Whether that is true in a particular case turns on a complex of ad hoc, empirical judgments, that is to say, on a type of inquiry that pushes beyond general categories to the terrain of social and historical context. Such an inquiry is inevitably embedded within and influenced by the moral and political world view of the investigator. In any event, while claims of efficiency may raise specific and important concerns for labor law reform, they present no general theoretical obstacle to a program of radical market reconstruction. The market reconstruction approach is not open to the criticism that it disregards efficiency concerns.

D. *Self-Limiting Market Reconstruction*

A workplace democracy approach to labor law must be sensitive to the claims of individual autonomy and efficiency, as these concerns make themselves felt in specific social settings. Neither value represents a general, *ex ante* obstacle to democratic revision of the institutional structures of employment. Accordingly, there is no reason why democracy-enhancing market reconstruction should not proceed indefinitely, through all of the contexts constituting or linked to the world of work.

The New Deal's ratification of the market reconstruction approach was a watershed event in American legal as well as political history. Since that time, however, proponents of labor law reform have not sought to extend market reconstruction indefinitely. Indeed, the dominant liberal conceptions of collective bargaining often seem committed, Pandora-like, to restraining the potentially limitless scope of the approach.

The industrial philosophy of New Deal and postwar labor law may be characterized as a commitment to *partial* or *self-limiting market reconstruction*. Federal labor policy embodies the basic market reconstruction idea. Congressional policy is to "encourag[e] the practice and procedure of collec-

88. *See* McPherson, *supra* note 14, at 364-68.

tive bargaining . . . ."[89] Yet federal labor policy has also always adhered to distinct, principled, and antidemocratic limitations on the scope and goals of the market reconstruction it endorses. For example, the New Deal/postwar model contains significant restrictions on protected, concerted activity; fundamentally accepts that work must be organized on an authoritarian basis; and holds that there is a "core of entrepreneurial control"[90] from which employee participation is excluded. The model takes for granted a background legal regime that treats managerial prerogative as "inherent in" the employer; this unduly limits the scope of employee participation in enterprise governance.

This is a negative way of describing New Deal labor law's philosophy of self-limiting market reconstruction. A more positive version holds that labor law is committed to the *autonomy* of collective bargaining. Labor law's greatest postwar theorists generally shared a commitment to this autonomy perspective.[91] The familiar theory is that law should set up the process and

89. NLRA § 1, 29 U.S.C. § 151 (1982).

90. Fibreboard Paper Products Corp. v. NLRB, 379 U.S. 203, 223 (1964) (Stewart, J., concurring).

91. *See generally* Cox, *The Duty to Bargain In Good Faith*, 71 HARV. L. REV. 1401 (1958); Cox & Dunlop, *Regulation of Collective Bargaining By the National Labor Relations Board*, 63 HARV. L. REV. 389 (1950); Feller, *The Coming End of Arbitration's Golden Age*, 29 PROC. NAT'L. ACAD. ARB. 97 (1976)[hereinafter Feller, *Golden Age*]; Feller, *General Theory*, *supra* note 3; Shulman, *Reason, Contract, and Law In Labor Relations*, 68 HARV. L. REV. 999 (1955).

Professor Summers has provided the following excellent summary of the autonomist view embodied in federal labor policy:

> The most obvious function of collective bargaining was of course its market function, to provide a better balance of bargaining power. The workers' economic weakness in individual bargaining, when confronted with the collective economic power of the employer, produced socially unacceptable results. The inequality of the individual labor market was to be remedied by creating a collective labor market . . . . A market, so constructed, would not guarantee socially desired outcomes but would leave market forces free to produce socially acceptable results.
>
> Collective bargaining, however, was conceived as much more than a market mechanism; it was prized as a process for extending constitutional values by bringing 'an element of democracy into the government of industry.' . . .
>
> . . . .
>
> Beyond these specific constitutional values, collective bargaining, as conceived by the Wagner Act, contributed to the underlying principle of limited government. . . . By replacing the individual labor market with the collective labor market, regulation of terms and conditions of employment could be left to market forces, and legal intervention could be limited to constructing the collective market. Workers would obtain sufficient bargaining power, the constitutional values of participation and due process would be enriched, and reliance on market forces retained.

Summers, *The Privatization of Personal Freedoms and Enrichment of Democracy: Some Lessons From Labor Law*, 1986 UNIV. ILL. L. REV. 689, 697-98 (footnote omitted). In current debate, Professor Weiler has offered the most probing and illuminating reconsideration of the

provide the groundrules, but otherwise recede into the background and play a minimalist role.[92] Beyond setting up the bargaining process, labor law is not and should not be designed to steer the substantive content or results of collective bargaining. To do so would be inconsistent with the basic ideal of party autonomy.[93] In particular, labor law is said to embody no preference for democratic, as opposed to authoritarian, forms of organization within the firm. To the contrary, by accepting the status quo, labor law often works *against* the democratization of firm governance procedures.[94]

The New Deal/postwar model of collective bargaining and labor law represents a highly effective effort to humanize work and extend democracy to working people by establishing and nurturing an "autonomous" rule of law in the workplace. Labor law at its best reflects a genuine societal commitment to the principle that employees have the right to participate in workplace governance. But the model of workplace democracy embodied in our labor law is a "defensive" or "reactive" conception. Employees can use concerted activity and collective bargaining procedures to bargain for general terms and to react to or protest management action, but they are not invited to participate directly and continuously in the firm's decisionmaking processes. In this sense, collective bargaining is not and never has been autonomous. It is an enclave of reactive due process in a sea of economic inequality and managerial power. Moreover, the autonomy of collective bargaining, implying as it does a minimalist role for law in market reconstruction, has permitted market segmentation to flourish, with profoundly damaging consequences to the interests of unrepresented and unpaid workers.

Of course, the Wagner Act was not the only important New Deal statute. The law has been committed to reconstruction of labor markets in other

---

market reconstruction approach. He has utilized its insights to advocate significant democratizing reforms, e.g., in the areas of strike replacements and secondary boycotts. *See generally* Weiler, *Striking A New Balance*, *supra* note 40, at 412-19; *see also* P. WEILER, LAW AT WORK, *supra* note 25. While Professor Weiler's position goes well beyond the customary restraint of the traditional approach, he too stops short of endorsing systematic market reconstruction.

92. *See, e.g.*, H.K. Porter Co. v. NLRB, 397 U.S. 99, 107-08 (1970) ("It is implicit in the entire structure of the Act that the Board acts to oversee and referee the process of collective bargaining, leaving the results of the contest to the bargaining strengths of the parties.").

93. *See, e.g.*, NLRB v. Insurance Agents' Int'l Union, 361 U.S. 477, 490 (1960) ("Our labor policy is not presently erected on a foundation of government control of the results of negotiations. . . . Nor does it contain a charter for the National Labor Relations Board to act at large in equalizing disparities of bargaining power between employer and union.").

94. This phenomenon is exemplified by NLRB v. Yeshiva University, 444 U.S. 672 (1980), in which the Supreme Court held that, because professors allegedly had significant input into policymaking at Yeshiva University, they were therefore excluded from the rights accorded employees under the NLRA. *Id.* at 686-90.

ways. Obvious examples of this commitment include wage and hour regulation, social security, and unemployment insurance, programs which provide a minimum social wages and benefits package. Conceding that perhaps it is all a matter of degree, I would nonetheless argue that even these crucial programs reflect an ambivalent, partial, and self-limiting conception of market reconstruction. Minimalism is the whole point of United States social welfare policy. Labor standards enactments have always set the floor sufficiently low as to leave ample room for thriving secondary labor markets. The problems of standards minimalism and market segmentation have been tragically, if unwittingly, exacerbated by labor's postwar success in creating a private welfare system through collective bargaining. As a result, unions saw less need to press government for a universal welfare system. Nor has minimum standards legislation been designed to generate wage pressure on backward employers, thereby inducing them to modernize by adopting high productivity techniques. As a general matter, our social policy has been designed to provide a safety net for those permanently or temporarily unable to function in prevailing labor markets. By contrast, particularly since World War II, many of our trade rivals have viewed social welfare policy as, at least to some extent, an investment in protecting and upgrading human capital. Insofar as these nations view generous and egalitarian social welfare programs as an investment in the quality of the workforce, their public policies dramatically and continuously alter both the supply and demand sides of the labor market equation.

In recent years, American employment law has begun to move beyond minimalism.[95] The self-limitations of New Deal market reconstruction have been breached, not so much by enhancing collective bargaining as such,[96]

95. *See supra* note 7 and accompanying text.

96. Recent legislative efforts to effect major changes in collective bargaining law have failed, notably in the case of the Labor Reform Act of 1977. *See infra* notes 111, 125 and accompanying text. However, there has been a significant extension of the coverage of collective bargaining law to new categories of employees. This includes non-profit health care employees, see Health Care Amendments of 1974, Pub. L. No. 93-360, 88 Stat. 395 (1974) (amending NLRA); and agricultural employees, *see, e.g.*, California Agricultural Labor Relations Act, 1975 Cal. Stat. 4013 (codified at CAL. LAB. CODE §§ 1140-1166 (Deering 1976)). Another area of expanded coverage is the public sector, although typically public employees are not granted the right to strike. Public employee unionism in the United States dates as early as the 1830s, however, the major expansion has occurred since the 1960s. The process was encouraged by legal reforms. At the federal level, the watershed event was President Kennedy's Exec. Order No. 10,988, 3 C.F.R. § 521 (1959-1963), which led, through a process of evolution, to the Civil Service Reform Act of 1978, Pub. L. No. 95-454, 92 Stat. 1192 (1978) (codified at 5 U.S.C. §§ 7101-7135 (1982 & Supp. IV 1986)). *See also* Postal Reorganization Act, Pub. L. No. 91-375, 84 Stat. 719, 728 (1970) (codified at 39 U.S.C. §§ 1001-1209 (1982 & Supp. IV 1986)) (collective bargaining rights of postal employees). Many states have also enacted collective bargaining statutes covering state civil servants. *See, e.g.*, ILL. ANN. STAT.,

although this did occur,[97] as by raising the baseline of labor standards. Significant early departures include: the Equal Pay Act (1963);[98] Title VII of the Civil Rights Act of 1964;[99] section 304 of the Consumer Credit Protection Act (1968);[100] the Occupational Safety & Health Act (1970);[101] and the Employee Retirement Income Security Act (1974).[102] Recent years have witnessed one of the most remarkable changes in modern common law history, the sudden, widespread emergence of contract and tort remedies for wrongful discharge.[103]

The strategy of democratizing labor markets by raising the social minimum wage and benefits package seems hardly to have run its course, although Reaganism has slowed its pace. Since I delivered the original version of this paper, Congress has enacted legislation on plant closing notification[104] and on polygraph testing.[105] Congress is currently considering or has recently considered legislation on parental leave,[106] mandatory health benefits,[107] and whistleblowers' protection.[108] State legislatures have also been active in raising the social floor of the employment relationship. Though knotty and difficult preemption issues remain, surely the United States Supreme Court's recent permissive holdings will encourage this trend at the

---

ch. 48, §§ 1601-1622 (Smith-Hurel 1986); MASS. GEN. L., ch. 150E, §§ 1-15 (1976); MINN. STAT. ANN. § 179A.01-.025 (West 1988).

97. *See generally* Modjeska, *Labor and the Warren Court*, 8 INDUS. REL. L. J. 479 (1986) (progressive interpretations of NLRA during Warren Court era).

98. 29 U.S.C. § 206(d) (1982).

99. 42 U.S.C. §§ 2000e - 2000e-17 (1982 & Supp. IV 1986).

100. 15 U.S.C. § 1674 (1982) (restricting discharge from employment due to wage garnishment).

101. 29 U.S.C. §§ 651-678 (1982 & Supp. IV 1986).

102. 29 U.S.C. §§ 1001-1461 (1982 & Supp. IV 1986).

103. *See supra* note 73.

104. Worker Adjustment & Retraining Notification Act, Pub. L. No. 100-379, 102 Stat. 890 (1988) (to be codified at 29 U.S.C. §§ 2101-2109).

105. Employee Polygraph Protection Act of 1988, Pub. L. No. 100-347, 102 Stat. 646 (to be codified at 29 U.S.C. §§ 2001-2009); Daily Lab. Rep. (BNA), June 28, 1988, at G1.

106. S. 2488, 100th Cong., 2d Sess. (1988) (required employers to grant unpaid leave to parents of new-born, newly adopted, or seriously ill children); H.R. 925, 100th Cong., 2d Sess. (1988) (similar to Senate bill but included more generous leave period). Parental leave legislation died in the Senate on October 7, 1988, although sponsors promised to revive the proposal in the next session. *See* 2 LAB. REL. WEEK (BNA) 970 (1988).

107. S. 1265, 100th Cong., 2d Sess. (1988) (minimum health benefits for all workers); H.R. 360, 100th Cong., 2d Sess. (1988) (similar to Senate bill).

108. S. 508, 100th Cong., 2d Sess. (1988) (designed to provide more protection to federal employees who report waste and fraud); H.R. 25, 100th Cong., 2d Sess. (1988) (similar to Senate bill). Final congressional passage of S. 508 occurred on October 7, 1988. *See* 142 CONG. REC. 15,328-29 (daily ed. Oct. 7, 1988). President Reagan pocket-vetoed the measure on October 26, 1988. 24 WEEKLY COMP. PRES. DOC. 1377 (Oct. 26, 1988).

state level.[109]

These steps beyond minimalism sit in an uneasy relationship with collective bargaining. The Supreme Court's preemption docket is but one symptom of the tension. Another is the continuing debate over the arbitrator's role, if any, in enforcing law external to the contract. Advocates of collective bargaining generally applaud minimum standards legislation, and they are often instrumental in getting it enacted. But there is a lingering disquiet that, beyond a certain point, the expanding role of statutes is a threat to the autonomy of collective bargaining. Some unionists fear that legislative and judicial developments may suggest to unorganized employees that eventually the political process will protect their rights without need of resort to the arduous and risky challenges of concerted activity and collective bargaining. For example, in some labor circles there has been hesitancy about expanding protections for non-organized at-will employees, although the AFL-CIO has officially endorsed such protections.[110] Perhaps for these or similar reasons, some of the most eloquent and creative contemporary advocates of workplace democracy hesitate to endorse open-ended, systematic market reconstruction.

While I ardently support "labor law reform" in the specific sense of improving collective bargaining law, I find this ambivalence about market reconstruction, or hesitancy to go further with it, puzzling. In retrospect, the emphasis on the autonomy of collective bargaining in the works of its leading labor law theorists appears to be not a necessary assumption, but, indirectly, a reflection of the decline of social unionism and the political isolation of the labor movement in the postwar era, leading to its failure or inability to mount a successful political challenge to the background legal regime of managerial prerogative. While the self-imposed limitations on market reconstruction contained in the New Deal conception of industrial democracy are understandable in historical and political terms, they cannot be defended from the standpoint of democratic principles. I therefore offer an alternative perspective favoring expansive market reconstruction.

III. Democracy-Enhancing Market Reconstruction

Proponents of industrial democracy have frequently and unnecessarily

109. *See* Lingle v. Norge Div. of Magic Chef, Inc., 108 S. Ct. 1877 (1988) (no preemption of state law remedy for retaliatory discharge); Fort Halifax Packing Co. v. Coyne, 107 S. Ct. 2211 (1987) (no preemption of state mandatory severance pay program); Metropolitan Life Insurance Co. v. Massachusetts, 471 U.S. 724 (1985) (no preemption of state mandatory mental health coverage).

110. AFL-CIO, Statements Adopted by the AFL-CIO Executive Council 44 (1987), *reprinted in* 34 Daily Lab. Rep. (BNA), Feb. 23, 1987, at E1.

blunted their case by confining it to arguments about the need to correct for bargaining or market failure, that is, arguments located on the terrain of efficiency analysis. In effect, collective bargaining is defended as a public good. This approach is quite helpful as far as it goes, but for too long it has suppressed the distributive dimension of labor law debate. Even equity arguments aimed at rectifying bargaining inequality are often somewhat euphemistically couched in the idiom of efficiency (e.g., "true liberty of contract," "establishing equality of bargaining power"). We need to reopen the discourse to frankly redistributive arguments. Power sharing is and should be on the agenda in the era of postindustrial transition.

My proposal, in essence, is to take the market reconstruction logic of New Deal labor law reform beyond its self-imposed limitations. *In the next cycle of labor law reform, the market reconstruction approach should be systematically mobilized to enhance democracy in every aspect of the employment relationship and the world of work.* The method of market reconstruction should be deployed to enhance collective bargaining, to democratize the governance structures of firms, and to democratize labor markets in both the organized and unrepresented sectors. Within collective bargaining law, market reconstruction should reduce the risks and increase the benefits of collective bargaining to employees. Law should strengthen employee bargaining power and remove certain built-in limitations of collective bargaining from the standpoint of democratic theory. With respect to firm governance, law should make an unambiguous commitment to democratic as opposed to hierarchical structures. Both for reasons of political theory and for practical business reasons, public law can no longer afford to be indifferent to the debilitating effects of hierarchy in working life. In labor markets, particularly the unorganized sector, law should redistribute power in favor of employees, raise the social minimum wage and benefits package, and mitigate labor market segmentation.

Democratic progress in work will require both legislative change and institutional reforms accomplished through enterprise-centered concerted activity. Political mobilization by employees and their allies and collective action within enterprises and industries are not antagonistic or alternative methods of achieving workplace democratization; they are fundamentally linked. In some cases, legislation can directly establish foundational democratic standards and conditions in work, as, for example, in the prohibition of race and gender discrimination. In general, law shapes the terrain upon which employee concerted activity takes place. Thus, the political process is, and must be, a vital arena of employee participation. Legislation can be an important register of gains from concerted activity. But my proposal is also oriented to the enterprise level, which, particularly in the United States, often offers a more accessible forum for employee participation. This is significant in light of the participatory conception of democracy that informs my proposal. Democracy—in work as in civic life—is something that needs to be won, created, and periodically reenvisioned. It is inherent in the concept of workplace democracy that it must, in a large part, be fashioned by employees themselves on an ongoing basis. Therefore, enterprise-centered employee concerted activity and collective bargaining must continue to play a central role in democratizing work. My call is not for government determination or imposition of all of the terms of the employment relationship, but rather for systematic revision of the background legal context in which employees participate through self-organization and otherwise in making the decisions that affect their working lives.

The remainder of this Article surveys potential areas of labor law reform and describes changes consistent with an expansive market reconstruction approach. The program of democratization through market reconstruction has possible implications for all aspects of the legal process, including further elaboration of common law remedies; the interpretation and administration of collective bargaining agreements and existing statutes by arbitrators, courts, and agencies; new legislation; and revised constitutional doctrine. The approach poses complex federalism and jurisdictional questions. Likewise, there is a wide array of subject matter areas to which democracy-enhancing market reconstruction could be applied. Here I present only some examples for purposes of launching the discussion, no attempt being made to cover the entire ground. Systematic elaboration of the program must necessarily be a long-term, collaborative project. Many of the specific reform proposals discussed here are well known. My hope is that the market reconstruction focus will link disparate areas of concern into a unified approach to law reform that will, in turn, suggest new areas of potential legal and institutional innovation.

A. Enhancing Collective Bargaining

Collective bargaining law creates a background legal regime that does more than affect the likely success of employees in organizing and collectivizing wage bargaining. As I have argued earlier, this background legal regime also affects the distribution of power within collective bargaining relationships, and, usually indirectly, the substantive outcomes of the process.

The emphasis in discussion of and proposals for labor law reform has been almost entirely on the organizing process and on boosting union chances for success in representation elections and in obtaining first contracts. There is no doubt that employer violations of the letter and spirit of the NLRA during organizing campaigns have been a potent barrier to the exercise by employees of their collective bargaining rights. I therefore strongly support reforms of the type contained in the ill-fated Labor Reform Act of 1977.[111]

Nonetheless, the time has come to acknowledge that labor law reform is also needed in aspects of collective bargaining that are often thought by its friends to be working rather well. The evidence suggests that even if the labor movement had won 100% of the elections it entered in recent years, union density would *still* be in decline.[112] Not only in the representation process, but throughout collective bargaining law and the law of internal union democracy, reform is needed to increase the value and decrease the risks of collective bargaining to employees.

Let me begin with a simple example, designed to bring the market reconstruction perspective into focus. The topic is how the law of waiver[113] interacts with legal regulation of the weapons of self-help. An issue that arises in strike situations is whether the employer may grant artificial or "superseniority" to strikebreakers. Such superseniority provides dramatically enhanced protection against future layoffs and is therefore a powerful incentive to cross picket lines. A common law regime creates no major barriers to the grant of superseniority, thus allowing the employer a potent economic weapon. By contrast, the Warren Court's brave decision in *NLRB v. Erie Resistor Corp.*[114] held that the grant of superseniority to strikebreakers is "inherently destructive" of employee rights under the NLRA, and therefore unlawful absent a showing of overriding business justification.[115] *Erie Resistor* was a high-water mark of liberal market reconstruction.

A subsequent NLRB decision, *Gem City Ready Mix Co.*,[116] shows how the device of waiver can undercut such a holding. Suppose that, in violation of *Erie Resistor*, the employer uses the superseniority tactic with a ven-

111. The Labor Reform Act of 1977 amended the NLRA, but never became law. S. 2467, 95th Cong., 2d Sess. (1977); H.R. 8410, 95th Cong., 1st Sess. (1977) (passed the House of Representatives on October 6, 1977); *see* 123 CONG. REC. 32,613 (1977).

112. *See* T. KOCHAN, H. KATZ, & R. MCKERSIE, *supra* note 2, at 47-80; Dickens & Leonard, *Accounting For the Decline in Union Membership, 1950-1980*, 38 IND. & LAB. REL. REV. 323 (1985).

113. On the doctrine of waiver, see Phillips, *The Contractual Waiver of Individual Rights Under the National Labor Relations Act*, 31 N.Y.L. SCH. L. REV. 793 (1986).

114. 373 U.S. 221 (1963).

115. *Id.* at 231-32. In an unusually frank departure from the dominant autonomy rhetoric, *see, e.g.*, *supra* notes 91-93 and accompanying text, the Court noted that often labor cases will turn on the "delicate task . . . of weighing the interests of employees in concerted activity against the interest of the employer in operating his business in a particular manner . . . ." *Id.* at 229.

116. 270 N.L.R.B. 1260, 116 L.R.R.M. (BNA) 1266 (1984).

geance, thereby bringing the union to its knees. Suppose also that in the strike settlement the defeated strikers agree to waive any right to challenge the employer's conduct. *Gem City* suggests, although it does not precisely hold, that the waiver would be honored, even if the defeated strikers did not understand or appreciate their relevant legal rights.[117] Validating the waiver reconstructs the market nearly full circle back to the common law, to the distinct advantage of employers.

Whatever one's substantive view of *Erie Resistor*, which I see as a victory for employee self-determination, it is fairly obvious that whenever a court or the Board proscribes the use of a particular bargaining weapon, the resulting legal rules will adjust power relations. But waiver is a complex and thorny area of labor law, and its implications for the structure of bargaining relationships are often more obscure. The waiver of rights seems something unremarkable, indeed, a "natural" feature of a system of "autonomous" collective bargaining. Most collective contracts routinely waive the right to strike. Despite possible Fourth of July overtones, a rhetoric of "inalienable rights" faces an uphill battle in the labor law context, as against the instinctive appeal of "free contract," "employee free choice," and limited government intervention in bargaining. That is, a prohibition of waiver seems "regulatory," whereas the authorization of waiver suggests the absence of government involvement.

Both prohibition and authorization reflect regulatory choices. In the typical labor market context of gross economic inequality, loose and unquestioning authorization of the waiver of employee statutory rights may crush rather than affirm worker autonomy and self-determination. Accordingly, my first proposal for democracy-enhancing reform is that labor law adopt a much more suspicious and grudging attitude toward the waiver of employee rights than hitherto. *Gem City* was wrong on the element of knowledge alone, but in any event it should be strictly confined to the narrowest reading of its facts, if not overruled on the substantive point of its inconsistency with the principles of *Erie Resistor*. Likewise, a general no-strike clause should not be deemed a waiver of the right of sympathetic observance of picket lines.[118] Assuming that the right to strike should under some circumstances

117. *Id.* at 1260-61, 116 L.R.R.M. at 1267-68. The Board's brief opinion in *Gem City* treats the superseniority question there as having arisen only as a part of a strike settlement, not as a cause of the union's defeat in the strike as in the hypothetical offered in the text.

118. Accordingly, the NLRB's doctrine in Indianapolis Power & Light Co., 273 N.L.R.B. 1715, 118 L.R.R.M. (BNA) 1201 (1985), *rev'd and remanded sub nom.* Local 1395, IBEW v. NLRB, 797 F.2d 1027 (D.C. Cir. 1986), should be overruled. (The Board's decision in this particular case was reversed and remanded for reconsideration of certain evidentiary issues).

be expressly waivable, it should never be subject to implied waiver.[119] An arbitration clause should surely never be deemed to waive the right to strike over nonarbitrable grievances, much less over grievances as to which the union has reserved freedom of action.[120] I question whether the right to strike over serious unfair labor practices should ever be waivable,[121] and I would be extremely reluctant to conclude that employees have waived the right to refuse unsafe work.[122] Unions should not be permitted to waive employees' statutory rights without, at a minimum, their consent having been manifested through ratification after full and adequate discussion. The law presently permits unratified union waivers of rights statutorily vested in employees, most notably and routinely the right to strike.[123]

Another area long overdue for reform is the question of access to and use of the workplace for employee self-organization and concerted activity.[124] In particular, nonemployee union organizers should be guaranteed some access to the workplace so that employees may have at least minimal opportunities to learn about collective bargaining.[125] Existing cases recognize that

119. Therefore, Local 174, Teamsters v. Lucas Flour Co., 369 U.S. 95 (1962), in which a no-strike obligation was implied, was wrong and should be overruled.

120. The "*Gateway Coal* presumption" should be abandoned. Gateway Coal Co. v. United Mine Workers, 414 U.S. 368 (1974), holds that an arbitration clause gives rise to an implied no-strike obligation that must be expressly negated in order for the union to preserve the right to strike. *Id.* at 382. This doctrine was applied in Goya Foods, Inc., 238 N.L.R.B. 1465 (1978), which held that a typical arbitration clause waives the right to strike after contract expiration over grievances arising during the contract term. *Id.* at 1467. *Goya* is another case that should be overruled.

121. The Board announced it would uphold this type of waiver in Reichhold Chemicals, Inc., 277 N.L.R.B. 639, 640, 120 L.R.R.M. (BNA) 1339, 1341 (1985), *vacated on other grounds*, 288 N.L.R.B. No. 8, 127 L.R.R.M. 1265 (1988) (supplemental opinion). In its supplemental opinion, the NLRB reaffirmed its view that the right to strike over unfair labor practices is waivable, 127 L.R.R.M. at 1268, but held that an employer may not insist to impasse on a prospective waiver of the right to seek redress from the NLRB or other tribunals regarding discipline imposed on replaced strikers under a contractual no-strike clause. *Id.* However, the Board did not determine whether a waiver of access to the Board is a permissive or an illegal subject of bargaining. *Id.* at n.18.

122. Another questionable decision is American Freight System v. NLRB, 722 F.2d 828 (D.C. Cir. 1983), ruling that contract language permitting employees to refuse unsafe work if "justified" waives any right under the NLRA to refuse work because of good faith safety fears. *Id.* at 832.

123. *See also* Prudential Insurance Co., 275 N.L.R.B. 208, 119 L.R.R.M. (BNA) 1073 (1985), holding that unions may waive employees' statutory right to assistance at disciplinary investigation interviews. *Prudential* should also be overruled.

124. *See generally* Gresham, *Still As Strangers: Nonemployee Union Organizers On Private Commercial Property*, 62 TEXAS L. REV. 111 (1983); Korn, *Property Rights and Job Security: Workplace Solicitation By Nonemployee Union Organizers*, 94 YALE L. J. 374 (1984); Summers, *supra* note 91, at 704-08.

125. The Labor Reform Act of 1977 proposed that the NLRB issue regulations providing minimal organizer access rights, so as to guarantee some opportunity to respond to employer

the workplace is the natural locus of work-related communication,[126] and that "[t]he right of self-organization depends in some measure on the ability of employees to learn the advantages of self-organization from others."[127] Decisionmakers should give life to these basic democratic principles in interpreting existing rules and entitlements.

At a minimum, rules that violate these principles, thereby impeding employee self-determination, should be overruled, beginning with the doctrine of *NLRB v. Babcock & Wilcox Co.*[128] and its progeny. Prior to that case, the Court had decided *Republic Aviation Corp. v. NLRB*,[129] a classic example of market reconstruction. *Republic* holds that under the NLRA the employer must suffer certain employee concerted activity (e.g., solicitation on behalf of the union) to occur on its property, unless the employer can establish that such activity interferes with a specific managerial interest.[130] According to *Republic* and subsequent cases, these interests include efficiency, productivity, safety, public image, and like concerns. The Court's decision is phrased as though the employer's common law ownership rights "give way" in the face of the competing statutory rights of employees. But a more accurate formulation is that the meaning of property ownership has been redefined so that the employer's ownership rights are more limited to start with than they were under the pre-existing common law.

Babcock & Wilcox dealt with access by *nonemployee* union organizers, which the Court treated as posing a different case from on-site *employee* concerted activity. While it has never been satisfactorily explained why this presents a different case, the Court did not follow *Republic* with respect to nonemployee access. Instead, it held: "[A]n employer may validly post his property against nonemployee distribution of union literature if reasonable efforts by the union through other available channels of communication will

"captive audience" speeches. *See* H.R. 8410, 95th Cong., 1st Sess., § 3 (1977). The measure passed the House on October 6, 1977. *See* 123 CONG. REC. 32,613 (1977). The bill died in the Senate the following year.

126. *See* Gale Prod. Div. of Outboard Marine Corp., 142 N.L.R.B. 1246, 1249 (1963) (acknowledging unique status of workplace as locus of communication among employees), *enf. denied*, 337 F.2d 390 (7th Cir. 1964). The relevant portion of *Gale Products* was cited with approval by the Supreme Court in Eastex, Inc. v. NLRB, 437 U.S. 556, 574 (1977), and NLRB v. Magnavox Co., 415 U.S. 322, 323-24 (1973).

127. NLRB v. Babcock & Wilcox Co., 351 U.S. 105, 113 (1956).

128. *Id.* at 112-14 (employer may exclude nonemployee union organizers).

129. 324 U.S. 793 (1945).

130. *Id.* at 803-04 & n.10 (citing Peyton Packing Co., 49 N.L.R.B. 828 (1943)). While *Republic Aviation* is an admirable decision, it is by no means beyond criticism. The Court's approval of the Board's famous dictum, "[w]orking time is for work," was an unnecessary and regrettable endorsement of a limiting, productivist conception of work. *Id.*

enable it to reach the employees with its message . . . ."[131] In practice, the alternative channels rule "has hardened into a near conclusive presumption that nonemployee union organizers can lawfully be excluded from the workplace."[132] For present purposes, the key point about *Babcock & Wilcox* is that the employer is *not* required to establish that the proposed on-site communication activity will interfere with any management interest. Rather, the *Babcock & Wilcox* conclusion is said to derive from a process of balancing or accommodating the employees' statutory rights and the employer's nonmanagerial "property rights."[133]

The law of organizer access rests upon a basic conceptual error of the sort exposed by the Legal Realists many years ago. In order to "balance" organizational and ownership rights, there must first *be* ownership rights; that is, these rights must have some source in law. There are no natural or preconventional rights of property ownership. "Property" is an emblem for the conclusion that, for reasons of social policy, the law enforces certain relationships and powers. Whether law ought to do so in a particular case or category of cases depends on whether there exist reasons of ethics or social policy indicating that law should play that role. However, the moment *Babcock & Wilcox* distinguished *Republic*, every legitimate concern for which "property" is a surrogate (e.g., efficiency, safety) was eliminated from the analysis. *Babcock & Wilcox* therefore rests on the erroneous premise that some ownership rights exist in the abstract, apart from any plausible instrumental consideration that might induce society to enforce property rights.[134]

But suppose there is some content to the employer's property interests apart from the managerial considerations. Even so, *Babcock & Wilcox* involves an element of circularity. The balancing test assumes that before balancing we know or can determine the respective weights of the employer's ownership and the employees' statutory rights. In effect, the balancing test assumes that we can calibrate the gravity of the employer's property rights apart from considerations of labor policy, and that policy enters only at the point of comparison between the two sets of rights. But because property entitlements are conventional rather than natural, we cannot possibly know the extent of the employer's rights until we consider, among other things, the implications of a national labor policy committed to encouraging collective

131. *Babcock & Wilcox*, 351 U.S. at 112. Additionally, the employer must not discriminate against the union by allowing other distribution. *Id.*

132. Gresham, *supra* note 124, at 114-15.

133. *Babcock & Wilcox*, 351 U.S. at 112. The distinction between managerial and other property interests is carefully maintained in a thoughtful recent case. *See* Dt. Lodge 91, International Ass'n of Machinists v. NLRB, 814 F.2d 876 (2d Cir. 1987).

134. There is also the dubious assumption that Congress intended to protect such abstract rights.

bargaining. The circularity of *Babcock & Wilcox* is that a balancing process is supposed to resolve the cases, but the balancing called for cannot be performed until the employer's rights take shape in light of labor policy; that is, until after the case is over.[135]

The proper approach to cases of this kind is to determine the maximum level of organizational and communication activity that can occur on-site consistent with reasonable "time, place, and manner" restrictions. Such restrictions may reflect considerations of productivity, safety, customer service, privacy, and the like, but should accord no weight to the employer's abstract property interests or desire to oppose unionization. The often ignored point of *Republic* is that the physical space of the workplace does not "belong" to the employer in the sense that the employer is privileged to exclude as a trespass protected activity that does not unduly interfere with operations.

This analysis has a constitutional law parallel. In *Perry Education Association v. Perry Local Educators' Association*,[136] Justice White upheld on mere reasonableness scrutiny a public employer's exclusion of dissenting union communications from school mailboxes.[137] His theory was that since the school mailboxes are not a "public forum," i.e., they are not dedicated to expressional activity by members of the public, only the most minimal scrutiny applies to the government employer's exclusion of the dissenting speech.[138] One would think that some showing of a plausible managerial concern should be required to justify the exclusion of nondisruptive, site-related speech on public property because of the identity or message of the speaker. Predictably, however, the Court's review of the employer's reasons for the exclusion was so superficial as to be meaningless. There is also an element of circularity in *Perry Education Association*. Justice White assumed that the mailboxes were not a public forum because the dissenting union (and other members of the "public") had no right of access to the mailboxes. However, the precise purpose of the case was to determine whether the first amendment and/or the equal protection clause afforded the dissenters a right to such access.

From a democracy-enhancement perspective, the proper first amendment test should track the approach to section 7 of the NLRA.[139] Namely, the

135. For a similar argument, *see* Gresham, *supra* note 124, at 161-73. The illogic of *Babcock & Wilcox* is exacerbated by the Board's recent refinement of access doctrine in Fairmont Hotel Co., 282 N.L.R.B. No. 27, 123 L.R.R.M. (BNA) 1257 (1986).

136. 460 U.S. 37 (1983).

137. *Id.* at 46-54.

138. *Id.* at 46-49.

139. 29 U.S.C. § 157 (1982); *see also supra* text following note 135.

first amendment should be interpreted to permit public employees to engage in the maximum amount of on-site expressional activity consistent with proper performance of the agency's functions. Seen in this light, *Perry Education Association* was wrongly decided. The Court's decision to favor the employer was arbitrary and insensitive to democratic values. It is inconceivable, on the record described by the Court, that the speech at issue could interfere either with school business or the proper performance of collective bargaining duties by the incumbent union. Conceivably the speech would enrich workplace democracy in that setting. The Constitution should protect it.

Another priority area for reform is the aspects of collective bargaining and arbitral law that deal with managerial prerogative, capital mobility, and successorship. In these matters, labor law has been deeply influenced by a certain common law conception of property entitlement. This notion is that the owner of a business has inherent, plenary authority to organize operations and make strategic decisions, unless the owner surrenders those rights in collective bargaining. Upon this foundation are erected a series of crucial doctrines that unduly limit the scope of industrial democracy: the mandatory/permissive distinction, the "reserved rights" doctrine of arbitral law, and the right of an employer to go completely out of business in retaliation against unionization.[140]

Collective bargaining is the primary institutional mechanism through which American private sector employees obtain a voice in matters of enterprise governance. But their input is artificially limited by the notion that topics falling within the "core of entrepreneurial control" are inherently decisions for management and therefore are not mandatorily bargainable.[141] Rarely is an attempt made to explain why certain business decisions are inherently unsuitable for discussion with employees. When such efforts are made, they are wholly unconvincing. They often reveal inappropriate and elitist attitudes regarding workers' alleged ignorance, immaturity, or shortsightedness.[142] But the true basis of the entrepreneurial core limitation on industrial democracy is a deep, often unarticulated belief, pervasive in the discourse of labor law, that it is simply inherent in the nature of private property that management is endowed with ultimate decisionmaking authority. Although Congress in 1935 enacted the NLRA, a statute designed to

140. Textile Workers Union v. Darlington Mfg. Co., 380 U.S. 263, 269-74 (1965).

141. The "core of entrepreneurial control" dictum appeared in Fibreboard Paper Products Corp. v. NLRB, 379 U.S. 203, 223 (1964) (Stewart, J., concurring). Current Supreme Court doctrine is set forth in First Nat'l Maintenance Corp. v. NLRB, 452 U.S. 666 (1981).

142. These attitudes are exposed and criticized in J. Atleson, Values & Assumptions in American Labor Law 111-35, 143-59 (1983).

foster industrial democracy,[143] democratic claims still apparently have to justify themselves in light of the cultural premise and presumption of employer sovereignty.

But managerial prerogative is not inherent in the concept of private property, much less in the nature of things. Managerial prerogative is a social convention. It can and should be altered and redefined. The mandatory/permissive distinction should be abandoned. In a democratic conception of labor law, any topic relevant to the strategic future of the enterprise or to employee job security should be presumptively bargainable. It follows that any information—including confidential financial data—relevant to this broad conception of the scope of bargaining should be mandatorily disclosable, subject to an appropriate system of such protective orders as are necessary to preserve trade secrets and the like.

It is often said that if strong unions are permitted to bargain about investment decisions, then weak unions must be forced to accept bargaining concerning internal union affairs. This logic escapes me. The proposal is to expand indefinitely bargaining over issues of concern to *enterprise* governance. *Union* governance forms no part of that agenda. Union democracy needs legal protection, but not through employer "bargaining." Union autonomy from managerial influence and domination is an essential component of any system of workplace democracy. But there need be no concern that abolishing the mandatory/permissive distinction must logically lead to exposing weak unions to the sort of illicit pressures involved in the *NLRB v. Wooster Division of Borg-Warner Corp.*[144] case. The rule should be that any topic related to governance of the enterprise is bargainable. A significant democratization of firms would be achieved by subjecting capital investment and disinvestment decisions to mandatory bargaining and information disclosure.[145]

Another important step to which the market reconstruction approach points is abolition of the arbitral doctrine of "reserved rights." This is a

143. *See* NLRA § 1, 29 U.S.C. § 151 (1982); *see also supra* text accompanying note 89.

144. 356 U.S. 342 (1958) (employer unlawfully insisted that collective bargaining agreement include "ballot clause" regarding internal union decisionmaking processes).

145. Skeptics argue that this change would be of little significance, because a union strong enough to exploit decision bargaining could achieve all or most of its realistic goals through bargaining over the effects of entrepreneurial decisions. Effects bargaining is mandatory. *See generally* Feller, *The Structure of Post-War Labor Relations: Response*, 11 N.Y.U. REV. L. & SOC. CHANGE 136, 138-39 (1982-83); Kohler, *Distinctions Without Differences: Effects Bargaining in Light of* First National Maintenance, 5 INDUS. REL. L. J. 402 (1983). While there is some force in these arguments, for reasons beyond the scope of this paper, I disagree. There are many situations in which predecision notice and opportunity to bargain can be of strategic and political significance to unions.

variant of the theme of "inherent managerial prerogative." According to this view, before the onset of collective bargaining, an employer possesses the prerogative to make strategic decisions for the firm and to direct operations. Therefore, even after collective bargaining commences, the employer retains such rights except and only to the extent that it surrenders them in the collective agreement. Employer prerogative is also subject to the union's right to protest management action by strike if, but only if, the union has retained a right to strike over such action in any contract in effect. As Professor Feller succinctly summarizes the theory:

> The agreement governs by its silence as well as its words. To the extent that a dispute as to management's right to take action affecting the employment relationship is not subject to arbitration, the agreement, if it does not permit a strike in protest against that action, establishes that management's action is final just as much as if that proposition were spelled out in words.[146]

Management's prerogative is said to be "inherent" or "reserved" unless surrendered, as though that way of ordering authority and power were a fact of nature. This is not correct. Management has this power not because this is the nature of things but because relatively recent political and social judgments were embodied in the common law to structure property entitlements this way. This is one of many reasons why talk of the "autonomy" of collective bargaining and arbitration, though descriptively plausible, is analytically unsound. Collective bargaining was never autonomous from the general legal regime, not even during Professor Feller's "golden age of arbitration." Collective bargaining has always been deeply embedded in and drawn some of its central norms from the common law of property entitlements.

There is no reason why collective bargaining and arbitration must assume an inherent managerial prerogative. Law easily could, and in my view should, substitute a different baseline assumption.[147] The norm should be that *employees* enjoy an inherent or vested right to participation in workplace decisionmaking. A situation vesting management with exclusive decisionmaking authority should be the exception requiring special justification as a departure from the basic commitment to democracy in firm governance. The presumption should be against waivers of participation rights. If the agreement is silent on, say, subcontracting or plant relocation, a democratic labor law would assume that management has failed in bargaining to achieve unilateral authority over that matter and that unilateral action is therefore

146. Feller, *Golden Age*, *supra* note 91, at 103.

147. *See generally* Langille, *"Equal Partnership" in Canadian Labour Law*, 21 Osgoode Hall L. J. 496 (1983).

either prohibited or, at a minimum, that any proposed course of action is now subject to bargaining.

A conception of collective bargaining based on a presumption that employees are entitled to some form of democratic participation in the decisions that affect their working lives would also call for revision of many doctrines having to do with capital mobility. Again based essentially on a common law notion of the "inherent" rights of the owner, the Supreme Court ruled in *Textile Workers Union v. Darlington Mfg. Co.*[148] that an employer may visit job loss, the ultimate punishment of industrial life, on employees simply because they have exercised their statutory right to organize.[149] There is no reason why private property ownership must be understood to include this privilege, and many reasons of social policy and democratic theory why it should not. Ownership rights should be redefined to exclude this power to use one's property so purposefully and unjustifiably to harm the vital interests of others. More generally, the legal definition of property should be revised so that the obligation of a successor to bargain with an incumbent union is guaranteed. Some Canadian provinces have statutes that point in this direction.[150] Successors' bargaining rights should not be left to rest on the shifting sands of current doctrine.[151] Moreover, the right of employees to make a fair price "buy out" of the enterprise upon employer disinvestment should also be guaranteed as an incident of the law of property.

Some readers may ask whether legislatures and/or courts can alter and redefine the basic social understanding of property in this way. In fact, it is not at all uncommon in American legal history for legislatures and courts to make such changes. The definition of property is regularly revised by legal reform, both in small and quite dramatic ways. While the *politics* of each situation varies, from the standpoint of legal process, there is no great difference between, on the one hand, promulgating a strong successor's duty to bargain or a mandatory buy-out option and, on the other, a legislative decision to abolish prospectively the common law tenancy by the entirety;[152] a court's declaration of public access entitlements vis-a-vis beachfront proper-

148. 380 U.S. 263 (1965).

149. *Id.* at 273-74.

150. *See, e.g.*, Ontario Labour Relations Act, ONT. REV. STAT., ch. 228, § 63 (1980) (as amended) (successor rights).

151. *See generally* Silverstein, *The Fate of Workers In Successor Firms: Does Law Tame the Market?*, 8 INDUS. REL. L. J. 153 (1986).

152. *See* West v. First Agricultural Bank, 382 Mass. 534, 549-52, 419 N.E.2d 262, 271-72 (1981) (discussing the 1979 amendments to MASS. GEN. LAWS ANN., ch. 209, § 1 (1958 & Supp. 1980)); Robinson v. Trousdale County, 516 S.W.2d 626, 629-32 (Tenn. 1974) (discussing the effect of the 1919 amendments to the Tennessee Code) (amendments currently codified at TENN. CODE ANN. §§ 36-3-504 to 505 (1984)).

ties;[153] a court's conclusion that owners of real property do not have the right to exclude government workers or legal services attorneys on official business seeking to visit migrant farmers temporarily staying on the owner's land;[154] or a court's ruling that an actionable nuisance is not enjoinable, so that the neighbor must suffer an inverse condemnation of a portion of his or her property for the polluter's private use.[155] In the labor context, two well-known property-revision cases are *Republic Aviation*,[156] and California's decision to open private shopping malls to political and labor activity.[157]

These are all classic instances of market reconstruction. Such decisions hardly guarantee substantive conditions: city dwellers are not guaranteed a vacation on the beach, migrant farmers are not guaranteed counsel, wives are not guaranteed an estate. But such legal changes are intended to and do shake up power relations, e.g., between husbands and wives or between growers and migrant workers. I by no means minimize the political and social questions raised by my proposals: my purpose is to invite such debate. But purely from the standpoint of legal form, the proposals are unremarkable.

B. Democratizing Firms

Labor law should be committed to democratizing the organizational structure of firms. Steps in this direction can be achieved simply by changes in the existing framework of collective bargaining law. One of the most promising sources of movement toward democratizing work is employee concerted activity, as found both in collective bargaining innovation and in the establishment of worker-owned businesses.

An important reform needed to encourage these processes is to remove the threat contained within existing doctrine that if employees achieve democratic forms of work organization or firm governance structures, they will bargain themselves right out of the protections of collective bargaining law.

153. *See, e.g.*, Matthews v. Bay Head Improvement Ass'n, 95 N.J. 306, 471 A.2d 355 (public trust doctrine), *cert. denied*, 469 U.S. 821 (1984); State *ex. rel.* Thornton v. Hay, 254 Or. 584, 462 P.2d 671 (1969)(custom). These cases are discussed in Singer, *The Reliance Interest In Property*, 40 STAN. L. REV. 611, 673-75 (1988).

154. *See* State v. Shack, 58 N.J. 297, 307, 277 A.2d 369, 374 (1971).

155. *See* Boomer v. Atlantic Cement Co., 26 N.Y.2d 219, 223-28, 257 N.E.2d 870, 872-75, 309 N.Y.S.2d 312, 315-19 (1970).

156. 324 U.S. 793 (1945); *see supra* notes 129-35 and accompanying text.

157. In PruneYard Shopping Center v. Robins, 447 U.S. 74 (1980), the Supreme Court upheld a California constitutional provision which, as interpreted, allows expressional activity on private shopping mall property. *Id.* at 80-88. Justice Rehnquist, whose relentless positivism sometimes leads him to unpredictable conclusions, wrote for the Court, rejecting first amendment and property rights challenges.

For example, *NLRB v. Yeshiva University*[158] suggests that the possession of governance powers and participation rights is inconsistent with "employee" status under the Labor Act. *College of Osteopathic Medicine*,[159] a post-*Yeshiva* NLRB decision, takes this antidemocratic absurdity to its logical conclusion by holding that, if statutory employees successfully utilize collective bargaining to obtain a direct, participatory voice in firm governance, they therefore cease to be covered employees and the employer becomes free to disavow its collective bargaining commitments.[160]

As I have argued elsewhere, in this period of historic transformation, workplace democracy requires both "adversary" and "participatory" institutional structures.[161] Given the pervasive inequality in labor markets and the ineradicable conflicts between employer and employee interests, the adversary or conflict-based system of collective bargaining is essential to guarantee employees the right to combine their voices and strength in autonomous, self-directed organizations. At the same time, if employees are to play a direct and continuous role in firm governance, participatory structures are needed so that the employees can become informed and have their input registered. *Yeshiva* and its progeny reflect a deep-seated distrust of democratic workplace organization. Such doctrine has no place in the democratic labor law of the future. Collective bargaining should not be restricted to the employees of authoritarian firms. Labor law should not only permit, but encourage, employees to use the collective bargaining process to obtain direct participation in firm governance.

Consistent with this view, the law should permit employees to achieve representation on corporate boards of directors through collective bargaining. Although this has been done, for example, at Chrysler Motors Corporation,[162] it is not yet entirely clear whether the NLRA contains obstacles to employees achieving significant or controlling positions on corporate boards. Collective bargaining also has an essential role to play in worker-owned businesses of any significant size. Yet substantial questions exist as to whether the owner-employees in such businesses have rights under the NLRA. Doubts should be promptly resolved in favor of coverage.[163]

The logic of the market reconstruction position is to favor statutorily mandated employee participation on corporate boards of directors, such as exists in some European systems. Difficult and challenging institutional is-

158. 444 U.S. 672 (1980).
159. 265 N.L.R.B. 295, 111 L.R.R.M. (BNA) 1523 (1982).
160. *Id.* at 297-98.
161. *See generally* Klare, *supra* note 10.
162. Wash. Post, Mar. 3, 1981, at F1, col. 1.
163. On these points, see Stone, *supra* note 14, at 120-31.

sues would arise in working out the precise role of employee representatives and the precise relationship between them and the union in organized plants. For present purposes, I simply insist on the desirability of inserting a right to participation in firm governance into the minimum social wage and benefits package. This right should be guaranteed whether or not employees choose to be represented by a labor union. Of course, fundamental changes in corporate as well as labor law would be required to accomplish such a result.

C. *Democratizing Markets*

As a general matter, the democracy-enhancing perspective endorses a redistribution of power in labor markets in favor of employees by raising the social minimum wage and benefits package. The specific goals of democracy-enhancing labor law over the next twenty or thirty years ought to be the protection of employee security in this period of economic restructuring; promotion of a human capital strategy for economic growth; reduction and eventual elimination of the discriminatory effects of labor market segmentation; and the creation of genuine, not just formal equal employment opportunity for women and minorities.[164] In order to expand women's opportunities for economic advancement and self-determination through paid work, it is essential to promote flexible entry and exit to paid employment by reducing the work week, establishing full-time equivalent benefits for part-time workers, including mandated flexitime in the social minimum wage and benefits package, and vastly increasing the provision of childcare services.

Democratic theory and a hopeful economic future demand linking American minimum employment standards policy with a strategy for upgrading

164. The area of discrimination in employment represents a crucial field for democratic reconstruction of labor markets. Although there is doctrine to the contrary, some current cases expressly or implicitly hold that existing market "realities" may excuse discrimination, even where such market forces are patently tainted by past or continuing racism, sexism, or other forms of invidious discrimination. For example, in AFSCME v. Washington, 770 F.2d 1401 (9th Cir. 1985) (Kennedy, J.), the employer based its compensation levels on prevailing market rates, even though the employer's own studies showed these rates to embed and carry forward past discrimination. *Id.* at 1403. The court held that the employer's wage practices were not subject to legal attack. *Id.* at 1405-08. Cases like this are inconsistent with what should be a fundamental purpose of our civil rights laws to reconstruct labor markets so that they are purged of the effects of past and current invidious discrimination. Such cases should be disapproved.

Fuller treatment of these issues would require a separate article. For discussions of the market reconstruction implications of feminist equality theory, see Finley, *Transcending Equality Theory: A Way Out of the Maternity & the Workplace Debate*, 86 COLUM. L. REV. 1118 (1986); Frug, *Securing Job Equality For Women: Labor Market Hostility to Working Mothers*, 59 B. U. L. REV. 55 (1979); Frug, *Sexual Equality & Sexual Difference In American Law* (unpublished manuscript).

and enhancing human capital. The normative dimension is the promotion of self-realization. From an economic standpoint, this linkage is a vital step in building a post-Fordist business system capable of organizational flexibility, rapid market response, and high quality outputs. As noted earlier, my assumption is that the know-how, creativity, and morale of American workers is the most important, growth-oriented asset in the economy.

I use "minimum standards" in a very broad sense. I include not only minimum wage and benefits legislation as such, but all programs that affect the "social wage." To promote a highly skilled, conceptually and interpersonally flexible, and confident workforce for the era of postindustrial transition, we will need massive investment in subsidized adult education and retraining, not only for technologically displaced employees but for all individuals who wish to alter their life paths. Educational sabbaticals must become as much a fixture in industry as they are in academia.

Education and training, both on the job and in schools, represent one side of the issue. There is another important facet to the economy's ability to enhance and draw upon employee problem solving capacities, namely, creating a climate of confidence among employees and respect for their job and income security. Without basic security, why should American workers be expected to participate willingly, let alone creatively, in the process of economic restructuring? Social policy and labor law must promote a climate of openness to change grounded on a baseline sense of job and income security.

Certain steps seem obvious. A democratic labor law must at a minimum provide for advance notice of mass layoffs and adequate transitional support in the event of plant closings or technological displacement. At the least this should include retraining allowances and mandatory severance pay. The new Worker Adjustment and Retraining Notification Act[165] represents an important initial step, but much remains to be done. In addition, public policy should encourage worker buyouts and worker-owned businesses through funding programs, loans, and favorable tax treatment.

It is important to note that welfare legislation and other spending programs are not the only ways to protect income security in periods of economic transition. It is also possible to restructure the background legal regime so as to compel businesses to internalize the economic and social dislocation costs of capital mobility. This could be accomplished by creating common law actions through which employees can protect their investment in human capital in plant closing situations.[166] As I assure my first-year

165. Pub. L. No. 100-379, 102 Stat. 890 (1988) (to be codified at 29 U.S.C. §§ 2101-2109).

166. The case for a legally protected reliance interest in property in plant closing situations is elegantly made in Singer, *supra* note 153.

students every year, this idea is fully consistent with the long-standing policy of tort law to design liability rules so as to correct for market failure due to the existence of externalities or third party effects. The goal of many tort rules is to force enterprises to internalize the costs of the physical injuries and environmental harms they cause. Transferring this well-established tort policy to the labor arena, it is obvious that cases like *United Steel Workers, Local 1330 v. United States Steel Corp.*,[167] which deny all common law remedies for capital flight, are wrongly decided. It should be a tort for an employer unilaterally to close a viable business vital to a community solely to make higher profits elsewhere without accounting for the social dislocation costs of capital mobility, a classic form of externality. The employer should be compelled by the threat of tort liability to discount alternative investments to the extent of potential liability for reparations to the abandoned community. The proposed tort rule for plant closings would require this calculus.

Reform is also urgently needed with respect to the problem of individual discharge. Almost all the advanced industrial nations now provide some form of public law protections against wrongful discharge. The United States is uniquely backward in this area. Until recently, and apart from special groups such as academics, there were two primary mechanisms for American employees to obtain such protections: civil service laws and collective bargaining. Perhaps American collective bargaining's greatest contribution, certainly one of its most significant, is to have introduced "just cause" protections into the private sector. But the time has come for the fundamental law of our society to guarantee protection against unjust dismissal for all employees. This protection should be a basic right, an aspect of the social minimum wage and benefits package.[168] Wrongful discharge pro-

167. 492 F. Supp. 1 (N.D. Ohio), *aff'd in part and vacated and remanded in part*, 631 F.2d 1264 (6th Cir. 1980).

168. At present, there is no federal constitutional right to job security, as there should be in a democratic society. For one thing, constitutional rights are not ordinarily applicable in the so-called "private sector," although it seems an easy case to argue that a large corporate employer's discharge of an employee is "state action." Even in the public sector, however, constitutional doctrine does not guarantee full just cause protections. Under current constitutional law, a discharged public employee has at most a claim of entitlement to procedural due process if and only if he or she can establish a "property interest" in the job (or the impairment of a "liberty interest"). *See* Bishop v. Wood, 426 U.S. 341 (1976); Arnett v. Kennedy, 416 U.S. 134 (1974); Perry v. Sindermann, 408 U.S. 593 (1972); Board of Regents v. Roth, 408 U.S. 564 (1972). *But see id.* at 588 (Marshall, J., dissenting)("[i]n my view, every citizen who applies for a government job is entitled to it unless the government can establish some reason for denying the employment"). Under current doctrine, state and local employers can circumvent constitutional due process simply by placing public employment on an at-will basis. At a minimum, constitutional doctrine should be revised so that all public employees are afforded due process

tections should be built into the floor of collective, as well as individual, bargaining, so that unions do not have to expend resources to obtain "just cause."

To achieve this goal, the underlying legal regime upon which individual and collective bargaining are erected should be revised.[169] Currently, the starting assumption is that employment is at-will unless modified. Instead, the assumption should be that absent an express modification, the employer cannot discharge without just cause. This protection should be waivable only under the most exceptional circumstances; it should never be waivable respecting discharges that violate public policy. The proposed change in the background legal regime could be achieved through judicial decision, legislation, or even constitutional amendment, or a combination of such actions.

Making "just cause" protections universally applicable would pose no threat to either the labor movement or to collective bargaining institutions. Although protections against arbitrary discharge and discipline are among the central benefits of organization, unions offer many other things of value to employees. The breadth of their contribution can be expected to expand in the next decades, particularly in the area of firm governance. Even in the area of discharge and discipline, much would remain to be done through collective bargaining even if basic just cause protections were guaranteed by law as is the minimum wage. Unions play and will continue to play a vital role in giving meaning and content to general legal rights in the particular setting of each workplace. Even with the proposed reform, unions would bargain for a jurisprudence, procedures, and remedies superior to those guaranteed to unrepresented employees. The presence of a union is often the best assurance that employee rights guaranteed on paper will actually be translated into meaningful enforcement at the workplace level. Moreover, were just cause protections mandated on a society-wide basis, unions might be relieved of the terrible dilemma they sometimes now face of choosing either to expend precious resources on weak grievances or to risk fair representation suits. Therefore, unions and the collective bargaining system have little to lose and much to gain from a basic societal commitment to prohibiting unjust discharge.

Much is made of the allegedly intractable conflict between the collective bargaining and arbitration system, on the one hand, and emergent state law

---

in discharge cases, regardless of whether the employee has a legal claim to the job under local law.

169. For an argument that principles long recognized in the common law already provide foundations for general wrongful discharge protection, see Minda, *The Common Law of Employment At-Will In New York: The Paralysis of Nineteenth Century Doctrine*, 36 SYRACUSE L. REV. 939 (1985).

remedies for wrongful discharge, on the other. An extreme version of the argument is that generous state law remedies will render arbitration less attractive and thereby undermine the congressionally preferred system of workplace dispute resolution. Hence, the supremacy of federal labor policy constitutionally bars the states from offering these remedies, at least with respect to employment in or affecting commerce. A softer and somewhat more plausible version claims that the states are barred only with respect to unionized employees.

Usually such arguments are put forth by employer counsel defending wrongful discharge suits. However, even friends of labor sometimes express concern that the common law/arbitration conflict with respect to unionized employees poses genuine dilemmas for workplace democracy. If state tribunals are permitted to pronounce whether an employee was discharged with or without just cause, it is feared that this will inevitably and directly interfere with the orderly and binding arbitral interpretation of just cause provisions in collective bargaining agreements. Likewise, there is concern that if unionized employees can circumvent and obtain remedies outside the arbitral process, the union's role as coauthor of the law of the shop will be undermined.[170]

While these are not simple issues, I am persuaded they can be resolved in favor of permitting the states to enact general wrongful discharge remedies as a basic component of the social minimum wage and benefits package. (There can be, of course, no preemption objection to Congress enacting such remedies pursuant to the commerce power.) The following is just an overview of preferred lines of development. Many tricky legal issues will need to be worked out in the years ahead. If the discussion illustrates anything it is that preemption doctrine may well become a crucial market reconstruction battlefield in the near future.[171]

Taking the problem a step at a time, let us first consider what seems a relatively easy issue, particularly after the Supreme Court's unanimous decision in *Lingle v. Norge Division of Magic Chef, Inc.*[172] The question arises as to whether a state is preempted from promulgating, by statute or decision, a tort remedy on behalf of employees who are discharged in violation of an important state policy. This issue could be raised, for example, in defense to a suit by an employee who is fired for filing a workers compensation claim or

---

170. *See* Vaca v. Sipes, 386 U.S. 171, 191 (1967).

171. For general overviews of the preemption doctrine, see F. Bartosic & R. Hartley, Labor Relations Law in the Private Sector 37-57 (2d. ed. 1986); J. Getman & B. Pogrebin, Labor Relations: The Basic Processes, Law & Practice 333-61 (1988).

172. 108 S. Ct. 1877, 1881-83 (1988) (state tort remedy held not preempted by § 301 of the LMRA).

for refusing to accede to the employer's request to do something illegal. This type of case is commonly known as a "retaliatory discharge" case.

Retaliatory discharge remedies should not be preempted, nor should they be waivable. There is no reason of collective bargaining policy why the states should be barred. Nor is there any evidence that Congress intended in section 301 of the Labor Management Relations Act[173] to preclude the states from protecting significant public policies by forbidding retaliatory discharges, any more than Congress intended to prevent states from forbidding race or gender discrimination in employment. A state tort rule creating a cause of action in favor of an employee fired in retaliation for exercising a legal right, performing a civic duty, or refusing to break the law, is simply one aspect of the basic civil rights law of the jurisdiction, which Congress in 1947 gave no hint of intending to disturb. The collective bargaining process can supplement, enlarge, and enforce these policies as it does other basic civil rights protections, but it should not be permitted to compromise or dilute them. Accordingly, the *Lingle* decision against preemption was correct.[174]

More difficult problems arise if the state promulgates "general" wrongful discharge remedies or "general" just cause protections.[175] "General" wrongful discharge or just cause protections go beyond remedies for retaliatory discharge. The employer is not only required to refrain from discharge in violation of public policy (i.e., discharge for a "bad" or forbidden reason). General just cause protections require the employer to refrain from *any* discharge unless the employer possesses and relies upon a "good" or "just" reason for its action. Such "general" remedies may sound either in tort, for illicit invasion of a valued interest or expectancy, or in contract, for breach of an implied-in-law just cause term in all employment contracts.

Opponents of general just cause protections challenge the power of the states to enact such remedies at all, with respect to employment in or affecting commerce. At any rate, they question the power of the states to afford

173. LMRA § 301(a), 29 U.S.C. § 185(a) (1982).

174. *Lingle* was awaiting decision when I delivered the original version of this paper. Not surprisingly, I took a position in favor of the result subsequently announced by the Court.

175. *See, e.g.*, MONT. CODE ANN., § 39-2-901 to 914 (1987). Montana's wrongful discharge statute breaks exciting new ground. However, Montana avoided the precise set of preemption issues discussed in the text. *See id.* at § 39-2-912(2) (exempting employees covered by written collective bargaining agreements from wrongful discharge remedies). While the exemption for unionized employees most likely eliminates a preemption challenge arising from the federal policy of uniformity with regard to collective bargaining agreements, *see infra* text accompanying notes 186-87, the fact that unionized employees are treated adversely on the face of the statute may constitute a discrimination that, somewhat ironically, raises a preemption issue under the *Machinists* doctrine. *See infra* notes 180-82 and accompanying text.

such remedies to employees covered by a collective bargaining agreement. The gist of the attack is that Congress has preempted the field of employer/employee relations which operate in or affect commerce, and that intrusive state remedies must therefore give way under the supremacy clause.[176] Congress has determined that voluntary arbitration is the preferred method of workplace dispute resolution.[177] Because the state just cause remedies will undermine arbitration, they are barred. A curious tension appears at this point in the discussion of exactly why the state scheme undermines the objectives of federal labor policy. One theory—a somewhat ironic one for employers to advance—is that the availability of state just cause remedies will render collective bargaining itself less attractive, in violation of the congressional policy of promoting collective bargaining to achieve industrial peace. The alternative theory is that automatic state remedies would give unions a head start at the bargaining table. The effect would be to make collective bargaining *more* attractive to employees, in violation of the congressional command that state law not alter the balance of power between management and labor.

These arguments for preemption are wholly unpersuasive. They reflect the basic pre-Realist error, discussed throughout this paper, of "naturalizing" the common law. The basic assumption is that the background legal regime *must* be authoritarian, it *must* permit discharge without just cause, as though the employer's power wrongfully to discharge were a datum of natural law. Moreover, the arguments are ultimately circular. Precisely what needs to be proved in these cases, precisely what is open to question, is *whether* the common law is required by federal labor policy to authorize discharge without cause. One cannot very well assume that in advance, as is implicitly done by the preemption challenges to just cause protections.

Underlying the preemption challenges is the erroneous assumption that in 1935 or 1947 Congress declared that only two workplace regimes can exist: the authoritarian regime of largely unbridled employer power or the collective bargaining regime. To be sure, Congress is on record as preferring the latter.[178] But there is no indication that Congress was of the view that these are the only two possibilities. Implicit also in the preemption challenges is the equally mistaken belief that collective bargaining can only be built on a foundation of authoritarian employer power. In the United States that is the typical case historically. Employees ordinarily seek to unionize in response to the felt disadvantages of unrestrained employer power. But there is noth-

176. U.S. CONST. art. VI.

177. *See* LMRA §§ 203(d), 29 U.S.C. §§ 173(d) (1982).

178. NLRA § 1, 29 U.S.C. § 151 (1982).

ing in the nature of collective bargaining that says this must be so or that collective bargaining is inconsistent with a more democratic background legal regime. Collective bargaining thrives elsewhere in the world where just cause and other rights are granted by positive law. While I have argued that the conception of collective bargaining enshrined in federal labor policy contains certain antidemocratic elements, there is no evidence that Congress ever determined that the unorganized workplace *must be* authoritarian or that employees have a choice only between traditional collective bargaining or no protection.

Let us now consider the challenges to general just cause protections in doctrinal terms.[179] Does a state violate the supremacy clause by promulgating and enforcing a basic right of all employees to be immune from wrongful discharge? Did Congress preempt the states from declaring just cause to be a fundamental human right?

One line of attack is based on "*Machinists*-preemption."[180] The concern of this doctrine is to prevent the states from upsetting the scheme of federal labor policy by regulating in an area that Congress intended to be left "unregulated." Outcomes in this zone are to be left to private ordering based on the "free play of economic forces."[181] For example, the *Machinists* case held that Wisconsin is federally preempted from regulating concerted refusals to accept overtime, which are neither protected nor prohibited under the NLRA.[182] Employers argue that state wrongful discharge remedies are preempted under *Machinists* for either one of two reasons. First, management may contend that such remedies interfere with the employer's self-help options, for example, its right to terminate employees who concertedly refuse overtime. The second, broader argument is that, by granting employees a

179. For a detailed discussion of the doctrinal issues that reaches similar conclusions, see Herman, *Wrongful Discharge Actions After* Lueck *and* Metropolitan Life Insurance: *The Erosion of Individual Rights and Collective Strength?*, 9 INDUS. REL. L. J. 596 (1987). For an opposing view stressing the primacy of arbitration in federal labor policy, see Wheeler & Browne, *Federal Preemption of State Wrongful Discharge Actions*, 8 INDUS. REL. L. J. 1 (1986).

180. *See generally* Lodge 76, International Ass'n of Machinists & Aerospace Workers, AFL-CIO v. Wisconsin Employment Relations Comm'n, 427 U.S. 132 (1976). I have set aside another issue that I regard as relatively easy, the question of "*Garmon* preemption." The essence of the *Garmon* problem is to secure the exclusive, primary jurisdiction of the NLRB. As a protective rule, cases even arguably subject to Board jurisdiction may not be heard in the first instance by any other tribunal, state or federal. *See* San Diego Bldg. Trades Council v. Garmon, 359 U.S. 236, 244-45 (1959). Cases alleging matters proper for Board adjudication in the first instance can be channeled there as in the past. This does not seem to me to present a significant barrier to permitting the states to proceed in other cases.

181. *Machinists*, 427 U.S. at 140 (*quoting* NLRB v. Nash-Finch Co., 404 U.S. 138, 144 (1971)).

182. *Id.* at 148-51, 155.

crucial right they ordinarily seek in bargaining, state law has given them an unfair head start, thereby interfering with the "free play of economic forces" that is supposed to underpin collective bargaining.

Both forms of argument are based on the fallacy of assuming a preconventional legal order. Both assume a natural, neutral background regime in which employers have a power to discharge without cause. This image of the background regime is necessary in order to perceive wrongful discharge remedies as a departure from baseline, as an intervention in the free play of economic forces. But, like all legal powers, the right to discharge is conventional and therefore subject to revision. The absence of wrongful discharge remedies is no less "regulatory" than their presence. Indeed, the common law conception of at-will employment is of quite recent vintage. As for the neutrality of the at-will rule, I am reminded of an apt phrase used by my labor law professor (in another context): the at-will rule is "neutral on the side of the employer." If an employer's *Machinists* argument were valid, so too must be the employee's opposite argument that the employer's common law *right* to discharge without cause is preempted under *Machinists* as a radical and harmful intrusion upon what should be the "unregulated" zone.

Moreover, the employer's "self-help option" argument is circular. The employer's argument *assumes* that in a free market employers can discharge without cause, but this is precisely what the employer seeks to prove. "Preemption" is a label for the conclusion, sought to be drawn, that the states cannot divest employers of the power to discharge without cause. One cannot logically use as a reason for that conclusion the premise that employers must have that power in the first place.

The broader *Machinists* argument also fails. A unanimous Court (Justice Powell not participating) recently stated in *Metropolitan Life Insurance Co. v. Massachusetts*[183] that:

> No incompatibility exists . . . between federal rules designed to restore the equality of bargaining power, and state or federal legislation that imposes minimal substantive requirements on contract terms negotiated between parties to labor agreements, at least so long as the purpose of the state legislation is not incompatible with [the] general goals of the NLRA.[184]

We may assume this statement applies to state common law rules as well as to legislation. Just cause remedies no more interfere with labor-management relations than any other form of minimum standards legislation. The only way to avoid this conclusion, and, therefore, the conclusion under *Metropoli-*

183. 471 U.S. 724 (1985).

184. *Id.* at 754-55. The great significance of the *Metropolitan Life* case is developed in Herman, *supra* note 179, at 625-39.

tan Life that just cause guarantees are not preempted, is to assume that, unlike the wage rate, rules about discharge cannot be altered. Minimum standards legislation simply sets the floor of assumptions upon which the collective bargaining process builds. To distinguish discharge rules from, say, wage rates, we would have to assume that collective bargaining *cannot* be erected upon a just cause foundation. But that is to assume, wholly without warrant, that collective bargaining can only thrive where the background legal regime is hostile to industrial justice.[185]

For the reasons stated, neither the NLRA nor the LMRA preempts general just cause protections. This brings us to the final challenge, the more focused argument that general just cause protections are at least preempted with respect to *unionized* employees, because of the unavoidable institutional conflicts between common law and arbitral remedies. The doctrinal claim arises under "section 301 preemption."[186] The goal of this doctrine is to provide uniformity in the law governing the interpretation and enforcement of collective bargaining agreements. Accordingly, as the Court stated in *Lucas Flour*: "in enacting § 301 [of the LMRA] Congress intended doctrines of federal labor law uniformly to prevail over inconsistent local rules."[187] Arguably, application of state remedies for wrongful discharge to unionized employees threatens to disrupt uniform administration of collective bargaining contracts, specifically of the just cause clause found in the typical agreement.[188] In a sense, this focused version of the section 301 preemption problem—how to combine the virtues of collective bargaining with other needed legal foundations of employee self-determination—is symbolic of all the problems facing the market reconstruction perspective discussed in this paper.

As noted above, the focused section 301 preemption issue is not simply an employer argument to evade wrongful discharge liability. Conflicts between legal and arbitral remedies may raise genuine issues for workplace democ-

185. It should go without saying that just cause meets the *Metropolitan Life* test of being not incompatible with the general goals of the NLRA. *See supra* text accompanying note 184.

186. *See* Local 174, Teamsters v. Lucas Flour Co., 369 U.S. 95 (1962).

187. *Id.* at 104.

188. While most collective bargaining agreements contain a clause prohibiting discharge except for "just cause," no provision of labor law requires the insertion of such a term. Presumably the § 301 preemption claim is arguable, if at all, only where the applicable contract contains a just cause clause. Indeed, it may be that § 301 preemption claims are further restricted to cases in which the parties intend to administer the just cause provision through a so-called "exclusive grievance procedure." *See* Vaca v. Sipes, 386 U.S. 171, 184 & nn. 9, 10 (1967) (indicating that the rules created there pursuant § 301 to apply only where an exclusive grievance procedure is intended); Republic Steel Corp. v. Maddox, 379 U.S. 650, 657-58 (1965) (similarly restricting application of the rule of that case).

racy. A common error in the way the question is discussed, however, is to confuse potential future issues with present-day concerns.

If just cause were recognized as a basic civil right, like protection against race and gender discrimination, collective bargaining about job security and discipline would start with just cause as the floor and build upwards. Employees would not have to expend bargaining chips to get elementary just cause protections. They might still seek to negotiate arbitral protections against unjust discharge, however, because arbitral jurisprudence, procedures, and remedies might be superior to those available under local law. Even today, unions often bargain hard to incorporate protections against race and gender discrimination in collective bargaining agreements to obtain swifter, less costly enforcement and better remedies than those available at law.

If in the future unions were to negotiate superior discharge protections on top of a just cause legal foundation, and if these protections were democratically chosen by employees, it might then be appropriate to implement preemptive doctrines of attempted exhaustion of and deferral to arbitration similar to those now existing under the law of section 301.[189] That is, arguably general just cause protections, as distinct from retaliatory discharge protections that implicate basic public policies, should be waivable if a democratically ratified collective bargaining agreement provides superior or at least equal remedies.[190] Even then, however, I would place an outer limit on waivability. I would not permit a waiver of all access to industrial due process in a discharge case. If the union cannot or in good faith will not invoke the collective bargaining remedies on behalf of a discharged employee, he or she must be free to invoke the minimal state remedies.[191]

All of that is for the future. It does not describe our situation now. At

189. *See Vaca*, 386 U.S. at 171 (exhaustion of grievance procedure); *Republic Steel Corp.*, 379 U.S. at 650 (requirement of attempt to exhaust grievance procedure); United Steelworkers v. Enterprise Wheel & Car Corp., 363 U.S. 593 (1960)(judicial deference to arbitral awards).

190. The Montana Wrongful Discharge From Employment Act exempts all employees covered by a written collective bargaining agreement from state wrongful discharge remedies. *See* MONT. CODE ANN., § 39-2-912(2) (1987). However, the statute does not in turn require that the exemption-triggering collective bargaining agreement satisfy minimum protective standards, such as the inclusion of a just cause clause subject to arbitral enforcement. *See id.* In theory, an employee could be barred from state remedies by the exemption, yet not have just cause protections under the contract. This gap should be closed by amendment or interpretation. A collective bargaining contract that fails to meet minimum protective standards should never trigger an exemption from state remedies.

191. To this extent, the contrary rule of *Vaca* should not be carried forward. Under *Vaca*, if without a fair representation breach the union declines to process a grievance to arbitration, the employee is precluded from any contractual remedy for wrongful discharge. *See Vaca*, 386 U.S. at 185-92.

present, just cause is not anything close to a universally recognized civil right in the United States. It is not the floor of bargaining (at least outside the public sector). It is something fought for and won by employees through concerted activity, often at a high price in terms of risk, effort, and alternative rights traded or benefits foregone at the bargaining table. To say that section 301 preemption now bars states from extending just cause to unionized employees is to make the wholly unjustified and inappropriate assumption that, by adopting section 301 in 1947, Congress intended to penalize employees who choose to bargain collectively by making them pay for elementary industrial justice at the bargaining table, even though a state grants it free of charge and as a matter of right to nonunionized employees. This reasoning assumes that Congress intended to make collective bargaining unattractive, to make unionized employees second-class citizens who have to pay for basic human rights available to first-class citizens at no cost. Section 301 should not be given this absurd interpretation.

For the reasons canvassed in the previous pages, I do not believe federalism concerns pose any insuperable barriers to the market reconstruction program, at least with respect to individual employee job security. In now concluding this survey of areas for democracy-enhancing labor law reform, I turn from constitutional constraints to constitutional guarantees implicated by the program of reconstructing labor markets.

As one example, the workplace democracy perspective should be a source of equal protection doctrine. This may be illustrated by examining the recent case of *Lyng v. International Union, United Automobile Workers.*[192] The Supreme Court there upheld, against substantial first amendment and equal protection challenges, a congressional policy denying food stamp benefits to strikers. *Lyng* turns on several arguments, but I wish to focus particularly on the Court's conclusion that striker ineligibility serves the legitimate governmental objective of avoiding favoritism in private labor disputes.[193] This position is reminiscent of the fallacious assumption that managerial prerogative is "inherent" or that property owners have an "inherent" right to exclude expressional activity irrespective of privacy or productivity concerns.[194] It cannot withstand serious scrutiny. Only the highest formalism could treat government withdrawal of benefits as "neutrality" in labor disputes, but deem the grant of such benefits an act of support for one side. Surely Justice Marshall's dissent in *Lyng* has it right:

> [T]he 'neutrality' argument reflects a profoundly inaccurate view

192. 108 S. Ct. 1184 (1988).

193. *Id.* at 1192-93.

194. *See supra* notes 131-35 and accompanying text (discussing property rights); and notes 140-51 and accompanying text (discussing "inherent" managerial prerogative).

> of the relationship of the modern federal government to the various parties to a labor dispute. Both individuals and businesses are connected to the government by a complex web of supports and incentives. . . . When viewed against the network of governmental support of both labor and management, the withdrawal of the single support of food stamps . . . cannot be seen as a 'neutral' act.[195]

The fallacy of the *Lyng* majority is the same, basic pre-Realist error of assuming that government is neutral with respect to the background legal regime.[196] A theme of this Article throughout has been that governmental action establishing the background regime of rights and entitlements implicates government and law in the distribution of wealth and the enjoyments of life. A Constitution committed to equality therefore demands that legislation be framed and interpreted so as to counteract inequality in the "private" sphere that inhibits the exercise of democratic rights. Strikers should receive food stamps not only because withdrawal of the benefit is a governmental act inhibiting the exercise of statutory and first amendment rights. *Lyng* should also be overruled because, under the equal protection clauses, employees should be at least minimally subsidized in self-organization and concerted activity.

This is not an argument that the Constitution requires Congress to see to it that employees always win strikes. The claim is the narrower one that our notions of constitutional freedom should minimally guarantee that basic democratic rights can be exercised without fear that one's family will suffer nutritional deprivation. Perhaps I am wrong in believing that the Constitution requires government minimally to subsidize the exercise of certain constitutional rights. At the least, however, in cases such as *Lyng* and *Harris*, which test funding program exclusions, equal protection should bar government from enacting exclusions that inhibit or prevent the exercise of basic freedoms and civil rights.

---

195. *Lyng*, 108 S. Ct. at 1198 (Marshall, J., dissenting).

196. A similar error underlies Justice Stewart's opinion in Harris v. McRae, 448 U.S. 297 (1980). In upholding the constitutionality of government's decision to subsidize childbirth, but not abortion, Justice Stewart wrongly argues that:

> [A]lthough government may not place obstacles in the path of a woman's exercise of her freedom of choice, it need not remove those not of its own creation. Indigency falls in the latter category. The financial constraints that restrict an indigent woman's ability to enjoy the full range of constitutionally protected freedom of choice are the product not of governmental restrictions on access to abortions, but rather of her indigency.

Id. at 316.

IV. Conclusion

The preceding discussion suggests the range and concerns of an expansive market reconstruction approach to labor law reform. The reform agenda is founded on the central premise that labor law should promote and enhance democracy at every level of working life: within firms, in collective bargaining, in unorganized labor markets, and in the institutional relationships between paid employment and the other aspects of social life. Programs of this kind are criticized in general terms as interfering with autonomy and as being inefficient. These same complaints are also frequently lodged against more moderate programs of legal encouragement of collective bargaining, such as that contained in federal labor policy. As I have attempted to show, these criticisms are unpersuasive. However, even friends of employee rights may question whether an expansive program of democracy-enhancing market reconstruction would threaten the autonomy of collective bargaining. To the contrary, the proposed law reform agenda is fully consistent with the enduring values of collective bargaining. The proposals have the potential to enhance collective bargaining's contribution to the continuing project of creating a democratic workplace. The next cycle of labor law reform must re-envision and advance that project.

[6]

IN DEFENSE OF EMPLOYEE OWNERSHIP

ALAN HYDE*

I. INTRODUCTION: THE RECENT POPULARITY OF MODIFIED EMPLOYEE OWNERSHIP

Our inquiry is into the economic success or failure of the business owned in the majority, and actually controlled, by the people who work there. There are very few such businesses in actual operation, and those few have already been studied microscopically by the political scientists and sociologists, and then over-theorized about by the economists, whose work is cited in the pages that follow.[1] Nevertheless, there are at least four reasons for a fresh look at their success and potential.

First, the vision of an economy of worker-owned businesses is an old and resilient one; it is, in fact, one of the things meant by "communism" in political discourse until an analyst named Marx argued that such an economic vision was "utopian" unless joined with a program for capture of political power.[2] The worldwide disenchantment with all or part of Marx's alternative program—a disenchantment that long predates 1989—has assisted a fresh look at the "utopian" vision he rejected—a

* Professor, School of Law—Newark Rutgers The State University of New Jersey. This is an expanded version of the Kenneth M. Piper Lecture originally given at IIT Chicago Kent College of Law on March 19, 1991. Thanks to Samuel Bowles, William Bratton, Oliver Hart, Douglas Kruse, Brian Langille, Louis Putterman, William Simon and Clyde Summers for comments on earlier drafts.

1. There are probably only about 2000 American companies of any size that are owned entirely or in the majority by their employees, and this number does not seem to be growing rapidly. The number is larger if one includes as "employee-owned businesses", as some scholars do, professional partnerships such as law firms and accounting firms. RAYMOND RUSSELL, SHARING OWNERSHIP IN THE WORKPLACE 143-67 (1985); Henry Hansmann, *When Does Worker Ownership Work? ESOPs, Law Firms, Codetermination, and Economic Democracy*, 99 YALE L.J. 1749 (1990). My argument applies to professional partnerships as well as industrial or service firms and I am thus happy to join the now ritualized footnote observing that "employee ownership" and "worker ownership" are used interchangeably and that neither refers only to blue collar workers. *Id.* at 1752, n. 4; JOSEPH BLASI & DOUGLAS KRUSE, THE NEW OWNERS: THE MASS EMERGENCE OF EMPLOYEE OWNERSHIP IN PUBLIC COMPANIES AND WHAT IT MEANS TO AMERICAN BUSINESS 91 (1991) [hereinafter BLASI & KRUSE].

2. MICHAEL SONENSCHER, WORK AND WAGES: NATURAL LAW, POLITICS AND THE EIGHTEENTH-CENTURY FRENCH TRADES 371-72 (1989); A DICTIONARY OF MARXIST THOUGHT 95 (Tom Bottomore ed., 1983) ("There is no systematic treatment of cooperation in the sense of the cooperative movement or particular forms of cooperative production in Marx's and Engel's work, but there are more references to the subject, and more favorable ones, than is sometimes supposed .... The comparative idea itself is not condemned, only deformations of it .... Cooperation could never defeat monopoly unless it was developed to national dimensions.") citing T. LOWIT, MARX ET LE MOUVEMENT COOPERATIF (1962).

vision that always had particular resonance in the resolutely pro-capitalist, anti-socialist segments of the American working class.[3]

Second, in the past decade, the prospect of mass employee ownership has passed decisively from utopian proposal to big business. Several hurdles have been jumped here. One common argument against the utopian cooperative vision was that such worker owned firms could never attain any size. However, there are now very large and successful companies that are over seventy percent owned by employees, such as Weirton Steel, ranking 288 on the Fortune 500, and Avis Corporation, now privately held but (as everyone knows) America's Number 2 car rental company. "Employees own a majority of the stock in three of the country's ten largest integrated steel manufacturers, two of the ten largest private hospital management companies, two of the three largest shipbuilders, two of the ten largest construction companies, and many others."[4]

Third, the spread in popularity in the United States of Employee Stock Ownership Plans (ESOPs) has suddenly created the possibility of an economy of firms in which the employees are in most cases the dominant shareholders. Already there are more Americans working for firms, more than 4 percent owned by their employees, than there are represented by labor unions. If, as is often asserted, a 15 percent ownership stake permits dominance, "[b]y the year 2000, more than a quarter of the companies traded on the New York Stock Exchange, the American Stock Exchange and Over-the-Counter Market will be more than 15 percent owned by *their* employees."[5]

Now a firm with an ESOP, even an ESOP that owns 15 or 25 or 75 percent of stock, is not necessarily a firm that workers control or manage. The ESOP, as envisioned by attorney Louis Kelso and later sanctioned by statute,[6] was carefully designed to permit companies to donate stock to employees without necessarily parting with any control.[7] To-

3. DANIEL RODGERS, THE WORK ETHIC IN INDUSTRIAL AMERICA 1850-1920 at 40-45 (1978); Derek C. Jones, *U.S. Producer Cooperatives: The Record to Date*, 18 INDUS. REL. 342 (1979). An ambitious recent attempt to capture and restate a distinctive vision of "social-republican property," held by private individuals but requiring active participation in the group of property holders and egalitarian intervention within the group, is William H. Simon, *Social-Republican Property*, 38 UCLA L. REV. 1335 (1991)[hereinafter Simon]. Simon's two leading examples are producer cooperatives, such as employee owned businesses, and housing cooperatives.

4. Corey Rosen, *Employee Ownership: Performance, Prospects, and Promise*, *in* UNDERSTANDING EMPLOYEE OWNERSHIP, 2 (Corey Rosen & Karen M. Young eds., 1991).

5. BLASI & KRUSE, *supra* note 1, at 3, provide a thorough analysis of the phenomenon of public companies with substantial employee ownership through ESOPs and other stock bonus plans.

6. I.R.C. § 4975 (West Supp. 1991).

7. JOSEPH BLASI, EMPLOYEE OWNERSHIP: REVOLUTION OR RIPOFF? 15-28, 122-57 (1988)(reviewing legislative history). This philosophy animates the ESOP deals actually concluded

day, the typical ESOP is a stock savings plan in which shares are held in trust for employees and voted by a trustee appointed by corporate management.[8] The company continues to be managed traditionally, and on the whole is *less* likely than a conventionally investor-owned firm to experiment in worker involvement of various kinds.[9] Until quite recently, sincere believers in worker management wanted nothing to do with ESOPs, which were seen as *inevitably* associated with control by conventional managers.[10] Their preferred institutional model was the cooperative, highly democratic, perhaps organized without any supervisors or leaders, and with jobs rotating.[11]

by Kelso and his firm. In the words of his associate, Joseph Schuchert: "Our programs are the antithesis of workplace democracy . . . . We've been criticized for not giving workers more participation, but we believe workers are natural shareholders, not natural managers." *Employee Stock Plans Turn Into Management Boon*, BOSTON GLOBE, January 2, 1985, *as quoted in* DAVID ELLERMAN, THE DEMOCRATIC WORKER-OWNED FIRM: A NEW MODEL FOR THE EAST AND WEST 105 (1990). In the words of experienced ESOP observer Brian Freeman, "These are just deals, not social programs." Brian Freeman, *Employee Buyouts*, 15 INST. ON SEC. REG. (PLI) 33, 48 (1984).

8. These include the "ripoffs" discussed by Blasi in his earlier book, cited *supra* note 7. Positioning shares in the hands of a trustee loyal to management encouraged the widespread adoption of ESOPs to discourage corporate takeovers, discussed in BLASI & KRUSE, *supra* note 1, at 139-210. Their recent survey of companies with substantial employee ownership—what they call the "Employee Ownership 1000"—reveals 60 to 75 percent that treat employee ownership simply as a vehicle for employee savings, and an additional 20 to 30 percent of firms they call "feudal" who administer employee stock ownership with no regard whatever for employee interests. *Id.* at 221-27.

9. Patrick M. Rooney, *Worker Participation in Employee-Owned Firms*, 22 J. ECON. ISSUES, 451, 453 (1988), surveyed firms with substantial employee stock ownership—47% of stock in the median firm—and found very little involvement of employees through meetings, quality of work life groups, or collective bargaining, let alone participation in investment decisions or the distribution of profits.

10. The supposed contrast between the democracy of the cooperative and the hierarchy of the ESOP dominated much of the popular literature on employee ownership, particularly from a left perspective, up until the middle of the 1980's. *See*, Jonathan Prude, *ESOP's Fable: How Workers Bought a Steel Mill in Weirton, West Virginia, and What Good it Did Them*, 14 SOCIALIST REV. 27, 38 (1984), for an interesting journalistic account of the Weirton buyout, spectacularly wrong on its predictions, largely because of hostility to the ESOP form; Henry M. Levin, *ESOPs and the Financing of Worker Cooperatives*, *in* WORKER COOPERATIVES IN AMERICA 245 (Robert Jackall & Henry M. Levin eds., 1984); David Ellerman, Notes on the Co-op/ESOP Debate (available from the Industrial Cooperative Association) (1982).

11. The most thorough academic treatments of such workplaces are by sociologists and political scientists interested in testing whether such a degree of democracy was feasible, and generally concluding that it wasn't. JANE T. MANSBRIDGE, BEYOND ADVERSARY DEMOCRACY (1984); JOYCE ROTHSCHILD & J. ALLEN WHITT, THE COOPERATIVE WORKPLACE: POTENTIALS AND DILEMMAS OF ORGANIZATIONAL DEMOCRACY AND PARTICIPATION (1986) (both studying cooperative clinics, schools, or other collectives founded in the very early 1970's).

There is some very skeptical theoretical economic analysis of such highly democratic organizations. Michael C. Jensen & William H. Meckling, *Rights and Production Functions: An Application to Labor-managed Firms and Codetermination*, 52 J. BUS. 469, 475-91 (1979) (analyzing a "pure rental" firm in which no one, not even employees, owns anything); Oliver E. Williamson, *The Organization of Work: A Comparative Institutional Assessment*, 1 J. ECON. BEH. AU. & ORG. 5 (1980) (analyzing "peer group" firm without any supervision and with job rotation). Even at the time, these were somewhat caricatured versions of employee ownership, as critics pointed out. Louis Putterman, *On Some Recent Explanations of Why Capital Hires Labor*, 22 ECON. INQUIRY 171 (1984) [hereinafter *Why Capital Hires Labor*]; Louis Putterman, *The Organization of Work: Comment*, 2 J.

It is possible, perhaps likely, that most of today's ESOPs will never amount to more than savings plans, in which case the subject of this Article—the genuinely worker-owned and managed firm—will evolve apart from the literature on ESOPs, as of course it did for the century and a half between the origins of utopian socialism and the maturity of Louis Kelso.

There are good reasons however to think that a significant number of the ESOPs of the 1980's will evolve during the 1990's into a new and exciting form of partial worker control. In the next few years the loans that established these leveraged ESOPS will be paid off, more stock will vest in employees, and the sheer quantity of employee-held stock creates interesting possibilities, for example, of alliance with pension funds and other institutional investors.[12] Meanwhile, a corps of lawyers, bankers, and other professionals experimented with combining workplace democracy with ESOP organization, and discovered that the ESOP is *not* inevitably associated with hierarchical management; indeed, there are ESOPs as "democratic" as the wildest cooperative.[13] It is likely in the 1990's

ECON. BEHAV. & ORGANIZATION 273 (1981); *see also* S.R. Jones, *The Organization of Work: A Historical Dimension*, 3 J. ECON. BEHAV. & ORGANIZATION 117, 125-36 (1982); Raymond Russell, *Employee Ownership and Internal Governance*, 6 J. ECON. BEHAV. & ORGANIZATION 217, 217-18 (1985) [hereinafter *Employee Ownership*]. As of 1991, it is apparent that little of the Williamson and Jensen & Meckling analyses applies to observable employee ownership, with its wide range of variation in who owns stock and how the firm is managed. However, in fairness to Williamson and to Jensen & Meckling, one must remember how rapidly the real world scene changed in the 1980's. At the time of their articles, the kind of purist democracy they analyzed was a subject of some practical and academic interest, as the books by Mansbridge and Rothschild show. Some readers of this article may have participated in food cooperatives or other highly democratic cooperatives at that time.

12. This is the theme, meticulously traced out, of BLASI & KRUSE, *supra* note 1.

13. There are still no comprehensive introductions to the new "democratic" ESOPs. One highly democratic ESOP is at Seymour Specialty Wire, *see* GARY B. HANSEN & FRANK T. ADAMS, SAVING JOBS AND PUTTING DEMOCRACY TO WORK: LABOR-MANAGEMENT COOPERATION AT SEYMOUR SPECIALTY WIRE, BUREAU OF LABOR-MANAGEMENT RELATIONS AND COOPERATIVE PROGRAMS, U.S. DEP'T OF LABOR, LABOR-MANAGEMENT COOPERATION BRIEF NO. 11, (1987); or the journalistic account in Jeremy Brecher, *Upstairs, Downstairs: Class Conflict in An Employee Owned Factory*, 1 ZETA (No. 2), Feb. 1988, at 68-74, *reprinted in* BUILDING BRIDGES: THE EMERGING GRASSROOTS COALITION OF LABOR AND COMMUNITY 274 (Jeremy Brecher & Tim Costello eds., 1990). Other brief introductions to "democratic" ESOPs include BLASI & KRUSE, *supra* note 1, at 227-30; Steve Newman & Mike Yoffee, *Steelworkers and Employee Ownership*, 3 J. EMPLOYEE OWNERSHIP L. & FIN. 51 (1991) (companies in which workers represented by the United Steelworkers hold substantial ownership); Catherine J. Ivancic & John Logue, *Democratizing the American Economy: Illusions and Realities of Employee Participation and Ownership*, *in* MANAGING MODERN CAPITALISM: INDUSTRIAL RENEWAL AND WORKPLACE DEMOCRACY IN THE UNITED STATES AND WESTERN EUROPE 232-40 (M. Donald Hancock, et al. eds., 1991) (same); Peter Pitegoff, The Democratic ESOP (available from Industrial Cooperative Association) (Jan. 1987); Craig Livingston, *Lessons from Three UAW Locals*, 6 LAB. RES. REV. 35 (1985); and the as-yet unpublished paper by my student Alex Kress, *Realizing the Potential for Democratically-Controlled Companies* (unpublished manuscript, on file with author). A weakness of Blasi's excellent book on Employee Stock Ownership Plans, cited *supra* note 7, was his failure to include information on "democratic"

that many firms with ESOPs will evolve somewhere in between, with workers exercising the kind of control that shareholders with 15 percent stakes do, though not the kind of control associated with worker cooperatives.[14] This trend makes more pressing a fresh look at the economic desirability of worker management.

Fourth, as I said, the few existing examples of real employee ownership have generated a large academic literature. However, that literature is not marked by consensus. It is a very ideological literature that is marked by a search for the "smoking gun" that will demonstrate decisively that economic ownership is (either, depending on the politics of the researcher), always a good idea for everybody, or could never possibly work for anybody. Since neither of these positions is consistent with the past decade's experimentation with multiple forms of *partial* employee ownership, it seems time for a fresh look at the literature from a policymaker's point of view, to determine the potential success and failure of genuine employee ownership.[15]

The Article that follows is an attempt to review the literature on the productivity of worker-owned businesses from the perspective of "efficient wage" models of labor contracting; "transaction costs" or "information costs" models of the firm; and theories of internal or "X"-inefficiency. The clearest conclusion is that models of the productivity of worker ownership must be *firm-specific*; there will never be a "smoking gun" that proves that worker ownership either always works or never works.

More particularly, I shall argue that worker ownership is likely to be highly positive for productivity where local histories of mistrust pre-

ESOPs. The "ripoffs" that Blasi discusses must be understood as typical, but not inevitable, results of ESOP organization.

14. BLASI & KRUSE, *supra* note 1, at 244-55.

15. Other points of view than the policymaker's are of course possible and perhaps even preferable. My friends and colleagues in the Critical Legal Studies Movement have often alerted us to the deadening effect that legal or economic models of reality may have on our abilities to imagine alternatives. On this view, the task of the scholar of employee ownership would be to demolish the legal and economic assumptions that appear to count against it, such as our very concepts of "property" and "market", and imagine fresh alternatives. This strategy is particularly indicated where, as here, the state of economic knowledge is particularly flimsy, and resort to economics to "prove" the inevitability of the status quo particularly likely to be ideological. Examples of excellent scholarship applying this perspective to problems of labor regulation include Karl E. Klare, *Workplace Democracy & Market Reconstruction: An Agenda for Legal Reform*, 38 CATH. U. L. REV. 1 (1988); and Joseph W. Singer, *The Reliance Interest in Property*, 40 STAN. L. REV. 611 (1988).

As will probably be evident in the pages that follow, I have a great deal of sympathy for any reader who, having worked through the academic literature on worker ownership, decides that sanity lies in freeing her mind from it and imagining alternatives. However, in this Article I want to speak directly to the versions of that literature that have shown up in the law reviews, since I believe that a more economically sound model of worker ownership is possible, even within recognized modes of economic analysis.

vent workers and managers from concluding cooperative arrangements that would in fact improve firm productivity, but will not be adopted because of low trust, high probability of opportunism, or high information costs. In this common but not universal scenario, an ownership stake for workers can decrease information costs and increase trust, and be positive for firm productivity. By contrast, a firm without such a history of low trust will almost surely not suffer by increasing employee ownership, but may not experience major productivity gains either. The case for employee ownership in such a firm is political, parasitic on theories of democracy, but is not distinctively economic.

The result, if the Article succeeds, should be an advance in how we think about employee ownership, namely shifting the level of analysis from The Firm to individual firms, and a modest defense of the role of employee ownership, and thus of public policies that advance it.

II. Current Academic Literature on Employee Ownership

The format of this Article does not permit a careful and comprehensive treatment of everything that has been written about worker ownership, and I shall be forced to caricature in order to explain how the model of employee ownership proposed here differs from its predecessors. As a general introduction, let me separate the "conceptual" literature, by economists, political theorists, and lawyers influenced by each, from the "empirical" literature by sociologists and political scientists.

A. Conceptual Models of Employee Ownership

The conceptual literature is notable for its simplified, indeed oversimplified, models of employee-owned firms. These never bore much relationship to observable real-world phenomena, and resemble them less over time. In particular, economists do not seem familiar with the idea, now bread-and-butter for attorneys practicing corporate finance, that a firm may be significantly owned by employees in combination with other investors. Yet these simplified models have their point, all the same. They permit the researcher to evade the eponymous question tellingly asked by Professor Hansmann in his recent article in the *Yale Law Journal*: "When Does Worker Ownership Work?"[16]

It is not really an exaggeration to say that the existing economic, political science, and legal literature answers that question in one of two ways. The answer is either "always" or "never." Here are slightly cari-

16. Hansmann, *supra* note 1.

catured—but really, only slightly—explanations of the "always" and "never" simplified models of employee ownership that dominate the conceptual literature by political theorists and some economists.

The model that suggests that employee ownership is just about always good for just about everybody does so because it sees employee ownership as the solution to more or less universal problems experienced by employees of modern industrial or service firms: loss of control of work, alienation, an experience of passively following orders.

The "always" model of the employee-owned firm has changed surprisingly little since its origins in the nineteenth century. Both its description and defense are largely in the vocabulary of political theory. A standard trope is the alleged disjuncture between the economic and political realms. Democracy is justified for reasons standard in political theory since Aristotle: many heads are better than one, perhaps, or the one wearing the shoe knows where it pinches, or as a solution to the problem of obedience to law, that bases it on the consent of the governed. The argument for democracy at work is then parasitic on the general political defense of democracy. The employee-owned firm is painted very vaguely, but prominent in the palette are tones of participation and responsiveness. The books end with a call for employee ownership, without too much in the way of specifics.[17]

17. Robert A. Dahl, A Preface to Economic Democracy (1985); Carol Gould, Rethinking Democracy 247-56 (1988); Martin Carnoy & Derek Shearer, Economic Democracy: The Challenge of the 1980s 125-94 (1980); Stephen R. Munzer, A Theory of Property 346-57 (1990).

The most economically sophisticated version of the "always" argument came to my attention after this speech was given. In an unpublished paper, Samuel Bowles and Herbert Gintis defend employee ownership as likely to be positive for the efficiency of all firms, drawing heavily on both the "efficiency wage" models of the labor market and "information costs" models of the firm. When published, theirs should be the standard defense of worker ownership in any anthology of economic writing on the subject. Their analysis parallels my own in many respects, and its economic sophistication much greater than my impressionistic account; I shall be drawing on it below. Nevertheless, it is still an "always" model; it has no scope for arguing that employee ownership might be a good idea for some firms but not others. This is accomplished, as is customary in economic analysis, through a set of simplifying assumptions, forthrightly identified by the authors but which nevertheless disable them from developing a firm-specific theory. Among these are that workers within the firm provide identical services and have no conflicts of interest, and that supervision of workers, here, as often in this literature, called "monitoring", involves no human labor and thus no agency problems in motivating or supervising the monitor. Samuel Bowles and Herbert Gintis, *The Democratic Firm: An Agency-Theoretic Evaluation*, *in* The Microfoundations of Political Economy: Participation, Accountability, and Efficiency (S. Bowles, H. Gintis, & B. Gustafsson eds., forthcoming) [hereinafter Bowles & Gintis]. (Page citations are to a manuscript version on file with the *Chicago-Kent Law Review*). Since the potentially interesting variations among firms are smoothed out, it becomes literally impossible within their model to argue that employee ownership might work some places but not others.

Bowles and Gintis argue that democratic firms can always attain efficient allocations of wage rates and worker effort that are unavailable to capitalist firms. While I will argue below that this is often the case, it is not clear to me why it should always be the case; why democratic firms must

A similarly rosy "always" model of employee ownership, rosy in the sense that it suggests that every or nearly every imaginable enterprise would benefit from employee ownership, is presented by Jaroslav Vanek, particularly when he is popularizing his own work. For example, Vanek presents an extremely appealing picture of an economy dominated by employee-owned firms: firms would be small, as there would be no incentive to expand beyond the point at which economies of scale are no longer realized; there would thus be more competition; less wasteful expenditure on promotion and advertising; full employment; and less environmental pollution, as plants are owned by those who work in and live near them.[18]

Across the Library, perhaps, in the economics section, lies a competing body of theoretical literature that suggests that employee ownership cannot possibly ever work for anybody.[19] In this version, employee

always reach this point and why capitalist firms never can. Bowles and Gintis rely on a different, and less clearly stated, set of simplifying assumptions here. In assuming the existence of more efficient wages, they draw a line in which worker output increases for each increase in wages. Surely this line must trail off after some level of worker effort. The capitalist is assumed to be indifferent to any point on this line, but is assumed not to be able to reach a hypothetical point, off the line, "at which efficiency has unambiguously increased: production is the same, while monitoring inputs have been reduced . . . and could be reallocated to productive purposes. In addition, worker welfare has risen because effort is unchanged, monitoring and hence dismissal probability is reduced, and wages are higher." *Id.* at 25. I will argue below that such a lovely move is sometimes possible, making a case for employee ownership, and present a theory explaining why some, perhaps most, capitalist firms will not reach this point without employee ownership. But I do not understand, and will not argue here, why no capitalist firm could ever reach this lovely point.

Perhaps as a result of these simplifying assumptions, the authors, though they believe they have shown that the democratic firm is "unambiguously more efficient," *id.* at 34, than the capitalist firm, still rely in places of their argument on the kinds of "political theory" arguments identified in text. "Our first claim is that in a capitalist economy the employment relationship gives the employer power over the worker, that on democratic grounds this power should be democratically accountable, and that a workplace democracy is a means towards securing this democratic accountability." *Id.* at 13; *see also id.* at 13-21 (developing this argument). Now as it happens I agree with this. However, one who doesn't would thus probably have to conclude that Bowles and Gintis have failed to demonstrate that employee ownership is always preferable to capitalist ownership.

My thanks to Duncan Kennedy for making this stimulating paper available to me.

18. JARSOLAV VANEK, THE PARTICIPATORY ECONOMY: AN EVOLUTIONARY HYPOTHESIS AND A STRATEGY FOR DEVELOPMENT 21-38 (1971). Vanek's more technical work displays awareness of inefficiencies of pure employee ownership, including tendencies toward underemployment, JAROSLOV VANEK, GENERAL THEORY OF LABOR-MANAGED MARKET ECONOMIES 193-96 (1970) [hereinafter GENERAL THEORY], and underfinancing, Jarsolav Vanek, *The Basic Theory of Financing of Participatory Firms*, *in* THE LABOR-MANAGED ECONOMY 186 (1977), that are much less prominent in the popularized treatment.

19. In addition to the Williamson and Jensen & Meckling articles cited *supra* note 11, *see* Eirik G. Furubotn, *The Long-Run Analysis of the Labor-Managed Firm: An Alternative Interpretation*, 66 AM. ECON. REV. 104 (1976); Eugene F. Fama & Michael C. Jensen, *Separation of Ownership and Control*, 26 J. L. & ECON. 301 (1983); Eugene F. Fama & Michael C. Jensen, *Agency Problems and Residual Claims*, 26 J. L. & ECON., 327 (1983). Like the Williamson and Jensen & Meckling articles, this literature models a factitious employee firm that bears very little resemblance to any observable firm.

While this literature is fairly well-known in law schools, due, no doubt, to the influence of the

owners would (like other neoclassical economic actors) maximize their current income, so that every dollar that comes in would be paid out in wages;[20] the firm would never plan or invest;[21] it would never expand, since each new employee would just divide this static income stream into a smaller rivulet;[22] the firm could generate no internal funds for investment, while no sane outside investor would ever finance such a firm;[23] which would go to a speedy grave unless imposed on the unwilling through force of law.

Journal of Law and Economics and to Professor Williamson's law school teaching, there is a substantial critique of it within the economics journals which to my knowledge has never been cited in any law review. In the notes that follow I shall cite both the critiques of employee ownership and the critiques of the critiques.

An outstanding survey of the economic literature is JOHN BONIN & LOUIS PUTTERMAN, ECONOMICS OF COOPERATION AND THE LABOR-MANAGED ECONOMY (1987).

20. This assumption was originally made by soi-disant friends of employee ownership. J.E. Meade, *The Theory of Labor-Managed Firms and of Profit Sharing*, 82 ECON. J. (SUPP.) 402 (1972); Benjamin Ward, *The Firm in Illyria: Market Syndicalism*, 48 AM. ECON. REV. 566 (1958); JAROSLAV VANEK, THE GENERAL THEORY OF LABOR-MANAGED MARKET ECONOMICS (1970).

21. In part this is just the corollary of the assumption that the employee-owned firm would maximize members' incomes by paying out every dollar of revenue as wages. The literature sometimes suggests additional reasons that employee-owned firms would prefer consumption to investment, and this has become known as the "horizon problem". *Furubotn, supra* note 19. The empirical literature on employee owned firms fails however to illustrate any "horizon problem"; if anything, worker owners have rather longer horizons than today's investors! Hansmann, *supra* note 1, at 1774; David P. Ellerman, *Horizon Problems and Property Rights in Labor-Managed Firms*, 10 J. COMP. ECON. 62 (1986).

22. A surprising and counterintuitive result of the early models of employee ownership was that such firms would never expand beyond the original group of employees. Ward, *supra* note 20; JAROSLAV VANEK, GENERAL THEORY, *supra* note 18. This too lacks empirical support and turns out not to be theoretically sound either. BONIN & PUTTERMAN, *supra* note 19; Katrina V. Berman & Matthew D. Berman, *An Empirical Test of the Theory of the Labor-Managed Firm*, 13 J. COMP. ECON. 281 (1989); Kathryn Nantz & Roger Sparks, *The Labor-Managed Firm under Imperfect Monitoring: Employment and Work Effect Responses*, 14 J. COMP. ECON. 33 (1990); J. Michael Montias, *On the Labor-Managed Firm in a Competitive Environment*, 10 J. COMP. ECON. 2, 7 (1986) ("safety of employment may provide the strongest incentive for individuals to join LMF's"); Branko Horvat, *The Theory of the Worker-Managed Firm Revisited*, 10 J. COMP. ECON. 9, 12 (1986) (same "absurd results" of falling supply in the face of rising prices would obtain if profit-maximizing firms are treated as maximizing profit per unit of capital); A.A. Brewer & M.J. Browning, *On the Employment Decision of a Labour-managed Firm*, 49 ECONOMICA 141 (1982); Alfred Steinherr & J.-F. Thisse, *Are Labor-Managers Really Perverse*, 2 ECON. LETTER 137 (1979). Hajïme Miyazaki & Hugh M. Neary, *The Illyrian Firm Revisited*, 14 BELL J. ECON. 259 (1983), assume by contrast that workers in a worker-managed firm would not maximize current payout but would rather contract among themselves to increase the value of their membership, in particular, their "income-employment security." Under this not implausible assumption, the firm ends up creating an internally-financed scheme of income insurance. With incomes insured, employee-owners accept work sharing and bear all other risks of firm nonperformance.

23. *See* Jensen & Meckling, *supra* note 11, at 473. This is true definitionally (but only definitionally) if the employee-owned firm is defined in advance as a firm with nothing to sell or pledge to investors. In the real world, employees can sell shares in any form they like. Benedetto Gui, *Basque Versus Illyrian Labor-Managed Firms: the Problem of Property Rights*, 8 J. COMP. ECON. 168 (1984). In recent years in the United States some employee-owned firms have reduced the level of employee ownership through public offerings, such as at Weirton Steel, or through simple sale to private investors. *See infra* note 46 and accompanying text.

B. Empirical Literature on Employee Ownership

The most important point to emerge from study of the empirical literature on employee ownership is that neither conceptual model—neither "always" nor "never"—could possibly be correct.[24] Let me sum up six of the most significant findings, and the challenges they present to the competing conceptual models. These are the central facts about employee ownership, which a more convincing model will eventually have to explain.[25]

First, there are in fact a great many successful, long-lived, employee-owned and managed firms in the United States and elsewhere. These firms have survived without government subsidy, often in hostile environments. This fact alone should give pause to one drawn to the "never" school.

Second, such genuine employee-owned businesses succeed in almost any imaginable industry, with all types of employees. Among those studied in the greatest depth include: plywood manufacturing cooperatives;[26] refuse collection;[27] the Weirton Steel Corporation, for a time the best-performing company in the American steel industry;[28] professional partnerships, such as law and accounting firms;[29] taxi cab collectives;[30] con-

24. Stephen Munzer makes a similar point in STEPHEN R. MUNZER, A THEORY OF PROPERTY 336-43 (1990). An outstanding attempt, not yet published, to correlate the theoretical and empirical literature from an economic point of view is John Bonin et al., Theoretical and Empirical Studies of Producer Cooperatives: Will the Twain Ever Meet?, Working Paper No. 91 /4, Department of Economics, Hamilton College. My thanks to Professor Putterman for sharing this paper with me.

25. Nearly all the literature referred to in this section deals with genuine employee-owned and controlled firms. As we have seen, *supra* notes 7-10, there is little reason to anticipate that a standard American ESOP to date will have behaved differently from a standard firm, since it *is* a standard firm, plus a savings plan. The few articles in this section that deal with ESOPs are clearly identified.

26. KATRINA BERMAN, WORKER-OWNED PLYWOOD FIRMS: AN ECONOMIC ANALYSIS (1967); EDWARD GREENBERG, WORKPLACE DEMOCRACY: THE POLITICAL EFFECTS OF PARTICIPATION 28-64 (1986); CHRISTOPHER GUNN, WORKERS' SELF-MANAGEMENT IN THE UNITED STATES 99-131 (1984).

27. STEWART E. PERRY, SAN FRANCISCO SCAVENGERS: DIRTY WORK AND THE PRIDE OF OWNERSHIP (1978); RUSSELL, *supra* note 1, at 71-104.

28. Corey Rosen, *The Record of Employee Ownership*, 19 FIN. MGMT. 39, 44-45 (1990); Michael Schroeder & John Hoerr, *Has Weirton's ESOP Worked Too Well?*, BUS. WK., Jan. 23, 1989, at 66. Weirton Steel's earnings are down sharply in the 1991 recession, of course, although this appears to reflect general economic downturn; internal efficiency remains high. *See* the Bear, Stearns report on Weirton Steel, July 29, 1991, available in Infotrac, General Business File; *see also* Moria Mallory, *How Can We Be Laid Off if We Own the Company*?, BUS. WK., Sept. 9, 1991, at 66; *Weirton Cutbacks*, N. Y. TIMES, April 24, 1991, at D4.

29. MARC GALANTER & THOMAS PALAY, TOURNAMENT OF LAWYERS: THE TRANSFORMATION OF THE BIG LAW FIRM 138 (1991) ("Compared to other business services, law remained relatively unconcentrated, decentralized, unbureaucratic, and worker-managed."); RUSSELL, *supra* note 1, at 143-67; Ronald S. Gilson & Robert H. Mnookin, *Sharing Among the Human Capitalists: An Economic Inquiry into the Corporate Law Firm and How Partners Split Profits*, 37 STAN. L. REV. 313 (1985).

struction companies;[31] artisanal manufacturing;[32] supermarkets;[33] the complex of industrial enterprises at Mondragon, Spain.[34]

In short, successful employee ownership and management is found in the production of goods and services; among educated and less-educated employees; performing tasks both simple and complex; in enterprises as large as several hundred workers and in some cases larger.[35]

30. GUNN, *supra* note 26, at 152-72; RUSSELL, *supra* note 1, at 105-41.

31. While few sizable American construction companies are owned collectively, perhaps ten percent of Italian building and construction is carried on through employee collectives, including the fifth largest construction company in Italy. MARK HOLMSTRÖM, INDUSTRIAL DEMOCRACY IN ITALY: WORKERS CO-OPS AND THE SELF-MANAGEMENT DEBATE 22 (1989).

32. HOLMSTRÖM, *supra* note 31, *passim*.

33. DENNIS CLARK & MERRY GUBEN, FUTURE BREAD: HOW RETAIL WORKERS RANSOMED THEIR JOBS AND LIVES (1983); ARTHUR HOCHNER, ET AL., JOB-SAVING STRATEGIES: WORKER BUYOUTS AND QWL (1988); Sherman L. Kreiner, *Worker Ownership as the Basis for an Integrated Proactive Development Model*, 15 N.Y.U. REV. L. &. SOC. CHANGE 227 (1986).

34. WILLIAM WHYTE & KATHLEEN K. WHYTE, MAKING MONDRAGON: THE GROWTH AND DYNAMICS OF THE WORKER COOPERATIVE COMPLEX (1988); KEITH BRADLEY & ALAN GELB, WORKER CAPITALISM: THE NEW INDUSTRIAL RELATIONS (1983); HENK THOMAS & CHRIS LOGAN, MONDRAGON: AN ECONOMIC ANALYSIS (1982).

35. I am therefore at a loss to explain Hansmann's statement, following a similar summary, that: "The types of industries in which worker-owned firms are found, and the structures those firms assume, are remarkably similar everywhere." Hansmann, *supra* note 1, at 1759 (footnote omitted).

Hansmann's is practically the only attempt in the literature to develop a theory that explains the actual observed success of employee ownership, and as such is an enormous step forward, although for reasons to be developed I am not convinced by the theory that Hansmann eventually works out. For Hansmann, the chief cost that employee ownership imposes on a firm is the cost of inefficient internal governance. As a result, employee ownership is likely to succeed only "when there is minimal opportunity for conflicts of interest among the worker-owners." *Id.* at 1784. Essentially, for employee ownership to succeed, there must be only one level of worker, relatively homogeneous, capable of being compensated at equal rates or (like taxi drivers or lawyers) with time inputs that are easily and uncontroversially metered.

I share with Hansmann a desire to develop a theory that actually explains the observable patterns of employee ownership. Moreover, I agree with him to the extent that conflicts of interest, internal to the firm, will play a large explanatory role in the theory I develop here.

While this whole article is in a sense a response to Hansmann, it may be helpful to state briefly why I was not convinced by his theory. (1) Hansmann simply does not deal with employee-owned factories, involving several different job descriptions and hierarchies, except for an analysis, with which I largely agree, as to why Mondragon is not really employee-controlled, *id.* at 1790-94. Perhaps Weirton Steel has not been employee-owned and successful long enough to permit generalization, or even inclusion on the list of successful employee ownership. *See supra* note 28. However, Hansmann should have done much more with Italy, the Western country with the largest proportion of cooperatively-owned firms, where long-standing cooperatives run profitable factories employing several hundred workers. *See* HOLMSTRÖM, *supra* note 31; Derek C. Jones and Jan Svejnar, *Participation, Profit Sharing, Worker Ownership and Efficiency in Italian Producer Cooperatives*, 52 ECONOMICA 449 (1985). Hansmann is dismissive of both the size of the co-ops, Hansmann, *supra* note 1, at 1759, though most Italian factories are small, and, for reasons I cannot determine, their internal democracy, *id.* at 1795. He also treats them as subsidized, *id.* at 1794, which is somewhat exaggerated. *See* ROB PATON, RELUCTANT ENTREPRENEURS: THE EXTENT, ACHIEVEMENTS AND SIGNIFICANCE OF WORKER TAKEOVERS IN EUROPE 80-84 (1989); Michael A. Conte, *Entry of Worker Cooperatives in Capitalist Economies*, 10 J. COMP. ECON. 41, 44-5 (1986)

(2) Hansmann errs in asserting that employee ownership only survives where employees are prepared to be treated equally. His own example shows successful employee ownership in firms of decidedly unequal compensation. Hansmann's chief (virtually only) example, to which he devotes five pages (1785-90), is the alleged practice among large law firms of "sharing the partnership's

Few of these firms are subsidized. In short, the "never" models have a tough time explaining the successes of employee ownership.

Third, however, we do not observe entire industries that are dominated by employee-owned firms, except where alternative arrangements are legally prohibited, such as law firms. This is a significant and embar-

earnings equally among all partners of a given age, regardless of individual productivity," Hansmann, *supra* note 1, at 1785. Hansmann cites Gilson & Mnookin, *supra* note 29, at 341, who identified three "sharing" firms, and hypothesized that this would be efficient law firm practice. Gilson & Mnookin did not make the empirical claim that Hansmann attributes to them, namely that all or most professional partnerships "share" equally by seniority. In fact, as Gilson & Mnookin make clear from their numerous counterexamples, *id.* at 351, 352, 387, it is rare for partners to be compensated equally. See also ROBERT L. NELSON, PARTNERS WITH POWER: THE SOCIAL TRANSFORMAtion of the Large Law Firm 190-204 (1988); MARC GALANTER & THOMAS PALAY, *supra* note 29, at 31, (citing ROGER SIDDALL, A SURVEY OF LARGE LAW FIRMS IN THE UNITED STATES 43-48 (1956) and MARTIN MAYER, THE LAWYERS 336 (1966)).

(3) The practical and empirical literature on employee ownership does not suggest that devising internal governance structures is the big deal that Hansmann makes it. After all, it's not as if conventionally-owned firms fall into simple patterns of internal organization.

In fact, employee involvement in the conventional firm is a source of enormous ferment now. One observes complex patterns of quality of work life groups, quality circles, collective bargaining, employee works councils of various kinds, employee representation on boards, teams, etc., all designed to solve problems of internal information costs and governance. *See generally* CHARLES C. HECKSCHER, THE NEW UNIONISM: EMPLOYEE INVOLVEMENT IN THE CHANGING CORPORATION (1988); THOMAS A. KOCHAN, ET. AL., THE TRANSFORMATION OF AMERICAN INDUSTRIAL RELATIONS (1986).

Employee-owned firms provide the same range of variation. *See generally Employee Ownership*, *supra* note 11, at 220-23. For example, the Ohio manufacturing companies discussed in J. Bado & John Logue, *Hard Hats and Hard Decisions*, 3 J. EMP. OWN. L. & FIN. 3, 14-33 (1991), utilize work teams, joint problem solving groups, worker representation on Boards of Directors, collective bargaining, and conventional management—the same range of decision-making institutions utilized by firms with conventional ownership. I am simply unaware of any literature, practical or theoretical, suggesting that employee-owned firms, as compared with conventional firms, face unique or distinctive problems in designing internal governance structures, and Hansmann does not cite any.

Again, Italian cooperatives provide an interesting test. Mark Holmström, whose book is cited *supra* note 31, is an anthropologist whose particular interest is in democratic governance structures, and who does not underestimate the practical difficulties in designing effective, efficient, meaningful participatory democratic structures. The point is that the co-ops he studies employ precisely the same kinds of institutions that comparable conventional Italian firms would: collective bargaining, elected works councils, employee meetings, decentralized teams. They may have more difficulty designing satisfactory organization, since their aspirations for participation are higher than the conventional firm's. But they do not appear distinctly inefficient in governance structure compared with conventional Italian firms.

(4) Hansmann's theory, linking employee ownership with homogeneity of workforce, suggests that there should be industries dominated by employee-owned firms and industries with none. This is just what we do not observe. In other words, Hansmann's is still an "always" or "never" theory, but limited to kinds of workforces. The task seems to me rather to develop theories to explain the appeal of employee ownership *to some firms, but not other firms*, involving similar work processes and work forces.

(5) The above factors convince me that Hansmann's theory is weak as a *descriptive* theory of worker ownership; its patterns are not what Hansmann claims and governance costs do not explain the patterns we see. To the extent that Hansmann's is a *normative* theory counseling us against worker ownership, it is weaker yet, as William Simon has observed. "If workforce heterogeneity tends to increase decisionmaking costs, there are two possible responses: we can try to narrow the range of worker decisionmaking, or we can try to decease worker heterogeneity." Simon, *supra* note 3, at 1395.

rassing fact for the "always" school, which tends to explain the low spread of employee ownership in terms of the weight of tradition, cognitive awareness of options, cultural factors that limit employee ownership to extreme risk-takers, high start-up costs in training a democratic workforce, free-rider and coordination problems, and similar factors.[36] Without denying these, it is harder to explain why, even after successful employee ownership, there are so few industries in which it is the dominant form. In countries and industries that have seen successful employee ownership, there would then be cognitive awareness of options, a break with tradition and other cultural factors, lower training costs. Yet even here one sees plenty of investor-owned plywood companies, steel mills, Italian artisanal factories, and (in medicine and accounting) professional partnerships.[37]

Fourth, substantial anecdotal evidence links the adoption of employee ownership to substantial productivity gains *in individual firms*.[38]

Fifth, however, large-scale comparisons of employee-owned firms with controlled groups of conventional firms reveal a more mixed, but basically positive, picture on productivity.[39] There do not appear to be

36. *See, e.g.*, Bowles & Gintis, *supra* note 17, at 35-42; Louis Putterman, *Some Behavioral Perspectives on the Dominance of Hierarchical over Democratic Forms of Enterprise*, 3 J. ECON. BEHAV. & ORGANIZATION 139 (1982).

37. Bowles & Gintis, *supra* note 17, at 34, who believe that democratic firms are "unambiguously more efficient," explain the prevalence of capitalist organization most importantly due to wealth inequality, the inability of workers to found businesses or borrow to do the same. While the first is true for the United States, the second is overstated. Bank loans to ESOPs are subsidized through the tax laws, specifically, I.R.C. § 133 (West Supp. 1991), which since 1984 permits lenders to exclude from income half of the income received on loans to ESOPs. This section was initially highly successful, and major banks lent billions of dollars to ESOPs, setting up ESOP departments and acquiring significant experience in and commitment to ESOPs, partly because in such loans a commercial bank takes on some of the functions of an investment bank. Alan Hyde & Craig Harnett Livingston, *Employee Takeovers*, 41 RUTGERS L. REV. 1131, 1141 n.30, 1142 n.34 (1989). Statutory amendments in 1989 restrict the exclusion to loans to ESOPs that own a majority stake in the company. It appears that bank loans to ESOPs fell off quite sharply after the restriction. BLASI & KRUSE, *supra* note 1, at 75. If Bowles & Gintis are correct, the banks' behavior is most surprising: having learned that ESOP loans are good, safe loans, why shouldn't they keep lending to "unambiguously more efficient" firms?

In all the literature on worker cooperatives, there has never appeared the kind of spontaneous growth "like mushrooms in a forest after rainfall" such as occurred with private farming and small business in formerly socialist Eastern Europe. János Kornai, *The Affinity Between Ownership Forms and Coordination Mechanisms: The Common Experience of Reform in Socialist Countries*, 4 J. ECON. PERSP. 131, 135 (1990).

38. *See* studies cited in BLASI, *supra* note 7, at 221, 269. Such stories are journalistic staples; the most recent example I have seen is Raju Narisetti, *Worker Input Helps an ESOP—and a Company—Work*; WALL ST. J., July 12, 1991, at B2. Note that managers typically attribute productivity increases to ESOPs *at their firm*, even where studies do not bear this out. *See*, *Most Managers Believe ESOPs Boost Productivity*, 43 EMPLOYEE BENEFIT PLAN REV., Dec. 1988, at 84; BLASI, *supra* note 7, at 232-36.

39. Excellent, skeptical reviews of the literature are BLASI, *supra* note 7, at 221-38 and 267-73, and J. Bonin et al., *supra* note 24, at 26-40.

any studies that find employee-owned firms clearly and significantly less productive than conventional firms, so the "never" school takes cold comfort from the empirical literature, and thus "never" discusses it.[40] The sharpest productivity differences between employee-owned and conventional firms occur in some of the long-lived firms listed above, firms with real employee control—not, typically, through an ESOP—over a long period of time.[41] Even this literature lacks the "smoking gun" that would be necessary to support the thesis of the "always" school, that all or just about all firms would benefit from employee ownership.[42] Moreover, if employee ownership is limited to shares in an ESOP, and there is

40. "There is no evidence that employee ownership hurts companies. Any claim that modern economic organization requires centralized ownership by individual capitalists or clear domination by managers insulated from absentee owners is simply unfounded." BLASI, *supra* note 7, at 231 (footnote omitted).

One recent study, published after Blasi's 1988 literature review, attempts to untangle the effects of employee ownership from employee participation and finds, uniquely to my knowledge, that substantial employee ownership (median 48 percent), unaccompanied by any device for participation, such as union representation, is positive for productivity only at low levels but then diminishes productivity for each added percentage of employee ownership. This is the only empirical study I have ever seen purportedly demonstrating negative productivity effects to employee ownership. On the other hand, the study confirms the now-conventional response that employee ownership together with employee participation is positive for productivity, although it is possible that the productivity effects come entirely from the participation and that ownership plays an insignificant role. Michael Conte and Jan Svejnar, *The Effects of Worker Participation in Management, Profits, and Ownership of Assets on Enterprise Performance*, *in* NEW DEVELOPMENTS IN THE LABOR MARKET: TOWARD A NEW INSTITUTIONAL PARADIGM 59 (Katherine Abraham & Robert McKersie eds., 1990).

If these results were to be confirmed in other studies, this would represent a significant negation of the theory I present here. Throughout this Article, I assume the more conventional result, discussed by Blasi and others, in which ownership without participation is neutral (not negative) for productivity, and ownership plus participation yields more productivity gain than participation alone. *See generally* Alan S. Blinder, *Introduction*, *in* PAYING FOR PRODUCTIVITY: A LOOK AT THE EVIDENCE 13 (Alan S. Blinder ed., 1990) [hereinafter PAYING FOR PRODUCTIVITY].

At the moment, I am not too troubled by the Conte and Svejnar paper. The sample was very small. Only forty firms were represented in the survey. The key category, of firms with employee ownership and no participation scheme, contained only five firms. Conte & Svejnar, *supra* at 72. There were no firms in the study that had participation plans and no employee ownership, so the respective effects of each were determined by regression. *Id.* at 69. All data were gathered in the recession year 1980-81, and, as the authors discuss, it is likely that endogenous variables explain the poor performance of the five firms with substantial ownership and no participation. "It may be, for example, that the presence of ESOPs with a high percentage of the firm's total assets is a consequence rather than a cause of inferior productive performance." *Id.* at 75. This must be at least partly correct; firms do not randomly adopt either participative or ownership schemes but do so in response to some endogenous factor. I await Conte and Svejnar's future research, in which they attempt to "tackle the endogeneity issue," *id.* at 75, with interest.

41. CARL J. BELLAS, INDUSTRIAL DEMOCRACY AND THE WORKER-OWNED FIRM: A STUDY OF TWENTY-ONE PLYWOOD COMPANIES IN THE PACIFIC NORTHWEST (1972); BERMAN, *supra*, note 26; HOCHNER ET AL., *supra* note 33, at 209-39; THOMAS & LOGAN, *supra* note 34; RUSSELL, *supra* note 1, at 71-104 (refuse collection collectives); Jones & Svejnar, *supra* note 35; Corey Rosen & Michael Quarrey, *How Well is Employee Ownership Working?*, HARV. BUS. REV., Sept.-Oct. 1989, at 126 (1987) (survey of companies; greatest growth in most participative companies).

42. Partly because of the endogeneity issue discussed *supra* note 40, it is not clear that firms that have never felt the need to experiment with employee ownership and participation would benefit that much from adopting it.

little direct employee participation, it is difficult to demonstrate much, or any, productivity gain *for whole groups of firms as compared with other whole groups of firms.*[43]

Sixth, employee-owned firms often go through a distinctive life cycle described by several economists.[44] Employee-owned firms often begin during economic recessions, when employees buy out failed or failing conventional firms. (Note how damaging is this simple fact to the "never" school; there are many examples of successful employee-owned firms where the identical firm, when conventionally owned, was failing or actually failed).[45] Such recession births succeed because workers will make concessions to themselves—lower wages, reduced staffing levels, other productivity gains—that they would not make to a management that might use them opportunistically. When the general economic climate improves, the employees sell the firm to private investors. (Obviously damaging to the "always" school. Yet employee-owned firms do indeed frequently sell out to private investors.)[46]

Now unfortunately this is an economist's model and corresponds imperfectly to the empirical reports; as such it belongs in this section only tenuously. Moreover, the economists build into their models certain dubious or counterfactual assumptions.[47] Nevertheless, I include this

43. *See* BLASI, *supra* note 7, at 221-38, and 267-73; Conte & Svejnar, *supra* note 40, at 76.

44. Avner Ben-Ner, *The Life Cycle of Worker-Owned Firms in Market Economies: A Theoretical Analysis*, 10 J. ECON. BEHAV. & ORGANIZATION 287 (1988); Avner Ben-Ner, *On the Stability of the Cooperative Type of Organization*, 8 J. COMP. ECON. 247 (1984); Hajime Miyazaki, *On Success and Dissolution of the Labor-managed Firm in the Capitalist Economy*, 92 J. POL. ECON. 909 (1984).

45. There were a number of such highly publicized cases in the early 1980's. Corey Rosen & Alan Cohen, *Employees to the Rescue: The Record of Worker Buyouts*, 6 J. L. & COM. 213 (1986); Deborah Groban Olson, *Union Experiences with Worker Ownership: Legal and Practical Issues Raised by ESOPs, TRASOPs, Stock Purchases and Cooperatives*, 1982 WIS. L. REV. 729, 753-80. Perhaps the five companies identified by Conte & Svejnar, *supra* note 40, with high employee ownership, low participation, and low productivity, fell into this group.

46. Schroeder & Hoerr, *supra* note 28; *Finance Briefs*, N.Y. TIMES, May 5, 1989, at D12 (both on Weirton Steel); RUSSELL, *supra* note 1, at 97-104 (scavenger companies); Jones, *supra* note 3 at 342, 349-50, 354-55 (1979); James P. Miller, *Some Workers Set Up LBO's of Their Own and Benefit Greatly*, WALL ST. J., Dec. 12, 1988, at A1 (on sale of employee owned businesses to public ownership).

47. Ben-Ner assumes, 8 J. COMP. ECON. at 258, that worker-owners have nothing they can sell as individuals should the firm become successful. This fortifies the conclusion that in such a case they would sell the whole firm. However, it does not accurately describe firms that are worker-owned through an ESOP, which can select any mix of employee or investor ownership, as occurred in May 1989 when the Weirton Steel Corporation made a public offering. BLASI & KRUSE, *supra* note 1, at 57-62, review public offerings of stock in companies substantially owned by ESOPs. The worker may have to put the stock to the ESOP rather than selling it on the market.

Miyazaki assumes, *supra* note 44, at 930, that the firm after worker ownership will experience no productivity growth. This is certainly possible, and suggests that *such* worker owners *should* probably sell to investors, who might manage the company better. It also suggests that Miyazaki's model has no application to the worker-owned firm that is becoming more productive and, *for that* reason, won't sell out to investors who won't manage it any better than the employees.

model here as a "fact" to be explained because it does correspond to a common, observable pattern in employee-owned businesses, though not an inevitable one.

It seems to me that the empirical literature on employee ownership is difficult if not impossible to interpret within the frameworks of the existing conceptual literature. The answer to the riddle of employee ownership simply cannot be, in our economy, either "never" or "always." This points out the need for newer models of the employee owned firm, that will better explain its pattern of successes. The answer to Professor Hansmann's question, "When Does Worker Ownership Work?", will have to start with the word "sometimes." In part III of this Article, I will sketch out the outlines of such a new model, confident that it will be far from the last word on the subject, but hopeful that it may inspire others to even more convincing accounts of employee ownership.

II. Recent Economic Analysis of Employment Contracts in the Modern Firm

Employee ownership is probably at its most appealing in those individual firms, where in addition to ordinary conflicts of interest between managers and employees, a history of management opportunism has led to low trust of management among employees. A likely employee response in such cases is to withhold information that management would like to have, so as to forestall further management opportunism. Management is now faced with some combination of uncertainty or very high information costs. In these circumstances, it is likely that management and employees will conclude employment contracts that are suboptimum both for individuals and the firms. Introducing employee ownership in such firms, where accompanied by institutions for genuine employee control, offers the prospect of reduced conflict of interest and supervision cost, increased information, fewer Prisoner's Dilemmas, and thus more efficient long term labor contracting for individuals and the firm.

In such firms, however identified, employee ownership should indeed be positively associated with productivity increases. In firms not initially suffering from such internal inefficiency, the introduction of employee ownership may realize some savings in supervision costs and information costs but is unlikely to result in dramatic productivity increases.

Ultimately, one's position on whether, as a matter of public policy, widespread employee ownership should be encouraged, should depend on one's estimate of the amount of internal inefficiency in contemporary firms.

That, in a nutshell, is my proposed new "information costs" model of employee ownership. I put it forward confident at this point that the reader of this Article will make nothing of it, unless he or she is familiar, as many legal readers now are, with three distinct and rarely related bodies of economic literature on employment contracts in modern firms: "efficiency wage" models of the labor market; the "property rights" analysis of information costs in modern firms; and theories of internal or "X"-inefficiency. None of this literature is specifically focussed on employee-owned firms; none of the theorists is an identified advocate of employee ownership, and at least some strongly oppose it. Nevertheless, I believe that the insights that these schools contribute to our understanding of labor contracts go a long way toward solving the problem of employee ownership.[48]

48. This might be an appropriate spot for a disclaimer that rarely appears in law review articles; perhaps it should appear more often. I am not an economist and have no training in economics or mathematics beyond undergraduate level courses. In citing articles below, I have not necessarily worked through all the equations and am not vouching for their accuracy. My goal throughout is to synthesize an economic model that makes sense of the empirical literature on employee ownership, *supra* notes 25-47, which is not usually the goal of economists. I cite economics articles for two purposes. First, as stimuli to our own thoughts, provided by scholars who have thought about these problems from different frames of reference than those in which I was trained. When I do that, I'm not really interested in then checking out all the author's equations; rather, I stop and ask myself whether his view is consistent with what I know about the world.

Second, I want to convey to legal readers some sense of the range of variation in economic approaches to these subjects. At the moment in American law schools an unhealthy situation obtains in which scholars on the political right frequently cite economics articles, while scholars on the left rarely do. This often gives a misleading picture of the state of economic knowledge on particular issues. Young legal scholars these days often attempt to refute what they term the "standard economic analysis" of a particular subject, when they are instead refuting a neoclassical analysis that is found principally in articles by lawyers and would barely be taken seriously by professional economists.

For example, virtually every article on employee ownership ever published in an American law review cites the classic article by Jensen & Meckling, *supra* note 11, which "proves" that labor-managed businesses would be so inefficient that no investor would ever lend money to them. I believe this Article is the first ever to cite the substantial critique of Jensen & Meckling within economics journals, *supra* notes 19-25. In citing this critique, I am performing both functions mentioned above. I am not vouching for the critique's superiority as economic analysis, nor am I competent to award such an accolade. I am performing the service of citing economics articles not otherwise cited in law reviews, which complicate a picture often presented as unduly simple. And I am advancing a model which seems to me closer to observable behavior, since, at least given certain subsidies, banks fall all over each other trying to lend money to Employee Stock Ownership Plans. *See, e.g.*, David Neustadt, *Lenders Court Employee Stock Plans: Tax Breaks, Loan Packaging Help Make Them Popular*, AM. BANKER, Sept. 2, 1987, at 22; Daniel Bell & Mark Keating, The Lending Environment for ESOP Companies: The Ohio Bank Study (*Northeast Ohio Employee Ownership Center, Department of Political Science, Kent State University*, 1987). (I am of course aware that these loans are subsidized and thus do not refute Jensen & Meckling. They do suggest, along with all the other evidence marshalled throughout this Article, that Jensen & Meckling's model, like all "never" models, must simply be too bleak.)

All three bodies of literature have arisen to explain why one or another observed feature of firm or labor market behavior deviates from a neoclassical model of firm behavior. In a neoclassical model, all firms hire inputs, and produce outputs, efficiently, so that competitive markets for all inputs and outputs will clear. As applied to labor contracts, firms will hire workers so long as wages do not exceed the value of marginal product added; workers not hired will decrease their demands; and eventually labor markets, like all others, will clear, irrespective of any idiosyncrasies of any firm's particular production function. As we shall see, in diverse ways, labor markets deviate from this model.[49]

Part II of this Article aims to provide concise summaries of this literature. Part III attempts to synthesize them into a theory of employee ownership.

A. *"Efficiency wage" models of the labor market: why firms employ long-term labor contracts*

"Efficiency wage" models of the labor market arose to explain "the key problem in macroeconomics . . . the explanation of unemployment, which is seemingly involuntary and varies with aggregate demand. Most

49. "The history of labor economics reflects a shifting pattern of relations between labor students and economic theorists that is only partially the result of the not-infrequent expressions of dissatisfaction with traditional labor market analysis by labor economists." PAUL MCNULTY, THE ORIGINS AND DEVELOPMENT OF LABOR ECONOMICS: A CHAPTER IN THE HISTORY OF SOCIAL THOUGHT 5 (1980). One can write the history of labor economics—McNulty has—as an account of the battle between classical or neoclassical and other models. Neoclassical models are supplemented in the ways discussed infra in text, and further supplemented with such factors emphasizing the institutional or political character of labor markets that prevent actors from behaving as neoclassical maximizers, *see*, e.g., JOHN T. DUNLOP, WAGE DETERMINATION UNDER TRADE UNIONS (1944); or the "ideal" or "moral" factors that influence perceptions of what employees "should" be paid, e.g., ROBERT SOLOW, THE LABOR MARKET AS A SOCIAL INSTITUTION 5-21 (1990).

Meanwhile, extreme deviants have even questioned whether workers are actually paid the value of their marginal products. PETER D. MCCLELLAND, THE AMERICAN SEARCH FOR ECONOMIC JUSTICE 371-80 (1990); Robert H. Frank, *Are Workers Paid Their Marginal Products?*, 74 AM. ECON. REV. 549 (1984); James L. Medoff & Katherine G. Abraham, *Experience, Performance, and Earnings*, 95 Q. J. ECON. 703 (1980).

Of course, the mere fact that a model has been discredited in its discipline of origin does not keep it from finding a home in the law reviews, the Museum of Discredited Models. For purely neoclassical analyses of labor markets, *see* Richard L. Doernberg & Jonathan R. Macey, *ESOPs and Economic Distortion*, 23 HARV. J. ON LEGIS. 103, 141 (1986) ("Why would the employees have lost their jobs upon a sale? Would they be replaced by more efficient workers?"); Richard Epstein, *In Defense of the Contract at Will*, 51 U. CHI. L. REV. 947 (1984), and Richard Epstein, *Agency Costs, Employment Contracts, and Labor Unions*, *in* PRINCIPALS AND AGENTS: THE STRUCTURE OF BUSINESS 140 (John W. Pratt and Richard J. Zeckhauser eds., 1985)("When one employee is wrongfully discharged, another will typically be hired in his place, so that the personal hardship of one is offset by the benefits that are conferred upon another."). This is true, of course. It is equally true, within a neoclassical framework, that there is no such thing as unemployment; that labor markets clear; and that the wrongfully discharged worker will therefore immediately obtain another position that pays precisely what his old job did. Of course, one must remember here that "true" is being used here, as economists do, to mean "assumed".

markets seem to clear, but not the labor market. Why?"[50]

The "efficient wage" hypothesis is that firms may and do find it efficient for their own purposes to pay wages only *above* the rate that unemployed workers would accept. Thus, new workers will not be hired, labor markets will not clear, and there will be unemployment.

Why on earth would firms insist on overpaying workers in this way? Theorists of efficient wages have by now generated quite a long list of ways in which labor productivity to the firm may *increase* with the wage paid, not all of which are germane to our purposes today.[51] In most versions of "efficient wage" models, the workers, who are being paid more than the wage the firm could get away with paying new hires, are comparatively senior employees, who receive their "efficient" wage as part of a long-term package designed to tie them to the firm.[52] In some accounts, these workers were paid less than their productivity when they were newly-hired; like law firm associates, they subsidized senior employees. The implicit bargain is that their wages will increase as they stay at the firm, irrespective of whether their productivity increases, and even if it decreases.[53]

50. George A. Akerlof & Janet L. Yellen, *Introduction*, in EFFICIENCY WAGE MODELS OF THE LABOR MARKET 1 (George A. Akerlof & Janet L. Yellen eds., 1986).

51. Some explanations for "efficient" (above market) wages that are not particularly relevant to present purposes include the idea that such wages may: (1) attract "better" workers with higher, though unobservable, human capital, Andrew Weiss, *Job Queues and Layoffs in Labor Markets with Flexible Wages*, 88 J. POL. ECON. 526 (1980); (2) forestall union formation or labor strife, William Dickens, Wages, Employment, and the Threat of Collective Action by Workers, Working Paper No. 1856, National Bureau of Economic Research, March 1986; and (3) displace shirking or absenteeism into increased rates of grievance filing, Peter Cappelli & Keith Chauvin, *A Test of An Efficiency Model of Grievance Activity*, 45 INDUS. & LAB. REL. REV. 3 (1991). The theory seems to have originated in the context of developing economies, where a wage above market levels may be necessary in order for the worker to receive enough nutrition to function. HARVEY LEIBENSTEIN, ECONOMIC BACKWARDNESS AND ECONOMIC GROWTH 58-76 (1957).

52. These labor economists often use the term "contract" to refer to this arrangement, and I have followed that usage here. *See generally* Sherwin Rosen, *Implicit Contracts: A Survey*, 23 J. ECON. LITERATURE 1144 (1985). Until recently, the usage was metaphorical, as much of the package would not have been legally enforceable by one employed "at will." Today, increasingly, such promises may constitute a legal "contract." Indeed, we may be approaching the point at which an employer, absent a quite specific disclaimer, is normally understood as contractually obligated to observe whatever of its procedures employees reasonably regard as normal and customary. *See, e.g.*, Wilkerson v. Wells Fargo Bank, 212 Cal. App. 3d 1217, 261 Cal. Rptr. 185 (1989); Garvey v. Buhler, 146 Wis. 2d 281, 430 N.W.2d 616 (Wis. Ct. App. 1988), in both of which employees were permitted to get to the jury with claims of discharge in breach of an "implied" contract, where the only evidence of the contract was the testimony of other employees or former supervisors as to the employer's ordinary practice. However, I shall use the term without regard to questions of legal enforceability.

53. Richard A. Ippolito, *The Labor Contract and True Economic Pension Liabilities*, 75 AM. ECON. REV. 1031 (1985); Edward P. Lazear, *Why Is There Mandatory Retirement?*, 87 J. POL. ECON. 1261 (1979).

Professor Paul Weiler explores the implicit employment contract identified by this economic literature, and its implications for the law of wrongful dismissal and other problems in contemporary

Why does the firm want to tie workers over the long term in this way? Some firms don't, of course; firms located in what "dual labor market" theorists call the "secondary" sector.[54] The literature suggests many reasons that long-term contracts with increasing wages, not tied to marginal productivity, might be an efficient arrangement for the firm, particularly (though not necessarily) the "primary sector" firm. An employee who is being paid right at the value of his marginal product has few reasons not to goof off (or "shirk", as these writers have it); he may not be detected, and if he is, and is fired, the loss to him is not so great and another, equally-poorly paid job may be available. Paying employees a premium will increase the costs to them of shirking, or of voluntary quitting, or striking.[55] The firm will also benefit if the premium wages are perceived as fair by workers and pay off in higher morale and higher voluntary effort.[56]

Why do workers agree to such long-term employment contracts? Economists have not studied this question as carefully as the question of firm efficiency.[57] One can certainly see why employees might prefer an arrangement that provides them greater security against wage reductions in their later years, although one cost that these employees will pay for the arrangement, where legal, is the institution of mandatory retirement.[58] Still, these long term contracts pose some obvious dangers to employees. The firm receives some of its biggest benefits "up front" and may well have incentives to behave opportunistically late in the game, by

labor law, in PAUL C. WEILER, GOVERNING THE WORKPLACE: THE FUTURE OF LABOR AND EMPLOYMENT LAW 63-71, 134-52 (1990).

See also Marleen A. O'Connor, *Restructuring the Corporation's Nexus of Contracts: Recognizing a Fiduciary Duty to Protect Displaced Workers*, 69 N.C. L. REV. 1189, 1203-18 (1991) (summarizing economic literature on implicit employment contracts).

54. PETER B. DOERINGER & MICHAEL T. PIORE, INTERNAL LABOR MARKETS AND MANPOWER ANALYSIS 163-83 (1971).

55. Guillermo A. Calvo & Stanislaw Wellisz, *Hierarchy, Ability, and Income Distribution*, 87 J. POL. ECON. 991 (1979); Steven C. Salop, *A Model of the Natural Rate of Unemployment*, 69 AM. ECON. REV. 117 (1979); Carl Shapiro & Joseph E. Stiglitz, *Equilibrium Unemployment as a Worker Discipline Device*, 74 AM. ECON. REV. 433 (1984).

56. George A. Akerlof, *Labor Contracts as Partial Gift Exchange*, 97 Q. J. ECON. 543 (1982); George A. Akerlof, *Gift Exchange and Efficiency Wage Theory: Four Views*, 74 AM. ECON. REV. PROC. 79 (1984).

57. One recent survey revealed strong preferences for receiving increasing wages over time, even after respondents were exposed to economic arguments suggesting that they should rationally prefer greater payments up front that then decline over time. Respondents' verbal explanations revealed that they derive positive utility just from feeling that their wages are going up; respondents also mentioned concern about inflation, desire to maintain or improve living standards, and the like. George Loewenstein & Nachum Sicherman, *Do Workers Prefer Increasing Wage Profiles?*, 9 J. LAB. ECON. 67 (1991).

58. Lazear, *supra* note 53, at 1264. That is, the firm might retain some senior employees if it could reduce their wages, but won't if it must pay them at rates well above the marginal product they contribute.

attempting to fire employees, or deprive them of their earned benefits.[59]

B. *The Firm as a "Nexus of Contracts": opportunism and strategic behavior among parties to relational contracts*

Concern over just such opportunism is an important feature of a second body of literature on modern employment contracts, the literature conceptualizing the firm as a nexus of relational contracts.[60] To be sure, these authors worry obsessively about "shirking" or opportunism by employees, and seem blithely unconcerned about possible opportunism by managers.[61] We, however, may overcome this omission and learn much about the contours of modern employment contracts in doing so.

Many readers of law reviews are now familiar with the analysis of firms as the locus of long-term relational contracts among investors, managers, and other employees.[62] On this view, the firm is a "legal fiction"[63]; ontologically prior are these contracts among factors of production.

This conception of the firm originated in order to correct a factitious distinction between "firms" and "markets." Ronald Coase had raised

59. WEILER, *supra* note 53, at 66-67. Lazear, *supra* note 53, at 1271 asserts that the firm has no incentive to cheat on the contract since such cheating will affect its reputation among the next generation of workers, who will simply demand more. *See also* Edward P. Lazear and Robert L. Moore, *Incentives, Productivity, and Labor Contracts*, 99 Q. J. ECON. 275 (1984). This seems wildly optimistic, not merely because of the anecdotal refutation offered by the many "unjust discharge" cases brought by employees on the losing end of such employer opportunism. There is little reason to think that the danger to their reputation could really discourage employers from such opportunism. Shapiro & Stiglitz, *supra* note 55, at 442; *cf.* Benjamin Klein & Keith B. Leffler, *The Role of Market Forces in Assuring Contractual Performance*, 89 J. POL. ECON. 615 (1981); WEILER, *supra* note 53, at 73-78; David Charny, *Nonlegal Sanctions in Commercial Relationships*, 104 HARV. L. REV. 373, 417-20 (1990).

60. It is interesting, to this noneconomist observer, how seldom these two bodies of literature: "efficiency wage" models of the labor market, and the new economic theory of the firm, link up, despite some obvious points of intersection: both use the metaphor of "contract" to describe long-term relations and both offer significant correction to simple neoclassical models. For example, Lloyd R. Cohen, *The Firm: A Revised Definition*, 46 So. ECON. J. 580 (1979), a meditation on the Coase and Alchian & Demsetz controversy, defines the firm as an economic entity whose internal purchases of factor inputs, such as labor, are at rates other than the value of their marginal product. Yet Cohen does not cite any of the "efficiency wage" literature, that makes the same point. Nor does that literature cite Cohen.

61. Gregory K. Dow, *The Function of Authority in Transaction Cost Economics*, 8 J. ECON. BEHAV. & ORGANIZATION 13, 21 (1987).

62. An excellent introduction prepared for legal audiences, on which the next few paragraphs draw, is Oliver Hart, *An Economist's Perspective on the Theory of the Firm*, 89 COLUM. L. REV. 1757 (1989). *See also* William W. Bratton, *The New Economic Theory of the Firm: Critical Perspectives from History*, 41 STAN. L. REV. 1471 (1989); William W. Bratton, *The "Nexus of Contracts" Corporation: A Critical Appraisal*, 74 CORN. L. REV. 407 (1989); *Symposium: Contractual Freedom in Corporate Law*, 89 COLUM. L. REV. 1395 (1989).

63. Michael C. Jensen & William H. Meckling, *Theory of the Firm: Managerial Behavior, Agency Costs and Ownership Structure*, 3 J. FIN. ECON. 305, 310 (1976).

the question of when production takes place through contracts that link market participants, and when within the boundaries of a firm. He identified the firm with authority relations, and concluded that relations within a firm will be efficient when concentrating bureaucratic authority is more efficient than the "transaction costs" associated with markets.[64]

Armen Alchian and Harold Demsetz later argued that Coase's contrast between the firm's authority relations, and the market's free contracting, was overdrawn. Certainly, within the firm, the boss may order an employee to do something, and if the employee doesn't, she will be fired. On the other hand, that is just the way market actors can enforce their will, if at all: threatening to terminate, then terminating, the relationship. The firm may be regarded as a series of coordinations of various inputs; it is not so different from a market. The ordinary aspects of firm organization that we observe—shareholders ("residual claimants"), professional managers, supervisors—do not demonstrate any superiority for hierarchy as such, but rather efficient reduction of information costs, here the costs of "metering input productivity and metering rewards."[65]

Now most people sympathetic to working people, whether liberals or leftists, will be tempted to dismiss this account as a mystification, for reasons of which I am well aware but which I shall relegate to a footnote.[66] Let us instead treat this account as the beginnings of a more

64. Ronald H. Coase, *The Nature of the Firm*, 4 ECONOMICA 386, 386 n.5 (1937). Coase's appreciation that markets are not always automatically the most efficient ways to accomplish things has not always been remembered in Chicago.

65. Armen A. Alchian & Harold Demsetz, *Production, Information Costs, and Economic Organization*, 62 AM. ECON. REV. 777, 778 (1972).

66. Hierarchies don't arise just because they are efficient and may perpetuate themselves long after they have ceased to be efficient at all, because people in power enjoy having power and do not give it up willingly. One thing that people with power and money are particularly good at doing is getting intellectuals to make up funny stories explaining why it is just and proper for people with money and power to retain those attributes; such stories must always be regarded with suspicion. Alchian and Demsetz don't just model the firm in a particular way because it is "true"; recall that economists use "true" to mean "assumed". All generalizations are to some extent normative (including my own); Alchian and Demsetz's generalizations are not merely implicitly legitimatory, they are expressly so. A model of the firm as "just" a nexus of "voluntary" contracts, like those between a grocer and his customer, eliminate any claim that firms have "power" over others. Conservative political commentators now frequently invoke this picture as a definitive defense of the legitimacy of the corporation. *See, e.g.* ROBERT R. HESSEN, IN DEFENSE OF THE CORPORATION (1979). No doubt this frankly legitimatory goal has turned many political liberals and leftists away from encounter with the "property rights" or "transaction costs" school. I think this has been a mistake, and that there is room for very valuable dialog between this school and others. Victor Goldberg made the same point in a very interesting discussion of similarities and differences between "radical" and "transaction costs" accounts of employment contracts. Victor P. Goldberg, *Bridges Over Contested Terrain: Exploring the Radical Account of the Employment Relationship*, 1 J. ECON. BEHAV. & ORGANIZATION 249 (1980). *See also* Katherine Van Wezel Stone, *Labor and the Corporate Structure: Changing Conceptions and Emerging Possibilities*, 55 U. CHI. L. REV. 73, 151-72 (1988). For example, as we have seen, most contemporary labor economists similarly model employment relations in

complete explanation for the prevalence of private ownership and hierarchical organization, and see how to make it more convincing.

For my purposes, the most valuable insight of the "nexus of contracts" school is their continuing insight that contracts in modern firms, though (on their view) on balance an efficient way of coordinating inputs compared to other institutional forms, do not really settle anything.[67] The contracts are entered into under informational uncertainty, possibly with assymetries of information, and there is an ever-present danger that one side will "shirk" its obligations. Contractual parties must therefore monitor each other's performances, while the monitoring itself imposes "agency costs."[68] In some cases, of course, a solution is to renegotiate particular contracts after unanticipated surpluses or losses have appeared, the firm being, after all, just a nexus of such contracts. However, as Oliver Williamson has shown, for parties in long term relationships, the transaction costs of such renegotiations will be staggering, and out of desperation they may select one dominant party to impose a solution which, as Williamson does not point out, simply raises the agency costs of monitoring the authoritarian manager.[69]

Let me put this sensitivity to agency costs together with the litera-

the firm as a series of implied contracts, without any legitimatory purpose, and, perhaps, without the sensitivity to transaction costs that members of that school bring to their work.

In this Article, I focus on the contrast between hierarchical and democratic organization *within* firms. I am not pursuing Coase's question of firm organization versus market organization. Those interested in Coase's question must conclude that Alchian and Demsetz do not really answer it. "[I]t is unclear why the problems of joint production and monitoring cannot also be solved through the market [i.e., via a contract]. In fact one does not need to look far to see examples of market solutions to these problems, such as auditing between independent contractors." Hart, *supra* note 62, at 1762.

67. The one exception that the transaction cost theorists make to this generalization is not adequately defended by them and does not sit well with their theory. Ownership of shares of a company becomes, in their view, a contract made by a "residual claimant" who thus has incentives to monitor the performance of all other actors. What has never been successfully explained is why the "residual claimant" doesn't act under the same uncertainties, with the same incentives to opportunism or shirking, that other actors do. Dow, *supra* note 61. In truth, there is a fundamental and unresolved conflict between the views that "firms must be [both] ownable and saleable if they are to be operated efficiently" and the view of the firm as merely the site of numerous individual contracts. Louis Putterman, *The Firm as Association versus the Firm as Commodity: Efficiency, Rights, and Ownership*, 4 ECON. & PHIL. 243 (1988).

68. "Agency costs" are the sum of (1) monitoring expenditures by the principal; (2) bonding expenditures by the agent; and (3) all residual losses. Jensen & Meckling, *supra* note 63, at 308.

69. Once parties are locked into each other, for example a highly-trained senior employee and a firm, external markets will not provide a proper evaluation of each party's opportunity costs. The only feasible kind of "ex ante" contract setting out each side's obligations will have to be so flexible as to leave much room for later negotiation. Yet there are costs associated with such later negotiation: the simple costs of negotiation; the sheer waste of distributional negotiations as each side tries to capture ex-post surpluses not clearly allocated by their underlying agreement, or to redistribute ex-post losses; inefficient initial allocation of investments, as each party tries to avoid being held up later on, at the ex-post stage. OLIVER E. WILLIAMSON, THE ECONOMIC INSTITUTIONS OF CAPITALISM 163-205 (1985).

ture on efficient wage contracts, to show some of the much-commented, intensely real-world problems that are likely to result in modern, primary sector firms. These fall into two main groups: problems of managerial opportunism, and poor incentives for employee performance.

First, under long-term employment contracts, as we have seen, employees bear substantial risks of managerial opportunism. Later in their careers, employees are, according to the contract, to be paid more than the value of their contemporaneous marginal product. Management will have incentives to shirk on these payments. For example, management may exploit the employees' location-specific investments; that is, it may extort modifications in the long-term contract by threatening disinvestment or relocation, or may actually disinvest or relocate.[70] Management may (and does) overstate the assets in the pension fund, then remove them for its own purposes, or terminate the pension plan.[71] Management, as in the recent strike at the *New York Daily News*, may have incentives to force workers into striking, so that management may avoid having to pay those pensions that the workers themselves have paid for. Finally, employees bear the risk of takeovers, in which the acquirer may (and, all during the 1980's, did) renege on the firm's earlier implied promise of longevity.[72]

Second, under the standard efficient wage contract, employees, who are paid gradually increasing wages irrespective of their contribution to productivity, may lack adequate incentives to work fully. "Work fully" here includes at least two aspects of employee performance. The first,

70. The extensive law review literature addressing this issue demonstrates how such managerial opportunism is immune from legal challenge. JAMES B. ATLESON, VALUES AND ASSUMPTIONS IN AMERICAN LABOR LAW 111-35 (1983); Robert A. Gorman, *The Negligible Impact of the National Labor Relations Act on Managerial Decisions to Close or Relocate*, 58 TUL. L. REV. 1354 (1984); Staughton Lynd, *Investment Decisions and the Quid Pro Quo Myth*, 29 CASE W. RES. L. REV. 396 (1979); Stone, *supra* note 66, at 151-72.

71. According to Howard Weitzmann, executive director of the Association for Private Pension and Welfare Plans, about 15,856 defined-benefit pension plans were terminated in 1989, 37 percent more than had been terminated the previous year. *Beware: Pensions Are an Endangered Species*, L.A. TIMES, July 30, 1990, *quoted in* BLASI & KRUSE, *supra* note 1, at 107.

72. Goldberg, *supra* note 66, at 267 n.38, predicted this. The Supreme Court encouraged it with its holding in NLRB v. Burns Int'l Sec. Services, Inc., 406 U.S. 272, 281-91 (1972), unanimous on this point, that a successor owner of a business, even one who retains the predecessor's workforce, takes free and clear of any existing collective bargaining agreements, rejecting the contrary doctrine of the National Labor Relations Board. A later holding made clear the implication that the acquirer is also normally free to discharge any or all of the unionized workforce without arbitrating the discharges. Howard Johnson Co., v. Detroit Local Joint Executive Bd., 417 U.S. 249 (1974). This was undoubtedly one of many factors behind the wave of corporate takeovers in the 1980's and specifically why acquirers could make money by liquidating other companies, or run them more "efficiently" than their earlier owners. *See* Andrei Shleifer & Lawrence H. Summers, *Breach of Trust in Hostile Takeovers*, *in* CORPORATE TAKEOVERS: CAUSES AND CONSEQUENCES 33, 41 (Alan Auerbach ed., 1988) (associating hostile takeovers with situations in which shareholders will benefit *ex post* from renunciation of compensation arrangements that were *ex ante* efficient).

extensively modelled by both "efficient wage" and "transaction cost" theorists, involves choosing to work hard rather than to shirk. This is a rather offensive and insulting way of putting the point, and runs the risk of making the theory seem unreal, since the many observers of the chronic lagging productivity growth of the American economy rarely observe much sheer goofing off or consider it an important aspect of low productivity.[73]

In my opinion, "shirking," as used by the economists, should be more accurately and less offensively understood as referring to a second phenomenon, in my view unquestionably more important economically. This involves active contribution to improving firm productivity—as the consultants say, "working smarter, not just working harder"—through active suggestions, participation in work reorganization, productivity monitoring, and the like. For example, employees face choices whether or not to invest their own time in education and training. The firm's pay structure will provide incentives for such investment if it rewards employees, or reimburses them, or permits them to share in resulting productivity gain. In a standard wage structure, however, education really is its own reward.

Whatever one understands to be meant by "shirking," everyone can see that a scheme in which wages are hardly tied at all to individual or small group productivity does not create incentives for avoiding it. Firms could theoretically solve this problem by flexibility in wages, directly tying wages to performance, but for all the reasons explored by both schools of economists this is rarely efficient. The inefficiencies have mostly to do with conflicts of interest between managers and employees. For example, piece rate systems of compensation seem to theoretical economists to be efficient incentive schemes, since they tie remuneration to productivity. But, as is well known, they rarely work out that way in practice. Employees develop ways of beating the system. They mislead the expert setting the rates, hide new work methods, and sanction socially those who work beyond socially approved rates. Moreover, such systems are complicated and require a great deal of expensive management time.[74]

In the models of both the "efficiency wage" and "transaction cost"

73. In my experience as an observer of the world of employment, academics are rarely in a position to lecture working people about "shirking."

74. *See generally*, EDWARD LAWLER, PAY AND ORGANIZATIONAL EFFECTIVENESS (1971); WILLIAM F. WHITE, ET AL., MONEY AND MOTIVATION: AN ANALYSIS OF INCENTIVES IN INDUSTRY (1955); Daniel J. B. Mitchell, et al., *Alternative Pay Systems, Firm Performance, and Productivity, in* PAYING FOR PRODUCTIVITY, *supra* note 40, at 36-42.

school, firms have basically only one way to prevent shirking: by creating bosses, who monitor employee performance and discharge nonperforming employees.[75] This scheme creates costs of its own. First, the direct cost of paying the bosses.[76] Second, it is well known that hierarchical organization often demotivates employees.[77] Finally, it creates new costs, the costs of preventing shirking by the bosses.

I find this a depressingly realistic picture of employment relations in many American firms. Employees bear substantial risks of job loss, pension loss, and other management opportunism; the incentives for top performance by employees are inadequate and inefficient; there is too much emphasis on the negative incentives of monitoring and job loss; and overall there is too much aggregate involuntary unemployment.

C. *Information costs and externalities: why inefficient employment contracts arise and persist*

Transaction cost theorists do not deny the existence of these costs; they seem to take a perverse pleasure in modelling the inside of a firm as a Hobbesian war of all against all, where anyone who promises to do anything for anyone immediately tries to figure out how to get out of it. They do tend to assert, however, that whatever the costs of this scheme,

75. In the original statement by Alchian & Demsetz, *supra* note 65, at 781-87, the monitor of employee performance is a private owner (or "residual claimant"), whose residual claim to firm earnings gives him incentives to monitor others' performance. Alchian and Demsetz forthrightly "assume" that monitoring by a single individual is more efficient than monitoring by a team, *id.* at 786. They do not consider another alternative, monitoring by an individual, who holds the monitoring position for periods in a rotation, then relinquishes it to others; this might be equally efficient. *See* James A. Mirrlees, *The Optimal Structure of Incentives and Authority Within an Organization*, 7 BELL J. ECON. 105 (1976); *see also* Louis Putterman, *On Some Recent Explanations of Why Capital Hires Labor*, 22 ECON. INQUIRY 171, 173 (1984).

Later treatments locate the monitoring function in supervisors hired by the residual claimants, e.g. OLIVER E. WILLIAMSON, MARKETS AND HIERARCHIES: ANALYSIS AND ANTITRUST IMPLICATIONS (1975); Guillermo A. Calvo & Stanislaw Wellisz, *supra* note 55; Joseph E. Stiglitz, *Incentives, Risk and Information: Notes Towards a Theory of Hierarchy*, 6 BELL J. ECON. 552 (1975). This is certainly a more realistic picture of the firm, but creates the unsolved riddle of how firms prevent shirking by the supervisors, who are of course just employees of a sort. "Other questions are: what makes the monitor honest?; if monitoring is observable, why can't it be hired on a fee-for-service basis, and if it isn't, how does it induce effort? When is mutual monitoring, motivated by profit sharing, superior to hierarchical monitoring with possible worker resistance?" Louis Putterman, *After the Employment Relation: Problems on the Road to Enterprise Democracy*, *in* MICROFOUNDATIONS, *supra* note 17, at n.2.

76. On the expanding numbers of supervisors and managers since World War II, *see* SAMUEL BOWLES, ET AL., BEYOND THE WASTE LAND: A DEMOCRATIC ALTERNATIVE TO ECONOMIC DECLINE 254-55 (1983). On the expanding gap between the compensation of managerial and production workers, see GRAEF S. CRYSTAL, IN SEARCH OF EXCESS: OVERCOMPENSATION OF THE AMERICAN EXECUTIVE (1991).

77. Haig R. Nalbantian, *Incentive Compensation in Perspective*, *in* INCENTIVES, COOPERATION, AND RISK SHARING: ECONOMIC AND PSYCHOLOGICAL PERSPECTIVES ON EMPLOYMENT CONTRACTS 14 (Haig R. Nalbantian ed., 1987).

it must be efficient, or something different would be observed.[78]

As a would-be reformer of this scheme, I deny the last assertion, which has been called "Economic Darwinism."[79] The arrangements described might persist despite being suboptimum both for individuals and firms. There are at least five broad classes of reasons why this is so.

The first three basically accept the "Economic Darwinism" framework, but show how parties can adopt arrangements which either appear to reduce costs for them, or actually reduce costs for them, yet are suboptimum because of costs imposed on others, or costs that the parties pay but do not recognize.

The first stems from the very kind of transaction and information costs to which these theorists have drawn our attention. Briefly, the division of the workforce into managers and employees, each with opportunities to cheat, leads to all contracts being made in very low levels of information. Parties have incentives to withhold information and no incentives to pay the price necessary to obtain the other's information. In other words, parties may think that longterm fixed employment contracts with high levels of supervision are efficient, and they may actually be efficient, within a framework that treats as fixed the high information costs stemming from the division of the workforce into supervisors and employees. This constraint however is far from fixed, and, if lifted, may result in efficiency gains.[80]

Second, the externalities of this scheme mean in effect that the public subsidizes it, so its greatest cost—continued aggregate unemployment—is not experienced as a cost by the parties. Third, even if each side shared more information, pervasive low trust will lead to Prisoner's Dilemmas in which cooperative, maximizing solutions will be rejected.

Of course, there are other classes of reasons that suboptimum bargains may arise and persist that traditionally have been of less interest to

78. *See, e.g.*, the contributions to the *Symposium*, *supra* note 62, by such "contractarians" as Frank H. Easterbrook & Daniel R. Fischel, *The Corporate Contract*, 89 COLUM. L. REV. 1416, 1444 (1989), or Fred S. McChesney, *Economics, Law, and Science in the Corporate Field: A Critique of Eisenberg*, 89 COLUM. L. REV. 1530, 1539-45 (1989). Recall that economists use efficient in a precise way: no one can be made better off unless someone else is made worse off. There is no such thing as an arrangement being more efficient than another.

79. *Why Capital Hires Labor*, *supra* note 11, at 185-86.

80. This is the central point of Bowles & Gintis, *supra* note 17, at 21-35. *See also* Oliver D. Hart, *Optimal Labour Contracts under Asymmetric Information: An Introduction*, 50 REV. ECON. STUD. 3 (1983); Martin L. Weitzman & Douglas L. Kruse, *Profit Sharing and Productivity*, *in* PAYING FOR PRODUCTIVITY, *supra* note 74, at 95, 104: "The defense of profit sharing and worker participation largely involves challenging the basic assumptions of the property rights school. In less extreme settings than perfectly costless monitoring and supervision finding the optimal degree of profit sharing becomes an extraordinarily complicated problem in the theory of the second or third best." (footnote omitted).

economists but which we cannot exclude. Suboptimum arrangements (such as investor ownership) may serve the political interests of those who have acquired political power and suppressed alternatives.[81] Or such suboptimum arrangements may have become conventional, creating very high entry costs to anyone seeking to challenge the convention.[82]

1. The high information costs of hierarchy

In the models of the "transaction cost" school, hierarchy arises "naturally" in order to provide information that the firm, or its owners, can use to monitor employee performance and sack the nonperformers. These models omit the costs of hierarchy in preventing firm managers from having access to information.

Employees, in my experience, typically regard *none* of the above package as optimal from their perspective. They would prefer not to bear such heavy risks of layoff, corporate takeover, or managerial opportunism with their pensions or other savings. They do not regard the level of supervision to which they are subjected as optimum either.[83] As they do not plan to shirk, certainly not in the sense of goofing off, they would much prefer a scheme in which they promise not to shirk and to work up to certain levels, and to assume the risk of some work sharing if necessary, in exchange for management's promise not to layoff and to reduce

81. Mark J. Roe, *A Political Theory of American Corporate Finance*, 91 COLUM. L. REV. 10 (1991) (political factors explain American pattern of widespread investor share ownership, as opposed to concentrated institutional ownership); *see also* Charles Sabel & Jonathan Zeitlin, *Historical Alternatives to Mass Production: Politics, Markets and Technology in Nineteenth-Century Industrialization*, PAST & PRESENT, Aug. 1985, at 133, for a historical study of the driving out of efficient alternatives.

82. This concept is particularly important in the work of the economist Harvey Leibenstein, discussed *infra* 102-13 and accompanying text. "Even the survival of an economic enterprise does not depend on efficiency in an absolute sense. At most, all that matters is the *relative* efficiency of firms vis-a-vis each other. Furthermore, there are a variety of sheltering mechanisms, and various ways in which an organization can operate under sheltered circumstances. Some organizations can themselves contribute to increasing the degree of shelter from competitive forces. Hence, stability, survival, and INEFFICIENCY can all persist for long periods of time." HARVEY LEIBENSTEIN, INSIDE THE FIRM: THE INEFFICIENCIES OF HIERARCHY 4 (1987)[hereinafter INSIDE THE FIRM]. *See also* David I. Levine & Laura D'Andrea Tyson, *Participation, Productivity, and the Firm's Environment*, *in* PAYING FOR PRODUCTIVITY, *supra* note 40, at 183, 204-35 (discussing systematic bias of the market system against efficient participatory workplaces); Jon Elster, *From Here to There; or, If Cooperative Ownership is So Desirable, Why Are There So Few Cooperatives?*, 6 SOC. PHIL. & POL'Y 93 (1989) (explaining paucity of cooperatives through importance of convention, adverse selection, free rider problems and the like).

83. There have been numerous recent experiments with varieties of team production or other ways of reducing the density of supervision. In every account I've seen, employees are quite happy to be less supervised. *See, e.g.*, HECKSCHER, *supra* note 35, at 138-46; SHOSHANA ZUBOFF, IN THE AGE OF THE SMART MACHINE: THE FUTURE OF WORK AND POWER 245-310 (1988); GREENBERG, *supra* note 26, at 40-50, 78-81.

levels and intensity of monitoring. If management is indifferent to this choice, why won't it let the employees have their way?

I think that Alchian and Demsetz, Jensen and Meckling, Williamson and others are basically right to see this problem as partly one of information costs.[84] Employees are simply not in a position to make a credible promise to supply enough effort to compensate management for assuming greater risk.[85] Management, under conflict of interest,[86] will assume that insuring employees against risks of layoff and job loss will create the "moral hazard" familiar from insurance, where insuring against an event creates incentives for its occurrence.[87] "Hence, the outcome of this bargaining situation (or contract) is what economists call 'second best.' The deviation from a first-best solution (optimum) and the resulting misallocation of risk is the true cost of the information imperfections that characterize the typical employment situation."[88]

As set out here, the problem in designing optimum employment contracts is partly the problem well-studied by economists of the proper tradeoff between incentives and risk. It seems generally accepted that efficient solutions to this tradeoff cannot be found under conditions of asymmetric information.[89] Yet that is precisely the process of employment contracting under conflicts of interest. Efficient tradeoffs would require that management know employees' preference for risk, maximal feasible work effort, and all employees' other ideas for improving productivity. Employees will, however, never volunteer this information to a management that will surely use it opportunistically. Management has no other way of acquiring the information at reasonable cost, so manage-

84. "Partly" because I would broaden their approach to include the kinds of internal or "X" inefficiency resulting from low trust that is associated with the work of Harvey Leibenstein, discussed *infra* Part IID. For comparisons with the "information costs" school, *see* Harvey Leibenstein and Klaus Weiermair, *X-Efficiency, Managerial Discretion, and the Nature of Employment Relations: A Game-Theoretical Approach*, *in* MANAGEMENT UNDER DIFFERING LABOUR MARKET AND EMPLOYMENT SYSTEMS 79 (G. Dlugos, et al. eds., 1988) [also in Leibenstein's Collected Essays].

85. Perhaps management would be indifferent if employees could post a bond against their future shirking. Lorne Carmichael, *Can Unemployment Be Involuntary?: Comment*, 75 AM. ECON. REV. 1213 (1985) suggests that such a bonding scheme should reach employment equilibrium without unemployment. However, real world employees obviously do not have the resources to post such a bond. Moreover, existing compensation schemes tying workers to firms are not good substitutes for such a hypothetical bond. George A. Akerlof & Lawrence Katz, *Workers' Trust Funds and the Logic of Wage Profiles*, 104 Q. J. ECON. 525 (1989).

86. Bowles & Gintis, *supra* note 17, at 7, call this "contested exchange."

87. The friends of the born nurse
Are always getting worse.

W. H. Auden, *Shorts*, in COLLECTED SHORTER POEMS 1927-1957 42 (1975).

88. Nalbantian, *supra* note 77, at 11-12.

89. Bengt Holmström, *Moral Hazard and Observability*, 10 BELL J. ECON. 74 (1979); Hart, *supra* note 80. *But cf.* Jacques H. Dreze, *Some Theory of Labor Management and Participation*, 44 ECONOMETRICA 1125 (1976).

ment supervises and monitors instead of seeking cooperation, and the resulting mix of risk bearing and incentives is optimum for no one.

2. Externalities and subsidies

Probably the biggest single cost of the current regime of efficient wage contracts is the cost of continuing involuntary unemployment.[90] Because firms are divided into supervisors and employees, they will adopt rigid pay scales and high supervision rather than flexible wages, work sharing, incentive pay, and low supervision. Because wages are not flexible, we have mandatory retirement;[91] excessive risk of discharge and layoff;[92] and unwillingness to hire potential workers who would be happy to be paid the value of their marginal product or even less.

Firms do not experience this cost as a cost at all. Employees experience the constant anxiety of job loss. The bulk of the cost, however, is born by the chronically unemployed, and to a lesser extent by the society that pays, through transfer payments, and through such destructive behaviors associated with chronic unemployment as mental illness, violence towards self and others, crime, alcoholism, and disease.[93]

I wish to stress this point, since, when we turn our attention back to employee ownership, we will see that much is made of the subsidization of employee ownership through ESOP legislation and tax treatment of cooperatives.[94] I do not deny such subsidization,[95] but also wish to point out the extremely heavy social subsidization given the current regime of employment contracts, in which, as so often occurs, costs are socialized while profits are private.[96]

90. Akerlof & Yellen, *supra* note 50; Joseph E. Stiglitz, *The Design of Labor Contracts: The Economics of Incentives and Risk Sharing*, *in* INCENTIVES, COOPERATION AND RISK SHARING: ECONOMIC AND PSYCHOLOGICAL PERSPECTIVES ON EMPLOYMENT CONTRACTS 3 (Haig R. Nalbantian ed., 1987).

91. Lazear, *supra* note 53.

92. *Supra* Part II B.

93. MEYER HARVEY BRENNER, MENTAL ILLNESS AND THE ECONOMY (1973); NORMAN T. FEATHER, THE PSYCHOLOGICAL IMPACT OF UNEMPLOYMENT (1990). High wages, in a very real sense, are subsidized by the families of the chronically unemployed.

94. Richard L. Doernberg and Jonathan R. Macey, *ESOPs and Economic Distortion*, 23 HARV. J. ON LEGIS. 103 (1986); William R. Levin, Note, *The False Promise of Worker Capitalism: Congress and the Leveraged Employee Stock Ownership Plan*, 95 YALE L. J. 148 (1985).

95. I don't want to overstate it either. A major theme of BLASI & KRUSE, *supra* note 1, at 88-138, is that employees typically pay for all or most of their ESOP, through restructuring of wages and benefits, such as wage concessions, elimination of defined-benefit pensions, profit sharing, or health benefits. *But see* Susan Chaplinsky & Greg Niehaus, *The Tax and Distributional Effects of Leveraged ESOPs*, 19 FIN. MGMT. 29, 37 (1990), finding that 48.2% of ESOPs increase employee compensation; 39.8% leave employee compensation unchanged; 6.0% decrease overall employee compensation.

96. In his oral comments to these remarks when given as the Piper Lecture, Professor Macey observed that such "subsidies" as transfer payments, unemployment benefits, and the social costs of

The work of the "efficiency wage" and "transaction costs" theorists helps us see the subtle as well as the obvious ways that the public, and the unemployed, subsidize "efficient wage" contracts. The obvious subsidy, central to all varieties of "efficient wage" theory, is that wages exceed marginal productivity, so labor markets do not clear, unemployment is created as an externality, and the public and the unemployed pay for the unemployment.[97]

The subtle subsidy is that, by paying for the externalities created by "efficient wage" contracts, the public inhibits the private adoption of solutions to unemployment. There is no shortage of proposals to mitigate unemployment, or (more narrowly) layoffs during recessions, through work sharing, in which firms would respond to downturns through shared salary and wage cuts, not layoffs.[98] Of course, unions are already free to negotiate such plans, and employers free to adopt them voluntarily; why are they so unusual? Efficiency wage theory provides one answer: labor productivity will drop if wages drop, as good workers leave, or for other reasons.[99] In Professor Weitzman's proposal, workers would be compensated for the income lost under work-sharing by profit-sharing, permitting the workers to recapture some of the productivity gained.[100] The "transaction costs" school explains why workers will never agree to this: workers, particularly workers without unions, are in no position to monitor company reporting and administration of profits.

unemployment, are neutral as between employee-owned and capitalist-owned firms and therefore cannot be said to subsidize the latter. This is formally true but, if the models of the "efficient wage" theorists are correct, untrue in practice. Most economic models of employee ownership, as well as empirical studies, *supra* note 22, find that such firms in practice would take great pains to avoid involuntary unemployment, and would thus rarely occasion the payment of the various social subsidies for unemployment. It is just as if the state built a highway system and then asserted that it was neutral, subsidizing neither trucking nor railroads.

97. In this example, we see clearly the economists' use of "efficient": typical employment contracts are "efficient" if neither workers nor the firm could be made better off except at the expense of the other, even if this "efficiency" imposes direct costs on the unemployed and on society. So often, "efficiency" is just a euphemism for the old British army expression "I'm all right, Jack." (The expression is implicitly completed by a common two-word imperative expression, left unspoken).

98. One that attracted considerable attention among economists and in the popular press is MARTIN L. WEITZMAN, THE SHARE ECONOMY: CONQUERING STAGFLATION (1984). Not only would such arrangements be fair, macroeconomically sounder, and popular with Harvard economists; until 1977 they would arguably have helped insulate companies and unions from potential liability under the Civil Rights Act of 1964. *See, e.g.*, Alfred W. Blumrosen & Ruth G. Blumrosen, *The Duty to Plan for Fair Employment Revisited: Work Sharing in Hard Times*, 28 RUTGERS L. REV. 1082 (1975); Clyde W. Summers & Margaret C. Love, *Work Sharing as an Alternative to Layoffs by Seniority: Title VII Remedies in Recession*, 124 U. PA. L. REV. 893 (1976). Still, they were rarely encountered at that time or afterward.

99. David Levine, *Efficiency Wages in Weitzman's Share Economy*, 28 INDUS. REL. 321 (1989); Andrew Weiss, *Job Queues and Layoffs in Labor Markets with Flexible Wages*, 88 J. POL. ECON. 526 (1980).

100. WEITZMAN, *supra* note 98, at 82-95.

Absent such monitoring, the company would be "tempted to cheat."[101]

D. *Internal or "X"-Inefficiency: How low trust leads to the persistence of inefficient labor contracts*

The combined models of the "efficient wage" and "transaction costs" school present what I find a compelling picture. At least in some firms (and so far we need form no estimation of their quantity), patterns of labor contracting may exist in which employees, rightly fearing management holdups and opportunism, withhold efforts or information that might improve firm productivity. The resulting employment contracts are suboptimum for firms (in terms of reduced productivity and losses from excessive supervision and labor unrest) and employees (in terms of inefficient allocations of the risk of job loss and incentives for better performance). Understanding the dynamics of this process in individual firms is enhanced by studying yet a third body of economic literature, the somewhat controversial literature on "internal" or "X"-inefficiency.[102]

The concept of internal or "X"-inefficiency was developed to explain the fact that sometimes individual firms experience very large gains in productivity. This fact is commonplace to management consultants, who make their living through bringing about such gains, and to the economists who study enterprise in developing countries and who first devel-

101. Clive Bull, *Business Cycles and Wage Determination in the United States*, *in* INCENTIVES, COOPERATION, AND RISK SHARING: ECONOMIC AND PSYCHOLOGICAL PERSPECTIVES ON EMPLOYMENT CONTRACTS 226 (Haig R. Nalbantian ed., 1987).

While this Article favors experimentation with employee ownership as a device for lowering information costs, this particular information cost, the workers' cost of acquiring accurate information about company finance, could be lowered considerably with modest reforms to the law under Section 8(a)(5) of the National Labor Relations (Wagner) Act, 29 U.S.C. § 158(a)(5). That section creates an employer's obligation to bargain in good faith, which includes an obligation to share information with the union that is extraordinarily modest in comparison with most European practice. *Compare* Leslie K. Shedlin, *Regulation of Disclosure of Economic and Financial Data and The Impact on The American System of Labor-Management Relations*, 41 OHIO ST. L. J. 441 (1980) *with* Washington Materials, Inc. v. NLRB, 803 F.2d 1333 (4th Cir. 1986) (no duty to disclose financial statements despite company claim that it was losing bids); ACL Corp. d/b/a Atlanta Hilton and Tower, 271 N.L.R.B. 1600 (1984) (no duty to disclose financial records).

Low trust and high information costs are not the only reason unions so rarely negotiate work-sharing and flexible pay arrangements. State programs of unemployment insurance typically compensate only victims of total unemployment, not those partially unemployed due to work sharing. Under principles of moral hazard, such insurance programs help bring about total unemployment. *See generally* SHORT-TIME WORK COMPENSATION: A FORMULA FOR WORK SHARING (Ramelle MaCoy & Martin Morand eds., 1984).

102. The controversy lies in these economists' relaxation of the postulate that economic actors maximize satisfaction; this redefinition of rationality is controversial among economists. *See* Leibenstein & Weiermair, *supra* note 84.

The basic works on internal inefficiency are the following works by Harvey Leibenstein: COLLECTED ESSAYS OF HARVEY LEIBENSTEIN (1989); INSIDE THE FIRM, *supra* note 82; BEYOND ECONOMIC MAN (1976). *See also* ROGER R. FRANTZ, X-EFFICIENCY: THEORY, EVIDENCE, AND APPLICATIONS (1987).

oped the theory. They report productivity gains of fifty percent or more after "simple reorganizations of the production process, e.g., plant-layout reorganization, materials handling, waste controls, work methods, and payments by result."[103] Such gains are, however, deeply puzzling to neoclassical economists who assume that all firms use inputs efficiently and experience what neoclassical economists call "inefficiency" (and Leibenstein calls "allocative inefficiency") only because of regulation, monopolies, cartels and the like. Internal or "X"-inefficiency is simply the name for all inefficiencies that distinguish two plants that purchase identical inputs, at identical prices, with identical knowledge of the state of the art, and nevertheless produce different output.[104]

Of course, even employee-owned firms will have internal inefficiencies. However, I want to focus on the particular form of internal inefficiency that Professor Leibenstein has emphasized in his recent work: the inefficiency that results from low trust between contracting parties, and the group processes that subsequently institutionalize the suboptimum arrangement, which may persist despite being suboptimum for all affected individuals and the firm.

1. The inefficiency of hierarchy: low trust and suboptimum deals

We have seen how the "transaction costs" school explains some suboptimum employment contracts as resulting from asymmetries of information that cannot efficiently be remedied. Leibenstein has illustrated another variety of suboptimum contract that may result, despite perfect information, simply from low trust between parties.

His initial illustration involves the bargaining in the second act of the opera *Tosca*.[105]

103. Harvey Leibenstein, *Allocative Efficiency vs. "X-Efficiency,"* 56 AM. ECON. REV. 392, 399 (1966)[hereinafter *Allocative Efficiency*].

104. Harvey Leibenstein, *Aspects of the X-efficiency Theory of the Firm*, 6 BELL J. ECON. 580 (1975). It includes "(1) intra-plant motivational efficiency, (2) external motivational efficiency, and (3) nonmarket input efficiency." Leibenstein, *Allocative Efficiency*, *supra* note 103, at 406-07.

Leibenstein believes that internal inefficiency does not merely supplement allocative efficiency but dwarfs it; internal inefficiency is much more important economically despite the emphasis of professional economists on allocative inefficiency. To the extent that the economic literature on worker ownership, *supra* notes 19-23, focuses solely on such issues of allocative inefficiency as allocation of employment and investment, it reinforces Leibenstein's point. "Whereas theorists studying the [Labor-Managed Firm] concern themselves mainly with allocative issues . . . , empirical researchers view questions of internal organization (e.g., x-efficiency) and variations in the productivity of a given group of resources as being at least as important from a policy standpoint." Bonin et al., *supra* note 24, at 26.

105. Libretto by Luigi Illica and Giuseppe Giacosa after the play by Victorien Sardou, music by Giacomo Puccini. Anatol Rapoport originally adapted this incident in *The Use and Misuse of Game Theory*, SCI. AM., Dec. 1962, at 108, 113.

The main protagonists are Tosca, a beautiful singer, and Scarpia, chief of police in Rome during the Napoleonic occupation. At the point relevant to our purposes, Scarpia has captured Tosca's lover, who has been sentenced to be shot. Scarpia makes Tosca an offer she cannot refuse. If she will sleep with him, he will substitute fake bullets for the real one. She accepts. On the way to the rendezvous, Tosca discovers a dagger which she can use to kill Scarpia, if she so chooses. Let us now stop the story in its tracks, so to speak, to consider the options. Scarpia can (1) stick to the agreement and order blank bullets used, or (2) he can leave the real bullets in and get rid of his rival for Tosca's affections. Tosca now has two options: she can honor the agreement and sleep with Scarpia, or she can use the dagger on Scarpia, and maintain her honor. Table 5.1 shows the payoffs in terms of utilities.

		SCARPIA	
		Fake	Real
TOSCA	Sleep	I 50 50	II 500 -600
	Dagger	III -600 500	IV -500 -500

TABLE 5.1

In cell I Tosca sleeps with Scarpia and Scarpia uses the blanks. This has a relatively low but positive payoff for both. While Tosca saves her lover, she yields to the hated Scarpia. Similarly Scarpia enjoys Tosca, but he does not get rid of his rival. Cell II is the best for Scarpia since he enjoys Tosca and gets rid of his rival. This had a high payoff for Scarpia (+500 utils), and the lowest possible payoff for Tosca since she loses her loved one and yields to Scarpia. Cell III is the reverse of cell II. Here Tosca is best off since she gets rid of the hated Scarpia and saves her lover. Cell IV is clearly inferior to cell I for both. For Scarpia it is worse since he gets killed. For Tosca it is worse since her lover is killed.

How will they choose? If each tries to choose independently we can see that the Prisoner's Dilemma outcome (cell IV) occurs. Consider Scarpia's logic: if Tosca will succumb he might as well get rid of his rival and not substitute the blank bullets. If he thinks Tosca will refuse or might kill him then he certainly has no reason to substitute the blanks. Hence he opts for the real bullets. Tosca's logic is similar. If Scarpia sticks to his bargain and has given the order to substitute the blanks then there is no point in yielding to him. She might as well use the dagger. If Scarpia has not given the order, then of course, she will kill him for revenge, rather than submit. Obviously, this type of thinking on both their parts results in the Prisoner's Dilemma outcome. Since the opera is a tragedy, it follows the logic of the situation. In the end, all the main characters go to their doom. The final scene has Tosca throwing herself off the rampart of the Castel Sant'Angelo after killing Scarpia, and upon learning of the death of her loved one.

For economics, the *Tosca* example of the Prisoner's Dilemma is more fundamental than the original Prisoner's Dilemma story. In the original, the fact that the two prisoners did not *communicate* was of the essence. In *Tosca* distrust is of the essence. In *Tosca*, the contending parties could, and did, communicate. In fact, they had worked out a satisfactory contract. What they did not have was mutual trust, and the *mutual incentives* to keep the contract. Present self-interest based on distrust made both parties worse off than would have been the case under the contract. Thus, the *Tosca* story is a member of a class of Prisoner's Dilemmas, which is essentially a mutual distrust dilemma.[106]

The remainder of Leibenstein's book is concerned with analogous bargaining between employees and managers. Employees may decide not to perform to the maximum, not trusting management to reward them for additional effort.[107] Management may not reward employees or improve the quality of work life, reckoning that such gifts to employees will not be reciprocated.[108] A cooperative solution that maximizes payoffs to all affected individuals will be rejected.

Now it is not news that low trust often describes relations between employers and employees. Alan Fox showed some time ago how much of the institutional apparatus of employment relations is explained by

106. INSIDE THE FIRM, *supra* note 82, at 44-46.

107. Here, as throughout this Article, I would urge that this be understood *not* primarily as a reference to "working harder", loading more sacks onto a truck, in the famous example of Alchian & Demsetz, *supra* note 65. The more interesting Prisoner's Dilemma involves whether employees will "work smarter"; suggest improvements; monitor productivity losses through poor decisions by supervisors or fellow employees; think about what they are doing. *See supra* note 74.

Of course, in particular settings the incentive problem is indeed to produce incentives for "working harder." In law firms, the problem is not really to induce associates to "work smarter." Law firm associates are screened carefully for personalities and academic records of working very smart indeed. Gilson & Mnookin, *supra* note 29, at 376-78. What large private law firms routinely induce, that government agencies and public interest offices do much less successfully, is indeed "working harder," in terms of exceptionally large quantities of sheer hours worked. Worker ownership is a substantial component of this incentive to "work harder": the winners will make partner.

108. Of course, where management believes, as a result of what it knows about workplace norms and conventions, that such gifts will be reciprocated, it will make them. Leibenstein is carrying forward, and describing the outer limits to, the process described in George A. Akerlof, *Labor Contracts as a Partial Gift Exchange*, 97 Q. J. ECON. 543 (1982).

this fact.[109] Leibenstein's work goes further in two respects. First, it shows how such low trust is strictly economically inefficient; it imposes high information and supervision costs and leads to inefficient bargains. Second, it is the firm-specific theory we have been looking for; it suggests that the inefficiencies due to low trust will vary from firm to firm.[110]

It is probably unnecessary to point out all the ways we have already seen that managerial opportunism contributes to low trust. We have already seen that management may exploit location-specific investments by threatening, or undertaking, capital mobility or disinvestment; by laying off; by lack of accountability to employees; by monkeying with pensions. Low trust may also reflect miscellaneous idiosyncratic reasons, such as a history of incompetence.[111]

2. Conventions: the perpetuation of suboptimum bargains

"Transaction costs" economists do not reject the idea that low trust may lead to Prisoner's Dilemmas and suboptimum bargains, but their models tend to assume that someone—the firm's residual claimant, for example—will have incentives to push the suboptimum bargain to an efficient outcome, so that the suboptimum bargain will not persist. The great contribution of Leibenstein's work on conventions is to show that this is not the case.

Briefly, as Alchian and Demsetz say, firms exist to coordinate productive inputs.[112] Just about any "coordination point" is better than no coordination. The suboptimum bargain resulting from the Prisoner's Dilemma will persist over time as the coordination point. In order to change the convention, a given individual will have to challenge peer groups and convince large numbers of people to change their behavior. It is rare for any individual to be in a position to do this.[113]

109. ALAN FOX, BEYOND CONTRACT: WORK, TRUST AND POWER RELATIONS (1974).

110. While the variation may be one of degree, the amounts may be substantial. I would not be inclined to argue with someone who claims, like Bowles & Gintis, *supra* note 17, that all capitalist firms experience such inefficiencies of contested exchange, low cooperation, low trust, high information costs. Nevertheless, the amount of such inefficiency will vary from firm to firm, and I would not rule out the possibility that there may be capitalist firms with comparatively rather low internal inefficiency resulting from low trust. For example, Professor Leibenstein believes that many Japanese firms have substantially surmounted this problem, INSIDE THE FIRM, *supra* note 82.

111. For a darkly hilarious ethnography, *see* TOM JURAVICH, CHAOS ON THE SHOP FLOOR: A WORKER'S VIEW OF QUALITY, PRODUCTIVITY, AND MANAGEMENT (1985). Anyone entranced by the starry-eyed vision of small-batch custom manufacturing in MICHAEL J. PIORE & CHARLES F. SABEL, THE SECOND INDUSTRIAL DIVIDE: POSSIBILITIES FOR PROSPERITY (1984), should immediately read this book as an antidote.

112. Alchian & Demsetz, *supra* note 65, at 778.

113. INSIDE THE FIRM, *supra* note 82, at 60-97. For example, an individual who favors reducing hierarchy as a public good will probably not challenge that hierarchy for reasons familiar from the

The convention story is familiar to anyone familiar with any institution, certainly including employee relations. There is scant if any evidence that firms administer their employee relations policies to achieve anything like the economist's "efficiency." For example, firms adopt the same benefits programs that everyone in their region and industry does, even if they would benefit from something different.[114] Firms don't administer their ESOPs for maximum financial advantage.[115] Leibenstein's work on conventions explains these behavioral findings much better than a neoclassical theory that assumes that all firms produce efficiently, or theories that assume that a private owner as residual claimant can efficiently, without high information or transaction costs, break a convention and push a firm to efficiency.

III. A Firm-Specific Model of Successful Employee Ownership

We are now in a position to describe (or model, if you like) a particular type of firm in which employee ownership might succeed.[116] Employee ownership can be an attractive solution to a firm experiencing:

1. high conflicts of interest between managers and employees.
2. low trust between managers and employees, as a result of ideological, cultural, or firm-specific factors.
3. suboptimum employment contracting as a "solution" to these problems; that is, employment "conventions" that institutionalize:
    a. low incentives for employee productivity, or
    b. high unnecessary supervision costs; or
    c. inefficient allocation of risks.

In Leibenstein's language, the firm in question will be experiencing high levels of internal or "X"-inefficiency due to some combination of information asymmetries or low trust between employees and managers,

public choice literature. A challenge would come only if some individual developed a preference for democracy as a private good, which doesn't seem too likely.

Challenging hierarchy becomes less likely yet under the quite plausible scenario "that a mature system of worker-run enterprise would be absolutely preferred to a capitalist system by the majority of the workforce who are non-managerial employees under the hierarchical system, and that most of the managerial workers would themselves be at worst indifferent between the two. . . . [T]his hypothesis could be true, yet, at the same time, it could be the case that a *transitional* worker-run enterprise would produce few immediate benefits for most of its members, and would involve significant sacrifices for any managerial personnel who joined it." Louis Putterman, *Some Behavioral Perspectives on the Dominance of Hierarchical Over Democratic Forms of Enterprise*, 3 J. Econ. Behav. & Organization 139, 151 (1982).

114. Allen Cheadle, *Explaining Patterns of Profit-sharing Activity*, 28 Indus.Rel. 387 (1989).

115. Chaplinsky & Niehaus, *supra* note 95, at 36.

116. Recall that we defined our task, *supra* note 48, as a "sometimes" theory of successful employee ownership that fit with the observable pattern of successful employee ownership.

or, if already successfully employee-owned, such as a law firm, would experience such high internal inefficiency if it converted from employee to investor ownership.

The essence of the concept of internal inefficiency is that it explains observed variations within an industry, variations among firms purchasing similar inputs in similar markets to produce similar outputs. Consequently, it is not easy to generalize about the shared characteristics of "firms with high internal inefficiency due to low trust." However, three common patterns of "low trust between employees and managers" go a long way toward explaining nearly all observable successful employee ownership, and explain that pattern much better than Professor Hansmann's rather reductionist, and readily falsifiable, theory, that limits successful employee ownership to easily metered service employees.[117] These are patterns, not causes-and-effects; they help identify the sorts of situations for which employee ownership is promising.

A. *"Low trust" as the common thread in employee ownership*

First, employees may not trust managers because they are *professional* employees who have been socialized into deep distrust of managerial types. What, after all, is a "professional" but one who, on the basis of specialized learning, can successfully command respect and autonomy from most managerial or nonprofessional authority?[118] When we deal with employee-owned law firms, we deal with an institution close to the experience of many readers of these pages, so I ask you whether you think law firms would be more efficient if organized as corporations, with shareholders, Boards of Directors, career managers. All my experience

117. Hansmann, *supra* note 1, at 1783-84.

118. The large literature on the supposed conflict between "professional autonomy" and "bureaucratic management" includes: ELIOT FREIDSON, PROFESSIONAL POWERS: A STUDY OF THE INSTITUTIONALIZATION OF FORMAL KNOWLEDGE 158-84 (1986); ALVIN W. GOULDNER, THE FUTURE OF THE INTELLECTUALS AND THE RISE OF THE NEW CLASS (1979); MAGALI SARFATTI LARSON, THE RISE OF PROFESSIONALISM: A SOCIOLOGICAL ANALYSIS 178-244 (1977) (noting the growth of an ideology of autonomy of professionalism as professional work conditions become threatened by bureaucratic or managerial authority); RICHARD ABEL, AMERICAN LAWYERS 199-200 (1989) (The historic independence of lawyers from bureaucratic management may be declining as law firms are increasingly managed by full-time professional managers.). *See also* David M. Rabban, *Distinguishing Excluded Managers from Covered Professionals Under the NLRA*, 89 COLUM. L. REV. 1775, 1832-52 (1989). I agree with ROBERT L. NELSON, PARTNERS WITH POWER: THE SOCIAL TRANSFORMATION OF THE LARGE LAW FIRM 233 (1988) that "professional autonomy" has often been used in contradictory ways. I use it here to note, as Nelson does, that firm lawyers are not really subject to "deskilling" or "proletarianization," that they "exercise considerable discretion and control over the work process," *id.* at 188; and in particular are supervised only by other professionals, not professional managers. In particular I am not suggesting that there is any substantial autonomy from *clients*, *id.* at 223, nor am I rejecting Nelson's observation, which seems right to me, that in large law firms *both* the values of "partnership" *and* the values of "management" serve as vehicles for the projection of power by dominant partners. *Id.* at 78-79, 121-22.

tells me that they would lose efficiency; that lawyers would never put in the hours, the effort, the initiative for managerial types that they will for a firm owned by themselves or where a future ownership stake is part of the motivational package. Just ask who works harder and smarter, the lawyers who own their own firms or the lawyers working under bureaucratic management.[119]

Second, employee ownership may succeed, at least comparatively, where employees for whatever political or cultural reason simply will never accept or trust managerial authority.[120]

Third, nonprofessional, nonpolitical employees may distrust management for deep if idiosyncratic reasons: they believe that *this* management has through *this* opportunism messed up *this* company, and they will not trust that management any more. For example, the firm may, as a result of conventional capitalist management, be bankrupt or on the verge of bankruptcy.[121]

This third pattern is of the greatest economic interest but is the least intuitively obvious. After all, if cranky professionals or far-out countercultural types won't work for anyone but themselves, then somebody should design situations in which they *will* work, but without any sense that any wider economic questions hang in the balance. What is the connection between internal inefficiency in the typical industrial firm, and work organization or employee ownership?

B. Employee ownership and information costs

Let me answer this question in two steps. First, common to a great deal of observable real world employee relations is a managerial effort to induce employees to share information with management. Second, it is easily demonstrable that, at least in some situations, an ownership stake will induce such information-sharing that other, competing forms of inducing employees will not.

1. What employees know:

To my mind, Karl Marx never wrote anything more beautiful than the famous discussion of the architect and the bee. At the risk of alienating readers who may conclude that an article quoting Marx cannot possibly be for them, let me quote the passage.

119. Nelson, *supra* note 118, at 184-88.

120. This may explain the cooperatives studied by Mansbridge and Rothschild & Witt, *supra* note 11.

121. Recall the cycle in which employee ownership is born in recessions. *See, e.g.*, Ben-Ner, *supra* note 44; Miyazaki, *supra* note 44.

> A spider conducts operations which resemble those of the weaver, and a bee would put many a human architect to shame by the construction of its honeycomb cells. But what distinguishes the worst architect from the best of bees is that the architect builds the cell in his mind before he constructs it in wax. At the end of every labour process, a result emerges which had already been conceived by the worker at the beginning, hence already existed ideally.[122]

For over a century, theorists of work and management, whether of the right or left, have often embarked from just this starting point: the idea that employees hold a great deal of knowledge that their employers do not have and would like to get. This was of course true of nineteenth century craft workers, who, through their control of the production process, had more effective control of the pace and quantity of production. This lead to the first great managerial campaign to acquire employee knowledge, the "scientific management" program of Frederick Winslow Taylor, in which employees were minutely observed, and their jobs then broken down into comparatively unskilled, repetitive jobs, the holders of no single one of which would be in a position to hold up or restrict production.[123]

Remarkably, however, even after Taylorist "deskilling," ordinary industrial workers today still control information that management lacks. The uneducated machine operator is likely to be the only one in the place who knows exactly how to operate that particular machine, how to keep it maintained and functional, long after management has refused to put any more money into it and the manufacturer has ceased to make replacement parts.[124]

From this perspective, the common thread among quality circles, quality of work life programs, and team production, all popular management reforms, is that all seek to create environments in which employees will share information with management that they will never share under conventional labor relations. At their most benign, the groups may engender suggestions about safer or more productive work processes, although even this kind of information sharing goes too far for some employee advocates, particularly if the productivity suggestions result in job

122. 1 KARL MARX, CAPITAL 284 (Fowkes trans. 1976).

123. DAVID NELSON, MANAGERS AND WORKERS: ORIGINS OF THE NEW FACTORY SYSTEM IN THE UNITED STATES 1880-1920 (1975); MARX, *supra* note 122; DAVID M. GORDON ET AL., SEGMENTED WORK, DIVIDED WORKERS: THE HISTORICAL TRANSFORMATION OF LABOR IN THE UNITED STATES (1982); HARRY BRAVERMAN, LABOR AND MONOPOLY CAPITAL: THE DEGRADATION OF WORK IN THE TWENTIETH CENTURY (1975).

124. JURAVICH, *supra* note 111; KEN C. KUSTERER, KNOW-HOW ON THE JOB: THE IMPORTANT WORKING KNOWLEDGE OF "UNSKILLED" WORKERS (1978).

loss.[125] At their most sinister, they may engender information about employee union sentiments and become the vehicles for psychological manipulation of employees, destroying employee solidarity to facilitate management control.[126] Their ultimate potential either for capitalist efficiency, or employee participation, remains unclear.[127]

2. Efficiency advantages of employee ownership:

If the chief efficiency advantage of employee ownership then is overcoming low trust and lowering information costs, it cannot be shown, necessarily to yield efficiency gains over a capitalist-owned firm which extensively employs team production or quality circles.[128] For example, Professor Leibenstein's preferred institutional arrangement for overcoming internal inefficiency appears to be, not employee ownership, but rather variants on Japanese employee relations.[129]

However hard to demonstrate, there may in theory be several ways in which structuring an ownership stake for employees in a participatory workplace will induce higher trust and lower information costs than simple resort to quality circles or team production without an ownership stake.[130]

125. MIKE PARKER, INSIDE THE CIRCLE: A UNION GUIDE TO QWL (1985); James Rinehart, *Appropriating Workers' Knowledge: Quality Control Circles at a General Motors Plant*, 14 STUD. POL. ECON. 75 (1984).

126. GUILLERMO J. GRENIER, INHUMAN RELATIONS: QUALITY CIRCLES AND ANTI-UNIONISM IN AMERICAN INDUSTRY (1988).

127. For an excellent discussion, see Karl E. Klare, *The Labor-Management Cooperation Debate: A Workplace Democracy Perspective*, 23 HARV. C.R.-C.L. L. REV. 39 (1988). A strong case that worker participation, especially if adopted by all firms, would be associated with improved productivity, is Levine & Tyson, *supra* note 82, at 183-243.

128. This is the crux of my disagreement with Bowles & Gintis, *supra* note 17. Of course, this pertains only to the efficiency case for employee ownership, leaving intact the political theory case. Moreover, the difference may be purely theoretical if capitalist firms do not in practice otherwise realize the efficiency gains that they would under worker ownership.

129. INSIDE THE FIRM, *supra* note 82, includes an extensive discussion of Japanese management practices. By contrast, I do not believe that Leibenstein has ever discussed employee ownership.

130. This is consistent with the empirical literature associating productivity gains with the combination of employee ownership and participation that could not be achieved by either individually. *See* Rosen, *supra* note 4, at 30, and sources cited therein. Jon Hyman has suggested one important theoretical reason why this might be so. As Robert Axelrod and others have shown, whether "low trust" will move to "cooperation," avoiding Prisoners' Dilemmas, depends strongly on whether games are repeated or not. ROBERT AXELROD, THE EVOLUTION OF COOPERATION 15-69 (1984). Whatever the theoretical potential of quality of work life groups for achieving such cooperation, in practice in the United States they rarely survive long enough to have any such effect; most peter out within five years. EDWARD COHEN-ROSENTHAL & CYNTHIA BURTON, MUTUAL GAINS: A GUIDE TO UNION-MANAGEMENT COOPERATION 122 (1987); C. HECKSCHER, *supra* note 35, at 133.

a. Workers may disclose even more information for productivity, work smarter, since the result will not necessarily be layoff, and anyway they can determine the result.

Critics of quality of work life programs have discussed extensively the fact that management normally retains complete discretion over whether or not to implement the suggestions of the participants.[131] This might seem to place an upper limit on the kind of productivity suggestions that astute employees will adduce. With an ownership stake, employees will reveal no less information, and may disclose more.[132] At the same time management loses incentives to misrepresent firm profitability to workers if those workers are also shareowners.[133]

b. Workers will reveal preferences on risk-bearing.

A basic idea of the "efficiency wage" school, also familiar in practice, is that in *some* workplaces, workers would be willing to adopt a more flexible wage system in which at least some wages would be tied directly to individual or group productivity. Such a scheme should in theory be more efficient, since it provides better incentives to employees to work hard and smart, and permits firms to adjust to economic downturns with wage adjustments rather than layoffs. However, in low trust workplaces, workers will not trust management to administer such schemes, and therefore withhold information on their willingness to assume more risk. They continue to withhold such information in QWL groups where they fear management opportunism. They will share such information with themselves.[134] Or in other words, an employee-owned company is a company in which the Board of Directors always has, essentially without cost, information on employee preferences.[135]

131. PARKER, *supra* note 125, at 44-45; DONALD WELLS, EMPTY PROMISES: QUALITY OF WORKING LIFE PROGRAMS AND THE LABOR MOVEMENT 68 (1987).

132. Simon, *supra* note 3, at 1344, points out that ". . . impediments to easy exit from the community create inducements for internally participatory efforts to improve the community" (citing ALBERT O. HIRSCHMAN, EXIT, VOICE AND LOYALTY: RESPONSES TO DECLINE IN FIRMS, ORGANIZATIONS AND STATES (1970)).

133. Dan Kovenock & Roger Sparks, *An Implicit Contract Approach to Employee Stock Ownership Plans*, 14 J. COMP. ECON. 425 (1990).

134. Hansmann, *supra* note 1, at 1765-68.

135. Some readers have objected that most shareholders are in no position to monitor management and there is no reason to expect employee shareholders to do a better job. Obviously the empirical picture is far from clear, but there are numerous structural reasons that employee shareholders might effectively monitor management: they are physically at the point of production; they may have union or other organization to overcome collective action problems; their information costs are lower; they are disposed to voice over exit.

c. Workers will be willing to bear the risk of tying between performance and wages since they don't have to trust management.

This has been a feature of every one of the well-publicized, perhaps over-publicized, worker buyouts of failing firms in order to preserve jobs.[136] It always turns out that workers will make concessions to themselves, mostly tying compensation to firm performance, that they would not and did not make to management.[137]

d. One of the best-documented, clearest advantages of employee-owned firms is substantial savings in the number of supervisors.[138]

This is highly significant, as many new computerized work processes have created the technological possibility of eliminating useless supervisors and replacing them with teams of workers, all working on the same data base and monitoring each other. It appears that employee-owned firms will be at a substantial advantage over conventionally-owned firms in realizing these savings.[139]

e. Workers with an ownership stake should be likelier to invest in firm-specific education or other investments of their time, energy, or savings that are specific to the firm.[140]

f. There is a possibility that an ownership stake may motivate workers through diffuse psychological mechanisms.

We are not on firm ground here; the literature does not clearly demonstrate any such relationship in observable employee-owned firms.[141] This fact is puzzling, however, and may simply reflect gaps in

136. Over-publicized because these were never either typical or the most promising occasions for employee ownership.

137. BLASI & KRUSE, *supra* note 1, at 88-138.

138. GREENBERG, *supra* note 26 at 43-44.

139. For a fascinating study of conventionally-owned paper mills that experimented with just such team production, *see* ZUBOFF, *supra* note 83. Despite substantial savings, increased productivity, and increased worker job satisfaction, the experiment was terminated by managers fearful for their positions. *See also* LARRY HIRSCHHORN, BEYOND MECHANIZATION: WORK AND TECHNOLOGY IN A POST-INDUSTRIAL AGE (1984).

140. The assumption, that "ownership of" or "property rights" in an asset will create incentives for further marginally productive investment, is central to the literature typified by Oliver Hart & John Moore, *Property Rights and the Nature of the Firm*, 98 J. POL. ECON. 1119 (1990).

141. I share Hansmann's skepticism, *see* Hansmann, *supra* note 1, at 1769-70. The unpromising psychological literature includes: J. Lawrence French & Joseph Rosenstein, *Employee Ownership, Work Attitudes, and Power Relationships*, 27 ACAD. MGMT. J. 861 (1984) (finding no relationship between share ownership and job satisfaction, at least in company where management owned most of stock and no visible efforts made at participatory culture); Tove Helland Hammer et al., *Absenteeism When Workers Have a Voice: The Case of Employee Ownership*, 66 J. APPLIED PSYCHOL. 561 (1981) (no change in absenteeism rates after conversion to employee ownership); Richard T. Long, *The Relative Effects of Share Ownership vs. Control on Job Attitudes in an Employee-Owned Com-*

techniques of motivation. It would seem that over time, employee-owned firms *should* be able to design cultures of motivation that are more effective than in conventional firms and would also pay off in terms of job satisfaction.

These, then, are the potential efficiency and productivity advantages of the employee-owned firm. Are there any ways in which employee ownership would be negative for productivity?[142] I would say no, for a simple reason: employee-owned firms are always free to be as hierarchical as they like. Workers can of course select any structure of management hierarchy they like, since it is responsive to them.[143] Employee ownership need not resemble food co-ops. If they need managers, they can and do hire them.

This glib conclusion could be challenged if anyone could identify some structural feature of worker-run businesses that would make them unwilling to hire managers, even where those managers would contribute marginal product above the cost of hiring them. This problem just flips around all our earlier models of the firm. The neoclassicist would have to concede that the employee-owned firm will hire the manager at once.[144] The transaction costs school would point out the cost of monitoring the manager, but, once these costs are added in, the manager will still be hired if it is efficient to do so. Only the internal inefficiency school might be concerned that conventions of team production would impede adoption of the more efficient managerial hire. I suppose that they might; however since this problem cannot be documented for real world employee-owned firms it appears that such conventions are weak, if they exist at all. Indeed, employees in our culture are so conditioned to accept managers that it would seem that the conventions would run the other way.

In conclusion, then, the efficiency or productivity case for employee ownership seems to me both empirically and conceptually very strong,

pany, 31 HUM. REL. 753 (1978) (comparison of employees who owned stock with similar employees who did not revealed no differences in motivation and weak differences in integration and satisfaction; however, comparison not clear since many nonshareholders intended to buy into ownership in the near future). On the other hand, both GREENBERG, *supra* note 26, at 65-114, and HOCHNER ET AL., *supra* note 33, at 181-82, report increased job satisfaction after conversion to employee ownership, although in the Hochner study, non-owners who participated in Quality of Work Life programs were more satisfied than owners.

142. Recall that the literature, with perhaps one exception, fails to identify any such cases; *see supra* note 40.

143. Putterman, *supra* note 11, at 274.

144. "Labor-managed cannot mean that labor owns the firm in the traditional sense, that is, it cannot mean that tradable residual claims on the firm are held by employees. If that is all it means we are back to the traditional profit maximizing firm." Jensen & Meckling, *supra* note 11, at 475.

although likely to be a different case for each firm, and stronger in some firms than others.

C. *The Problem of Risk Allocation*

There is one very strong argument against an ownership stake for many workers, and that is the problem of allocation of risk. As we have seen, most working people in the primary sector of the contemporary American economy already are tied to their employer by implicit long-term employment contracts that leave them with a great deal of firm-specific and location-specific investment. What investments do working people have? They do not own stocks or bonds and do not have much savings. They may own a home, but in smaller communities the value of that home will not be independent of the economic strength of the leading employers. To an extent unique in the industrialized world, their access to health care and retirement security will also be a function of their employer's health.

These background facts are not inevitable, and may even be internationally deviant, but they are facts about the American economy today, and it cannot be said that there is any strong political likelihood at present of change to a more Western European-style welfare state. Under the circumstances, it is rational for most employees, who already bear quite substantial risks of their firm's poor performance, to take on no risks other than those imposed by the background system.

This fact explains for me both the historic low incidence of worker ownership in most industries, and the tendency of worker owned firms to revert to private ownership. In order to understand this, we must look quite closely at the actual risks born by employees under various common arrangements.

From the time collective bargaining over pensions became common at the end of the Second World War until the recession of the early 1980's, primary sector employees attempted to reduce any risk they bore of their employer's poor performance, through negotiated packages of benefits. These either were actually negotiated by labor unions, or awarded by employers mimicking the union sector, often trying to keep unions out. Some of these benefits, such as supplemental unemployment benefits, were funded by the employer and thus not really free of risks of employer nonperformance. The jewels of the crown, however, were the defined benefit pension, and the health insurance plan. Employers and employees paid for these plans, of course, but the money paid would then be invested by insurance companies and plan trustees in a portfolio of investments, so that benefits could thereafter be paid to employees irrespective of their employer's fortunes.

I cannot cite attitude surveys of American workers or their leaders from the 1950's through 70's, but the many conversations I have had with labor people over the years about employee ownership, and my own sense of rationality, convinces me that this kind of risk aversion explains much of labor's lack of interest in worker ownership during those years. The experiences of the Great Depression shaped these attitudes. Employee stock ownership was all the rage in the 1920's, and by 1930 about 2.5 percent of the workforce had bought shares valued at over $1 billion, roughly the equivalent of the value of ESOP holdings in the early 1980's—shares mostly worthless after the 1929 crash.[145] Moreover, I think that working people and their organizations were right to pursue security from risk during the postwar period, and if such a deal were actually available, would be right to pursue it again.

With the advantage of 1991's hindsight, it is now clear that the pension and health arrangements of the 1950's through 70's did not provide the security for which working people hoped. If the "efficiency wage" people are right, the difficulty of downward wage adjustment may have led to a readiness to lay off workers and a wariness about hiring new ones.[146] Pension funds became easy prey for both corporate and union leader greed; federal regulation came too little, too late, guarantees neither the continued existence nor financial health of pension plans, makes no real effort to enable working people to monitor their pensions and does not even purport to permit them to control them.[147] None of

145. Rosen, *supra* note 4, at 4-5; STUART D. BRANDES, AMERICAN WELFARE CAPITALISM, 1880-1940, at 86 (1976); LIZABETH COHEN, MAKING A NEW DEAL: INDUSTRIAL WORKERS IN CHICAGO, 1919-1939, at 175, 194-95 (1990).

146. *See supra* notes 53-59 and accompanying text.

147. Tales of the looting of pension plans are common enough in the popular press though seem to lack comprehensive academic treatment at present. The most recent example of the former I've seen is Peter Appelbone, *Mill Town Pensioners Pay for Wall Street Sins*, N.Y. TIMES, July 30, 1991, at A1, detailing the recent 30 percent reduction in pension payments to 12,900 retirees of Cannon Mills. The pension plan had been terminated by a California businessman who purchased the company in 1982, kept for himself around $30 million in "surplus" assets, and, as legally required, procured $67 million worth of individual annuity contracts from a California insurance company itself heavily invested in "junk bonds" and now bankrupt. *See also* Nancy Peckenham, *Out in the Cold at Cannon Mills*, THE NATION, Sept. 16, 1991, at 298. *See generally* Staughton Lynd & Alice Lynd, *Labor in the Era of Multinationalism: The Crisis in Bargained-For Fringe Benefits*, 93 W. VA. L. REV. 907 (1991).

When Jensen & Meckling, *supra* note 11, at 473 observe: "Given a choice, potential investors will not voluntarily put their wealth in the hands of codetermined firms; and this includes labor itself, even though many unions in the United States could easily do just that by buying entire companies with their [sic] pension funds," they are so at odds with reality as to make it difficult to attend seriously to the rest of their argument.

these legal background considerations is inevitable; they simply reflect the political weakness of working people and their organizations.

Professor Hansmann reflects these developments in observing that the risk of layoffs makes working for an investor-owned firm rather risky too. (He does not mention the risks of disinvestment, capital mobility, or sheer discriminatory discharge).[148] He concludes that: "In short, there is good reason to believe that risk-bearing is not in itself a major obstacle to worker ownership and that it does not play a strong role in explaining the distribution of worker ownership that we observe."[149] I cannot accept this conclusion, for which no authority is cited. I guess Hansmann and I have been talking to different people. No goal has shaped union bargaining behavior more over the last fifty years than the protection of employees from risk and insecurity. The fact that the arrangements they negotiated turned out not to be such effective protection does not demonstrate that they were motivated by anything other than a desire to eliminate risk, or that the rejected paths, including tying employee security to firm performance, were not rejected precisely because of their riskiness.

I mentioned before that the 1980's saw worker buyouts in which it emerged that workers were willing to assume *more* risk.[150] These are very important, but must be seen in context. After the scales have fallen from their eyes, after the company is on the ropes, the pension plan revealed to be underfunded, concessions inevitable, sale to a raider probable—then workers may be willing to accept a different sort of risk, particularly if they acquire some control in the process.[151] Still, imagine that a good fairy could present working people or their leaders with a choice: a risk-free environment in which a welfare state or employers provided iron-clad promises of health, unemployment, disability, and retirement security; or, on the other hand, an economy in which all enterprise was owned and controlled by employees, but there were few public benefits providing a floor, and few opportunities for diversifying investments. Of course the votes would divide, but who is confident that the second alternative would be decisively preferred?

I believe that risk aversion is the single greatest problem with em-

148. On the extent and importance of the last, *see* WEILER, *supra* note 53, at 63-78.

149. Hansmann, *supra* note 1, at 1773.

150. *Supra* note 45.

151. This is nearly always the scenario in that small minority of employee ownership deals with heavy union involvement, such as the deals discussed in Steve Newman & Mike Yoffee, *Steelworkers and Employee Ownership*, 3 J. EMPLOYEE OWNERSHIP L. & FIN. 51, 59-60 (1991). BLASI & KRUSE, *supra* note 1, and Rosen, *supra* note 4, are right to observe that this is an overcommented, tiny minority of employee ownership deals. However, they are the only deals with much union involvement; in other deals, one can be certain that employee ownership serves primarily management interests and will not be structured to serve maximally employee interests.

ployee ownership and the single greatest obstacle to its wider spread. This conclusion is fortified by examining the pattern so commonly observed in which businesses become employee owned in recessions, make dramatic recoveries, and sell to private investors.[152] Why do they sell out? Hansmann, as usual discussing few actual examples, answers: "The most likely explanation is that worker ownership is not an efficient mode of organization for the firms involved."[153] This conclusion is preposterous, given that in nearly all such cases studied a firm driven to the brink of bankruptcy by management opportunism and investor ownership has experienced incredible revival under employee ownership to the point where outside buyers are attracted who never were under investor ownership.

The reason they sell out is no secret. It is mentioned publicly in nearly every case of sale to private ownership, including Weirton Steel, the one actual case that Hansmann mentions: risk diversification for employees. This includes at least two components, depending on whether the employees are currently employed, or facing retirement.

First, the company may need more capital, to modernize or expand, and employees simply do not want so much concentrated risk; they seek a partnership with an outside investor in furtherance of their original goals, and for the same reason anyone else would.[154]

A second component is the problem of repurchase liability. By law, ESOPs must stand ready to repurchase the shares of employees, partly so that employee ownership is diluted only by group, not individual decision, and partly to permit employees to diversify their own investments.[155] If the company has really turned around under employee ownership, such repurchase liability can be very expensive, in some cases

152. *See* the accounts of Weirton Steel, *supra* note 28. On the theory, *see* Ben-Ner, *supra* note 44; Miyazaki, *supra* note 44.

153. Hansmann, *supra* note 1, at 1778.

154. One of the reasons Weirton undertook a partial public offering was that the employees vested in the ESOP did not want to risk undertaking a $500 million expansion of capacity all by themselves. Myron S. Scholes & Mark A. Wolfson, *Employee Stock Ownership Plans and Corporate Restructuring: Myths and Realities*, 19 FIN. MGMT. 12, 19 (1990) (citing Michael Schroeder, *Has Weirton's ESOP Worked Too Well?*, *supra* note 28, at 66). Similarly, the Copper Range Company went from 100 percent to 20 percent employee owned in order to raise funds for modernization. Workers each received around $50,000 for their shares, and the purchaser, a German company, retained the same Board of Directors, with heavy employee representation. Newman & Yoffee, *supra* note 151, at 59-60.

155. Employees who have participated in an ESOP for ten years or who have reached the age of 55, whichever comes later, have the right to sell their stock back and diversify their stock holdings. 26 U.S.C. § 401(a)(28). Employees who have received nonpublicly traded shares have the right to put these to the company. 26 U.S.C. § 409(h)(1)(B). *See generally* ROBERT W. SMILEY, JR. & RONALD J. GILBERT, EMPLOYEE STOCK OWNERSHIP PLANS 17 (1989).

requiring nearly all the company's cash.[156] Yet requiring such repurchases is necessary lest employees be left with an intolerable assumption of risk, in which they would approach the retirement years invested in a solitary investment.

Risk diversification is thus in both theory and practice the most serious problem with employee ownership as now practiced in the United States. It explains why rational employees will normally want only a partial ownership stake in their employer: in order to protect their retirement and health security. Risk diversification also explains why it is so hard to observe majority employee ownership selected by employees without preexisting professional or political disposition towards employee ownership. Essentially, only employees faced with risks of job and benefit loss, that in the particular case outweigh the risk of having retirement and health benefit funds so heavily invested in a single employer, will voluntarily select majority employee ownership. (It further explains once again why theories of employee ownership must be firm-specific). Finally, it explains why we observe both a strong theoretical and empirical case for the efficiency of majority employee ownership, and yet so few firms attempting to achieve those efficiency gains. Once again, economists would describe this as a tradeoff between incentives for performance and allocation of risk.

In my opinion, advocates of employee ownership have given insufficient attention to solving the problem of risk diversification. Partial solutions to this problem exist. There are a number of ways that ESOP investment may be made less risky for employees.[157] Others are not le-

156. One early example of such a case has frequently been discussed at ESOP meetings, though so far as I know not written about anywhere. A small chain of Midwestern discount retail stores, listed on the New York Stock Exchange, became in 1981 100 percent owned by an ESOP. Management was committed to a participatory culture and involved employees heavily in training in running profitable stores. The chain did spectacularly well. Theft dropped to one-tenth of the industry average; employees made no concessions of any kind. Moreover, stock prices rose generally after 1981. The private valuation of the stock rose from $19 million at the time it went private to $165 million. Share repurchases from retiring or departing employees were taking all the company's cash. In the spring of 1985, the ESOP sold its stock for $170 million to a venture capitalist who retained no employee ownership. The average employee of the discount stores received $300,000! The stock has continued to rise in value, and while new ESOPs have been studied, they are now too expensive. Charles Smith, Economic Democracy and Employee Stock Ownership Plans, Presentation at the Walt Whitman Center for the Culture and Politics of Democracy, Rutgers University (April 25-27, 1991).

157. Scholes & Wolfson, *supra* note 154, at 19, discuss several currently-practiced techniques for reducing employee risk. The most common appears to be to have employees hold convertible voting preferred stock, generally less risky than common. Another less common technique is to have the ESOP invest in assets other than company stock. By law, the ESOP must invest "primarily" in employer stock, and while the Department of Labor and Internal Revenue Service have never defined this phrase, most professionals assume that the ESOP need only invest half its assets in the

gally permissible, but could become so with regulatory change.[158] As employee ownership spreads, other devices for reducing employee risk would become feasible.[159] Ultimately, however, there is a plain conflict between having the bulk of employee savings and benefits trust funds invested in their own employer, and security for those employees.

My personal preference would be to decouple employee ownership from retirement and health security entirely. It is purely historical accident, and a distinctively American accident, that they have anything to do with each other at all.[160] I would prefer to see employee ownership in large enterprises understood in the terms of this Article, that is, as that ownership stake large enough to permit employee control (in connection with other investors), communication and implementation of employee preferences regarding risks and incentives so as to optimize firm performance, and protection against unnecessary job loss or relocation. To me this makes most sense if layered on top of retirement and health security provided through public benefits plans. Since there is no practical way of realizing this particular plan in America in the near future, employee ownership will remain self-limiting, to employees willing to accept either a very small stake, or a much larger stake accompanied by fairly great risk.

sponsoring employer's stock. In practice, however, four-fifths of ESOPs invest over 75 percent of their assets in stock of the sponsoring employer.

Finally, the ESOP could be combined with another defined contribution benefit plan invested entirely in bonds. All these techniques inevitably make the ESOP safer for employees, yet less potent as a control device, since employees will end up owning less common stock. There is simply no way of having both sides of this dilemma.

158. Before 1987, it was possible to combine an ESOP with a defined benefit plan that provided a floor, guaranteeing, say, 50 percent of terminal salary, but distributed only if the ESOP failed to meet the goal. Scholes & Wolfson, *supra* note 154, at 19.

159. For example, one could imagine pensions and health benefits plans in which trust assets were administered by a bank or insurance company, owned partly by its own employees and partly by the employees of other employers whom it served. That bank would invest funds in a portfolio of employee-owned and community-owned businesses. Although the bank's owning shares in these businesses would obviously dilute the control exercised by their own employees, one suspects that for ideological reasons such a bank would normally support the strategies of the local employee-owners, as well as providing a way for *them* to bear less risk. Something like this scheme exists among the complex of employee-owned businesses in Mondragon, Spain; *see* THOMAS & LOGAN, *supra* note 34, at 155-58. *See also* Simon, *supra* note 3, at 1378-80.

160. Today we are predisposed, by the models of the legislative process of the public choice school, to understand any legislation benefiting (say) employees as an example of their rent-seeking. In fact, the favorable tax treatment of deferred compensation, which is deductible to the employer as a business expense when contributed, though not taxable income to the employee until distributed later, had a different origin. In 1939, the Vandenberg-Herring Subcommittee, Senate Subcommittee of the Committee on Finance, issued its Survey of Experiences in Profit Sharing and Possibilities of Incentive Taxation, 84 CONG. REC. 7401, declaring profit sharing to be "essential to the ultimate maintenance of the capitalist system." *Id.* at 7402. Elite concession during perceived crisis, not rent-seeking, explains the bulk of pro-employee legislation. I try to generalize this into a theory in Alan Hyde, *A Theory of Labor Legislation*, 38 BUFF. L. REV. 383 (1990).

IV. Policy Implications

The public policy case for modest subsidization of employee ownership stakes thus depends on two propositions, both deriving from earlier defenses of employee ownership, but neither one previously articulated in this form.

First, employee ownership is a potentially attractive device for improving productivity in those firms routinely overinvesting in supervision due to some combination of low trust and conventions of excessive supervision. This seems to me the convincing variation on the constant theme of advocates of employee ownership, that employee ownership improves firm productivity, a claim that, when reduced to that kind of stark form (starker than sophisticated advocates of employee ownership would put it), must be treated skeptically.[161]

On the other hand, one cannot simply ignore the steady stream of anecdotal reports of businesses completely turned around under employee ownership. It is time to begin tentative generalization about these businesses, mindful that the nation's experience with employee ownership is expanding quickly and that our generalizations will become richer and better over the next decade. Given today's empirical record, the best I can do for my own purposes is that employee ownership seems associated with a particular set of productivity gains: overcoming low trust; reducing supervision levels; permitting employee incentive systems linked efficiently to firm performance; and increasing communication of employee productivity suggestions and preferences regarding risk and incentives.

No doubt over the next decade we will form a clearer picture of the firms for which employee ownership will be positive for productivity. The time is past, however, for "always" or "never" theories, and one would hope that scholars of employee ownership might join hands in constructing firm-specific theories that are consistent with observable reality.

Now this first defense of employee ownership depends entirely on its productivity impact within individual firms and is bound to raise the economist's question: since such firms should be expected to operate efficiently on their own, why subsidize employee ownership? This Article has answered that question. Public policy funds numerous activities in the hopes of increasing the productivity of private firms: job training, a functioning financial market, various tax subsidies and disincentives.

161. *See, e.g.*, Blasi, *supra* note 7; Hansmann, *supra* note 1, at 1763 n.54.

The power of conventions, cultural familiarity with inefficient levels of supervision, and the desire of those exercising power to hold on to it, all lead to a kind of market failure in which individuals who might desire and benefit from employee ownership as a public good cannot procure it through private initiative.[162] Modest inducements to experiment with employee ownership shares—the tax treatment of ESOPs and cooperatives—have been quite effective in overcoming convention, management opportunism, and related market failure.

The case for continuing or expanding this level of public support is not independent of the level of serious "X"-inefficiency in American firms, that is, what proportion of lagging American productivity is explained by these factors *that firms left alone will never do anything about.* I know of no way of forming a reliable estimate of this figure, but can only signal my intuitive sense that Leibenstein has this one just about right.[163]

My second defense of employee ownership is a macroeconomic defense that has not previously been made. I think that partial employee ownership is the road to a "share economy" that might reduce continued high unemployment. If the "efficiency wage" scholars are correct, high unemployment results in significant part from wages that do not adjust downward in recessions and yet are not incentives for optimum performance either. Let us be very clear about whose wages those are. After the "givebacks" and concession bargaining of the 1980s, it cannot seriously be maintained that the union wages of working people resist downward adjustment.[164] It is even more the salaries of managers and supervisors, often socially unnecessary to begin with, that routinely soar above market-clearing levels.

Considerable empirical evidence supports the idea that employee ownership is associated with sharply reduced levels of supervision, concessions by employees, and greater assumption of risk by employees.

162. Elster, *supra* note 82, at 108-10; Simon, *supra* note 3, at 1401-03.

163. *Allocative Efficiency*, *supra* note 103, at 397. Leibenstein's estimates, from studying tariffs and monopolies, that the welfare costs of "allocative" inefficiency (monopolies, cartels, regulation) are "trivial"—perhaps one tenth of one percent—while inefficiency internal to firms, and resulting from low trust, convention, poor motivation, and the like, is responsible for far greater welfare losses. On the other hand, corporate law types are painfully familiar with the general tale of efficiency gains unlocked due to reductions in agency costs—the tale that figured in all the defenses of 1980's corporate takeovers, though which turns out to be difficult to establish one way or the other (Bill Bratton made this point to me).

164. Here again the law may have played a facilitative role, due to doctrines of the National Labor Relations Board that require employers to negotiate about corporate transformations such as subcontracting, relocation, and partial closure only when these "turn on labor costs", that is, where the bargaining will turn to labor concessions and givebacks. Dubuque Packing Co., 303 N.L.R.B. No. 66, 1991-1992 NLRB Dec. (CCH) ¶ 16,687 (June 14, 1991).

Widespread adoption of employee ownership stakes could well facilitate more flexible wage structures, less reliance on the negative incentives of monitoring and supervision, more positive incentives tied to firm performance, and thus more entry level jobs at market wages.[165] Employees would be irrational to trust management to administer a "share economy"; but they can and will do so themselves. This macroeconomic case for encouraging employee ownership shares has little or nothing to do with individual firm productivity improvements, though as I have said those will come too.

Conclusion

While the current literature on employee-owned and managed firms would certainly not support on economic grounds a law imposing such structures on all firms, it provides good reason to think that America gets its money's worth with modest subsidies to acquire practical knowledge and expertise in employee ownership. This subsidization would be even more valuable if it could be targeted, as it is not now, on those firms for which employee ownership offers greatest promise, and on those participatory varieties of employee ownership that reduce low trust and involve workers in combatting internal inefficiency.

A generation from now, if current trends continue, we will be able to look back with pride at our policies that enabled working people to own their own jobs.

165. Miyazaki & Neary, *supra*, note 22, show how a labor-managed firm can create efficient, internally-financed income insurance. With incomes insured, employee-owners will accept work-sharing and be willing to bear other risks of firm performance.

Part III
Interdisciplinary Feminist Theory and Theological Perspectives

[7]

BOSTON COLLEGE LAW REVIEW

VOLUME XXXIII | MAY 1992 | NUMBER 3

IMAGES OF POWER IN LABOR LAW: A FEMINIST DECONSTRUCTION†

*Marion Crain**

INTRODUCTION

A central task of feminist legal scholars is to deconstruct systematically, from a feminist perspective, existing law and the institutions that it creates.[1] The effort to reveal and to challenge the male-centered attitudes that structure the law has as its goal the introduction of women's perspectives and a consequent transformation of the law.[2] An underlying premise of some feminist efforts, including this one, is that such a transformation will not only render

---

* Associate Professor of Law, The University of Toledo. B.S., 1980, Cornell; J.D., 1983, UCLA. The Fund For Labor Relations Studies and the University of Toledo College of Law provided research support. Thanks go to Meg Gehrke and D.B. Deck for their able research assistance, and to Ken Matheny for his insightful critique of an earlier draft.

[1] *See* Judith Resnik, *On the Bias: Feminist Reconsiderations of the Aspirations for Our Judges*, 61 S. CAL. L. REV. 1877, 1906 (1988). "A major shared premise [of feminist work] is that knowledge of the world is constructed from one's viewpoint and that what has been assumed (by some) as a universal viewpoint is, in fact, a viewpoint of some men, who have articulated a vision of reality and claimed it to be true for us all." *Id.*

[2] *See* Kathryn Abrams, *Gender Discrimination and the Transformation of Workplace Norms*, 42 VAND. L. REV. 1183, 1185, 1192 (1989). Katherine Bartlett describes feminist method as asking "the woman question":

> The woman question asks about the gender implications of a social practice or rule: have women been left out of consideration? If so, in what way; how might that omission be corrected? What difference would it make to do so? In law, asking the woman question means examining how the law fails to take into account the experiences and values that seem more typical of women than of men, for whatever reason, or how existing legal standards and concepts might disadvantage women.

Katherine T. Bartlett, *Feminist Legal Methods*, 103 HARV. L. REV. 829, 837 (1990).

the law more inclusive of the experiences of previously marginalized groups,[3] but also assure that the law is, in some overriding sense, fairer.[4]

In this article, I undertake a feminist deconstruction of the labor laws and the activities of the institutions created by them, labor unions.[5] Some scholars might question the relevance of such

---

[3] Abrams, *supra* note 2, at 1247–48 (feminist task of transforming workplace norms seeks to teach men to "see beyond a workplace made in their own image, to numerous inhabitants who are not (male)").

[4] *See, e.g.*, Leslie Bender, *Feminist (Re)Torts: Thoughts On the Liability Crisis, Mass Torts, Power, and Responsibilities*, 1990 DUKE L.J. 848, 888 (applying feminist analysis to mass tort disputes and suggesting rules or techniques to equalize the parties' power, ultimately increasing the likelihood of just results); Carrie Menkel-Meadow, *Toward Another View of Legal Negotiation: The Structure Of Problem-Solving*, 31 UCLA L. REV. 754, 840–41 (1984) (arguing that following a problem-solving approach in legal negotiations rather than engaging in a traditional adversarial negotiation process produces a broader array of solutions and, ultimately, more satisfactory resolutions, because the focus of problem solving is on addressing the underlying real needs of the parties rather than on winning the game; this problem-solving approach enables parties to negotiate more equitable solutions that meet their long- and short-term interests and hence produces a greater commitment to abide by the agreement reached); *see also* Carrie Menkel-Meadow, *Portia In A Different Voice: Speculations On A Women's Lawyering Process*, 1 BERKELEY WOMEN'S L.J. 39, 52–58 (1985) (observing the connection between the development of Alternative Dispute Resolution and cooperative forms of negotiation, and the scholarly development of a feminist perspective, and arguing that importing feminist insights into the law and legal institutions potentially benefits all lawyers).

[5] The phrase "labor law" refers to the National Labor Relations Act, 29 U.S.C. §§ 141–187 (1988). This article builds upon previous work in which I issued a call to feminist scholars to begin deconstructing the labor laws. *See* Marion Crain, *Feminizing Unions: Challenging The Gendered Structure of Wage Labor*, 89 MICH. L. REV. 1155, 1159 (1991). Aside from my own work, the only legal scholarship that has addressed sex equality arguments in the context of the labor law (as opposed to employment discrimination or employment law) has been in the area of pay equity. *See, e.g.*, Paul Weiler, *The Wages of Sex: The Uses and Limits of Comparable Worth*, 99 HARV. L. REV. 1728, 1798–1801 (1986) (arguing that comparable worth might be made a subject of collective bargaining). Most of this work is not explicitly feminist in orientation or method. *See id.* Although many feminist legal scholars have written on the subject of male-centered workplace norms, all have done so in the context of employment discrimination, and consequently have focused on title VII or on constitutional law rather than on the labor laws. *See, e.g.*, CATHARINE A. MACKINNON, SEXUAL HARASSMENT OF WORKING WOMEN—A CASE OF SEX DISCRIMINATION 4–6 (1979) (analyzing workplace sexual harassment as a form of sex discrimination that reinforces and expresses women's traditional subordinate role in the work force, and outlining legal arguments for reform under title VII and the Equal Protection Clause of the Fourteenth Amendment); Abrams, *supra* note 2, at 1186 (analyzing sexual harassment and the relationship between career advancement and parenting responsibilities in context of the "primary litigation tool," title VII); Ruth Colker, *Anti-Subordination Above All: Sex, Race, and Equal Protection*, 61 N.Y.U. L. REV. 1003, 1004–08 (1986) (comparing and contrasting the efficacy of principles of anti-subordination and anti-differentiation in affirmative action cases under the Equal Protection Clause); Lucinda M. Finley, *Transcending Equality Theory: A Way Out of the Maternity and the Workplace Debate*, 86 COLUM. L. REV. 1118, 1122–42 (1986) (examining treatment of maternity issues in the workplace under title VII); Mary Joe Frug, *Securing Job Equality for Women: Labor Market Hostility to Working Mothers*, 59 B.U. L. REV. 55, 58–61 (1979) (analyzing title VII and equal

an inquiry, in view of the rapidly dwindling share of the work force represented by labor unions.[6] I have argued elsewhere that unions

protection doctrine for strategies to challenge employment policies that burden working mothers); Sylvia A. Law, *Rethinking Sex and the Constitution*, 132 U. PA. L. REV. 955, 1002, 1008–13 (1984) (proposing strict constitutional analysis of sex-based laws and laws governing reproductive issues in the workplace where laws operate to perpetuate sex inequality); Vicki Schultz, *Telling Stories About Women and Work: Judicial Interpretations of Sex Segregation in the Workplace in Title VII Cases Raising the Lack of Interest Argument*, 103 HARV. L. REV. 1749, 1754–69 (1990) (examining judicial treatment under title VII of phenomenon of sex segregation in occupations); Joan C. Williams, *Deconstructing Gender*, 87 MICH. L. REV. 797, 800–02 (1989) (challenging relational feminists' theory and description of gender differences, showing how employers have turned relational feminist theory against women under title VII, and proposing gender neutral reforms designed to alter the existing vision of the ideal worker, which is constructed around male norms, while simultaneously refusing to institutionalize a correlation between gender roles and biological sex differences).

It is possible that the dearth of feminist legal scholarship in this area is attributable primarily to the paucity of female labor law professors. Women are also underrepresented on industrial relations faculties. *See* Lois S. Gray, *Professional Careers for Women in Industrial Relations*, *in* WORKING WOMEN: PAST, PRESENT, FUTURE 225, 239 (Karen Shallcross Koziaria et al. eds., 1987) (only 12% of members of Industrial Relations Research Association involved in research, teaching or administration in industrial relations were women). In fields where women are more commonly found teaching, such as sociology, much has been written on the subject of the relationship between feminism and labor unions. *See* U.S. BUREAU OF THE CENSUS, STATISTICAL ABSTRACT OF THE UNITED STATES: 1990, at 389, Table No. 645 (47.6 % of all social scientists and urban planners are women, but only 19.3 % of lawyers are women); *see, e.g.*, DIANE BALSER, SISTERHOOD AND SOLIDARITY: FEMINISM AND LABOR IN MODERN TIMES (1987); LINDA M. BLUM, BETWEEN FEMINISM AND LABOR: THE SIGNIFICANCE OF THE COMPARABLE WORTH MOVEMENT (1991); ALICE KESSLER-HARRIS, OUT TO WORK (1982); RUTH MILKMAN, GENDER AT WORK: THE DYNAMICS OF JOB SEGREGATION BY SEX DURING WORLD WAR II (1987).

Nevertheless, the failure of feminist legal scholars to concentrate on a body of law primarily affecting the rights of working class women, and their tendency to prefer to engage in analyses of workplace norms that primarily affect middle- and upper-class professionals and semi-professional women (usually white women), raises the familiar specter of essentialism in feminist theory. *See* BLUM, *supra*, at 15 (mainstream feminist movement has overlooked centrality of class in determining women's experiences); BELL HOOKS, FEMINIST THEORY: FROM MARGIN TO CENTER 34–35 (1984) (failure to emphasize necessity for mass-based feminist movement addressing concerns of poor women and women of color helped marginalize feminism; a fundamental change in strategy and focus of feminist movement is required if it is to realize its transformative potential); Angela P. Harris, *Race and Essentialism in Feminist Legal Theory*, 42 STAN. L. REV. 581, 585 (1990) (arguing that the work of feminists Catharine MacKinnon and Robin West relies on gender essentialism, "the notion that a unitary, 'essential' women's experience can be isolated and described independently of race, class, sexual orientation, and other realities of experience"). *See generally* ELIZABETH SPELMAN, THE INESSENTIAL WOMAN: PROBLEMS OF EXCLUSION IN FEMINIST THOUGHT (1988) (examining essentialism in feminist theory).

[6] Union density has declined dramatically over the last four decades: between 1953 and 1989, density in the private sector fell from 35 percent to 12 percent. Robert J. LaLonde & Bernard D. Meltzer, *Hard Times For Unions: Another Look At the Significance of Employer Illegalities*, 58 U. CHI. L. REV. 953, 953 (1991). In 1991, private sector union density stood at 11.9%. *Union Membership Unchanged At 16.1 Percent of Employment in 1991*, Daily Lab. Rep. (BNA) No. 28, at B-1 (Feb. 11, 1992). This figure is projected to drop below 10 percent by

should be relevant, particularly to the women's movement, because they are properly situated to effect significant economic, political and social advances for working women.[7] Moreover, even if unions themselves are irrelevant, the issues raised by their decline are not.[8] The labor laws that have shaped the course of union representation for workers are modeled on the larger political structure of representative democracy, serving as a "charter of industrial democracy" for workers.[9] Consequently, "labor law as a representative democracy promises the same rewards and confronts the same problems as its parent and archetype, liberal democracy."[10]

Although a few scholars[11] and labor leaders[12] have advocated the abolition of labor law, the vast majority remain committed to the philosophy and structure of labor law in the United States, and advocate its reform and transformation, rather than its abolition.[13]

---

the year 2000. Paul Weiler, *Hard Times For Unions: Challenging Times For Scholars*, 58 U. CHI. L. REV. 1015, 1017 (1991).

[7] *See* Crain, *supra* note 5, at 1156.

[8] CHARLES HECKSCHER, THE NEW UNIONISM: EMPLOYEE INVOLVEMENT IN THE CHANGING CORPORATION 12 (1988).

[9] *See* Steven L. Willborn, *Industrial Democracy and the National Labor Relations Act: A Preliminary Inquiry*, 25 B.C. L. REV. 725, 725 (1984).

[10] *Id.*

[11] *See* Richard A. Epstein, *A Common Law for Labor Relations: A Critique of the New Deal Labor Legislation*, 92 YALE L.J. 1357, 1357 (1983) (proposing that "a sensible common law regime relying heavily upon tort and contract law" should replace the NLRA) [hereinafter Epstein, *A Common Law For Labor Relations*]; Richard A. Epstein, *In Defense of the Contract At Will*, 51 U. CHI. L. REV. 947, 982 (1984) [hereinafter Epstein, *Contract at Will*] (championing the adequacy of protection afforded individual employees by idealized, freely functioning labor market); *see also* Charles Fried, *Individual and Collective Rights in Work Relations: Reflections on the Current State of Labor Law and its Prospects*, 51 U. CHI. L. REV. 1012, 1019 (1984) (advocating reconsideration of the premise that the best protection of worker interests is accomplished through restructuring of the market, with guaranteed access to the process of bargaining in which the strength of workers' position is assured through the monopolistic principle of exclusive representation; Fried proposes direct imposition of minimal standards and removal of the governmentally sheltered status of labor unions); Richard A. Posner, *Some Economics of Labor Law*, 51 U. CHI. L. REV. 988, 999–1002 (1984) (labor law and unionization function to cartelize the labor supply at the expense of productivity, competition, consumer welfare and the remainder of the labor market).

[12] *See* Richard L. Trumka, *Why Labor Law Has Failed*, 89 W. VA. L. REV. 871, 871, 877 (1987) (United Mineworkers president advocates repeal of labor law; unions should wage battles in state courts and in political arenas); *Kirkland Says Many Unions Avoiding NLRB*, 132 Lab. Rel. Rep. (BNA) 13 (Sept. 4, 1989) (AFL-CIO president Lane Kirkland would prefer no labor law because current law "forbids us to show solidarity and direct union support").

[13] Most propose incremental reforms. *See, e.g.*, PAUL WEILER, GOVERNING THE WORKPLACE: THE FUTURE OF LABOR AND EMPLOYMENT LAW 185 (1990) [hereinafter WEILER, GOVERNING THE WORKPLACE] (proposing reforms designed to realign the balance of power in the union organization phase and to expand protection for union economic weapons); Charles B. Craver, *The Vitality of the American Labor Movement in the Twenty-First Century*, 1983

I join the chorus of voices defending the philosophy of American labor law, but for a fundamentally different reason.[14] I argue that

U. ILL. L. REV. 633, 635–36 (1983) (arguing that unions must organize white-collar workers and those who work with new technology, and include these highly educated workers in expanded participatory management schemes, as well as attend to the need to adapt to a global economy); David L. Gregory, *Proposals to Harmonize Labor Law Jurisprudence and to Reconcile Political Tensions*, 65 NEB. L. REV. 75, 82–84 (1986) (advocating the formation of a federal Labor Court of Appeals to hear all NLRB cases in order to coordinate and centralize NLRB jurisprudence and end inter-circuit conflicts); Theodore J. St. Antoine, *Federal Regulation of the Workplace in the Next Half Century*, 61 CHI.-KENT L. REV. 631, 658–62 (1985) (arguing that state and local government workers should be governed by a national employment law and that employee participation in workplace management should be mandatory); Clyde Summers, *Past Premises, Present Failures, and Future Needs in Labor Legislation*, 31 BUFF. L. REV. 9, 19 (1982) (suggesting that the use of collective bargaining should be expanded and encouraged and, in the absence of a union, alternative forms of worker representation should be implemented); Paul Weiler, *Promises To Keep: Securing Workers' Rights to Self-Organization Under the NLRA*, 96 HARV. L. REV. 1769, 1805 (1983) [hereinafter Weiler, *Promises To Keep*] (proposing union certification on basis of signed authorization cards rather than after prolonged organizing campaign and election); Paul Weiler, *Striking A New Balance: Freedom of Contract and the Prospects for Union Representation*, 98 HARV. L. REV. 351, 404–19 (1984) [hereinafter Weiler, *Striking a New Balance*] (suggesting recourse to compulsory arbitration of deadlocks in first union contracts, reversal of rule allowing permanent replacement of strikers, loosening of secondary boycott restrictions, and increased union power to discipline members).

Others, especially Critical Legal Studies scholars, focus on the original radical potential of the Wagner Act, and argue that judicial interpretation of the Act has undermined it; accordingly, transformative, re-radicalizing efforts are required. *See, e.g.*, JAMES B. ATLESON, VALUES AND ASSUMPTIONS IN AMERICAN LABOR LAW 143–60, 171–80 (1983); Karl E. Klare, *Judicial Deradicalization of the Wagner Act and the Origins of Modern Legal Consciousness, 1937–41*, 62 MINN. L. REV. 265, 270, 336–39 (1978) [hereinafter Klare, *Judicial Deradicalization*]; Karl E. Klare, *Labor Law as Ideology: Toward A New Historiography of Collective Bargaining Law*, 4 INDUS. REL. L.J. 450, 459, 465, 481–82 (1981) [hereinafter Klare, *Labor Law as Ideology*]; Karl E. Klare, *Workplace Democracy & Market Reconstruction: An Agenda For Legal Reform*, 38 CATH. U. L. REV. 1, 5, 16–17 (1988) [hereinafter Klare, *Workplace Democracy & Market Reconstruction*]. *See generally* Peter E. Millspaugh, *America's Industrial Relations Experiment: Legal Scholarship Assesses the Wagner Act*, 32 ST. LOUIS U. L.J. 673, 673–74, 711 (1988) (summarizing critiques of labor law and proposals for its reform advanced in the last decade).

The commitment of these scholars is especially clear with regard to the following attributes of labor law created by the Wagner Act: an individual rights-based system of protection for employees; an adversarial structure with a balance of power between capital and labor as the goal; industrial democracy, with unions serving as the voice of employees; and collective bargaining in the individual workplace. *But see* HECKSCHER, *supra* note 8, at 254–56 (arguing for evolution of unionism toward "associational unionism," a new, more flexible form of unionism for which it is necessary to "turn the Wagner Act upside down").

[14] I share with some of the scholars cited at note 13, *supra*, a focus on increasing employee empowerment through participation in the process of workplace governance, rather than through the safeguarding of individual entitlements, or rights. *See* Klare, *Judicial Deradicalization*, *supra* note 13, at 336–39; Klare, *Labor Law as Ideology*, *supra* note 13, at 481–82; *see also* Cass R. Sunstein, *Rights, Minimal Terms, and Solidarity: A Comment*, 51 U. CHI. L. REV. 1041, 1058–59 (1984) (significance of Wagner Act is that it creates a right to a process of workplace decisionmaking; goal is to generate employee participation). I identify that commitment to ensuring voice, rather than ensuring rights, as more consistent with a commu-

the Wagner Act was a jurisprudentially unique attempt to construct a system of representative government to institutionalize the dynamics of a communitarian social order, the labor movement.[15] Both the communitarianism typified by the early labor movement and modern relational feminism envision an individual's fulfillment as achieved through connection and community, rather than through separation and autonomy.[16] Moreover, collective action is consistent with a radical feminist theory of economic and political empowerment.[17] Thus, the Wagner Act is consistent in its basic philosophy with women's values and experience, and offers an effective route to collective empowerment for working women.

Unlike the system of individual rights created by liberal legal theory as a check on government power, the effort by labor law to protect group rights and to codify the experience of direct self-government is fundamentally compatible with feminist method and theory. The Wagner Act was intended to advance the larger political democracy by empowering workers and by promoting industrial

---

nitarian system of power allocation in the workplace than it is with the existing republican/liberal focus on individual rights, increasingly reflected in labor law jurisprudence and scholarship. See *infra* notes 160–90 and accompanying text for a discussion of the republican/liberal system of power allocation.

[15] The Wagner Act was the original piece of federal labor legislation that established the federally protected status of unions; encouraged employees to organize collectively to counterbalance the economic power of employers; granted statutory protection for concerted employee activity, including the right to strike; and prescribed a legal framework favoring collective bargaining between unions and employers. National Labor Relations (Wagner) Act, Pub. L. No. 74–198, 49 Stat. 449 (1935) (codified as amended at 29 U.S.C. §§ 151–187 (1988)). The Wagner Act and its subsequent amendments, see The Labor-Management Relations (Taft-Hartley) Act, 1947, Pub. L. No. 80–101, 61 Stat. 136 (1947) (codified as amended at 29 U.S.C. §§ 141–197 (1988)), and The Labor-Management Reporting and Disclosure (Landrum-Griffin) Act of 1959, Pub. L. No. 86–257, 73 Stat. 519 (1959) (codified as amended at 29 U.S.C. §§ 153–187 (1988)), are collectively referred to as the National Labor Relations Act, and are codified at 29 U.S.C. §§ 141–187 (1988).

[16] *Compare* Gregory S. Alexander, *Dilemmas of Group Autonomy: Residential Associations and Community*, 75 CORNELL L. REV. 1, 32 (1989) (communitarian conception of the common good emphasizes the importance of participating as a group member to process of self-realization) *with* CAROL GILLIGAN, IN A DIFFERENT VOICE 148 (1982) (describing decision-making, in a context where interests conflict, from a cultural feminist perspective, as "the process of making decisions with care, on the basis of what you know, and taking responsibility for choice while seeing the possible legitimacy of other solutions") *and* Robin West, *Jurisprudence and Gender*, 55 U. CHI. L. REV. 1, 14, 17 (1988) (feminist works focus on connection and relationships, rather than on separation and autonomy, as the fundamental difference between (respectively) female and male perspectives).

[17] *See* Jeanne L. Schroeder, *Abduction From the Seraglio: Feminist Methodologies and the Logic of Imagination*, 70 TEX. L. REV. 109, 195 & n.272 (1991) (describing radical feminists, particularly MacKinnon, as supporting collective action by women because it is an effective political strategy for empowerment).

democracy in the workplace.[18] These goals rested upon the assumption that the union's ability to influence decisionmaking in the workplace would emanate from its power as the employees' majority representative to speak on behalf of its members. The union's power, then, derived from the community of workers, and its strength rested directly on the bonds between community members.[19] Union power was effectuated through protection of the collective right to "engage in concerted activity for mutual aid or protection," a "translation into law of the labor movement concept of 'solidarity.'"[20]

Nevertheless, the Wagner Act is also riddled with patriarchal assumptions about power and its allocation that are fundamentally incompatible with feminist method and theory. The primary goal of the Wagner Act was to create ("restore") a "balance of power" between capital and labor in order to ensure industrial peace.[21] This goal rested on an image of management-labor relations as inherently adversarial, necessarily entailing a struggle for power that could only be resolved when one succeeded in dominating and controlling the other. Because the employer's role as the senior "partner" in the relationship with labor was assumed, labor's role as the junior subordinate "partner" was inevitable.[22] Such a concept of power relations, which I have defined elsewhere as "patriar-

---

[18] *See* ATLESON, *supra* note 13, at 41; Willborn, *supra* note 9, at 725.

[19] As Staughton Lynd put it, because union members perceived that "'an injury to one is an injury to all,'" they were willing to place their own jobs in jeopardy to protect another member's rights. Staughton Lynd, *Government Without Rights: The Labor Law Vision of Archibald Cox*, 1981 INDUS. REL. L.J. 483, 494.

[20] *See* National Labor Relations Act, § 7, 29 U.S.C. § 157 (1988); Lynd, *supra* note 19, at 494.

[21] National Labor Relations Act, § 1, 29 U.S.C. § 151 (1988). Section one provides:

> The inequality of bargaining power between employees . . . and employers . . . substantially burdens and affects the flow of commerce . . . . Experience has proved that protection by law of the right of employees to organize and bargain collectively safeguards commerce from injury . . . by removing certain recognized sources of industrial strife and unrest . . . and by restoring equality of bargaining power between employers and employees.

Id.; *see also* SELIG PERLMAN, A HISTORY OF TRADE UNIONISM IN THE UNITED STATES 279 (1923) ("[T]he social order which the typical American trade unionist considers ideal is one in which organized labor and organized capital possess equal bargaining power.").

[22] First Nat'l Maintenance Corp. v. NLRB, 452 U.S. 666, 676 (1981) ("Congress had no expectation that the elected union representative would become an equal partner in the running of the business enterprise in which the union's members are employed."); *see also* PERLMAN, *supra* note 21, at 279 (noting that the American trade unionist, while desiring an equal voice with the employer in fixing wages and working conditions, did not aspire to the task of "running industry without the employer").

chal,"[23] is inconsistent with a feminist understanding of power. Feminist power is conceived of as a relation between people; it is based in community and is exercised as energy, ability or capacity, rather than through domination and control of another.[24]

The purpose of this article is to expose how these contradictory underlying assumptions about power cause tension between labor law's twin goals of industrial democracy and industrial peace, to show how these assumptions are reflected in the National Labor Relations Act ("NLRA") and its jurisprudence, and to suggest how the NLRA might be altered to become a more significant tool in a feminist agenda challenging the economic, political and social disempowerment of working women. Today, the predominant image of power reflected in the NLRA and perpetuated in labor law jurisprudence is the patriarchal vision of power as domination and control. Such a limited understanding of power affects the way power is exercised as well as who exercises it.[25] Ultimately, it ensures that worker solidarity and power is never truly realized, and that capital retains control.[26]

In this article, I describe the patriarchal vision of power (domination and control) that pervades labor law, examine how it affects labor law jurisprudence, and inquire how the law might differ if the alternative image of power (community-centered), which is also present in the NLRA, assumed preeminence. I argue that a com-

---

[23] *See* Marion Crain, *Feminism, Labor, and Power*, 65 S. CAL. L. REV. (forthcoming May 1992) (manuscript at 12–13, on file with the BOSTON COLLEGE LAW REVIEW) (patriarchal definition of power revolves around a hierarchical paradigm in which one dominates and another submits, one controls and another is controlled; because it is founded on a material base and controls the dispersion of the fruits of capitalism in a sexist hierarchy where women occupy the bottom rungs, its exercise ultimately oppresses women). It is not surprising to find a patriarchal understanding of power reflected in law, since the essence of law itself is patriarchal: "The whole structure of law—its hierarchical organization; its combative, adversarial format; and its undeviating bias in favor of rationality over all other values—defines it as a fundamentally patriarchal institution." Diane Polan, *Toward A Theory of Law and Patriarchy*, *in* THE POLITICS OF LAW: A PROGRESSIVE CRITIQUE 294, 301 (David Kairys ed., 1982); *see also* Janet Rifkin, *Mediation From A Feminist Perspective: Promises and Problems*, *in* 2 LAW & INEQUALITY: A JOURNAL OF THEORY AND PRACTICE 21, 22 (1984) (patriarchal paradigm of law is hierarchy, combat and adversarialism).

[24] Crain, *supra* note 23, at 55–56.

[25] *See* Jane S. Jaquette, *Power As Ideology: A Feminist Analysis*, *in* WOMEN'S VIEWS OF THE POLITICAL WORLD OF MEN 9, 10–11 (Judith W. Steihm ed., 1984).

[26] Our continued reliance on an adversarial paradigm of labor law serves as an effective barrier to transforming the law. *See* William B. Gould IV, *Reflections on Workers' Participation, Influence, and Powersharing: The Future of Industrial Relations*, 58 U. CIN. L. REV. 381, 383 (1989) ("A major obstacle in reshaping relationships in this country . . . has been our adherence to traditional adversarial attitudes, and the fact that labor law has based its assumptions upon the model of conflict.").

munitarian-based theory of power allocation is more likely to produce worker empowerment, particularly for women workers, than the predominant liberal/republican paradigm of power allocation. Section I describes the patriarchal ideology of power that shapes our adversarial system, and more particularly, the republican system of power allocation reflected in our labor laws and jurisprudence.[27] Section II articulates a feminist theory of power, assesses its compatibility with communitarian theory, and examines its foundations in Wagner Act jurisprudence.[28] Section III analyzes other proposals for labor law reform that call for reconsideration of its adversarial nature, and contrasts those proposals with the feminist/communitarian perspective described in Section II.[29] Section IV sets forth a blueprint for a labor law jurisprudence that would reflect this alternative conception of power and further worker participation and empowerment.[30]

I. Patriarchal Images of Power in Labor Law

The law both articulates and reflects patriarchy: "it is both real and ideal; it both constructs reality and mirrors it; it is both determined and determining."[31] Zillah Eisenstein argues that, because the law controls the dynamics of patriarchy and so helps to maintain the status quo, the law is a proper target for feminists who seek to change patriarchy.[32] With that end in mind, I turn to a deconstruction of the patriarchal images of power that are embedded in the structure of labor law.

A. *The Patriarchal Conception of Power*

Political theorists and sociologists, assuming that conflict of interests and goals is inevitable in a materialistic society possessing scarce resources, have equated power with domination, control and

---

[27] *See infra* notes 31–146 and accompanying text.

[28] *See infra* notes 147–222 and accompanying text.

[29] *See infra* notes 223–40 and accompanying text.

[30] *See infra* notes 241–76 and accompanying text.

[31] Zillah R. Eisenstein, Feminism and Sexual Equality: Crisis in Liberal America 97 (1984).

[32] *Id.* Although Eisenstein concedes that challenges to the law are alone insufficient to dethrone patriarchy in society, she argues that struggles within the law are an essential part of the process of challenging patriarchal privilege because changing the law changes patriarchy as it *presently* exists. *Id.* at 100.

coercion.[33] Often conceptualized as "power over" others because of its relative nature, such power usually is dispersed through and exercised within a hierarchical, competitive system.[34] The key to power in a materialistic society is the possession of or access to scarce resources.[35] Ultimately, because power brings increased access to resources, power itself becomes a scarce resource.[36]

Feminist theory posits that an understanding of power as domination, control and coercion is patriarchal because it is materially based and is exercised within a hierarchical paradigm in which one person or group dominates and another submits.[37] This vision of power is predicated on the following assumptions:

> that there exists a fixed quantity of resources that all desire equally, creating an inherent conflict of interest which is exacerbated by existing power differentials; that resources are distributed according to a hierarchical power structure; that one's position in the hierarchy is achieved through competition characterized by overt conflict; that such competition takes the form of dominating those less powerful than oneself; and that the desire to dominate is natural, inevitable, and is sex itself.[38]

The patriarchal definition of power has shaped law generally, particularly its adversarial character.[39] Patriarchal notions about power

---

[33] *See* Crain, *supra* note 23, at 17; *see also* NANCY C.M. HARTSOCK, MONEY, SEX AND POWER: TOWARD A FEMINIST HISTORICAL MATERIALISM 2 (1983) (summarizing Bertrand Russell's view of power as "the ability to compel obedience"); STEVEN LUKES, POWER: A RADICAL VIEW 23–24 (1974) (most insidious exercise of power is to influence and shape people's perceptions so that "they accept their role in the existing order," thus preventing conflict from arising in the first instance); DENNIS H. WRONG, POWER: ITS FORMS, BASES AND USES 23–35 (1979) (power takes one of four distinct forms: force, manipulation, persuasion and authority); Talcott Parsons, *On The Concept of Political Power*, *in* POLITICAL POWER: A READER IN THEORY AND RESEARCH 251, 256 (Roderick Bell et al. eds., 1969) (power is defined as "the generalized capacity to secure the performance of binding obligations").

[34] *See* STEWART CLEGG, THE THEORY OF POWER AND ORGANIZATION 65–67 (1979) (discussing work of theorists who conclude that power distribution is "zero-sum" and therefore necessarily entails competition and conflict); MARILYN FRENCH, BEYOND POWER: ON WOMEN, MEN AND MORALS 506–07 (1985) (noting propriety of the "power over" label).

[35] Crain, *supra* note 23, at 14.

[36] *See* Anthony Giddens, *Power in the Recent Writings of Talcott Parsons*, 2 SOCIOLOGY 257, 264–65 (1968). In more colloquial terms, "the rich get richer."

[37] Such a paradigm is patriarchal even when it exists between and among men. Heidi Hartmann, *Capitalism, Patriarchy, and Job Segregation By Sex*, *in* CAPITALIST PATRIARCHY AND THE CASE FOR SOCIALIST FEMINISM 206, 232 n.1 (Zillah R. Eisenstein ed., 1979).

[38] Crain, *supra* note 23, at 17.

[39] Labor law provides a particularly clear illustration of the adversarial nature of law. *See infra* notes 120–46 and accompanying text.

also have been instrumental, however, in structuring systems of power allocation and management, otherwise known as political theory. Because an understanding of the political model for labor law is essential to the illumination of the role of power in framing adversarial labor law, I address the political model of labor law first.

B. *The Republican Model of Power Dispersion*

Labor law has been justified and legitimated through an analogy to the larger political democracy. The National Labor Relations Act functions as the constitution in this "mini-democracy," providing the organizational structure and ensuring basic individual rights for workers.[40] Under its auspices and the watchful eye of the National Labor Relations Board ("NLRB"), workers elect unions to represent them in the "legislative process" of collective bargaining.[41] The labor agreement, once negotiated, becomes the industrial code applicable to the particular workplace.[42] Private arbitrators serve as the judiciary to resolve disputes arising under the labor agreement.[43] In short, the NLRA was modeled after a republican system of government, with power dispersed through a representative democracy.[44]

1. Republican Systems of Power Allocation in the Larger Political Context

Republicanism, by which I mean the political theory of power dispersion and management on which our political structure is based, is currently undergoing a "revival" among legal scholars and political theorists.[45] This revival has brought to light new insights

---

[40] Willborn, *supra* note 9, at 729.

[41] *Id.* at 728–29.

[42] *See* United Steelworkers of Am. v. Warrior & Gulf Navigation Co., 363 U.S. 574, 578 (1960) ("The collective bargaining agreement . . . is more than a contract; it is a generalized code to govern a myriad of cases which the draftsmen cannot wholly anticipate."); J.I. Case Co. v. NLRB, 321 U.S. 332, 334–35 (1944) ("Collective bargaining . . . negotiations between union and management result in what often has been called a trade agreement, rather than in a contract of employment.").

[43] Willborn, *supra* note 9, at 728.

[44] *Id.* at 731.

[45] The theory is so trendy that the *Yale Law Journal* recently devoted an entire issue to a symposium on republicanism and its revival. *See* Frank Michelman, *Law's Republic*, 97 YALE L.J. 1493 (1988); Cass R. Sunstein, *Beyond the Republican Revival*, 97 YALE L.J. 1539 (1988). See also the comments following the principal articles, at 97 YALE L.J. 1591–1723. The dialogue has occupied some of the most "provocative and insightful constitutional [and other] scholars." *See* Richard H. Fallon, Jr., *What Is Republicanism, and is it Worth Reviving?*, 102

about the advantages and disadvantages of republicanism for oppressed groups within the citizenry. Republicanism is a philosophical doctrine concerning the distribution of power among the citizenry and in politics. This doctrine is associated with the work of Pocock and Shalhope.[46] There exists no unitary conception of politics that can be described as republican.[47] The underlying assumption of all republican theory, however, is that freedom can be best attained through participation in a community, wherein citizens place the public good above their individual interests.[48] By contrast, liberalism seeks freedom through negative means, and assumes that true freedom inheres only in autonomy, or the right to be let alone.[49]

Scholars have identified two distinct forms of republicanism, classical republicanism and Madisonian republicanism. Classical republicanism focuses on the deliberative process of politics as the means of freedom for a participating citizenry.[50] Decisionmaking under classical republicanism occurs through a process of dialogue

---

HARV. L. REV. 1695, 1695 (1989). Most of the scholars who have engaged in this debate have contrasted republicanism (sometimes erroneously confused with communitarianism because of the centrality of the republican value of civic virtue, or the good of the community) with liberalism, and its focus on individual rights. Because individual rights are "conflict notions," they arguably have no place in an intimate or harmonious community; indeed, recognizing individual rights may actually have a deleterious effect on the commitment of individuals to the community. *See* Suzanna Sherry, *Civic Virtue and the Feminine Voice in Constitutional Adjudication*, 72 VA. L. REV. 543, 544 (1986) (feminine jurisprudence might embrace and adapt "communitarian and virtue-based framework of Jeffersonian republicanism"); Cynthia V. Ward, *The Limits of "Liberal Republicanism": Why Group-Based Remedies and Republican Citizenship Don't Mix*, 91 COLUM. L. REV. 581, 583 (1991) (republican revivalists draw upon "communitarian aspirations for public-spirited citizenship"); *see also* John Tomasi, *Individual Rights and Community Virtues*, 101 ETHICS 521, 521–22 (1991) (articulating the tension between rights and community, but concluding that individual rights are compatible with the virtues of community); *cf.* James G. Pope, *Republican Moments: The Role of Direct Popular Power in the American Constitutional Order*, 139 U. PA. L. REV. 287, 296 (1990) (emphasizing "political design features" of republicanism rather than its ethical foundations, and therefore contrasting republicanism with interest group pluralism rather than liberalism in the abstract).

[46] *See* Fallon, *supra* note 45, at 1696 n.9 (attribution of theory); *see also* Michael A. Fitts, *Look Before You Leap: Some Cautionary Notes on Civic Republicanism*, 97 YALE L.J. 1651, 1655 (1988) ("result (if not goal) of republican approach is dispersion of power within the political process").

[47] Sunstein, *supra* note 45, at 1547; Ward, *supra* note 45, at 584.

[48] *See* Pope, *supra* note 45, at 296–97. The "allure" of republicanism lies in its hope of a "'constitutive' community." Fallon, *supra* note 45, at 1721 (quoting MICHAEL J. SANDEL, LIBERALISM AND THE LIMITS OF JUSTICE 150–51 (1982)). Such a community is one in which there exists "a deep and ongoing political dialogue through which we open ourselves to others, shape and are shaped by others, and experience an enriching and ennobling integration of self and community." *Id.*

[49] Pope, *supra* note 45, at 296.

[50] Sunstein, *supra* note 45, at 1547–48.

in politics conducted by citizens who participate as equals, in pursuit of a common good.[51] "Civic virtue" is a "central organizing feature" of classical republicanism.[52] The assumption is that every citizen is virtuous, or has the potential to be so, and hence will strive toward realization of the common good. Indeed, participation in politics is assumed to be self-actualizing for the citizenry.[53]

Madisonian republicanism, by contrast, envisions participation through the deliberation of virtuous representatives elected by the people, but far enough removed from them to avoid the tyrannies of faction and corruption.[54] Madison eschewed direct citizen participation in the processes of government, believing that national representatives of the populace, "operating above the fray," would possess the virtue necessary to further an "objective" conception of the public good.[55] Representatives were made accountable to the polity through the imposition of political checks, including electoral supervision and other safeguards.[56] Republican revivalists have tended to focus on Madisonian republicanism rather than on classical republicanism.[57]

Cass Sunstein describes four attributes of republicanism that give it a "contemporary appeal." First, republicanism offers an opportunity for deliberation in government. Such deliberation would allow existing desires to be revised according to collective discussion, in light of alternative perspectives and additional information that may arise. Republicanism uses deliberation to arrive at a decision that will best serve the community in general, based on notions of civic virtue.[58] Second, republicanism requires political equality; that is, all individuals and groups must be afforded access to the political process.[59] Third, republicanism seeks universality of norms, or

---

[51] Michelman, *supra* note 45, at 1503.

[52] MARK TUSHNET, RED, WHITE AND BLUE: A CRITICAL ANALYSIS OF CONSTITUTIONAL LAW 10 (1988) (in its classical form, republican theory mandates participation among virtuous citizens "who draw their understandings of themselves and the meaning of their lives from their participation with others in a social world that they actively and jointly create"); Sunstein, *supra* note 45, at 1548.

[53] *See* Michelman, *supra* note 45, at 1503. Hannah Arendt argues that the Aristotelian pursuit of civic action is good for the soul. *See* HANNAH ARENDT, THE HUMAN CONDITION 7–8, 10, 175–81 (1958); HANNAH ARENDT, ON REVOLUTION 15 (1963).

[54] Cass R. Sunstein, *Interest Groups in American Public Law*, 38 STAN. L. REV. 29, 38–48 (1985).

[55] *Id.* at 42.

[56] *Id.* at 46–47, 85.

[57] *See, e.g.*, *id.* at 30.

[58] Sunstein, *supra* note 45, at 1549–50.

[59] *Id.* at 1552. For some, but not all, republican theorists, the commitment to political equality also includes a commitment to economic equality. *Id.* at 1552–53.

agreement as a regulative ideal. Rather than suggesting that there exists a common understanding of a unitary public good, Sunstein argues that universality refers to a belief in the process of mediating differing views of the public good through dialogue.[60] The final attribute is the significance of citizenship, specifically the right to participate in the political process, with the purpose of monitoring the behavior of representatives. Small, decentralized republican systems have been considered most likely to be true to the deliberative process.[61] Although Sunstein's vision of the deliberative process is representative, and therefore Madisonian in nature, he advocates direct participation of the citizenry at the local level.[62]

Sunstein notes that a serious shortcoming of republicanism is its historical strategy of exclusion of the non-propertied—women, Blacks and other minorities; he notes that the common good was defined in relation to these practices of exclusion.[63] The assumption that a unitary common good exists ignores the needs and interests of those who, because of their disempowerment, do not participate at any level in defining the public good.[64] Classical republicanism is especially hostile toward women; it "is militaristic, . . . associating political behavior with warfare, and valuing in politics the characteristics prized during times of battle."[65] Moreover, classical republicanism is consistent with the existence of rigid social hierarchies, and emphasizes the role of tradition in according status within them.[66] Finally, it is a highly rationalistic political theory, emphasizing deliberation as a means of transcending the affective side of humanity, and devaluing the private sphere as part of "nature."[67]

Nevertheless, Sunstein defends a form of liberal republicanism with a new twist. He argues that the principles of this liberal republicanism provide the basis for reform that could support a theory of social subordination reinforcing constitutional protections against discrimination.[68] He proposes proportional representation

---

[60] *Id.* at 1554–55.

[61] *Id.* at 1555–56.

[62] Cass R. Sunstein, *Constitutionalism After the New Deal*, 101 HARV. L. REV. 421, 429 (1987).

[63] Sunstein, *supra* note 45, at 1539.

[64] *Id.* at 1540.

[65] *Id.* at 1564.

[66] *Id.* at 1565.

[67] *Id.*

[68] *Id.* at 1580–81. This is apparently an oblique reference to the work of feminist legal scholars, in particular Catharine MacKinnon, who have constructed equality arguments—under the Constitution and title VII—on a theory of social and economic subordination. *See*

in government of disadvantaged groups in order to remedy the problem of access to the deliberative process.[69]

Sunstein's defense of modified republicanism is incomplete, however, particularly on the question of the fate of the rights of oppressed groups under the "new republicanist" tradition. Republicanism's search for a "common good" assumes a moral consensus on values, and ignores the fact that republicanism is by nature hostile to those whose voices threaten disruption of its normative unity. In an incisive critique, Derrick Bell and Preeta Bansal note that the emphasis on reasoned deliberation, with its aura of passionless objectivity, is distinctly male and distinctly white.[70] They point out that the backdrop of "shared values" against which decisions concerning the public good have been made include a belief in the propriety or naturalness of the inferior, subordinate position that Black Americans have occupied relative to whites.[71]

Kathleen Sullivan dubs the Sunstein version of republicanism (shared in its significant respects by Frank Michelman) "rainbow republicanism," to capture the idea that the heterogeneity of the modern populace and its variety of perspectives could be a virtue of republicanism, rather than a vice.[72] Sullivan eschews rainbow

---

Catharine A. MacKinnon, Feminism Unmodified 40–41 (1987) (arguing that an equality question is a question of power and its distribution; thus, sex equality issues are raised by the socially situated subordination of women accomplished through women's assignment to low-paying sex-segregated work, the high incidence of sexual violence directed against women, including rape, sexual assault, domestic violence, and sexual harassment, and the continued growth of industries trafficking in female flesh, including prostitution and pornography); *see also* Colker, *supra* note 5, at 1007–16; Robin West, *Equality Theory, Marital Rape, and the Promise of the Fourteenth Amendment*, 42 Fla. L. Rev. 45, 59–61 (1990) (summarizing arguments of feminist anti-subordinationists, notably Catharine MacKinnon, Mary Becker and Ruth Colker, that the social subordination of women by men is the target of the Equal Protection Clause, and substantive equality its goal).

[69] *Id.* at 1588.

[70] *See* Derrick Bell & Preeta Bansal, *The Republican Revival and Racial Politics*, 97 Yale L.J. 1609, 1610 & n.4 (1988) (citing feminist critiques by Carol Gilligan, Catharine MacKinnon and Suzanna Sherry).

[71] *Id.* at 1611. This "common good" sanctioned slavery for centuries, and continues to promote racial domination through a consensus ideology that, while promising non-discrimination, reinforces the racial disadvantages of our blatantly racist past. *See id.*; *see also* Ward, *supra* note 45, at 604–05. Ward argues that proportional representation of disadvantaged groups in governmental bodies is incompatible with republicanism. *Id.* She argues that such group representation accepts the notion that the political interests of racial and ethnic minorities are "irreducibly opposed" to those of the white (male) majority, and that only members of those disadvantaged groups can represent the groups' interests in government. *Id.* In contrast, Ward notes that republicanism's goal is "dialogic empathy between equal citizens" working together toward some common good; thus, group representation is "communo-pathic." *Id.*

[72] Kathleen M. Sullivan, *Rainbow Republicanism*, 97 Yale L.J. 1713, 1713–14 (1988).

republicanism because of its focus on immutable differences—sex, race, physical disability, sexual orientation—and its consequent tendency to institutionalize involuntary group cleavages in politics.[73] The historian Linda Kerber points out that the exclusion of oppressed, non-propertied groups was "*essential* to the republican view of the world, not an easily correctable accident."[74] Thus, despite the efforts of republican revivalists to offer up a republican theory shorn of its exclusionary aspects, the relationship between the politics of patriarchy and republican tradition is too complex and too intertwined to be so easily dismissed.[75] As Kerber explains, both patriarchy and the institution of slavery (or racial subordination) reinforce republicanism: "the [male] head of the family represents the family [and its servants and slaves] in its relationship to the state."[76]

Richard Epstein reinforces these critiques in his argument that republican theory, though portrayed by Michelman and Sunstein as procedural, actually assumes certain substantive norms and values.[77] For example, Epstein argues that Sunstein assumes that "correct" deliberation on anti-discrimination legislation will show the value of government regulation.[78] Epstein contends that because serious deliberation might actually yield the opposite result, a possibility that Sunstein ignores, Sunstein's theory is actually substantive, rather than solely procedural. Yet Sunstein makes no explicit defense of his theory's substantive assumptions, that is, that race and gender discrimination are evils that should be addressed through the political process.[79] In other words, Sunstein assumes that a definition of the public good will be conducted by reference to shared social norms that are liberal in character, rather than market-oriented.

In short, exclusion of subordinated groups is itself a shared social norm, although it is rarely acknowledged. The social reality is that subordinated groups do not possess, and have not possessed,

---

[73] *Id.* at 1716. Sullivan proposes a philosophy of normative pluralism that would avoid any quest for agreement upon a single common good and would instead emphasize *voluntary* group affiliations, independent of the state, as the relevant centers of value formation and social interaction. *Id.* at 1714.

[74] Linda K. Kerber, *Making Republicanism Useful*, 97 YALE L.J. 1663, 1665 (1988).

[75] *See id.* at 1668.

[76] *Id.*

[77] *See* Richard A. Epstein, *Modern Republicanism—Or the Flight from Substance*, 97 YALE L.J. 1633, 1639–43 (1988).

[78] *Id.* at 1646.

[79] *Id.*

an equal right of access to the community of participation and deliberation.[80] Their exclusion from access begins in patriarchal institutions such as the family, is reinforced by a hierarchically structured workplace featuring white men in positions of power—with women, Blacks and other subordinated groups in servile roles[81]—and is continued by republican political theory reinforcing the isolation of the populace from their representatives (who, of course, are predominantly white males). The federal legislative process, distant as it is from the daily experience of most citizens, is unlikely to alleviate this exclusion.[82] Indeed, Madisonian republicanism has historically emphasized the insulation of representatives from the populace, in order to protect representatives from public pressure and to foster deliberation rather than an "unreflective representation of popular will."[83]

The inherent elitism in republican theory makes republicanism an unlikely vehicle for eliminating the subordination of oppressed groups. As James Pope has argued, the initial Michelman/Sunstein approach of locating republicanism in the judiciary, despite Michelman and Sunstein's personal aversion to elitism, demonstrates how elitism is hopelessly intertwined with republican theory.[84] If our goal is to recast the role of popular participants in decisionmaking for the community, "it seems odd to look for primary guidance from the courts."[85] Reliance on the judiciary as the watchdogs of republicanism impacts most heavily on women, Blacks and other oppressed groups because the judiciary is predominantly comprised of white males.[86]

Subsequent proposals by Michelman and Sunstein to place republican self-government in local communities and other intermediate groups also evidence elitist attitudes, although in more subtle

---

[80] *See* Kerber, *supra* note 74, at 1671.

[81] *See* ROSABETH M. KANTER, MEN AND WOMEN OF THE CORPORATION 4–5 (1977) (analogizing corporate structure to stereotypical family patriarchal structure).

[82] Kathryn Abrams, *Law's Republicanism*, 97 YALE L.J. 1591, 1604 (1988).

[83] Fitts, *supra* note 46, at 1653.

[84] *See* Pope, *supra* note 45, at 300–01 ("To suggest that judges, who are typically white, male, and rich, can virtually represent the rest of us is to forget the legacy of legal realism, something that I doubt Michelman intends.") (footnote omitted).

[85] Abrams, *supra* note 82, at 1604.

[86] *See* THE FEMINIST MAJORITY, THE FEMINIZATION OF POWER: WOMEN IN THE LAW 3 (1990) (women represent only 7.2% of state court full-time judges (25 states have no woman serving on the state supreme court), 7.4% of the full-time federal judges, 9.5% of the U.S. circuit judges, and 11.1% (1 out of 9) of the United States Supreme Court justices; statistics for African-American women are even lower).

form.[87] For example, the Michelman/Sunstein formulation of republicanism relies upon the judiciary to help ensure that legislators do not "reflexively" follow their constituents' interests.[88] Similarly, Sunstein's description of the process of deliberation reveals his continuing preoccupation with the need for representatives who are more likely to make "intelligent and virtuous decisions for the public good than is the public itself,"[89] a concept of deliberation that is inconsistent with his concern for broad participation in the political process.[90] In short, modern republicanism continues the tradition of an insulated, representative democracy,[91] thus reinforcing the social realities of patriarchy and racial subordination.

2. The Republican Model in Labor Law

The Wagner Act, modeled on the larger political democratic structure, imports a republican model of representative government into the workplace. Although the drafters of the Wagner Act were concerned primarily with establishing a balance of power between individual employees and employers in order to avoid strikes and the consequent interruption of commerce, they were also interested in empowering workers economically and in promoting workplace democracy, which was thought to enhance political democracy.[92]

---

[87] *See* Pope, *supra* note 45, at 302 & n.66.

[88] Fitts, *supra* note 46, at 1653.

[89] H. Jefferson Powell, *Reviving Republicanism*, 97 YALE L.J. 1703, 1708 (1988).

[90] *Id.*

[91] *See* Fitts, *supra* note 46, at 1653.

[92] Some commentators have argued that Congress's primary concern in enacting the NLRA was the protection of employee rights, rather than the prevention of industrial strife. *See* Note, *Participatory Management Under Sections 2(5) and 8(a)(2) of the National Labor Relations Act*, 83 MICH. L. REV. 1736, 1759 (1985). The Act's legislative history and historical context, however, make this position "virtually indefensible." Shaun G. Clarke, Note, *Rethinking The Adversarial Model in Labor Relations: An Argument for Repeal of Section 8(a)(2)*, 96 YALE L.J. 2021, 2033 (1987); *see also* Marion Crain, *Building Solidarity Through Expansion of NLRA Coverage: A Blueprint For Worker Empowerment*, 74 MINN. L. REV. 953, 965–66 (1990) (preserving industrial peace and flow of commerce was basis for congressional jurisdiction to legislate in the area and key to political feasibility of its passage).

Whatever can be said about Congress's original intent, the Supreme Court has made it clear that the attainment of industrial peace takes precedence over protecting employee rights or insuring workplace democracy. The Court has consistently resolved the tension between protecting employee rights, and preserving industrial peace and the uninterrupted flow of commerce, in favor of the latter. *See, e.g.*, First Nat'l Maintenance Corp. v. NLRB, 452 U.S. 666, 679 (1981) (no duty to bargain over management decision to partially close business when burden placed on conduct of business outweighs benefit to collective bargaining process); Local 174, Teamsters v. Lucas Flour Co., 369 U.S. 95, 104–06 (1962) (no-strike clause implied in collective bargaining contract containing arbitration clause to preserve

Like its prototype, republican democracy, the Wagner Act assumed that democracy was best attained through a militaristic, win-lose competition between the interests of the relevant constituencies—here, employers and employees engaged in a struggle for control of the workplace, production and the distribution of profits. With the explicit goal of copying republican, representative democracy, Congress established an adversarial system of rights, rules and processes within which the contest was to be waged, and authorized representatives on each side (managers for the companies, unions for the employees) to conduct the battle. To help even out the economic scales, individual employees were afforded a right to organize against employers "organized in the corporate [form],"[93] and a right to engage in "concerted activities for the purpose of collective bargaining or other mutual aid or protection."[94]

Collective bargaining was chosen by Congress as the preferred means for resolving conflicts between workers and employers.[95] Collective bargaining is directly analogous to the legislative process in the larger political democracy. Its primary goal is the efficient management of the enterprise, which in turn leads to industrial peace and uninterrupted production. The underlying assumption is that the workplace is hierarchically ordered and that workers, who occupy the bottom rungs on the hierarchy, must be con-

---

industrial peace); NLRB v. Fansteel Metallurgical Corp., 306 U.S. 240, 256 (1939) (sitdown strikes unprotected by Act because they interrupt production); NLRB v. Mackay Radio & Tel., 304 U.S. 333, 345–46 (1938) (employer may permanently replace striking employees in order to continue business).

[93] National Labor Relations Act, § 1, 29 U.S.C. § 151 (1988). Section one states:

> The inequality of bargaining power between employees who do not possess full freedom of association or actual liberty of contract, and employers who are organized in the corporate or other forms of ownership association substantially burdens and affects the flow of commerce . . . . [P]rotection by law of the right of employees to organize and bargain collectively . . . promotes the flow of commerce . . . by restoring equality of bargaining power between employers and employees.

Id.

[94] National Labor Relations Act, § 7, 29 U.S.C. § 157 (1988). As one writer summarized the Act's approach:

> The essential idea embodied in the [Wagner] Act is that worker representation involves *balancing* the power of management by building a parallel organization of workers. One behemoth, according to this logic, can best be controlled by another one. The concept requires the drawing of a series of lines to establish the field of battle: one defining workers as opposed to management, another defining the issues about which they must bargain, and a third marking legitimate tactics in the contest.

HECKSCHER, *supra* note 8, at 7.

[95] *See* National Labor Relations Act, § 1, 29 U.S.C. § 151 (1988).

trolled.[96] The concept is made more palatable through the use of democratic rhetoric: the workplace is a place that must be "governed," and the workers may "choose" their "representative" in the legislative process.[97]

Scholars associated with the Critical Legal Studies movement have argued persuasively that collective bargaining law "aims to legitimate and justify unnecessary and destructive hierarchy and domination in the workplace," and that it has "evolved an institutional architecture . . . that reinforces this hierarchy and domination."[98] Accordingly, labor law "promises a modicum of democratic participation to encourage worker acceptance of," and consent to, the hierarchical and authoritarian character of the workplace.[99] "Liberal labor theory," as Karl Klare has dubbed the legislative analogy and the assumptions supporting it, thus utilizes collective bargaining law as a means of coopting the labor movement into a "junior partnership" role with management.[100]

Perhaps most strikingly reminiscent of republican tradition, the Wagner Act sought to ensure an autonomous representative for employees—the labor union—exclusively through which employees would advance their interests.[101] Congress defined who was covered by the NLRA (and so who might organize);[102] regulated when,

---

[96] Some scholars have assumed that authoritarian structure and hierarchy in the workplace are "inevitable," because such a structure emanates from the very "nature of the modern industrial enterprise." David E. Feller, *A General Theory of the Collective Bargaining Agreement*, 61 Cal. L. Rev. 663, 721 (1973).

[97] *See id.* at 726, 742; Klare, *Labor Law as Ideology*, *supra* note 13, at 460.

[98] *See* Klare, *Labor Law as Ideology*, *supra* note 13, at 452.

[99] *Id.* at 459–60 (1981) (quoting United Steelworkers of Am. v. Warrior & Gulf Navigation Co., 363 U.S. 574, 578, 582 (1960)).

[100] *See id.* at 455 n.17; *see also* Atleson, *supra* note 13, at 8.

[101] *See* National Labor Relations Act, § 7, 29 U.S.C. § 157 (1988) ("Employees shall have the right to . . . bargain collectively through representatives of their own choosing . . . .").

[102] The Taft-Hartley Act of 1947 effectuated management's need for faithful agents to represent it by excluding supervisors from the definition of "employee" in the Act. *See id.* § 2(3), 29 U.S.C. § 152(3) ("The term 'employee' . . . shall not include . . . any individual employed as a supervisor."). The Supreme Court, reasoning that because managerial employees were higher in the authority structure than supervisors, has held that managerial employees and confidential employees with a "labor relations nexus" were also representatives of the employer rather than "employees" covered by the Act. *See* NLRB v. Hendricks County Rural Elec. Membership Corp., 454 U.S. 170, 187–88 (1981) (confidential employees assisting or acting in a confidential relation to persons exercising managerial functions in the field of labor relations); NLRB v. Bell Aerospace Co., 416 U.S. 267, 283–84 (1974) (managerial employees). *See generally* Crain, *supra* note 92 (arguing that attempt to draw the line between covered employees and excluded supervisors, managers and confidential employees stratifies the laboring class and undermines labor solidarity).

where, and by whom organizing might be accomplished;[103] and established an election system to determine whether a particular union represented a majority of the employees.[104] Finally, Congress enacted section 8(a)(2), which ensured that unions were free from employer domination or assistance, and section 9(a), which afforded unions exclusivity in representing employees on issues of wages, hours, and terms and conditions of employment.[105] Both sections advanced the notion, typical of republicanism's aspirations of achieving the public good, that the good of the group takes precedence over the good of individuals.[106]

---

[103] *See, e.g.*, Lechmere, Inc. v. NLRB, 112 S. Ct. 841, 848 (1992) (rejecting Board's *Jean Country* balancing test and reaffirming and narrowing *Babcock & Wilcox* rule: no balancing of employees' Section 7 rights against the employer's property rights is appropriate unless non-employee union organizers lack reasonable access to employees outside the employer's property; such access is absent only where the location of the plant and the living quarters of the employees place them beyond the union's reach, and not where access is merely cumbersome or difficult, as in a large metropolitan area); NLRB v. Babcock & Wilcox Co., 351 U.S. 105, 112 (1956) (non-employee organizers may not trespass on employer's property in order to communicate information about the union to employees unless there exists no other means of access); Republic Aviation Corp. v. NLRB, 324 U.S. 793, 802 n.8, 803 (1945) (upholding NLRB determination that employees may organize before and after working hours, during rest periods and lunch breaks, but not during "working time").

[104] Section 9 of the Act establishes the electoral procedure for selection of the union authorized to represent the employees. *See* 29 U.S.C. § 159(a) (1988) ("Representatives designated or selected for the purposes of collective bargaining by the majority of the employees in a unit appropriate for such purposes, shall be the exclusive representatives of all the employees in such unit for the purposes of collective bargaining . . . .").

[105] *Id.* §§ 158(a)(2), 159(a).

[106] *See* J.I. Case Co. v. NLRB, 321 U.S. 332, 338 (1944) (invalidating individual contracts of employees with employer where they served as limits on rights of the employees under the collective bargaining agreement). The *J.I. Case* Court stated that "[t]he very purpose of providing by statute for the collective agreement is to supersede the terms of separate agreements of employees with terms which reflect the strength and bargaining power and serve the welfare of the group." *Id.* The strength of this principle has been reinforced in the duty of fair representation cases, where the courts have consistently held that, although the union does owe a duty of fair representation to its individual members, the union's primary duty is to serve the good of the membership in general, rather than the individual. *See* Vaca v. Sipes, 386 U.S. 171, 190, 195 (1967) (breach of union's duty of fair representation "occurs only when a union's conduct toward a member of the collective bargaining unit is arbitrary, discriminatory, or in bad faith"; thus, individual employee has no absolute right to have his grievance taken to arbitration); Steele v. Louisville & Nashville R.R. Co., 323 U.S. 192, 204 (1944) (if union is to enjoy the cloak of exclusivity conferred by section 9(a), it owes a correlative duty to represent all employees within the bargaining unit "without hostile discrimination, fairly, impartially and in good faith").

This principle is referred to by students in my labor law classes as the "Spock" rule, in reference to a statement made by Spock during one of the *Star Trek* movies, as he sacrificed his own life (temporarily, as sequels later disclosed) to save the crew of the starship Enterprise. Spock justified his own demise with the declaration that "the good of the many outweighs the good of the few . . . or the one." STAR TREK II: THE WRATH OF KHAN (Paramount Pictures 1982).

Once the union is authorized to serve as the employees' exclusive representative, the Wagner Act imposed an obligation to bargain in "good faith" over "wages, hours, and other terms and conditions of employment,"[107] and otherwise left the parties to the "'free play of contending economic forces'" in negotiating a labor contract.[108] Nevertheless, the NLRA undertakes to regulate the use of economic weapons by both parties by affording protection to some employee activities (the primary strike),[109] leaving others unprotected (the sitdown strike,[110] wildcat strikes,[111] and the slowdown),[112] and prohibiting certain others (secondary boycotts,[113] organizational or recognitional picketing,[114] and hot cargo

---

[107] National Labor Relations Act, § 8(d), 29 U.S.C. § 158(d) (1988).

[108] *See* Lodge 76, Int'l Ass'n of Machinists v. Wisconsin Employment Relations Comm'n, 427 U.S. 132, 140 n.4 (1976) (quoting Howard Lesnick, *Preemption Reconsidered: The Apparent Reaffirmation of* Garmon, 72 COLUM. L. REV. 469, 478 (1972)). The Court also quoted with approval the following remarks by Archibald Cox regarding the congressional intent behind the NLRA:

> An appreciation of the true character of the national labor policy expressed in the NLRA [National Labor Relations Act] and the LMRA [Labor Management Relations Act] indicates that in providing a legal framework for union organization, collective bargaining, and the conduct of labor disputes, Congress struck a balance of protection, prohibition, and laissez-faire in respect to union organization, collective bargaining, and labor disputes.

Id. at 140 n.4 (quoting Archibald Cox, *Labor Law Preemption Revisited*, 85 HARV. L. REV. 1337, 1352 (1972)).

[109] *See* National Labor Relations Act, § 7, 29 U.S.C. § 157 (1988) ("Employees shall have the right to . . . engage in other concerted activities for the purpose of collective bargaining or other mutual aid or protection . . . ."); *see also id.* § 13, 29 U.S.C. § 163 ("Nothing in this Act . . . shall be construed so as to interfere with or impede or diminish in any way the right to strike . . . .").

[110] *See* NLRB v. Fansteel Metallurgical Corp., 306 U.S. 240, 254–55 (1939) (illegal sitdown strike by trespassing employees in response to employer unfair labor practices removes the right to reinstatement that employees would otherwise possess).

[111] Wildcat strikes—strikes that are unauthorized by the union, although otherwise lawful—are characterized as unprotected activity in some circuits, either because they derogate from the union's status as exclusive representative, or because they undermine the institutionalized collective bargaining structure. *See, e.g.*, NLRB v. Shop-Rite Foods, 430 F.2d 786, 791 (5th Cir. 1970) (stating that an unauthorized walkout to protest an employee's discharge "could only undermine the goals of democracy in the union and effective labor adjustment through the bargaining process"). *See generally* ATLESON, *supra* note 13, at 77–81; Gould, *The Status of Unauthorized and Wildcat Strikes Under the NLRA*, 52 CORNELL L.Q. 672 (1967).

[112] *See* Elk Lumber Co., 91 N.L.R.B. 333 (1950) (slowdown in work production not protected concerted activity). *But see* NLRB v. Insurance Agents Int'l Union, 361 U.S. 477 (1960) (slowdowns, while unprotected, do not constitute bad faith bargaining; nevertheless, employer can sanction employees by discharging them).

[113] *See* National Labor Relations Act, § 8(b)(4), 29 U.S.C. § 158(b)(4) (1988).

[114] *See id.* § 8(b)(7), 29 U.S.C. § 158(b)(7).

agreements).[115] Similarly, although the NLRA explicitly forbids employers from utilizing certain economic weapons (discriminatory or retaliatory discharges),[116] the Supreme Court has protected certain employer activities designed to maintain production in the face of employee unrest. These activities include the right to permanently replace economic strikers,[117] the right to close a business completely without liability for discrimination,[118] and the right to purchase a business without assuming its labor contract.[119]

In short, Congress's initial assumption, that employees and employers possess a fundamental conflict of interest in how the workplace is to be run and how the profits of the enterprise are to be distributed, dictated an adversarial approach to the process of allocating power between employees, the union and the employer. Judges attempting to interpret the labor laws have necessarily focused on creating rules and drawing lines to enhance the fairness of the adversarial game; hence, the insistence upon drawing a line between employer and employee, between when and where union organizing may and may not take place, between when employer anti-union campaigns may and may not be conducted, between mandatory and permissive subjects of bargaining under the NLRA, between good faith and bad faith bargaining, and between what is and what is not protected economic activity.

C. *The Adversarial Model of Power Allocation Under Labor Law*

The Department of Labor has described the framework of United States labor law as "tending to produce collective bargaining relationships that are legalistic, rule-driven, and confrontational."[120]

---

[115] *See id.* § 8(e), 29 U.S.C. § 158(e).

[116] *See id.* §§ 8(a)(3), 8(a)(4), 29 U.S.C. §§ 158(a)(3), 158(a)(4).

[117] *See* NLRB v. Mackay Radio & Tel. Co., 304 U.S. 333, 345–46 (1938) (despite the explicit protection afforded the right to strike in the Act, an employer does not lose "the right to protect and continue his business by supplying places left vacant by strikers. And he is not bound to discharge those hired to fill the places of strikers, upon the election of the latter to resume their employment, in order to create places for them.").

[118] *See* Textile Workers Union v. Darlington Mfg. Co., 380 U.S. 263, 269 (1965) (decisions to end a business are "so peculiarly matters of management prerogative that they would never constitute violations of § 8(a)(1), whether or not they involved sound business judgment, unless they also violated § 8(a)(3)").

[119] *See* NLRB v. Burns Int'l Sec. Servs., Inc., 406 U.S. 272, 288 (1972) (Court refused to "saddle" new employer with terms and conditions of employment contained in its predecessor's labor contract because to do so might discourage the transfer of capital).

[120] Bureau of Labor-Management Relations and Cooperative Programs, U.S. Dep't of Labor, U.S. Labor Law and the Future of Labor-Management Cooperation: Final Report 141 (1989).

At the heart of the labor laws is a belief that the interests of labor and capital are necessarily adverse, and that labor and capital are therefore adversaries. The assumption that the employer and the employees have antithetical interests is reflected in three basic tenets of the NLRA: first, the division of workers into two categories, "employees," who are represented by the union, and "supervisors" or "managers," who represent the employer; second, the definition of a labor organization by reference to its dealings with the adverse party, the employer, and an accompanying proscription against employer domination or support of labor organizations; and third, the principle of exclusive representation of employees by the labor organization.

1. The Definition of "Employees" Covered Under the NLRA

Under the NLRA, collective bargaining is carried out between two independent players with inevitably conflicting interests: the employer, represented by supervisory and managerial personnel, and the union, representing the other employees. In the adversarial model of the NLRA, the centrality of separation of the competitors is clear; strict separation between the parties to collective bargaining must be maintained for bargaining to be fair.[121]

The separation between employees and employers is maintained at the individual level through the definition of "employee" in section 2(3) of the NLRA, which excludes supervisors from the definition of "employee."[122] The rationale for the exclusion of supervisors is the employer's need for front-line representatives in its dealings with employees; it was considered vital that supervisors' loyalties not be divided between the employer and the union.[123] The

[121] The NLRA's adversarial model and the separation of parties that it requires has received a great deal of criticism from scholars. *See, e.g.*, Michael C. Harper, *Reconciling Collective Bargaining With Employee Supervision of Management*, 137 U. Pa. L. Rev. 1, 7–9 (1988); Thomas C. Kohler, *Models of Worker Participation: The Uncertain Significance of Section 8(a)(2)*, 27 B.C. L. Rev. 499, 513–16 (1986); Clarke, *supra* note 92, at 2022 & n.7; Note, *Collective Bargaining as an Industrial System: An Argument Against Judicial Revision of Section 8(a)(2) of the National Labor Relations Act*, 96 Harv. L. Rev. 1662, 1673–80 (1983) [hereinafter *Collective Bargaining as an Industrial System*]. *See generally* Robert A. McCormick, *Union Representatives As Corporate Directors: The Challenge to the Adversarial Model of Labor Relations*, 15 U. Mich. J.L. Ref. 219 (1982) (discussing limitations the adversarial model imposes on union influence on business decisions, and considering implications for employees of affording labor a broader role in corporate governance).

[122] Section 2(3) of the NLRA provides: "[t]he term 'employee' . . . shall not include . . . any individual employed as a supervisor." 29 U.S.C. § 152(3) (1988). The term "supervisor" is defined in § 2(11), 29 U.S.C. § 152(11).

[123] *See* Crain, *supra* note 92, at 972–73.

exclusion was later expanded to include employees acting in managerial or confidential capacities.[124] As I have argued previously, this division of the work force siphons off some of the most educated and most powerful members of the work force, factionalizing the work force and hampering effective collective resistance to employer power.[125]

2. The Definition of a Labor Organization by Reference to Its Dealings with the Opposition and to the Proscription Against Employer Domination or Support

The exclusion of supervisory and managerial employees from the union ranks is balanced by section 8(a)(2) of the NLRA, which makes it an unfair labor practice for an employer to "dominate or interfere with the formation or administration of any labor organization or contribute financial or other support to it."[126] Section 8(a)(2) was designed to eradicate the "company union," a company-controlled organization instituted by employers to pacify employees and thereby stave off union organizing efforts, especially those conducted on a multi-shop scale.[127]

Since section 8(a)(2) applies only to employer domination, interference or assistance with a "labor organization," a threshold

---

[124] *See* NLRB v. Hendricks County Rural Elec. Membership Corp., 454 U.S. 170, 187–90 (1981) (confidential employees who assist or act in a confidential relation to persons exercising managerial functions in the field of labor relations are excluded from NLRA coverage); NLRB v. Bell Aerospace Co., 416 U.S. 267, 283–84 (1974) (managerial employees implicitly excluded from coverage under NLRA because they are higher than supervisors in the authority structure of the workplace).

[125] Crain, *supra* note 92, at 1006 (labor laws ensure that the most powerful employees are alienated and isolated from the laboring class). The ideology of individualism reflected in the Taft-Hartley Amendments to the NLRA is perhaps the Act's most harmful legacy for American workers. *See id.* at 1008, 1013 & n.346 (nonunionized middle-level employees vulnerable to discharge are victims of their own individualistic philosophy); *see also* Joel Rogers, *Divide and Conquer: Further "Reflections on the Distinctive Character of American Labor Laws,"* 1990 Wis. L. Rev. 1, 8–9, 144 (arguing that the Taft-Hartley Amendments codified and furthered the weakness of American unions because they fragmented organized labor by imposing limits on coordinated bargaining strategies, and encouraging the pursuit of particularistic bargaining strategies; Rogers dubs this approach the "divide and conquer" strategy).

[126] National Labor Relations Act, § 8(a)(2), 29 U.S.C. § 158(a)(2) (1988).

[127] *See* 78 Cong. Rec. 3443 (1934), *reprinted in* 1 NLRB, Legislative History of the National Labor Relations Act, 1935, at 15–16 (1949) (statement of Senator Wagner). Senator Wagner was especially concerned with the possibility that company unions would limit employee collective action to a single shop, operating to deprive workers of the "wider cooperation [across employer units] which is necessary . . . to stabilize and standardize wage levels . . . ." *Id.*

issue is the status of an entity as a labor organization. The term "labor organization" is identified by reference to a group's dealings with the employer. Section 2(5) of the Act defines a labor organization as "any organization of any kind, or any agency or employee representation committee or plan, in which employees participate and which exists for the purpose, in whole or in part, of dealing with employers concerning grievances, labor disputes, wages, rates of pay, hours of employment, or conditions of work."[128]

In recent years, many employers have initiated "participatory management" schemes in an effort to forestall worker dissatisfaction and to increase productivity. These organizations take various forms, each tailored to the employer's primary goal in implementing it. The three most popular are Quality Control Circles, which are organized on a department level and focus on increasing production and improving product quality; Quality-of-Work-Life programs, which give employees a limited hand in shaping their immediate work environments, and which typically originate as an effort to generate loyalty and stem dissatisfaction; and Board of Director Participation programs, which place a worker representative on a company's board of directors, usually with the goal of obtaining concessions from labor by nominally involving it in the strategic corporate planning process.[129]

The courts, torn between striving to prevent the resuscitation of the company union by another name and the desire to encourage efforts at cooperation between parties that have historically been hostile, have carefully scrutinized these organizations to determine whether they qualify as "labor organizations" under the NLRA. They have developed three methods of determining status as a labor organization under section 2(5): looking to the form it assumes, the subject matter it deals with, or the function it serves.[130] To be classified as a labor organization, an entity may assume virtually any structure, must deal with the employer over "conditions of work" (broadly construed), and must exist to represent its member-employees.[131]

The circuit courts are split in applying the standard. The Seventh and Second Circuit courts construe the term labor organization

---

[128] National Labor Relations Act, § 2(5), 29 U.S.C. § 152(5) (1988).

[129] *See* Andrew A. Lipsky, Comment, *Participatory Management Schemes, The Law, and Workers' Rights: A Proposed Framework of Analysis*, 39 AM. U. L. REV. 667, 673–75 (1990).

[130] *Id.* at 688–89.

[131] *Id.* at 689–90.

very broadly, finding labor organization status even in the absence of formal structure, constitution or bylaws, officers, dues requirements or continuing existence.[132] This broad construction of section 2(5) operates to disestablish many participative management schemes because they involve employer domination or assistance that violates section 8(a)(2) of the NLRA. By contrast, the Sixth Circuit Court of Appeals has imposed a more restrictive definition of a labor organization, resulting in the conclusion that many employee committees are not section 2(5) labor organizations, but merely part of an "enlightened personnel policy"; hence, they do not violate section 8(a)(2).[133]

The legislative history of section 8(a)(2) indicates that Congress intended to promote communication between management and labor.[134] Nevertheless, it is clear that Congress also intended to limit the realm in which permissible cooperation between capital and labor might occur.[135] Cooperation was to be accomplished by good faith bargaining between two independent entities—employer and union—over terms and conditions of employment.[136] The courts have struggled with application of the section 8(a)(2) "domination or support" test where employers have sought to cooperate directly with employees in cooperative management programs that fit within the definition of a labor organization under section 2(5) of the Act.

In *Newport News Shipbuilding & Drydock Co.*, the Supreme Court originally interpreted section 8(a)(2) very strictly, mandating the disestablishment of employer-assisted representation plans regardless of the employees' satisfaction with the plan and the employer's

---

[132] *See* NLRB v. Ampex Corp., 442 F.2d 82, 84 (7th Cir. 1971) (informal, randomly chosen "communications committee" that employer claimed acted as glorified suggestion box, was deemed to be a labor organization); Pacemaker Corp. v. NLRB, 260 F.2d 880, 883 (7th Cir. 1958) (lack of officers does not prevent finding of section 2(5) status); NLRB v. Stow Mfg. Co., 217 F.2d 900, 903–04 (2d Cir. 1954) (informal monthly meeting sufficient to indicate section 2(5) labor organization), *cert. denied*, 348 U.S. 964 (1955); NLRB v. Indiana Metal Prods. Corp., 202 F.2d 613, 620–21 (7th Cir. 1953) (lack of constitution or bylaws does not preclude finding of section 2(5) labor organization status); NLRB v. American Furnace Co., 158 F.2d 376, 378 (7th Cir. 1946) (finding labor organization status despite lack of continuity); Wyman-Gordon Co. v. NLRB, 153 F.2d 480, 482 (7th Cir. 1946) (finding labor organization status despite absence of dues).

[133] *See* NLRB v. Streamway Div. of Scott & Fetzer, 691 F.2d 288, 295 (6th Cir. 1982).

[134] *See* Lipsky, *supra* note 129, at 697–98 (congressional committee eliminated proposed terms "initiate" and "influence" in drafting section 8(a)(2), which demonstrates that Congress intended to permit communication and to promote cooperaton accomplished through collective bargaining).

[135] *Id.*

[136] *See* National Labor Relations Act §§ 8(a)(2), 8(d), 9(a), 29 U.S.C. §§ 158(a)(2), 158(d), 159(a) (1988); Lipsky, *supra* note 129, at 696–97.

motives in establishing it.[137] Subsequently, however, the circuit courts have again split on the question of how to treat employer-initiated employee participation plans. The First, Sixth, Seventh and Ninth Circuits, reasoning that courts should encourage cooperative labor-management relations, have refined the Supreme Court's test. These courts have upheld participatory plans where there is no evidence of anti-union animus on the employer's part, and no employee dissatisfaction with the plan.[138] A few circuits have followed a more traditional approach, striking down such employee participation plans in the absence of clear anti-union animus or employee dissatisfaction with the employee committee.[139]

Section 2(5) and 8(a)(2) are instrumental in shaping the structure and culture of organized labor along oppositional lines. By defining labor unions as "other," and by setting them up in opposition to organized capital, the law ensures that labor unions will

---

[137] 308 U.S. 241, 251 (1939).

[138] *See* NLRB v. Northeastern Univ., 601 F.2d 1208, 1214 (1st Cir. 1979) (changing conditions in labor-management relations suggest need to allow alternatives to traditional adversary model); Hertzka & Knowles v. NLRB, 503 F.2d 625, 631 (9th Cir. 1974) (condemnation of cooperative model reflecting employees' free choice would condone adversarial model of labor relations); Modern Plastics Corp. v. NLRB, 379 F.2d 201, 204 (6th Cir. 1967) (assistance from employer not necessarily tantamount to support or domination); Chicago Rawhide Mfg. v. NLRB, 221 F.2d 165, 167–68 (7th Cir. 1955) (cooperation between labor and management is primary goal of NLRA).

[139] *See, e.g.*, Irving Air Chute Co. v. NLRB, 350 F.2d 176, 180–81 (2d Cir. 1965) (finding 8(a)(2) violation where there was employer support, but no domination). The question of how to interpret sections 2(5) and 8(a)(2) is currently before the Board in the Electromation, Inc. case, N.L.R.B. No. 25–CA–19818. In that case, an administrative law judge ruled that "employee action committees" formed by the employer in response to employee discontent, for the purpose of providing input on mandatory bargaining subjects (overtime, tardiness, wages, bonuses, attendance, bereavement leave, sick leave and incentive pay), were labor organizations within the meaning of section 2(5) of the Act. *See* Charles J. Morris, *National Labor Policy: Worker Participation and the Role of the NLRB*, Daily Lab. Rep. (BNA) No. 43, at E–1, E–2 (Mar. 4, 1992) (containing text of speech presented February 6, 1992, at the 1992 Southern California Labor and Employment Law Symposium, Los Angeles, California). The administrative law judge also concluded that the employer had violated section 8(a)(2), reasoning that the employer had unlawfully dominated and supported the action committees by initiating them; choosing the employee representatives who would sit on them; determining the subject matter to be discussed; determining size and composition of the committees; paying employees for attendance at committee meetings; holding all meetings on company premises and providing company support services; and continuing to encourage the joint-committee process during and after the union organization and election process. *Id.* at E–3. As Morris points out, *Electromation* should be an "easy case" because it does not involve the sort of worker participation entailed in work teams, quality circles or groups concerned with the manner of job performance. *Id.* at E–1. Morris predicts that the Board "will have no choice but to uphold the administrative law judge's determination," despite an aggressive campaign by the organized management community to influence the Board to reverse the administrative law judge's decision. *Id.* at E–1, E–3.

strive to conform to the structure and function of capital. Otherwise, unions would risk becoming marginalized. In effect, the law establishes an organizational norm—that of a bureaucratic, militaristic organization where power is centralized—to which unions must adhere if they desire to compete with capital on the legal playing field. Sociological studies show that unions have done exactly that.[140] Because unions' source of power has historically been the sense of solidarity and community inspired by working together toward a common, positive end (producton of goods or the provision of services), power has been expressed in a decentralized, spontaneous form. The shift to reliance on centralized decisionmaking and to the exercise of power in a militaristic fashion has altered the character of the modern union, straitjacketing unions into corporate bureaucratic styles and, ultimately, disempowering them.[141]

3. Exclusive Representation of Employees by the Union

Section 9(a) of the NLRA completes the foundation of the adversarial model; it guarantees that only bargaining units approved by the NLRB may bargain with employers on behalf of employees over "rates of pay, wages, hours of employment, or other conditions of employment."[142] Under the so-called "exclusivity doctrine" established by section 9(a), a duly certified union is the sole representative with which the employer may deal concerning mandatory subjects of bargaining.[143] Its corollary, the duty of fair representation owed by the union to its members individually and collectively, is designed to deter discrimination against minority interests within the union.[144]

Section 9(a) thus affords unions monopolistic status as the voice of employees. Operating against the backdrop of an exclusionary and discriminatory union structure,[145] section 9(a) ensures that the

---

[140] Crain, *supra* note 23, at 24–28 (parallelism in organizational philosophy, structure and tactics of oppositional groups within a common legal environment is predictable; organizations will tend to model themselves after more legitimate, successful oppositional organizations, particularly where one organization is dependent on another).

[141] *See id.* at 28–31.

[142] National Labor Relations Act, § 9(a), 29 U.S.C. § 159(a) (1988).

[143] Lipsky, *supra* note 129, at 702–08.

[144] *See* Vaca v. Sipes, 386 U.S. 171, 177 (1967) ("[T]he exclusive agent's statutory authority to represent all members of a designated unit includes a statutory obligation to serve the interests of all members without hostility or discrimination toward any . . . .").

[145] There can be no doubt that modern union structure continues a tradition of discrimination against women and minorities, systematically excluding them from representation and power. *See* Dan La Botz, Rank and File Rebellion 79 (1990) (describing sweetheart

most oppressed workers—typically women and minorities—will have no voice at all in the workplace.

These three fundamental principles, embodied in four sections of the Act—section 2(3), defining individuals as employees or representatives of the employer; section 2(5), defining a labor organization and the subject matter over which it is to deal; section 8(a)(2), prohibiting employer domination and interference with labor unions; and section 9(a), conferring exclusive representative status on NLRB-certified labor unions—collectively represent Congress's conclusion that channeling conflict into collective bargaining is the surest route to industrial peace.[146] These provisions reflect underlying assumptions that the interests of employees and employers are necessarily in conflict, that confrontation over the division of scarce resources is inevitable, and that such conflicts are best resolved exclusively through participation in an adversarial process of decisionmaking. In my view, these assumptions are all based upon a patriarchal understanding of power.

II. A Feminist Theory of Power and Its Allocation

The labor laws, as well as the history of labor unionism, help to institutionalize what one commentator has dubbed the "adversarial culture in American labor-management relations."[147] As I discuss in this section, American labor law essentially translated the early communitarianism of the labor movement into two separate and opposing communities—a community of workers and a community of managers—and sanctified them by law. Because theories of community are implicitly theories of power,[148] I turn first to an examination of an alternative theory of power that would support a more liberating restructuring of workplace communities.

---

deals in Teamsters Union contract negotiations in which the rights of women and racial minorities were compromised in return for benefits to white male majority members); Crain, *supra* note 5, at 1168–69, 1183–84 (gender stereotypes held by union members are reflected in a paucity of women in the ranks of union officers and organizers, as well as in the failure to close the wage gap between the sexes in collective bargaining).

[146] *See Collective Bargaining as an Industrial System*, *supra* note 121, at 1678.

[147] Clarke, *supra* note 92, at 2042. Indeed, the adversarial stance taken by unions operating under the labor laws has led some commentators to conclude that American unions and unionism are fundamentally incompatible with cooperative approaches designed to enhance productivity and insure industrial peace. *See, e.g.*, *id.* at 2039–49 (advocating repeal of section 8(a)(2) to facilitate labor-management cooperation).

[148] *See* Hartsock, *supra* note 33, at 3.

A. *A Feminist Theory of Power*

Feminists who have undertaken a reevaluation of the concept of power have uniformly rejected understandings of power that focus on domination and control.[149] Instead, feminists have defined power as referring to energy, ability, capacity and freedom.[150] This vision of power, often referred to in the sociological and political literature as "power to," as distinguished from "power over,"[151] is uniquely feminine because it is a product of women's experience of power through motherhood. As mothers, women create life and nurture children; consequently, women develop a form of female power that is creative, beneficent and generative.[152] I refer to this understanding of power as feminist because its focus is on empowerment, whether achieved through the direct production of ideas or art, through stimulating productive effort in others, or through heightening vitality.[153]

In contrast to patriarchal forms of power, which are grounded upon material resources, feminist power is a capacity or relation between people, and thus draws its legitimacy from the existence of a community.[154] Power in the community emanates horizontally and is distributed in a web-like pattern; those who exercise power are positioned at the center of the group, where they act to mobilize others.[155] Such a structure exists in marked contrast to patriarchal distributions of power, which are typically envisioned as hierarchical, with the power-wielders positioned at the top of a pyramidal structure.[156]

Finally, feminist power is realized by acting collectively through communities to accomplish change. Feminine leadership is empowering and participatory in nature.[157] Grassroots feminist mobilization has followed this pattern of collective empowerment, empow-

---

[149] *Id.* at 225–26.

[150] *See, e.g.*, Jean B. Miller, Toward A New Psychology of Women 116 (2d ed. 1986) (power may be defined as "the capacity to implement," or the ability to influence others without controlling, limiting or destroying them).

[151] *See* French, *supra* note 34, at 505.

[152] *See* Adrienne Rich, Of Woman Born: Motherhood As Experience and Institution 73 (1976); Haunani-Kay Trask, Eros and Power: The Promise of Feminist Theory 149 (1986).

[153] *See* Crain, *supra* note 23, at 55–56.

[154] Hannah Arendt, On Violence 44, 52 (1969).

[155] Crain, *supra* note 23, at 66–71 (describing empirical evidence of existence of distinctly feminine style of exercising power).

[156] French, *supra* note 34, at 299–300; Crain, *supra* note 23, at 18.

[157] Crain, *supra* note 23, at 68.

ering individual women through group consciousness-raising that examines women's position within their families, within their social units, and ultimately, within the larger political context.[158] The development of a bond between women based upon common membership in a marginalized and oppressed group has helped to prevent the replication of patriarchal concepts and practices of power. Women's awareness of the reality of interdependence and women's experience with caring and nurturing tends to result in an assumption of responsibility for others, rather than an urge to dominate them.[159]

B. *The Communitarian Model of Power Dispersion*

Feminist power, with its emphasis on community, connection and cooperation, is most consistent with communitarianism, a theory of power allocation that favors similar values.[160] Some scholars have characterized the cultural feminist work of Gilligan as itself embodying an articulation of a communitarian philosophy because it privileges values of connection and caring, and thus contains an implicit critique of individualism.[161]

---

[158] *See* CATHARINE A. MACKINNON, TOWARD A FEMINIST THEORY OF THE STATE 83–90 (1989) (describing process of consciousness-raising through which contemporary feminist analysis of women's social condition has been shaped and shared).

[159] *See* GILLIGAN, *supra* note 16, at 30. Of course, this has not been universally true. For example, the white, middle and upper class women's "equal opportunity" movement has historically excluded women of color and working class women. *See supra* note 5 and accompanying text. In the process, it has often replicated the patriarchal practice of power by privileging some women (white, middle and upper class women) at the expense of others (women of color and working class women) who occupy lower status positions in the social hierarchy. *See* Crain, *supra* note 23, at 77.

[160] A number of writers have noted the similarity between cultural feminist values (such as those articulated by Carol Gilligan and her disciples) and communitarian values. *See, e.g.*, Marilyn Friedman, *Feminism and Modern Friendship: Dislocating the Community*, 99 ETHICS 275, 275–77 (1989) (anti-individualist developments in feminist thought are strikingly similar to those in new communitarianism); Linda J. Lacey, *Introducing Feminist Jurisprudence: An Analysis of Oklahoma's Seduction Statute*, 25 TULSA L.J. 775, 783 (1990) (much feminist jurisprudence is communitarian, emphasizing ideals of cooperation and connection instead of competition and autonomy); Joan C. Williams, *Feminism's Search for the Feminine: Essentialism, Utopianism, and Community*, 75 CORNELL L. REV. 700, 708–09 (1990) (feminism, like communitarianism, struggles to resolve tension between value of connection and tendency toward essentialism and devaluation of diversity); *see also* Alex M. Johnson, *The New Voice of Color*, 100 YALE L.J. 2007, 2054 n.198 (1991) (arguing that critical race theory, like the "difference" strand of feminist theory, is communitarian).

[161] *See* Stephen L. Pepper, *Autonomy, Community and Lawyers' Ethics*, 19 CAP. U. L. REV. 939, 941–42 (1990) (Gilligan's message resonates with and reinforces the message of communitarians that connection and relation are as important as freedom and independence).

Communitarians perceive the self as a being shaped and defined by its attachments, including its social relationships, family and community ties, and its historical context.[162] The self is contextual, and the individual "is viewed as part of the community, simultaneously shaping the community to which [s]he belongs and being shaped by it" through a continuing dialogue.[163]

The "new communitarianism" that has spawned such popular books as *Habits of the Heart: Individualism and Commitment in American Life*[164] has evolved largely as a critique of possessive individualism. The essence of communitarianism is described as "a *deemphasizing* of *individualism* and *individual rights*—which are so important for the liberal view of self—and privileging of the individual's role in the community so as to realize the attainment of right actions that lead to good consequences within the larger community."[165] Communitarians acknowledge the inherent potential for tension between the larger good and self-interest, and suggest that our contemporary understanding of love is predicated on an individualism so deeply ingrained that it shapes the very meaning of love, creating conflict where there may be none.[166] They posit a form of individualism that is fulfilled in community rather than against it.[167]

Some feminists have criticized communitarian theory because its historical focus on traditional communities, particularly the family, condones traditional communal norms of gender subordination.[168] Nevertheless, communitarian theory retains sufficient appeal to justify efforts at re-conceptualizing it within the context of chosen, voluntary communities, rather than limiting it to the traditional communities of family, neighborhood, school and church.[169] Marilyn Friedman goes further, displaying a willingness to demarcate pro-active[170] communities by reference to immutable

---

[162] *See* Michael Sandel, Liberalism and the Limits of Justice 179–81 (1982); Friedman, *supra* note 160, at 275–76; Alexander, *supra* note 16, at 23; *see also* Alasdair MacIntyre, After Virtue 6–21 (1981); Amy Gutman, *Communitarian Critics of Liberalism*, 14 Phil. & Pub. Aff. 308, 310 (1985).

[163] Johnson, *supra* note 160, at 2056.

[164] Robert N. Bellah et al., Habits of the Heart: Individualism and Commitment in American Life (1985).

[165] Johnson, *supra* note 160, at 2055.

[166] *See* Bellah et al., *supra* note 164, at 108.

[167] *Id.* at 162.

[168] *See* Friedman, *supra* note 160, at 280–81.

[169] *Id.* at 287–88. Kathleen Sullivan has expressed similar ideas in the context of republican theory. *See* Sullivan, *supra* note 72, at 1714.

[170] By "pro-active" I refer to chosen, voluntary communities; but it means more than

traits such as sex and race. To this end, Friedman defines a "community of choice" as "a community of people who share a common oppression."[171]

Indeed, gender subordination norms have been so central to communitarianism that the characteristics that distinguish it from republicanism, which shares a similar exclusionary history, are often overlooked.[172] Suzanna Sherry has argued that a feminine perspective is most consistent with a classical republican (Jeffersonian) system of power allocation, in contrast to a masculine perspective, which parallels pluralist liberal theory.[173] Sherry uses the terms "republicanism" and "communitarianism" interchangeably, ignoring fundamental differences between the two traditions.[174] In com-

---

that here—it connotes the formation of groups initiated by their members for the purpose of ending oppression.

[171] Friedman, *supra* note 160, at 289–90. Sullivan disagrees with such an approach in republican theory because it tends to institutionalize involuntary group cleavages in politics. *See supra* note 72 and accompanying text.

[172] *See supra* text accompanying note 63.

[173] *See, e.g.*, Sherry, *supra* note 45, at 543. Sherry is careful to distinguish a "feminine" perspective from a "feminist" perspective. In her view, the former refers to the theory of women's moral and psychological development articulated by Carol Gilligan, Nel Noddings and Jean Baker Miller. *See id.* at 580 n.168. The latter, exemplified by the work of Zillah Eisenstein, Jean Bethke Elshtain, Catharine MacKinnon and Diane Polan, is associated with a political agenda. *See id.* at 583 & n.172.

[174] *See id.* at 592, 601, 604. Sherry is not alone. See also Johnson, *supra* note 160, at 2011, who uses the two terms together as synonyms ("communitarian/republican"). Johnson acknowledges that a "semantic distinction" can be drawn between communitarianism as a political philosophical theory of the individual's role within a community, and republicanism as a vision of participatory government that is grounded in communitarianism. *Id.* at 2054 n.195.

Sherry describes the republican value of community and argues that republicanism is group-focused, exalting the "good of the whole over the good of its individual members." Sherry, *supra* note 45, at 551. The anti-pluralist nature of republicanism follows inevitably from its anti-individualism; an important object of republican government is to structure a shared, common value system for the community. *Id.* at 555. Thus, a republican system of government has as its primary purpose the definition and prioritization of community values and the creation, through education of the citizenry, of the public and private virtue necessary to achieve those values. *Id.* at 551–52.

Although citizens in the republic have a right to participate in defining the public good, their means of participation is not so clear. *See id.* at 555. Because Sherry favors the concept of direct popular representation that is central to classical republican theory, she eschews the "elitist, anti-egalitarian" features of Madisonian republicanism. *Id.* at 552 n.26. Nevertheless, she acknowledges the value of "wisdom and judgment" in government, and thus necessarily accepts along with it the elitist assumption that only certain citizens are sufficiently virtuous to serve as representatives of the populace in government. *See id.* at 555. Eventually, Sherry argues, both Hamilton and Jefferson came to doubt the capacity of the common people for virtue; Hamilton sought to address the problem by limiting participation in government to the wealthy, who were ostensibly of better moral character than the poor, while Jefferson abandoned virtue altogether as the basis of good government, turning to a system of a

munitarianism, unlike republicanism, control is from the bottom up, rather than from the top down. Participatory government, rather than representative democracy, is the goal, and consensus, rather than majority rule, is the guiding principle. Further, instead being a means to an end—for example, establishing rules to govern the community or to further virtuous ideals that the government has selected—the process of participatory government *is* the end.

It is the process of decisionmaking in communitarian systems that renders communitarianism compatible with feminist theory. The process of participating fully and directly in community value-setting is itself a source of empowerment. This is a central tenet of both cultural and radical feminism.[175]

Perhaps it is understandable that legal theorists who have focused on republicanism have ignored the significance of participatory democracy, thereby blurring the distinction between republicanism and communitarianism.[176] Most theorists have considered communitarianism either as an ethical/jurisprudential concept,[177] or as political theory suitable for adoption in national government.[178] Undeniably, participatory democracy, focused as it is on the elimination of hierarchy and on decentralization, works best in small, homogeneous communities.[179] Size restriction enables the maintenance of collective control and the development of a sense of com-

---

balance of powers in government to maintain order among competing factions. *Id.* at 557–59. Ultimately, Sherry explains, the triumph of modern liberalism was the result of the Jeffersonian shift in focus from ennobling the human spirit to regulating conflicting interests characteristic of the "baser aspects" of human nature. *Id.* at 559–61.

[175] According to Gilligan, both men and women recognize the need for agreement on common values, but they see the process of reaching agreement as mediated in different ways: for men, the process is to be handled "impersonally through systems of logic and law," for women it must be achieved "personally through communication in relationship." Gilligan, *supra* note 16, at 29. According to MacKinnon, feminist efforts are directed not only toward obtaining for women the right to "play with the boys," but also toward obtaining the right to participate in the process of rule-making, "to question why the point and ethic of sports is competition." Catharine A. MacKinnon, Feminism Unmodified 28 (1987).

[176] *See* Pope, *supra* note 45, at 303 (as republicanists have moved toward a focus on direct participation by ordinary citizens in government, they have been confronted by the dilemma of size: "[h]ow are disempowered groups to engage in nationwide dialogue and law making?").

[177] *See, e.g.*, Sherry, *supra* note 45, at 592 (describing the feminine communitarian jurisprudence of Justice O'Connor).

[178] *See, e.g.*, Michelman, *supra* note 45, at 1493–94; Sunstein, *supra* note 45, at 1539; Sunstein, *supra* note 54, at 47–48; Sunstein, *supra* note 62, at 429.

[179] *See* Joyce Rothschild & J. Allen Whitt, The Cooperative Workplace: Potentials and Dilemmas of Organizational Democracy and Participation 137–41 (1986) (describing conditions that facilitate participatory democracy).

munity, while homogeneity fosters group cohesion and eases the process of consensus decisionmaking.[180]

Nevertheless, the possibility that communitarianism might function well in groups whose composition is determined through voluntary associations based upon common oppression[181] remains relatively uncharted territory.[182] Several characteristics suggest that the workplace might provide a fertile ground for such communities. Work is a primary source of civic virtue.[183] A primary goal of communitarianism in the context of the workplace would be the alteration of the meaning of work in our society, a "reappropriation of the idea of vocation or calling, a return in a new way to the idea of work as a contribution to the good of all and not merely as a means to one's own advancement."[184]

---

[180] *Id.*; *accord* Staughton Lynd, *Prospects For the New Left*, *in* STAUGHTON LYND & GAR ALPEROVITZ, STRATEGY AND PROGRAM: TWO ESSAYS TOWARD A NEW AMERICAN SOCIALISM 1, 25 (1973).

[181] *See supra* text accompanying note 169.

[182] Such voluntary associations based upon a common oppression are typically organized on a model of participatory democracy. In a limited-scope empirical study of workplace collectives and cooperatives, Rothschild and Whitt describe the following structural attributes as typical of these communitarian groups: (1) authority resides in the collective as a whole, rather than attaching to individuals by virtue of their status in the hierarchy; (2) compliance with the group's goals is determined by consensus of the collective, rather than by fixed rules implemented by leaders; (3) there exists a practice of addressing problems on an ad hoc, individualized basis, guided by ethics, rather than a practice of resolving dilemmas by application of fixed and rigid rules; (4) social control is maintained through personal or moral appeals rather than through standardized rules and sanctions; (5) an ideal of community, rather than of impersonality, is observed; (6) solidarity incentives are primary, while material incentives are secondary; (7) employment is based on socio-political values and personality, rather than upon formal credentials; (8) there exists a lack of hierarchy, characterized by an egalitarian structure; and (9) division of labor and segmentation of role or function are minimized, replaced by wholistic roles. *See* ROTHSCHILD & WHITT, *supra* note 179, at 50–64; *see also* Joyce Rothschild-Whitt, *The Collectivist Organization: An Alternative to Rational-Bureaucratic Models*, 44 AM. SOC. REV. 509, 519 (1979) (table outlining dimensions).

[183] *See* BELLAH ET. AL, *supra* note 164, at 288.

[184] *Id.* at 287–88. The authors' concern is with worker isolation and alienation. Where work is interesting but lacks social utility (e.g., that done by many professionals), we must cultivate a sense of the institution's contribution to the public good. Where routine work is involved, it can be improved by affording workers a voice in the running of their enterprises. *Id.* at 288.

In this regard, the authors echo the concerns of Karl Klare, Erich Fromm and Michael Lerner. *See* ERICH FROMM, THE SANE SOCIETY 121–22 (1955) (modern workers' lack of control over what is made, how it is made and how it will be used causes them to be alienated from their work); MICHAEL LERNER, SURPLUS POWERLESSNESS 101, 333–34 (1986) (roots of occupational stress lie in lack of power workers have to control production); Karl E. Klare, *The Labor Management Cooperation Debate: A Workplace Democracy Perspective*, 23 HARV. C.R.-C.L. L. REV. 39, 44 (1988) (advocating goal of active self-actualization and realization in work, an experience of work that is developmental).

Second, employer opposition to the organization of workplace communities of employees would strengthen, rather than weaken, such an organization: the community's solidarity and sense of purpose tend to solidify in response to opposition, rendering it an ideal "alternative" form of organization.[185] Third, communitarism is most likely to succeed where it is combined with a social movement orientation, such as the labor movement, because orientation to a larger movement lessens the risk of cooptation.[186] Finally, participation in cooperative institutions organized around a communitarian perspective itself educates members and generates further participation by positively reinforcing earlier efforts.[187] Direct action participation in such organizations teaches members how to participate effectively in governance. Once they become accustomed to self-governance, they will want more, and will generalize their experience to the national level.[188] Unlike the defensive nature of participation in a republican system of representative government, which exists to protect private interests, direct participation is power-generating.[189] Consequently, communitarianism holds greater transformative potential to redistribute power to working people, particularly women, than does republicanism.[190]

C. *The Communitarian Model in Labor Law Jurisprudence*

The original craft unions typical of the early labor movement were communal in character, and sought to advance egalitarian values and radical social ideals.[191] The communitarian character of the labor movement continued into the late nineteenth century, encompassing unskilled worker organizations.[192] By the late nineteenth century, however, labor leaders had abandoned their original communal structure in favor of a bureaucratic structure that mir-

---

[185] RICK FANTASIA, CULTURES OF SOLIDARITY: CONSCIOUSNESS, ACTION AND CONTEMPORARY AMERICAN WORKERS 25 (1988).

[186] ROTHSCHILD & WHITT, *supra* note 179, at 140.

[187] *Id.* at 14.

[188] *See id.* at 13.

[189] *Id.*

[190] Because of their commitment to providing working models for future society, members of cooperatives and collectives see themselves as engaged in a process of "'pre-revolutionary structure-making.'" *Id.* at 17 (quoting MARTIN BUBER, PATHS OF UTOPIA (1960)). They are "'creating organizations of people's power'" in opposition to capitalism. *Id.* (quoting a subject in the author's study of communitarian groups).

[191] HECKSCHER, *supra* note 8, at 16–17; Crain, *supra* note 23, at 20.

[192] HECKSCHER, *supra* note 8, at 16–17.

rored the large corporations they opposed.[193] Along with this change in structure came a shift in labor's philosophy of unionism towards a focus on wage gains and concrete benefits, and away from radical political goals.[194]

Some commentators believe that the shift away from communitarianism as the system of power allocation, became inevitable as the labor movement aged and grew. James Morone has theorized that Americans feel a "democratic wish," the motivating force that drives us toward communal democracy and results in institution-building, but is nevertheless ultimately destined to fail.[195] Morone describes the "democratic wish" as a vision of "a single, united people, bound together by a consensus over the public good which is discerned through direct citizen participation in community settings."[196] Ironically, although it is our suspicion of state power that propels our democratic impulse, our efforts toward achieving direct democracy have, in the end, only served to strengthen the bureaucracy of government.[197] However radical they may be at their outset, the institutions we create only succeed in further bureaucratizing and empowering the government.

Though it makes for powerful rhetoric, "the people" is merely a political fiction, the "democratic wish" a utopian vision that cannot be achieved; thus, communal democracy is a myth.[198] It accomplishes "large changes but small victories."[199] Morone explains this process of de-radicalization through invocation of the "democratic wish." In his analysis, pressure for government action is blocked by the checks of a liberal state; entrenched interests mobilize conservative allies by raising the specter of socialism, and existing bureau-

---

[193] *See* Crain, *supra* note 23, at 21.

[194] *See id.*

[195] JAMES A. MORONE, THE DEMOCRATIC WISH: POPULAR PARTICIPATION AND THE LIMITS OF AMERICAN GOVERNMENT 5, 7 (1990). According to Morone, Americans experience simultaneous dread and yearning with regard to the allocation of power; we dread the power of the state, which poses a threat to individual liberty, while we yearn for direct, communal democracy. *Id.* at 1.

[196] *Id.* at 7. The democratic wish has four components: an image, a method, an assumption and a setting. *Id.* at 5–7. The image is of the people as a single, united political entity, an alternative locus of political authority. *Id.* at 5. The method is direct citizen participation in politics, filtered through small republics. *Id.* at 5–6. The assumption is that the people form a homogeneous body with a consensus about the shared public interest. *Id.* at 6. The setting is the community. *Id.* at 7.

[197] *Id.* at 1.

[198] *Id.* at 4.

[199] *Id.* at 9.

cracies limit the possibilities for government action.[200] Reformers overcome the standoff by calling on the people, thereby invoking the "democratic wish."[201] The issues are returned to the relevant "community," which implements new programs, only to have the imagined consensus of the people deteriorate into a clash of interests, with previously suppressed groups vying for political legitimacy.[202] Retrenchment follows, as the imperatives of organizational maintenance replace the enthusiasm of mobilization.[203] Ultimately, the new groups are incorporated into the existing structure, and the administrative power of the government is extended still further.[204]

Applying his analysis to the organized labor movement, Morone argues that President Roosevelt's call to the people, using rhetoric drawn from the republican tradition, triggered the mobilization of workers into labor unions.[205] The union structure reconfigured patterns of representation within the labor movement, and the issue of the conflict between the interests of labor and capital was returned to the workplace, with "industrial democracy" framed as the common goal.[206] The search for community yielded conflicts between workers as well as between capital and labor, and the newly-created administrative organizations wielded new state authority in labor relations.[207] Ultimately, a new class of political participant was legitimated: the labor union.[208] Class struggle was transformed into a dispute over representation.[209] The workers themselves were induced to restructure the labor movement, and to create the bureaucracy that now restrains them.[210] Labor unions now fight for "marginal gains, their own stability and the preservation of the new institutional status quo."[211]

---

200 *Id.* at 27.
201 *Id.* at 27–28.
202 *Id.* at 28.
203 *Id.* at 28–29.
204 *Id.* at 29.
205 *Id.* at 146.
206 *See id.* at 145–85.
207 *Id.*
208 *Id.* at 184.
209 *See id.* at 145–85.
210 *Id.* at 184–85.
211 *Id.* at 185. In the end, Morone says, "a less grandiose democratic conception might offer more real power to real people." *Id.* at 7. Morone calls for a refocusing on communitarian values, which he contends are more fragile than individualistic values. *Id.* at 335. Despite the fact that the communal impulse has not yet found a permanent home at the center of our political institutions, the democratic wish has endured, constantly resurfacing

Nevertheless, labor law itself continues to reflect the "democratic wish." In contrast to liberal political theory, with its focus on individual rights, the labor laws revolve around a qualitatively different kind of right: workers' right, guaranteed in section 7 of the NLRA, "to engage in . . . concerted activities for . . . mutual aid or protection."[212] As Staughton Lynd has described it, the right guaranteed in section 7 is a "translation into law of the labor movement concept of 'solidarity.'"[213] That right resonates with its communitarian underpinnings.

The National Labor Relations Board originally held that an employee covered by a collective bargaining agreement engages in protected concerted activity whenever she exercises a right guaranteed by the agreement, whether she acts on her own or in connection with others.[214] Subsequently, the NLRB concluded that, even in the absence of a collective bargaining agreement, the efforts of a single worker could constitute protected activity if the worker sought to address safety concerns that all employees might reasonably be expected to share.[215] These NLRB rulings captured the essence of the group right protected in section 7: one person's enjoyment or exercise of a collective right does not subtract from another's enjoyment or exercise of the same right.[216]

In the 1980s, however, the NLRB reversed itself, ruling that a solitary employee's action is not concerted unless it is engaged in "with or on the authority of other employees."[217] The Board reasoned that the NLRA requires "some linkage to group action" in order for an individual employee's activity to be deemed "con-

---

in the shape of a new social movement. *Id.* at 336–37. We must, Morone suggests, search for a more workable form of popular participation that will "marr[y] democratic wishes to contemporary institutions." *Id.* at 335–36.

[212] 29 U.S.C. § 157 (1988).

[213] Lynd, *supra* note 19, at 494; *see also* Richard M. Fischl, *Self, Others, and Section 7: Mutualism and Protected Protest Activities Under the National Labor Relations Act*, 89 COLUM. L. REV. 789, 850–51 (1989) (elaborating on the origin of section 7's "mutual aid or protection" language in the labor movement and its ethos of class-based solidarity).

[214] *See* Interboro Contractors, Inc., 157 N.L.R.B. 1295, 1301–02 (1966) (holding that complaints concerning working conditions covered by the collective bargaining agreement were protected activity).

[215] *See* Alleluia Cushion Co., 221 N.L.R.B. 999 (1975) (solitary employee's complaints about safety conditions in workplace, where no collective agreement was in effect, were protected activity).

[216] *See* DENNIS CHONG, COLLECTIVE ACTION AND THE CIVIL RIGHTS MOVEMENT 2–4 (1991) (goals such as civil rights, women's rights and peace are public goods, and the benefits of these goods are not susceptible to "crowding").

[217] Meyers Indus., Inc., 268 N.L.R.B. 493, 497 (1984) (*Meyers I*).

certed."[218] The D.C. Circuit Court of Appeals affirmed the Board's interpretation of the NLRA;[219] the Second Circuit has concurred.[220]

The NLRA's statutory right to engage in collective action, unique in our jurisprudence, is central to the essence of what labor unions are, or could be, about. I join Staughton Lynd in suggesting that this right should serve as a building block in a new movement to restore "from below" the vigor of the labor movement.[221] The right to engage in collective action is a clear reflection of Morone's "democratic wish," although it remains dormant as a result of union complacency, powerlessness, and the NLRA interpretations that have undermined its efficacy. An infusion of new ideas, strategies and goals is required to resuscitate it, lest the labor movement sink further into stagnation.[222]

III. Critiques of the NLRA and Proposals for Reform

Labor scholars have mounted numerous critiques of the labor laws, the system of collective bargaining and labor unions themselves.[223] The vast majority of these critiques either accept the fundamental premises and values of the adversarial system—hierarchy, competition and linear, bi-polar thinking—or they proceed from an individualistic, rights-based approach that necessarily entails privileging the rights of one individual or group "over" those of another, which is a more subtle form of hierarchy.[224] Thus, both lines of analysis revolve around a partriarchal conception of power as one individual's ability to control another.[225] Neither critique is predi-

---

[218] Meyers Indus., Inc., 281 N.L.R.B. 882, 883–84 (1986) (*Meyers II*) (on remand from the D.C. Circuit Court of Appeals, which had required further explication of the Board's reasoning and its basis in the NLRA, in Prill v. NLRB, 755 F.2d 941, 956–57 (D.C. Cir.), *cert. denied*, 474 U.S. 948 (1985)).

[219] Prill v. NLRB, 835 F.2d 1481, 1485 (D.C. Cir. 1987).

[220] *See* Ewing v. NLRB, 861 F.2d 353, 361 (2d Cir. 1988).

[221] *See* Lynd, *supra* note 19, at 494–95; *see also* Staughton Lynd & Alice Lynd, *Labor in the Era of Multinationalism: The Crisis in Bargained-For Fringe Benefits*, 93 W. Va. L. Rev. 907, 912, 944 (1991) (advocating a "rebuilding of the labor movement from below by grassroots direct action," "in the spirit of 'an injury to one is an injury to all'").

[222] *See* Chong, *supra* note 216, at 197.

[223] *See supra* note 13 and sources cited therein.

[224] The sole exception is the communitarian critique articulated by Staughton Lynd. *See supra* notes 19, 180, 213 and accompanying text, and works of Staughton Lynd cited therein.

[225] Indeed, both theories can be conceptualized as dealing with an individual's or group's entitlement to property or resources over and against another's entitlement. *See* Lynd, *supra* note 19, at 494.

cated on the feminist conception of power described in Section II.A.[226]

A. *The Adversarial Theory*

Adversarialists picture the interests of labor and management as inherently conflicting, and either support collective bargaining as an appropriate mechanism for channeling that conflict, or criticize it for masking and defusing workers' power. In either event, they view labor-management relations as a struggle for control: over the production process, over working conditions, and ultimately, over distribution of the profits.[227]

Adversarialists who defend the collective bargaining system as a proper channeling of the inevitable conflict between employers and employees typically propose incremental reforms in the labor laws.[228] Paul Weiler is a well-known incrementalist. He articulates coherent proposals for repair of existing labor laws that are nonetheless loyal to the adversarial underpinnings of the NLRA.[229] Clyde

---

[226] *See supra* notes 149–59 and accompanying text.

[227] *See, e.g.*, Barbara Reisman & Lance Compa, *The Case for Adversarial Unions*, HARV. BUS. REV., May-June 1985, at 22, 30 (healthy conflict is organic to capitalist system).

[228] *See* Millspaugh, *supra* note 13, at 697–98 (incrementalists do not challenge fundamental assumptions of existing regime, preferring to focus on adjustments to existing structure). Some adversarialists, of course, do not propose any changes at all. *See, e.g.*, *Collective Bargaining as an Industrial System*, *supra* note 121, at 1680 (defending adversarial model of labor relations because it confines industrial strife within "relatively stable bounds," and advocating strict judicial construction of section 8(a)(2) to promote necessary separation between employer and workers). The author of the above-cited work worries that even incremental reforms may undermine the adversarial nature of the Act. *See id.* at 1682 ("The courts that have attempted to reinterpret section 8(a)(2) [to permit cooperative employee representation plans] have failed to recognize that pulling this single thread may ultimately threaten the entire fabric of the Act.").

[229] *See* Fried, *supra* note 11, at 1017–18. Fried cites and briefly discusses two of Weiler's works: *Promises To Keep*, *supra* note 13 (suggesting reform modeled on Canadian labor law to allow union certifications based upon authorization card counts), and *Striking a New Balance*, *supra* note 13 (proposing compulsory arbitration over deadlocks in first union contracts, reversal of the *Mackay Radio* rule allowing permanent replacement of strikers, relaxed rules against secondary boycotts, and firmer union controls over workers through increased power to discipline members). *Id.*

In his most recent work, Weiler continues to defend the collective bargaining system, attributing unions' decline primarily to two factors: increased employer opposition and cumbersome legal procedures blocking unionization. *See* WEILER, GOVERNING THE WORKPLACE, *supra* note 13, at 108–18. Although Weiler also makes brief reference to changes in popular attitudes toward unions, and calls for the union movement itself to "refurbish its own structure, platform, and image," he apparently sees union structure and image as a problem only with respect to the "new breed" of worker (white-collar, technical, administrative and professional employees) to whom the traditional union is unappealing. *Id.* at 106–08. As one commentator has noted, Weiler's focus on employer anti-union efforts and legal

Summers, another prominent incrementalist, advocates shoring up the collective bargaining system in unionized workplaces, and extending it to cover non-unionized employees.[230]

Other adversarialists, sometimes contradictorily referred to as "cooperationists," are critical of the collective bargaining system *because* it promotes confrontational behavior on the part of unions.[231] They too subscribe to the underlying assumption that a struggle for control between employers and workers is inevitable; their position is that openly confrontational strategies promote unnecessary hostility between management and labor, ultimately leading to inefficiency.[232] Cooperationists strive to make the inevitable struggle between labor and management "kinder and gentler" by

---

obstacles to unionization prevents him from examining more closely unions' failure to adapt to changing workplace realities. *See* Samuel Issacharoff, *Reconstructing Employment*, 104 HARV. L. REV. 607, 630 (1990) (book review). Ultimately, Weiler concedes that incremental labor law reform may be insufficient to accomplish the broader goal of an independent employee voice in the corporate system, but remains optimistic about the potential of the combined effects of social and institutional changes and serious statutory reform. *See* WEILER, GOVERNING THE WORKPLACE, *supra* note 13, at 275–79.

[230] *See* Summers, *supra* note 13, 19–34.

[231] By "cooperationists," I refer to those who advocate new forms of cooperative ventures in which "management forms a long-term partnership with labor and engages labor's input in the early stages of planning, decision-making, and development," but that leaves the ultimate decisionmaking power with management. *See* Lori M. Beranck, Comment, *The Saturnization of American Plants: Infringement or Expansion of Workers' Rights?*, 72 MINN. L. REV. 173, 179 (1987). *See also infra* note 234 and accompanying text.

[232] Adversarialists and cooperationists are often portrayed in the industrial relations literature as having antithetical positions. The adversarial versus cooperation debate usually takes the form of disagreement over the interpretation of section 8(a)(2). *See supra* note 121 and accompanying text. Many commentators have assumed that the adversarial and cooperative models are distinct, alternative and fundamentally incompatible. *See* Clarke, *supra* note 92, at 2021, 2023 (describing the cooperative model as "diametrically opposed" to the adversarial model, and proposing that workers be offered the choice between adversarial or cooperative representation); Kohler, *supra* note 121, at 499–500, 513, 517–18. As others have pointed out, however, the polarization between the two positions is exaggerated, and reforms that blend the two are possible. *See, e.g.*, Klare, *supra* note 184, at 51, 60 ("[P]roductive cooperation *requires* the existence of autonomous, collective organization of workers, a central feature of adversarialism."); Lipsky, *supra* note 129, at 669–70 ("The adversarial model, based on scientific management theories, and the cooperative model, based on humanistic theories, are not mutually exclusive.").

In short, the adversarial and cooperative models, rather than being antithetical, are correspondent. Differences between them are superficial. Adversarialists posit "pure conflict"—that the interests of labor and management are irreconcilable, and therefore favor direct confrontation. Cooperationists purport to ignore the conflicts and argue that "pure consensus" exists—that the interests of labor and management in such matters as efficiency and productivity are identical. *See* Joel Cutcher-Gershenfeld, *The Impact on Economic Performance of a Transformation in Workplace Relations*, 44 INDUS. & LAB. REL. REV. 241, 242 n.1 (1991). A few, more sophisticated commentators acknowledge the simultaneous possibility of a conflict and a convergence of interests. *See* Klare, *supra* note 184, at 62.

proposing modifications to, or broader interpretations of, NLRA section 8(a)(2) in order to pave the way for cooperative ventures.[233] Many cooperationists assume that the employer is entitled to control the workplace as a matter of right; participatory methods are utilized to make this reality more palatable for employees.[234] Other cooperationists simply value profitability, and the ability to compete internationally, more highly than the minimal additive value of the opportunity to express their hostility at the bargaining table.[235]

---

[233] *See, e.g.*, David H. Brody, Note, *The Future of Labor-Management Cooperative Efforts Under Section 8(a)(2) of the National Labor Relations Act*, 41 VAND. L. REV. 545, 574 (1988) (arguing for relaxed judicial interpretation of section 8(a)(2) that would permit cooperative employee committees that promote employee free choice); Clarke, *supra* note 92, at 2022, 2023 (proposing congressional repeal or modification of section 8(a)(2) to facilitate cooperative representation and worker participation plans, while harnessing section 8(a)(1) as a vehicle to prevent employer domination or coercion); Lipsky, *supra* note 129, at 670, 716–19 (1990) (proposing legislative and judicial changes to accommodate two-tiered "cooperative" structure with labor representatives on board of directors, with traditional adversarial relationship during bargaining at the board of director level, and cooperative, yet organized structure on the shop floor).

[234] *See* Kohler, *supra* note 121, at 547 (cooperative model is merely subtle tool for management subjugation of worker self-determination; participatory associations are "more manipulative than democratic in intent"); Sar A. Levitan & Clifford M. Johnson, *Labor and Management: The Illusion of Cooperation*, HARV. BUS. REV., Sept.-Oct. 1983, at 8 (in its present form, participative management is a placebo that "gives workers the trappings of decision-making power"); *Collective Bargaining as an Industrial System*, *supra* note 121, at 1662 n.2 (many union supporters "consider even 'benign' employee representation plans a management device to undermine union solidarity").

In effect, then, many forms of participative management only seek to sugarcoat the gap between the interests of labor and management with goodwill and improved communication. *See* Levitan & Johnson, *supra*, at 7. Indeed, some participative management schemes are inherently inconsistent with the spirit of genuine cooperation because management retains the ultimate control, exercising its power to ignore labor's demands when they conflict with profit-maximization goals. *Id.* at 9. Genuine cooperation would require that labor contribute not only to the solution of problems, but also to their perception and definition. *Id.* at 16. Karl Klare expresses the weaknesses of the pure cooperative model most succinctly, suggesting that it is characterized by "an overly exclusive focus on efficiency at the expense of the other dimensions of the employment relationship; overemphasis on attitudes, which prevents the cooperationists from seeing the historical basis of adversarialism; and failure to take account of the true structure of power within the firm." Klare, *supra* note 184, at 61.

[235] *See, e.g.*, BUREAU OF LABOR-MANAGEMENT RELATIONS AND COOPERATIVE PROGRAMS, *supra* note 120, at 141 (describing review of labor laws conducted by Department of Labor to determine whether labor laws impede efforts at labor-management cooperation; Department believes such cooperation is necessary for America to return to predominance in the world market); Klare, *supra* note 184, at 58–60 (describing call for cooperative approach to industrial relations as stressing cessation of hostilities in order to increase productivity and competitiveness of the firm; goal is to achieve voluntary alignment of the individual worker's loyalties with the objectives of the firm, as ultimately defined by management).

B. *Individual Rights Theorists*

Individual rights theorists also assume an inevitable conflict of interest between management and labor, but approach the issue on an individual level rather than on a group or class-based level. These theorists argue for radical, innovative reform that purports to give maximum rein to individual employees in realizing their interests. The conservative line of critical attack is led by Richard Epstein, who advocates deregulation and proposes that the NLRA be replaced by a common law regime based on tort and contract law.[236] Another prominent conservative, Charles Fried, proposes replacing collective bargaining with improved legislation setting minimal terms of employment, thus specifically conferring rights on individual employees.[237]

At the opposite end of the political spectrum, but nevertheless equally concerned with individual employee rights, are the Critical Legal Studies scholars. These academics oppose deregulation and privatization because such reforms effectively reinforce pre-existing disparities in power between management and labor.[238] Although supportive of unionism and collective bargaining as tools to further workplace democracy, Critical Legal Studies proponents are troubled by the lack of efficacy of these tools in the context of the existing legal and social structure.[239] Nevertheless, such scholars share the assumption that the interests of labor and capital conflict, and believe that a rights-based system offers the best form of protection in a society where power between capital and labor is unbalanced. Accordingly, Critical Legal Studies writers propose reforms, based on direct governmental intervention guaranteeing individual rights to employees and substantive protections to unions

---

[236] *See* Epstein, *A Common Law for Labor Relations*, *supra* note 11. *See generally* Epstein, *In Defense of the Contract at Will*, *supra* note 11 (defending contract of employment at will, arguing that evolving doctrine of wrongful discharge undermines basic individual liberty of contract).

[237] *See* Fried, *supra* note 11, at 1036–37.

[238] *See* Katherine Van Wezel Stone, *The Future of Collective Bargaining: A Review Essay*, 58 U. CIN. L. REV. 477, 487 (1989) (book review).

[239] Karl Klare summarizes the common themes running through the work of Critical Legal Studies advocates, as follows:

> First, we argue that collective bargaining law articulates an ideology that aims to legitimate and justify unnecessary and destructive hierarchy and domination in the workplace. The second theme is that collective bargaining law has evolved an institutional architecture, a set of managerial and legal arrangements, that reinforces this hierarchy and domination.

Klare, *Labor Law as Ideology*, *supra* note 13, at 452.

under labor law, that are designed to alter the power imbalance between employees and employers.[240]

In the next section, I articulate a "re-vision" of labor law that is predicated upon a feminist conception of power. Because I begin with the assumption that the process of empowerment is as important as the immediate substantive outcome, I reject reforms accomplished solely through government intervention. My concern is not only with correcting the imbalance of power, but with defining and building a new form of power.

IV. An Alternative Vision

In a companion article, I argue that unions must forge a solidarity that stretches across class, gender and race boundaries to re-radicalize the labor movement.[241] In that article, as in this one, I suggest that a labor movement allied with the feminist movement and organized around a feminist conception of power would bring new vitality to unions as they struggle to empower workers, particularly women.[242] The other piece of the program for this revitalization is explored in this section: the labor laws must be altered to foster a new understanding of the exercise and allocation of power between labor and capital.

The feminist vision of power outlined above suggests different, and more radical, transformative possibilities for legal reform. The intervention strategies suggested by those who subscribe to a patriarchal understanding of power are based upon a paternalistic model, in which protectionist strategies are employed in aid of the disempowered group, labor. In this model, labor continues to be

---

[240] *See, e.g.*, Klare, *Workplace Democracy & Market Reconstruction*, *supra* note 13, at 3, 13 (proposing market reconstruction at the governmental level in support of collective bargaining); Katherine Van Wezel Stone, *Labor and the Corporate Structure: Changing Conceptions and Emerging Possibilities*, 55 U. Chi. L. Rev. 73, 152–61 (1988) (arguing that the law should be modified to give labor access to conventional levers of power, including representation on corporate boards and expanded rights to deal with corporate creditors, so that labor can pursue its interests in competition with the other constituencies of the corporation).

[241] *See* Crain, *supra* note 23, at 113–15. A simultaneous challenge to class, gender and race barriers is likely to be even more powerful than the sum of its parts. A community cannot be dealt with apart from its context, and class is not the only linkage, or even the most important linkage, among workers in a particular community. Suzanne Goldberg, *In Pursuit of Workplace Rights: Household Workers and a Conflict of Laws*, 3 Yale J.L. & Feminism 63, 102 (1991). My focus here is on gender, a context that has historically been overlooked by the labor movement. *See* Crain, *supra* note 5, at 1159–84.

[242] *See* Crain, *supra* note 23, at 115. Some express hope that the feminization of unions will initiate a new "social unionism" reminiscent of the radical, communitarian union spirit that pervaded the 1930s. *See, e.g.*, Blum, *supra* note 5, at 11.

overpowered or controlled, but it is the government rather than the employer that exercises control. By contrast, a model of intervention based on a feminist vision of power utilizes power-balancing strategies that facilitate the disempowered party's efforts to empower itself.[243] The feminist model is preferable because it enhances opportunities for autonomy, dignity, choice and decisionmaking, rather than simply substituting the court's power for that of the unempowered party, and because it is fairer, in a distributive sense.[244]

In this section, I outline the foundation of a feminist program for the feminization of the labor laws.[245] I describe a system in which (1) rights of individual workers are expanded but also are collective in nature; (2) workers could join together in decentralized "unions" only vaguely resembling those with which we are now familiar; (3) such unions would reject the narrow goal of commercial empowerment for workers in favor of a broader goal of economic, social and political empowerment; (4) participatory democracy would be the norm rather than the exception; (5) decisions would be made by persuasion and consensus rather than majoritarian vote; and (6) unions would deal with the employer in a coordinated fashion on all subjects that concern capital and labor, cooperating where possible to avoid conflict and confronting conflicts where they do exist.

Because the labor laws are explicitly designed to strike a balance of power between labor and capital, I begin with the deconstruction of the patriarchal concept of power that lies behind the labor laws. In general, I suggest abandoning the rigid, adversarial, "win-lose" mindset underlying the labor laws, in favor of a more flexible, cooperative, "win-win" philosophy. At the heart of my argument is an assumption that the interests of labor and capital are not always,

---

243 Bender, *supra* note 4, at 892–93. Leslie Bender has made a similar argument in the context of protecting plaintiffs in tort law. *See id.* at 890–91. In *Feminist Re (Torts)*, Bender advocates that courts adopt a feminist strategy of power-balancing (through burden-shifting rules, rebuttable presumptions concerning liability, and immediacy of remedy) that would empower plaintiffs in mass tort cases who face corporate defendants with greater resources, knowledge and access to information. *Id.* at 893–94. Bender refers to this feminist modality of power as "'empowering or power-balancing,'" and contrasts it with a masculine modality of power, which she terms "'overpowering or controlling/protecting.'" *See id.* at 892; *see also* Leslie Bender, *Changing the Values in Tort Law*, 25 TULSA L.J. 759, 762–63 (1990) (synthesis of same arguments).

244 *Id.* at 890–91.

245 This proposal builds on the general outlines I suggested for the feminization of labor law in a previous work. *See* Crain, *supra* note 5, at 1214–19.

inevitably, in conflict. Thus, it is simultaneously possible for them to share some common goals and to clash over others, or to agree on goals but disagree on the means of achieving them. My argument also assumes that the relationship between labor and capital is far more complex than the simplistic adversarial cast it has acquired through tradition and law. In short, I suggest that the law should reflect the reality that the relationship between employer and employees, like any continuing relation, is multi-faceted and entails both conflict and cooperation.

My paradigm of a reconstituted labor law overlaps with some of the suggestions made by others; however, it differs in significant ways because of my focus on eliminating the patriarchal norms of power and power allocation, which are encoded as republicanism in the labor laws. The proposal that is most compatible with a feminist re-visioning is that advanced by Charles Heckscher. Heckscher is critical of the "balance of power" ideology that permeates labor law. He contends that the balance created by establishing two parallel adversaries is rigid, slow to adapt, and ill-suited for dealing with diversity among workers.[246] Heckscher advocates in its place a more flexible form of unionism, "associational unionism."[247]

A key feature of associational unionism is its tolerance for multiple forms of worker representation that would coordinate diversity within unions, thereby capitalizing on workers' ties with other social movements, such as the women's movement.[248] Another characteristic of associational unionism that is consistent with a feminist model is its mechanism for resolution of disputes, which includes extended negotiation, direct participation, deliberate clarification of values and interests, and aspirations toward consensus-building.[249]

Nevertheless, Heckscher's proposal places the burden solely on unions to transform themselves; he makes no concrete suggestions as to how the law ought to be modified in order to accommodate associational unionism. This is of particular concern because, as he acknowledges, the energy for change is centered in groups located outside the traditional labor relations system.[250] Many of these groups, such as Blacks and women, already shoulder the additional

---

[246] HECKSCHER, *supra* note 8, at 7.
[247] *See id.* at 8.
[248] *Id.* at 177, 189–90.
[249] *Id.* at 193–94.
[250] *Id.* at 191, 256.

burden of fighting oppression based on gender and/or race. Thus, Heckscher's system would place the responsibility for initiating change on these groups, rather than shifting the onus onto unions to mobilize for change through institutional restructuring.

James Pope has offered a more concrete suggestion in support of associational unionism.[251] Because the law has traditionally maintained a rigid division between labor activities (covered by the NLRA) and community protests (for which First Amendment protection is available), Pope urges a reexamination of the law to accommodate labor-community boycotts.[252] He believes that labor-community boycotts could provide a source of economic power for unions because such boycotts are a vehicle for unions to engage allies from other social movements, such as the women's and the civil rights movements, to put pressure on employers.[253] He envisions these boycotts as a practical "testing ground" for the viability of Heckscher's associational unionism.[254] Nevertheless, rather than proposing change in the labor laws or directly challenging the artificial dichotomy in the law's treatment of industrial and community activism, Pope advocates classifying labor-community boycotts in the political sphere, and according them expanded First Amendment protection because they are more political and less coercive in nature than traditional labor boycotts.[255]

Paul Weiler has articulated some useful arguments for a feminist reconstructive reform of the labor laws. Weiler accepts the balance of power ideology and adversarial assumptions behind the law, and proposes legal reforms designed to shift the balance of power toward labor's side of the equation.[256] Although Weiler does

---

[251] James G. Pope, *Labor-Community Coalitions and Boycotts: The Old Labor Law, the New Unionism, and the Living Constitution*, 69 TEX. L. REV. 889 (1991).

[252] *Id.* at 897.

[253] *Id.* at 912–13. Pope points out that both movements boast networks of experienced, committed activists that could be effective in conducting boycotts and in appealing to workers to join unions. *Id.*

[254] *Id.* at 913.

[255] *Id.* at 919–20, 973; *cf.* James G. Pope, *The Three-Systems Ladder of First Amendment Values: Two Rungs and a Black Hole*, 11 HASTINGS CONST. L.Q. 189 (1984) (describing artificial dichotomy in First Amendment law and arguing for expanded First Amendment protection for labor speech).

[256] *See* WEILER, GOVERNING THE WORKPLACE, *supra* note 13, at 275 (arguing for redesign of representation process and process by which unions negotiate first contracts). Weiler refers to this type of labor law reform as "reconstructive," in the sense that the changes proposed would "reconstruct" the background labor law, and contrasts it with a regulatory model, which, in his view, entails excessive reliance on external NLRB or judicial regulation. *Id.* at 253. The reconstructive model is superior because it enlists the workers themselves in the struggle to gain fundamental rights. *Id.*

not mount a challenge to the definition of power itself, some of his proposed reforms have the potential to modify the culture of the union and the way in which it exercises power. For example, his proposals with regard to restructuring first contract negotiations[257] and providing recognition through card counts rather than resorting to elections[258] are consistent with a feminist modality of empowerment. These proposals could establish conditions facilitating mobilization, while leaving the process of empowerment in the hands of the workers.

On the other hand, Weiler has also suggested a "constitutive" model of change, in which government legislation would guarantee all employees access to a basic level of participation in a specified range of workplace decisions.[259] I disagree with this approach because it reinforces patriarchal power and disregards the significance of the organizing process itself. Moreover, Weiler's approach devalues the process of establishing and nurturing relationships, building a community, and developing a collective rapport. These aspects of the organizing process are central to the empowerment process.[260]

A. *Eliminating the Adversarial Premise*

In order to alter the understanding of power in the labor laws at the most fundamental level, I begin with the cornerstones of the adversarial labor law system: the definition of an employee (NLRA section 2(3)), the definition of a labor organization and its relationship to the employer (NLRA sections 2(5) and 8(a)(2)), and the exclusivity provisions limiting employee voice (NLRA section 9(a)). These are the constitutive aspects of labor law, and they are the places in the law where the line-drawing that reinforces the adversarial system is anchored. All are predicated on a conception of power as domination and control, and its exercise as creating a hierarchical relation.

---

[257] *See* Weiler, *Striking A New Balance*, *supra* note 13, at 405–12; *see also*, Weiler, *Promises to Keep*, *supra* note 13, at 1805.

[258] *See* Weiler, *Promises to Keep*, *supra* note 13, at 1805.

[259] WEILER, GOVERNING THE WORKPLACE, *supra* note 13, at 282. Weiler proposes adoption of Employee Participation Committees ("EPC's"), modeled on the West German Works Council. *Id.* at 284. In such a system, the Works Council deals directly with management within the individual enterprise about the application of industry-wide standards contained in umbrella agreements negotiated by unions. *See id.* at 293–94. In Weiler's vision, EPC's would serve as a safety net for the vast majority of unorganized, unrepresented employees, and could coexist with unions to reinforce worker rights. *Id.* at 282–95.

[260] *See* Crain, *supra* note 23, at 89–96.

I have argued elsewhere that the NLRA's definition of employee should be modified to encompass the entire laboring class.[261] My explicit premise was that there exists no natural, inevitable "line" between management and labor, or insurmountable conflict of interest for managers who simultaneously seek to protect their own interests while serving those of the employer.[262] Accordingly, section 2(5) would be modified to include organizations of "employees," as newly defined in section 2(3). These changes would result in the broadest possible definitions of employees and labor organizations, enhancing the potential for worker solidarity and bringing as many workers and worker organizations as possible under the umbrella of the NLRA.

Section 8(a)(2), prohibiting employers from dominating, interfering with or assisting the formation or administration of a labor organization, should be repealed. It reinforces the "line" between employer and employees, and essentially further divides them by blocking efforts at cooperation. Moreover, section 8(a)(2) incorporates a paternalistic assumption that labor unions will not be capable of remaining loyal to their members if subjected to pressure and/or temptation from the employer. While the repeal of this section might be of some concern in the context of a dichotomy between employees and managers, and a system of exclusive union representation that encourages entrenched, centralized power, it should not present a danger to workers in a modified environment of broader NLRA coverage and non-exclusive representation.

Repeal of section 9(a)'s principle of exclusive representation is essential to a feminist reform of the labor laws. The "tight solidarity of collective action" is neither feasible nor desirable in a work force as heterogeneous as the current and projected population of workers. Consequently, unions must forego the security of exclusive representation in order to accommodate multiple, overlapping communities of workers within the same workplace unit.[263] The prin-

---

[261] *See* Crain, *supra* note 92, at 1015–20 (proposing amendment to delete exclusion of supervisors, managerial employees and confidential employees from NLRA coverage).

[262] *See id.* at 983–92.

[263] *See* Heckscher, *supra* note 8, at 183; *see also* Craver, *supra* note 13, at 655 (noting tension between the increasing heterogeneity of the work force and the section 9(a) exclusivity provision, and suggesting either repeal of section 9(a) or modification to provide a limited veto power for minorities, overridable only by a weighted majority); George Schatzki, *Majority Rule, Exclusive Representation, and the Interests of Individual Workers: Should Exclusivity Be Abolished?*, 123 U. Pa. L. Rev. 897, 938 (1975) (suggesting that abolition of exclusivity rule, particularly in light of the context of a Board unit determination process that neglects

ciple of majoritarian representation does not adequately safeguard the interests of women and minorities, given their history of exclusion from, and continuing lack of power in, labor unions. A system of coordinated diversity will contribute to a decentralized union structure and help to ensure participatory democracy rather than the re-creation, in union structure, of the hierarchical, exclusionary structure of capital. Repeal of section 9(a) will require corresponding changes in the duty of fair representation doctrine, a requisite corollary to the exclusivity doctrine under existing law.[264] The duty of fair representation, if it continued to exist at all, would likely evolve into an equal protection model of representation.[265]

B. *Additional Reforms*

Although it will not be clear exactly what further reforms are needed to conform labor law to the new unionism until these fundamental changes have been made and we gain some experience with this new unionism, I outline below some reforms that appear necessary in light of the experience of a few feminized unions. Although many of the doctrines or provisions discussed below appear to reflect neutral values, their interaction with the disparate economic power of capital and the current nature of male-dominated unions produces a decided "tilt" against a new form of union that includes previously marginalized workers, particularly women.[266]

1. Organizing

It is obvious that unions require increased access to workers in order to organize them. The existing doctrine governing union access to employees for organizational purposes gives exaggerated weight to the employer's interests in maintaining control over its property, blocking effective union access to the vast majority of

employees' community of interest, would democratize unions, make them more responsive to members' concerns, and relieve the Board of its election responsibilities).

[264] *See* Vaca v. Sipes, 386 U.S. 171, 190 (1967).

[265] *See* Michael C. Harper & Ira C. Lupu, *Fair Representation As Equal Protection*, 98 HARV. L. REV. 1211, 1216–17 (1985) (arguing that politically weak or unpopular minorities can be protected in democratic unions through application of a coherent theory of equal protection as the model for the duty of fair representation).

[266] *See* WEILER, GOVERNING THE WORKPLACE, *supra* note 13, at 228; *see also* Bender, *supra* note 4, at 884–85 (exploring concept of "equality-before-the-law," which ignores the realities of power differences and employs "neutral" rules that are "blind" (like justice) to these power imbalances).

employees.[267] It is no accident that initial success with clerical workers has been achieved in the university setting; the distinctive openness of the academy for employees and outside organizers has been a significant factor in the ability of union organizers to reach women workers, who often find it difficult to attend after-work meetings because of their double burden of child care and domestic responsibilities.[268]

Paul Weiler's suggestion that we abandon the election system in favor of instant recognition based on a super-majority card count would be helpful here.[269] The current election system is consistent with an adversary system based upon an individualistic ethic of justice. The system assumes that those who did not wish to be represented by a union will be content to live with one because the election process was fair.[270] This misconstrues the goal of unionism: an association of workers who are bound together by a perception of common interest and a feeling of community, rather than by the application of legal principles of majoritarian rule. A system of instant recognition based upon a super-majority card count, in combination with abolition of the exclusive representation principle, would be more consistent with a feminist method of empowerment and participatory democracy, which relies on consensus as the source of group power and cohesiveness. Under this system, non-signers would be free to change their minds and join the recognized group following recognition, or to form a separate organization, or to form none at all. In this way, the incentive for the organizer to

---

[267] The doctrine respecting access by outside union organizers accords undue deference to the employer's rights to control its physical property, and to protect it against trespass. *See* Lechmere, Inc. v. NLRB, 112 S. Ct. 841 (1992) and NLRB v. Babcock & Wilcox, 351 U.S. 105 (1956), discussed *supra* note 103. The law governing solicitation by employees on company property permits undue employer control over workers' labor—viewed by the Court as another form of company "property"—through no-solicitation rules. *See* Republic Aviation v. NLRB, 324 U.S. 793 (1945), discussed *supra* note 103.

[268] *See* Craig Becker, *Unions on Campus: Lessons of the Harvard Drive*, THE NATION, Feb. 12, 1990, at 196.

[269] *See* WEILER, GOVERNING THE WORKPLACE, *supra* note 13, at 253–61. Some unions have successfully utilized an 8(b)(7) strategy to obtain an expedited election, which accomplishes the goal of avoiding a lengthy campaign period while simultaneously exerting economic pressure. Once the union has enough signed authorization cards to suggest likely success in an election, it demands recognition, and when the employer refuses, the union establishes a picket with non-employees, and instructs employees to continue working. Within thirty days of the commencement of the picketing, the union files a petition for an election, validating the continuation of the picketing under § 8(b)(7)(C). *See* Bernard L. Samoff, *What Lies Ahead for the NLRB?*, 38 LAB. L.J. 259, 266–67 (1987).

[270] *See* Robin Leidner, *Stretching the Boundaries of Liberalism: Democratic Innovation in a Feminist Organization*, 16 SIGNS 263, 283 (1991).

build a large community remains intact, but the inevitable dissidents do not remain to dilute the union's power by undermining solidarity.

2. Bargaining

Two areas of reform are immediately apparent in the process of bargaining. First, as multilateral negotiation techniques are developed in order to accommodate bargaining between multiple parties, the dynamics of bargaining will change.[271] Concepts such as the duty to bargain "in good faith" must evolve in order to be meaningful in a multi-party situation. Bargaining "to impasse," for example, which normally means negotiating until the parties' positions become fixed and a stalemate occurs,[272] would take on an entirely different meaning because multiple parties would be much less likely to polarize. Because bargaining to impasse is the prerequisite to the employer's ability to implement unilateral changes in working conditions (mandatory subjects),[273] it has been a vital tool in determining the extent of employee participation in workplace governance.

Second, the implicit restrictions that the NLRA places on bargaining, by explicitly including some subjects and implicitly excluding others (the mandatory/permissive subject dichotomy), must be eliminated. These implicit restrictions are contained in section 2(5) (defining labor organizations as those that deal with employers "concerning grievances, labor disputes, wages, rates of pay, hours of employment, or conditions of work"), section 8(d) (defining duty to bargain collectively in good faith only "with respect to wages, hours, and other terms and conditions of employment"), and section 9(a) (specifying that a labor organization is the exclusive representative for the purpose of bargaining "in respect to rates of pay, wages, hours of employment, or other conditions of employment"). The subjects limitation of the NLRA serves not only to remove some of the most important decisions from the collective bargaining process, but also reinforces prevailing patterns of power in industrial life

[271] *See* HECKSCHER, *supra* note 8, at 200 (multilateral negotiation is not just a bigger form of bilateral collective bargaining).

[272] *See generally* David G. Epstein, Comment, *Impasse in Collective Bargaining*, 44 TEX. L. REV. 769, 777 (1966) (impasse requires (1) a deadlock in negotiations and (2) good faith bargaining, with particular attention to factors such as use of a mediator, changes in bargaining position, desire to continue negotiations and the frequency of bargaining negotiations).

[273] *See* NLRB v. Katz, 369 U.S. 736, 741–43 (1962).

and, ultimately, limits our imagination in rethinking issues of workplace governance.[274]

3. Concerted Activity As a Means of Economic Pressure

The collective right to engage in "concerted activities . . . for mutual aid or protection" afforded employees by section 7 of the NLRA is at the heart of the NLRA's communitarian basis. This right is an attempt to codify the experience of solidarity, and should be construed as broadly as possible. A broad construction of the "concert" requirement would recognize the industrial reality that the action of an individual worker is experienced by other workers as one in which they have a long-term stake.[275] A broad construction of the "mutual aid or protection" requirement would pave the way for innovative strategies of collective economic resistance.[276]

Conclusion

Labor law and labor unionism are at a crossroads. Pressure from employers and from competition with foreign businesses has ensured that "[t]he labor movement does not have the luxury of continuing with business as usual, even if it could somehow induce its disillusioned membership to do so."[277] I suggest that organized labor must build a new form of solidarity that is not solely class-based, but is instead forged in the common experience of oppression across race, gender and class. Feminist visions and practices of power, exercised within communitarian structures of power allocation, provide a hospitable environment for constructing the

---

274 *See* Note, *Subjects of Bargaining Under the NLRA and the Limits of Liberal Political Imagination*, 97 HARV. L. REV. 475, 479 (1983).

275 *See* Staughton Lynd, *Communal Rights*, 62 TEX. L. REV. 1417, 1426 (1984); *see also* Robert A. Gorman and Matthew W. Finkin, *The Individual and the Requirement of "Concert" under the National Labor Relations Act*, 130 U. PA. L. REV. 286, 329 (1981) (calling for broad reading of concert requirement in section 7); B. Glenn George, *Divided We Stand: Concerted Activity and the Maturing of the NLRA*, 56 GEO. WASH. L. REV. 509, 511 (1988) (same). *But cf.* Cynthia L. Estlund, *What Do Workers Want? Employee Interests, Public Interests, and Freedom of Expression Under the National Labor Relations Act*, 140 U. PA. L. REV. 921, 942, 967 (1992) (arguing for interpretation of section 7 that would protect the rights of employees to communicate and protest about matters beyond the terms and conditions of their employment; under this proposal, the concert requirement would remain intact, but determination of appropriate subjects of employee concern would be left to employees).

276 *See* Estlund, *supra* note 275, at 967; Pope, *supra* note 251, at 912–13; Crain, *supra* note 23, at 107–13.

277 Lynd & Lynd, *supra* note 221, at 944.

bridge of empathy that must serve as the connecting and stabilizing element in this new solidarity.

In a previous article, I articulated a feminist strategy for empowerment that unions might adopt in organizing, bargaining and exerting economic pressure.[278] A critical factor in its success, however, is a legal environment that facilitates, or at least is not hostile to, such routes to empowerment.[279] In this article, I have sketched the outlines of a labor law framework that would facilitate the feminization and re-radicalization of labor unions. In particular, I have argued that the current republican system of allocation, with its overlay of representation and exclusivity predicated on both internal and external union hierarchies, reinforces and perpetuates the internal division and factionalization of the labor movement. In its place, I propose the adoption of a communitarian structure, wherein multiple and overlapping communities of workers can cooperate with one another in the process of direct action empowerment.

Such a "re-visioning" of labor law will require major structural changes in the present labor laws. This is not unique to a feminist approach; in the context of the current labor crisis, most scholars agree that fundamental change is necessary.[280] What is unique about the feminist strategy I have advanced is that it proposes transformation, rather than reform; it questions fundamental, underlying assumptions about the nature of power and its exercise as reflected in our labor laws and, ultimately, in our larger political democracy. Grounded in concrete, grassroots activism, it proposes that working people "shatter the self-reflecting world which encircles [them] and . . . project [their] own image onto history" by re-visioning their own power in a revolutionary way.[281]

Perhaps what is most needed in the labor movement is a combination of revolutionary vision, anger and strength of heart. The working class movement, after all, is a social movement; its ends—political, economic and social empowerment—are far broader than the narrow "business" unionism, with its singular focus on obtaining marginal economic gains, that is commonplace in labor unions today. Unions must inspire workers by appealing to more than their

---

[278] *See* Crain, *supra* note 23.

[279] *See* CHONG, *supra* note 216, at 173–74 (noting that a sympathetic government or one that is perceived as responsive will encourage collective action).

[280] *See, e.g.*, sources cited *supra* note 13.

[281] *See* MACKINNON, *supra* note 158, at 84.

economic rationality. Instead, an appeal must be made to their emotional, affective side, and workers must be persuaded to undertake the difficult task of empowering themselves from the inside out.[282] The concept is eloquently expressed in this excerpt from a poem by Donna Kate Rushin, written for women of color:[283]

> [B]reathe
> Before you suffocate
> Your own fool self
>
> Forget it
> Stretch or drown
> Evolve or die
>
> The bridge I must be
> Is the bridge to my own power
> I must translate
> My own fears
> Mediate
> My own weaknesses
>
> I must be the bridge to nowhere
> But my true self
> And then
> I will be useful

[282] *See* Alan Hyde, *Endangered Species*, 91 COLUM. L. REV. 456, 471 (1991) (reviewing WEILER, GOVERNING THE WORKPLACE, *supra* note 13). Hyde points out that unions cannot survive or flourish if they limit themselves to economic appeals, because rational workers will choose "free ridership." *Id.* Idealistic, visionary appeals have constructed a strong collective identity, succeeding where more limited, rational approaches failed. *Id.*

[283] Donna K. Rushin, *The Bridge Poem*, *in* THIS BRIDGE CALLED MY BACK: WRITINGS BY RADICAL WOMEN OF COLOR at xxi, xxii (Cherrié Moraga & Gloria Anzaldua eds., paperback ed. 1983).

[8]

FEMINISM, LABOR, AND POWER*

MARION CRAIN**

I. INTRODUCTION

Debate rages in scholarly publications about the future relevance of labor unions.[1] Scholars have devoted significant energy to ascertaining why organized labor's represented share of the work force has declined so drastically over the last fifteen years.[2] Most assume that the answer to

---

** Associate Professor of Law, The University of Toledo; B.S. 1980, Cornell; J.D. 1983, UCLA. I am grateful for the research support provided by the Fund For Labor Relations Studies and by the University of Toledo College of Law. Thanks go to D.B. Deck and Meg Gehrke for their able research assistance and to Ken Matheny for his thoughtful critique of an earlier draft.

1. *See, e.g.*, PAUL WEILER, GOVERNING THE WORKPLACE: THE FUTURE OF LABOR AND EMPLOYMENT LAW 185 (1990) [hereinafter WEILER, GOVERNING THE WORKPLACE] (arguing that "union representation is as attractive a form of [workplace] governance [as] we have yet been able to devise" and proposing reforms designed to realign the balance of power in the representation phase and in the process by which unions negotiate first contracts); Robert J. LaLonde & Bernard D. Meltzer, *Hard Times for Unions: Another Look at the Significance of Employer Illegalities*, 58 U. CHI. L. REV. 953, 955-56 (1991) (challenging Weiler's assertion that employer illegalities during organizational-campaign and first-contract negotiations have been a major factor in the decline of unions and presenting empirical evidence suggesting otherwise); Paul Weiler, *Hard Times For Unions: Challenging Times for Scholars*, 58 U. CHI. L. REV. 1015, 1029-32 (1991) [hereinafter Weiler, *Hard Times for Unions*] (responding to LaLonde & Meltzer critique and arguing that their empirical evidence corroborates his original thesis that employer reprisals have been one significant reason for the decline in private sector union representation); Charles B. Craver, *The Vitality of the American Labor Movement in the Twenty-First Century*, 1983 U. ILL. L. REV. 633, 695 (arguing that in order for unions to survive, they must adapt to changing demographic trends, technological advances, and the internationalization of the world economic market); Karl E. Klare, *Workplace Democracy & Market Reconstruction: An Agenda for Legal Reform*, 38 CATH. U. L. REV. 1, 2 (1988) (arguing that current economic, political, and legal climates are hostile to labor law and that to counter this employee advocates must "rethink old assumptions," confront current problems, and enlarge the concept of workplace democracy); Theodore J. St. Antoine, *Federal Regulation of the Workplace in the Next Half Century*, 61 CHI.-KENT L. REV. 631, 661-62 (1985) (concluding that if unions continue to decline, governmental intervention, in the form of federal labor legislation, is unavoidable). *See generally* Julius Getman, *Is Labor Law Doing Its Job?*, 15 STETSON L. REV. 93, 93-94 (1985) (reporting widespread disillusionment with labor law in the academic community); Peter E. Millspaugh, *America's Industrial Relations Experiment: Legal Scholarship Assesses the Wagner Act*, 32 ST. LOUIS UNIV. L.J. 673 (1988) (summarizing critiques of labor law and major proposals for its reform advanced in the last decade).

2. Over the past 37 years, the percentage of the work force belonging to unions has dropped from 34.7% (in 1954) to 16.1% (in 1991). *Union Membership Unchanged at 16.1 Percent in 1991*,

the riddle of labor's numerical decline illuminates the course for rebuilding labor power and propose reforms tailored to fit their assessment of the problem.[3] Apparently believing that labor power has a material base (i.e., that increased union membership translates into financial power through the imposition of dues, and consequently into greater ability to exercise economic and political clout), critics have focused on reforms designed to increase organized labor's numbers. These critics assume that if labor's numbers increase, its power will as well.[4]

In this Article, I suggest that labor scholars have unnecessarily cabined the discussion by adopting a patriarchal vision of power as materially based, and of its exercise as synonymous with domination and control.[5] This narrow understanding of power has caused us to ignore other, less readily quantifiable potential bases of labor power. Because I believe

---

Daily Lab. Rep. (BNA) No. 28, at B-1 (Feb. 11, 1992). The bulk of the decrease in the percentage of the total work force (public and private) who are union members has occurred during the last 16 years: Union membership as a percentage of employed workers was 28.9% in 1975, compared with 16.1% in 1991. U.S. DEP'T OF COMMERCE, STATISTICAL ABSTRACT OF THE UNITED STATES 408 (1987); Marvin J. Centron, *Into the Twentieth Century*, THE FUTURIST, July-Aug. 1988, at 29, 35.

Union membership in the private work force is even lower: In 1991, only 11.9% of employees in the private sector were union members, a significant drop from the 25% who were members in 1973. *Union Membership Unchanged at 16.1 Percent in 1991*, *supra*; *Union Coverage of Private Workforce Predicted to Fall Below 5 Percent by 2000*, 3 Lab. Rel. Wk. (BNA), at 1185 (1989) [hereinafter *Union Coverage*]. The forecast for the next decade is gloomier still: Two labor economists have predicted that the percentage of the private sector work force that is unionized may fall below five percent by the year 2000. *Id.*

3. *See* sources cited *supra* note 2.

4. In fact, the decline in union membership is both a cause and an effect of organized labor's lack of power. *See* Marion Crain, *Building Solidarity Through the Expansion of NLRA Coverage: A Blueprint for Worker Empowerment*, 74 MINN. L. REV. 953, 954 (1990). In this Article, I focus on its significance as an effect rather than as a cause.

5. *See* Robin West, *Feminism, Critical Social Theory and Law*, 1989 U. CHI. LEGAL F. 59, 61-62 (observing that patriarchal power is "profoundly negative [and] censorial," has a material base, encourages hierarchical relations between men, and ultimately oppresses women). The patriarchal vision to which I refer throughout this article has elsewhere been described as a "patriarchal paradigm characterized by hierarchy, linear reasoning, the resolution of disputes through the application of abstract principles, and the ideal of the reasonable person. Its fundamental aspiration is objectivity, and to that end it separates public from private, form from substance, and process from policy." Trina Grillo, *The Mediation Alternative: Process Dangers for Women*, 100 YALE L.J. 1545, 1547 (1991).

Such a patriarchal understanding of power is not surprising among legal scholars. Indeed, the essence of law itself is patriarchal: "The whole structure of law—its hierarchical organization; its combative, adversarial format; and its undeviating bias in favor of rationality over all other values—defines it as a fundamentally patriarchal institution." Diane Polan, *Toward a Theory of Law and Patriarchy*, *in* THE POLITICS OF LAW: A PROGRESSIVE CRITIQUE 294, 301 (David Kairys ed., 1982); *see also* Janet Rifkin, *Mediation from a Feminist Perspective: Promises and Problems*, 2 LAW & INEQ. J. 21, 22 (1984) (arguing that the patriarchal paradigm of law is hierarchy, combat, and adversarialism).

that a broader conception of the source of labor's power is key to understanding and curing its weakness,[6] I advance here an alternative vision of power and its exercise in and by labor unions, informed by feminist theory and by the experience of woman-centered labor unions.[7]

At its inception, the labor movement was radical. It was socialist in nature, and its goals were far-reaching; some factions sought to challenge directly the capitalist system that distributed the bulk of the profits to capital owners.[8] The source of its power was "solidarity," which meant

---

6. The notion that power and vulnerability have the same origin is one that feminists, particularly feminists of color, have advanced. *See, e.g.*, ELIZABETH V. SPELMAN, INESSENTIAL WOMAN: PROBLEMS OF EXCLUSION IN FEMINIST THOUGHT 124-25, 132 (1988) (maintaining that being black is a source of pride as well as an occasion for being oppressed; black history and identity are cause for celebration and potential sources of power and liberation).

This concept is expressed nowhere more clearly and poignantly than in Adrienne Rich's poem *Power*:

> Living in the earth-deposits of our history
> Today a backhoe divulged out of a crumbling flank of earth
> one bottle amber perfect a hundred-year-old
> cure for fever or melancholy a tonic
> for living on this earth in the winters of this climate
>
> Today I was reading about Marie Curie:
> she must have known she suffered from radiation sickness
> her body bombarded for years by the element
> she had purified
> It seems she denied to the end
> the source of the cataracts on her eyes
> the cracked and suppurating skin of her finger-ends
> till she could no longer hold a test-tube or a pencil
>
> She died a famous woman denying
> her wounds
> denying
> her wounds came from the same source as her power

Adrienne Rich, *Power*, *in* THE DREAM OF A COMMON LANGUAGE 3 (1978).

7. Not all of the female-dominated unions discussed in this Article would be comfortable referring to themselves as "feminist" unions. Some prefer to distance themselves from the negative connotations associated with the feminist movement, particularly its more radical factions. For example, Kris Rondeau of the Harvard Union of Clerical and Technical Workers prefers the less politically loaded term "feminine" to describe the Harvard Union style of organizing. Interview with Kris Rondeau, Regional Director of AFSCME, in Boston, Mass. (June 19, 1990); *see* Minouche D. Kandel, Note, *Finding a Voice Through the Union: The Harvard Union of Clerical and Technical Workers and Women Workers*, 12 HARV. WOMEN'S L.J. 260, 268 n.49 (1989). Accordingly, although I regard as feminist any union that has as its central goal increasing female power in the workplace, *see* Marion Crain, *Feminizing Unions: Challenging the Gendered Structure of Wage Labor*, 89 MICH. L. REV. 1155, 1207-08 (1991), I will refer to such unions, and their tactics, as "woman-centered."

8. *See* MICHAEL HARRINGTON, SOCIALISM: PAST & FUTURE 28-59 (1989) (maintaining that early utopian socialism was committed to transformation of work); Martha A. Ackelsberg & Kathryn Pyne Addelson, *Anarchist Alternatives to Competition*, *in* COMPETITION: A FEMINIST TABOO? 221, 228-29 (Valerie Miner & Helen E. Longino eds., 1987) (explaining that the Industrial Workers of the World attempted to raise workers' class consciousness in order to challenge the capitalist order).

commitment to common goals, an allegiance to a community, and a tradition of participatory democracy and consensus-style decision making.[9] Since the enactment of the Wagner Act,[10] however, unions have become deradicalized;[11] most unions now mirror the hierarchical, authoritarian structure and operation of capital in the belief that this structure will enable them to battle more effectively with capital over the distribution of wealth. In the process, unions sacrificed the solidarity that once served as the source of workers' empowerment. Lacking a sense of connection and empathy with other workers in the union, members lost trust; lacking the feeling of empowerment that comes with the experience of directly effecting change, members lost faith. Trust and faith are essential to a solidarity that enables people to take risks, both economic and emotional, in a political movement.

Unions must shoulder a significant portion of the responsibility for the decline of labor.[12] Unions erred in allowing their understanding of power to be limited by the dominant patriarchal vision of power reflected in our labor laws, particularly the adversarial culture and history the labor laws reify. Motivated by self-interest, labor leaders have pursued a course destined to erode the base of labor power: solidarity. Labor economists and statisticians agree that only "exceptional increases in overall organizing activity could offset the growth in the [nonorganized service

9. *See* HARRINGTON, *supra* note 8; Staughton Lynd, *Prospects for the New Left*, *in* STAUGHTON LYND & GAR ALPEROVITZ, STRATEGY AND PROGRAM: TWO ESSAYS TOWARD A NEW AMERICAN SOCIALISM 1, 23-24 (1973).

10. Wagner Act, ch. 372, 49 Stat. 453 (1935).

11. Karl Klare has made a parallel argument with regard to the deradicalization of the Wagner Act itself. *See* Karl E. Klare, *Judicial Deradicalization of the Wagner Act and the Origins of Modern Legal Consciousness, 1937-1941*, 62 MINN. L. REV. 265 (1978).

12. Others have also placed blame on organized labor for contributing to its own decline. *See, e.g.*, STANLEY ARONOWITZ, WORKING CLASS HERO: A NEW STRATEGY FOR LABOR 125-70 (1983); Julius Getman, *Ruminations on Union Organizing in the Private Sector*, 53 U. CHI. L. REV. 45, 45-46 (1986). I do not contend that organized labor should bear the sole burden to "refurbish its own structure, platform, and image in order to make itself more appealing to the new breed of worker . . . ." *See* WEILER, GOVERNING THE WORKPLACE, *supra* note 1, at 107. Because unions took (and continue to take) their cue in understanding power from the labor laws themselves, fundamental and constitutive labor law reform is imperative. I argue this position in more detail in Marion Crain, *Images of Power in Labor Law: A Feminist Deconstruction* 33 B.C. L. REV. (forthcoming May 1992). Nevertheless, because changes in union structure and philosophy can be accomplished *now*, within the confines of the existing system, and because the political pressure exerted by reradicalized unions will be vital to accomplishing labor law reform, I view union reform as prior to before (though integrally linked with) labor law reform.

sector] labor force and the declining employment in unionized establishments" and halt the downward spiral in union density.[13] In short, the labor movement is "in crisis."[14]

Demographic trends in the labor force—the influx of traditionally disadvantaged groups, such as women and minorities, and their employment in disproportionate numbers in the rapidly growing, largely non-unionized service industry—have motivated unions to target women and minority workers in organizing efforts.[15] However, unions that target women and minority workers in a desperate effort to increase their numbers risk repeating past errors with a different population. A renewed commitment to communitarian values, participatory democracy, and consensus-style leadership is necessary to restore solidarity to the labor movement.

An alliance with feminism could revitalize labor solidarity and hence labor power, because feminism values connection, community, and shared decision making. Further, the major systems of oppression—

---

13. *Union Coverage, supra* note 2. Weiler has noted that even this may not be enough. He observes that despite the surge of unionism among government employees and the success of some unions in improving private-sector organizing efforts, unions are still unsuccessful in translating employee interest into certification and collective agreements. *See* Weiler, *Hard Times for Unions, supra* note 1, at 1018-19. Weiler argues that employer resistance is a major part of the answer to this puzzle. *Id.* at 1019.

While I agree that employer resistance is a significant factor in the decline of labor union membership, it is not a complete answer to the phenomenon of waning labor power that Weiler describes. For the increasing numbers of women workers who are government and private-sector employees targeted by unions in organizing drives, the significance of employer resistance lies in the oppositional culture of unionism that it helps create. Wavering employee commitments to unionism during organizing, at the voting booth, or in supporting the union in collective bargaining are the result of shortsighted, goal-oriented organizing tactics that ignore the necessity of building a network of connections among workers and serve as the glue of solidarity in place of class-based identification. *See infra* part III.C.1.

14. CHARLES C. HECKSCHER, THE NEW UNIONISM: EMPLOYEE INVOLVEMENT IN THE CHANGING CORPORATION 3 (1988).

15. Service-sector workers have historically been ignored by unions. *See* Harry Bacas, *In Unions There Is Weakness*, NATION'S BUS., Apr. 1985, at 29; James Green & Chris Tilly, *Service Unionism: Directions for Organizing*, 38 LAB. L.J. 486 (1987). Women will constitute approximately 63% of the new entrants into the labor force between 1985 and 2000, and many of them will enter the service sector. Centron, *supra* note 2, at 35. The Bureau of Labor Statistics estimates that women will represent almost 60% of the entire work force by the year 2000. *Id.* Some unions, painfully aware of their decreasing share of labor force participation, have recently begun to show considerable interest in organizing women in an effort to boost their sagging fortunes. *See* Constance Gustke, *Unions Move to Recruit Women*, MGMT. REV., Feb. 1988, at 52 (describing efforts by unions to organize women, including clerical workers, garment workers, and flight attendants); Kevin Kelly & Hazel Bradford, *Labor May Have Found an Rx for Growth*, BUS. WK., Feb. 22, 1988, at 62 (discussing efforts to organize female health care workers); Michael A. Pollock, *Pink-Collar Workers: The Next Rank and File?*, BUS. WK., Feb. 24, 1986, at 116 (describing efforts by the Service Employees International Union to organize office workers).

racial, sexual, heterosexual, and class—are interlocking.[16] Many feminists who work against the synthesis of these oppressions are socialists who advocate the destruction of capitalism as well as patriarchy.[17] Whether or not capitalism must fall for sex equality to flourish, a simultaneous challenge to class and gender oppression within the capitalist patriarchy is likely to be more powerful than the sum of its parts. Thus, integrating a feminist conception of power into union philosophy, structure, and praxis would alter the culture of unionism and ultimately reradicalize it.

In this Article, I uncloak the patriarchal conception of power observed by unions in formulating strategy. I then advance an alternative feminist conception of power that holds transformative possibilities for revitalizing labor unions and empowering workers. To illustrate my thesis, I focus on three areas of vital concern to labor: organizing, bargaining, and wielding economic power. In Part II, I describe the traditional patriarchal vision of power as control, domination, and hierarchy that structures capital and, increasingly, unions.[18] In Part III, I argue that labor unions have bought into the patriarchal concept of power by mimicking the structure of capital, and I examine union tactics that embody this vision of power.[19] In Part IV, I articulate an alternative feminist concept of power as energy, competence, and influence; present evidence of its existence and operation within corporate hierarchies; and address criticisms that might be advanced against it.[20] In Part V, I argue that importing a feminist understanding of power into labor unions would provide the foundation for an alliance between feminism and labor that would reradicalize unions, set forth a vision of how a woman-centered union might operate, and contrast the strategies employed by woman-centered unions with the strategies adopted by male-dominated labor unions.[21]

16. The Combahee River Collective, *A Black Feminist Statement*, *in* CAPITALIST PATRIARCHY AND THE CASE FOR SOCIALIST FEMINISM 362, 365 (Zillah Eisenstein ed., 1979).

17. *See, e.g.*, *The Berkeley-Oakland Women's Union Statement*, *in* CAPITALIST PATRIARCHY AND THE CASE FOR SOCIALIST FEMINISM, *supra* note 16, at 355-57; *see also* BELL HOOKS, FEMINIST THEORY: FROM MARGIN TO CENTER 58 (1984) (arguing that women must accept the need for redistribution of wealth in order to forge a sisterhood that transcends class divisions).

18. *See infra* part II.

19. *See infra* part III.

20. *See infra* part IV.

21. *See infra* part V.

II. PATRIARCHAL IMAGES OF POWER

Traditionally, political theorists and sociologists have defined power as a relationship with others that entails the ability to control their actions, often conceptualized as "power over" others.[22] A typical influential definition is that articulated by Max Weber: "[W]e understand by 'power' the chance of a man or a number of men to realize their own will in a social action even against the resistance of others who are participating in the action."[23] Others have focused on the qualities that enable one to impose his will upon another, defining power as "a property possessed by an actor that enables him to alter the will or actions of others so that they conform to his will."[24]

Most interpret the "property" of power as having the capacity to impose penalties or to coerce compliance.[25] Others have been even clearer about equating power and coercion, rejecting altogether voluntary compliance as an example of the exercise of power.[26] Writers vary on the subject of the source of power; some imagine power as conferred primarily by external authority or status,[27] and others view it as an innate personal characteristic.[28]

Not all define power so narrowly. Dennis Wrong describes power as "the capacity of some persons to produce intended and foreseen effects on others," a definition that avoids the equation of power with the ability to impose sanctions and includes instances in which someone voluntarily complies with the intentions of the power holder.[29] Wrong defines four distinct forms of power: force (any use of the physical self to restrict

22. *See* Marilyn French, Beyond Power: On Women, Men and Morals 506-07 (1985).

23. Dennis H. Wrong, Power: Its Forms, Bases and Uses 21 (1979) (quoting Max Weber, 2 Economy and Society 926 (Guenther Roth & Claus Wittich eds., 1986). Wrong notes that the word "even" is often omitted from Weber's definition, which has the effect of making "coercion and conflict of goals and interests inherent in the very nature of power." *Id.* at 261 n.1.

24. French, *supra* note 22, at 505 (citing Talcott Parsons, *On the Concept of Political Power*, *in* Political Power: A Reader in Theory and Research 251, 256 (Roderick Bell et al. eds., 1969)).

25. *See* Wrong, *supra* note 23, at 21, 261 n.1.

26. *See id.* at 22 (citing Peter Bachrach & Morton S. Baratz, *Decisions and Nondecisions: An Analytical Framework*, 57 Am. Pol. Sci. Rev. 632, 633-34 (1963)).

27. *See, e.g.*, Wrong, *supra* note 23, at 21 (phrasing conventional understanding as "the capacity to impose, or to threaten successfully to impose, penalties or deprivations for noncompliance").

28. *See, e.g.*, Nancy Hartsock, Money, Sex and Power: Toward A Feminist Historical Materialism 2 (1983) (summarizing Bertrand Russell's view of power as "the ability to compel obedience").

29. Wrong, *supra* note 23, at 21.

another's actions, including physical force exercised against another's body and nonviolent uses of one's own body as a physical object to prevent or restrict actions); manipulation (deliberate and successful efforts to influence another's response in which the power holder conceals his intent from the power subject); persuasion (presenting arguments, appeals, or exhortations to convince another, who, after independently evaluating their content in light of his own values and goals, accepts the communication as the basis of his own behavior); and authority (successful ordering or forbidding, the issuance of commands that are followed because of their source without regard to their content).[30]

Nevertheless, these conceptions of power share a common understanding of power as relative; one's power has meaning only when compared with the power of others. I categorize these definitions of power as patriarchal because all revolve around a hierarchical paradigm in which one dominates and another submits; one controls and another is controlled.[31] Even persuasion, seemingly the most benign form of power described by Wrong, envisions power as the substitution of the view of the power holder for that of the overpowered.[32] The assumption is that the conflict of will between autonomous, independent beings is inevitable because there exists a conflict of interests and goals. This conflict can be resolved only by a choice between the two wills that privileges one at the expense of the other.

In this system of human relations, the key to power is an individual's access to resources: When an individual possesses scarce resources

30. *Id.* at 23-35.

31. Patriarchy as a system can exist between and among men as well as between men and women. *See* Heidi Hartmann, *Capitalism, Patriarchy, and Job Segregation by Sex*, *in* CAPITALIST PATRIARCHY AND THE CASE FOR SOCIALIST FEMINISM, *supra* note 16, at 206, 232 n.1.

32. Indeed, the supreme exercise of power may take the form of persuasion or manipulation rather than force:

> A may exercise power over B by getting him to do what he does not want to do, but he also exercises power over him by influencing, shaping or determining his very wants. Indeed, is it not the supreme exercise of power to get another or others to have the desires you want them to have—that is, to secure their compliance by controlling their thoughts and desires? . . . . [Indeed] the most effective and insidious use of power is to prevent such conflict from arising in the first place.

STEVEN LUKES, POWER: A RADICAL VIEW 23 (1974). Lukes concludes that the most insidious exercise of power is

> to prevent people, to whatever degree, from having grievances by shaping their perceptions, cognitions and preferences in such a way that they accept their role in the existing order of things, either because they can see or imagine no alternative to it, or because they see it as natural and unchangeable, or because they value it as divinely ordained and beneficial . . . .

Id. at 24. Thus, one of the most effective uses of power, though on its surface the most benign, is to keep potential issues out of politics altogether. *Id.*

that are needed by others, he necessarily exercises control over their lives.[33] The underlying assumption is that the needed resources are scarce; thus, competition for the scarce resources is inevitable. All men[34] are assumed to be engaged in a consuming, warlike competition for scarce resources: "[I]f any two men desire the same thing, which nevertheless they cannot both enjoy, they become enemies; and in the way to their end, which is principally their own conservation, and sometimes their delectation only, endeavor to destroy, or subdue one another."[35] Ultimately, because positions of power offer tangible benefits and psychological rewards, having power means potentially having access to the valued scarce resources, and so power itself becomes a scarce resource.[36]

Overt conflict is inevitable in this hierarchical, competitive power structure. Power distribution is "zero-sum" in nature, meaning that power is a fixed, finite property over which power seekers fight; whatever is not allocated to one is redistributed to another.[37] Thus, power differentials themselves are thought inevitably to entail a conflict of interest.[38] Overt conflict is the predictable outcome because a "lust for power" is assumed to be a universal, basic human drive.[39] The primitive impulse

33. *See* DAVID KIPNIS, THE POWERHOLDERS 3 (1976).

34. Because of their lower aggressive drive, women in this system are presumptively excluded from the status of power wielder. *See* WRONG, *supra* note 23, at 221-22 (relying on Freud's work in support of the finding that aggression is one of the basic human drives). The phenomenon is reflected in sex stereotypes that define leadership positions in terms of stereotypically male qualities. *See* ANN-MARIE RIZZO & CARMEN MENDEZ, THE INTEGRATION OF WOMEN IN MANAGEMENT 10 (1990) (maintaining that the model of a successful manager in our culture is masculine: A good manager is "aggressive" and "competitive"). The authors catalogue sex-role stereotypes derived from research on power dimensions for men and women managers and report that such character traits as aggression, assertiveness, confidence, toughness, and forcefulness are more typical of men than women, who display such "feminine" characteristics as emotionality, sentimentality, submissiveness, and tender-mindedness. *Id.* at 16-17.

35. THOMAS HOBBES, LEVIATHAN 105 (Bobbs-Merrill 1958) (1651); *see also* WRONG, *supra* note 23, at 219.

36. *See* Anthony Giddens, *"Power" in the Recent Writings of Talcott Parsons*, 2:3 SOCIOLOGY 264-65 (1968).

37. *See* STEWART CLEGG, THE THEORY OF POWER AND ORGANIZATION 65-67 (1979) (discussing TALCOTT PARSONS, SOCIOLOGICAL THEORY AND MODERN SOCIETY 297 (1967)).

38. *See id.* at 67 (discussing Giddens, *supra* note 36, at 264-65).

39. *See* WRONG, *supra* note 23, at 218-19. The idea of an inherent lust for power as a universal and fundamental element of human nature is primarily attributable to Machiavelli and Hobbes. Machiavellians insist that in all societies, the many are ruled by the few; consequently, either the ruling elite possess exceptionally strong power drives or the majority (the ruled) yield to a complementary desire to submit. *Id.* at 218. Hobbes maintained that men seek power primarily for defensive reasons: They must continually strive for more power in order to secure the advantages they have already attained. *Id.* at 219.

from which this elemental lust for power originated is thought to be the propensity for aggression.[40]

The use of the term "lust" in connection with the description of the innate drive for power is no accident; the concept of power as domination has itself become sexualized. The literature on power is replete with references to the connection between power conceived as domination and manliness or virility.[41] Some of the most significant advances made by feminists studying the relationship between power and sex have addressed the fact that power (synonymous with domination) is so sexualized in our society that its exercise is often confused with a sexual act.[42] This is because "sexuality in our society is defined almost exclusively in masculine terms, and . . . hostility and domination are central to the construction of masculine sexuality."[43]

---

40. WRONG, *supra* note 23, at 221.

41. *See* HARTSOCK, *supra* note 28, at 6. Hartsock quotes philosopher Bertrand de Jouvenel ("a man feels himself more of a man when imposing himself and making others the instrument of his will"), Robert Penn Warren ("masculinity is closely tied to every form of power in our society"), and Henry Kissinger ("Power is the ultimate aphrodisiac."). *Id.*

The connection between power and sex is revealed even in the more expansive definitions of power articulated by male scholars. For example, Wrong describes his vision of power as capability, potency, or mastery ("power to" rather than "power over"). WRONG, *supra* note 23, at 219. Two of these three terms reflect the sexual understanding of power as domination: potency connotes male virility, while mastery conjures up a master-servant, command-authority relation. *But cf.* FRENCH, *supra* note 22, at 505 (describing power "to" in neutral terms as "ability, capacity, and . . . a kind of freedom"). *See generally infra* part IV.A.1.

42. Catharine MacKinnon has been a pioneer in identifying the link between sex and power. She has argued that male dominance is sexual and that men sexualize hierarchy. Thus, acts perceived as purely sexual or purely violent are revealed as acts of dominance, acts of intrusion on those who are less powerful, which are experienced as sexually arousing. CATHARINE A. MACKINNON, TOWARD A FEMINIST THEORY OF THE STATE 127 (1989). She cites feminist work supporting this assertion in the areas of rape, battery, sexual harassment, sexual abuse of children, prostitution, and pornography. *See id.* at 276-79 n.2.

The example of rape provides a compelling demonstration of this link between sex and power. A growing body of literature documents the revelation that rape is an act of domination and power rather than of sex; yet, the act of domination itself is sexual. *See, e.g.*, SUSAN BROWNMILLER, AGAINST OUR WILL: MEN, WOMEN AND RAPE 196, 256 (1975) (stating that the purpose of rape is humiliation and degradation rather than eroticism and that all rape is exercise of power). Brownmiller illustrates her point (in part) by reference to the phenomenon of prison rape. She points out the fallacy of the view that prison homosexuality is the result of placing men in a situation where they have no heterosexual outlet for their physical needs; she identifies the ideology of prison rape as the need to prove mastery through physical and sexual assault and to establish a coercive hierarchy of the strong on top of the weak. *Id.* at 267. Brownmiller argues that rape is "a conscious process of intimidation by which *all* men keep *all* women in a state of fear." *Id.* at 15; *see also id.* at 209 ("That *some* men rape provides a sufficient threat to keep all women in a constant state of intimidation; forever conscious of the knowledge that the biological tool must be held in awe for it may turn to weapon with sudden swiftness borne of harmful intent.").

43. HARTSOCK, *supra* note 28, at 7 (citation omitted).

In short, the patriarchal vision of power is predicated on an assumption that there exists a fixed quantity of resources that all desire equally, creating an inherent conflict of interest that is exacerbated by existing power differentials; that resources are distributed according to a hierarchical power structure; that one's position in the hierarchy is achieved through competition characterized by overt conflict; that such competition takes the form of dominating those less powerful than oneself; and that the desire to dominate is natural, inevitable, and is sex itself. Consequently, the property of power is synonymous with the ability to coerce, dominate, or control others who occupy lower positions in the hierarchy.[44]

III. THE PATRIARCHAL PHILOSOPHY, STRUCTURE AND STRATEGY OF LABOR POWER

Patriarchal structures tend to be hierarchical and pyramidal in arrangement, with the majority of people (the less powerful) clustered at the bottom.[45] Weber dubbed the hierarchical form of organization "bureaucratic" and theorized that this form of organization was superior to all others.[46] Power in such an organization is transmitted vertically, either from bottom to top (lower-level people generate power by contributing their work), or from top to bottom (higher-level workers apply the power provided from below, make policy, and oversee those below).[47]

Capital, organized in the corporate form, and labor, organized as a union of workers, have been mentioned as the prototypical examples of

44. The adversarial model on which our legal system is based is a product of a patriarchal understanding of power. The values underlying the adversarial model are advocacy, persuasion, hierarchy, competition, and binary results (win/lose). Carrie Menkel-Meadow, *Portia In A Different Voice: Speculations on a Women's Lawyering Process*, 1 BERKELEY WOMEN'S L.J. 39, 50-51 (1985). Transposing hierarchies of power into hierarchies of values is thought to help defuse disagreements by framing them as an impersonal conflict of rights. *See* CAROL GILLIGAN, IN A DIFFERENT VOICE 32 (1982). Such a hierarchical ordering of claims carries with it powerful imagery of winning and losing on the basis of the application of objective, impersonal rules. Such a structure is designed to contain and suppress the "natural" male tendency to resort to violence to resolve conflict. *See supra* notes 34-35 and accompanying text.

45. *See* FRENCH, *supra* note 22, at 299-300.

46. MAX WEBER, THE THEORY OF SOCIAL AND ECONOMIC ORGANIZATION 337 (A.M. Henderson & Talcott Parsons trans., 1947) ("Experience tends universally to show that the purely bureaucratic type of administrative organization . . . is . . . capable of attaining the highest degree of efficiency and is in this sense formally the most rational known means of carrying out imperative control over human beings. It is superior to any other form in precision, in stability, in the stringency of its discipline, and in its reliability.").

47. FRENCH, *supra* note 22, at 301.

the hierarchical distribution and operation of power. John Kenneth Galbraith describes the modern corporation as dependent on its effectiveness in producing and selling its products, for which it in turn depends on the quality and degree of its internal organization. Its internal organization is, simply, the "extent and depth of the submission of its employees."[48] The labor union operates on the philosophy that the collective interest of workers outweighs their individual interests.[49] According to Galbraith, the union's power depends upon the internal submission of its members.[50]

The patriarchal structure and exercise of power in and by organized labor is the result of the militaristic, adversarial culture of the capital-labor relation. In this section, I trace the historical development of this oppositional culture, describe a sociological perspective on its role in shaping union philosophy and structure, and detail the impact of the resulting patriarchal vision of power on union strategy in the areas of organizing, bargaining, and applying economic pressure.[51]

A. The Historical Development and Deradicalization of Labor Unions

At their inception, unions were both democratic and radical. The original craft unions typical of the nineteenth century were informal

48. John Kenneth Galbraith, The Anatomy of Power 58 (1983). Stewart Clegg, in his Marxist analysis of power and structure, puts the same idea a little less bluntly: "The qualities of the person are disregarded in favour of their quantification as factors of production having a specific value. The bureaucracy is built up on this basis—it is materially supported by virtue of the specific value accruing from the appropriation of labour power." Clegg, *supra* note 37, at 93.

49. Galbraith, *supra* note 48, at 57.

50. *Id.* Galbraith explains: "If union solidarity, the synonym for effective internal discipline or submission, is high, then the chance of winning union demands or of successful strike action is good." *Id.* at 57-58.

51. The adversarial culture of the labor-management relation is reinforced by and reflected in the labor laws. Scholars have described the framework of American labor law as "tending to produce collective bargaining relationships that are legalistic, rule-driven, and confrontational." Bureau of Labor-Management Relations and Cooperative Programs, U.S. Dep't of Labor, Pub. No. 134, U.S. Labor Law and the Future of Labor-Management Cooperation 141 (1989). Although this Article discusses particular provisions of the labor laws that operate to reinforce union strategies of organizing, bargaining, and economic pressure predicated on patriarchal assumptions about power, it does not address the patriarchal view of power embodied in the National Labor Relations Act as a whole. I undertake that task, which I view as integral to an understanding of the operation of the patriarchal norm of power on labor, in a companion article to this one. *See Crain*, *supra* note 12.

communities that controlled the tools and knowledge necessary for production.[52] Even the unskilled-worker organizations of the late nineteenth century were communal in character, with egalitarian values and radical social ideals typical of preindustrial farming cultures.[53]

However, the rise of large corporate organizations and their characteristic bureaucratic structure transformed the workplace and ultimately altered the character of worker associations from communal to bureaucratic. Large corporations brought with them hierarchy in organization and opposed the fledgling craft unions with hostility and violence.[54] By the late nineteenth century, labor leaders had abandoned the communal form of action, with its "glue" of solidarity, for the bureaucratic foundation of current unions, held together by clear goals, a chain of command, and formal mechanisms.[55]

The alteration of the organizational culture and structure of unions was part of a larger shift in the American Federation of Labor's philosophy of unionism. The relatively narrow "business unionism" conceived by the AFL entailed the following key changes: (1) rejection of all grand visions of social reform that might divide the membership (such as those espoused by the Knights of Labor) and development of a narrowed list of goals to which specific action could be tailored;[56] (2) development of an internal system of union discipline, with centralized authority in the hands of international officers;[57] and (3) a focus on tangible benefits designed to tie the workers to the organization.[58] The shift was considered necessary in order to wage an effective battle with capital over the distribution of profits.

---

52. *See* HECKSCHER, *supra* note 14, at 16.

53. *Id.* at 17.

54. *Id.*

55. *Id.* at 18-19.

56. *Id.* at 18-19. The AFL developed a "philosophy of pure wage consciousness," signifying "a labor movement reduced to an opportunistic basis, accepting the existence of capitalism and having for its object the enlarging of the bargaining power of the wage earner in the sale of his labor." SELIG PERLMAN, A HISTORY OF TRADE UNIONISM IN THE UNITED STATES 78 (1922).

57. HECKSCHER, *supra* note 14, at 19.

58. *Id.* The AFL's shortsighted and narrow focus sacrificed solidarity for wage gains and ultimately led to the creation of a partnership of organized labor and capital that supported exclusionary policies against marginalized workers, including women. *See* ALICE KESSLER-HARRIS, OUT TO WORK 152 (1982); LINDA M. BLUM, BETWEEN FEMINISM AND LABOR: THE SIGNIFICANCE OF THE COMPARABLE WORTH MOVEMENT 12-13 (1991). *See also* PERLMAN, *supra* note 56, at 266-67. Perlman explains that American workers refused to accept Marxian revolutionary goals; they perceived themselves narrowly, as bargainers desiring to strike the best wage bargain. They focused their attention on the menaces they encountered as bargainers, for these were the forces on which the employer's bargaining advantage rested. Accordingly, "their impulse [was] . . . to suppress those

The strategy of opposition employed by capital in the struggle for industrial control was instrumental in shaping the structure and culture of organized labor. Capital's adoption of scientific management techniques—"Taylorism"—in the early twentieth century reinforced its bureaucratic, hierarchical structure while simultaneously imposing it on labor.[59] Taylorism weakened craft unions, creating a new social grouping of unskilled workers.[60] The Congress of Industrial Organization unions developed as a response to the needs of the increasing number of unskilled workers. The CIO unions grouped together workers who, lacking a uniting craft community, were linked only by their common position at the bottom of the firm hierarchy.[61] These unions were even more centralized, hierarchical, and bureaucratic than the AFL craft unions.[62]

The oppositional culture of labor-management relations put unions in "the essentially contradictory situation" of being "associations trying to act like organizations."[63] Historian Melvyn Dubofsky describes the catch-22 as follows:

> [U]nions have to be understood as peculiarly contradictory institutions. They are . . . simultaneously town meetings and military formations. In one guise, unions are marked by rank and file participation where policy decisions are reached only after open democratic debate. In the other guise, they are fighting machines struggling for survival or victory through discipline, absolute loyalty to command and unbroken solidarity.[64]

Attempts to strengthen the organizational structure of a union in order to make it more responsive in an adversarial crisis tended to weaken the

---

competitive menaces, be they convict labor, foreign labor, 'green' or untrained workers working on a machine, and so forth." *Id.*

59. Taylorism, the brainchild of Frederick Winslow Taylor, advocated the application of "scientific" methods to control the production process. *See* HARRY BRAVERMAN, LABOR AND MONOPOLY CAPITAL: THE DEGRADATION OF WORK IN THE TWENTIETH CENTURY 112-19 (1974). Its basic tenet was the separation of conception from execution in the labor process in order to increase efficiency. The ultimate design was to break the hold over the production process that skilled workers possessed by virtue of their knowledge. *See id.* at 114; DAVID MONTGOMERY, WORKERS' CONTROL IN AMERICA 9 (1979).

60. HECKSCHER, *supra* note 14, at 22.

61. *Id.* at 23-24. Heckscher identifies two distinct types of solidarity: "mass" solidarity, enjoyed by the industrial unions, and "community" solidarity, present in the craft unions. *Id.*

62. *Id.*

63. *Id.* at 26. By this Heckscher means that unions, though voluntary associations whose power lies in the active participation of their membership, try to behave like disciplined organizations managing a long-term battle with employers. *Id.* at 16.

64. Melvyn Dubofsky, *Legal Theory and Workers' Rights: A Historian's Critique*, 4 INDUS. REL. L.J. 496, 500 (1981).

commitment of the membership, which historically had been the source of union power.[65] In short, unions' strength became their weakness.

B. Sociological Perspectives on Union Philosophy and Structure

Some writers theorize that countermobilization to bureaucracy will necessarily assume a bureaucratic form.[66] This phenomenon of parallelism in the organizational philosophy, structure, and tactics of two organizations that operate in opposition to one another is known as isomorphism.[67] Sociologists posit that organizations competing with one another in the same field, facing the same set of environmental conditions, tend to become more homogeneous, or similar to one another.[68] A chief contributing factor to this process of homogenization, or isomorphism, is the existence of a common legal environment.[69] Another factor is uncertainty; when the environment creates symbolic uncertainty, organizations tend to model themselves after other organizations, particularly those that they perceive to be more legitimate or successful, borrowing their practices and innovations.[70] Isomorphism is particularly likely to occur when one organization is dependent upon another, both organizations are dependent on a common source of support for vital resources, or both organizations must transact with agencies of the state on a regular basis.[71]

Labor leaders, operating in a setting in which all of these factors were present, accepted the strategy of counterorganization and began "trying to meet their opponents (capital) at their own level by establishing a balance of power."[72] The parallelism between labor and capital

65. *Id.*

66. *See* WEBER, *supra* note 23, at 338 ("When those subject to bureaucratic control seek to escape the influence of the existing bureaucratic apparatus, this is normally possible only by creating an organization of their own which is equally subject to the process of bureaucratization."). Others believe that oppositional culture has little to do with the tendency toward bureaucratization. According to this view, any organization that begins with a democratic philosophy and subsequently experiences an increase in size will invariably degenerate into a bureaucracy; growth will necessarily generate an increasingly complex and impersonal bureaucratic structure. *See* ROBERT MICHELS, POLITICAL PARTIES: A SOCIOLOGICAL STUDY OF THE OLIGARCHICAL TENDENCIES OF MODERN DEMOCRACY, 32-40 (1959) (positing an "iron law of oligarchy").

67. *See* Paul J. DiMaggio & Walter W. Powell, *The Iron Cage Revisited: Institutional Isomorphism and Collective Rationality in Organizational Fields*, 48 AM. SOC. REV. 147 (1983).

68. *Id.* at 149.

69. *Id.* at 150.

70. *Id.* at 151-52.

71. *Id.* at 154-56.

72. HECKSCHER, *supra* note 14, at 19; *see* GALBRAITH, *supra* note 48, at 72-88 (maintaining that society is in equilibrium between those who exercise power and those who counter it; dissent's

extended beyond the structure of the organizations to the *sources* of their power and the instruments of its exercise. Galbraith articulates a theory of symmetry that explains the tendency of organizations in opposition to one another to rely upon similar sources and strategies of power.[73] Using the "classic struggle" between capital and labor as an illustration of the principle, he traces the early role of personality as a source of power in both capital and labor, describes the transition to property as a source of power, and concludes that bureaucratic, hierarchical organization has replaced personal leadership as a source of power in corporations and unions:

> With some important exceptions, personal leadership ceased to be a central factor; violence diminished or disappeared. At first, property, in the form of the strike fund, became an important source of union power, bringing with it the ability on the union side to extend and last out a strike. Then a solid organization became even more important, and from this came an answering skill in negotiation and an answering capacity to carry the unions' case to the public. . . . The strike—the comparative test of property resources—became a symbol of failure. Overwhelmingly, the source of power on both sides was organization.[74]

The tactical advantage of bureaucratic structure as a source of power in an oppositional setting is its amenability to deployment in times of crisis. The sterner the internal discipline, the more potent the organization will be vis-a-vis external forces.[75] Heckscher observes that

resort to countervailing power similarly structured is predictable). The assumption that "[o]ne behemoth . . . can best be controlled by another one," HECKSCHER, *supra* note 14, at 7, is central to labor law. *See* National Labor Relations Act, § 1, 29 U.S.C. § 151 (1988) ("protection by law of the right of employees to organize and bargain collectively safeguards commerce . . . by restoring equality of bargaining power between employers and employees").

The concept of offsetting power with opposing power probably has its origin in the irrationality (stemming from fear, guilt, greed, excessive pride, revenge, etc.) of those who have wielded it; the fear is that if power is not sufficiently checked, it will assume demonic form and impose an irrational will on the world. This concern about the potential illogical or irrational exercise of power is premised on an experience of the world as ordered by rights, logic, or justice in order to protect the underlying values of autonomy and freedom. *See* GILLIGAN, *supra* note 44, at 164, 174; *infra* part IV.A.3.

73. GALBRAITH, *supra* note 48, at 74-75. Although Galbraith acknowledges that the symmetry of the exercise of power is neither inevitable nor necessary (he later mentions several examples, including the resistance movements led by Gandhi and Martin Luther King, wherein exercises of countervailing power have depended for their effectiveness on *asymmetry*), he believes that symmetry may "generally be assumed." *Id.* at 79-80.

74. *Id.* at 77.

75. *See id.* at 58.

> [t]he main reason that organization triumphs over community is that the former can count on much stricter discipline than the latter. Commands [typical of a bureaucracy] get obeyed most of the time because they are backed up by sanctions; but influence [characteristic of communal structures] is often disregarded because each individual may think he or she knows best.[76]

The natural tendency of individuals operating within the hierarchy to strive to keep power reinforces the status quo once it is established.[77]

Thus, union structure—hierarchical, bureaucratic, formalistic—has come to mimic the structure of the large companies in opposition to which unions were formed. The effects are increased power at the top; decreased power among the rank and file; retention of formal control by union officials over the means of communication, thus restricting rank and file members' free speech rights; and the monopolization of political power and leadership skills by union leaders.[78] Like corporate structure, union structure is exclusionary and discriminatory. Recurring efforts to democratize or reform labor unions provide eloquent testimony to the lack of democracy experienced by most workers in today's hierarchical, impersonal unions.[79]

Union members, deeply disillusioned with their unions, feel isolated from the top union leadership whom their dues support and powerless to affect the content of the labor contracts that are nevertheless negotiated with the aid of economic pressure applied through their work stoppage.[80] Michael Lerner argues that unions, by adopting a "We do it all for you"

---

76. HECKSCHER, *supra* note 14, at 18.

77. *See* MARILYN BOYD, WOMEN'S LIBERATION IDEOLOGY AND UNION PARTICIPATION: A STUDY 25 (1981) (arguing that desire of union officials to maintain power and to make their tenures permanent exacerbates and maintains union hierarchy).

78. *Id.* at 25.

79. *See* RICHARD EDWARDS, CONTESTED TERRAIN: THE TRANSFORMATION OF THE WORKPLACE IN THE TWENTIETH CENTURY 215 (1979) (maintaining that broad segments of the working class are demonstrating an interest in redemocratizing Steelworkers, Teamsters, and United Mine Workers); DAN LA BOTZ, RANK AND·FILE REBELLION (1990) (chronicling movement within Teamsters Union by Teamsters for a Democratic Union). La Botz illustrates the lack of democracy and the discriminatory culture within the Teamsters Union with the example of "sweetheart" deals in labor contract negotiations, in which the rights of women and racial-minority Teamsters were compromised in exchange for benefits to white male majority Teamsters. *Id.* at 79.

80. MICHAEL LERNER, SURPLUS POWERLESSNESS 63 (1986). The Executive Committee of the AFL-CIO is completely isolated from democratic control by members. Similarly, many of the large international unions do not elect union leaders by democratic vote; instead, union locals select representatives to attend national conventions, where the representatives vote for national leaders. *Id.* National contracts are often negotiated with very little, if any, input from members, who are asked to ratify them without the opportunity to suggest or debate alternatives, frequently *after* they have already returned to work following a strike. *Id.*; *see also* Weiler, *Hard Times For Unions*, *supra* note 1, at 1018 ("popular impression is that unions are large, bureaucratic organizations, led by

slogan, have created a "culture of passivity." Rather than empowering workers, union membership actively operates to disempower them, derailing militancy and discouraging participation in union affairs and the larger political arena.[81] Lacking any sense of connection and meaning in their work lives, many workers vainly seek a sense of meaning in their personal lives; their failures in this area serve only to further isolate and disempower them.[82] Lerner concludes that unions have lost the solidarity built on trust and the sense of connection with fellow members that is essential to persuade members to take risks in a political movement.[83] In the process of deradicalization, unions lost their power base.

---

remote leaders who are unrepresentative, and out of touch with, the new breed of American workers").

81. *See* LERNER, *supra* note 80, at 68-70. In particular, women and minorities, underrepresented in union leadership, have been denied any opportunity to shape the labor movement's political agenda—which often consists primarily of general social legislation of great interest to them, such as civil rights legislation, antipoverty legislation and programs, and family leave legislation. *See* Alice H. Cook, *Introduction* to WOMEN AND TRADE UNIONS IN ELEVEN INDUSTRIALIZED COUNTRIES 1, 15-16 (Alice H. Cook et al. eds., 1984) (arguing that unions can serve as agents of social change for women). *But cf.* RICHARD B. FREEMAN & JAMES L. MEDOFF, WHAT DO UNIONS DO? 191-206 (1984) (concluding that although unions have a great deal of political power and influence over the passage of general social legislation, they have been unsuccessful in using this power to obtain favorable special-interest legislation); M. Neil Browne & Andrea M. Giampetro-Meyer, *The Overriding Importance of Market Characteristics for the Selection of Pay Equity Strategies: The Relative Efficacy of Collective Bargaining and Litigation in the Nursing Industry*, 11 INDUS. REL. L.J. 414, 433 (1989) (arguing that unions have been ineffective in all major industrialized countries as agents of social change for women).

Moreover, workers who are deprived of the opportunity to affect their day-to-day work lives are less likely to exercise political power on an individual basis in the larger arena. *See* ROBERT A. DAHL, WHO GOVERNS? DEMOCRACY AND POWER IN AN AMERICAN CITY 286-87 (1978) (arguing that an individual who is relatively confident of success in influencing decisions is more likely to make the attempt than one who fears failure; the striking characteristic of a political activist is belief that what she does matters).

82. LERNER, *supra* note 80, at 98. The situation is particularly acute for women. Trapped in oppressive, low-paying jobs and frequently burdened with child care responsibilities, both single and married women become more vulnerable to sexual and emotional exploitation by men. Lerner theorizes that women's emotional need for a sense of connection and meaning, coupled with their economic fragility, causes single women to form and pursue relationships they otherwise would not, *see id.* at 97, and married women to remain in oppressive marriages. *Id.* at 105.

83. *See id.* at 97, 99. Lerner's theory is that many people involved in the labor movement today—or in other social-change movements—have a deep emotional commitment to losing, to being isolated, and to remaining powerless. Their assumption that no one will take them seriously or listen to them shapes their tactics and strategies, leading them to follow paths that ensure failure. Lerner refers to this mind-set as "surplus powerlessness." *Id.* at 1.

C. Union Strategies Exemplifying a Patriarchal Vision of Power

By mimicking the confrontational, adversarial stance and authoritarian, top-down structure of the employers they oppose, unions acquired a patriarchal understanding of power: Specifically, unions strove to compel obedience, to dominate, and to control employers and union members. In this patriarchal system of power relations, unions view themselves as engaged with employers in a warlike competition for scarce resources, from which only one side can emerge victorious (the "zero-sum" mentality).[84] The labor movement has been deradicalized as unions have systematically sabotaged the source of their power—rank-and-file solidarity—by treating member-employees and prospective members as fungible soldiers in the hierarchy of the union ranks. The operation of a patriarchal norm of power and consequent deradicalization are reflected in three primary areas of union activity: organizing, bargaining, and exercising economic pressure.

1. *Organizing*

The traditional model[85] of union organizing begins with an outside union organizer responding to a call for help from an employee inside the target workplace. The initiating call from a disgruntled worker to a local

84. *See supra* text accompanying note 37.

85. My description of the "traditional model" of union organizing is based upon interviews conducted during 1990 and 1991 with directors of organizing for nine major unions: American Federation of State, County, and Municipal Employees (interview with Paul Booth, in Washington, D.C. (July 10, 1990)); Association of Flight Attendants (interview conducted by Dr. Joyce Rothschild with John Schmidt, in Washington, D.C. (June 14, 1991)); Communications Workers of America (interview with Larry Cohn, in Washington, D.C. (July 11, 1990)); International Brotherhood of Teamsters, Chauffeurs, Warehousemen, and Helpers of America (interview with Vicki Saporta, in Washington, D.C. (July 12, 1990)); International Ladies' Garment Workers Union (interview with Joe Danahy, in Washington, D.C. (July 12, 1990)); Service Employees International Union (interview with Andy Stern, in Washington, D.C. (July 11, 1990)); United Automobile, Aerospace and Agricultural Implement Workers of America (interview with Ben Perkins, in Detroit, Mich. (Aug. 15, 1990)); United Food and Commercial Workers International Union (interview with Dwayne Carman, in Washington, D.C. (July 11, 1990)); United Steelworkers of America (interview with Bernard Hostein, in Pittsburgh, Pa. (June 25, 1990)). I also conducted telephone interviews with 30 organizers drawn primarily from those unions and an interview with Richard Bensinger, Director of the AFL-CIO Organizing Institute, in Washington D.C. (July 11, 1990) (all transcripts on file with author). The empirical results of these interviews are reported in more detail in Marion Crain, Gender and Union Organizing (1992) (unpublished manuscript, on file with author). Although individual procedures vary, the basic process followed by each union is sufficiently uniform that I have presented here a composite of the traditional organizing process. For more detailed but similar descriptions of the traditional model, *see* Getman, *supra* note 12; Green & Tilly, *supra* note 15; Richard W. Hurd & Adrienne McElwain, *Organizing Clerical Workers: Determinants of Success*, 41 Indus. & Lab. Rel. Rev. 360 (1988).

or regional union office prompts the union to research the feasibility of organizing the workplace of that particular employer. The feasibility study examines such factors as the employer's financial situation, whether the employer is likely to move away or close, and its past response, if any, to organizing activity. If the employer looks organizable, the call is referred to an on-staff, paid organizer. The organizer, typically a previous rank-and-file member who aspires to move up through the union hierarchy,[86] visits the town in which the workplace is located and attempts to ascertain whether the employees have sufficient interest in union organization. The organizer will then ask the interested employees to form an in-plant committee, which will be responsible for most of the early organizing activity. In addition to supplementing the committee's activities directly by leading informational mass meetings, the organizer serves in an advisory capacity until the committee is ready to solicit the signed authorization cards in preparation for either a National Labor Relations Board-ordered election or a request for voluntary recognition by the employer.

Once the in-plant committee has garnered sufficient support (defined by the number of people attending meetings, the number of cards signed, or other objective methods), the organizer moves in, takes control of the organizing campaign, and leads the committee through the remaining phases of the campaign. After the election is held, win or lose, the organizer leaves town and severs his connection with the committee.

A modified form of the conventional organizing model is the "blitz" approach. The blitz model, developed in response to management's increasingly sophisticated antiunion campaigns, is based on an explicit analogy between organizing a union and waging a war; the union seeks to gain the upper hand in the campaign before the employer can mount an antiunion attack.[87] The blitz model differs from the conventional model

86. In virtually all unions, the union organizer occupies an entry-level, low-status position in the union hierarchy. Organizers must endure a trial by fire—organizing is replete with travel, long hours, low pay, unpredictability, and frustration—before being considered for a position with better working conditions and wages, further up the union ranks. *See generally* Paul F. Clark, *Organizing the Organizers: Professional Staff Unionism in the American Labor Movement*, 42 INDUS. & LAB. REL. REV. 584, 587 (1989) (documenting the fact that organizing staff, disturbed about job security, wages, benefits, and lack of input into formulation of union policy, are organizing themselves). Even the few unions who recruit college-educated, non-rank-and-file organizers subscribe to this view of organizers' status.

87. The blitz model was developed by Richard Bensinger, a former organizer for the Amalgamated Clothing and Textile Workers Union. Bensinger, with the help of the AFL-CIO, recently founded the AFL-CIO Organizing Institute, whose mission is to develop more effective organizing strategies, train organizers, and professionalize the occupation. Interview with Richard Bensinger, Director of the AFL-CIO Organizing Institute, in Washington, D.C. (July 11, 1990) (transcript on

primarily in the timing of the allocation of union resources to organizing: Instead of committing the time of one organizer to a campaign for a period of several months, unions commit multiple organizers at the outset. Thus, rather than leaving control of the campaign in the hands of the employees until some critical mass of support has been gained and later wresting it away, the blitz organizers[88] take control of the campaign from the beginning. The organizing phase is condensed into a very short period of time—sometimes as brief as one weekend—and the employer is presented with the fait accompli of signed cards, often combined with a threatened work stoppage, before the employer becomes aware of the campaign's existence and has a chance to call its lawyer and set the anti-union campaign in motion.

The basic assumption underlying both the blitz method and the conventional method is that employees can be categorized at the outset as either "with" the union on a political or philosophical level or against it. If they are politically and spiritually in sync with the union, the union views them as "organizable"; while there may be work for the union to do to overcome workers' fears of employer retaliation or to educate them about the particular union recruiting them, their organizability is established.[89] Although the Blitz Manual cautions organizers not to burn bridges by arguing with skeptical workers they encounter during house calls because "[t]he skeptics and anti's may come around later,"[90] it touts the advantage for the union of assessing the possibility of campaign success "[w]ithin a few days."[91] The manual warns against going forward with the campaign if the house calls detect too many skeptics.[92]

Further, although the blitz model acknowledges the importance of developing a sense of ownership among potential union supporters, the manual does not instruct organizers how to accomplish this within a few days.[93] In fact, the manual relies exclusively upon the sense of momentum, enthusiasm, and excitement generated by the blitz, rather than any

file with author). The AFL-CIO Department of Organization and Field Services has produced a manual describing the blitz method. *See* AFL-CIO, THE BLITZ: A MANUAL FOR ORGANIZERS ON HOW TO RUN FAST-PACED PRE-PETITION CAMPAIGNS [hereinafter THE BLITZ MANUAL].

88. The Blitz Manual recommends five "blitzers" for every 100 workers. THE BLITZ MANUAL, *supra* note 87, at 12.

89. As I have previously argued, unions often rely on erroneous stereotypes in characterizing workers as "unorganizable" and so ignore fertile sources of potential membership. *See* Crain, *supra* note 7, at 1162-84.

90. THE BLITZ MANUAL, *supra* note 87, at 15.

91. *Id.* at 9.

92. *See id.* at 21.

93. For example, the manual advises:

sense of ownership or community, to sustain the union after the organizers leave.[94] Finally, the Blitz Manual advises organizers to keep the number of "contact" employees within the company down, particularly during the preblitz planning phase, and warns against "getting too many people involved . . . too fast."[95] Otherwise, both the secrecy of the campaign and its calculated choreography are at risk.

Thus, conventional organizing strategy—and even some progressive methods developed to meet employer antiunion campaigns—proceed from the premise that the union is engaged in a war with the employer for scarce resources. In the organizing phase of the union's activity, the workers are the scarce resources. Workers are either with the union and, presumably, "against" the company, or they are aligned with the employer. Initial assessments of a worker's allegiance are made after a minimal investment of time by organizers, and no effort is made to build a community spirit among workers; the primary goal is to drum up enough enthusiasm to get through the organizing and election phases. To that end, control of the campaign is retained by the organizers, who shape the issues after the initial meeting with disgruntled employees and determine campaign strategy. The employees are relegated to doing the day-to-day practical work of passing the word, gathering names, and getting cards signed. The traditional strategy assumes that once an election has been won, the organizing task is over.[96] The employees are handed the reins of control for the first time—subject, of course, to controls imposed by the international union. Alternatively, the election is lost, the organizers leave, and the union's interest in the workers ends.[97]

> The primary message to convey to the workers is that they are forming their own union, to meet their own needs, with their own leadership. The union is not an outside "third party," it is the people themselves. This understanding is important both to develop a strong base for the organizing drive, and for the long-run vitality of the union. It is also a critical way to inoculate against the inevitable company campaign.

Id. at 15.

94. *See id.* at 7, 21, 24.

95. *Id.* at 10.

96. *See* Green & Tilly, *supra* note 15, at 487.

97. Strict adherence to this model of organizing was certainly not present among all the directors and organizers interviewed. Indeed, in Part V of this Article I discuss a few of the radically different (and, in my view, far more promising) philosophies of organizing that I encountered in conducting this empirical research. Perhaps the most compelling evidence of the existence of the assumptions to which I allude in the text were the comments of individual organizers who expressed regret at the inability of the union structure to accommodate what they felt would be more effective techniques. Nevertheless, this goal-driven philosophy—and particularly its reflection within the blitz model—were articulated frequently and in sufficiently concrete terms to support the generalizations I have made in aid of my point. Other empirical research supports my observations. *See, e.g.*, Getman, *supra* note 12, at 60 (observing that unions lost elections because of such campaign errors as "working almost exclusively with one or two people on the employee committee" and "not getting

The goal-oriented approach favored by unions is reinforced by the provisions of the National Labor Relations Act that govern the conduct of elections.[98] Once the union gathers the requisite number of signed authorization cards,[99] it is in a position either to request voluntary recognition from the employer[100] or to file a petition for a certification election. The election, if ordered, is generally scheduled within twenty-five to thirty days following the direction of election, which occurs once the regional director of the NLRB resolves any disputes concerning the appropriate unit or the validity of the authorization cards and determines that a question concerning representation exists.[101] Employers frequently delay the election by challenging the unit composition, affording themselves time to mount an impressive antiunion campaign. Once the necessary number of cards are signed, however, the union will be entitled to an election. Therefore, the immediate goal of any union organizing campaign is to obtain sufficient numbers of signed authorization cards.

If the union is fortunate enough to prevail at the election, it is protected from decertification petitions or petitions by rival unions for one year. The employer is required to recognize that union as the representative of its work force for the same period; the theory is that this time is necessary to stabilize industrial relations and to give collective bargaining a chance to work.[102] If the union is fortunate enough to win a collective

to know the rank-and-file members"—both of which take time); Hurd & McElwain, *supra* note 85, at 371 (finding that election delay has no significant negative impact on union organizing success because of the relatively slow organizing process typical of successful clerical campaigns); Green & Tilly, *supra* note 15, at 487 (stating that if a quick victory seems unlikely, union organizers are likely to ignore the shop).

98. National Labor Relations Act, 29 U.S.C. §§ 151-168 (1988).

99. Section 9(c)(1)(A) of the Act provides that a petition for an election must be supported by a "substantial number of employees." 29 U.S.C. § 159(c)(1)(A). National Labor Relations Board rules define "substantial" to mean at least 30%. *See* NLRB Rules and Regulations and Statements of Procedure, Series 8, § 101.18 (1987). Requests for voluntary recognition by an employer must be supported by signed authorization cards from a majority of employees in the appropriate unit. *See infra* note 100.

100. *See* NLRB v. Gissel Packing Co., 395 U.S. 575, 596-97 (1969) (holding that union authorization cards, if obtained from a majority of employees without misrepresentation or coercion, are sufficiently reliable to provide a valid, alternate route to majority status triggering a bargaining obligation).

101. NLRB Rules and Regulations and Statements of Procedure, *supra* note 99, at § 101.21(d).

102. *See* National Labor Relations Act § 9(c)(3), 29 U.S.C. § 159(c)(3) (1988) (forbidding holding an election within 12 months of a preceding valid election); Brooks v. NLRB, 348 U.S. 96, 98-99, 104 (1954) (holding that absent unusual circumstances, an employer must recognize a union for the entire "certification year" even if it has evidence of the union's loss of majority status). A similar but more time-limited rule protects unions that achieve recognition voluntarily. *See* Keller Plastics Eastern, 157 N.L.R.B. 583, 587 (1966) (ruling that once employer voluntarily and validly agrees to recognize union, the parties have a "reasonable time"—typically, three weeks—to negotiate a collective bargaining agreement).

bargaining agreement within that time frame, the contract-bar doctrine prevents a rival union from holding an election for a period of up to three years.[103] Thus, the law encourages unions to achieve Board certification or employer recognition as quickly as possible and then insulates the union from attack immediately following certification or recognition. This reinforces the notion that the organizing and community-building period ceases upon certification or recognition. For many unions relying upon the initial momentum and enthusiasm of the blitz approach, however, the process of building solidarity and a sense of community among workers has just begun.

The goal-oriented approach favored by the majority of unions thus eschews the *process* of empowering the workers through building solidarity and community in favor of the goal of adding another union local to the international union's membership. This approach leaves employees vulnerable to powerful emotional counterattacks by savvy employers who are well aware that campaign momentum is critical and have become adept at delaying certification elections.[104] Moreover, even if majority support sustains the employees through the election process, the lack of solidarity hobbles the union at the bargaining table. For example, if the union lacks strong rank-and-file support for work stoppage or the use of other economic weapons in support of demands made at the bargaining table, the employer may call the union's bluff. The threat of permanent replacement may be enough to shake the faith of workers who lack the emotional support from the community to take the significant economic risk of replacement.[105]

Finally, employees who were motivated only by the enthusiasm and momentum of a blitz campaign are unlikely to feel sufficiently empowered to have a voice in the union once it is in place. This is particularly true when the union has stressed secrecy rather than urging employees to

103. The contract must be in writing, must contain a valid union security clause, and must be of fixed duration, although three years is the maximum bar period for petitions by rival unions. *See generally* 1 THE DEVELOPING LABOR LAW 361-76 (Charles J. Morris ed., 2d ed. 1983).

104. *See* Paul Weiler, *Promises To Keep: Securing Workers' Rights to Self-Organization Under the NLRA*, 96 HARV. L. REV. 1769, 1777-78 (1983) (observing that employers emphasize to employees the risks of supporting the union, such as more stringent supervisory practices, loss of special benefits, hefty union dues and fines, the risk of lost wages due to strikes, the likelihood of jobs lost to replacement workers, and the threat of employer relocation); Getman, *supra* note 12, at 53 (noting that many professional antiunion campaign managers routinely delay elections in hopes that time will cool the employees' ardor for the union).

105. *See* NLRB v. MacKay Radio & Tel. Co., 304 U.S. 333, 345 (1938) (ruling that workers striking in support of economic demands may be permanently replaced).

publicly voice their support for the union,[106] or when the outside organizer has exercised strong control over the organizing drive, depriving the employees of the experience of organizing themselves. Blitz organizing campaigns deprive employees of the process of organizing, building a community, and realizing that what was previously conceived of as personal is, in fact, political. Thus, such union organizing strategies favor the ends (election wins) over the means (building a community of workers who are empowered by their solidarity) and continue the cycle of alienation. The union becomes simply one more layer in the hierarchy between the individual and the employer, rather than the collective voice of the workers.

2. *Bargaining Strategies*

The bargaining strategy employed by most labor unions is the traditional adversarial approach to negotiation. Variously referred to as "win-lose," "zero-sum," and "distributive" bargaining,[107] the adversarial bargaining model is linear in nature, and its strategy and tactics have been likened to a football game.[108] After an initial offer, the negotiations follow a pattern of offer-counteroffer or demand-concession until a compromise is reached somewhere within the bargaining range, which is the area of possible theoretical agreement between the parties' goals, or target points, and outside of their bottom lines, or resistance points.[109] Such a negotiating style affects both the substance of the bargain (because compromise, split-the-difference resolutions are often unsatisfactory when issues in the negotiation are multiple and varied) and the subsequent relationship between the parties. The latter is of particular concern in an area such as labor-management relations, where the quality of the parties' relationship in the future is at least as important as the immediate bargain struck.

---

106. *See* Getman, *supra* note 12, at 76 (describing the extremely effective dynamic of the Yale organizing campaign wherein the union printed a poster resembling the Declaration of Independence, bearing the signatures of hundreds of union supporters).

107. The phrases "zero-sum," "win-lose," and "distributive" bargaining refer to the view that what one party gains the other must give up. The assumptions underlying this view are that resources are scarce, both parties desire the same resources, and therefore they are in conflict that can only be resolved through division of the resource according to their relative power; the "winner" of the negotiation will receive more of the resource. Carrie Menkel-Meadow, *Toward Another View of Legal Negotiation: The Structure of Problem-Solving*, 31 UCLA L. REV. 754, 756, 764-65 (1984); *see supra* text accompanying note 37.

108. Menkel-Meadow, *supra* note 107, at 769-70.

109. *Id.*

This adversarial bargaining pattern is reinforced by the labor laws. Once a union has been certified as the exclusive representative of the employees in a particular unit, the NLRA imposes an obligation to bargain "in good faith" over "wages, hours, and terms and conditions of employment."[110] The Supreme Court has construed the Act as establishing two categories of bargaining subjects: "mandatory" subjects over which the parties must bargain (wages, hours, and working conditions) and "permissive" subjects, upon which neither party may insist at the bargaining table.[111] Refusal to bargain over mandatory subjects or insistence upon permissive subjects exposes the employer or the union to unfair labor practice charges.[112] The Act requires that the parties bargain "to impasse" over mandatory subjects, which normally means negotiating until the parties' positions become fixed and stalemate occurs.[113] Thus, the Act reifies the adversarial bargaining model by fixing the subjects of bargaining and by defining the bargaining obligation in a way that operates to encourage positional, goal-driven bargaining that terminates in impasse or agreement.

The first vice of adversarial negotiating strategies is that they lead to limited, competitive thinking that narrows the range of solutions, resulting in bargains that may be satisfactory to neither party.[114] Carrie Menkel-Meadow gives the simple example of two children arguing over a piece of chocolate cake. The linear compromise of cutting the piece of cake in half will be unsatisfactory to both children if "one prefers the cake and the other the icing."[115] The adversarial paradigm assumes "first, that there [exists] only one issue . . . and second, that both parties desire equally and exclusively the thing by which that issue is measured."[116] In multidimensional negotiations, such assumptions are not

110. The National Labor Relations Act, 29 U.S.C. § 158(d) (1988). The good-faith bargaining requirement has been construed with a focus on the requirement that the parties "bargain," rather than with a focus on their good faith. The courts view evidence of positional bargaining behavior—i.e., offers and counteroffers on mandatory subjects, with concessions made on both sides—as indicative of good faith. *See generally* 1 THE DEVELOPING LABOR LAW, *supra* note 103, at 579-93 (describing criteria used by courts as indicia of good-faith bargaining).

111. *See* NLRB v. Wooster Div. of Borg-Warner Corp., 356 U.S. 342, 349 (1958).

112. Sections 158(a)(5) and 158(b)(3) make it an unfair labor practice for an employer or a union, respectively, to refuse to bargain collectively with its adversary. National Labor Relations Act, 29 U.S.C. §§ 158(a)(5), 158(b)(3) (1988).

113. *See* David G. Epstein, Comment, *Impasse in Collective Bargaining*, 44 TEX. L. REV. 769, 770 (1966) (noting that courts consider an impasse, or deadlock, as a defense to the charge of refusal to bargain). Bargaining to impasse is the legal prerequisite to the employer's ability to implement unilateral changes in working conditions. *See* NLRB v. Katz, 369 U.S. 736, 741-42 (1962).

114. *See* Menkel-Meadow, *supra* note 107, at 775-76.

115. *Id.* at 771.

116. *Id.* at 784.

only unfounded but are counterproductive. As Menkel-Meadow has argued in the legal negotiation context, these assumptions foreclose creative solutions to complex problems that could broaden the range of possible solutions and maximize both parties' gains.[117]

In the labor context, adversarial assumptions about bargaining serve to remove some of the most important decisions from the collective bargaining process and limit the parties' ability to think creatively about the issues and solutions.[118] Bargaining sessions conducted according to an adversarial model are typically influenced by the "shadow of the court" (or, in this case, the NLRB)—meaning that negotiators assume that they are limited to what would be available if the court (or Board) were to resolve the dispute.[119] Thus, union negotiators may concentrate their efforts on mandatory subjects of bargaining since these are the only ones on which the employer can be legally compelled to bargain to impasse.[120] Such an adversarial, legalistic focus is likely to stifle the development of creative, innovative, or idiosyncratic solutions to problems that would be more satisfactory to all parties, thus preventing such disputes from proceeding to adjudicative levels (the Board and the courts).[121]

The second flaw in the adversarial method of negotiation is its effect on the parties' future relationship. First, the argumentative offer-counteroffer form of discussion typical of traditional adversarial bargaining may lead to competitive strategies that escalate hostility levels and

---

117. *See id.* at 789. This is a concept that feminists, particularly feminists of color, have explored in the context of conflicting demands by oppressed groups for liberation. In an impassioned argument against the identification of other oppressed groups as the enemy in a struggle for a scarce resource (liberation), Andrea Canaan writes:

> It's as if we think liberation a fixed quantity, that there is only so much to go around. That an individual or community is liberated at the expense of another. *When we view liberation as a scarce resource, something only a precious few of us can have, we stifle our potential, our creativity, our genius for living, learning and growing.*

Andrea Canaan, *Brownness*, *in* THIS BRIDGE CALLED MY BACK: RADICAL WRITINGS BY WOMEN OF COLOR 232, 235 (Cherríe Moraga & Gloria Anzaldua eds., 1981).

118. *See* Note, *Subjects of Bargaining Under the NLRA and the Limits of Liberal Political Imagination*, 97 HARV. L. REV. 475, 479 (1983); *see also* JAMES B. ATLESON, VALUES AND ASSUMPTIONS IN AMERICAN LABOR LAW 120 (1983) (arguing that creation of a permissive category of subjects undermines the bargaining obligation imposed by the Act).

119. *See* Menkel-Meadow, *supra* note 107, at 789.

120. *See supra* note 113 and accompanying text.

121. *See* Menkel-Meadow, *supra* note 107, at 790-92; *see also* Andrew A. Lipsky, Comment, *Participative Management Schemes, the Law, and Workers' Rights: A Proposed Framework of Analysis*, 39 AM. U. L. REV. 667, 709 (1990) (arguing that mandatory-permissive doctrine has hobbled the "development of creative bargaining techniques that participative management schemes require"). Menkel-Meadow points out that lawyers may actually prefer the "shadow of the court" limited conception of negotiations because it makes it easier to evaluate alternatives and predict likely outcomes for clients. Menkel-Meadow, *supra* note 107, at 791.

contribute to inefficiency by taking more time and costing more money.[122] Second, the combined effect of traditional admonitions to refuse to disclose one's true interests and goals and the debate-style structure of the discussions serves to preclude the asking of questions and exchange of information that would reveal additional issues and possible solutions.[123]

The adversarial model of bargaining reflects a patriarchal vision of power: It assumes an overt conflict of interest over equally desired scarce resources, typically characterized as the profits of the workers' labor, and posits a competitive win-lose method for determining the "winner" of the dispute. The model is inefficient and counterproductive in the labor context, where the parties' interests are often in harmony and the debate concerns only the methods for achieving the goal (increased profits); where there exist multiple issues and many permutations of their possible resolution; and where the maintenance of the parties' ongoing daily relationship may be more important than the deal struck. Thus, the application of patriarchal norms of power to union bargaining strategy operates to constrain the parties' ability to "make and remake industrial life."[124]

3. *Strategies of Economic Pressure*

The primary economic weapon wielded by conventional unions is work stoppage, or the strike. Historically, the strike was effective when employed by unions whose members were skilled, difficult-to-replace craftspeople who lived in union towns, where the social pressure against scabs was sufficient to deter many from taking union jobs during a strike. In today's urban service-sector economy, unskilled replacement workers are plentiful; the threat of poverty looms larger than the social pressure exerted against scabs, who may be immigrant workers with little to lose in the way of social acceptance and who can vanish into the anonymity of a large city at the end of the workday. Thus, the strike weapon is not only ineffective, it is costly: Workers go without pay, often in the absence of an adequate strike fund, and risk losing jobs in an increasingly depressed labor market. From the union's perspective, using the strike weapon puts everything on the line for the organization and its members,

122. *See* Menkel-Meadow, *supra* note 107, at 794. In labor law, such inefficiency is sometimes justified as "therapeutic" because it helps to release the inevitable hostility between management and labor. In addition to assuming that labor-management hostility is natural and inevitable, this argument is unpersuasive because it is typically the lawyers for each side that are releasing their hostilities or, at the most, one or two high-level management representatives and a union business agent.

123. *Id.* at 780-82.

124. Note, *supra* note 118, at 494.

exacting a heavy toll on members' loyalty and morale in the event of failure.[125] In short, "[a] strike for a union is like a sting for a bee—painful for the enemy, but often more damaging to the attacker in the end."[126]

Again, the law reinforces unions' focus on strikes as the primary economic weapon. Other than the limited protection the law affords picketing and boycotting, the strike is the only employee economic weapon explicitly protected by the NLRA.[127] Alternative economic weapons that halt or slow production and can be narrowly tailored to achieve the ends desired, such as the sitdown strike or the secondary boycott, are not protected under the Act because they are too effective: They challenge the employer's assumed right to unilateral control over the production process.[128] Thus, they carry the risk of permanent job loss and civil or criminal sanctions.[129] Occasional innovative efforts by unions to engage in passive resistance outside the workplace have been punished swiftly.[130] Thus, the law operates to continue to ensure unions'

---

125. *See* LERNER, *supra* note 80, at 30-31.

126. *Id.* at 30.

127. *See* National Labor Relations Act, §§ 7, 13, 29 U.S.C. §§ 157, 163 (1988). *See also* §§ 8(b)(4), 8(b)(7)(C) (provisos), 29 U.S.C. §§ 158(b)(4), 158(b)(7) (1988) (permitting limited organizational and informational picketing and observance of primary boycotts).

Of course, even the protection afforded striking workers is quite limited: although employers may not fire strikers, they may "permanently replace" them in order to continue production. *See* NLRB v. MacKay Radio & Tel. Co., 304 U.S. 333, 345-46 (1938).

128. *See* Archibald Cox, *The Right to Engage in Concerted Activities*, 26 INDUS. REL. L.J. 319, 339 (1951) (arguing that slowdowns and similar on-the-job disobedience "are too effective to permit them to be part of the employees' arsenal"); *see also* ATLESON, *supra* note 118, at 58.

129. The sitdown strike is unlawful and may expose participants to job loss and civil and criminal penalties. *See* NLRB v. Fansteel Metallurgical Corp., 306 U.S. 240, 252 (1939). Employers who are victims of illegal secondary boycotts may seek compensatory damage awards against the union in federal court. *See* Labor Management Relations Act, § 303(b), 29 U.S.C. § 187(b) (1988). The slowdown, although it is not unlawful and so does not subject workers to civil or criminal penalties, is also unprotected under the Act; it carries the risk of job loss or employer discipline. *See* NLRB v. Elk Lumber Co., 91 N.L.R.B. 333, 336 (1950).

130. For example, severe sanctions were imposed on the United Mineworkers and individuals acting in support of the passive resistance effort employed by the union in aid of its 1989-90 strike against the Pittston Coal Company in Virginia and Kentucky. During the strike, Virginia Gov. Gerald Baliles ordered state troopers to provide armed escorts to coal-truck convoys. G.L. Marshall, *Jackson Lends Support to Miners*, UPI, Apr. 30, 1989, *available in* LEXIS, Nexis Library, UPI File. "Sister Bernadette Kenny, a 50-year-old Catholic nun, was arrested by a federal marshal for driving her mobile health clinic too slowly in front of a coal truck." She was jailed on federal charges; the charges were later dismissed. Michael deCourcy Hinds, *Bitter Coal Strike May Be at End, but Ripples from Dispute Are Widely Felt*, N.Y. TIMES, Dec. 23, 1989, § 1, at 17. The United Mineworkers Union was fined $9 million in one week in October, 1989, for slowing down coal traffic on Virginia highways. *See* Marianne Lavelle, *The New Coal Wars*, NAT'L L.J., Nov. 20, 1989, at 1. Total fines assessed against the union for using massive sitdown demonstrations, placing spikes in the road to halt coal-truck traffic, and taking over a production plant for four days were at least $52

reliance on the strike weapon as the primary means of exerting economic pressure.

Moreover, unions themselves have a stake in eschewing unconventional "self-help" weapons in favor of the strike. Because unconventional economic weapons vest power in the rank and file and are local rather than centralized in nature, they undermine the union's hierarchical structure of control.[131] They typically involve the affected workers directly, according them more accountability and responsibility. Many are flexible and their use and timing can be tailored to fit the goal desired. For example, sick-outs have proved effective in a few cases in exerting pressure in response to specific management actions.[132] Ultimately, such methods are more empowering than a top-down, militaristic strike.

Similarly ignored by most unions are limited forms of collective shop-floor resistance, which are typically lower risk and lower gain creative struggles waged by workers who cannot risk losing their jobs but seek to limit the employer's control over production.[133] Such strategies include collective pacing, griping, humming while working, and other shop-floor antics.[134] These resistance strategies, like slowdowns and sick-outs, are amenable to use by the rank and file, can be conceived spontaneously, do not require centralized organization and planning, and

million. *Mineworkers Head Calls for U.S. Energy Independence*, DAILY LAB. REP. (BNA) No. 181, at A-9 (Sept. 18, 1990).

It is questionable whether all of the United Mineworkers' resistance efforts were truly "passive"—many appear to have involved violence or threats of violence. *See McGothlin to Hold Hearings on Fines*, UPI, Jan. 4, 1990, *available in* LEXIS, Nexis Library, UPI File (detailing that during a nine-month walkout there were 212 felony arrests, most of which involved "violence," ranging from placing jack rocks in the roads to throwing objects into vehicles). Nevertheless, government administrators and courts that became embroiled in the controversy appear to have viewed the primary harm as the interruption of business; the vast majority of arrests were for road-blocking sitins or rolling roadblocks. *See id.*; Hinds, *supra*; Lavelle, *supra*.

131. *See* ATLESON, *supra* note 118, at 47 ("[U]nity might be undercut by 'well-intentioned but uncoordinated' actions at local levels.").

132. Telephone interview with Julie Kushner, UAW District 65 Director of Organizing for the Division of Technical, Office and Professional Employees (July 1991) (notes on file with author).

133. *See* Nina Shapiro-Perl, *Resistance Strategies: The Routine Struggle for Bread and Roses*, *in* MY TROUBLES ARE GOING TO HAVE TROUBLE WITH ME: EVERYDAY TRIALS AND TRIUMPHS OF WOMEN WORKERS 193, 194 (Karen Brodkin Sacks & Dorothy Remy eds., 1984).

134. *Id.* at 197-202. Most recently, the UAW District 65 disrupted business at a Hudson's department store in Michigan by staging a rally in the parking lot, marching inside singing "Solidarity Forever," and tying up cash registers for long periods by purchasing merchandise with pennies, nickels, and dimes and then returning it. Joann Muller, *UAW Uses Disruptive Tactics Against Hudson's*, DET. FREE PRESS, July 24, 1991, at 1E. The protest was intended to pressure Hudson's into bargaining with employees at another Hudson's store, who had voted in the union more than a year previously; the employer had delayed bargaining by filing appeals. *Id.*

can be narrowly tailored to challenge specific shop-floor practices. Hence, they too challenge the union's hierarchical power structure.

Unions' reliance on the strike weapon, encouraged by the law, serves to reinforce existing union hierarchy and limit worker resistance against employers. The patriarchal view of power reflected in unions' concern with controlling the workers through the strike weapon also prevents unions from recognizing and capitalizing on the potential for uncoordinated worker militance in the workplace; it constrains our imagination about the possible forms worker resistance may assume.[135] Whether unions' failure to utilize these resistance strategies reflects the desire to preserve union power over workers, organized labor's co-optation by capital in the control of workers, or simply a limited imagination, the range and efficacy of employee economic resistance is restricted.

IV. A FEMINIST THEORY OF POWER

Feminists in all disciplines have observed that many women conceptualize power differently from men. According to Gloria Steinem,

> We as women . . . tend to define power as the ability to use our own talents and to control our own lives. . . . [W]omen's conviction that

135. A poem by feminist Adrienne Rich makes a poignant plea that our different understandings of each other's gestures of anger or rebellion should not prevent us from ultimately recognizing our similarities. She writes:

> Someday if someday comes we will agree
> that trust is not about safety
> that keeping faith is not about deciding
> to clip our fingernails exactly
> to the same length or wearing
> a uniform that boasts our unanimity
>
> Someday if someday comes we'll know
> the difference between liberal laissez-faire
> pluralism and the way you cut your hair
> and the way I clench my hand
> against my cheekbone
> both being possible gestures of defiance
>
> Someday if there's a someday we will
> bring food, you'll say I can't eat what you've brought
> I'll say Have some in the name of our
> trying to be friends, you'll say What about you?
> We'll taste strange meat and we'll admit
> we've tasted stranger
>
> Someday if someday ever comes we'll go
> back and reread those poems and manifestos
> that so enraged us in each other's hand
> I'll say, But damn, you wrote it so I
> couldn't write it off You'll say
> I read you always, even when I hated you

Adrienne Rich, *Negotiations*, *in* TIME'S POWER 9 (1989).

> power has to be earned . . . leads to an emphasis on individual excellence, knowledge, and learning. . . . When women work in groups instead of being dispersed through existing structures . . . . [h]ierarchies are usually weaker, more likely to be based on who does the most work, and less likely to be based on status in the outside world. . . . Perhaps most distinctive of all, these networks often state a goal that few Establishment groups would consider—"empowerment," that is, giving power to other women.[136]

The difference between a patriarchal conception of power and a feminist view of power is one of substance: A feminist conception of power results in a differing identification of *issues*.[137] Ultimately, the way power is defined affects not only the way it is used but who can use it and to what ends.[138]

---

136. GLORIA STEINEM, OUTRAGEOUS ACTS AND EVERYDAY REBELLIONS 226-28 (Holt, Rinehart and Winston 1983). Steinem acknowledges that these positive attributes originated in women's conformity with gender stereotypes; she notes that when women "are tempted to act out power's traditional meaning of dominance, the cultural punishments for such 'unfeminine' behavior are so great that we tend to pull back." *Id.* at 227. Nevertheless, she concludes that although women could benefit from learning the useful parts of the hierarchical, masculine style of exercising power, there exists much about women's definition of power to celebrate and embrace. *Id.* at 227-28. Chief among its attributes is our perception of the empowerment of other women as a "reciprocal gift." *Id.* at 228.

137. The significant distinction between patriarchal and feminist theories of power is

> *not the way of seeing power . . . but that which they will see. . . . [I]t is not a question of competing "views" at all, but an issue of different vistas. [The difference lies in] the criteria of significance which they attach to what it allows them to see. . . .* This is because it is not so much their concept of power, as such, which differentiates them, as the issues in which they will see it. And the criteria of what constitutes an issue are embedded in the respective *uses* to which the concept of power is put.

CLEGG, *supra* note 37, at 60 (contrasting male theoreticians Bachrach and Baratz with Dahl).

138. *See* Jane S. Jaquette, *Power as Ideology: A Feminist Analysis*, *in* WOMEN'S VIEWS OF THE POLITICAL WORLD OF MEN 9 (Judith Hicks Stiehm ed., 1984).

The significance of power in defining issues is exemplified by the public/private spheres dichotomy, identified by feminists as a key ideological culprit in maintaining women's subordination. The relegation of women to the primary role of mother sidelines them to the private sphere of home and family, dismissing them from the public realm. More subtle forms of patriarchal organization derive from this gendered hierarchical social structure, including the sexual division of labor in the workplace and the ideological separation of political and family life. ZILLAH R. EISENSTEIN, FEMINISM AND SEXUAL EQUALITY: CRISIS IN LIBERAL AMERICA 33 (1984). *See also* Crain, *supra* note 7, at 1178-79, 1184 (arguing that labor unions' categorization of issues directly affecting women, such as child care, maternal leave, and parental leave, as personal or private has contributed to women's economic subordination in the market); Drude Dahlerup, *Overcoming the Barriers: An Approach to How Women's Issues Are Kept from the Political Agenda*, *in* WOMEN'S VIEWS OF THE POLITICAL WORLD OF MEN, *supra*, at 33 (analyzing how the issue of women's suffrage in Denmark was raised or suppressed from the political agenda); Lucinda M. Finley, *Transcending Equality Theory: A Way out of the Maternity and the Workplace Debate*, 86 COLUM. L. REV. 1118, 1118-19 (1986) (arguing that the public-private split between home and workplace has fostered the economic and social subordination of women); Martha Minow, *Words and the Door to the Land of Change: Law, Language, and Family Violence*, 43 VAND. L. REV. 1665, 1671-92 (1990) (arguing that the law contributes to the problem of domestic violence when judges believe that such violence is part of the private sphere

A. Defining Power

1. *Power as Ability*

Feminist thinkers who have examined the concept of power have conceived of it as energy, ability, capacity, and freedom.[139] The Latin root of the word "power" is *posse*, which means "to be able."[140] Feminist power is a form of creative energy; it is exercised through competence and effectiveness, whether in the direct production of ideas or art, through stimulating activity in others, or through heightening vitality. This form of power, though considered a personal attribute, is primarily a capacity or a relation among people and assumes its full meaning only when it is realized by acting through communities or networks supporting individuals.[141] It is sometimes referred to as "power to,"[142] referring in a social context to the ability to cause or prevent change.[143]

Feminists reject the patriarchal understanding of power as domination.[144] Although the feminist concept of power is relational, the awareness of the connection among people fostered by women's experience[145] gives rise to an assumption of responsibility for others rather than an urge to dominate them.[146] Feminists perceive others as "members of a network of relationships on whose continuation they all depend"[147] rather than as opponents in a contest of rights. Communication is viewed as the best mode of conflict resolution, and persuasion, not compulsion, is the means to initiate action.[148] Power is exercised "with" rather than "over" another; cooperation is generated by raising others'

---

and does not belong in court); Frances E. Olsen, *The Family and the Market: A Study of Ideology and Legal Reform*, 96 HARV. L. REV. 1497, 1498 (1983) (arguing that social reform to eliminate subordination of women has been limited by the public-private dichotomy between market and family).

139. *See, e.g.*, JEAN BAKER MILLER, TOWARD A NEW PSYCHOLOGY OF WOMEN 116 (2d ed. 1986) (asserting that power may be defined as "the capacity to implement" or the ability to influence others without controlling, limiting, or destroying them); HARTSOCK, *supra* note 28, at 225-27 (noting that whenever a feminist has reexamined assumptions about power, she has emphasized an understanding of power that focuses on energy and ability rather than on domination).

140. Ann Weick, *Issues of Power in Social Work Practice*, *in* WOMEN, POWER, AND CHANGE 173, 174 (Ann Weick & Susan T. Vandiver eds., 1981).

141. *See* FRENCH, *supra* note 22, at 505; HARTSOCK, *supra* note 28, at 222-24 (describing the work of Dorothy Emmet).

142. This is to distinguish it from the concept of "power over." *See* FRENCH, *supra* note 22, at 505; *see supra* notes 22-24 and accompanying text.

143. *See* Weick, *supra* note 140, at 174.

144. *See* HARTSOCK, *supra* note 28, at 225-26.

145. *See infra* part IV.A.3.

146. *See* GILLIGAN, *supra* note 44, at 30.

147. *Id.*

148. *Id.* at 30-31.

morale and stimulating productive effort rather than by molding their opinions or practices through force, coercion, or psychological pressure.[149]

Thus, power and community are closely connected in feminist thought: Community is the source of power. Hannah Arendt makes clear that power is not property, not a thing one can possess, but a function of the relationship among people.[150] Its legitimacy derives from the community's existence: "*Power* corresponds to the human ability not just to act but to act in concert. Power is never the property of an individual; it belongs to a group and remains in existence only so long as the group keeps together."[151] Thus, rather than having a material base, feminist power is founded on the nature and strength of the connection among group members.

2. *Power as Nurturant*

A number of feminist writers have emphasized the nurturant aspect of power. The focus on the nurturant property of female power derives from its association with mothering. Woman as mother gives birth and nurtures, creating life and transmitting "culture, language, love, and community."[152] Adrienne Rich describes women's power as beneficent and generative, incorporating the biological capacity of reproduction as the source of a magical, transcendent power.[153] For Rich and many other feminists, women's much-heralded ability to care stems from this power; feminist power is strong and resilient, "a power attuned to the rhythm of the life instincts."[154] Nevertheless, such power has " 'no mere will to mastery, only care for the many-lived unending forms' of life."[155]

These descriptions of power are closely tied to prepatriarchal images of power in goddess cults and concepts of power in matriarchal societies. Rich writes that the goddess cults taught women "that power, awesomeness, and centrality were theirs by nature, not by privilege or miracle; the

---

149. HARTSOCK, *supra* note 28, at 222-24 (summarizing the work of Dorothy Emmet).

150. HANNAH ARENDT, ON VIOLENCE 44 (1969).

151. *Id.*

152. HAUNANI-KAY TRASK, EROS AND POWER: THE PROMISE OF FEMINIST THEORY 149 (1986).

153. ADRIENNE RICH, OF WOMAN BORN: MOTHERHOOD AS EXPERIENCE AND INSTITUTION 73 (1976).

154. TRASK, *supra* note 152, at 150 (discussing commonalities among the works of Robin Morgan, Jill Johnston, Mary Daly, and Adrienne Rich).

155. *Id.* at 147 (quoting Rich).

female was primary."[156] Rather than appearing as a mysterious, hostile force that must be harnessed and shaped by culture, nature becomes a positive force, a "prototype for harmonious growth and balance."[157]

There is no question that these conceptions of female power as nurturant have a biological basis. Robin Morgan's focus on the celebration of the female body and women's physical as well as emotional role in mothering is typical.[158] Audre Lorde links feminist power with eros, urging women to reconnect with their erotic, biological selves as a source of inspiration, creativity, and strength: "Within the celebration of the erotic in all our endeavours, my work becomes a conscious decision—a longed-for bed which I enter gratefully and from which I rise up empowered."[159] For Lorde, the erotic is the "sensual bridge which connects the spiritual and the political."[160]

A focus on the biological source of women's power is essential in order to overcome "somatophobia." Somatophobia is a tradition of Western culture that devalues the physical body and its tasks and advocates "transcending" the body and aspiring to more highly valued intellectual pursuits.[161] Somatophobic theories have appeal for some feminists because women's identification with the body—particularly its capacity to bear children—has been instrumental in our oppression.[162]

156. RICH, *supra* note 153, at 94. Power among tribal peoples is "conceived of as being supernatural and paranormal. It is a matter of spirit involvement and destiny. Woman's power comes automatically, by virtue of her femaleness, her natural and necessary fecundity, and her personal acquaintance with blood." PAULA GUNN ALLEN, THE SACRED HOOP: RECOVERING THE FEMININE IN AMERICAN INDIAN TRADITIONS 254 (1986). Some feminists believe that patriarchy is the product of our universal fear of female power. Men, afraid of women's power, instituted a system of sexual domination in which women willingly collaborate in their own subordination. The argument is that our absolute dependency as infants on our mothers results in a fear of female power, and consequently all humans, male and female, engage in a struggle to "keep [female power] under control and harness it to chosen purposes." DOROTHY DINNERSTEIN, THE MERMAID AND THE MINOTAUR 161 (1976).

157. TRASK, *supra* note 152, at 158.

158. *See* Robin Morgan, *The Child* and *The Self*, *in* LADY OF THE BEASTS 78-88 (1976) (celebrating the biological connection between mother and child and concluding that "[t]here is nothing I have not been, and I am come into my power. There is nothing I cannot be."). *See also* Robin West, *Jurisprudence and Gender*, 55 U. CHI. L. REV. 1, 20-21 (1988) (describing women's relational capacity as biologically based in the physical capacity to bear children and nurture them); Marie Ashe, *Zig-Zag Stitching and the Seamless Web: Thoughts on "Reproduction" and the Law*, 13 NOVA L. REV. 355, 359-71 (1989) (describing her experience of the birthing process of each of her children and its relationship to the depth of her connection with each child).

159. Audre Lorde, *Uses of the Erotic: The Erotic as Power*, *in* SISTER OUTSIDER: ESSAYS AND SPEECHES 54-55 (1984).

160. TRASK, *supra* note 152, at 94 (describing Lorde's work).

161. *See* SPELMAN, *supra* note 6, at 126.

162. *Id.*

Therefore, prominent feminists have argued that the source of our liberation lies in sundering the connection between women and their bodies by making it possible to conceive and bear children outside the womb, and by disassociating ourselves from the thankless tasks of the body.[163] This strategy is shortsighted because it does not alter the negative attitude toward the body and its tasks, which are, after all, essential for human existence. If we do not challenge somatophobia, we ensure that women's liberation will be predicated on the oppression of some other group—probably defined by race or class—who will then be assigned to do the body's work.[164] Therefore, a truly transformative feminist theory of power must recognize the biological source of women's power.

3. *Understandings of Power Shaped by Women's Experience*

The nurturant aspect of women's power is also grounded in women's cultural experience: women in our society are uniquely focused on affiliative relationships of care.[165] Women's role in a capitalistic society is dualistic: We labor inside and outside the home (in housework and wage work), in a complete immersion in the world of production; in addition, we reproduce human beings.[166] These dual roles result in the construction of women's entire existence around relationships, typically with men. In performing housework, women directly serve the needs of

---

163. *See id.* (describing the work of Betty Friedan, Shulamith Firestone, and Simone de Beauvoir).

164. *See id.* at 127-28.

165. Although I agree with Robin West that women's bodily structure and function predispose us toward connection with others, *see* West, *supra* note 158, at 2-3, 14 (arguing that female experiences of menstruation, coitus, pregnancy, childbirth, and lactation all challenge the male norm of bodily boundaries), I believe that a confluence of social, economic, and biological factors contributes to women's particular concern with affiliative relationships of care.

However, women's economic, political, and social subordination in our postindustrial society is purely cultural (or, in MacKinnon's terms, it is purely political). My favorite vignette illustrating this point is a story about the women of Juchitan, Mexico, that appeared in a *Wall Street Journal* article. Matt Moffett, *The Strong Women of a Mexican Town Crush Stereotypes*, WALL ST. J., Apr. 2, 1991, at A1. The women of Juchitan dominate both the local economy and the men. The Juchitan people descend from the Zapotec Indians, a tribe with Amazonian traits. *Id.* The Juchitan women are physically dominant over men (in terms of size and strength), and they possess an arm lock on the local market. *Id.* Women are the primary breadwinners, while men assume most of the child care responsibilities. *Id.* at A4. Women in this isolated town take their preeminent position for granted, assuming that female superiority is "only natural." *Id.*

166. *See* EISENSTEIN, *supra* note 138, at 235-37.

their husbands and children,[167] while sex segregation in wage work confines us to repetitive, servile types of labor.[168]

Women in our culture have been taught to define and experience themselves relationally, as many feminists have eloquently explained.[169]

167. As the primary character in Marilyn French's novel THE WOMEN'S ROOM describes the experience, "[w]ashing the toilet used by three males, and the floor and walls around it, is, Mira thought, coming face to face with necessity." MARILYN FRENCH, THE WOMEN'S ROOM 150 (1977).

168. *See* ROBERTA GOLDBERG, ORGANIZING WOMEN OFFICE WORKERS: DISSATISFACTION, CONSCIOUSNESS, AND ACTION 26 (1983). Goldberg describes eloquently the similarities for clerical workers between their work at home and their work in the office:

> Filing is like washing dishes and induces the same sense of frustration. Typing a perfect letter is as transient an achievement as cooking an egg. These things are done with little conscious attention; the routine becomes automatic, and the mind wanders into its own escapist paths. . . . Both kinds of work take place when the master is away; most of his presence is spent giving orders for the next round of work.

Id. (quoting M. BENET, SECRETARY: ENQUIRY INTO THE FEMALE GHETTO 74-75 (1972)); *see also* ROSABETH MOSS KANTER, MEN AND WOMEN OF THE CORPORATION (1977) (demonstrating how the sexual hierarchy is reproduced in the modern corporation). For women of color, the similarities have been even more pronounced: For many, the wage work available replicates housework. *See* HARTSOCK, *supra* note 28, at 236.

169. *See, e.g.*, GILLIGAN, *supra* note 44; NEL NODDINGS, CARING: A FEMININE APPROACH TO ETHICS AND MORAL EDUCATION (1984). Gilligan's work has been extremely influential. For a sampling of legal and nonlegal works that apply Gilligan's analysis, see Leslie Bender, *From Gender Difference to Feminist Solidarity: Using Carol Gilligan and an Ethic of Care in Law*, 15 VT. L. REV. 1, 1-3 n.2 (1990).

Gilligan and Noddings have been careful to point out the cultural origins of women's concern with relationships and connections. They note that although this characteristic (or "voice") is empirically observable primarily in women, this is the result of women's common experience of the world rather than any function of biology. *See* GILLIGAN, *supra* note 44, at 2 (asserting that the "different voice" she describes is characterized by theme rather than gender, but admitting that her study traces the development of this voice primarily through women's voices); NODDINGS, *supra*, at 8 (claiming to resist temptation to generalize based on sex, but referring to the ethic of caring as "characteristically and essentially feminine" because of its origins in women's experience). Despite their explicit comments, their work contains considerable ambivalence and can be read as assigning significance to the role of biology in shaping women's experience. The risk of asserting a biological basis for women's experience of the world is that differences in women's economic, political, and social condition will be reinforced as the product of biology and therefore seen as natural and inevitable.

Others have embraced the biological origins of difference and sc have not been afraid to generalize by sex. *See* Alice Rossi, *A Biological Perspective on Parenting*, DAEDALUS No. 2, Spring 1977, at 4 (rejecting egalitarian ideology that denies the reality of biological differences); West, *supra* note 158, at 3 (arguing that experiences of menstruation, intercourse, childbirth, and lactation define women's perspective on world).

In feminist legal scholarship, the debate has been couched in terms of sameness versus difference. Feminist gender-difference theories recognize gender difference as a salient point for analysis and argue for the inclusion and appreciation of gender differences typically associated with women. *See* Bender, *supra*, at 3. Equality feminists reject acknowledgement of gender differences because of the risk of resurrecting a dangerous "separate spheres" ideology. *See id.* at 4. Radical feminists are critical of gender-difference theory because it valorizes voices of women that are the product of gender hierarchies that subordinate women. *See id.* Critical race theorists are concerned with the

In her famous study of female development and its relationship to concepts of identity, morality, and the process of making life choices, Carol Gilligan concluded that women tend to value intimacy and connection to others, while men value separation and autonomy.[170] Consequently, women are guided by an ethic of care and responsibility for others, while men subscribe to an ethic of rights or of justice in order to protect individual autonomy.[171] This translates, ultimately, into different world images for the two sexes: for men, a hierarchy of values; for women, a web of relationships.[172]

---

essentialism inherent in generalizing about sex because it obscures differences of race, class, sexual preference, and ethnicity. *See id.* at 5.

While I do not intend to engage in that debate here, my reliance on Gilligan's work might lead some to conclude that I am a gender-difference theorist. To the contrary, I have serious concerns about the strategies employed by many difference theorists and confess to an ongoing process of internal debate about its validity. Nevertheless, I agree with Bender that gender differences are a reality today and that the theory can be useful in transforming law and building feminist solidarity *now*. *See id.* at 48. For example, as Linda Blum has noted, comparable-worth strategy carries the risk that by seeking to value sex-stereotyped "women's work" in the market by comparing it to sex-stereotyped "men's work," we implicitly reinforce the sex stereotyping of work and do not directly address the problem of sex segregation in the workplace. BLUM, *supra* note 58, at 18. Nevertheless, it is a valuable and potentially effective strategy because it contests women's devaluation, has proved effective in mobilizing women, and exemplifies a potentially transformative vision of the future in which both difference and equality might be embraced. *Id.* at 19.

170. *See* GILLIGAN, *supra* note 44, at 160-61, 164. In this work, Gilligan summarizes conclusions drawn from three studies: the "college student study," which explored identity and moral development in early adult years among 25 college students enrolled in a course on moral and political choice; the "abortion decision study," which considered the relation between experience and the role of conflict in development among 29 women who were in the first trimester of pregnancy and were considering abortion; and the "rights and responsibilities study," which compared conceptions of self and morality, experiences of moral conflict and choice, and judgments on hypothetical moral dilemmas among 144 males and females at nine age points across the life cycle. *See id.* at 2-3.

171. *Id.* at 164, 174.

172. *Id.* at 32. This difference in men's and women's perception of situations has sometimes been referred to as a difference in their "ways of knowing." Literature is rich with examples. One compelling illustration is found in Susan Glaspell's short story *A Jury of Her Peers*. Susan Glaspell, *A Jury of Her Peers*, *in* IMAGES OF WOMEN IN LITERATURE 370-85 (Mary A. Ferguson ed., 1973). Glaspell describes the interchange between two women, wives of the sheriff and the county attorney, who accompany their husbands to the home of a man who was allegedly murdered by his wife. While their husbands examine the physical evidence at the scene of the killing in an effort to ascertain the motive for and circumstances of the killing, the two women remain in the kitchen, investigating its contents and discussing "trifles." They focus on the relationship between the couple, noting the change in the accused murderess, Minnie Wright, following her marriage to John Wright. Subsequently, they discover a partially pieced quilt with stitching that suddenly becomes erratic and uneven, an empty bird cage with a broken door, and a dead canary—whose neck had been wrung—wrapped carefully in silk and placed in Mrs. Wright's sewing box. By relying on their own experience and integrating many small observations that provide clues about the incipient violence within the relationship, the women are able to discern a truth that is hidden from the men. Meanwhile, the forensic investigation has been unproductive, and their husbands are stumped as to the motive; it

Gilligan recognized that women's life experience resulted in a difference in women's orientation toward power. Her studies indicate that women are quicker than men to recognize their own interdependence, equate power with giving and care, and see acts of nurturing as acts of strength.[173] Gilligan's findings reinforce Jean Baker Miller's analysis of women's attitudes toward power.[174] According to Miller, women's positions as caretakers in relationships of temporary inequality (i.e., parent-child) and as subordinates in relationships of permanent inequality (husband-wife) situate us so as "to observe the potential in human connection both for care and for oppression."[175] Consequently, women interpret maternal power as a responsibility to care for the unempowered, to teach and to empower, and are likely to avoid revisiting their own experience of oppression on another.[176]

4. *Summary*

Thus, a feminist theory of power rejects the understanding of power as domination, focusing instead on ability, competence, and the capacity to influence others. Power exercised in a community emanates horizontally, expanding outward in a weblike fashion, rather than vertically. Power belongs to the group rather than to an individual. Those who

---

appears that their inability to hear Mrs. Wright's story—the consequence of their devaluing of relationships—will ultimately result in Mrs. Wright's freedom.

As one literary critic has commented, the men in this story not only lack the ability to "read" the text that is placed before them, "they literally can not recognize it as a text because they can not [sic] imagine that women have stories." Judith Fetterley, *Reading About Reading: "A Jury of Her Peers," "The Murders in the Rue Morgue," and "The Yellow Wallpaper," in* GENDER AND READING: ESSAYS ON READERS, TEXTS, AND CONTEXTS 147, 147-48 (Elizabeth A. Flynn & Patrocinio P. Schweickart eds., 1986). This is because they are bound by a set of preconceptions that limit them to their own (male) story, a "story they are familiar with" and "can recognize as a text." *Id.* at 148.

173. GILLIGAN, *supra* note 44, at 167-68 (citing DAVID C. MCCLELLAND, POWER: THE INNER EXPERIENCE (1975)).

174. *Id.* at 168 (citing JEAN BAKER MILLER, TOWARD A NEW PSYCHOLOGY OF WOMEN (1976)).

175. *Id.*

176. *See* Leslie Bender, *Feminist (Re)Torts: Thoughts on the Liability Crisis, Mass Torts, Power, and Responsibilities*, 1990 DUKE L.J. 848, 892 ("It is the very awareness of the inequality of power that prompts or produces the responsibility to protect, to enable, and to give care, rather than to overwhelm or control.") (citing West, *supra* note 158, in support of her conclusions); *but cf. infra* notes 208, 216-17 and accompanying text (critiquing these conclusions).

Perhaps the basic difference between the patriarchal concept of power and the feminist theory of power is that they rest upon divergent perceptions of human nature. A patriarchal understanding of human nature is profoundly negative; therefore, patriarchal exercises of power tend to be censorial. *See supra* note 5. A feminine view of human nature tends to be positive and the exercise of power by women more affirming. Such a fundamental optimism in a group that has been colonized and oppressed, often in very violent ways, is remarkable and perhaps accounts for the certainty of many feminists that we are unlikely to exercise power in the same way that our oppressors have.

exercise power may be visualized as positioned at the center of a group, from where they are able to mobilize others. Women's experience plays a crucial role in shaping our understanding of power. The source of feminist power is a passionate caring, grounded in recognition and celebration of the link between mind and body and the capacity to generate and nurture life.

B. Woman-Styled Power Within a Hierarchical System

Empirical support for the existence of a distinctly feminine or female style of exercising power is emerging. Observers of the corporate culture have noticed a change in leadership style that seems to correspond with the assumption of positions of leadership by increasing numbers of women.[177] Management experts, always alert to ways of maximizing production and efficiency, have attended to gender difference and have begun to study its implications for the improved performance of corporate structures. Several have identified a particular style of management that they associate with women.

Judy Rosener, who conducted a survey on leadership styles in management, concluded that the "command-and-control leadership style associated with men is not the only way to succeed."[178] Indeed, Rosener observes that successful women managers are "succeeding because of—not in spite of—certain characteristics generally considered to be 'feminine' and inappropriate in leaders."[179] Rosener identifies two management styles: "transactional," usually associated with males, and "transformational," usually associated with females.[180] In a transactional leadership model, the manager views job performance as a series of transactions with subordinates; performance of each transaction by the subordinate is rewarded or punished. Transactional leaders rely heavily

177. A *New York Times* article reports that some white male workers have observed that women managers tend to adopt a more democratic approach to management; according to the article, many workers welcome the freedom from the old oppressive ways. Peter T. Kilborn, *How a Workforce Responds when Equal Rights Is a Goal*, N.Y. TIMES, May 12, 1991, § 1, at 1. One senior vice president at Pacific Gas & Electric describes workers' feelings succinctly: "Some people see a door closing on them . . . [b]ut some of us look at it as a door being properly positioned." *Id.* at 13.

There is some evidence that corporate structure is beginning to change in a direction that may facilitate feminine styles of exercising power, although it is not clear that a causal connection exists between the two phenomena. *See* ROBERT B. REICH, THE WORK OF NATIONS: PREPARING OURSELVES FOR 21ST CENTURY CAPITALISM (1991) (describing the shape that corporations are beginning to assume as "weblike," characterized by less hierarchical, more decentralized structure).

178. Judy B. Rosener, *Ways Women Lead*, 68 HARV. BUS. REV., Nov.-Dec. 1990, at 119.

179. *Id.* at 120.

180. Rosener is careful to note, however, that many women succeed by adhering to the traditional model of leadership and that some men use the transformational style. *Id.* at 125.

on power that derives from their position in the organizational hierarchy—their "formal authority."[181]

By contrast, transformational leaders motivate subordinates to transform their own interest into the interest of the group by building concern for a broader goal. Transformational leaders derive power primarily from "personal characteristics like charisma, interpersonal skills, hard work, and personal contacts."[182] Rosener's interviews with women leaders who utilize a transformational style of leadership reveal an interactive leadership in which managers actively sought to make their interactions with subordinates positive, encouraged participation, shared power and information, attempted to build self-worth and to energize subordinates, and generally pursued a "win-win" strategy in which both employee and organization benefited.[183] A vital part of this leadership style is its power-sharing, participatory nature. For example, women leaders ask for suggestions from subordinates before reaching conclusions and test and modify decisions before implementing them, thereby creating loyalty, maximizing their access to needed information, and ensuring support for the decision once reached.[184] In addition, such a style promotes employees' self-worth and enthusiasm for work.[185]

Rosener attributes the origin of the transformational leadership style to women's experience: a style that is cooperative, supportive, understanding, and gentle seems "natural" for women.[186] Further, women's access to formal power in the workplace has been limited by discrimination; consequently, they have "by default" been compelled to find other ways to attain credibility—chiefly through individual merit and performance.[187]

Similar findings were reported by Sally Helgesen, who conducted an in-depth study of four successful women leaders.[188] These leaders described their management structure as a web or a series of circles arranged in an expanding series of orbits, in contrast to the conventional hierarchical pyramid.[189] This facilitated inclusion as well as power and

181. *Id.* at 120.

182. *Id.*

183. *Id.*

184. *Id.* at 122-23.

185. *Id.* at 123.

186. *Id.* at 124.

187. *Id.* at 124-25.

188. *See* SALLY HELGESEN, THE FEMALE ADVANTAGE: WOMEN'S WAYS OF LEADERSHIP (1990).

189. *Id.* at 44-45.

information sharing. These women described their role as being in the center rather than at the top, and they thought of themselves as reaching out rather than down.[190] Helgesen notes the similarity between these descriptions and Gilligan's findings on the different ways men and women tend to structure relationships and view the world, particularly the feminine value of connection.[191]

According to Helgesen, women leaders tend to be more reflective than their male counterparts and tend to take a longer view, or bigger-picture perspective, on their organization and its relationship to society.[192] Consequently, women have an advantage during times of rapid technological change.[193] Earlier feminist work had identified a "beta" style of leadership as typical of women; beta-style "leadership focuses on long-range issues, values, and goals" and is an integrative, multidimensional style that adapts well to change.[194] By contrast, the "alpha" style of leadership, associated with men, is highly competitive, is characterized by "analytical, rational, quantitative thinking and relies on hierarchical relationships."[195] It has a narrow, detail- and task-oriented focus.[196] Leaders with the alpha style perceive change as disruptive and chaotic because it interferes with achievement of short-term goals.[197]

Despite the many advantages of the female style of leadership, it is indisputably difficult to maintain within the confines of a hierarchical, rule-bound organization. For women who invade male bastions of power, the temptation to assimilate is strong. For years, women were instructed either to become like men in order to succeed in the workplace[198] or to learn to play the game according to men's rules.[199] Betty Harragan, the author of two books advising women on how to play a

190. *Id.* at 45-46.

191. *Id.* at 49-50, 223 ("The images of hierarchy and web, drawn from the texts of men's and women's fantasies and thoughts, convey different ways of structuring relationships and are associated with different views of morality and self."). *Id.* at 50 (quoting GILLIGAN, *supra* note 44, at 62).

192. *Id.* at 25-26.

193. Rosener also notes the efficacy of a female leadership style in organizations that have experienced fast growth and change. *See* Rosener, *supra* note 178, at 125.

194. *See* ELIZABETH NICKLES & LAURA ASHCRAFT, THE COMING MATRIARCHY: HOW WOMEN WILL GAIN THE BALANCE OF POWER 174-76 (1981).

195. *Id.* at 175.

196. *Id.*

197. *Id.*

198. *See, e.g.*, MARGARET V. HIGGINSON & THOMAS L. QUICK, THE AMBITIOUS WOMAN'S GUIDE TO A SUCCESSFUL CAREER at vii (1975) (advising women who want to be upwardly mobile to be "more aggressive, alert, shrewd, and determined" than their male counterparts).

199. *See* BETTY LEHAN HARRAGAN, GAMES MOTHER NEVER TAUGHT YOU: CORPORATE GAMESMANSHIP FOR WOMEN (Rawson Associates 1977) [hereinafter HARRAGAN, GAMES MOTHER NEVER TAUGHT YOU]; BETTY LEHAN HARRAGAN, KNOWING THE SCORE: PLAY-BY-

man's game, likened the modern corporate structure to the military and urged aspiring women managers to educate themselves about the military mind-set and to study the dynamics of such team sports as football.[200] Harragan, displaying barely concealed contempt for men, also urged women to "play to [men's] weak side" by capitalizing on sex stereotypes; for example, older bosses can be "jollied along" indefinitely by ambitious women whom they see as daughters, and younger males can be controlled by women who assume a mother image and "crack the whip."[201]

Finally, such books are filled with "dress for success" advice geared toward assimilating the woman manager into male managerial culture.[202] Aspiring women were to assume the conservative uniform of their male counterparts and to avoid at all costs the secretarial dress style so as not to risk identifying themselves with the clerical ranks rather than the executive ranks.[203] Women were advised to ensure that skirts were long enough to avoid triggering "the innate [male] impulse to look between your legs"[204] and to eschew handbags and other "uniquely female" accessories that might remind men of their gender.[205] Harragan and other writers of her ilk justified their advice by pointing out that most women, because of social conditioning and discriminatory barriers, were oblivious to the reality of [male] corporate gamesmanship and needed to be educated; after all, Harragan argued, "[y]ou can't change a game until you can play by the rules that exist."[206]

PLAY DIRECTIONS FOR WOMEN ON THE JOB (1983) [hereinafter HARRAGAN, KNOWING THE SCORE]; MARGARET HENNIG & ANNE JARDIM, THE MANAGERIAL WOMAN (1976).

200. HARRAGAN, GAMES MOTHER NEVER TAUGHT YOU, *supra* note 199, at 37-95. *See also* HENNIG & JARDIM, *supra* note 199, at 39 (advocating study of football in order to focus women on goal achievement rather than process).

201. HARRAGAN, GAMES MOTHER NEVER TAUGHT YOU, *supra* note 199, at 126-31.

202. *See, e.g., id.* at 336-47.

203. *Id.* at 337-38.

204. *Id.* at 339. After all, wrote Harragan, "[i]f the shoeshine man comes around and you don't dare put your foot up to join in the ritual because of your 'immodesty,' [the short skirt] is no good as a work uniform." *Id.*

205. *Id.* at 343-47.

206. *Id.* at 383; *see also* HARRAGAN, KNOWING THE SCORE, *supra* note 199, at 75-76 (urging a black woman engineer experiencing discrimination in the workplace to "go down to defeat gracefully if you are overridden when presenting expert opinions to your superiors," and explaining that "accommodation tactics work well for blacks and women who want to progress in a male environment").

More-recent books are devoted to helping the male or female subordinate learn to deal with a female manager who has become "a clone of the men." *See, e.g.*, PAULA R. BERN, HOW TO WORK FOR A WOMAN BOSS, EVEN IF YOU'D RATHER NOT (1987). Bern claims to be convinced that women "wield power in very much the same way as men," see *id.* at 35, although she concedes that women must become like men in order to compete in the corporate world—hence, she implicitly acknowledges a difference in styles. *Id.* at 37.

Some feminists have been openly critical of such survival strategies. Suzanne Gordon worries that women who strove to assimilate in the male marketplace have succeeded too well; she argues that many women leaders have adopted traditional male attitudes of disdain for care-giving activities of women. Ultimately, these women have become "prisoners of men's dreams."[207] Gordon points out the short-sightedness of pursuing "equal opportunity feminism," a co-opting ideology that ultimately produces women who imitate men in wielding power.[208] Instead, she urges women to strive for "transformative feminism," to "organize for care," to resurrect empathy and caring as valued traits, and to pursue a program for change in the workplace and the home.[209] Bella Abzug also believes women leaders have a responsibility to change society: "I, personally, am not interested in having women in power unless they're going to change the nature of power as it is manifest today in our nation. I believe women should change the nature of power rather than have power change the nature of women."[210]

---

207. SUZANNE GORDON, PRISONERS OF MEN'S DREAMS: STRIKING OUT FOR A NEW FEMININE FUTURE 3 (1991).

208. *Id.* at 7-9. Gordon is especially critical of the shift toward individualism in the feminist movement. Transformative feminism would challenge patriarchy and capitalism; equal-opportunity feminism channels women toward individual achievement, which results in collective disempowerment. *Id.* at 75. The original idea behind equal-opportunity feminism was that the problem of the undervaluation of women's work would be solved when enough individual women went into previously male-dominated fields and altered the institutional personalities of those fields: As women gained power, "female subordinates would benefit from sisterly solidarity of a trickle-down sort." *Id.* at 160. But as Gordon points out, it is not necessarily true that women, because they have themselves been victims of oppression, will never oppress other women, particularly where differences of race or class exist; generalized moral superiority among the oppressed is a myth. *Id.* at 160-61; *see also* Kanter, *supra* note 168, at 189 (describing findings of Karen Horney and Rollo May that within a hierarchical context persons who "are rendered powerless in the larger arena" may tend to dominate "those over whom they have even a modicum of authority").

209. *Id.* at 273-96. Gordon has been criticized, as have other cultural feminists, for adding a third responsibility to working women's existing "double shift"—the moral responsibility for preserving the "soul" of our society. *See* Erica Munk, *That Classic Female Trait*, N.Y. TIMES, Jan. 13, 1991, § 7, at 20 (reviewing Gordon's *Prisoners of Men's Dreams*).

210. BERN, *supra* note 206, at 6 (quoting from a telephone interview with Bella Abzug); *see also* HOOKS, *supra* note 17, at 83-93, discussed *infra* notes 215-17 and accompanying text.

Guidance is available for women who wish to wield power in a caring way. One author, after describing women's "paths to power" in terms very different from men's (power as effectiveness rather than power as forcefulness), urges women to remain true to their conception of power, first by empowering themselves and then by sharing power and empowering others. *See* NATASHA JOSEFOWITZ, PATHS TO POWER: A WOMAN'S GUIDE FROM FIRST JOB TO TOP EXECUTIVE 4-5 (1980). She stresses caring and responsibility as key attributes of an effective leader. *Id.* at 200-02.

C. Critiques of a Feminist Theory of Power

Some criticize the feminist theory of power advanced above as unrealistic because it ignores the fact that power can and does assume the form of systematic domination.[211] Nancy Hartsock worries that feminists' exclusive focus on women's oppression has caused us to neglect the vital task of analyzing how power operates today—for example, how men's dominance is constructed and maintained.[212] Alternatively, feminist power theories are said to reflect a fear of power, originating in women's history of oppression.[213] Consequently, feminist power theorists are criticized for having failed to grapple with the problems of changing the world and the possibility of doing harm to others in the process. Others put the same critique more positively, noting that women are often uncomfortable with power because it requires accepting risk and the possibility of failure, actions that in turn depend upon a sense of self-worth—"something women are only just beginning to achieve."[214]

These criticisms—particularly those that assert that a fear of power lies at the root of feminist power theory—repeat patriarchy's assumption of a male norm of power by comparing a woman-centered vision of power to the patriarchal norm and, inevitably, finding it lacking because it is "other," "different," and therefore inferior. The implication is that if women desire equality with (white) men, they must demonstrate an equal facility at dominating and controlling others.[215] While it is true that women must deal with the reality of patriarchal institutions that are premised on a patriarchal vision of power, the central paradox of feminism (as with any potentially transformative social movement) is the problem of operating within an existing system without being deradicalized or coopted by the pressure to assimilate and the resulting rewards. Accepting the "natural" superiority of patriarchal norms of power and exploiting those forms of power, in theory or in practice, even for the avowed purpose of working to eliminate oppression, undermines the radical nature

211. *See, e.g.*, Hartsock, *supra* note 28, at 255.

212. *Id.* at 1.

213. *See* Weick, *supra* note 140, at 183. Although Weick recognizes the existence of positive expressions of power, she argues that we cannot ignore the prevalence of negative expressions of power (i.e., exploitation, manipulation, and competition) in the bureaucratic models of our institutions, and she urges women who must function within the constraints of such institutions to learn to use these forms of power. *Id.* at 183-84.

214. Nickles & Ashcraft, *supra* note 194, at 171, 173.

215. *See* hooks, *supra* note 17, at 83-85.

of the movement because the patriarchal hierarchy will inevitably privilege those who do at the expense of those who don't.

Others level a related but more fundamental criticism: How can women, acculturated to patriarchal norms of power, avoid repeating the pattern if and when they do gain power? Such criticisms assert that feminist power theories are the product of women's socialization to accept their "difference" from men; the feminist power theories themselves are the construct of women's experience of oppression and thus can only operate to reinforce the status quo.[216] This is, indeed, a significant risk for a white, upper- and middle-class women's "equal opportunity" feminist movement. The successes of these individual women come at the expense of others who occupy places on the lower rungs of the patriarchal hierarchy because of their race, class, or sexual orientation. Affirming and exploring alternative visions of power is possible only in a truly transformative feminist movement that seeks the eradication of domination in all human relationships. Such a bottom-up movement, combining the interests of those oppressed by sex, race, class, and sexual orientation, would be truly radical; it would teach women that they could "reject the powerful's definition of their reality"[217] and begin to define it for themselves.

Because feminist theories of power are grounded in the experience of oppression, they are more accurately labeled theories of *empowerment*. On a day-to-day basis, feminism is a process, concerned first with empowering the individual, then the individual within her family, then the individual within her social unit, with the circles of empowerment "rippling more widely and inclusively as they go."[218] Only "by adopting a vantage point located in women's life activity" is it possible to construct a feminist theory of power that will ground a critique of the institutions and ideology that constitute the capitalist form of patriarchy and

216. *See, e.g.*, *id.* at 84-87; *see also* Linda Miller Atkinson, *Feminism & Political Theory*, TRIAL MAG., Sept. 1991, at 76, 78 (pointing out that notions of gender-based differences in the exercise of power operate to reinforce women's oppression by using sexual differences to justify excluding women from positions of power in existing hierarchy) (reviewing FEMINISM & POLITICAL THEORY (Cass R. Sunstein ed., 1990)).

217. HOOKS, *supra* note 17, at 90; *see also* KANTER, *supra* note 168, at 190-91 (predicting that those who have confidence in their ability will be more likely to use persuasion than domination as a means of influencing others).

218. ROBIN MORGAN, GOING TOO FAR: THE PERSONAL CHRONICLE OF A FEMINIST 9 (1977).

ultimately support the constitution of a more complete human community.[219] Thus, whatever the strategic risk of acknowledging and celebrating our biologically and culturally constructed femaleness, we must do so in order to empower ourselves.

Feminist power theory, like theories of racial and class power, offers the perspective of a marginalized group.[220] It is our differences—the asserted reasons for our marginalization—that constitute our strength and hold the possibility of radical transformation. A feminist theory of power *must* draw its strength from the essence of our differences, biological and cultural, if it is to avoid re-creating, in "a higher register,"[221] the system of power devised by men. Further, the rejection of hierarchy and domination in the structuring of human relationships necessarily aligns such a truly radical feminist theory with social movements that resist oppression based on race, class, and sexual orientation because all of these movements also challenge the existing hierarchical order. Their strength also lies in their "differences," the cause of their oppression and marginalization.

V. AN ALTERNATIVE MODEL OF LABOR POWER

Labor power in conventional unions is centralized. It follows a hierarchical pattern, devolving from the top (the national or international level) down. Rank-and-file workers are disempowered; they have little say in the day-to-day operation of their union or in its larger political decision making. Consequently, such unions serve only to reinforce the

219. *See* HARTSOCK, *supra* note 28, at 9-12, 231. Hartsock draws an explicit analogy to the perspective of the proletariat and argues that feminist theory, like Marxist theory, holds the potential to aid in deconstructing capitalist patriarchy so that "theory and practice can be redirected in more liberatory directions." *Id.* at 231. She characterizes a feminist critique, however, as "deeper-going" than a Marxist critique because the male worker is subordinated "only during the time his labor power is being used by the capitalist." *Id.* at 234. At home, however, he "strides in front, while a third person, not specifically present in Marx's account of the transactions between capitalist and worker (both of whom are male) follows timidly behind, carrying groceries, baby, and diapers."

220. This is the primary reason why those who have advocated Gilligan's "ethic of care" have labeled it feminist rather than humanist. Because women have been silenced and ignored for so long, the explicit recognition of gender difference and its consequences for law is important to avoid the "co-optation of being reabsorbed, resilenced, and resubmerged into a newly invisible system of male dominance." Bender, *supra* note 169, at 40; *see also* Ellison v. Brady, 924 F.2d 872, 876-78 (9th Cir. 1991) (holding that a "female plaintiff states a prima facie case for hostile environment sexual harassment under title VII when she alleges conduct which a reasonable woman would consider sufficiently severe or pervasive to alter the conditions of employment and create an abusive working environment. . . . [S]ex-blind reasonable person standard tends to be male-biased and ignores the experiences of women." *Id.* at 879; *accord* Robinson v. Jacksonville Shipyards, Inc., 760 F. Supp. 1486, 1522-23 (M.D. Fla. 1991).

221. *See* CATHARINE A. MACKINNON, FEMINISM UNMODIFIED 39 (1987).

status quo by co-opting union leaders and channeling and containing rank-and-file conflict. In this part, I present an alternative vision of a labor union as a participatory democracy structured in a cooperative way that is consistent with a feminist understanding of power. Such a union would be organized from the bottom up and would draw its strength from direct action supported by a renewed concept of labor solidarity that cuts across race, sex, and class boundaries.

Cooperatively structured, woman-centered labor unions can be a particularly effective agent of change because they pose a challenge to systems of oppression based upon class, sex, and race. Consequently, I urge the exploration of new forms of power within such compatible institutional structures. Notwithstanding the widely held view that bureaucracy is inevitable and will eventually dominate our social structure,[222] some islands of anarchy have flourished within the sea of hierarchy. Those that are feminist in character have traditionally been closely associated with issues of concern to women in gaining power: for example, reproductive freedom (the organizing principle behind abortion referral and family-planning clinics); violence against women (rape crisis centers and domestic-violence centers); and economic benefits for working women (women's unions). These institutions are explicitly organized around feminist principles of participatory democracy, decentralized power, and grass-roots control; they practice nonhierarchical, noncompetitive ways of organizing their work.[223]

The congruity of goals between such feminist institutions and the individual women leaders within them (i.e., information sharing, empowerment) eliminates the tension caused by attempting to transform a patriarchal, hierarchical organization from the inside out.[224] In feminist institutions, the individual exercise of female power is intertwined with the structure of the institution, both of which work toward the common goal of female empowerment. Such cooperatively structured institutions

222. MAX WEBER, ECONOMY AND SOCIETY 228 (1978).

223. *See* Ackelsberg & Addelson, *supra* note 8, at 221, 230; Robin Leidner, *Stretching the Boundaries of Liberalism: Democratic Innovation in a Feminist Organization*, 16 SIGNS 263, 268-69, 281 (1991). For example, the National Women's Studies Association is committed to a "flat" structure that maximizes grass-roots control and avoids the inherently inegalitarian relations of a hierarchical structure. *Id.* at 281. The NWSA has established some "convoluted procedures" in order to create a structure that reflects the feminist value of care. *Id.* at 283.

224. *See* Ackelsberg & Addelson, *supra* note 8, at 221, 230. The authors observe that competition in a hierarchical institution serves to legitimate differentials of wealth and power; most people believe that the competition is fair and efficient and that their place in the hierarchy is deserved. *Id.*

challenge the meritocratic roots of the liberal tradition of the competitive, hierarchical model and hence represent the possibility of more transformative change.[225]

Such unions must be constructed outside of the entrenched union hierarchy in order to prevent their co-optation and deradicalization.[226] International or national union structure must be fluid enough to facilitate freedom of action by smaller constituent groups; otherwise, the bureaucratic, hierarchical union will succeed only in making "a revolution in its own image."[227] A new form of labor solidarity would bind together the heterogeneous workers represented in these constituent groups or worker associations.[228] The smaller associations would function as communities—groups of people who are socially interdependent, share certain practices or traditions, and participate together in discussion and decision making[229]—and the collective power of the larger union would be based on the power conferred upon it by these communities.

A. The New Solidarity

The key to labor power is solidarity. Solidarity is not new to the labor movement. As Staughton Lynd has explained, the well-being of the individual worker and that of the group as a whole (the union) are

225. *Id.* at 230.

226. Staughton Lynd made a similar argument in the '70s with regard to the reradicalization of labor unions through the energies of the "New Left." *See* Lynd, *supra* note 9, at 33-39 (arguing that unionists who work within a union hierarchy are ultimately ineffective and that the best strategy for the union radical is to hold a low-level office within the union hierarchy and simultaneously be active in grass-roots organizational forms outside the union structure).

227. *Id.* at 42-43. Lynd suggested that the New Left could most effectively influence labor unions by operating through groups similar to shop committees, "keeping one foot within the circle of the larger organization." *Id.* at 40. In this way, Lynd believed, the labor movement could reap the benefits of the Old Left's mass organization as well as the New Left's vitality and commitment. *See also* Rick Fantasia, Cultures of Solidarity, Consciousness, Action and Contemporary American Workers 19 (1988) (arguing that the routinized, bureaucratic institutional union structure channels conflict and limits solidarity and suggesting that workers must circumvent usual channels and rely upon mutual solidarity as the source of their power if they are to be effective).

228. *See* Heckscher, *supra* note 14, at 254-56 (advocating an associational union structure able to embrace diverse types of members, deal with long-term strategic concerns and day-to-day shop-floor issues, utilize a range of tactics tailored to the situation, and accommodate the type of solidarity characteristic of semiprofessional work forces).

229. *See* Habits of The Heart: Individualism and Commitment In American Life 333 (Robert N. Bellah et al. eds., 1985) [hereinafter Habits of The Heart].

not antagonistic.[230] Instead, workers feel together: An injury to one is an injury to all.[231] Lynd expresses the concept of solidarity most eloquently:

> I do not scratch your back only because one day I may need you to scratch mine. Labor solidarity is more than an updated version of the social contract through which each individual undertakes to assist others for the advancement of his or her own interest. . . . When you and I are working together, and the foreman suddenly discharges you, and I find myself putting down my tools or stopping my machine before I have had time to think—[it is] because, as I actually experience the event, your discharge does not happen only to you but also happens to *us*.[232]

Traditional labor solidarity was class based. This limited sense of solidarity has proved to be a significant barrier to mobilizing white-collar workers, women, and people of color, who do not share the traditional (white male) working-class identity that grounded labor solidarity. Something more than traditional class-based solidarity is required. In order to create a bond among today's urban, isolated, and alienated workers, unions must build a community, alerting workers to their connection with one another and to their commonality of interests. The seemingly irreconcilable conflict of interests among diverse workers can be addressed by importing a new ingredient into this revisioning of solidarity: empathy. The bridge, or link, between these heterogeneous groups is the ability of each to empathize with the others.

Feminists define empathy as a "feeling with" another.[233] It involves caring for one another, and so receiving and sharing another's feelings.[234] The empathic process entails a motivational shift: The "one-caring," in

230. *See* Staughton Lynd, *Communal Rights*, 62 TEX. L. REV. 1417, 1426 (1984).

231. Staughton Lynd, *Government Without Rights: The Labor Law Vision of Archibald Cox*, 4 INDUS. REL. L.J. 483, 494 (1981). Lynd explains:

> In place of the conception of rights otherwise prevalent in our society and jurisprudence, in which one person's right subtracts from, or at most is separate from, another person's right, here the qualitatively different vision is set forth of a right which is diminished when another person's exercise of the same right is inhibited.

Id.

232. Lynd, *supra* note 230, at 1427. Lynd analogizes the relationship among workers to the relationship among family members. *Id.* However, his "family at work" example includes only male members (father and son). As Marilyn Friedman has cautioned, communitarian theory is a "perilous ally" for feminism because it focuses on the family—which has been instrumental in subordinating women—as a model of community. *See* Marilyn Friedman, *Feminism and Modern Friendship: Dislocating the Community*, *in* FEMINISM & POLITICAL THEORY 143, 145 (Cass R. Sunstein ed., 1990).

233. *See* NODDINGS, *supra* note 169, at 30-31.

234. *Id.* at 31. Lynne Henderson has offered the following more analytical definition of empathy: 1. The capacity to perceive others as having one's own goals, interests, and affects; 2. imaginative experience of the situation of another; and 3. the distress response that accompanies this

Nel Noddings's terminology, allows her motivational energy to flow toward the other and perhaps toward her ends.[235] The ability to receive another's being into oneself, and to feel with another, is quintessentially feminine.[236]

I suggest that woman-centered labor unions, forging a link among class, race, and gender movements, offer the potential for radical change.[237] Transformed labor unions could capitalize on empathy as the source of labor solidarity. They could then utilize their heterogeneity as a strength—a force facilitating growth and change—rather than experiencing it as a weakness.[238] Because it is the combination of the dynamics of work *and* family life that results in alienation and feelings of powerlessness among many workers, the labor movement must take on issues in the private sphere—family life—that are central to mobilizing workers to tackle issues in the public sphere; the personal *is* the political.[239] A revisioning of the connection between work and family would heal the split between the public and private spheres, permitting women to participate more fully in the work force and men to assume an equal role in home obligations and child care.[240]

Although legal changes aimed at strengthening workers' status in the employment relationship are also important, they are unlikely to transform the nature of work in the absence of a fundamental change in the worker's own sense of empowerment. Unless workers internalize a sense of empowerment, any legally imposed right or advantage on the workers' side of the balance will likely result in the relinquishment of

---

experiencing—which may (but not must) lead to action to ease the pain of another. Lynne Henderson, *Legality and Empathy*, 85 MICH. L. REV. 1574, 1579-82 (1987). True empathy, as distinguished from sympathy, entails an ability to receive and share another's feelings even if they are dissimilar to one's own. *See id.* at 1579 (noting that experiencing the distress of another functions as a catalyst for action).

235. NODDINGS, *supra* note 169, at 33.

236. *See id.* at 40. Noddings specifically rejects the masculine definition of the term proffered by the *Oxford Universal Dictionary*: "The power of projecting one's personality into, and so fully understanding, the object of contemplation." *Id.* at 30 (quoting THE OXFORD UNIVERSAL DICTIONARY ON HISTORICAL PRINCIPLES (James A. Murray ed., 3rd ed. 1955)). *But cf.* Toni M. Massaro, *Empathy, Legal Storytelling, and the Rule of Law: New Words, Old Wounds*, 87 MICH. L. REV. 2099, 2102 (1989) ("Gender per se does not seem to affect empathic capacity.").

237. *See* Crain, *supra* note 7, at 1207-08; *see also* BLUM, *supra* note 57, at 183-202 (arguing that comparable worth, because it combines class and gender movements, offers radical possibilities).

238. *See* Gar Alperovitz, *Notes Toward a Pluralist Commonwealth*, *in* STRATEGY AND PROGRAM: TWO ESSAYS TOWARDS A NEW AMERICAN SOCIALISM, *supra* note 9, at 49, 59.

239. *See* LERNER, *supra* note 80, at 101-02.

240. *Id.* at 288; *see also* Crain, *supra* note 7, at 1171, 1210-11. The utopian goal should be the humanization of society, the primacy of a focus on love and caring, and attention to the pain of family life, including sexism. *See* LERNER, *supra* note 80, at 101, 103-15, 333-34.

another right or advantage when the inevitable request for a concession comes from the employer.[241] Meaningful protective legislation must coincide with extralegal empowerment of the community itself through its own actions.[242]

Consequently, the woman-centered unions that have achieved success or empowered themselves within the structure of existing laws are an important subject for study. Their success indicates that a prerequisite to meaningful legal change has occurred or is occurring, and their philosophy and methodology may furnish insights concerning fruitful avenues of legal change. The law should be structured to facilitate the culture and activities of successful unions rather than allowing the law to determine the culture, structure, and methodology of unions. In the next section, I articulate an alternative union culture that already exists within woman-centered unions and address how the feminist conception of power in such unions impacts on organizing, bargaining, and using economic weapons.

B. Strategy and Method in Woman-Centered Unions

In general, woman-centered unions are characterized by a different culture, or style, than conventional male-dominated labor unions. Women's experience as caretakers and nurturers causes female unionists to focus on interpersonal dynamics and relationships, seeking to build a community based on trust, openness, and direct communication. Woman-centered unions tend to the emotional lives of their members as well as to the economic aspects of workers' lives.[243] They tend to be structurally decentralized, with a grass-roots style of organization that is reinforced by a separation from their parent union.[244] In Heckscher's phraseology, they show "associational behavior,"[245] representative of a

241. *See* Suzanne Goldberg, *In Pursuit of Workplace Rights: Household Workers and a Conflict of Laws*, 3 YALE J.L. & FEMINISM 63, 103 (1991).

242. *Id.*

243. *See* BLUM, *supra* note 58, at 11 (citing studies by Roberta Lynch and Ruth Needleman); LERNER, *supra* note 80, at 103-15, 333-34.

244. HECKSCHER, *supra* note 14, at 187. Heckscher mentions the women's pressure group Nine to Five (affiliated with SEIU Local 925) and District 1199 of the Service Employees' International Union as examples. Additional examples are the Harvard Union of Clerical and Technical Workers, affiliated with AFSCME, and District 65 at Columbia University, affiliated with the UAW.

245. *Id.* Rick Fantasia expresses a similar idea, describing "cultures of solidarity," which are not coterminous with unions; they are, instead, "bounded groupings that may or may not develop a clear organizational identity and structure, but represent the active expression of worker solidarity within an industrial system and a society hostile to it." FANTASIA, *supra* note 227, at 19.

strategy of "coordinated diversity."[246] In the following subsections, I detail exactly how this woman-centered culture is reflected and re-created in the common union activities of organizing, bargaining, and exercising economic influence. My examples are drawn primarily from the experiences of three university clerical unions, all of which are affiliated with conventional labor unions: the Harvard Union of Clerical and Technical Workers (affiliated with AFSCME), the Yale Union (affiliated with the Hotel and Restaurant Employees Union), and the Columbia Union (affiliated with the UAW, District 65).

1. *Woman-Centered Organizing*

Perhaps the most important part of creating a union that exists as a community of workers is the process of its formation. It is during the organizing drive that the union's character, or culture, is formed. Although the goal of a union organization drive is to win the representation election, the union's subsequent bargaining power depends upon its character, cohesiveness, and degree of solidarity. These attributes are created during the organizing drive; thus, "a successful union election represents the institutionalization of that which brought it about—namely, a praxis of worker solidarity."[247] Furthermore, the organizing phase has significance independent of the union organizing drive's success, for the process of organization is the key to the empowerment of the workers.[248]

A characteristically female form of exercising power and influence in the community of the workplace has been identified in some union organizing efforts. In contrast to the hierarchical male norm of a leader

246. HECKSCHER, *supra* note 14, at 177. Paul Weiler envisions a similar union structure: The form of worker organization that can accommodate diversity is one "whose role is confined to providing resources and assistance to constituent units of a loose union confederation." WEILER, GOVERNING THE WORKPLACE, *supra* note 1, at 309.

247. FANTASIA, *supra* note 227, at 131. Fantasia observes that the union culture often forms with opposition as its central, defining feature. *Id.* at 138. While this is certainly true of many unions, it need not necessarily be so. Indeed, such an adversarial model of community building may ultimately lead to isomorphism and the very bureaucratization and suppression of conflict of which Fantasia is critical. The Harvard Union, for example, specifically rejected an adversarial, oppositional approach and has been hailed as a model example of a union culture of solidarity. *See infra* notes 258-67 and accompanying text.

248. This is a feminist concept. As Gloria Steinem has written: "Power can be taken, but not given. The process of the taking is empowerment in itself." STEINEM, *supra* note 136, at 402.

as a spokesperson and orator,[249] female styles of leadership within a community tend to assume a weblike pattern, with those who are most powerful and influential at the center rather than the front. "Centerwomen" exercise leadership without possessing any real "authority" by serving simultaneously as the "repositories of others' opinions and keepers and shapers of the consensus" and by initiating change.[250] They are often expert at such feminine, family-oriented skills as interpersonal mediation, conflict resolution, and providing emotional support and advice.[251] Their typically feminine focus on the preservation of relationships readily lends itself to the building of the work-based social networks upon which a union is predicated.[252]

The Harvard Union recently won a representation election in a large unit after a seventeen-year organizing campaign and two unsuccessful elections. The Harvard Union used "innovative organizing strategies," eschewing written literature, relying primarily on a one-to-one contact technique, and utilizing organizers from within the work force.[253] Organizers stressed issues of power, self-respect, dignity, and self-representation and urged the workers to focus on their relationship to one another rather than on their relationship as individuals to the union.[254] Community and responsibility for others were the themes around which organizing was conducted.[255] This focus enabled workers to see that issues previously perceived as personal, such as low salaries, were in fact institutionalized and were therefore political and subject to change through collective organization.[256] Participation in the organizing effort was encouraged, and employees began to conceive of themselves as agents of change. According to the union, participatory democracy was key if the union was to be more than a simple replacement for the employer as an authority figure.[257]

249. *See* KAREN BRODKIN SACKS, CARING BY THE HOUR: WOMEN, WORK AND ORGANIZING AT DUKE MEDICAL CENTER 140-41 (1988).

250. *Id.* at 137-38.

251. *Id.* at 132.

252. *Id.*

253. *See* Kandel, *supra* note 7, at 265.

254. *Id.* at 265-66.

255. *Id.* at 269.

256. *Id.* at 273-274 & n.70. Yale workers experienced a similar politicization of issues during the organizing campaign there. Molly Ladd-Taylor, *Women Workers and the Yale Strike*, 11 FEMINIST STUD. 465, 476 (1985).

257. Kandel, *supra* note 7, at 268.

Kris Rondeau, lead organizer for the union, describes the organization as more than a workplace organization, "a social, political, and educational entity."[258] For Harvard employees, issues were secondary; the main focus of the organizing campaign was on building a community, decreasing isolation, and empowering workers to participate and to represent themselves in workplace decision making.[259] Rondeau describes a two-part approach to organizing: an emotional appeal and an intellectual appeal.[260] The emotional appeal consists of building bonds of trust and credibility among the workers and establishing common values and interests, a task made easier if the organizers are insiders.[261] The emotional connection, once established, creates a foundation on which workers rely when the employer's antiunion campaign begins and employees experience that "kicked-in-the-stomach" feeling that often causes them to doubt the union's utility.[262] The intellectual aspect of organizing consists of educating the workers regarding their legal rights and the union's philosophy, stance, and potential to accomplish change.[263] Rondeau is convinced that both aspects of organizing—the emotional appeal and the intellectual appeal—are necessary for every worker, but that some workers respond better to one appeal first, some to the other.[264]

In addition, Rondeau observes that the ethic of care instilled in the community as it is built contributes to the general mental health of the workers. A number of the Harvard workers lacked traditional support systems. Many had little self-esteem, and few perceived themselves as capable of effecting change in the outside world. Identification with a community provided them with a source of emotional support, decreased their sense of isolation, and increased self-esteem.[265]

---

258. *Harvard University Union, Management Have Working Relationship, Parties Say*, DAILY LAB. REP. (BNA) No. 66, at A-4 (Apr. 5, 1990).

259. *Id.*

260. Interview with Kris Rondeau, Regional Director for the American Federation of State, County and Municipal Employees, in Boston, Mass. (June 19, 1990).

261. *Id.* Rondeau described organizing methods that were far different from conventional methods. For example, organizing meetings consisted of conversations over meals with exchanges of personal information, discussions about family and day-to-day job issues, etc.

262. *Id.* This aspect of organizing is ignored by most unions. Many unions utilize a polling process to ascertain initial organizability of a potential target work force. If the work force is categorized as predominantly wary of a union, the organizing effort is abandoned. According to Rondeau, many of the workers whom she successfully organized at Harvard would have appeared to be antiunion on an initial poll. However, the emotional ties established during the organizing drive were often successful in altering an employee's initial reluctance toward unionization. *Id.*

263. *Id.*

264. *Id.*

265. *Id.*

Finally, the union assumed a nonadversarial approach to organizing: its slogan was "It's not anti-Harvard to be pro-union."[266] Instead, the union stressed empowerment, dignity, and the right to participate in workplace decision making. The union pointed out that it was possible to be assertive and to participate in workplace governance while still caring about Harvard as an institution. In this respect, the union's conception of power is consistent with a feminist concept of power as ability or competence rather than as domination—power "to" rather than power "over." Some might argue that the nonadversarial posture of the union is mere rhetoric and misleading rhetoric to boot. After all, they might say, the union's reason for being is to assert the employees' economic interests, which are opposed to the employer's economic interests; therefore, joining the union constitutes disloyalty to the employer. Alternatively, the union's nonadversarial approach might be interpreted as a reluctance to confront issues of power and inequality head-on.

Both criticisms miss the point. The union's reason for being is empowerment. Only one aspect of that empowerment is economic. Political and social empowerment will flow from unionization whether or not an improvement in the economic conditions within that particular workplace is achieved. Since the ultimate goal of unions is the redistribution of power (and wealth), it is shortsighted to consider only the ramifications within the particular workplace being unionized. More sweeping change may occur at national or state political levels as workers come to appreciate their own power to effect change. Moreover, the critiques proceed from a black-and-white, zero-sum approach to the world that is characteristically masculine: You're for either the union or the employer. As Gilligan's research indicates, the male preoccupation with cataloguing and characterizing information is not typical of women's approach, which is more contextual and tolerant of ambiguity.[267]

Finally, the interests of capital and labor are not inevitably opposed to one another. Indeed, they are inseparably linked.[268] Capital is nothing more than "the result of the heritage of human labor . . . labor that

266. Carol Kleiman, *Feminine Model of Union Organizing Brings Access to Power*, CHI. TRIB., July 9, 1990, at C5.

267. *See* Gilligan, *supra* note 44, at 16-17, 58-59. As Robin West has observed, there exists a fundamental experiential contradiction between invasion and intimacy in women's lives, which enables us to embrace an ethic of care while simultaneously fighting for rights of individuation, physical privacy, and freedom. It also explains why, despite the fact that they rest on flatly contradictory premises, we can read the work of Carol Gilligan and Andrea Dworkin and experience a shock of recognition of a part of our experience in each account. *See* West, *supra* note 157, at 54-56.

268. *See* GREGORY BAUM, THE PRIORITY OF LABOR 119 (1982) (quoting from the appendix, *Laborem exercens, Encyclical Letter of Pope John Paul II*).

has become instrument."[269] Its current posture of opposition to labor is the result of an erroneous conception of human beings as economic units whose behavior predictably follows the rules of the market.[270] As Pope John Paul II has argued, this conception ignores the spiritual side of man, ultimately limiting [his] potential.[271]

The Harvard Union proceeds from the perspective that the interests of workers and the employer are not ultimately opposed. Despite Harvard's hostility toward the union during the organizational phase, the union was successful in maintaining a caring, cooperative approach while still fighting hard for recognition—a stance that seems counterintuitive to many conventional unions. Indeed, the union found it impossible to affiliate with the UAW because of disagreements about tactics and power; "the clash of cultures was simply too great."[272] In the next subsection, I examine the impact of this unique culture on bargaining tactics and assess the contract that resulted.

2. *Bargaining*

The Harvard Union has also been credited with having developed one of the most "innovative labor-management [cooperative] arrangements in the country."[273] At the core of the bargaining relationship between the union and Harvard University lies an attitude of fundamental cooperation, a commitment to build consensus, and a focus on solving problems. The negotiators believe that the contract language is second in importance to a commitment to resolve differences. Indeed, the ultimate goal is to establish a relationship and a pattern of dealing that is so habitual that the contract itself becomes irrelevant.[274] Ben Fischer, expert negotiator and scholar, describes a labor-management-relations utopia as the day

---

269. *Id.* at 23-24 (critiquing encyclical).

270. *Id.* at 25.

271. *Id.* at 120-21 (describing the error of "economistic" perspective). In his commentary on the Pope's encyclical, Baum is critical of the insensitivity displayed toward the women's movement and notes that the encyclical reflects a male world, typified by constant references to "man," "his work," and "his world." *Id.* at 78. Further, he writes, the encyclical is deficient in its failure to acknowledge the institutional injustices to which women are subject, to analyze their effect on women's lives, and to inquire into the beneficiaries of their subjugation. *Id.* at 79.

272. Robert Kuttner, *A Beachhead for the Beleaguered Labor Movement*, BUS. WK., July 17, 1989, at 14.

273. *Harvard Now Shares Management Role with Clerical Union It Once Fought*, DAILY LAB. REP. (BNA) No. 215, at C-1 (Nov. 6, 1990).

274. *Id.* This is not as novel an approach as it might first appear. John Dunlop, chief negotiator for Harvard, recalls a system used in the clothing industry in New York in the '20s. A team of umpires resolved all problems. According to Dunlop, the contract became so irrelevant after the

> when there will be no need for a labor contract as we know it. After all, the labor contract is really a truce, absent warfare you do not need a truce. Union and management representatives should have an ongoing relationship which addresses issues as they arrive and review what exists, whenever it appears that change may be appropriate.[275]

Building such a relationship within the confines of an adversarial culture is difficult. In the past, cooperative relationships were typically prompted by economic necessity, and unions sought cooperation from a position of weakness.[276] At Harvard, however, the situation is different: The Harvard Union proposed the concept after successfully battling more than a decade of employer hostility by one of the richest and most powerful universities in the country. The reluctant party, Harvard, "came to 'accept the desirability' " of the process, and appointed John Dunlop, well known for his fairness and focus on consensus building, as chief negotiator.[277]

The Harvard Union and Harvard University first devised a set of simple rules designed to further a cooperative relationship. They agreed to tell each other the truth, be direct, and treat each other with kindness and respect. In addition, the parties decided to maintain confidentiality, allow members on both sides to change their minds, build awareness of overlapping interests, and avoid political solutions.[278] Rondeau describes this approach as consistent with a feminine model of resolving problems through moral reasoning; Dunlop apparently considers it consistent with his consensus-building approach.[279] The relationship is predicated upon

---

first decade of the relationship that the parties couldn't find a copy of the agreement; "[i]f they had a problem, they sat down." *Id.*

Similarly, the Saturn-UAW contract, the product of another cooperative relationship, is largely irrelevant. As expert negotiator Ben Fischer has commented, the union activists and employer representatives in the Saturn plant do not carry a copy of the contract; the ultimate contract is their common interest in making automobiles. Ben Fischer, *Developing Human Resources: Participative Management and Employee Involvement: Slogans and Reality?*, 16 CAN.-U.S. L.J. 137, 143 (1990).

275. *Id.*

276. *Harvard Now Shares Management Role with Clerical Union It Once Fought*, *supra* note 273.

277. *Id.*

278. *Id.*

279. *Id.* Rondeau is referring to more than the mere fact that women served as the chief negotiators for the union. While some have argued that there exist sex differences in negotiating style, specifically that women tend to utilize a more accommodating, cooperative style and men tend to be more competitive, others have found no significant differences. *See* Charles B. Craver, *The Impact of Gender on Clinical Negotiating Achievement*, 6 OHIO ST. J. ON DISP. RESOL. 1, 18 (1990). Rondeau's reference is to the broader concept that the cooperative, participatory approach followed by the Harvard Union is consistent with women's experience. Telephone Interview by Dr. Joyce Rothschild with a member of the Harvard Union (July 27, 1991) (transcript on file with author); *see*

recognition by the employer and the union that they have a great deal more in common than they do in conflict. The parties considered this principle so important that they memorialized it in a four-paragraph "Understanding" that appears on the second page of their labor agreement.[280]

The assumption that the parties to a labor contract have more in common than they do in conflict is not new. To the extent that capital and labor are in competition for scarce resources, Walter Reuther has advocated that "instead of waging a struggle to divide up scarcity, we ought to find ways of cooperating to create abundance and then intelligently find a way to share in that abundance."[281] Recent scholarship in the area of negotiation theory describes a "problem-solving approach"

Kandel, *supra* note 7, at 269 n.50 (noting the similarity between Rondeau's use of the term "feminine style" and Carol Gilligan's concept of women's distinctive voice).

280. The "Understanding," negotiated on February 13, 1989, as a prelude to contract negotiations, reads as follows:

> We have learned, during the transition, that we share numerous hopes and concerns. It is our common purpose, through the framework of this Understanding, to work together to advance the long-term role of Harvard University as a premier center of learning, research and teaching. It is commonly understood that Harvard has come to be governed, in the broadest sense of the term, through a cooperative process among governing boards and administrators, faculty, students and alumni, in which each plays a role. This Understanding welcomes the support staff in libraries, in laboratories, and in academic and administrative offices and centers, represented by HUCTW, as a valued and essential participant in this process.
>
> We have also learned that we agree about the value of decentralization. The creation of knowledge and its dissemination through scholarship and teaching are decentralized at Harvard, with responsibility distributed to the various faculties and in turn to academic groups, libraries, museums and laboratories. We can agree that some matters affecting the support staff and their work environment need to be consistent across the University, while other questions are better left to joint discussion in the separate and diversified units and departments. Indeed, it is our common view that insofar as it is practical and equitable, constructive relations in the individual workplace are to be encouraged as the focus of problem solving.
>
> Finally, we have learned that we share a commitment to the processes of reasoned discourse in resolving problems and issues that may arise within separate departments and units, as well as in contract negotiations and University-wide problem-solving. We agree to listen to each other persistently and pay careful attention to relevant facts and concerns from all corners. We further dedicate ourselves to training and developing these problem-solving skills in the administrators and supervisors of the University and in the officers and representatives of HUCTW.
>
> In sum, we have learned that we can begin to agree on principles and standards which can apply well and reasonably to every part of this diverse and historic institution. We are optimistic about a future which continues in that vein.

Agreement on Labor-Management Cooperation, July 1, 1989-June 30, 1992, Harv. Univ.-Harv. Union of Clerical & Technical Workers, AFSCME, AFL-CIO, at 3 [hereinafter Harv.-HUCTW Agreement] (on file with author).

281. Irving Bluestone, *Representation of Employees and the Role of Unions in the United States and Canada: The Union Response to Change in a Competitive Context*, 16 CAN.-U.S. L.J. 157, 158 (1990) (quoting from address by Reuther before the University of Virginia Law School).

designed to capitalize on common interests and to minimize distributional conflicts. Roger Fisher and William Ury have developed a principled approach to negotiation that urges separation of the relationship problems from the merits of the substantive dispute, focuses on the interests of the parties rather than on their positions, encourages inventing options to take advantage of potential joint gains, and applies objective standards in evaluating results.[282] The focus of their approach is on building a relationship that is conducive to decision making in the face of divergent interests, a point elaborated on in subsequent work by Fisher and Scott Brown.[283] The building of relations through negotiation is particularly important when the parties have an ongoing relationship; choices made today influence not only immediate outcomes but also later choices.

Indeed, despite the popular wisdom that management and labor are adversaries intent on fighting over the allocation of scarce resources, what labor unions really strive for is democratization of the workplace—the opportunity for employees to participate in decision making at work.[284] The right that unions seek to a voice in the conduct of industry is more fundamental than the right to negotiate over wages and working conditions, although that is the arena in which the voice is now heard. Unions strive for the right to identify issues in the first instance, and to determine the processes by which they will be resolved.[285] Such a right amounts to access to power at the point of its leverage. Like women seeking power in a male world, unions strive not just to be permitted to play the game, but to be able to participate in the construction of the rules by which it is played.[286]

In short, the key to successful bargaining is the process employed.[287] This is an insight shared by feminist theorists who have considered the

282. ROGER FISHER & WILLIAM URY, GETTING TO YES: NEGOTIATING AGREEMENT WITHOUT GIVING IN 10-14 (1981).

283. ROGER FISHER & SCOTT BROWN, GETTING TOGETHER: BUILDING A RELATIONSHIP THAT GETS TO YES 8-9 (1988).

284. Bluestone, *supra* note 281, at 158-59.

285. *See* Sar A. Levitan & Clifford M. Johnson, *Labor and Management: The Illusion of Cooperation*, 1983 HARV. BUS. REV., No. 5, 8, at 16 (asserting that genuine cooperation requires that management view workers as equal partners, not silent followers, and that unions must contribute to the perception and definition of problems as well as to their solution).

286. *See* MACKINNON, *supra* note 221, at 28 ("[Women want] not only to be allowed to play with the boys, but to question why the point and ethic of sports is competition.").

287. *See* Roger Fisher, *Comment to Essay Review: The Pros and Cons of "Getting to YES,"* 34 J. Legal Educ. 115, 121 (1984) ("The guts of the negotiation problem, in my view, is not who gets the last dollar, but what is the best process for resolving that issue.").

area of negotiation theory.[288] As in the case of building a union, the culture of the management-labor relationship is created by the process of decision making rather than by its result. The type of bargaining process used is another aspect of the Harvard negotiations that has been hailed as unique. Prior to the start of formal negotiations, the union and Harvard agreed to embark upon a sixty-day "transition period" with the assistance of a neutral facilitator, "to get acquainted, to explore mutual priorities and philosophies, to share all relevant statistical information, and to plan negotiations."[289] The parties worked toward agreement on a process of problem solving rather than a contract containing detailed sets of rules; they also decided to simultaneously revise an existing personnel manual, which would then serve as an adjunct to the contract.[290]

The system of problem solving by consensus was implemented through the creation of twenty-six joint councils and nineteen local problem-solving teams.[291] The joint councils make policy determinations affecting the staff collectively. Each school or administrative department has at least one joint council, which consists of an equal number of management and union representatives (elected by the membership), ranging from three to five each depending on the proportionality of the school or department to Harvard as a whole.[292] The University Joint Council oversees all of the joint councils, resolves issues on which the joint councils cannot reach consensus, and considers issues of universitywide significance. The University Joint Council is composed of three union representatives and three management representatives. It also operates on a consensus basis; in the event it is unable to reach a consensus, it may seek the assistance of a mutually acceptable mediator.[293]

288. *See, e.g.*, Menkel-Meadow, *supra* note 44, at 51; Menkel-Meadow, *supra* note 107, at 763-64 (advocating a problem-solving process in the legal context that "promotes and maximizes human interactions that are creative, enfranchising, enriching and empowering" and ultimately produces results that are tailored to the parties' needs and are more just).

289. Harv.-HUCTW Agreement, *supra* note 280, at 2.

290. *Harvard Now Shares Management Role with Clerical Union It Once Fought*, *supra* note 273, at C1. In fact, the personnel manual more closely resembles a traditional labor contract than does the atypical Agreement; the manual deals with employment classifications, hours, holidays, vacations, sick pay, layoffs, and overtime, among other subjects. *See* Personnel Manual, Harvard University and Harvard Union of Clerical and Technical Workers, AFSCME, AFL-CIO, July 1, 1989 (copy on file with author). Nevertheless, the Manual is replete with messages of cooperation similar to those contained in the Agreement. For example, it eschews arbitration in favor of mediation. Manual, *supra*, at 2.

291. *See* Harvard-HUCTW Agreement, *supra* note 280, at 3-8.

292. *Id.* at 5; *Harvard Now Shares Management Role With Clerical Union It Once Fought*, *supra* note 273, at C1.

293. Harv.-HUCTW Agreement, *supra* note 280, at 5-6.

Individual workplace problems are resolved at the local level, through the problem-resolution procedure specified in the contract. If no satisfactory solution is reached, the problem is referred to the Local Problem-Solving Team for review. The Local Problem-Solving Team consists of an equal number of union and management representatives, two of whom deal with individual complaints at any one time (one from the union, one from management).[294] If consensus cannot be reached, the problem is referred to the University Problem-Solving Team, also composed of an equal number of union and management representatives. Mediation is provided in the event it is unable to reach a consensus.[295]

The system has functioned well in the more than two years it has been in operation. The councils have established "a new policy allowing library workers to go home on hot summer days, agreements to refurbish staff lounges, satisfactory arrangements for avoiding workplace problems during construction, [and] agreements on how to handle work when vacancies arise."[296] The problem-solving teams have resolved 300 problems, twenty-five of which reached the University Problem-Solving Team level and only three of which went to mediation.[297]

The system ensures direct participation by an unusually large number of employees. More than 300 workers, or about ten percent of the bargaining unit, participate directly in workplace governance.[298] Nevertheless, it is well organized and functions efficiently, debunking a common argument that participative democracy is inefficient.[299] In fact, the contract negotiating team numbered sixty-five, yet the first contract negotiations were completed within four months of the first formal bargaining session.[300]

294. *Id.* at 7-8.

295. *Id.* at 8.

296. *Harvard Shares Management Role with Clerical Union It Once Fought*, *supra* note 273, at C1.

297. *Id.*

298. *Id.* One hundred employees serve on joint councils, 60 on local problem-solving teams, 100 as union representatives, and 30-40 on joint committees. In addition, the union has set up 35 organizing committees, whose function is to continue the process of building a community begun during the organizing drive. The union is governed by a 17-member executive board. *Id.*

299. *Id. See also* Joel Cutcher-Gershenfeld, *The Impact on Economic Performance of a Transformation in Workplace Relations*, 44 INDUS. & LAB. REL. REV. 241, 242 (1991) (concluding that transformational workplace relations, characterized by increased cooperation and improved dispute resolution, are more efficient and yield better economic performance than traditional adversarial labor-management relations.)

300. Interview by Dr. Joyce Rothschild with members of HUCTW, in Cambridge, Mass. (May 16, 1991).

The Agreement itself compares very favorably with other first contracts. It provides for raises in pay by thirty-two percent over three years, increasing the average salary from $19,900 to $26,400.[301] The Agreement also calls for an increased contribution by the university to health care costs, raising the previous sixty-six to seventy-two percent contribution to eighty-five percent of the premium.[302] Improvements in pension benefits, disability benefits, maternity- and parental-leave benefits, and a pilot child care program were also achieved.[303] In addition, clerical and technical employees were granted the right to use university athletic facilities.[304]

What can be gleaned from this description of an alternative process of bargaining? First, it was efficient—agreement was reached within four months. Second, it achieved a substantive result considered positive by both parties. Third, it established a working problem-solving, decision-making relationship ultimately intended to render the Agreement irrelevant. And finally, it was quintessentially feminine: cooperative, contextual, caring, and process oriented. I turn now to the question of whether such an approach is the product of weakness, bred by a fear of confrontation and conflict, or whether it can coexist with strength.

3. *Economic Pressure/Militance*

A question often raised about working women is whether their traditional reluctance to engage in confrontation and conflict precludes militance in the labor market.[305] Sometimes this view is expressed as a belief that women are more loyal to their employers than are men and are therefore more reluctant to challenge their employer's authority.[306] Alternatively, it is couched as an assertion that women tend to be uninterested in their work lives because they are preoccupied with families and domestic roles.[307] These stereotypes are exacerbated by the existence

301. *Agreement on First Contract Reached for 3,500 Clerical Workers at Harvard*, 123, DAILY LAB. REP. (BNA), No. 123 at A-5 (June 28, 1989).

302. *Id. See* Harv.-HUCTW Agreement, *supra* note 280, at 14.

303. *Agreement on First Contract Reached for 3,500 Clerical Workers at Harvard*, *supra* note 301, at A-5. Expanded maternity-leave provisions (permitting eight weeks of maternity leave at 70% of salary) and provisions allowing accumulated sick leave to be used to care for ill dependents were especially valuable to the more than 80% of the Harvard clerical and technical work force who are female. *See* Bruce D. Butterfield, *Labor '89: The Family Is Central to Agenda*, THE BOSTON GLOBE, Sept. 4, 1989, at 1; *see* Harv.-HUCTW Agreement, *supra* note 280, at 16-17.

304. *Agreement on First Contract Reached for 3,500 Clerical Workers at Harvard*, *supra* note 301; Harv.-HUCTW Agreement, *supra* note 280, at 14-15.

305. *See* Crain, *supra* note 7, at 1204-07.

306. *See id.* at 1183.

307. *See id.* at 1176-82; Shapiro-Perl, *supra* note 133, at 193.

of an historically male adversarial labor-management-relations norm. Cooperative relationships predicated on a feminist understanding of power are seen as different, inferior, adopted out of a position of weakness rather than strength.[308] Although cooperative styles have been subject to criticism when advanced by males,[309] when associated with a feminine style they are likely to be further devalued.[310]

Women unionists have not behaved in conformity with the stereotypical passivity with which they are credited. In fact, recent studies suggest that once organized, women are actually more militant than men.[311] Most recently, female workers at Columbia and Yale demonstrated their willingness to apply economic pressure to their employers by engaging in prolonged strikes. The Yale Union, Local 34 of the Federation of University Employees, an affiliate of the Hotel and Restaurant Employees Union, has a membership of secretaries, telephone operators, computer programmers, and other technical workers who are eighty-two percent female.[312] It has grass-roots, bottom-up origins and prevailed in a representation election after a two-and-a-half-year organizing drive (which followed two attempts by other unions during the preceding twelve years to organize Yale's clerical and technical workers).[313] The union then successfully waged a five-month battle, including ninety-one negotiating sessions and a lengthy strike in support of its pay-equity demands at the bargaining table.[314] The workers obtained a first contract with an across-the-board pay increase of 20.25% over three and a half years, a cost-of-living increase, and improved health benefits and maternity-leave provisions.[315] A sister blue-collar union, Local 35 of the

308. *See supra* note 213-14 and accompanying text.

309. James J. White, *Essay Review: The Pros and Cons of "Getting to YES,"* 34 J. Legal Educ. 115 (1984) (book review) (criticizing the theory of win-win negotiating advanced in *Getting To YES*).

310. STEINEM, *supra* note 136, at 382-83 (observing that qualities associated with an "inferior" group will be used to justify its plight of powerlessness); *see also* ANDREA DWORKIN, LETTERS FROM A WAR ZONE (1988) (maintaining that when women enter any occupation or industry in great numbers, the field itself becomes feminized, i.e., takes on the low status of women).

311. *See* Crain, *supra* note 7, at 1205-07; *see generally* MY TROUBLES ARE GOING TO HAVE TROUBLE WITH ME, *supra* note 133 (collection of essays on female militance in the labor market).

312. Mark Bittman & Bob Arnold, *Comparable Worth Is Put to the Test at Yale; A Bitter Strike May Determine Whether the Concept Gets a Foothold in the Private Sector*, BUS. WK., Nov. 26, 1984, at 92; Peter Perl, *"Pay Equity" Fight at Yale; Strike over Women's Salaries Is First Major Private-Sector Battle*, WASH. POST, Oct. 16, 1984, at A13.

313. Cynthia Saltzman, *Office Workers Hail a Victory*, N.Y. TIMES, June 26, 1983, § 11, at 22; William Serrin, *Union's Success at Yale: New Focus on White-Collar Women*, N.Y. TIMES, Apr. 10, 1984, at B24; *Clerical, Technical Employees at Yale Vote in Favor of Union Representation*, DAILY LAB. REP. (BNA) No. 99, at A-3 (May 20, 1983).

314. Paul Bass, *"Time of Healing" at Yale*, N.Y. TIMES, Jan. 27, 1985, § 11CN, at 23.

315. *Id.*

United Food and Commercial Workers Union, supported the strike by refusing to cross strike picket lines; this disrupted dining services and helped bring student and faculty pressure to bear on Yale.[316]

Similarly, clerical workers at Columbia University prevailed in a representation election following an organizing drive that spanned several years; they are now represented by District 65 of the United Automobile Workers Union.[317] District 65, a New York-based union that originated in the textile industry, has a reputation for aggressiveness which has aided it in organizing such purportedly nonunionizable workers as clericals, administrative and semiprofessional workers, and lawyers.[318] Like Harvard and Yale, Columbia strenuously resisted unionization by its clericals; a strike threat, backed by the UAW, was necessary to persuade the University to recognize and bargain with the union.[319] After a five-day strike, the Columbia Union won a contract guaranteeing workers a six percent general wage increase in each of the three years of the contract, along with a lowered deductible on the health care plan and remedial pay for those who had been victims of pay inequity.[320] As with the Yale strike, the Columbia strikers received support from sister unions (including the Yale Union), faculty, and students.[321]

Much female militance, however, may be difficult for male unionists to recognize because it does not take the conventional form of bursts of violence, picketing, and strikes. The women of the Harvard Union, for example, demonstrated their own brand of militance by persevering in a fourteen-year organizing drive that never became violent, maintaining a consistently cooperative attitude with management, and abiding by self-constructed tenets of kindness and compassion in their dealings with the

316. William Fitzgerald, *Yale-Union*, UPI, Dec. 3, 1984 available in LEXIS, Nexis Library, UPI File. The strike also resulted in class cancellations, and cockroach sightings in the dorms, and it ultimately provoked a $10 million suit by students charging Yale with failure to provide an education, custodial services, and dining services. Bittman & Arnold, *supra* note 312, at 92. Although student and faculty support was partially attributable to self-interest, hostility was directed at Yale rather than the union because Yale was perceived as "intransigent," "arrogant," and "pompous." *Id.*

317. Glenn Fowler, *Striking Clerical Workers Reach a Tentative Pact with Columbia*, N.Y. TIMES, Oct. 22, 1985, at B2.

318. William Serrin, *Office Union Confident of Victory at Columbia*, N.Y. TIMES, May 9, 1983, at B10.

319. William Serrin, *Columbia Faces Threat of Strike over Union Vote*, N.Y. TIMES, Dec. 31, 1984, § 1, at 28.

320. *Columbia University Clericals Accept Initial Contract, Ending Five-Day Strike*, DAILY LAB. REP. (BNA) No. 206, at A-3 (Oct. 24, 1985).

321. *No Progress Reported in Strike at Columbia*, N.Y. TIMES, Oct. 19, 1985, § 1, at 32.

employer.[322] Beneath their gentility and humanism, however, lies a steely determination to resist oppression. As Rondeau says, the Harvard Union is "as much a trade union as ever," and members are "wise enough never to forget" Harvard's prolonged and hostile antiunion campaign; according to Rondeau, "If they fight us, we'll fight; if we have to do it the old-fashioned way, we'll do it as well as anyone."[323]

Studies of shop-floor resistance show that women workers wage a daily struggle for "bread and roses" even though their style of militance does not conform to such traditional confrontational patterns as picketing, sitdowns, walkouts, and strikes.[324] Overlooking creative fight-back strategies such as pacing (a strategy of time calculation in which workers selectively hustle and idle during a day to serve their own best interests),[325] humming louder and louder while working,[326] and throwing goods produced by the company at one another[327] may result in the erroneous conclusion that workers are passively accepting their lot in the workplace.[328] These low-risk, low-gain nontraditional behaviors indicate that women workers are "*already* engaged in a silent struggle with management over control of the work process."[329] While not transformative, these individually based resistance strategies may reflect the seeds of class consciousness that could be harnessed to forge a collective effort by workers to gain control over their work lives.[330]

The problem runs deeper than a mere failure by unions to recognize and capitalize upon instances of female militancy in the workplace. As I have argued, feminine styles of exercising power are so different from male styles that they have been overlooked and, consequently, culturally silenced.[331] Our laws, which operate to contain and sometimes (as in the

---

322. *See supra* notes 278-80 and accompanying text.

323. *Harvard Now Shares Management Role with Clerical Union It Once Fought*, *supra* note 273, at C-1.

324. Shapiro-Perl, *supra* note 133, at 194.

325. *Id.* at 197-98.

326. *Id.* at 200.

327. *Id.*

328. *Id.* at 194.

329. *Id.*

330. *See id.*

331. In Native American culture, by contrast, female power in its many forms is revered. *See, e.g.*, *Okanogan Traditional: The Beginning and the End of the World*, *in* SPIDER WOMAN'S GRANDDAUGHTERS: TRADITIONAL TALES AND CONTEMPORARY WRITING BY NATIVE AMERICAN WOMEN 125 (Paula Gunn Allen ed., 1989) (presenting stories about [Native American] warrior women which portray them as capable of exerting great prowess, ruthlessness, and willingness to use what might and power they possess; they seldom display the helpless, meek and mild qualities usually attributed to women in Anglo-European fiction); *Iroquois (Mohawk) Traditional: The Woman Who Fell from the Sky*, *in* SPIDER WOMAN'S GRANDDAUGHTERS, *supra*, at 65 (creation story of

case of the labor laws) to distribute power, reflect this cultural silencing of women's experience of power. Ultimately, the labor movement's failure to recognize feminine styles of exercising power has reinforced the disempowerment of women, and, because they constitute an increasing percentage of wage workers, the working class.

VI. CONCLUSION

In this Article, I have explored the potential for building an alliance between the feminist movement and the labor movement. My thesis is that the emerging feminist concept of power, if integrated into labor unionism, could spawn a new form of solidarity that would stretch across class, sex, and race boundaries to revitalize and reradicalize an admittedly ailing labor movement. As Audre Lorde has written in words that apply with equal force to labor,

> [Survival] is learning how to take our differences and make them strengths. *For the master's tools will never dismantle the master's house.* They may allow us temporarily to beat him at his own game, but they will never enable us to bring about genuine change. And this fact is only threatening to those . . . who still define the master's house as their only source of support.[332]

Unions organized around a feminist concept of power would be decentralized, less hierarchical, and more participatory in nature than conventional unions. They would attend more closely to nurturing connection and community among members, which would increase union power by creating a new form of solidarity that is not solely class based. Ultimately, feminized unions could reshape the structure of the labor laws.[333]

This new form of solidarity, forged in difference, would draw on the common experience of oppressed groups to bring them together and to

---

Iroquois includes story of woman "who overcomes her enemy . . . through an act of great courage, power, and self-assertion [that] turns his [betrayal] into a new planet, Earth"); *Pretty Shield: A Woman's Fight, in* SPIDER WOMAN'S GRANDDAUGHTERS, *supra*, at 31 (narration of Crow story designed to inform white man that Crow women were "strong and self-defining," despite erroneous white male opinion attributing white women's characteristics to Crow women).

332. Audre Lorde, *The Master's Tools Will Never Dismantle the Master's House, in* THIS BRIDGE CALLED MY BACK, *supra* note 117, at 108, 109.

333. This point is further explored in my forthcoming work, *Images of Power in Labor Law: A Feminist Deconstruction*, *supra* note 12. As many have noted, women's unique perspective on law and jurisprudence holds promise for reforming areas of the law that are not traditionally thought of as having special relevance for women. *See, e.g.*, Suzanna Sherry, *Civic Virtue and the Feminine Voice in Constitutional Adjudication*, 72 VA. L. REV. 543, 581 (1986); Jane Byeff Korn, *Changing Our Perspective on Arbitration: A Traditional and a Feminist View*, 1991 U. ILL. L. REV. 67, 93-94.

redefine power. I have focused on the feminist movement as a force for change because a transformative feminism embraces an agenda that seeks to end domination in all human relationships, including sexism, racism, classism, and heterosexism. Further, women's experiences have resulted in a positive understanding of power based upon community and connection between people that is naturally suited to unionism. The creative nature of the power women possess is, as yet, untapped. As Jean Baker Miller has noted,

> [P]ower . . . has operated without the special values women can bring to it. . . . I am not suggesting that women should soften or ameliorate power—but instead that, by their participation, women can strengthen its appropriate operation. Women can bring more power to power by using it when needed and not using it as a poor substitute for other things—like cooperation.[334]

In return, an alliance with labor unions would provide a power base for the feminist movement. It would be easier to develop women's feminist consciousness in the context of their roles in the labor market than in the context of their roles as wives and mothers. Working women internalize capitalist values that purportedly reward individual merit and hard work; when they observe differential treatment in the market based upon their membership in a sexual class, they begin to develop a critical consciousness.[335] By contrast, sex inequality in the family, where relationships are supposedly regulated by love, is harder to admit and to confront. Nevertheless, as working women perceive the patriarchal structuring of opportunities in the market, the possibilities increase for feminist consciousness of and challenge to patriarchal control maintained in the home.[336]

To illustrate my argument I have sketched an outline of an alternative, woman-centered union methodology for organizing, bargaining, and invoking member support to exert economic pressure. The feminist concept of power is necessarily a product of the distinctive experience of women as a class. Nevertheless, it holds promise for all oppressed workers, male and female, black, brown, and white, who seek to harness the power of solidarity to help them achieve their own empowerment.

---

334. MILLER, *supra* note 139, at 118.

335. EISENSTEIN, *supra* note 138, at 51.

336. *Id.* at 52. The double workday of the typical married woman, who leaves her paid job to continue unpaid labor in the home, makes such an awakening especially likely in married wage-earning women. *Id.*

[9]

CATHOLIC LABOR THEORY AND THE TRANSFORMATION OF WORK

DAVID L. GREGORY*

INTRODUCTION

This essay addresses the tremendous interdisciplinary potential that the synergy of law and theology holds for labor law. No legal literature directly has examined the impact of theology on labor law. This essay examines the promise this fusion holds for transforming labor law. This essay serves as a preliminary assessment of the potential for the Catholic Church's social teaching on the world of work to accomplish what Marxist theory has failed to do. My essential purpose is to review a Catholic vision of labor theory that transcends capitalism and Marxism and promises to transform the world of work.

Catholic social teaching on labor incorporates and differs from both Marxist and capitalist teachings. Theology, understood in the broadest sense as incorporating Catholic social teaching as an important component, rather than Marxism alone, may hold the key to transforming and redeeming the world of work. I analyze the Catholic theology of work because the modern history of Papal encyclicals and Bishops' pastoral letters on labor is especially timely and is powerfully integrated in Pope John Paul II's 1981 labor encyclical, *Laborem Exercens,* and in the United States Catholic Bishops' 1986 pastoral letter, *Economic Justice for All.*

OVERVIEW

In the very act of creation God dignified work. The history of the world is the history of work. It is a history first eloquently told in the Torah, as the Jews moved from the toil of slavery in Egypt to the dignity of meaningful work as free people in a free land. In the New Testament Jesus continued to dignify work. Unfortunately, for much of humanity the world of work historically has been debased and denied in alienation. This

---

* Kenneth Wang Research Professor of Law, 1987-88, St. John's University. J.S.D. 1987, Yale University; LL.M. 1982, Yale University; J.D. 1980, University of Detroit; M.B.A. 1977, Wayne State University; B.A. 1973, Catholic University of America. I deliberately have written this article as an essay. It is somewhat amorphous, perhaps even speculative, offering thoughts on a vision of the world of work not yet in the making. Conventional law review stylistics of tight doctrinal categories and of heavy footnotes seem incongruous and perhaps even inappropriate here. I have endeavored to keep them to a minimum.

This article generously was supported by the Kenneth Wang Research Fund of St. John's University Law School. I thank Milner Ball, Gregory Baum, Maria Ciampi, Lawrence Joseph, Ronald Krietemeyer, Leo Penta, Robert Rodes, Thomas Shaffer, and Paul Surlis for their helpful comments reading prior drafts of this article.

is the tragedy of labor; tragic because alienation is unfair, undeserved, and remarkably intractable. This was the core insight of Karl Marx. Within the past century Catholic social teaching on labor, borrowing from Marxist analysis, has transcended Marxism and revivified the world of work.

Recent statements by Pope John Paul II and by the Catholic Bishops of the United States offer especially unique and powerful promise to reconstruct the world of work. This is not a Catholic message in any parochial sense. Rather, this is a universal "catholic" message to all of humanity. It is a message of particular relevance to workers, unions, employers, labor lawyers, and labor law theoreticians. Catholic labor theory is sophisticated and profound. It is an established intellectual movement, coinciding with the development of workers' movements in Western Europe and the United States since the late nineteenth century. This essay describes the potential for contribution by a very progressive Catholic social teaching to the legal theory, and one day, to the practice of work. This has special implications for labor law in the United States, ranging from improving the quality of work life, to worker democracy, to worker ownership—all designed to harness capital in the service of labor.

In Part One of the article, I adumbrate the roles of the individual and the community alienated within, and from, the world of work. Alienation cries out for redemption. Large complex societies, whether in late capitalist or controlled socialist economies, have not effectively coordinated the individual, the community, and the world of work. Consequently, community is badly fragmented, individuals are cast adrift in atomistic despair, and the tragedy of labor is further exacerbated. Catholic social teaching offers hope to both the individual worker and to the community.

Part Two of the article examines the entrenched and enduring problem of worker alienation. Within the minority of the world's population fortunate enough to be employed, a substantial portion of workers hate their working lives. Rather than ennobling and empowering lives of workers with dignity and meaning, work instead often has the opposite influence of debasing workers' lives. Consider two familiar characters in the tragedy of labor. The bitter factory worker, engaged in mindless, dangerous, repetitive tasks, seduced by the illusion of "profit sharing" or "employee ownership," and concerned about the endangered economic future of the enterprise, is an increasingly common figure. The young Wall Street lawyer routinely works ninety hours each week to earn a $70,000 annual starting salary. He carries an accumulated college and law school education loan debt approaching his annual salary. While proof reading documents at 2 A.M., he realizes that he, the highly paid technician, is for all practical purposes little more than an indentured servant. He may grow to despise his legal work as a debased means to a confused end of material comfort. He also may realize he lacks the call to the transformative vocation of law. The benumbed lawyer may eventually become materially wealthy and spiritually bankrupt.[1] These are profoundly disturbing scenarios.

1. *See* Kronman, *Living in the Law*, 54 U. CHI. L. REV. 835 (1987).

Whether a person is a lawyer or factory worker, devoting a working life to a cold, dry task that has no meaning other than as a means to accumulate wealth, is both tragic and pathetic indeed. It profits the worker nothing to gain the world if in the process he loses his soul.[2] Many workers are gravely wounded amalgams of the pathos of Willie Loman in *Death of a Salesman* and of the tragedy of Shakespeare's King Lear. Indeed it is probably most accurate to say that more workers are pathetic Lomans; fewer reach the tragic heights of Lear. Because the highly educated lawyer probably is intellectually more aware of opportunities to live a more socially meaningful working life than is the factory worker, he may be more like Lear. Studies reveal a pandemic level of work dissatisfaction among those lawyers who view the practice of law mainly as a technical means to make money,[3] rather than as a means to achieve greater collective human dignity and as a transformative vocation to further individual and social justice. Highly intelligent workers quickly can be reduced to cynical instrumentalists. Both the alienated factory worker and the alienated lawyer are victimized by succumbing to the fetishism of commodities, idolatrously worshipping the false god of materialism. As Karl Marx, Pope Leo XIII, and Pope John Paul II realized, the world of work will be transfigured only when labor is given priority over capital and material is harnessed to serve humanity. The Bishops' letter offers special hope for "workaholics"—people who work compulsively without reflection on the deeper meaning of life and of their actions. The quality and pace of work should be more human in scale, enabling people to experience the dignity and value of their work and giving them time for other duties, obligations, and, at least equally important, for leisure, play, and recreation. This balance is vitally important for sustaining the social, political, educational, and cultural structures of society.[4] Catholic social teaching may offer a way out of the capitalist insanity of commodification, which Lukacs called the "central, structural problem of capitalist society in all its aspects"[5] and characterized as containing within it "the whole of historical materialism."[6]

Part Three of the article comparatively will assess Marxist and Catholic alternatives, and the possible symbiotic amalgamation of their insights, to transfigure the world of work. Marxist historicism alone cannot redeem the world of work. Marxist labor theory removes from its debased ontology the transcendent yet simultaneously personal and immanent God and falsely substitutes the delusion of proletarian triumph of a workers' paradise in

---

2. *Luke* 9:25.

3. Hirsch, *Are You On Target?*, BARRISTER, Winter, 1985, at 17; Zinke, *Money Is Less Important Than Work*, NAT'L L.J., July 28, 1986, at 16, col. 1.

4. UNITED STATES NATIONAL CONFERENCE OF CATHOLIC BISHOPS, ECONOMIC JUSTICE FOR ALL: PASTORAL LETTER ON CATHOLIC SOCIAL TEACHING AND THE UNITED STATES ECONOMY 169 (1986) [hereinafter ECONOMIC JUSTICE].

5. LUKACS, *Reification and the Consciousness of the Proletariat*, in HISTORY AND CLASS CONSCIOUSNESS: STUDIES IN MARXIST DIALECTICS 83 (R. Liningston trans., 1971).

6. *Id.* at 170.

God's stead. This is necessarily an incomplete and imperfect nonsolution. Catholic social teaching instead provides a much more viable standard by which to begin to redeem the world of work from the tragedy of labor. The 1981 papal encyclical of Pope John Paul II, *Laborem Exercens*, and the 1986 pastoral letter of the United States National Conference of Catholic Bishops, *Economic Justice for All*, will highlight the analysis throughout the essay.

Part Three will not offer a concrete, positive agenda. There is no mechanical point-by-point plan capable of immediately transforming a very fallible, imperfect, and adversarial world of work. Thus far, there has been an unbridgeable gulf between the deeply flawed world of work and the utopian, idealized vision of many labor law scholars and theoreticians. Catholic labor teaching offers the most promise to bridge this abyss. Critical legal scholar Roberto Unger's brilliant new *Politics* trilogy, owing much to the Gospel message and to the communism of Chapter Four of the Acts of the Apostles,[8] offers the most comprehensive Christian romantic agenda for effectuation of transformative social democracy.[9]

A profound malaise of spirit afflicts many workers. Misery, meaninglessness, deep dissatisfaction, and often unarticulable impoverishment of purpose plague even many of the most "successful," especially if "success" is measured only by conventional norms of monetary remuneration in late capitalist society. It has long been axiomatic that most persons who work for a living, as distinguished from those peculiarly driven to "live to work," dread Monday morning. This poignantly simple description of the world of work encapsulates much of the contemporary tragedy of labor. Most workers continue to experience alienation in their working lives. Whether nonunionized, mid-level managers employed at will, or blue collar industrial "employees" as defined by Section 2 of the National Labor Relations Act[10] and

---

7. Roberto Unger's sweeping new work, POLITICS: A WORK IN CONSTRUCTIVE SOCIAL THEORY (1987), is comprised of three volumes: SOCIAL THEORY: ITS SITUATION AND ITS TASK; FALSE NECESSITY: ANTI-NECESSITARIAN SOCIAL THEORY IN THE SERVICE OF RADICAL DEMOCRACY; and PLASTICITY INTO POWER: COMPARATIVE-HISTORICAL STUDIES ON THE INSTITUTIONAL CONDITIONS OF ECONOMIC AND MILITARY SUCCESS. This trilogy was the subject of a major symposium immediately upon its publication. *See Roberto Unger's Politics: A Work in Constructive Social Theory*, 81 NW. U. L. REV. 589 (1987).

8. *Acts of the Apostles* 4:32-35 states:

> Now the company of those who believed were of one heart and soul, and no one claimed that any of the things which he possessed was his own, but they held everything in common. . . . There was not a needy person among them, for as many as were possessors of lands or houses sold them and brought the proceeds of what was sold and laid it at the apostles' feet, and distribution was made to each according to his need.

Id.

9. Following his Rubin lecture at Columbia Law School, March 30, 1988, Roberto Unger expressly acknowledged his common bond with much of Catholic labor teaching, especially with the labor encyclicals. However, Unger also maintained his agenda in his POLITICS trilogy was more complex and not so exclusively communitarian as the emphases of the encyclicals and related pastoral letters.

10. 29 U.S.C. § 152(3) (1982).

represented by a union, most workers do not find fulfillment in the world of work. True job satisfaction remains the relatively rare exception. Its absence proves the enduring rule of alienation almost a century and a half after Karl Marx first incisively analyzed the problem of alienated labor.[11]

As the United States approaches the close of the twentieth century, the relatively low official national unemployment rate[12] and the creation of new jobs offer little solace, especially from a "macro" perspective. Beneath these initially heartening statistics, entire regions of the country remain economically devastated by endemic and catastrophically high unemployment. Many other persons are underemployed, having involuntarily traded former high wage industrial jobs for minimum wage service sector positions,[13] as domestic merger activity and international competition steadily erode the high wage manufacturing sector of the United States economy.

Even in good times, "joblessness is becoming a more widespread and deep-seated problem in our nation."[14] As the United States National Conference of Catholic Bishops expressly noted in their November, 1986 pastoral

---

11. *See* K. Marx, *Alienated Labor*, in Economic and Philosophical Manuscripts of 1844, Collected Works (1975).

12. Of course, the current official unemployment rate of less than 6% in the United States would have been unacceptably high less than two decades ago. In April 1988, the 5.6% national unemployment rate reached a 14-year "low." "Full" employment in the post-World War II era had been measured at an unemployment rate below 4%. However, in 1987, even Japan, with previously miniscule unemployment, had 3% unemployment. Most Western European industrial nations have experienced double digit unemployment throughout the decade, significantly higher than the rate in the United States. *See generally* Europe's Economy in Crisis (R. Dahrendorf ed. 1982).

13. *See generally* B. Bluestone & B. Harrison, The Deindustrialization of America (1982); Committee On The Evolution Of Work, AFL-CIO, The Future Of Work (1983).

14. Economic Justice, *supra* note 4, at 69. Following the November, 1980 general meeting of the United States National Conference of Catholic Bishops, an ad hoc committee was appointed to draft a letter on the United States economy. Drafts were submitted and discussed in November, 1985, and June, 1986. The Letter was approved during the plenary session of the Bishops in Washington, D.C. in November, 1986. During the past two decades, the Bishops of several other nations have issued similar pastoral letters. *See* Canadian National Conference of Catholic Bishops, Ethical Reflections on the Economic Crisis (1983). The pastoral letter of the United States Bishops has been bitterly criticized as a pro-socialist and anti-capitalist delusion. The most prominent critic of the letter is Michael Novak. Novak maintains that capitalism is the system most consistent with the maximization of economic and human freedom. "The extensive effort underway to commit the church to 'economic rights' has the potential to become an error of classic magnitude. It might well position the Catholic Church in a 'preferential option for the State' that will more than rival that of the Constantinian period." Novak, *Economic Rights: The Servile State*, Catholicism In Crisis, Oct., 1985, at 10; Novak, *Socialists Circle Bishops*, Nat'l Rev., Apr. 5, 1985, at 46. Novak has repudiated his early work. *See* Novak, A Theology for Radical Politics (1969). Within the past decade, he has become both a powerful critic of what he perceives as the Catholic Church's dangerous shift to socialism and a premier apologist for the virtues of capitalism. *See also* Novak, Capitalism and Socialism: A Theological Inquiry (1979); Novak, Freedom with Justice: Catholic Social Thought and Liberal Institutions (1984); Novak, The Spirit of Democratic Capitalism (1982); Novak, Toward A Theology of the Corporation (1981).

letter, *Economic Justice for All*, "there are about 8 million people in the United States looking for a job [sic] who cannot find one."[15] When the underemployed and those not statistically recognized are added, such as the disheartened who have abandoned the search for work, and the homeless, perhaps one-eighth of the work force is directly affected adversely by unemployment. This is exacerbated by the fact that the majority of the unemployed do not receive any unemployment insurance monetary benefits.[16] The Bishops "call for a new national commitment to full employment. We say it is a social and moral scandal that one of every seven Americans is poor."[17]

Organized labor recently has shown some signs of resuscitation. The self defeating mentality, isolation, and union cooptation of the early nineteen eighties finally show some signs of fading. There has been some revival of labor class consciousness and corresponding aggressive collective bargaining. Nevertheless, more often than not, unionized workers continue to be cruelly deceived by the false promise of employee profit sharing and participatory workplace democracy. As I argued in an earlier article,[18] most of these ownership-initiated schemes of supposed workplace democracy have thus far deceived workers and have failed to halt the continued impoverishment of workers' spirits.

Members of the nonunionized eighty percent of the United States workforce are perhaps even more miserable with the alienation and meaninglessness of their working lives than are their unionized colleagues. After dedicating entire adult careers to one employer, senior managers employed at will often summarily are terminated. The profile of the typical plaintiff in litigation springing from termination of an at will employment relationship is a middle aged, mid-level, mid-career, male manager who has spent the majority of his adult life with the former employer.[19] His psychological devastation is often irreparable; legal remedies available in most state jurisdictions that have judicially or legislatively modified the traditional American rule of employment at will are often insufficient to repair the former worker's life. Once cast adrift by the now disembodied corporate abstraction, to which they had pledged their working lives as an almost filial act, these former managers can be the most pathetic and helpless of victims. The Age Discrimination in Employment Act is not sufficient to fill the breach.[20]

---

15. ECONOMIC JUSTICE, *supra* note 4, at 69; *see* Uchitelle, *America's Army of Non-Workers*, N.Y. Times, Sept. 27, 1987, at F1, col. 2.

16. ECONOMIC JUSTICE, *supra* note 4, at 70.

17. *Id.* at xii.

18. Gregory, *Lessons From Publius for Contemporary Labor Law*, 38 ALA. L. REV. 1 (1986).

19. *See* Gregory, *Toward Federalization of Protection Against Wrongful Discharge* (unpublished manuscript on file with author).

20. *See* 29 U.S.C. § 923 (1982) (codifying Age Discrimination in Employment Act of 1967).

The tragedy afflicting labor in the world of work transcends current academic debates over the perceived crisis[21] in labor relations law and over the viability of reforms in nonunionized, at will employment.[22] The tragedy of labor is a very complex and dynamic phenomenon, simultaneously spanning the worlds of work and unemployment as well as permeating the class ranks of labor, management, and ownership.

"Labor" always has been a complex term. This is especially true in contemporary capitalist and socialist economies. Labor can designate the class of organized employees represented by a union in conventional labor relations law. Labor, so understood, has a well recognized institutional meaning of class consciousness and connotes structural boundaries of legal ritual and formulae. Labor is also a broader term, encompassing all persons engaged in the world of work, without regard to whether they are represented by the institution of the union.

Labor also connotes the activity of work. Division of labor into performance of specific task functions is quite familiar. In Marxist terms the pernicious core consequence of the act of work in capitalist regimes is the alienation of the worker from the product and process of work.[23] Ownership elites, controlling means of production, artificially separate the worker from the work product. The worker becomes the object, rather than the subject, of work. Marxism promises embittered workers achievement of the ineluctable victory of the proletariat, the defeat of stratified capitalism, and the withering away of the capitalist state. Thus far the Marxist cure usually has been worse than the capitalist disease.

At the outset, it is important to acknowledge the deep problem of using generic labels of capitalism and Marxism. Laissez faire capitalism, if it ever existed as other than powerful mythic imagery, has long since evolved into corporate welfare statism. Georg Lukacs similarly suggests that Marxism "came to an end some time ago."[24] Likewise, "socialism" has a variety of

21. *See* Klare, *Traditional Labor Law and the Crisis of Collective Bargaining Law: A Reply To Professor Finkin*, 44 Md. L. Rev. 731 (1985); Weiler, *Promises To Keep: Securing Workers' Rights to Self Organization Under the NLRA*, 96 Harv. L. Rev. 1769 (1983) Professor Weiler writes, "Contemporary American labor law more and more resembles an elegant tombstone for a dying institution." 96 Harv. L. Rev. at 1769.

22. *See* Gregory, *supra* note 19.

23. *See* Marx, *supra* note 11.

24. Ferrarotti, *A Final Rethinking: Gyorgy Lukacs Talks with Franco Ferrarotti*, Soc. Pol'y., July-Aug., 1972, at 47. Lukacs states, "Marxism as a general theory of society has in fact undergone an interruption. It has stood still. One may say that Marxism, conceived as it should be conceived, as a general theory of society and of history, no longer exists, that it came to an end some time ago." *Id.* Roberto Unger, the premier critical legal studies scholar, has launched a devastating critique of Marxism in his new *Politics* trilogy. *See supra* note 7. For additional commentary on Lukacs, Habermas, the Frankfurt School, and the varieties of contemporary Marxism, see A. Feenberg, Lukacs, Marx, and the Sources of Critical Theory (1981); D. Held, Introduction to Critical Theory: Horkheimer To Habermas (1980); E. Lunn, Marx And Modernism (1982) (Marx and modernism meet through Lukacs); S. Spender, The Struggle Of The Modern: An Historical Study of Lukacs, Brecht,

meanings.[25] At one end of the spectrum is the totalitarian-perverted Leninism of the Soviet Union. Centrist welfare state models describe most Western European versions of democratic socialism. They eschew Soviet style totalitarianism.

The United States Bishops call for the effectuation of economic justice in the corporate welfare state of late capitalism. The Bishops subscribe to a social democracy quite similar to that of the centrist Western European regimes. Pope John Paul II, however, subscribes to a vision of social democracy substantially to the left of that espoused by the United States Bishops. Elements of Marxism are present in most, but not necessarily all, of these variants of socialism.[26] Socialism, capitalism, and Marxism carry heavy baggage of meaning today. I use these generics within their broad, popular, or conventional meanings.

Catholic labor teaching is deeply consonant with social democracy, the most powerfully shared political aspiration in the world today. Professor Roberto Unger particularly emphasizes the deep attraction of social democracy with his unique cogency:

> The single most attractive emergent model of social organization in the world today—the least oppressive, most respectful of felt human needs, and therefore also most likely to attract the most diverse support of the most thoughtful citizens—is social democracy. The supporters of social democracy do not paint it as Utopia, nor do they claim that all countries are equally ready for it. They recognize how hard it may be to achieve amid the extremes of poverty and ignorance when its achievement remains precarious in even the most favorable circumstances. They merely affirm that social democracy is the best that mankind can hope for, for an indefinite time to come.[27]

The attempted but deeply flawed actualization of Marxist theory usually has resulted not in the reconciliation of meaning in workers' lives, but rather in the exacerbation of the tragedy of labor. The Union of Soviet Socialist Republics and the People's Republic of China are Marxist labor disasters. Beyond the plain untruth of their "republicanism," the gulags and forced labor camps of totalitarian regimes represent the cruelest shat-

---

BENTAMIN, AND ADORNO (1963); THE UNKNOWN DIMENSION: EUROPEAN MARXISM SINCE LENIN (D. Howard & K. Klare eds. 1972); Standen, *Critical Legal Studies as an Anti-Positivist Phenomenon*, 72 VA. L. REV. 983 (1986).

25. The non-Marxist democratic socialism most consonant with Catholic social teaching on labor is outlined in G. DORRIEN, THE DEMOCRATIC SOCIALIST VISION (1986). *See also* W. TEMPLE, CHRISTIANITY AND THE SOCIAL ORDER (1942) (classic exposition of protestant socialism in Great Britain).

26. J. Cort, *Can Socialism Be Distinguished from Marxism?*, CROSS CURRENTS, Winter 1979-1980, at 29.

27. R. UNGER, FALSE NECESSITY: ANTINECESSITARIAN SOCIAL THEORY IN THE SERVICE OF RADICAL DEMOCRACY 25 (1987).

tering of the aspirations of workers in human history. The brutal suppression of Solidarity, a true workers' movement in Poland, is an especially heartbreaking example of the tragedy of labor in one of the client states of history's most notorious totalitarian regime. It has especially galvanized the ire and the eloquence of Pope John Paul II.

Within the last two decades, there has been an interesting fusing of Marxist theory and Catholic social teaching in liberation political theology.[28] Of course this popular terminology is somewhat redundant: theology is necessarily liberating and redemptive. In France, for example, the Catholic Church has a rich, modern tradition of worker priests.[29] The Church's contemporary liberation theologians in the Western hemisphere offer the promise of an especially powerful and coordinated vision for transforming the world of work.

Today's most interesting and promising development, with the potential to redeem the worker from the tragedy of labor, lies in the amalgamation of Marxist labor theory with Catholic social teaching and theology.[30] In his 1981 papal encyclical *Laborem Exercens* (On Human Work), Pope John Paul II unequivocally reaffirmed the Catholic Church's modern social teaching which expressly declares the priority of labor over capital and asserts the inherent dignity of work.[31] Pope John Paul II shares the core

---

28. The classic work of liberation political theology is G. GUTIERREZ, A THEOLOGY OF LIBERATION (1973). *See also* L. BOFF & C. BOFF, INTRODUCING LIBFRATION THEOLOGY (1987); A. FLORIDI & A. STIEFBOLD, THE UNCERTAIN ALLIANCE: THE CATHOLIC CHURCH AND LABOR IN LATIN AMERICA (1973); C. GUDORF, CATHOLIC SOCIAL TEACHING ON LIBERATION THEMES (1980); Baum, *Liberation Theology and Marxism*, THE ECUMENIST, Jan.-Feb., 1987, at 22. Throughout this essay, I will use the joint terminology of liberation political theology to symbolize its potential and to defuse some of the polarized hyperbole. Liberation theology is the usual reference in Central and South America. Political theology is the normal terminology in Europe and North America. I am not a professional theologian. As a Catholic, I am bound to take very seriously, and have been tremendously inspired by, the social and labor encyclicals of Pope John Paul II; his theological vision is political, holy, and certainly "liberating" in the best senses of those meanings.

29. *See* J. ROWE, PRIESTS AND WORKERS (1965); THE WORKER-PRIESTS: A COLLECTIVE DOCUMENTATION (J. Petrie trans., 1956).

30. *See* McGovern, *Marxism: An American Christian Perspective*, in MARXISM AND RADICAL RELIGION (1970).

31. POPE JOHN PAUL II, LABOREM EXERCENS (On Human Work) (1981) [hereinafter LABOREM EXERCENS]. I am particularly grateful for Gregory Baum's outstanding analysis of the encyclical. *See* G. BAUM, ON THE PRIORITY OF LABOR (1982); *see also* T. DONAHUE, A TRADE UNION PERSPECTIVE OF LABOREM EXERCENS (1982); WORK AND RELIGION (G. Baum ed. 1980). LABOREM EXERCENS commemorated the ninetieth anniversay of the landmark labor encyclical of the modern Papacy. Pope Leo XIII issued RERUM NOVARUM (On the Condition of Workers) in 1891. For additional Papal and Conciliar sources of Catholic social teaching on labor, economics, and social resources, see POPE PIUS XI, QUADRAGESIMO ANNO (On Reconstructing the Social Order) (1931); POPE JOHN XXIII, PACEM IN TERRIS (On Establishing Universal Peace in Truth, Justice, Charity, and Liberty) (1963); POPE JOHN XXIII, MATER ET MAGISTER (On Christianity and Social Progress) (1961); POPE PAUL VI, POPULORUM PROGRESSIO (On Promoting the Development of Peoples) (1967); POPE PAUL VI, OCTOGESIMA ADVENIENS (On the Occasion of the Eightieth Anniversary of the Encyclical *Rerum Novarum*) (1971);

insight of St. Thomas Aquinas, Hegel, and Marx that the human being must always be the subject, rather than the object, of work.

Gregory Baum maintains that this insight inspires much of the originality of John Paul II's labor encyclical. Because the person is the subject of work, the person always will be more important than the object produced by the work of the person subject.

> The dignity and honor which work communicates to people is derived not so much from the objective dimension, from their achievement, from the product of their hands and minds, as from the subjective dimension; it is ultimately man's engagement which counts, his fidelity to the call, his increasing sense of responsibility, his self realization. In labor the transformation experienced by the subject is of greater value and importance than the object produced.[32]

The illegitimate transmogrification of the worker into object rather than subject of work is one root aspect of the alienation of labor. This insight has energized Catholic labor teaching. But Catholic social teaching transcends Marxism, because, pursuant to Catholic labor theory, the worker can never be completely objectified. The worker's subjectivity shares in the image of God. This subjectivity never can be stripped completely away from the worker.[33] Marxism fails in its disavowal of man's core transcendent subjectivity.

In November 1986 the United States National Conference of Catholic Bishops issued a comprehensive and controversial pastoral letter, *Economic Justice for All.*[34] In the age of late capitalism, and in this particularly turbulent time in the history of the world's most powerful capitalist society, the Bishops' letter elucidates the tensions that contribute to the current tragedy of labor. By reiterating the Church's preferential option for the poor, the Bishops' letter complements Pope John Paul II's radical statements in support of worker movements throughout the world. The Bishops' letter

---

Pope John Paul II, Sollicitudo Rei Socialis (The Social Concerns of the Church) (1988); *Gaudism et Spes,* Documents Of The Second Vatican Council (1966). *See also* N. Betten, Catholic Activism and the Industrial Worker (1976); J. Calvez & J. Perrin, The Church and Social Justice (J.R. Kirwan trans., 1961); R. Camp, The Papal Ideology of Social Reform (1969); J. Cronin, Catholic Social Principles (1950); J. Cronin & H. Flannery, The Church And The Workingman (1965); D. Door, Option For The Poor: A Hundred Years Of Vatican Social Teaching (1983); J. Gremillion, The Gospel Of Peace And Justice: Catholic Social Teaching Since Pope John XXIII (1976); E. Kaiser, Theology Of Work (1966); E. McLean, Roman Catholicism And The Right To Work (1985); J. Moody, Church And Society: Catholic Social And Political Thought And Movements, 1789-1950 (1953); Renewing The Earth: Catholic Documents On Peace, Justice, and Liberation (D. O'Brien & T. Shannon eds., 1977). J. Ryan, The Church and Labor (1924).

32. G. Baum, On The Priority Of Labor 14 (1982).

33. *Id.* at 17.

34. *See supra* note 14 (discussing Economic Justice).

is much more moderate,[35] however, than Pope John Paul II's labor encyclical, which was overtly socialist in tone and spirit.

The Church's preferential option for the poor, coupled with the broad variety of liberation political theology practiced by many local churches in the United States, has certainly not yet come to fruition. However, if the world of work is to be transformed from bleak despair and alienation, the social teaching of the Catholic Church perhaps offers the most real promise. One serious problem may be whether Pope John Paul II's express call foi the priority of labor over capital can be effectuated fully within the republican system of government guaranteed by the Constitution of the United States, without simultaneously collapsing capitalist society. Thus, it is quite possible, ultimately, that even the best efforts to implement Catholic labor teaching on a wide scale will be frustrated by the very size and heterogeneity of society in the United States. Witness, for example, the wide support in the United States for labor initiatives in Poland, ironically coterminous with significant antipathy toward organized labor in this country. The Bishops' letter is very cognizant of this challenge. It is a challenge that labor lawyers can help translate into practice.

Other religious traditions eloquently have supported the dignity of work, the rights of labor, and the redemptive function of the law. From the perspective of Judaism, the late Professor Robert Cover was a particularly passionate advocate of the redemptive messianic power of the law.[36] Obviously, much of the Catholic Church's social teaching on work is rooted in Judaism and the Torah.[37]

I. INDIVIDUALS, COMMUNITY, AND THE WORLD OF WORK

Work, or at least the aspiration to work, is ubiquitous. Work permeates, and is often nearly synonymous with, much of both individual and social life. The individual person is dignified by work; the community is enriched by work. Society stands condemned by failure to provide meaningful work. In the Book of Genesis, God enjoined humanity to earn its living: "In the sweat of your face you shall eat bread."[38] By sin work was reduced to toil. Work became nothing more than a necessary means to the end of preserving life. Gradually, however, work as means was understood as affording its own intrinsic dignity as a limited end. As *Laborem Exercens* expressly

---

35. L. Penta, *The Economic Pastoral: On Empowerment,* 25 THE ECUMENIST, Nov.-Dec., 1986, at 1.

My understanding of the Bishops' Letter, ECONOMIC JUSTICE FOR ALL, has been singularly enriched by Rev. Penta's outstanding analysis.

36. *See* Cover, *Bringing The Messiah Through Law: A Case Study,* in NOMOS XXX: RELIGION, MORALITY AND THE LAW (forthcoming 1988); Cover, *The Supreme Court, 1982—Foreward: Nomos and Narrative,* 97 HARV. L. REV. 4 (1983). Professor Cover develops a notion of a "paideic community" formed by interpersonal bonding through shared commitment to moral tradition, and its process of redeeming life through evolving law.

37. *See Genesis* 3:19; *Psalms* 127-28; *Proverbs* 10:22; *Exodus* 1:8-14; *Jeremiah* 22:13.

38. *Genesis* 3:19.

recognizes, "there is no doubt that human work has an ethical value of its own."[39] Work helps us become more fully human.[40] The challenge now is to harmonize the limited end of dignified work with the broader end of human dignity.

How is "work" best defined? Work is a fundamental dimension of human existence. Understanding work is essential in order to understand our humanity. In *Laborem Exercens*, Pope John Paul II offers an excellent broad definition of work:

> Through work man must earn his daily bread and contribute to the continual advance of science and technology and, above all, to elevating unceasingly the cultural and moral level of the society within which he lives in community with those who belong to the same family. And work means any activity by man, whether manual or intellectual, whatever its nature or circumstances; it means any human activity that can and must be recognized as work, in the midst of all the many activities of which man is capable and to which he is predisposed by his very nature, by virtue of humanity itself. Man is made to be in the visible universe an image and likeness of God himself, and he is placed in it in order to subdue the earth. From the beginning therefore, he is called to work. Work is one of the characteristics that distinguish man from the rest of creatures, whose activity for sustaining their lives cannot be called work. Only man is capable of work, and only man works, at the same time by work occupying his existence on earth. Thus work bears a particular mark of man and of humanity, the mark of a person operating within a community of persons. And this work decides its interior characteristics; in a sense it constitutes its very nature.[41]

Unfortunately, most of the world never has known dignified work. Most of the world always has been desperately and inescapably poor. We are assured that the poor always will be with us. Catholic social teaching reinforces Jesus' call that all humanity join in solidarity with the poor; we are challenged to be "poor in spirit."[42] Without meaningful work, crushing poverty of both material and spiritual life is inevitable. The majority of the earth's population will never experience any work, let alone have working lives filled with dignity and hope. Productive work will remain incomprehensible, or, at most, an ineffable and unattainable dream for the majority of the earth's population. They will die prematurely, in ignorance, and in regimes where lives of unemployment and poverty are the established norm.

---

39. Laborem Exercens, *supra* note 31, at IV. For the reader's convenience, I use citations throughout to the headings and pages of the encyclical as set forth in Gregory Baum's outstanding book, On the Priority of Labor (1982).

40. Laborem Exercens, *supra* note 31, at II (6) and II (9).

41. *Prologue*, Laborem Exercens, *supra* note 31.

42. *Matthew* 25:35-40.

The European social theorist Ralf Dahrendorf maintains that "there is no cure for today's unemployment."[43] The Malthusian specter never has evaporated. Despite fragmented rich abundance of material resources in some nations, the world remains haunted by economic and spiritual destitution.

By this structural social sin[44] of mass collective omission from the world of work, most of humanity suffers daily. While the world of work is imperfect and fraught with deep alienation and division, nothing is more tragic than the complete absence of even the barest opportunity to work and the evil social ostracism of the unemployed. If one never can enter the world of work, one has much less opportunity to experience life. Obviously, one excluded also is deprived of any opportunity to contribute to any possible transformation of the world of work. One need not look to the Third or Fourth World to observe the nearly universal exclusion of entire populations from the world of work. The absence of meaningful work is especially pronounced in many economically devastated areas of the United States.[45] Compare, for example, the thriving professional working world of Manhattan with New York City's ever growing unemployed underclass and homeless population. Or, on a regional basis, compare the booming Northeast with the devastated energy belt.

Consider the role of a single transnational corporation in perpetuating and exacerbating the subordination of labor to capital. General Motors Corporation is effectuating sweeping plant closings throughout the United States. Despite the United Auto Workers Union's emphasis on labor contract job security, profit sharing, retraining programs, and rights of transfer to other facilities, thousands of General Motors workers, unionized and non-unionized alike, are being permanently exiled from the world of work. For all practical purposes, most will never work again.

For much of the world's population, and for a disturbingly high percentage of the United States' population, the pathos and the tragedy of labor lies in their structural exclusion from the world of work. Absent conscious collective participation in work, there is little possibility to contribute to the process of redeeming the world of work. Access to work is often controlled by capital. If labor is foreclosed from work, capital can continue to fragmentize the world of work and to subordinate labor indefinitely. If the world of work, with all its flaws, is ever to become accessible to the majority of the world's population, so that the hierarchy of capital over labor one day may be inverted, careful assessment of the grave collective social sin of deliberate omission from meaningful work is absolutely im-

43. Dahrendorf, *The End Of The Labor Society*, WORLD PRESS REV., March, 1983, at 28.

44. *See* G. BAUM, THE PRIORITY OF LABOR 67 (1982). "Contemporary ecclesiastical documents have taken up the notion of 'social sin.'" *Id.*

45. *See* Miller, *Toward Recognition of a Constitutional Right to a Job*, in POLITICS, DEMOCRACY, AND THE SUPREME COURT: ESSAYS ON THE FRONTIER OF CONSTITUTIONAL THEORY 319 (1985); Rubenstein, *The Elect And The Preterite*, 59 SOUNDINGS 357, 359 (1976) ("The threat of permanent economic superfluity now confronts millions").

perative. This evil is condemned in *Laborem Exercens. Pope* John Paul II summarizes:

> As we view the whole human family throughout the world, we cannot fail to be struck by a disconcerting fact of immense proportions: the fact that while conspicuous natural resources remain unused there are huge numbers of people who are unemployed or underemployed and countless multitudes of people suffering from hunger. This is a fact that without any doubt demonstrates that both within the individual political communities and in their relationships on the continental and world levels there is something wrong with the organization of work and employment, precisely at the most critical and socially most important points.[46]

The United States Bishops reinforce the papal observation. The Bishops argue that because "[f]ull employment is the foundation of a just economy . . . [t]he most urgent priority for domestic economic policy is the creation of new jobs with adequate pay and decent working conditions."[47]

Because employment is a basic right, society has a duty to protect it. Begin with the Book of Genesis. In the act of creation, God dignified work. God labored six days. But after the fall from grace, humanity was individually and collectively commanded to enter the debased world of toil. Throughout much of the ancient world, arduous manual labor was performed by slaves. Artisans and technicians performed more specialized functions. Truly free persons aspired to public lives of citizenship and, for the philosophers, to lives of contemplation in the Greek city states. The rigorous, demanding duties of public citizenship and the highest human aspiration of philosophical contemplation were made possible by being freed from the conventions of work. The free Greeks were the first to develop leisure, sport, and play. With the enactment of early labor codes, Jews in Egypt began to move from slavery to freedom.[48] Still, work largely was seen as a necessary evil. Only the privileged elites, freed from conventions of work, could aspire to pursue contemplation, to seek the good, and to engage in leisure. Work was redignified by Jesus the Carpenter, who was about his Father's business. His scriptural parables are replete with examples of good workers, as well as with those toilers who failed to appreciate the dignity of work. Gradually, the revelation of God in human history redeemed the world of meaningful work from the realm of toil. For example, use of the term "labor" to describe the process of giving birth marks the unique joy and satisfaction of productive creation. Jesus dignified labor from the inception, via the virgin birth.

But, now, what of those not at work? The unemployed are now suspect. In the Soviet Union, the otherwise able person who is unemployed risks

46. Laborem Exercens, *supra* note 31, at IV (18).
47. Economic Justice, *supra* note 4, at 69.
48. *See* L. Pfeffer, Religion, State, and the Burger Court (1984).

criminal prosecution for being a "parasite" on the state. The state defines what constitutes work. Boris Grebenshikov, the most popular folk rock musician in the Soviet Union, is not supported financially by the state. His musicianship is not officially recognized. He must avoid state sanction as an unemployed "parasite" by engaging in a transparent bureaucratic masquerade, claiming his officially recognized occupation as a "playwright."[49] The irony, of course, is that he is employed most productively, given the huge fanatic audience so desperately devoted to hearing his music.

This is the pernicious legacy of Marx's lack of sympathy for the unemployed. Marx placed his secular faith in the working class. The marginal and the unemployed underclasses he called "Lumpen," the German word for hoodlum. Of course, the irony now is that the unemployed masses far outnumber the relatively privileged working class in most post-modern economics.[50] The irony is about to be further compounded, with the purported restructuring of the Soviet economy, and the Soviet regime's threat to lay off millions of unproductive persons by the turn of the century, little more than a decade away. Again, we see the clear advantages of Catholic social teaching over Marxism. The former has a dynamic and affirmative appreciation of human solidarity of the masses of the poor with all workers. "The call for the solidarity *of* the poor and *with* the poor is truly a radical Christian principle. It is materialist and spiritual at the same time."[51]

Pathologies also circumscribe "work" in late capitalist societies. In the United States and Japan there is an almost manic desire to work, both for its own sake, and more often in order to make more money—an uncertain means to a perhaps forgotten end of greater human dignity. Work is one important element in, but not identical with, the whole of an integrated life. Social ostracism almost universally attaches to unemployment. This is especially the case of those unable to support themselves financially. The Bishops' letter confronts the sin of social victimization of the unemployed. The individual is debased and made to feel worthless. Unemployment leads to physical and psychological disease from increased incidence of crime, alcoholism, and drug use, to battery of spouses and children, and to increases in the federal deficit.[52]

Even the independently wealthy risk being labeled dilettantes if they do not work. Everyone is rightly troubled by growing numbers of persons rendered unemployable by insufficient education[53] and other limited opportunities. Persons who retire "early" often seek to reenter the world of work. Those few persons who might aspire to lives of contemplation in late

49. *See* Keller, *For Soviet Rock Musicians, Glasnost Is Angst,* N.Y. Times, April 9, 1987, at A1, col. 4.

50. G. Baum, The Priority of Labor 38 (1982).

51. *Id.* at 39.

52. Economic Justice, *supra* note 4, at 71-72.

53. *See generally* A. Bloom, The Closing of the American Mind (1987); E. Hirsch, Cultural Literacy (1987).

capitalist society are seen as bizarre or eccentric. Of course, the modern Western sense implicit here is that contemplation or leisure will be somehow "productive"—a definite capitalist twist to the Platonic ideal. Thus, one especially deep paradox is that in the United States, where the leisure class grows and opportunity for leisure abounds, leisure is still regarded as the exception, the rare luxury, the necessary periodic propaedeutic to renewed "productivity."[54] To do "nothing" is viewed with suspicion, unless it is a respite in cyclical renewal for more orthodox work.

The Bishops' letter, much more than the Papal encyclical,[55] recognizes the distinct importance of leisure, and the need for a proper balance between work and leisure in the integrated life.[56] The balance of work and leisure and culture in the Bishops' letter is primarily attributable to the influence of Archbishop Rembert Weakland of Milwaukee. A graduate of Julliard, he was the head of the Benedictine Order worldwide before becoming a bishop. *Economic Justice for All* reconciles humanity to the importance and the guiltless dignity of leisure and culture. After dignifying work in the act of creation, God also dignified rest.[57] While guarding against aimlessness, we must not be afraid to engage in leisure. The Bishops recognize the tensions this balance may pose.

> For disciples of Christ, the use of leisure may demand being countercultural. The Christian tradition sees in leisure, time to build family and societal relationships and an opportunity for communal prayer and worship, for relaxed contemplation and enjoyment of God's creation, and for the cultivation of the arts which help fill the human longing for wholeness.[58]

Perhaps in leisure time of re-creation the most important work occurs—the building of family, social, and community relationships. Witness, for example, the first miracle of Jesus' public life. He changed water to wine at the wedding feast of Cana, while at leisure among family and friends.

When individuals are stigmatized and ostracized because they cannot or do not work, this is another powerful manifestation of the tragedy of labor.

---

54. *See* J. Pieper, Leisure: The Basis of Culture (1952) (classic work on indispensability of leisure); *see also* J. Murphy, Concepts of Leisure: Philosophical Implications (1974).

55. *See* G. Baum, The Priority of Labor 13 (1982). Baum writes:

> The Pope does not recognize a place for a leisure class. . . . Is work really the appropriate mode for man's self-actualization? Are there not some signs that in the future there may not be enough work for everyone? Society may have to create a division of labor that allows people to work part-time and spend their energies on other activities. Is there not a disadvantage in defining man as worker? Does this not make it more difficult for people excluded from work to create their identity and live out of as yet hidden resources of their personalities? The encyclical is unperturbed by these questions.

Id. at 20.

56. Economic Justice, *supra* note 4, at 169-70.

57. *Genesis* 2:1-4.

58. Economic Justice, *supra* note 4, at 170.

On the flip side of this tragic coin are those who live to work; they unwisely confuse the limited ends of work with the broader true ends of a socially responsible, full, and dignified life in community with fellow humans. Work is a part of that equation, but it is not the whole sum of the dignified, redeemed life.

In the United States, the usual social and economic consequence for those who do not work, and who are otherwise without independent means of financial support, is consignment to the demeaning and insufficient government welfare scheme. The more ominous consequence of homelessness always lurks in the background. In the Soviet Union, the immediate social consequence is more even Draconian: unemployed "parasites" on the state are subject to imprisonment. Failed managers can be imprisoned or executed, rather than merely discharged. Neither capitalism nor Marxism is tolerant of those at the heart of the tragedy of labor, those who are involuntarily omitted from the world of work.

Labor is defined largely by community norms. Individuals removed from the world of work, virtually regardless of the reasons, but especially those not financially self-sufficient, are seen as aberrant. Orthodoxy places the social premium upon work and devalues the lives of the unemployed who are perceived as an economic drag upon the community. Community norms must be transformed to provide meaningful work and to end the ostracism of those who are unable to work.

Taking broad social, economic, and political steps to provide meaningful work to those who want to work and are now unable to find work, while simultaneously militating against the community's ostracism of those who do not work, would be powerful transformative steps to begin to redeem the world of work. Unfortunately, in the United States, with the rare exception of possible minimal child care and family care leave legislation,[59] steps at the federal level in this decade instead have been taken to punish further those absent from the world of work. This spring, the Supreme Court upheld denial of food stamps to strikers.[60] Consequently, one literally can be starved into returning involuntarily to work. The "social safety net" has been steadily unwoven by the federal government, and access to the world of work has been constricted. High wage industrial jobs disappear by the hundreds of thousands, while the federal government boasts of the lowest unemployment rate since, eerily enough—and fully consonant with Marxist critique of capitalism—the Vietnam War. Naturally, the government embarrassedly and unsuccessfully attempts to mask the former high wage unemployed factory worker by putting a cosmetic veneer on the face of the minimum wage, fast food emporia employee. Welding guns have been

---

59. *See* The Family and Medical Leave Act of 1987, H.R. 925, 100th Cong., 1st Sess. (1987) (co-sponsored by Rep. P. Schroeder and Rep. W. Clay); The Parental and Medical Leave Act of 1987, S. 249, 100th Cong., 1st Sess. (1987) (co-sponsored by Sen. C. Dodd and Sen. A. Specter).

60. Lyng v. International Union, 108 S. Ct. 1184, 1194 (1988).

traded for burger bags. McDonald's now employs more people in the United States than does the entire steel industry.[61]

The United States has a great deal to learn from Western European social democracies,[62] such as federal legislation to provide for paid, job-protected extended leaves for child and family care. This is but one example of legislation that can positively militate against the community stigmatizing those who do not or cannot work. Involuntary unemployment certainly can escalate from individual tragedy to epidemic social disaster.[63] But if everyone must work, this may debilitate the importance of leisure in a fully integrated life.[64]

The lessons to be learned by the United States pale in comparison to those that the international community now is teaching the Soviet Union. The Soviets' client states are the best teachers of their intransigent, unwilling pupil. The international tragedy of labor in the post-World War II period has been most courageously and best exemplified by the heroic martyrs of Solidarity, the free trade union initiative of Poland brutally suppressed by Soviet puppets.[65] Pope John Paul II's remarkable vision for labor in *Laborem Exercens* is deeply rooted in his identification with the aims of Solidarity. He expressly reiterates the unique importance of labor unions as mouthpieces for social justice.[66] There is a definite, important place for unions in the fulfillment of Catholic labor theory. Catholic social teaching, especially in its support of worker-initiated plans for worker democracy, can restructure labor union hierarchies, corporate bureaucracies, and the Church's own internal labor relations.

From the macro perspective of international law and politics, Marxist or capitalist prospects for transforming the world of work are bleak, absent a theology.[67] Individuals deviating from the orthodoxy of work are potentially susceptible to severe sanction by the community. This regrettable forced subordination of individual choice to community convention had been part of history. It is not peculiar to the late corporate welfare capitalist United States nor to the twisted Marxism of the Soviet Union.

Socrates and Jesus are timeless individual witnesses who deliberately rejected conventional community norms of "work." Instead, they chose to pursue their own eschatological visions. Why "work," as the prevailing community norms defined it, when one might choose the higher, more difficult, and inscrutable labor of teaching truth, asking the right, hard

---

61. *See supra* note 13 and accompanying text (discussing shift of employment opportunities from industrial sector to service sector).

62. *See generally* G. DORRIEN, THE DEMOCRATIC SOCIALIST VISION (1986).

63. LABOREM EXERCENS, *supra* note 31, at IV (18).

64. *See supra* note 54 and accompanying text (discussing indispensability of leisure).

65. *See* Sila-Nowicki, *The Role of the Catholic Church in Polish Independence*, 6 N.Y. LAW. SCH. J. OF INT'L. AND COMP. LAW 703 (1986).

66. LABOREM EXERCENS, *supra* note 31, at IV (20); *see also Pope Offers His Full Support to Organizers of Labor Unions*, N.Y. Times, May 9, 1988, at A11, col. 1.

67. *See* POPE JOHN PAUL II, SOLLICITUDO REI SOCIALIS (1988) [hereinafter SOLLICITUDO].

questions, redeeming the world, being the Messiah? Concomitantly, however, it is interesting that Jesus simultaneously dignified a wide variety of occupations in the world of work.[68] He first worked as a carpenter.[69] Later, when he embarked on his Father's business, he chose his closest followers from the working class, making fishers from Galilee "fishers of men." The Catholic Church honors Joseph the Carpenter, the earthly father of Jesus, as the patron of workers. Jesus, through the parables, dignified many occupations and forms of labor and described God the Father as the vinedresser.[70]

Socrates and Jesus were not punished for their occupational choices. Philosophers were recognized in Athens, rabbis in Jerusalem. Rather, they were punished for how they performed their occupations, and for the transformation of conventional occupations into transformative redemptive vocations.

It is not enough to seek work, or simply to work; the individual must work as the community mandates, or face potentially lethal sanction. Teach truth to the young people of Athens by confessing ignorance and by perpetual, difficult questioning; drink the hemlock. Walk away from the family carpentry business; make transcendent God immanent; be crucified. Individuals and community must be reconciled to one another if the world of work is to be redeemed from the tragedy of labor. As the Bishops' letter makes clear, individuals are fully dignified only in community. The person is both sacred and social.[71] The redemption of the world of work will reintegrate our needlessly bifurcated individual and social arenas of work. Many social theoreticians share this view.[72] Catholic labor theory can bring it into practice.

II. ALIENATION

Alienation in the world of work, exacerbated by the insidious fragmentation of community and individual working life, perhaps has reached its nadir. The challenge always has been to heal alienation. Alienation has been the single most enduring problem afflicting the world of work.[73] Most assuredly, the decade of the nineteen eighties has been overtly pro-ownership in tenor, philosophy, and practice.[74] Concomitantly, to some extent, the

68. *Id.* at V (26).

69. *Mark* 6:1-3.

70. *John* 15:1.

71. ECONOMIC JUSTICE, *supra* note 4, at ix.

72. *See* R. DAHRENDORF, LIFE CHANCES: APPROACHES TO SOCIAL AND POLITICAL THEORY (1979) (freedom and individual growth depend on developing community bonds that link autonomous individuals together as moral agents in community); R. DAHRENDORF, CLASS AND CLASS CONFLICT IN INDUSTRIAL SOCIETY (1959).

73. *See* MARX, *supra* note 11.

74. Gregory & Mak, *Significant Decisions of the NLRB, 1984: The Reagan Board's "Celebration" of the 50th Anniversary of the National Labor Relations Act*, 18 CONN. L. REV. 7 (1985).

decade has been anti-organized labor. The proportion of unionized workers in the United States workforce has fallen below twenty percent. Many influential union leaders and academic labor lawyers forcefully have asserted that organized labor is in crisis, perhaps irreversibly and terminally so.[75]

However, probably attributable to a residue of class consciousness, unionized employees have been better able than the nonunionized to cope with alienation in the world of work and to deal with the vicissitudes of ownership and the frightening uncertainty that increasingly has typified the mercurial national economy during the past few decades. Relatively low expectations of achieving meaningful work life, arms length cynicism and adversarial collective bargaining relationships with management, pessimism, and industrial realpolitik about the world of work, combine to cushion unionized employees against the seemingly inevitable cyclical downturns in the United States' late capitalist economy.

Meanwhile, however, nonunionized managers potentially have been far more severely victimized by the vicissitudes of capitalist economics. Lacking working class consciousness, individual managers who often are employed at the will of the employer are especially vulnerable to the psychological and economic devastation that can result when they involuntarily are separated from the world of work. Having closely identified with the philosophy of benevolent paternalism of the corporate family, these former managers, cast adrift by the now faceless, abstract, and impersonal corporation to which they had pledged almost filial personal allegiance, understandably feel especially betrayed. In this tragedy of labor, these Willie Lomanesque former managers are among the most pathetic figures forced to exit the stage.

The plight of the unsuccessful manager is infinitely worse in state-controlled economies of Marxist regimes. Given the self-interest of human nature—a trait powerfully realized and given rein by James Madison's ingenious device of factions in the Federalist Papers[76] and in the Constitution—workers in closely controlled statist economies, regardless of their individual place in the very definite hierarchy of purportedly nonhierarchical economies, have little for which to strive. There is no tangible prospect of individual gain to motivate them. Abstract historicist appeals to class ideology and to the promised triumph of the proletariat have been notoriously unable to inspire workers to complete commitment to their work for the good of the totalitarian state. Mr. Gorbachev is desperately attempting to motivate the Soviet work force through a combination of public jawboning and internal economic reforms. The world's most notorious state-controlled economies, the Soviet Union and China, cautiously are implementing limited forms of capitalism in some segments of their economies.[77]

75. *See supra* note 21 and accompanying text (discussing crisis in organized labor).

76. *See* THE FEDERALIST No. 10 (J. Madison).

77. Wren, *Comparing Two Communist Paths to Reform*, N.Y. Times, Sept. 6, 1987, at E2, col. 1. More than 80% of new restaurants, repair shops, and service outlets opened in China since the end of the Cultural Revolution in 1976 are privately owned. *Id.*

This injection of Madisonian capitalist economic self-interest into these totalitarian states is yielding tentatively positive results. Madison, in turn, owes a debt to Thomas Aquinas' insights; Aquinas realized private ownership had merit because it gave the individual a sense of individual worth and autonomy.[78]

Workers in the United States still are succumbing to the thus far generally pernicious ownership seduction of profit sharing and participatory management and experiments in purported workplace democracy. The problem is that relatively few of these initiatives emanate from the workers. Capitalist regimes in the United States temporarily are manipulating quasi-socialist forms of labor relations, unlike genuine restructuring of forms of workplace ownership as in, for example, Sweden.[79] Owner-generated experiments in worker ownership in the United States have proven very troubling. In return for the illusory promise of workplace democracy, worker concessions are demanded by ownership during adverse economic periods. At most, workers receive a disproportionately small share of profits in exchange for betraying and abandoning their class consciousness.[80] If workplace democracy initiatives emanate from ownership elites, and are not the true creatures of the workers, the initiatives probably will be pretexts designed by ownership to continue to manipulate labor. To their credit, the Bishops were very cognizant of this potential perversion of worker democracy by manipulative ownership elites, and they caution workers to beware. "Workers rightly reject calls for less adversarial relations when they are a smokescreen for demands that labor make all the concessions. For partnership to be genuine it must be a two-way street, with creative initiative and a willingness to cooperate on all sides."[81]

Meanwhile, the Japanese and South Korean economies are manifesting serious employee disenchantment with corporate and state paternalism, via increasing incidence of labor unrest and recent initiatives toward unionization.[82]

The profound malaise and alienation that afflict the world of work do not respect status, hierarchy, class, individual, or nation. Every individual and every economy is, to some very real extent, adversely affected by and inextricably bound up in the tragedy of labor. It remains especially difficult for labor law scholars to formulate an effective program to dissipate the alienation of the worker from the process and product of work. Analysis

---

78. THOMAS AQUINAS, SUMMA THEOLOGICA, II-II, 9.65, a.2.

79. For thorough discussion of the Meidner plan in Sweden, which designs collective capital control and full employment, see G. DORRIEN, THE DEMOCRATIC SOCIALIST VISION 144-50 (1986).

80. *See* Gregory, *supra* note 18.

81. ECONOMIC JUSTICE, *supra* note 4, at 150.

82. *See Koreans Warned On Labor Violence; Car Exports Off Sharply*, N.Y. Times, Sept. 6, 1987, at A4, col. 1. "Hundreds of thousands of workers demanding more pay and shorter working hours have taken part in more than 3,000 recent strikes throughout South Korea. The labor unrest has been the worst in the nation's history." *Id.*

of alienation has been Marxism's most important contribution to labor theory. However, Marxism alone inherently is unable to formulate an adequate solution to the core problem.

The alienation of the worker from the process and product of work is much more complex than Marx originally had imagined. Much has changed in a century and a half in heterogeneous post-industrial societies. Work has become increasingly intellectual; most tasks requiring brute physical force have been automated. But while the problem of alienation has grown much more complex, it may have grown even more intractable. In the fallible human condition, as long as we earn our living by the sweat of our brow, the world of work will never be perfected by secular theory alone. The Marxist dictatorship of the proletariat will remain just that—a statist dictatorship perhaps even more flawed than the capitalism it proposes to displace. Ultimately, for all practical purposes "the economy in the communist countries is not socialism but state capitalism."[83] Materialism perniciously objectifies the subject worker; it matters not whether the materialism is capitalist or Marxist. Because Marxist materialist historicism is deliberate, and its error of economism profound, Marxism especially is criticized by Catholic social teaching.[84] It is important for the worker to know that he is working "for himself," not merely for capitalist remuneration or for class-based anonymous contribution to bureaucratic statism.[85]

Consider again the bitter factory worker. Dull, dangerous, repetitive work often can be redesigned and automated. Worker skills can be upgraded. Current workers need not be displaced by automation. Workers can be retrained. The hyperefficiencies of Taylor's scientific management of the early assembly lines are now proving dysfunctional. As General Motors learned at their Lordstown, Ohio assembly plant in the early seventies,[86] and as Honda now is learning at its Marysville, Ohio assembly plant in the late eighties, the high speed Fordist assembly line breeds anonymity, physical and mental exhaustion, and heightened alienation. Employee involvement circles and quality of work life programs, if used legitimately and not merely as a management pretext to increase production, are positive steps that can be taken to actualize for the embittered factory worker some real degree of discretion, responsibility, and involvement in the process of work. Dangerous workplaces can be made safer. While alienation probably will not evaporate totally, it can be substantially mitigated, as workers achieve some autonomy and maturity in the world of work.

In *Laborem Exercens* Pope John Paul II repeatedly offers this redemptive vision. "In fact, in the final analysis it is always man who is the purpose of the work, whatever work it is that is done by man—even if the

83. G. Baum, The Priority of Labor 37 (1982).

84. *See generally* Laborem Exercens, *supra* note 31.

85. *Id.* at III (15).

86. D. Moberg, Rattling The Golden Chains: Conflict And Consciousness of Auto Workers (1978) (doctoral dissertation available at University of Chicago).

common scale of values rates it as the merest 'service,' as the most monotonous, even the most alienating work."[87] *Laborem Exercens* does not mandate specifically the form that the world of work with man as subject must take. The encyclical does not resolve whether joint ownership of the means of work or shareholding by labor in the management or profits of business will be the best route to ensure the recognition and actualization of worker as subject. However, Pope John Paul II concludes that ultimately "on the basis of his work each person is fully entitled to consider himself a part owner of the great workbench at which he is working with everyone else."[88] The anonymity of work can be reduced by organizing workers into smaller cells and units, both on the factory assembly line and the intellectual assembly line of the mega-law firm. Consider also the new Wall Street law firm associate. Rather than subordinate the ends of achieving greater dignity in life to the confused fetishized means of making a disproportionate amount of money for its own sake, law firm salaries can be stabilized, rather than continuously accelerated. Client fees can be moderated while client needs still can be met professionally. The relentless, frenzied quest for even more billable hours could then abate somewhat, the quality of work life enhanced, and the dignity of an integrated life made realistically capable of attainment.

Smaller work circles are mediating structures that positively can improve the quality of work life in the anonymity of the complex, large work place. This is the insight of the sociology of work.[89] But the inherent nature of complex organizational bureaucracy cannot be transformed completely by these smaller work units. The early Christians were radical classic communists. From Chapter Four of the Acts of the Apostles, we know that the early Christian communities pooled all resources earned by individuals into the service of the Christian community.[90] However, once Christianity became the state-sponsored, majoritarian religion of the Roman Empire, the nature of bureaucratic culture and complex organizational behavior displaced personalism with anonymity. Vatican City, the epicenter of the world's oldest and most sophisticated complex bureaucracy, is a far cry from the early Christian communes. It is interesting that the philosophy of personalism in the world of work is now so powerfully reintroduced in the pastoral letters of the Catholic heirarchy, and in the most recent (February, 1988) social encyclical of Pope John Paul II.[91]

Marxist labor theory reenergized the worker. The sociology of John Paul II and the philosophy of personalism of Dorothy Day and the Catholic Worker[92] owe much to the Daily Worker and to the worker philosophy of Peter Maurin. In turn, the motto *ora et labora,* pray and work, of the

---

87. Laborem Exercens, *supra* note 31, at II (6).

88. *Id.* at III (14).

89. G. Baum, The Priority of Labor 59 (1982).

90. *Acts of the Apostles* 4:32-35.

91. *See* Sollicitudo, *supra* note 67.

92. For a fine history of Dorothy Day and the Catholic Worker, see W. Miller, A Harsh and Dreadful Love (1973). *See also* R. Coles, Dorothy Day (1987).

fifteen hundred year old monastic Benedictine Order, presciently trumped Marxism by over a millenium. Unmasking and analyzing the reality of alienation in the world of work has been the most important, valuable, and enduring contribution of Marxist labor theory. Unfortunately, Marxist theory alone is congenitally incapable of articulating a realistic solution to alienation. Proletarian victory is not ontologically certain. In addition to failing to appreciate fully the complexity of alienation in even contemporary Soviet society, Marxist theory ultimately proves unable to defuse alienation because it proposes a secular statist false necessity.

Capitalist society in the United States is perhaps even less capable of unilaterally formulating a realistic solution to the problem of alienation. Marxist theory has an analytic advantage over capitalism in that Marxism has an intellectual history of wrestling with the fundamental nature of the problem of alienation.[93] In both theory and practice, capitalism lags Marxism, and is only now beginning to come to grips with problems of alienation in the world of work. Thus far, capitalism has made only a few tentative steps toward redesign of work from large corporate anonymity into smaller work cells. There is serious danger that even this positive first step may be compromised by confusing the problem of alienation with what ownership perceives as counter-productive adversarial labor relations. Fitful ill-advised steps toward purported "worker ownership" thus far have been little more than pretexts for seducing and coopting organized labor, robbing unionized workers of class consciousness, and increasing profits to ownership elites.

The synergy of law and theology best may redeem workers from the tragedy of labor.[94] This is the promise of Catholic social teaching, first adapting the positive contributions of Marxist labor theory, and then transcending Marxist historicism with a fuller teleology. Catholic social teaching, with its express teleological consciousness of spirituality and justice, trumps Marxism. Gregory Baum incisively highlights the advantages of Catholic labor theory:

> Only religion or religiously based convictions can make the unity of humankind a felt reality and motivating factor. We are responsible for one another before God.
>
> * * *
>
> Workers, oppressed people, and those in solidarity with them have made and are still making these sacrifices, but collective self-interest does not account for their motivation. Most of them do not ask why they take these burdens upon themselves. They feel it in their bones that they must wrestle for justice. Whether they realize it or not, their motivation is religious. Universal solidarity can only be based on faith—on a faith in man's promised destiny. In my mind,

93. *See* MARX, *supra* note 11.

94. G. BAUM, RELIGION AND ALIENATION (1975).

this is a materialistic argument for religion. In the most concrete, down to earth, bread-and-butter sense, God makes humanity possible.[95]

III. IMMANENCE, TRANSCENDENCE, AND ESCHATOLOGY: A PROLEGOMENON FOR LABOR THEORY

It has become the height of law review fashion to offer rarefied speculation concerning the metaphysics of law,[96] to cite, *de rigeur,* as Professor James Boyle puts it so aptly and wittily, litanies of famous dead European philosophers.[97] The tension posed by the imperative to rethink core labor theory and to redesign effective pragmatic tactics is especially pronounced for the academic labor lawyer. Labor law is grounded in the empirical, pragmatic, and very earthy real world.[98] Meanwhile, labor theory is compellingly conceptual. Today's theoretical discourse ineluctably dictates the shape of tomorrow's empirical reality. This is certainly as true in labor law as in other areas of the law. The prolegomenon broadly adumbrated here may never come to fruition in the world of work. There may never be a legally-driven redemption from the tragedy of labor. The possibility that, despite our best efforts, the world of work may never be transformed is a large part of the tragic aspect of the problem. Nevertheless, mindful of the Biblical truth that the Lord helps those who help themselves, human free will and the Gospel message mandate that we persevere.

Laborem Exercens recognizes the need for fluid, continual reassessment of the rapid and, as yet, unforeseeable changes in the world of work in order best to advocate realization of maximum human dignity.

> It is not for the Church to analyze scientifically the consequences that these changes may have on human society. But the Church considers it to be its task always to call attention to the dignity and rights of those who work, to condemn situations in which that dignity and those rights are violated, and to help guide the above-mentioned changes so as to ensure authentic progress by man and society.[99]

No mystical *deus ex machina* relief is promised to either workers or to labor scholars, nor should it be sought from the realm of the theologian. However, theology recently has been appreciated more by legal scholars.

---

95. G. Baum, The Priority of Labor 40, 70 (1982).

96. Peller, *The Metaphysics of American Law,* 73 Calif. L. Rev. 1151 (1985).

97. Boyle, *The Politics of Reason: Critical Legal Theory and Local Social Thought,* 133 U. Pa. L. Rev. 685, 738 (1985) ("a tale spun from the dry thread of epistemology and embroidered with the appropriately impressive names of 'famous dead Europeans who once wrote about ideology'").

98. Gregory, *The National Labor Relations Board and the Politics of Labor Law,* 27 B.C. L. Rev. 39 (1985).

99. Laborem Exercens, *supra* note 31, at 1 (1).

Hermeneutics has energized constitutional textual interpretation through analogous adaptation of the device of scriptural exegesis, for example.[100] Theology is helping lawyers better understand and thus more clearly pose the most fundamental issues of law, equity, and justice. Professor Burt has shown how religious parables enhance understanding of constitutional law.[101] In his eloquent recent book, *The Authoritative and the Authoritarian,*[102] Professor Vining concludes by analogizing the function of the lawyer to that of the priest. This suggests a wide range of roles. There are charismatic prophets, as well as ministerial priests. But, as Roberto Unger has argued, there are also pharisees who have lost their faith, who observe ritual and formula without belief, who sit in hypocritical ceremony at cold altars.[103] Prophets, true priests, and pharisees all share, to some extent, the concern with whether transcendent God will hear the prayer to enter into human relations. Over a decade ago, Roberto Unger presciently concluded his brilliant book, *Knowledge and Politics,* with a plea to hear the voice of God in human relations.[104]

In his book, *Passion: An Essay In Human Personality,* Professor Unger eloquently summarized the unique contribution of religion to positive reconstruction of social reality:

> The most significant articulation of existential projects can be found in the major religious and religiously inspired ethics of world history. For more than the abstract doctrines of moral and political philosophers, these legal and religious traditions embody visions and projects that have withstood the test of experience, enabling large numbers of people over long periods of time to make sense of their experience.[105]

---

100. Ciampi, *Applying Scriptural Exegesis to the Interpretation of Article III of the Constitutional,* 26 DUQ. L. REV. 13 (1987).

101. Burt, *Constitutional Law and the Teaching of the Parables,* 93 YALE L. J. 455 (1984).

102. J. VINING, THE AUTHORITATIVE AND THE AUTHORITARIAN (1986); *see* Ball, Book Review, 35 U.C.L.A. L. REV. 547 (1988); Joseph, Book Review, MICH. Q. REV. (forthcoming, Winter 1987); Miller, Book Review, 84 MICH. L. REV. 880 (1986).

103. Unger, *The Critical Legal Studies Movement,* 96 HARV. L. REV. 561 (1983) Professor Unger writes, "When we came, they were like a priesthood that had lost their faith and kept their jobs. They stood in tedious embarrassment before cold altars. But we turned away from those altars, and found the mind's opportunity in the heart's revenge." *Id.* at 675.

104. R. UNGER, KNOWLEDGE AND POLITICS 295 (1975).

> Desirous of faith, touched by hope, and moved by love, men look unceasingly for God. Their search for Him continues even when thinking must stop and action fail. And in their vision of Him they find the beginning and end of their knowledge of the world and of their sympathy for others. So is man's meditation on God a final union of thought and love—love which is thought disembodied from language and restored to its source.
>
> But our days pass, and still we do not know you fully. Why then do you remain silent? Speak, God.

Id.

105. R. UNGER, PASSION: AN ESSAY IN HUMAN PERSONALITY 47-48 (1984).

The world of work certainly needs to learn the lessons that the amalgamation of law and theology is best able to teach. Marxist historicism alone is an inadequate solution to the problem of alienation in the world of work. The tragedy of labor can not be ameliorated by a contradictory Marxist metaphysics that offers the idol of worker statism as telos. Rather than offer a truly transcendent vision for labor theory, Marxism exalts the means, and attempts to transmogrify the means of work into a labor eschatology. A Marxist metaphysics that answers immanence with immanence is doomed to frustration. Instead, viable labor theory must both meld the transcendence of theory with the immanence of action and preserve the distinction of means and ends. Marxism regards the worker as an economic creature. Unlike Marxism, Catholic labor theory highlights the spiritual dimension of the worker. In comparison, Marxist dialectical materialism and economic determinism as scientific historicist explanation of life in positivistic terms is inevitably impoverished.[106]

Fortunately, the positive contributions of Marxist labor theory, especially its perceptive analysis of the enduring problem of alienation, can be rechanneled by the fusion of Marxism and theology. Within the past two decades, liberation political theology has swept the world. It is now being translated into practice in myriad forms, in Europe, the Phillipines, and throughout the Americas. To be sure, liberation political theology can be deeply problematic. Its potential excess of reflecting more Marxism and little theology has been sharply and properly criticized by the Vatican.[107]

Broadly and properly understood, theology is inherently liberating, redeeming. The Catholic Church repeatedly has endorsed the dignity of work. The world of work in Genesis can be transformed. The Benedictine monastic order, founded in the sixth century, has offered a fifteen hundred year history premised on the indispensability of prayer and the dignity of work. The worker priests of Europe and the priest-advisors to the Solidarity free trade union movement in Poland offer powerful current witness to the power of theology to liberate the world of work. Poland's martyr priest, Jersy Popieluszko, was murdered in 1984 by state security agents because of his outspoken support of the now-outlawed free trade union Solidarity

---

106. G. Baum, The Priority of Labor 26 (1982); *see also* G. Dorrien, The Democratic Socialist Vision 161 (1986).

> Religion should inform and limit the ideology and politics of the Left. The religious sense of sin is a crucial restraint for any political movement, because it serves to remind activists that even the most humane politics cannot redeem human nature or give ultimate meaning to human efforts. If history has any meaning, that meaning is transcendental, not historical. It will not be found by creating socialism, any more than socialism will eliminate the effects of sin. The Left could have spared itself and others much agony in this century if only it had understood that its success would not bring the fulfillment or redemption of history.

Id.

107. *Instruction on Certain Aspects of the "Theology of Liberation"* (1984); *Instruction on Christian Freedom and Liberation* (1986); *see also* M. Novak, *The Case Against Liberation Theology*, N.Y. Times Magazine, Oct. 21, 1984.

movement. Salvadoran Bishop Oscar Romero and missionary nuns from the United States were likewise brutally murdered by right wing fascist death squads in El Salvador for their community work. They stand as contemporary Thomas Beckets, timeless thorns in the side of totalitarian regimes.

Phillipine Cardinal Jaime Sin was severely critical of the tyranny of the Marcos regime. Brazilian Archbishop Helder Camara has lived a life of courageous witness in opposition to military dictatorship and in support of workers' rights, sharing the tradition of the martyred Oscar Romero.

In the United States, churches politically have organized local communities, and have pressed for specific improvements in housing, immigration policy, schools, police protection, and employment opportunities. In Brooklyn, New York, the innovative Nehemiah program to increase the supply of moderately priced, privately owned homes was designed and implemented by the coalition of East Brooklyn Churches.[108] In 1987 the Nehemiah plan became the prototype for new federal housing legislation to support similar private housing construction initiatives in communities throughout the United States.[109] The late Dorothy Day and the Catholic Worker movement have an established history of translating Catholic social teaching into practice by service to the urban poor.

Pope John Paul II has been outspoken in his support of Solidarity and in support of worker democracy and labor rights throughout the world. His 1981 Papal encyclical *Laborem Exercens,* is a radical voice for workers and a powerful express call for the priority of labor over capital. He carries on the tradition of modern papal support for labor that was first notably articulated in 1891 by Pope Leo XIII in his papal encyclical *Rerum Novarum* (On New Things).

A. *The Special Challenge To Implement The Priority Of Labor In The United States*

In many statements, Pope John Paul II has severely criticized the false ideology of materialist values. This critique formed much of his seventh and most recent encyclical, *Sollicitudo Rei Socialis* (The Social Concerns of the Church), issued in February, 1988. Because of deliberate greed of ownership elites, materialism has infected capitalism. Capitalism is not inherently evil.[110] In conjunction with the politics of social democracy,

108. *See* J. Gittings, *East Brooklyn Churches and the Nehemiah Project—Churches in Community: A Place to Stand,* CHRISTIANITY AND CRISIS, Feb. 2, 1987; Roberts, *Despite Success, Housing Effort Still Struggling,* N.Y. Times, Sept. 24, 1987, at B1, col.1.

109. *Public Housing Bill Approved by House,* N.Y. Times, June 12, 1987, at A16, col. 1; *see generally* Malloy, *The Political Economy of Co-Financing America's Urban Renaissance,* 40 VAND. L. REV. 67 (1987); DePalma, *The Nehemiah Plan: A Success, But . . .,* N.Y. Times, Sept. 27, 1987, at R1, col. 1.

110. Pope John Paul II's attitude towards entrepreneurs is not inflexibly hostile. "The degree of well being which society today enjoys would be unthinkable without the dynamic

capitalism can be a powerful instrument for good. The challenge in the United States is to reform capitalism into proper means in service of the ends of labor. Pope John Paul II is not favorably disposed to capitalism in its present form; he is moving Catholic social teaching toward a socialist planned economy.[111] This is a dilemma for the United States National Conference of Catholic Bishops. In their 1986 pastoral letter, *Economic Justice for All*, the Bishops endeavor to integrate Catholic social teaching on work into a capitalist economic and governmental structure. The Bishops carefully disavow any particular economics, while respecting the traditional republican constitutional politics of the United States.

> In our letter, we write as pastors, not public officials. We speak as moral teachers, not economic technicians. We seek not to make some political or ideological point but to lift up the human and ethical dimensions of economic life, aspects too often neglected in public discussion. We bring to this task a dual heritage of Catholic social teaching and traditional American values. . . . The pastoral letter is not a blueprint for the American economy. It does not embrace any particular theory of how the economy works, nor does it attempt to resolve the disputes between different schools of economic thought.[112]

The Bishops expressly recognize the legitimacy of private property, reject ideological extremes, and appreciate that ours is a "mixed" economy.[113]

This is the conundrum faced by the Catholic Church in the United States—how to implement Catholic social teaching on the priority of labor

---

figure of the businessperson, whose function consists of organizing human labor and the means of production so as to give rise to the goods and services necessary for the prosperity and progress of the community." Address by Pope John Paul II, To Businessmen and Economic Managers of Milan, Italy (May 22, 1983), *reprinted in* L'OSSERVATORE ROMANO June 20, 1983, at 9:1 (English ed.). The Gospel root is Jesus' parable of God as the owner of the estate. Although the owner can "do as he pleases" with his money, he chooses to be generous and pays high wages to low seniority workers. *Matthew* 20:1-16.

111. In his first encyclical, Pope John Paul II advocated a planned central economy. *See* G. Baum, *A Pope from the Second World*, 18 ECUMENIST Jan.-Feb., 1980, at 25; G. BAUM, CATHOLICS AND CANADIAN SOCIALISM (1980); Baum writes, "The encylical recognizes that contemporary Western society is no longer defined by the free market, even if the old liberalism is still used for ideological purposes. Government is in fact deeply involved in the economy." G. BAUM, THE PRIORITY OF LABOR 33 (1982). Pope John Paul II and the premier contemporary socialist in the United States, Michael Harrington, share this aspiration. "The fundamental proposition in all of Harrington's books is that modern industrialized societies are moving ineluctably toward collectivism, and that the meaningful political question of our time is therefore not *whether* we should have planning, but *how* planning should be organized." G. DORRIEN, THE DEMOCRATIC SOCIALIST VISION 122 (1986) (emphasis added); *see also* M. HARRINGTON, DECADE OF DECISION: THE CRISIS OF THE AMERICAN SYSTEM (1980); M. HARRINGTON, THE TWILIGHT OF CAPITALISM (1976); HARRINGTON, *Corporate Collectivism: A System of Social Injustice*, in CONTEMPORARY READINGS IN SOCIAL AND POLITICAL ETHICS (1984).

112. ECONOMIC JUSTICE, *supra* note 4, at vii, ix.

113. *Id.* at xii.

within the capitalist motif of constitutional republicanism. True worker democracy potentially threatens both capitalism and republicanism. "Democracy at the workplace is at odds with capitalist theory."[114] Clearly, the popular mass perception in the United States of leftist calls for true worker democracy raise the specter of Marxism rather than the promise of spiritual redemption. In the United States capitalist republic, *Laborem Exercens* probably sounds uncomfortably more like Karl Marx than Pope John Paul II to most audiences. The capitalist power elites in the United States would be as threatened by the profound ramifications of the papal encyclical as by any Marxist tract.

The challenge for the Catholic Bishops in the United States is to preach implementation of Catholic social teaching on the priority of labor in a measured incremental way, without advocating the destruction of capitalism or its displacement with socialism. If possible, the Catholic Church in the United States must seek a methodology to implement Catholic social teaching on labor in a fashion consonant with capitalism and constitutional republicanism. Initially, the Church must open the ears of an alienated and divided society so it can hear the message. Ultimately, this may not be fully possible. The priority of labor over capital obviates the demise of laissez faire capitalism. It is not certain whether the socialism of worker democracy will likewise spell the end of constitutional republicanism. It may well be that the effectuation of Catholic social teaching in the constitutional republic of the United States will yield an as yet unanticipated higher, redeemed order of both economic capitalism and republican governmental structures.

Laissez faire capitalism in the United States evolved into welfare capitalism decades ago. The Bishops are working with welfare capitalism as a form of corporate statism that can mediate rather successfully between the interests of labor and ownership. The Bishops appreciate that, especially in the United States, labor cannot exist without capital and capital cannot exist without labor. This was the message of the first modern Papal encyclical on labor, *Rerum Novarum,* by Pope Leo XIII in 1891. Leo XIII's key perception was that the interests of labor and capital can be harmonized, but probably never equated. The Bishop's pastoral letter reflects the accuracy of Leo XIII's perception for the United States in its period of late capitalism, contrary to *Laborem Exercens'* pronouncement that labor and capital never can be opposed.[115] This was the policy insight of the National Labor Relations Act—a structural and institutional legal appreciation of the importance and necessity of independent organized labor, while preserving and respecting the legitimate role of ownership in the operation of the complex capitalist economy. The Bishops share that insight; they respect the distinction between management and labor. However, they caution that the adversarial relationship must not become extreme, and thus can avoid dysfunction.[116] Good faith collective bargaining is the basis upon which to

114. G. Baum, The Priority of Labor 24-25 (1982).
115. Laborem Exercens, *supra* note 31, at III (13).
116. Economic Justice, *supra* note 4, at 148.

build some forms of worker democracy and codetermination in a centrist corporate welfare state.

The United States Bishops face a formidable challenge. They must preach the implementation of Catholic social teaching in the world of work within the corporate welfare statism of contemporary late capitalism in the United States. Unlike the Polish philosopher Pope of the universal Church, the Bishops must work within a very mainstream American constituency. The Catholic model for effectuation of the priority of labor continues to appreciate the aphorism that labor needs capital as its means. Capital needs labor, because capital as means is designed to serve the labor ends of achieving human dignity in the world of work. Capital is the means, the important instrument of labor. In the United States, capitalism and constitutional republicanism are closely linked; both are premised on the Madisonian device of factions and the near sacrosanct status of private property elucidated in Federalist Paper 10. Because of this Madisonian linkage of capitalism and constitutional Republicanism, the challenge of Catholic social teaching is especially pronounced. *Laborem Exercens* expressly summarizes:

> Christian tradition has never upheld this right [of private ownership of property] as absolute and untouchable. On the contrary, it has always understood this right within the broader content of the right common to all to use the goods of the whole of creation. The right to private property is subordinated to the right to common use, to the fact that goods are meant for everyone.[117]

For Catholicism, the real issue is the use to which capital is put, rather than the ownership of capital. Catholicism thus dynamically transcends Marxism.[118] *Laborem Exercens* does not demand the "a priori elimination of private ownership of the means of production."[119] Statist collectivism as the alternative to capitalism does not necessarily guarantee true socialization of ownership.[120] Because it is important that the worker have a sense of working "for himself,"[121] and work not only for money or to contribute anonymously to bureaucratic statism, *Laborem Exercens* acknowledges that, as Thomas Aquinas originally recognized, private ownership of means of production may have value because it enhances this important sense of worker autonomy and worth.[122]

In their comprehensive pastoral letter, the Bishops reinforced Pope John Paul II's encyclical. The Bishops urge a preferential option for the poor, reaffirm the dignity of work, and also support initiatives for workplace democracy. But there is a prudent and deliberately measured tone to the Bishops' specific recommendations. They reject current levels of unemploy-

---

117. LABOREM EXERCENS, *supra* note 31, at III (14).
118. G. BAUM, THE PRIORITY OF LABOR 24-25 (1982).
119. LABOREM EXERCENS, *supra* note 31, at III (14).
120. *Id.*
121. THOMAS AQUINAS, SUMMA THEOLOGICA II-II, 9.65, a.2.
122. LABOREM EXERCENS, *supra* note 31, at III (15).

ment as unacceptable. They urge a national policy of meaningful full employment, based on coordination of fiscal, monetary, and tax policy, expansion of job retraining, and job creation to bring the marginally employed and the unemployed into the world of work.[123] The Bishops also expressly reiterate, however, the Church's established social teaching on the legitimacy of private ownership of property.[124] The Bishops urge that private ownership be enjoyed by the broadest segment possible of the population, and militate against undue concentration of ownership in only a few hands.[125]

Empowerment is at the heart of the Bishops' letter.[126] Widespread private ownership among as many persons as possible is one means by which capitalism can enhance social empowerment. Empowerment of workers, individually and collectively, without merely aping the pathologies of economic capitalist elites, may hold the answer to ameliorating the tragedy of labor and to redeeming the world of work.

The Bishops call for "the empowerment of people everywhere." Poverty is certainly one manifestation of powerlessness. Those excluded from the world of work often are simultaneously consigned to poverty and powerlessness. However, work alone, while it may be the means to escape economic poverty, may not relieve the even deeper problem of powerlessness. This insight partially explains the virtually intractable malaise of spirit that permeates the world of work, regardless of whether it occurs in a capitalist or a socialist economy, and without regard to whether one is a unionized rank and file worker or a manager.

Money alone is not power. Acquiring money, while it may enable escape from poverty, does not guarantee empowerment. Witness the upper-mid level manager with a six figure annual income. He is not economically impoverished, but he may still be, for all practical purposes, relationally powerless within the community, and therefore at the mercy of the ownership elite. Without relational power, the unemployed poor and highly skilled and well paid workers alike lack the ability to reconstruct the world of work and to alleviate the tragedy of labor.

The Bishops endorse an option for the poor as part of a broader appreciation of the linkage of poverty and powerlessness. The Bishops urge the working class and the middle class to realize that they, despite not being immediately and individually victimized by poverty, may otherwise be as powerless as the poor. Rather than simply ape the pursuit of money by the economic elite, the poor and the working class must realize that they are bonded in solidarity and are called to seek the true empowerment that transcends money. In the Sermon on the Mount, Jesus said "blessed are the poor in spirit."[127] This is the call of God throughout history for solidarity

---

123. ECONOMIC JUSTICE, *supra* note 4, at 78-83.

124. *Id.* at 57.

125. *Id.*

126. My analysis of empowerment in ECONOMIC JUSTICE FOR ALL draws heavily from Penta, *supra* note 35.

127. *Matthew* 5:1-6.

among all humanity poor in spirit, regardless of economic class distinctions. Jesus repeatedly cast his lot with the dispossessed. Redemption, both individual and collective, is premised on our solidarity with the poor; "for I was hungry and you gave me food, I was thirsty and you gave me drink . . . as often as you did it for one of my least brothers, you did it for me."[128] This is a radical call, make no mistake. It is not, as unfortunately it has often been illegitimately used, a basis for facile rationalizations by troubled elites seeking to preserve economic and political hegemony.

Relational community of action in solidarity with the poor, rather than futile emulation of the capitalist elites, holds the true promise of genuine empowerment. The Bishops share the Marxist insight that calls for collective relational power among people. This is sharply contrasted to seeking hierarchical and atomized power as sovereignty and dominion over those individuals with relatively less money.

The Bishops reflect a theology of justice shared among the empowered community, and reject a hierarchy of economically dominant monied individuals. "Establishment of minimum levels of participation in the life of the human community for all persons" is the key to the amelioration of individual and collective powerlessness. Poverty can be alleviated as an ancillary consequence of this universal participation in community.

This socialist understanding of relational power among the community, rather than the capitalist motif of hierarchical economic power of elite dominion, has the radical potential to fuse in solidarity the seemingly foreign amalgam of the poor unemployed and the managerial workers of the upper middle class. By better realizing the nature of powerlessness and the dynamics of empowerment, the unemployed may be better able to enter the world of work. Meanwhile, alienation of workers can be mitigated. Perhaps most important, through appreciating the Bishops' insight that money alone will not result in empowerment, workers can repudiate the idol of materialism and the fetishism of commodities. Workers can seek true empowerment, without aping the hierarchical behaviors of the monied elites.

This leads, logically enough, to the Bishops' endorsement of worker democracy. Heightened autonomy, discretion, and responsibility will lessen alienation and enhance the sense of relational power among workers and owners. To be truly empowering, worker democracy must be worker initiated, with workers as subjects, not objects, in relational power with ownership. Unfortunately, in the United States, this is a lesson not yet learned.[129] Most worker participation schemes have been management schemes, originally designed as pretexts to obtain worker concessions during periods of economic adversity. The Bishops are cognizant of this danger of ownership manipulation of workers. It is a delicate balance that the Bishops attempt to achieve. Worker democracy and codetermination unquestionably are positive contributions to greater human dignity in the world of work.

---

128. *Matthew* 25:35-40.
129. *See* Gregory, *supra* note 18.

However, the Bishops realize that they are proposing essentially socialist work relationships within a capitalist and usually hierarchical work structure. Thus, the United States Bishops stop short of Pope John Paul II's overt call for the priority of labor over capital. Just as Pope John Paul II reflects his socialist culture of Eastern Bloc Poland, so too do the United States Bishops reflect an understanding of their capitalist culture. The Bishops are seeking to reform, without ruining, the positive contributions of capitalism, which is the dominant economic and governmental motif in the United States. The Bishops offer an agenda for revivifying the world of work, short of the shared socialism of Pope John Paul II and of classic Marxism. Priority of labor over capital ultimately could lead to the confusion of the means of work with the end of greater human dignity, of which work, while important, is still only one component. Whether committed under the mantle of Marxism or of the Papacy, the raw indiscriminate advocacy of labor over capital can confuse work with teleology. Generally, failed worker ownership has been the unfortunate practical consequence of this confusion thus far in the United States.

The Bishops offer an agenda for redeeming the tragedy of labor without supplanting capitalism with socialism and without completely equating workers and ownership. By enhancing awareness of empowerment as incorporating yet transcending economic power, the Bishops helpfully broaden worker class consciouness without advocating unproblematic and indiscriminate worker ownership. Thus, the Bishops suggest how worker alienation can be reduced, how worker autonomy can be enhanced, and how workers' consciousness can be heightened, while simultaneously repudiating ownership behaviors that mistakenly equate amassing of money alone with empowerment. The Bishops seek to redeem the world of work and to heal the tragedy of labor while retaining the capitalist and republican constitutional order on which the economic and governmental structure of the United States is based. While it remains to be seen whether they will succeed, the Bishops evidence a deep understanding of the need for progressive, measured healing of the world of work, while avoiding a wholesale radical socialist displacement of the entire capitalist order.

The Bishops' core concept of relational empowerment will be quite familiar to organized labor, premised, as they both are, on the call for collective action. Both traditional modalities of collective bargaining and the Bishops' call for redemptive empowerment prioritize the collective action of relational political empowerment over forms of economic power. Economic power alone cannot determine effective political power. The Bishops' concept of empowerment shares a powerful commonality with the imperative of collective action and relational power at the heart of effective organized labor. The direct linkage between theology and labor law, and the redemptive implication for the world of work, is profound and unmistakable. Reverend Leo Penta cogently has summarized the possibilities of the Bishops' 1986 call for economic justice:

> What ultimately is at stake here can be seen to be the development of a long-term positive synthesis between democratic values of

> participation and equality and the Gospel values of love and justice. Such a synthesis would depend much more on a process of enabling action from below than upon changes in economic policy from above.[130]

It remains to be seen whether worker generated egalitarianism and middle class solidarity with the poor can occur in our closely linked capitalist and constitutional republic.

B. The Fusion of Law And Theology

These many examples, both within the United States and from the international community, convincingly demonstrate the merits of properly understood liberation political theology. The powerful fusion of the immanent world of work with the transcendence of theological vision has the potential to transform and redeem the world of work, to address the problem of alienation, and to salve the wounds of the tragedy of labor. As Professor Robert Rodes has suggested, this amalgamation of law and theology creates a jurisprudence of liberation,[131] the future rich potential of which we can now only barely begin to appreciate. Nowhere could the consequences of this new jurisprudence of liberation be more affirmative and healing than in the world of work. The Papacy, the international teaching magisterium, the hierarchy, and the grass roots worker priests and laity, both within the United States and throughout the world, consistently have supported the dignity of work and improvements in working life throughout the Church's modern history. The Catholic Church has offered a transformative, redemptive vision for the world of work. The relative failure of Marxism to afford a similar transformative vision of the world of work especially is revealed in the ruthless Soviet suppression of a free trade union movement in an environment that purports to offer the telos of a proletarian paradise. This plain irony of the ultimate workers' state summarily crushing worker aspirations is certainly one of the most profound manifestations of the continuing failure of Marxist practice. Catholic theology, not Marxist ideology, offers the best hope for transforming the world of work.

Gregory Baum best explains how Pope John Paul II, reflecting his Eastern Bloc Polish socialism, adapts and then transcends Marxism by contemporary Catholic social teaching on work. "Pope John Paul II permits himself to be impressed by certain Marxist insights. Yet in the discussion of these insights he opens them up, overcomes their rigidity, expands them toward new meaning, and thus produces a social philosophy that transcends Marxism from within."[132] While rejecting Marxism's atheism, authoritari-

---

130. *See* Penta, *supra* note 35.

131. R. Rodes, Law and Liberation (1986); *see also* M. Ball, Lying Down Together: Law, Metaphor and Theology (1985); T. Shaffer, On Being a Christian and a Lawyer (1981).

132. G. Baum, The Priority of Labor 3 (1982).

anism, and rigidity, liberation political theology, including *Laborem Exercens,* draws upon Marxist social insights.[133] In *Rerum Novarum* in 1891, Pope Leo XIII bitterly attacked the evils of socialism as an atheistic materialism at odds with Catholicism; by 1971, Pope Paul VI acknowledged certain forms of socialism were appropriate for Catholic participation. The objective of Catholic labor theory is actualization of justice in the world of work, not the victory of any particular class. Catholicism, partially inspired by Marxism, has dereified and personalized class struggle, and has transcended Marxism by offering a uniquely valuable theory of labor history in the world of work.[134] Catholic labor theory regards all humanity as struggling for justice, rather than against any particular class. The workers' struggle is essentially one based on a moral assault to overcome social sin of economic oppression in all its forms.[135]

Liberation political theology is in its infancy as both metaphysics and as praxis. It would be utterly futile and totally premature to more than broadly outline the possible eschatological implications of the fusion of law and liberation political theology. I am increasingly pessimistic of our ability to transform the world of work solely by the conventions of secular labor law scholarship. However, I also reject the passive fatalism that awaits some mystic, *deus ex machina* salvation from a labor law armageddon. Unfortunately, civilization will witness a parade of apocalyptic charlatans of every sort as the millenium fast approaches. Labor law theory and practice is troubled enough without buying snake oil elixirs. It is unlikely that theology will be able to energize labor theory if labor theoreticians and practitioners abandon the daily struggle to improve the world of work. This would be the danger of relying solely on theological eschatology as a passive salvation, to the complete exclusion of political action. The powerful contribution of Catholic social teaching on labor is that it requires human action to transform the world of work; workers cannot passively rely on religious abstractions. They must work in concert with the unemployed poor who aspire to enter the world of work. Simultaneously, Catholicism reminds humanity of the goal of justice and of the transcendent and spiritual—an eschatology that gives meaning to struggle.

As liberation political theology begins to influence positively the world of work and to heal the wounds of the tragedy of labor, labor law theoreticians better can appreciate theology's transformative and redemptive potential. If the world of work truly can be transformed by theology, the current conventions of labor theory may become obsolete. The tragedy of labor, affected by exclusion, alienation, and malaise of spirit, finally may be resolved. By the influence of theology and especially through Catholic social teaching, the tragedy of labor may not be as intractable as it has thus far proven to be in Marxist theory of history.

133. *Id.* at 5-6.
134. *Id.* at 31.
135. *Id.* at 57.

Liberation political theology, vis-a-vis its transformative potential for the world of work, will be better understood several years hence. The centennial of *Rerum Novarum* in 1991 will be an opportune moment for an assessment. However, I suspect that it will be an eschatology, not in the conventional sense of a final teleological culmination, but rather, an eschatology that more fully reflects and helps us to appreciate the immanence of the world of work. As the philosophy of phenomenology has demonstrated, from St. Augustine of Hippo through Husserl,[136] an immanentized eschatology, although it initially seems to be a contradition or at least a confusion in terms of immanence and transcendence, makes the most sense in the world of work. An immanentized eschatology collapses notions of anthropomorphicized time; eternity is suddenly defined by immanence, not by transcendence. Time is a quaintly constrained human notion. Instead, all that ever was, is, and will be is immanentized in Augustine's "ever present present." As God revealed to Moses in the burning bush in the Book of Exodus, "I am who I am"—the perfect eschatalogical immanentization of the transcendent.

Likewise, I suspect, liberation political theology, through Catholic social teaching, will share in, revivify, and reflect the daily struggle for greater dignity in the world of work in a thoroughly immanent way. Individual and collective salvation occur in almost imperceptible ways, living each day. Heaven is revealed more as the daily road toward heaven, than as a final destination. Unlike Marxism, Catholic social teaching does not seek the ultimate disappearance of class distinctions in the world of work. The contributions of Thomas Aquinas stop the magisterium shy of raw egalitarianism. Instead, Catholicism seeks to maximize human dignity in the world of work, regardless of the institutional structures that the world of work ultimately may take. Catholic social teaching on work also may transform the bureaucracy of the Catholic Church itself. While Pope John Paul II takes Marxism seriously, and borrows heavily from both Marxism and liberation political theology, the nonideological socialism of *Laborem Exercens* both transcends, and is distinct from, Marxism and liberation political theology. Indeed, the magisterium sharply has criticized liberation political theology because some theologians have questioned whether the Church itself has participated in forms of social oppression. There is no self-critique in *Laborem Exercens*. There are many pressing internal labor relations questions within the Church. How will it treat its own workers, ranging from clergy with AIDS, to nuns with insufficient retirement funds, to faculty seeking to unionize? Gregory Baum has suggested that the labor encyclical affirmatively can be utilized to realign institutional Church structures in the furtherance of redeeming the world of work.[137]

---

136. Husserl is widely recognized as the father of modern phenomenology. *See generally* E. Husserl, Cartesian Meditations (1960); E. Husserl, Ideas: General Introduction to Pure Phenomenology (1952); E. Husserl, Phenomenology and The Crisis of Philosophy (1965).

137. G. Baum, The Priority of Labor 77-78 (1982).

IV. CONCLUSION

Scholars have begun to suggest how the law of liberation positively and pervasively will influence the future. The current modes of labor theory, including even the considerable innovations respectively engendered by critical scholarship and by economic analysis, lack the transformative potential necessary to dignify fully the world of work and to cure the alienation and malaise at the heart of the still seemingly intractable tragedy of labor. The Catholic Church, from the original classic communism described in Chapter Four of the Acts of the Apostles, to the recent proclamations of Pope John Paul II and the Bishops of the United States, eloquently and consistently has supported the dignity of work and the hopes of workers for better lives, free of alienation and full of autonomy and responsibility. I am cautiously optimistic that this theology, understood in this very broad sense of incorporating Catholic social teaching, has the fullest potential to redeem the world of work from the tragedy of labor.

Within the past few years, incisive legal scholars as diverse as Roberto Unger, Robert Rodes, Milner Ball, and Joseph Vining have reminded us of the promise theology can hold for law. Although the contour of the effectuation of this transformation necessarily must await future scholarship, if we now listen carefully and quietly, we may sense the theological redemption of the world of work underway. If work can be transformed, achievement of justice and peace, goals of both law and religion, cannot be far away.[138] The priority of labor over capital, while preserving and respecting the legitimacy of the means of capital in the service of labor, certainly will further justice. Through Catholic social teaching, we finally may have a true spirituality of work,[139] to transfigure the human laws of work. Finally, through this immanentized labor eschatology, Roberto Unger's prayer of over a decade ago may be answered.[140] God is speaking.

---

138. LABOREM EXERCENS, *supra* note 31, at I (2). "Commitment to justice must be closely linked with commitment to peace in the modern world." *Id. See also* C. BLACK, THE HUMANE IMAGINATION 14-16 (1986).

139. LABOREM EXERCENS, *supra* note 31, at V (24).

140. *See* Unger, *supra* note 104, at 295. It is striking to witness how Unger's most recent trilogy, POLITICS (1987), begins to translate much of Christian theory into practice. Scholars are divided over whether Unger is a utopian or a true Christian romantic. "Unger maintains his earlier *Knowledge and Politics* is a 'Christian' book . . . *Passion,* and now *Politics,* may be claimed as 'Christian' in the same way. If they are Christian in some sense, however, they are not Christian in the biblical sense." Ball, *The City of Unger,* 81 NW. U. L. REV. 625, 660 (1987). "The human longing for infinity leads toward an encounter with God. . . . I cannot help wondering whether, in this replacing God with man, Unger is not placing more weight on the individual/social world than it can rightly bear." Galston, *False Universality: Infinite Personality And Finite Existence In Unger's* Politics, 81 NW. L. REV. 751, 764 (1987). "I do not mean to suggest that Unger is a secular leftist. A plausible argument can be made, I think, that his work is more fairly assimilated to the religious left." Perry, *Preface to Symposium, Roberto Unger's Politics,* 81 NW. L. REV. 589, 591 (1987). "Unger's viewpoint is motivated by explicit religious concerns—such as kinship with nature as seen in romantic love, or transcendence over nature as manifested in the hope for eternal life." West, *Between*

Academic labor lawyers, practitioners, and workers should be listening closely with theologians to discern and to immanentize God's transcendent words in the world of work. We cannot wait passively; we are also obliged to help one another toward a transformed world of work, finally free and fully redeemed from pathos and tragedy. Rather than await God's final messianic victory in history as sideline spectators, the more modest task today is to use Catholic labor teaching to make society better, more just, and more humane in the daily lives of all working people. This will unfold in a myriad of ways not yet known. It is good that the optimism of Catholic labor theory presently outpaces its implementation. Only then can today's inspiration become tomorrow's reality. Pope John Paul II would certainly share the core insight of Professor Unger:

> [I]n theory as in practice, insight and fecundity count for more than consistency. Every thinker betrays his most subversive intentions in the process of carrying them out. It is better to betray them less than to betray them more. But it is also better to let vision outreach theory building than to see and to say only what you can already formulate coherently and persuasively.[141]

Dewey and Gramsci: Unger's Emancipatory Experimentalism, 81 Nw. L. Rev. 941, 941 (1987).

Ultimately, it is best to let Professor Unger speak for himself. In a letter in response to a review of Knowledge and Politics, Unger stated that the reviewer failed to understand that Knowledge and Politics is Christian. Kronman, Book Review, 61 Minn. L. Rev. 167, 203-04 (1976). In addition to his earlier response to Professor Kronman's review of Knowledge and Politics in 1976, Unger said the substantive aim of Passion: An Essay in Human Personality, was to "restate the Christian-romantic image of man." R. Unger, Passion: An Essay in Human Personality, vii (1984).

At any rate, it will be interesting to see whether Unger's agenda in Politics (1987) will provide the international means for the translation of Catholic labor teaching into practice. The recognized potential for a singularly rich fusion is certainly there. *See supra* notes 7-9 and accompanying text; *supra* notes 104-05 and accompanying text (discussing Unger's work).

141. R. Unger, Social Theory: Its Situation and Its Task: A Critical Introduction to Politics, A Work in Constructive Social Theory 216 (1987).

Part IV
International and Comparative Law Perspectives

[10]

The Right to Unionize as a Fundamental Human and Civil Right

*David L. Gregory**

I. Introduction

Lawyers in the United States occasionally suffer from an intellectual myopia. There are powerful international theoretical and practical contributions to human and civil rights we may take for granted. Unfortunately, these international contributions to core rights are not always sufficiently appreciated. This is especially true in labor relations law. While multinational corporations have fostered consciousness of the need for "competitiveness," there is little, if any, corresponding awareness of the fundamental rights of workers in this calculus. Parochialism still afflicts the conventional labor and employment law regime in the United States today. Many civil rights lawyers may initially find the subject of this essay unproblematic. Of course, they would maintain, the right to unionize has always been regarded as a fundamental human and civil right in this country. Would that it were so!

To the contrary, I maintain that the right to unionize has had, at best, a fitful and tortured intellectual and practical history. This is true both in the United States and throughout the world. The right to unionize, as a human and civil right, has never been fully secured in either the United States or in the world public order.

The right to unionize has often been dismissed as an irrelevant or, more ominously, unwarranted socialist intrusion into the prerogatives of ownership elites. The struggle to translate the right to unionize from the realm of theory into the world of practice has always taught hard, bitter lessons. Attempts by workers to organize have always been met by powerful, and often ruthless and overwhelming, opposition from corporate elites. Even if, assuming arguendo, there were universal utopian agreement accorded to the theoretical right to unionize as a fundamental human and civil right, the sad truth would remain that, in many quarters, the right remains just that: an abstract, esoteric nicety, which can be cavalierly dismissed. One need only pause to consider the legacy of the Reagan era in order to appreciate this truth. The decade of the eighties will be long remembered for revealing the lie of supposed respect for the right to unionize.

---

*Professor of Law, St. John's University School of Law. J.S.D., Yale University, 1987; LL.M., Yale University, 1982; J.D., University of Detroit, 1980; M.B.A., Wayne State University, 1977; B.A., Catholic University of America, 1973. My faculty colleague Charles Biblowit provided many very helpful insights into the international law dimensions and sources of workers' rights.

Yet, despite this country's ambivalence toward the right to unionize as a fundamental human and civil right, the United States nevertheless has more real respect for the right to unionize than has been demonstrated by most other nations in this century. Unfortunately, this relative advantage has engendered an ominous complacency in the United States. When the right to unionize is taken for granted, as it has been, it is a civil right in peril.

After an overview of the embattled nature of the human and civil right to unionize, this article will briefly survey the intellectual history and the practical reality of the right to unionize in the United States. Comparative assessments of the theory and the practice in Great Britain, the Soviet Union, Poland, Nicaragua, South Korea, and South Africa will then be offered. While the right to unionize in the United States is fraught with difficulties, the international status of the right to unionize on every continent, and spanning a broad political spectrum, is much more bleak. In most other nations, the right to unionize is much more enfeebled, assuming it exists at all, than in the United States. While this country offers much of value to the international community by way of practical example, international law in turn offers theoretical insight to strengthen consciousness of this right in the United States.

The article will then examine two especially important international sources for the revitalization of the right to unionize. The International Labor Organization, under the auspices of the United Nations, offers a model to the world. Unfortunately, most labor lawyers in the United States have demonstrated little interest, understanding, or use of the International Labor Organization's two major Conventions, Nos. 87[1] and 98,[2] regarding the rights of workers. Of course, this is exacerbated by the United States' failure to ratify these ILO Conventions and by the United States' equivocal, fractured membership in the ILO. The United States was not a member, given the ILO's origin under League of Nations' auspices in 1919, until 1934. With the entry of the Soviet Union into the ILO in 1954, sentiment in the United States began to build for United States withdrawal, which occurred in 1977 and lasted until re-entry in 1980.

The article will conclude by examining the Catholic Church's social teaching of unequivocal support of the rights of workers and of labor unions. Building on the base of Pope Leo XIII's powerful encyclical, *Rerum Novarum* (Concerning New Things), in support of labor in 1891, the current Pope, John Paul II, courageously offers the single most eloquent international voice in the world today in support of the right to unionize as a fundamental human and civil right. These international models are potentially rich sources for the in-

1. Convention (No. 87) Concerning Freedom of Association and Protection of the Right to Organize, *adopted* July 9, 1948, 68 U.N.T.S. 17 (1948).

2. Convention (No. 98) Concerning the Application of the Principles of the Right to Organize and to Bargain Collectively, *adopted* July 1, 1949, 96 U.N.T.S. 257 (1949).

tellectual enhancement and pragmatic effectuation of this fundamental human and civil right.

The aphorism is worth reiteration at the outset: without the presence of a free union movement, no society can long remain free. History repeatedly offers graphic proof of this time-tested truth. Wherever the right to unionize is contemptuously violated, the regime is neither civil, nor humane, nor free. All lawyers in the United States should unequivocally support this fundamental human and civil right. By appreciation and creative use of the International Labor Organization's Conventions and by implementation of Catholic social teaching on the rights of workers to unionize, the right can be strengthened throughout the international community.

II. A Brief Overview of Intellectual History and Political Philosophy Regarding the Right to Unionize

According to the core tenets of classic political philosophy, human rights take on full true meaning only in the context of free, consensual participation in civil society. The purely private person, hermetically trapped in the solipsism of personal perception, cannot appreciate the meaning nor enjoy the fullness of civil rights. This was the insight of Plato's *Republic* and Aristotle's *Politics*; only citizens participating in public life can best understand civil rights. Human rights are fully vitalized in civil society. From the time Thomas Hobbes demanded from each private person the sacrifice of some individual rights to the Leviathan of government in order to make everyone's life less nasty, brutish, and short, civil life enjoyed by public citizens was stabilized; but the dynamic tension between the public and private spheres continues to dominate much of the discourse about law and political philosophy today.[3]

It is certainly true that the rights to associate,[4] to come together, to act in concert for mutual aid and protection, antedate the Constitution's first amendment and section 7 of the National Labor Relations Act.[5] The rights of persons to come together are independent of any positive law. The right to unionize has jurisprudential roots in natural law, transcending any secular legal conventions. The right to unionize, when understood as an aspect of the right to associate, is certainly a fundamental human right. Unionization is the social and political manifestation by workers of a most indispensable human right. Individuals yearn to join in community.

When persons decide to come together in union, they move from personal private life into the participatory political life of community. The right to un-

3. *See* Symposium, *The Public/Private Distinction*, 130 U. Pa. L. Rev. 1289 (1982).

4. The right to associate is an implicit core right within the first amendment. *E.g.*, NAACP v. Alabama *ex rel.* Patterson, 357 U.S. 449, 460-61 (1958).

5. 29 U.S.C. § 157 (1982). The right of employees to act in concert for mutual aid and protection is at the heart of the rights statutorily protected by section 7 of the National Labor Relations Act. *Id.*

ionize builds upon the human right of association and thus transforms initial pre-political individual choice. Because the act of unionization incorporates aspects of community and moves necessarily and deliberately into the realm of public political life, it is also a civil, as well as a human, right. Community is a compelling image and it can become a powerful reality. Workers seeking to act in concert have long appreciated the truth of the semantics; one cannot spell "community" without "unity"—and one cannot spell "unity" without "you" and "I". The effectuation of the fundamental human and civil right to unionize is an especially profound workplace empowerment of this truth.

III. THE RIGHT TO UNIONIZE IN THE UNITED STATES: THEORY AND PRACTICE

The Constitution of the United States does not expressly recognize a right to unionize, unlike some state constitutions[6] that protect the right to unionize and to bargain collectively. Like many other fundamental human natural rights, such as minimum food, clothing, shelter, and education, the right to unionize has no express federal constitutional source. Indeed, black letter parts of the Constitution can be read as directly antithetical to the right to unionize. Ownership elites opposed to worker unionization have historically cited the contracts clause, article I, section 10, "[n]o State shall pass any . . . Law impairing the Obligation of Contracts,"[7] to maintain that unionization is an unconstitutional interference with the constitutionally protected right of freedom of contract.[8] These ownership elites would compel a wholly artificial understanding of the employment relationship as the mythic, individual, good faith consensual negotiation between forces of rough parity on a relatively level playing field. In fact, in the world of employment, most employees, absent a union, are left atomized, individualized, and relatively quite helpless to influence the essentially adhesion contract terms unilaterally extended by powerful corporate employers.

Absent an express federal constitutional source, and in the alternative, as for so many other constitutionally unstated but fundamental rights, the right to unionize is constitutionally grounded in a creative jurisprudential amalgam of the preamble's welfare and security provisions and the press, speech, and petition and, implicitly, associational, rights found in the first amendment.

Political economy in the United States has been based upon the prevailing, still dominant, and historically, the often near-absolute, mythic capitalist motif

6. *See, e.g.*, N.Y. CONST. art. I, § 17.
7. U.S. CONST. art. I, § 10, cl. 1.
8. *E.g.*, Lincoln Fed. Labor Union v. Northwestern Iron & Metal Co., 335 U.S. 525, 531 (1949).

of the near-sanctification of private property[9] and of the ownership interests.[10] Therefore, it is not surprising that the political realities historically have been quite inimical to the right to unionize. Wholly peaceful and innocuous simple pickets were ruthlessly repressed by ex parte judicial injunctions, strikes were crushed,[11] and unionization efforts were disingenuously punished as violations of federal antitrust laws at the turn of this century.[12] Even after the Clayton Act of 1914 expressly exempted labor from the sanctions of the Sherman Anti-Trust Act of 1890, the reactionary Supreme Court judicially vitiated the Clayton Act labor exemption and speciously continued to subject unionization efforts to the draconian sanctions of the federal antitrust law.[13]

The anti-union legal and political environment was most notoriously and infamously judicially reflected in the Lochnerized era at the turn of this century. The Supreme Court repeatedly engaged in transparent substantive due process to strike down enlightened social and labor legislation as unconstitutional.[14]

During the Great Depression, the desperate condition of laborers and the vitiation of the right to unionize became completely untenable. The Norris-LaGuardia Act of 1932 broadly prohibited previously unrestrained federal courts from enjoining peaceful labor activities.[15] When the National Industrial Recovery Act was struck down as unconstitutional by the Court in the first term of President Franklin Roosevelt's New Deal Administration,[16] sufficient controls were built into the National Labor Relations Act of 1935 to withstand constitutional challenge. The Act was narrowly upheld as constitutional by the Supreme Court

9. In THE FEDERALIST No. 10 (J. Madison) (J. Cooke ed. 1961), James Madison recognized the intellectual and political heritage of Thomas Hobbes and John Locke. The protection of private property is perhaps the basic reason for private persons coming together as public citizens to constitute a civil government.

10. Acquisition and capitalist ownership has historically had very raw and immediate meaning. Adam Smith's WEALTH OF NATIONS, published in 1776, the year of the Declaration of Independence, is a genteel abstraction. The land mass of the continent was physically seized from the native population, which, in turn, was consigned to literal and cultural genocide. Strickland, *Genocide-at-Law: An Historic and Contemporary View of the Native American Experience*, 34 U. KAN. L. REV. 713 (1986). The "peculiar institution" of slavery was not terminated by the Constitution. On the contrary, continued importation was expressly allowed until 1808, by the terms of Article I. U.S. CONST. art. I, § 9, cl. 1.

11. The legal citations are voluminous. Perhaps the most poignant, recent illustration of the anti-labor history in the United States is the John Sayles' film, *Matewan* (Cinecom Int'l Films 1987), based on armed ownership's brutal repression of coal miners' unionization efforts in West Virginia and Kentucky during the 1920s.

12. Duplex Printing Press Co. v. Deering, 254 U.S. 443 (1921).

13. *Id.*

14. Lochner v. New York, 198 U.S. 45 (1905) (striking down New York state legislation regulating the working conditions and hours of bakers as interference with freedom of contract). For a thorough discussion of the notorious anti-labor cases of this era, see Casebeer, *Teaching An Old Dog Old Tricks:* Coppage v. Kansas *and At-Will Employment Revisited*, 6 CARDOZO L. REV. 765 (1985).

15. Norris-LaGuardia Act of 1932, 29 U.S.C. § 101 (1982).

16. A.L.A. Schechter Poultry Corp. v. United States, 295 U.S. 495 (1935). For a discussion of the salient nondelegation doctrine decisions of the Supreme Court, see generally Gregory, *The Congressional Response to* NLRB v. Bildisco *and the Constitutional Subtleties of the Nondelegation Doctrine*, 62 U. DET. L. REV. 245 (1985).

in *NLRB v. Jones & Laughlin Steel*[17] in 1937.

The National Labor Relations Act did not effect any sudden transformation of the anti-labor, capitalist regime into a workers' paradise. The Act itself was quickly debilitated by the courts, as Professor Karl Klare has so convincingly demonstrated in his landmark article, *Judicial Deradicalization of the Wagner Act and the Origins of Modern Legal Consciousness, 1937-1941.*[18] Most business interests were infuriated by the Act. Ownership interests largely regarded both the Act and the National Labor Relations Board as the instruments, agents, and dupes of ominous socialism.[19]

Even the judicially vitiated tepid protections afforded to labor proved too much for ownership to tolerate. In 1947, the National Labor Relations Act was further weakened by the Taft-Hartley amendments.[20]

The primary policy of the Act has always been the furtherance of industrial peace.[21] In the capitalist motif, this has been understood as the maintenance

17. 301 U.S. 1 (1937). For an interesting, pointed debate over the meaning and history of the NLRA, see Finkin, *Revisionism in Labor Law*, 43 MD. L. REV. 23 (1984); Klare, *Traditional Labor Law Scholarship and the Crisis of Collective Bargaining Law: A Reply to Professor Finkin*, 44 MD. L. REV. 731 (1985); Finkin, *Does Karl Klare Protest Too Much?*, 44 MD. L. REV. 1100 (1985); Klare, *Lost Opportunity: Concluding Thoughts on the Finkin Critique*, 44 MD. L. REV. 1111 (1985).

18. Klare, *The Judicial Deradicalization of the Wagner Act and the Origins of Modern Legal Consciousness, 1937-1941*, 62 MINN. L. REV. 265 (1978).

19. The intense anti-labor philosophy and frenzied lobbying effort mounted against the National Labor Relations Act are extensively discussed in Gregory, *Proposals to Harmonize Labor Law Jurisprudence and to Reconcile Political Tensions*, 65 NEB. L. REV. 75 (1986); Gregory, *The National Labor Relations Board and the Politics of Labor Law*, 27 B.C.L. REV. 39 (1985).

20. Labor Management Relations (Taft-Hartley) Act, 29 U.S.C. §§ 141-97 (1982) (amended 1984).

21. See 29 U.S.C. § 151 (1982) for the major policy provision of the NLRA:

> The denial by some employers of the right of employees to organize and the refusal by some employers to accept the procedure of collective bargaining lead to strikes and other forms of industrial strife or unrest, which have the intent or the necessary effect of burdening or obstructing commerce by (a) impairing the efficiency, safety, or operation of the instrumentalities of commerce; (b) occurring in the current of commerce; (c) materially affecting, restraining, or controlling the flow of raw materials or manufactured or processed goods from or into the channels of commerce, or the prices of such materials or goods in commerce; or (d) causing diminution of employment and wages in such volume as substantially to impair or disrupt the market for goods flowing from or into the channels of commerce.
>
> The inequality of bargaining power between employees who do not possess full freedom of association or actual liberty of contract, and employers who are organized in the corporate or other forms of ownership association substantially burdens and affects the flow of commerce, and tends to aggravate recurrent business depressions, by depressing wage rates and the purchasing power of wage earners in industry and by preventing the stabilization of competitive wage rates and working conditions within and between industries.
>
> Experience has proved that protection by law of the right of employees to organize and bargain collectively safeguards commerce from injury, impairment, or interruption, and promotes the flow of commerce by removing certain recognized sources of industrial strife and unrest, by encouraging practices fundamental to the friendly adjustment of industrial disputes arising out of differences as to wages, hours, or other working conditions, and by restoring equality of bargaining power between employers and employees.
>
> Experience has further demonstrated that certain practices by some labor organizations, their officers, and members have the intent or the necessary effect of burdening or obstructing commerce by preventing the free flow of goods in such commerce through strikes and other forms of industrial unrest or through concerted activities which impair the interest of the public in the free flow of such commerce. The elimination of such practices is a necessary condition to the assurance of the rights herein guaranteed.

of the smooth and uninterrupted profitable production process.[22] The protection and encouragement of the right to unionize, expressed in the section 7 NLRA right of workers to take concerted action for mutual aid and protection, and in the section 9 right of workers to select an exclusive bargaining representative in order to negotiate collectively with the employer, were severely compromised by the Taft-Hartley Act amendment to section 14(b) in 1947.[23] The NLRA was amended to permit individual states to enact legislation to prohibit union shop arrangements.[24] In a serious blow to principles of labor law stability and coherence that only a strong, centrally administered federal labor law can fully satisfy,[25] Congress shamefully endorsed a retreat to the atomized, romanticized, pre-Act employment regime of individualized employment relations, dominated by ownership elites and governed by discordant state law.

In 1976, in *Hudgens v. NLRB*,[26] the Supreme Court held that section 7 of the NLRA, and not the first amendment of the Constitution, was the source of organized laborers' rights of speech, press, petition, and association. As Justice Stewart, writing for the Court, expressly stated, "the rights and liabilities of the parties in this case are dependent exclusively upon the National Labor Relations Act."[27]

Thus, in "private" sector labor relations, the Constitution of the United States was, incredibly enough, relegated to subordinate, remote status, vis-a-vis section 7 of the NLRA, as the source of protection for workers' rights to engage in speech, press, and associational concerted activities for mutual aid and protection.

This is a wholly false dichotomy. Rather than so artificially bifurcate the National Labor Relations Act and the Constitution, in the typical "either-or" jurisprudence that so afflicts much of the law, the wiser jurisprudential choice, as Staughton Lynd has so incisively argued, would be the effective integration of the NLRA and the constitutional rights of workers into a synergistic construct greater than the sum of either of its two individual parts. Lynd points out the dangerous incoherence induced by the Court's fallacious "either-or"

> It is declared to be the policy of the United States to eliminate the causes of certain substantial obstructions to the free flow of commerce and to mitigate and eliminate these obstructions when they have occurred by encouraging the practice and procedure of collective bargaining and by protecting the exercise by workers of full freedom of association, self-organization, and designation of representatives of their own choosing, for the purpose of negotiating the terms and conditions of their employment or other mutual aid or protection.

22. Stone, *The Post War Paradigm in American Labor Law*, 90 YALE L.J. 1509 (1981).

23. 29 U.S.C. § 164(b) (1982).

24. *Id.* For a devastating critique of state "right to work" legislation, see St. Antoine, *National Labor Policy: Reflections and Distortions of Social Justice*, 29 CATHOLIC U.L. REV. 535, 545-47 (1979).

25. For comprehensive discussion of the labor preemption doctrine, generally supporting broad federal preemption of state law attempts to regulate major aspects of labor relations law, see Gregory, *The Labor Preemption Doctrine: Hamiltonian Renaissance or Last Hurrah?*, 27 WM. & MARY L. REV. 507 (1986).

26. Hudgens v. NLRB, 424 U.S. 507 (1976).

27. *Id.* at 521.

schematic and critiques its specious subordination of the Constitution to the already severely constrained section 7 NLRA rights. He argues for an alternative synergistic conception:

> A worker employed by a private corporation does not have on-the-job constitutional rights because the Constitution applies only to governments, not to private employers.
>
> . . . .
>
> . . . [I]f the rights associated with the First Amendment can be viewed as communal rights, it might be possible to celebrate and defend them along with the communal rights of workers, without weakening the critique of rights associated with private property. First Amendment rights would then be seen not as "bourgeois rights," to be cast aside along with private property, but as communal rights prefiguring the qualities of a future better society.[28]

With the forced false dichotomy between and the subordination of the Constitution to the already weakened NLRA, the Constitution and the Act have both been further dangerously debilitated as sources of workers' rights. During the tenure of the Reagan-appointed NLRB, the Board has severely constrained the meaning of section 7 concerted activity, especially in the case of non-unionized workers.[29] Most ominously, when workers not represented by a union are most in need of strong statutory protections of the right to act in concert for their mutual aid and protection, they are now left virtually unprotected by the Reagan NLRB in many key areas.[30] Concomitant with the Reagan Board's assault on section 7 protections, free market advocates have resurrected the ghost of the dissent in *NLRB v. Jones & Laughlin* and are again maintaining that the NLRA itself is an unconstitutional interference with freedom of contract.[31]

The myth that the United States historically has been completely receptive to the right to unionize as a fundamental human and civil right is unmasked by the harsh realities of law and politics. To the contrary, the right to unionize has always been tenuous, problematic, and embattled. It is not surprising that Professor Paul Weiler of Harvard Law School has termed the pathetic state of the National Labor Relations Act under the Reagan Administration's National Labor Relations Board as an inscription on a tombstone.[32]

---

28. Lynd, *Thesis and Antithesis: Section 7 of the NLRA, the First Amendment, and Workers Rights*, in A LESS THAN PERFECT UNION; ALTERNATIVE PERSPECTIVES ON THE U.S. CONSTITUTION 151, 163 (J. Lobel ed. 1988).

29. Prill v. NLRB, 835 F.2d 1481 (D.C. Cir. 1987). For a general discussion of the many controversial important pro-ownership decisions of the NLRB in the mid-eighties, see generally Gregory & Mak, *Significant Decisions of the NLRB, 1984: The Reagan Board's "Celebration" of the 50th Anniversary of the National Labor Relations Act*, 18 CONN. L. REV. 7 (1985).

30. E. I. DuPont, 289 N.L.R.B. No. 81 (1988) (non-unionized employees have no *Weingarten* right to a representative at an investigatory interview they reasonably believe may result in adverse action by the employer).

31. Epstein, *A Common Law for Labor Relations: A Critique of the New Deal Labor Legislation*, 92 YALE L.J. 1357 (1983).

32. Weiler, *Milestone or Tombstone: The Wagner Act at Fifty*, 23 HARV. J. ON LEGIS. 1 (1986).

Under even optimal circumstances, given the NLRA's restriction of its direct protections to those it defines as "employees" in section 2(11),[33] perhaps only half of the private sector workforce in the United States was ever potentially eligible for the Act's direct protections. Supervisors and managers are deprived of the section 2(11) status of "employees"; they are not eligible for the Act's direct protections should they choose to unionize. Small wonder, then, that little more than a third of the workforce was unionized in the 1950s, the zenith of unionization in this country. Given that supervisors and managers are deprived of such direct rights under the NLRA, that high water mark of unionization still was well in excess of two-thirds of the total of those potentially unionizable. With less than one-fifth of the workforce unionized today, this still represents approximately forty percent of all workers eligible for unionization.

Neither theory nor practice has consistently fostered the right to unionize as a fundamental human and civil right. Yet, in relentless struggle, workers continue to unionize. The public sector has witnessed especially strong growth in the unionization of government employees at the federal, state, county, and municipal levels. In 1987, 41,000 new members joined AFSCME, the American Federation of State, County, and Municipal Employees.[34] White collar workers increasingly are unionizing, including, significantly, the clerical workers at Harvard University in the spring of 1988.

Workers in the United States have always had to struggle to achieve and to protect their right to unionize. The legal and political climate has usually been ambivalent, at best, and, more likely, suspicious and grudging of the right, regarding it as a necessary evil to be endured in order to preserve "industrial peace," the code words for the uninterrupted profitable production process, which is the *raison d'etre* of capitalist political economy.

The labor movement in the United States has always reflected the most communal and social values possible in a capitalist society.[35] In turn, the organized labor movement historically has been one of the truest and most ambitious champions advocating the expansion of civil rights for all persons, often transcending the immediate agenda of organized labor. As Professor St. Antoine has concisely summarized:

> [Unions] act most nobly when they champion the cause of the unorganized and the oppressed in the public arena. It is frequently forgotten that the AFL-CIO and several international unions played major, possibly crucial, roles in the enactment of Title VII of the Civil Rights Act of 1964. Organized labor has also consistently fought for the extension of the minimum wage, for consumer protection, and similar social legislation, even when the interests of its own largely middle-class membership were marginally involved. It is in the furtherance of humane values in these various circumstances, then, and not in supposed economic tri-

33. 29 U.S.C. § 152(11) (1982).
34. 26 Gov't Empl. Rel. Rep. (BNA) 960 (June 27, 1988).
35. *See* Lynd, *supra* note 28.

umphs on behalf of working people, that organized labor finds its truest vindication.[36]

Workers in the United States must be constantly vigilant to protect their right to unionize. Having secured this fundamental human and civil right against powerful opposition by ownership elites, unionized workers have consistently demonstrated courageous initiatives to safeguard and to expand broader civil rights for all persons. This is dramatic proof that free unions are among the best means of ensuring the protections of a free society.

IV. COMPARATIVE ASSESSMENT OF THE RIGHT TO UNIONIZE IN OTHER NATIONS

Ironically, workers in the United States have the considerable advantage of unionizing without any illusions of any express constitutional solicitude of that right. The Constitution offers no such express protections, and the Supreme Court has made it clear that the NLRA, far more than the Constitution, directly determines the press, speech, and associational rights of private sector work force employees. In the United States, workers who seek to unionize know all too well what they are up against. Yet, with only modest legal protections, unionized workers in the United States have been able to accomplish a great deal with relatively little formal legal support.

The Union of Soviet Socialist Republics, history's most profound oxymoron, has no formal political or legal ambivalence concerning the right to unionize. The Soviet Constitution expressly recognizes the rights of workers in considerable detail, especially when compared to the absence of any express language in the United States Constitution. Indeed, the Soviet Constitution guarantees everyone employment. Unemployment purportedly is a contradiction in terms and was officially "abolished" in the Soviet Union on October 9, 1930.[37] Of course, the current efforts of Mr. Gorbachev to restructure the Soviet economy threaten to destabilize the ossified bureaucracy, with the dislocation of millions of workers within the next decade. Regardless of possible economic adjustments, the immediate fact remains: despite elaborate express guarantees of the rights of workers, the Soviet model of a workers' paradise has been a workers' nightmare.

In 1978, the World Confederation of Labor and the International Confederation of Free Trade Unions complained to the International Labor Organization (ILO) that the Soviet Union was violating ILO conventions 87 and 98, regarding the rights of association, unionization, and collective bargaining. Article 126 of the Soviet Constitution makes the Communist Party "the leading core of all the organizations of the working people."[38] Apart from this fact

36. St. Antoine, *supra* note 24, at 539.

37. Redden, *Soviet Union Bracing for Future Unemployed*, U.P.I., Jan. 19, 1988 (available on NEXIS).

38. KONST. SSSR art. 126.

of constitutionally guaranteed state domination and control of labor by the Communist Party, Amnesty International and unemployed Soviet workers alleged to the ILO in 1978 that workers who criticized bureaucrats and who resolved to form a new "Workers' Free Trade Union Association" were terminated from employment, arrested, and confined in the Gulag's notorious psychiatric hospitals.[39]

Consider also the desperate plight of unions in two of the Soviet Union's puppet client satellites, both prominent in international affairs. Rebellious Poland, despite the ruthless suppression of the Solidarity free workers' movement, remains a beacon of inspiration for all who value a free trade union movement. During the July, 1988 meeting of the Warsaw Pact Soviet satellites in Poland, Gorbachev and his puppet, General Jaruzelski, were badgered by continuing worker demands for dignity and for true state recognition of the fundamental right to unionize.[40] During Gorbachev's July, 1988 Warsaw Pact meeting, supporters of the outlawed Solidarity struck major steel and machinery works to demand the reinstatement of workers dismissed during major strikes in the spring of 1988. Now, in early 1989, the Solidarity movement may achieve significant official representation within the government and the national legislature.

Consider further the anti-labor actions of the Marxist-Leninist regime in Nicaragua. In ever-accelerating vicious downward spirals, the regime suspended all purported constitutional guarantees, suspended rights of speech and press, and closed all but governmentally-controlled newspapers and radio stations. LaPrensa, the major alternative newspaper, and the Catholic Church's radio station repeatedly have been closed by the regime's decree.[41] Despite elaborate express black letter constitutional guarantees, these totalitarian regimes have made the cruelest mockery of the right to unionize. In the United States, while the right to unionize is not so formally guaranteed, neither has it ever been so viciously destroyed. In the United States the formal guarantees have been very modest, but the hard-won incremental progress in achieving the right to unionize has been relatively stable and, finally, grudgingly accepted by government and ownership elites.

The prospects for the right to unionize are also very bleak outside the Soviet orbit. For example, South Korea's vaunted economic efficiency and international competitiveness has been purchased at a terrible price. The right to unionize is virtually non-existent. Sixty-hour work weeks are the norm, attributable at least as much to the ruthlessness of an authoritarian government as to any

39. Meron, *Violations of ILO Conventions by the USSR and Czechoslovakia*, 74 AM. J. INT'L L. 206 (1980).

40. Tagliabve, *Gorbachev Skirts the Issue of Solidarity*, N.Y. Times, July 14, 1988, at A8, col. 4. *See also* Wirth, *Trade Union Rights in the Workers' State: Poland and the ILO*, 13 DEN. J. INT'L L. & POL'Y 269 (1984); Note, *The Polish Labor Crisis of 1980: An Assessment of the Role of the International Labor Organization*, 8 BROOKLYN J. INT'L L. 177 (1982); Note, *The International Labor Organization and the Polish Independent Labor Movement*, 22 VA. J. INT'L L. 555 (1982).

41. Kinzer, *In Managua, No More Accommodation*, N.Y. Times, July 17, 1988, at E3, col. 1.

simplistic Western cultural stereotyping of Korean industrial sociology. With the right to unionize and the rights of workers consequently so enfeebled, the South Korean regime is now reaping the bitter fruit it has sown. Increasing civil and student strife periodically threaten to destabilize the government, and worker demands for lives of dignity and worth inexorably accelerate in scope and intensity. Major South Korean industries, such as the Hyundai car manufacturer, are thrown into turmoil by serious labor difficulties and continuing unrest.[42]

As a final prominent contemporary example of the struggle to preserve the right to unionize and of the unequivocal, direct relationship between the right to unionize and the enhancement of all civil rights in a free society, consider the situation in South Africa. The black trade unions, especially the National Union of Mineworkers, led by the young lawyer, Cyril Ramphosa, have been a primary force in the political and social struggle for civil rights and against apartheid.[43] The miners have demonstrated the inextricable fusion of organized labor's rights with the labor-led struggle for broader political rights. The authoritarian regime in South Africa is also fully aware of this linkage. Therefore, the government's ultimately futile current repression of the miners' union has been particularly ruthless. Viable and free unions not only further their own immediate labor agendae, increase their membership, and safeguard the right to unionize; historically, they also have enhanced the civil rights of the entire society.

These international and national struggles by workers against these totalitarian and authoritarian regimes in order to secure the right to unionize and to exercise fundamental civil rights are powerful witness to the core truth that the right to unionize is a fundamental human and civil right. Worker aspirations, even in the most trying circumstances of political repression, continue to spring eternal. All of these examples from contemporary international relations convincingly demonstrate the importance of a free union movement to ensure the freedom of the broader society. Even in the most repressive regimes, workers continue to seek freedom for everyone in the society. It is more than coincidence that the most totalitarian regimes in history, under Hitler and Stalin, quickly targeted free and independent union movements for extermination.

Obviously, the ambivalence toward the right to unionize in the United States has never even begun to approach the wholly repressive atmosphere labor has suffered under in many other nations. Because workers in the United States

42. Chira, *South Korea Swept by Labor Unrest*, N.Y. Times, June 3, 1988, at A3, col. 1.

43. The National Union of Mineworkers, the largest black labor union in South Africa with more than 250,000 members, has repeatedly struck to improve the working conditions and wages of its members. *See* Battersby, *Mine Strike's Lessons: South African Companies' Victory is Costly and Union Learns Limits of its Power*, N.Y. Times, Sept. 1, 1987, at A9, col. 1. The National Union of Mineworkers has also been a leader in the broader civil rights struggle against the apartheid policies of South Africa's racist regime. "Black unions like the mine workers, acting lawfully, offer the best remaining hope for a peaceful transition to democracy." *Solidarity with the Black Miners*, N.Y. Times, Aug. 11, 1987, at A22, col. 1.

have struggled successfully to achieve and to preserve the right to unionize, the panoply of broader civil rights enhanced by the efforts of organized labor and enjoyed in the United States has offered the world a dual positive model for emulation. However, workers and labor and civil rights lawyers in the United States cannot afford to rest on past successes, or to retreat to a bunker mentality, narrowly concerned only with preservation of past gains. Unless organized labor is ever-vigilant, its rights will erode. Witness, for example, the debilitation of organized labor in Great Britain under the Thatcher government, coupled with the concomitant anti-labor aggression of entrepreneurs such as Rupert Murdoch. With British labor intimidated, broad social benefit programs are now under assault.

I am not suggesting or advocating confrontation of ownership elites as the only instrument, or even as the most viable means, for organized labor to utilize today. But it is indisputable that organized labor must consciously, aggressively, and vigilantly guard against erosion of the right to unionize. Otherwise, inexorably, broader civil rights will also be debilitated throughout the larger society.

While unions in the United States continue to enjoy a preferred position compared to workers in most other nations today, all workers share a universal common bond in strengthening both the national and international dimensions of the right to unionize. Because of usually parochial national law, labor laws, where they exist in individual countries, generally offer workers little or no international protections against the institutional power and prerogatives of the multinational corporations.[44] At least in theory, the International Labor Organization offers a viable international model for the aspirations of all workers.

V. The International Labor Organization

The freedom of association is expressly recognized in both the Preamble and in the body of section two of the Constitution of the International Labor Organization. International Labor Organization Conventions 87 and 98 are, respectively, the freedom of association and protection of the right to organize

44. There have been several recent international initiatives under ILO auspices, to regulate the conduct of multinational corporations. *See generally* Blanpain, *Transnational Regulation of the Labor Relations of Multinational Enterprises*, 58 Chi.-Kent L. Rev. 909 (1982); Forde, *The European Convention on Human Rights and Labor Law*, 31 Am. J. Comp. L. 301 (1983); Gunter, *The International Labour Office Declaration of Multinational Enterprises and the International Code of Conduct Movement*, 4 Loy. L.A. Int'l & Comp. L.J. 1 (1981); Gunter, *Erosion of Trade Union Power Through Multinational Enterprises?*, 9 Vand. J. Transnat'l L. 771 (1976); Horn, *International Rules for Multinational Enterprises: The ICC, OECD, and ILO Initiatives*, 30 Am. U.L. Rev. 923 (1981); Sander, *Implementing International Codes of Conduct for Multinational Enterprises*, 30 Am. J. Comp. L. 241 (1982). *But see* Northrup, *Why Multinational Bargaining Neither Exists Nor is Desirable*, 29 Lab. L.J. 330 (1978).

and to bargain collectively.[45] These two salient ILO Conventions provide that workers have the right to establish and join unions of their own free choosing, without previous state or employer authorization or later interference. In turn, the unions have the right to form constitutions, to elect representatives, and to join in national and international labor confederations. Conventions 87 and 98 permit supervisors to unionize, and they apply to most workers in the public, as well as in the private, sectors. Obviously, this is far broader than the National Labor Relations Act, which does not fully extend to the public sector and does not afford direct protections to supervisors and managers. Convention 98 more specifically elaborates Convention 87, with special reference to rights of association and unionization for purposes of collective bargaining. Convention 98 also protects workers from anti-union discrimination and from union domination by employers. The ILO Conventions also restrict the scope of governmental prohibitions of the right to strike. Convention 98 has been ratified by the largest number of nations who are members of the ILO. More than 110 of the more than 150 nation members of the ILO have ratified Convention 98, while over ninety nation members have ratified Convention 87.[46] The ILO, the most prominent and most important international organization of representatives of management and labor from more than 150 nations, has expressly declared the right to unionize as a fundamental human and civil right.[47] Regrettably, the United States has not ratified either Convention 87 or Convention 98. The United States has ratified only seven of the more than 160 ILO Conventions, and none of those seven ratified Conventions pertain to collective bargaining rights.[48]

The United States became a member of the ILO in 1934 during the Roosevelt Administration, at the urging of Frances Perkins, Roosevelt's Secretary of Labor. This was fifteen years after the ILO was founded under League of Nations auspices in 1919. Beginning with the admission of the Soviet Union in 1954, following decades of Communist denunciation of the ILO as a tool of capitalism, the United States' commitment to the ILO grew increasingly ambivalent, culminating in the United States' withdrawal from the ILO in 1977, which was effective until its re-entry in 1980. Consequently, most lawyers in the United States are relatively ignorant of the ILO and of its objectives. Suffice it to say

---

45. The other three directly pertinent major ILO conventions are the abolition of forced labor, elimination of employment discrimination, and the right to equal pay for equal work. D. MORSE, THE ORIGIN AND EVOLUTION OF THE I.L.O. AND ITS ROLE IN THE WORLD COMMUNITY 58 (1969). The ILO has promulgated 162 Conventions and 172 Recommendations. When a nation member ratifies a Convention, it is formally committed to effectuate and observe the Convention in its national law and to be amenable to monitoring by the ILO regarding compliance. A Recommendation does not require ratification. Conventions are broad policy declarations; Recommendations are guidelines more specifically directed to particular problems.

46. *See* Note, *The Polish Labor Crisis of 1980: An Assessment of the Role of the International Labor Organization*, *supra* note 40, at 181. The United States has ratified only seven relatively minor ILO Conventions and has not ratified either Convention 87 or Convention 98. 128 Lab. Rel. Rep. (BNA) 376 (1988).

47. *See* D. MORSE, *supra* note 45, at 58.

48. *See supra* note 46.

that, at least theoretically, the ILO aims to further the dignity and human rights of all who work and of all who aspire to work.[49]

As David Morse, the former Director-General of the ILO, succinctly stated in his Cornell University lectures in 1968:

> The I.L.O.'s aim is not, in short, simply to protect workers from exploitation and injury. It is also to demonstrate the salutary effects that good, safe, and humane working conditions can have on the workers' morale and thus on the output and growth of the economy. We are passing from the *protection* of the worker to the *promotion* of a world-wide awareness of the importance—in both economic and social terms, in both developed and developing countries—*of treating the worker as a human being, of devising measures to meet his material and spiritual needs, and of respecting his human rights.*[50]

These have always been the broad goals of the ILO; the right to unionize is certainly an integral part of this construct.

The ILO has its historic and philosophic roots in socialist initiatives in late eighteenth century Europe. Its formal birth occurred in 1919, under the auspices of the League of Nations. Samuel Gompers, first president of the American Federation of Labor, was the first chairman of the Paris Peace Conference's Commission on International Labor Legislation. On October 29, 1919, the first meeting of the ILO was held in Washington, D.C. However, the United States did not become a member of the League of Nations; the Senate refused to ratify the treaty.

The United States finally joined the ILO in 1934. After World War II, West Germany and Japan joined the ILO in 1951; the Soviet Union joined in 1954. With the formation of the United Nations after World War II, the ILO has operated from its Geneva headquarters under United Nations auspices.

Almost simultaneous with the Soviet Union's entry into the ILO, in 1954, pressures immediately began to mount in the United States for withdrawal from the ILO. Within a decade thereafter, both the United Nations and the ILO were politically dominated by emerging nations no longer under the hegemony of the East-West superpowers.

In 1970, the United States withheld financial support from the ILO. The ILO's admission of the Palestine Liberation Organization to observer status in the mid-1970s, and its condemnation of Zionism, finally galvanized sufficient

---

49. *See generally* Gormley, *The Emerging Protection of Human Rights by the International Labour Organization*, 30 ALB. L. REV. 13 (1966).

50. *See* D. MORSE, *supra* note 45. For excellent general sources on the ILO, see generally G. KRUGLAK, THE POLITICS OF UNITED STATES DECISION-MAKING IN UNITED NATIONS SPECIALIZED AGENCIES: THE CASE OF THE INTERNATIONAL LABOR ORGANIZATION (1980); Alford, *The Prospective Withdrawal of the United States from the International Labor Organization: Rationales and Implications*, 17 HARV. INT'L L.J. 623 (1976); Vincent-Daviss, *Human Rights Law: A Research Guide to the Literature—Part III: The International Labor Organization and Human Rights*, 15 N.Y.U. J. INT'L L. & POL. 211 (1982); Wolf, *At the Apex of the Value Hierarchy—An International Organisation's Contribution*, 24 N.Y.L. SCH. L. REV. 179 (1979).

support for the United States' withdrawal from the ILO in 1977 until re-entry in 1980.

The undeniable politicization of the ILO, its anti-Zionist anti-Semitism, its recent and very troubling highly selective concern for human rights, and its acquiescence in denial of due process rights by totalitarian regimes compelled the United States, withdrawal in 1977, with most of the organized labor movement in this country supporting the decision of the Carter Administration.[51]

While the reality of the ILO has occasionally fallen short of its promise, the ILO remains the best established international instrument today for furtherance of the right to unionize and for the international expression of workers' aspirations.[52] Today, it has focused particular critical attention against the racist regime in South Africa. The ILO is an international leader in the struggle against apartheid.

Until Poland's withdrawal from the ILO in 1986, each Eastern European bloc Soviet client state was an ILO member and had ratified ILO Conventions 87 and 98.[53] The United States should certainly remain in the ILO, to serve, if nothing else, as a gadfly upon the epidermis of totalitarian communist regimes. United States ratification of ILO Conventions 87 and 98 seems long overdue. However, given the United States' current refusal to pay its $467 million in dues in arrears to the United Nations,[54] ratification of ILO Conventions is

---

51. George Meany, President of the AFL-CIO, stated: "We support and endorse the decision of President Carter to stand by the notice of withdrawal by the United States from the International Labor Organization." *U.S. Membership in ILO Ends*, AFL-CIO Free Trade Union News, Dec. 1977, at 6.

52. Of course, the ILO Conventions are not the only international sources to support workers' rights to form and to join free unions. The Universal Declaration of Human Rights, art. 23(4); the European Convention for the Protection of Human Rights and Fundamental Freedom, Nov. 11, 1950, art. 11, 213 U.N.T.S. 221; the European Social Charter, Oct. 18, 1961, art. I(5) and (6), 529 U.N.T.S. 89; the International Covenant on Civil and Political Rights, Dec. 19, 1966, art. 22, 999 U.N.T.S. 171; and the International Covenant on Economic, Social, and Cultural Rights, Dec. 19, 1966, art. 8, 993 U.N.T.S. 3, each provide similar guarantees.

Again, unfortunately, the United States is a party only recently to the Universal Declaration. While the Universal Declaration of Human Rights is not a treaty and is not binding, it has acquired recognition as international law by most of the world community. The Helsinki Accords, while also not a treaty, do not expressly refer to the right to unionize; but the Accords do incorporate by reference the Universal Declaration of Human Rights. The Madrid Conference following the Helsinki Accords explicitly recognized the right to unionize.

A worldwide union lobbying effort is now underway to pressure the General Agreement on Tariffs and Trade to authorize workers' rights clauses in international trade agreements. The union lobbying effort is being led by the International Metalworkers Federation in Geneva, which represents 14 million metal workers around the world. [Current Reports], Int'l Trade Rep. (BNA) 1068 (July 27, 1988).

53. *See* Wirth, *supra* note 40, at 273.

54. *Paying the Price of Peace*, N.Y. Times, Aug. 11, 1988, at A24, col. 1.

hardly at the top of the United States' international law agenda.[55] Even as a purely practical matter, the full flowering of the European Economic Community by 1992 compels our understanding of the ILO and of international labor dynamics.

It is significant that the ILO has been supported by the Catholic Papacy. Many of the ILO's most important Conventions directly reflect the spirit of the Catholic Church's landmark labor encyclical, *Rerum Novarum*, issued by Pope Leo XIII in 1891. On November 19, 1954, at a special audience, Pope Pius XII conferred the apostolic blessing on the ILO.[56] It is to the most universal, the most "catholic" of all sources of the right to unionize, that the article now turns: the papal labor encyclicals of the Catholic Church.

VI. The Contributions of Catholic Social Teaching

Unfortunately, labor lawyers in the United States are, if anything, even more unfamiliar with the transformative contributions of Catholic social teaching to the world of work than they are with the contributions of the International Labor Organization. The Catholic Church's strong theoretical support of the rights of workers has been most unequivocally set forth in two major labor encyclicals in 1891 and in 1981.

In 1891, nearly a half century before the passage of the NLRA, Pope Leo XIII unequivocally declared the social, moral, and theological imperative of parity and respect between ownership and labor. Workers and unions were entitled to full parity in the equation, as Pope Leo XIII courageously declared in *Rerum Novarum* (Concerning New Things). Labor and ownership need one another to achieve and to maintain respect, harmony, and peace. The encyclical unequivocally declared that capital ownership cannot exist without labor, and that labor needs capital. The spirit of the labor encyclical in 1891 permeated the policy provisions of the NLRA in 1935.[57]

In 1981, to commemorate the ninetieth anniversary of *Rerum Novarum*, Pope John Paul II issued the Catholic Church's second major labor encyclical, *Laborem Exercens* (On the Nature of Work). It is fitting that the present Pope,

55. The Third Restatement of Foreign Relations of the United States does not list the right to unionize among those enumerated in the international law of human rights. *See* Restatement (Third) of the Foreign Relations Law of the United States § 702 (1987).

While the United States is barely involved in the international law arena regarding its formal recognition of the right to unionize, it is not completely oblivious. Under United States law, duty-free treatment under the Generalized System of Preferences is denied to countries which do not take steps "to afford internationally recognized worker rights," defined as the right of association; the right to organize and to bargain collectively; prohibition of compulsory labor and of child labor; and furnishing "acceptable conditions of work with respect to minimum wages, hours of work, and occupational safety and health." 19 U.S.C. § 2462(a)(4) (1982 & Supp. IV 1986). The law is enforced by the U.S. Trade Representative through administrative proceedings. Chile, Romania, Paraguay, and Nicaragua have had their GSP beneficiary status suspended.

56. *See generally* A. Le Roy, The Dignity of Labor: The Part Played by Catholics in the Work of the International Labor Organization 67 (1957).

57. *See supra* note 21.

forced to work on a labor gang by the Nazis during World War II and now a champion of Poland's outlawed Solidarity movement, has moved Catholic social teaching on the rights of workers so dramatically beyond the labor and ownership class partnership theme first sounded by Pope Leo XIII in 1891. Pope John Paul II, while reaffirming that labor and ownership need one another's respect, has also unequivocally stated that capital remains only a means subordinated to the service of people. Capital can never be the end. This is a particularly important and timely message, when so much of the world has exactly reversed the means and the ends, improperly reifying people as expendable objects in the false pursuit of materialism. *Laborem Exercens* extensively develops several related themes, including the fundamental right of workers to unionize.[58] Catholic labor theory properly reminds the world that the natural law and theological roots of human collective action antedate even the classic Platonic and Aristotelian political philosophy that measured the quality of public life by the extent of participation by free citizens in the Greek city-states.

Pope John Paul II has repeatedly reiterated unequivocal support of the rights of workers. During his papal visit to several South American countries in the spring of 1988, he addressed the rights of workers and the rights of free unions. His talk in Meleo, Uruguay on May 8, 1988, was especially compelling and it was pointedly directed to the repressive government. He said that union organizers deserved unconditional support and encouragement: "with my words and my heart I am very close to those who dedicate themselves to union activities."

The rights of workers and of their unions were again reaffirmed in Pope John Paul II's major social encyclical issued in 1987, *Sollicitudo Rei Socialis* (On Social Concern). Reiterating some of the themes of *Laborem Exercens*, Pope John Paul II expressly reminded the world that the rights of workers and of unions are fundamental human rights. They cannot be atomized by supposedly free market principles or by totalitarian governments. Rather, they must be respected by the entire international community:

> Recognition that the "social question" has assumed a worldwide dimension does not at all mean that it has lost its *incisiveness* or its national and local importance. On the contrary, it means that the problems in industrial enterprises or in the workers' and union movements of a particular country or region are not to be considered as isolated cases with no connection. On the contrary, they depend more and more on the influence of factors beyond regional boundaries and national frontiers.[59]

The right to unionize is expressly regarded as a human right in Catholic social teaching. Pope John Paul II rhetorically asks, "The denial or the limitation of human rights—as for example the right to religious freedom, the right

58. The best book regarding *Laborem Exercens* is G. BAUM, THE PRIORITY OF LABOR (1982). *See also* Gregory, *Catholic Labor Theory and the Transformation of Work*, 45 WASH. & LEE L. REV. 119 (1988).

59. POPE JOHN PAUL II, SOLLICITUDO REI SOCIALIS 14 (1987).

to share in the building of society, *the freedom to organize and to form unions*, or to take initiatives in economic matters—do these not impoverish the human person as much as, if not more than, the deprivation of material goods?"[60]

Thus, Pope John Paul II joins in intellectual solidarity with some of the most radical and profound critiques of regimes that have denied the human and civil right of workers to unionize.[61] He concludes his most recent, and perhaps most insightful of all social encyclicals, by calling on the Catholic Church to "affirm her confidence in a *true liberation*."[62] Surely one important aspect of this true liberation theology is the support for persons to come together in community and in solidarity, including, certainly, the rights of workers to unionize and to act in concert for mutual aid and protection.

Catholic social teaching, especially as highlighted in the labor encyclicals of the Papacy spanning nearly the entire past century, is a remarkable and outstanding theoretical resource for supporting and revitalizing the fundamental human and civil right of workers to unionize.[63]

VII. CONCLUSION

Workers in the United States have had significant success in voluntary unionization. Despite the absence of an express federal constitutional right, the judicial tempering of section 7 NLRA statutory rights, and the ongoing social ambivalence toward unions, unionized workers in the United States have certainly had success in the achievement and maintenance of workers' rights at least equal, and more often quite superior, to those of workers in most other nations in most other periods in history. Certainly relative to the Soviet Union, Poland, Nicaragua, South Korea, and South Africa, the United States stands as a beacon and model of workers' hopes and aspirations.

However, as most of those in organized labor know all too well in this

---

60. *Id.* at 25 (emphasis added).

61. *See, e.g.*, R. UNGER, POLITICS: A WORK IN CONSTRUCTIVE SOCIAL THEORY (1987) (This important new trilogy shares the papal encyclical's utopianism and proposes alternatives to the current statist domination of human rights, whether capitalist or socialist.).

62. POPE JOHN PAUL II, SOLLICITUDO REI SOCIALIS 94 (1987).

63. *See* St. Antoine, *supra* note 24, at 536 (quoting Pope John XXIII, *Mater Et Magistra (Christianity and Social Progress)* (1961), in SEVEN GREAT ENCYCLICALS 219, 234, 238, 289 (W. Gibbons ed. 1963)):

> [E]mployees should have an active part in the affairs of the enterprise wherein they work, whether these be private or public . . . [i]t is of the utmost importance that productive enterprises assume the character of a true human fellowship whose spirit suffuses the dealings, activities and standing of all its members . . . . [T]his is achieved especially by collective bargaining between associations of workers and those of management.

Pope John's words parallel those of the principal architect of the original National Labor Relations Act of 1935, Senator Robert Wagner:

> Genuine collective bargaining is the only way to attain equality of bargaining power . . . .
>
> . . . [W]ider cooperation [among workers] is necessary, not only to uphold their own end of the labor bargain but to stabilize and standardize wage levels, to cope with the sweatshop and the exploiter, and to exercise their proper voice in economic affairs.

decade, workers and unions in this country have little reason to be smug or to rest content on past triumphs. The percentage of workers unionized in the private sector has fallen well below twenty percent during the decade, PATCO was dismantled, the social stigma has evaporated from strike breakers, and employers openly retain "union avoidance" strategists. Labor and civil rights lawyers in the United States have much to learn from such established but generally ignored sources as the Conventions and Declarations of the International Labor Organization and the Papal encyclicals of the Catholic Church. These sources can revitalize labor theory and, if their messages are heeded, can further assist in the practical protection and enhancement of the fundamental human and civil right of all workers to unionize.

When the right to unionize is protected, all of society benefits, and human dignity is tangibly advanced. As the late Walter Reuther, charismatic president of the United Autoworkers Union stated:

> The labor movement will become less of an economic movement and more of a social movement. It will be concerned with the economic factors, of course, but also with the moral, spiritual, the intellectual, and the social nature of our society, and all of this in terms of an ultimate objective—the fulfillment of the complete human being.[64]

The right to unionize is a key, but often regrettably overlooked, human and civil right. It deserves renewed attention, in both theory and in practice.

---

64. St. Antoine, *supra* note 24, at 556 n.95.

[11]

REFLECTIONS ON WORKERS' PARTICIPATION, INFLUENCE AND POWERSHARING: THE FUTURE OF INDUSTRIAL RELATIONS

*William B. Gould IV**

I. Introduction

A number of major developments promise to reshape industrial relations in established relationships between labor and management in this country. One of them is the rising expectations of workers which finds expression in many forms, wrongful discharge actions being one of them. For the past 200 years, there has been a considerable lag between society's willingness to accept political democracy, conceded in substantial part in the 19th century, and a similar acceptance of economic democracy in the corporation and the workplace. The most profound impact in recent years has resulted from changes in the relationship between employee and employer at the shop floor level, the most prominent example of which is the team method of work assignments and responsibilities which has found acceptance in much of basic manufacturing.

Worker directors on the board, whether union leaders or representatives or not, as well as employee-owned firms are ideas that have not caught on in this country except where an economic crisis dictates such a course of action because there is no alternative available.[1] This is hardly surprising given the fact that, aside from the obduracy of employers and their resistance to seating union or worker representatives, the trade union leadership, through much of the past decade or two during which such issues have been debated, has been critical of such ideas in an outspoken and derisive fashion.

Yet the principal significance of workers' participation in West Germany and to some extent Sweden lies in the sharing of authority at the shop floor level.[2] It is here that change has occurred in Europe and, if comparable reform is to be implemented in the United States, it is likely that the most visible shifts will come at the same

* Charles A. Beardsley Professor of Law, Stanford Law School. Professor Gould was co-chairman of the California State Bar Report on Termination-at-Will and Wrongful Discharge, which issued its report, *To Strike a New Balance*, on February 8, 1984.

1. For a general discussion of these and related issues in America and abroad, see Towards Industrial Democracy: Europe, Japan and the United States (B. Roberts ed. 1984).

2. *See* Summers, *Worker Participation in Sweden and the United States: Some Comparisons from an American Perspective*, 133 U. Pa. L. Rev. 175 (1984).

level here as well, notwithstanding what will likely be increased fascination with the kind of employee equity or ownership which seems to be emerging, for instance, in the airline industry.

There is a second factor of some consequence at work here as well, and this is an economic one. It is quite clear that the modern and industrially developed countries have become increasingly economically interdependent, a factor no doubt substantially responsible for the post-World War II prosperity enjoyed throughout the First World this past half century. As Brazil, South Korea and Taiwan have forged their way up the economic ladder, disrupting the previously established hierarchical order in industries like steel, it has become appropriate to speak of global interdependence and to focus greater attention upon such regions of the world as the Pacific Rim.

All of this, in turn, has meant competition for industries that have been traditionally among the most highly unionized in this country—a competition which accelerated furiously in the late '70s. Economic problems have been encountered particularly in the unionized sector of the economy in the late '70s and '80s in manufacturing as well as transportation and construction—the real union strongholds in this country. This has impelled both labor and management to rethink their relationships. The unions, as some of the left-wing critics of industrial democracy never cease to remind us, have not initiated the changes which confront the parties today. As noted above, those have been dictated by foreign competition from both Europe and Japan, and more recently, Korea, Brazil and other developing countries. Thus, since the early '80s it has been management which has been formulating the initiatives and making the demands—a phenomenon which, whatever the result which finally emerges, has been the driving force in the 1989 Eastern Airlines dispute as well as the concessions earlier negotiated, not only in transportation, but also in the auto and steel industries.

One of management's demands, as in the Eastern negotiations, has been for restraint and freezes or, indeed, the diminution of both wages and fringe benefits. This is the most obvious meaning of concessions. But another facet of the negotiations has involved even more important demands: namely, the revision of work rules, the reduction or broad-banding of job classification categories, and the establishment of mechanisms through which employee involvement in and understanding of the job and the company's business will be enhanced.

These "concessions" have been a significant factor in both the promotion of union and employee interest in greater participation and also employer willingness to accede to labor's demands. They have also promoted a measure of industrial democracy allowing for employee consultation, a sharing of power through both compensation—an area in which the Japanese have long pioneered[3]—and, more importantly, involvement in management decision making.

A major obstacle in reshaping relationships in this country, however, has been our adherence to traditional adversarial attitudes, and the fact that labor law has based its assumptions upon the model of conflict. With the exception of industrial relations in Great Britain, the American model of adversarial labor-management relations knows no equal throughout the world. It is a philosophy that is well summarized by the Supreme Court, speaking through Justice Brennan, in *NLRB v. Insurance Agents' International Union.*[4] There the Court said the following of collective bargaining:

> [U]nder a system where the Government does not attempt to control the results of negotiations, [it] cannot be equated with an academic collective search for truth—or even with what might be thought to be the ideal of one. The parties—even granting the modification of views that may come from a realization of economic interdependence—still proceed from contrary and to an extent antagonistic viewpoints and concepts of self-interest. The system has not reached the ideal of the philosophic notion that perfect understanding among people would lead to perfect agreement among them on values.[5]

II. The Law

A. *Company Assistance to Unions*

A major focal point for labor lawyers concerned with both law and policy in this arena is Section 8(a)(2) of the National Labor Relations Act (NLRA), the anti-company union unfair labor practice prohibition which disallows both financial assistance—other than time off with pay for negotiation during working hours—and employer domination of the labor organization. Much of America's history of industrial relations—especially the portion of it leading directly to the adoption of the National Labor Relations Act—witnessed the use of employee representation committees or company unions to suppress authentic and autonomous labor unions and thus free col-

3. *See* W. Gould, Japan's Reshaping of American Labor Law (1984).
4. 361 U.S. 477 (1960).
5. *Id.* at 488-89.

lective bargaining. Senator Wagner viewed the provision as a cardinal element of the Act,[6] indeed its most important provision.

Today the company union concept is virtually unknown. True, non-union employers have frequently instituted employee representation committees, quality of work life groups and circles and the like. The non-union sector has been the driving force in such changes.[7] But these committees and programs seem to be different in kind from the company unions that were instituted in the 1920's and which were the object of the anti-company union prohibitions contained in Section 8(a)(2).

Now, once again, employers are attempting to accomplish the same objective in the interest of warding off genuine trade unionism. But they are hardly likely to attempt to characterize the new entities as unions for the practical reason that the union is the last thing that the employer wants the worker to believe that he needs, let alone the fact that such a strategy works at cross purposes with the law. To the extent that the new entities are characterized as "labor organizations" any financial assistance not specifically authorized by Section 8(a)(2), i.e., payment for time spent negotiating during working hours, is prohibited.[8] But the real concern under the National Labor Relations Act is that new initiatives undertaken in the context of established bargaining relationships can implicate the prohibitions contained in Section 8(a)(2) relating to financial assistance.

Yet, beginning with the quality of work life programs sponsored by some of the UAW leadership and some elements within GM and Ford, it has been seen that such programs are frequently necessary. For instance, employees are provided time off with pay at Fremont's NUMMI joint venture to learn about how the product is marketed. UAW officials and represented employees have been provided with financial assistance to travel, for instance, to Japan to learn the work processes of Toyota. The NUMMI experiment has been chronicled

---

6. S. 2926, 73d Cong., 2d Sess., 78 CONG. REC. 3443 (1934) *reprinted in* 1 NLRB, LEGISLATIVE HISTORY OF THE NATIONAL LABOR RELATIONS ACT OF 1934, at 15-18 (1959).

7. T. KOCHAN, H. KATZ & R. MCKERSIE, THE TRANSFORMATION OF AMERICAN INDUSTRIAL RELATIONS (1986).

8. Section 158(a)(2) provides that,

> [i]t shall be unfair labor practice for an employer . . . to dominate or interfere with the formation or administration of any labor organization or contribute financial or other support to it: *Provided*, That subject to rules and regulations made and published by the Board pursuant to section 156 of this title, an employer shall not be prohibited from permitting employees to confer with him during working hours without loss of time or pay.

29 U.S.C. § 158(a)(2) (1982).

by the United States Department of Labor in its report on The Future of Labor-Management Cooperation.[9]

It would seem as though the financing of union representatives' air fare to Japan and other expenses is unlawful under the National Labor Relations Act and perhaps other federal statutes as well. Yet for the Board to declare such efforts illegal seems nonsensical, given the obvious benefits. It would seem that some amendments to the National Labor Relations Act are necessary if a literalistic view of the statute prevails.

Some of the courts of appeals have adopted the view that communications between employees and employers, even if fostered by financial assistance, are appropriate as long as it does not result in a paternalistic system which is designed or has the effect of eroding the union as bargaining representative in the collective bargaining process. These modern cases, which begin with the Seventh Circuit's decision in *Chicago Rawhide Manufacturing Co. v. NLRB* [10], seem to me to be an appropriate view of the relationship between labor and management in a cooperative environment.

To some extent, the law relating to Section 8(a)(2) intersects with the definition of an employee. Teamwork in manufacturing and in other sectors of the economy has become an essential element in redefining jobs and promoting competition, and, most important of all, the idea of responsibility and autonomy for employees in shaping their own responsibilities and tasks. Team leaders are those who are in charge of this effort, although they appear to operate on

---

9. U.S. Dept. of Labor, Bureau of Labor-Management Relations and Cooperative Programs, U.S. Labor Law and the Future of Labor-Management Cooperation 16-22 (BLMR 104, 1986). That report, and other writings, e.g., Gould, *Fifty Years Under the National Labor Relations Act: A Retrospective View*, 37 LAB. L.J. 235 (1986), discuss the problems posed by such programs for the NLRA. For analysis by the Board and the courts of some of the Section 8(a)(2) issues, *see generally*, Sparks Nugget, Inc., 230 N.L.R.B. 275 (1977) (management created employee-employer grievance council is not violative of 29 U.S.C. § 158(a)(2) as it is not a labor organization within the meaning of § 2(5) because council serves an adjudicatory function and therefore does not deal with employer); Mercy-Memorial Hosp. Corp., 231 N.L.R.B. 1108 (1977) (employee-employer grievance committee not a labor organization dealing with employer because committee established to give employees a voice in resolving grievances); General Foods Corp., 231 N.L.R.B. 1232 (1977) (job enrichment programs which are not established to head off organizing drives by outside unions or in response to any employee unrest are not violative of § 8(a)(2)); NLRB v. Streamway Div. of the Scott Fetzer Co., 691 F.2d 288 (6th Cir. 1982) (representation committee created by employer is not a labor organization since it did not deal with employer but was a way to determine employee attitudes regarding working conditions); Hertzka & Knowles v. NLRB, 503 F.2d 625 (9th Cir. 1974) (objectivity of NLRA to facilitate employee free choice and self organization requires balancing of concerns of employer domination with employee desires for employee-employer cooperation).

10. 221 F.2d 165 (7th Cir. 1955).

the basis of consensus. If problems relating to discipline, promotion and the like are placed in the hands of such individuals, it is possible that they could be regarded as supervisors or non-bargaining unit employees within the meaning of the Act. If this conclusion is reached by an administrative agency, questions would arise with regard to the union's autonomy and whether the presence of supervisors generally, within it makes it a subordinate entity with a kind of fifth column within its ranks—the exact opposite concern of corporate law where it is feared that union representatives will not possess a sufficiently fiduciary relationship with the shareholders to make them loyal and effective board members.[11]

Where teamwork is in fact practiced as planned, it would seem as though the leaders are not supervisors but rather employees, given the lack of any "independent" judgement[12] about key matters as well as an inability to discharge or discipline but rather reliance upon a kind of consensus. With this finding, the Board would not conclude that section 8(a)(2) has been violated.

B. "Employee" Defined

Other questions are posed by the status of those involved in new work processes as well. For instance, the Supreme Court in the landmark *NLRB v. Yeshiva University*[13] decision concluded, by a 5-4 vote, that the more autonomy and freedom that university professors possess, the more likely it was that they would be characterized as "managerial"[14] employees under the statute. The decision, while not logically applicable to other job categories in the work force, nevertheless, does not bode well for reform of the workplace and the way in which workers' functions are to be performed. The whole thrust of the so-called teamwork experiment in automobile and other areas of manufacturing has been designed to enhance flexibilty, to erode archaic work rules, and to increase employee interest in the job and its significance. The logical, if not practical (most employees are not as far up the corporate ladder as the Court imagined university professors to be) import of *Yeshiva* is that such

11. The problem and cases are discussed in such articles as Stone, *Labor and the Corporate Structure: Changing Conceptions and Emerging Possibilities*, 55 U. CHI. L. REV. 73 (1988) and Harper, *Reconciling Collective Bargaining With Employee Supervision of Management*, 137 U. PA. L. REV. 1 (1988).

12. Note, *The NLRB and Supervisory Status: An Explanation of Inconsistent Results*, 94 HARV. L. REV. 1713 (1981).

13. 444 U.S. 672 (1980).

14. NLRB v. Bell Aerospace Co., 416 U.S. 267, 275 (1974) (holding that Congress intended to exclude "managerial" employees from the protection of the National Labor Relations Act).

initiatives will undercut the collective bargaining process inasmuch as the employees involved will be more likely to be characterized as managerial and thus beyond the protection and coverage of the Act.

I have long thought that Justice Brennan's dissent on behalf of three other justices in *Yeshiva* was the better view in that case.[15] But, absent a reversal of the Court's 5-4 decision—a switch which does not seem likely to be implemented in the near future—the holding ought to be limited to the facts of its case so as to promote a teamwork approach. My own view has been that the modification of job classifications and work rules and a more flexible work assignment environment is one of the truly significant practices that we can learn from Japan.

On the other hand, the traditions of American collective bargaining require the establishment of certain safeguards. Among them is the continued use of seniority or some other objective measure which limits (but does not eliminate) management's discretion in assignments. This is an important response to some of the criticisms which have been aimed at shop floor workers' participation and the allegation that such programs, whether entered into with the union or not, allow management to play favorites and harass those who are out of step with the program, without protection—a charge that has been made both in the United States and Great Britain.[16]

C. *Worker and Union Representatives as Directors of the Board*

In *First National Maintenance v. NLRB*,[17] the Supreme Court, by a 7-2 vote, held that decisions to institute partial plant closures (and presumably complete plant closures as well) are not mandatory subjects of bargaining under the Act and therefore not issues over which employers are obliged to bargain with the unions to the point of impasse. The Court viewed certain subjects which could be properly characterized as "management prerogatives" as beyond the Act's duty-to-bargain obligation. It seems reasonably clear that unions would be precluded from insisting upon negotiating worker director provisions in a collective bargaining agreement or separate agreements inasmuch as this would be characterized as an internal management matter. True, the parties might be free to bargain such provisions (more about that below), but even if unions view this issue as an important one, it seems unlikely that most employers

15. *See* W. Gould, A Primer on American Labor Law 38 (2d ed. 1986).

16. *See* P. Bassett, Strike Free: New Industrial Relations in Britain (1986).

17. 452 U.S. 666 (1981).

would bargain on this matter voluntarily. Indeed, it is unlikely that European employers or their American counterparts would do so.

But even when the parties voluntarily negotiate employee members on the board, there are problems aplenty under Section 8(a)(2) of the Act. The General Counsel, however, has refused to issue a complaint regarding former United Auto Workers Union President Douglas Fraser's appointment to the board at Chrysler. Said the General Counsel:

> [T]here is no immediate danger of a conflict of interest based on the role of a union agent in management affairs. Indeed, such a conflict is far less likely than in [other NLRB precedent] where seven of 15 board members were union representatives and several other board members were representatives of employer-union trust funds . . . . [T]here are no Union loans to the employer and . . . Fraser himself owns no stock and has indicated that he will not personally accept any payments for his duties as a Director. The Union has no financial interest in the affairs of Chrysler, except to the extent that it, like any responsible union, has a vital interest in keeping the employer of represented employees financially healthy in order to preserve and promote jobs and job benefits. Further, Fraser has stressed publicly and in his proxy statement that his prime interest in being on the Board of Directors is to represent the interests of the employees he represents, particularly with respect to matters which affect terms and conditions of employment, *e.g.*, plant closings. There is nothing in Fraser's conduct which suggests that he has behaved inconsistently with this prime interest in representing employees. Nor is there anything in the reputation of Fraser or of the Union which would suggest that Fraser would use his position on the employer's board to compromise the interests of unit employees.
>
> Further, there is nothing to suggest that Fraser would utilize his twin roles to injure competitors of Chrysler and thereby the employees of such competitors. Although it is conceivable that the Union would take "harsh" positions in bargaining with other auto manufacturers for the purpose of injuring them and benefitting Chrysler, there is no evidence to indicate that the Union or Fraser has done that or plans to do that. Further, since the employees of such other manufacturers are also Union-represented, and since an injury to those manufacturers would harm these employees, it is unlikely that the Union or Fraser would pursue such a course. Finally, the whole relationship between the Employer and the Union has been free from infirmity. For many years, the Employer and

> the Union have been parties to "arms-length" *bona fide* collective bargaining relationship.[18]

In one respect, the Board's position seems to be legally appropriate and yet in another it contains deficiencies. Union representation on the board does not present an inherent conflict. So far, so good. Yet there is the implicit assumption that minority representation makes the anti-conflict of interest case a more persuasive one. My judgment is that the Bullock Commission was correct in its Committee of Inquiry Report on Industrial Democracy in noting that the conflict of interest problems of union representatives are not fundamentally disimilar from those of other representatives, such as creditors like banks who have their representatives on the board. Said Bullock:

> [T]he argument that employee representatives on the board, regardless of particular circumstances, will tend to push the company toward the high wages and high employment policy rests on the assumption that short term benefits to their constituents—higher wages or more jobs now—will seem more important than the long term benefits to the same constituents represented by profitable growth, i.e., secure or expanding employment in the future. The reasonableness of making such an assumption has received strong criticism in a number of submissions.
>
> . . . We do not see why a board comprising employee as well as shareholder representatives should be unable to strike an adequate balance between short term and long term interests. A board consisting of shareholder representatives is said to be able to strike the correct balance between the short and long term interests of equity investors in determining, for example, the size of dividends. If employee representatives are unable to strike a similar balance on wage and employment policies, it must either be because they or their constituents are more short-sighted than shareholders and their representatives, or because the real economic interests of employees lie, relatively speaking, in the short term and those of shareholders in the long term. Neither proposition is self-evident, let alone proved. To put it no higher, there does not seem any reason to believe that employee representatives will not have as clear a perception of where their constituents' best interests lie, or that the stake held by employees in the long term health of the company is less than that of the share holders.[19]

18. Advice Memorandum of General Counsel, 1980-81 NLRB Dec. (CCH) ¶ 20,269 (October 22, 1980).

19. Report of the Committee of Inquiry on Industrial Democracy at 53 (Dept. of Trade, U.K., 1977, Her Majesty's Stationery Office).

Yet there are areas which present genuine conflicts of interest for the unions. For instance, although the matter was addressed within the context of the anti-interlocking directorate provisions of the Sherman Antitrust Act, the problem arose when the United Auto Workers was about to negotiate a union representative on the board at American Motors, having already witnessed Fraser's election to the board at Chrysler. Under such circumstances there would be a genuine conflict of interest for a union leader under the conflict of interest themes sounded by the Board under Section 8(a)(2). It might be difficult for union representatives to avoid political pressure in two different contexts.

One situation would be the scenario which concerns the Board, i.e., that the union will gang up and have a less than arms-length relationship with the employer where it has a representative on the board of directors. But another possibility relates to pressure from employees in companies which are competitors of those in which union representatives sit and who bring pressure to bear upon such representatives so as to compromise them or to create the potential for their compromise in their representative capacity. One can very easily imagine rank and file in such companies, if they see wages and fringe benefits and job security lagging behind the worker director companies, pressuring for information which provides them with a basis for restoring some measure of parity. The pressures imposed upon American trade union representatives, in contrast to works council leaders who sit on the boards in Germany and company union leaders in Japan, stems from the political responsibility and unity of the union which overrides corporate lines.

One answer to this problem might lie in the enactment of worker director legislation which would apply with uniformity so that no employees would be in a worker directorless company and the potential for unions ganging up with employers in worker director companies would be diminished. The difficulty with this proposal is that it is politically impractical given the relatively low position assigned the issue by the unions as well as employer resistance. Another answer to some of the Section 8(a)(2) problems may lie in the election of employees to the boards who are not union representatives. This would not be very different from the practices of West Germany which has pioneered in the co-determination area and where representatives of works councils or union activists who may not hold top positions inside the union are frequently those who are promoted by labor for the position. Thus, unions play a role in this connection.

Another fundamental problem is one that made the British unions balk at the Bullock Report on Industrial Democracy and the co-determination idea, i.e., the representative role of employees who are not represented by unions at all. This, in itself, has been a sticky point for the West German unions which have taken the position that management employees should not be counted as labor representatives on their side of the board but are rather more properly identified with management itself. Similarly, the British unions wanted union representation on the board which would cover non-union employees as well. Given the shrinking sector which trade unions in the United States now occupy, this would be a formidable problem under any kind of industrial democracy pattern or procedures mandated by law.

D. *Job Security*

Finally, while few employers can guarantee that they will be able to produce their products and thus preserve jobs, an obvious part of the bargain for unions has to be some measure of job security. Agreements negotiated in basic manufacturing, particularly in the automobile industry in 1987 and before, move labor and management in this direction.

But the difficulty is that the duty to bargain cases, particularly *First National Maintenance* as well as a series of Supreme Court decisions involving the concept of successorship,[20] i.e., the question of whether employers must adhere to either statutory or contractual obligations undertaken by their predecessors relating to unions, generally has placed the unions on the short end of the stick. Indeed, the only circumstances under which unions may impose contractual obligations upon successful employers are where (1) provisions in their collective bargaining agreement with a predecessor allowed them to file a motion for a preliminary injunction against the predecessor where it is clear that the predecessor intends to enter into a sales agreement with a successor which does not incorporate the collective agreement in the latter's relationship or (2) where the successor hires a majority of the employees. One of the major ironies of contemporary American labor law—particularly given the purposes of the Workers' Adjustment and Retraining Act of 1988—is that there is an incentive for the successor not to

20. *See* John Wiley & Sons, Inc. v. Livingston, 376 U.S. 543 (1964); NLRB v. Burns Int'l Sec. Servs. Inc., 406 U.S. 272 (1972); Howard Johnson Co. v. Detroit Local Joint Executive Board, 417 U.S. 249 (1974).

hire employees of the predecessor where the successor employer is interested in shedding the union's contractual obligation.

E. Information

The other concern manifested by critics of shop floor workers' participation is that workers and unions have neither adequate information nor influence to avoid a co-optation in the worst sense of that word. In some bargaining relationships, management attitudes towards information sharing have changed enormously throughout the past decade. This is particularly true in the automobile industry where the United Auto Workers had no difficulty obtaining cost information upon which management and union demands are or ought to be predicated. But the law has lagged behind this kind of practice.

A divided Supreme Court has extolled the virtues of employer confidentiality in connection with the administration of the contract in the *Detroit Edison Co. v. NLRB*[21] case and the leading decision on disclosure remains the *NLRB v. Truitt Manufacturing Co.*[22] holding of more than thirty years ago that resistance to unions demands need not be verified by permitting the union to inspect corporate books and accounts unless the employer pleads inability to pay. Thus far, both the Board and the courts have been chary in applying this concept to situations where management is claiming that union demands or cost considerations will put it at a competitive disadvantage rather than that it will have to go belly-up or bankrupt if it accedes to the union's position.[23] Judge Posner of the Seventh Circuit, on the other hand, has attempted to fashion disclosure obligations so as to delineate on the basis an employer's *need* as opposed to a *want*.[24]

If the employer, according to Judge Posner's reasoning, would simply prefer to have particular employment conditions, there are no obligations to disclose. On the other hand, if it is a need—whether driven by the perils of bankruptcy or the competitive pressures of other companies—there is an obligation to verify through disclosure. This seems to me to be a sensible approach to the mat-

21. 440 U.S. 301 (1979).

22. 351 U.S. 149 (1956).

23. *See* ACL Corp., 271 N.L.R.B. 1600 (1984); Washington Materials, Inc., 276 N.L.R.B. 839 (1985), *enforced in part and denied enforcement in part*, 803 F.2d 1333 (4th Cir. 1986); Gould, *Fifty Years Under the National Labor Relations Act: A Retrospective View*, 37 LAB. L.J. 235, 240-41 (1986).

24. *See* Nielsen Lithographing Co. v. NLRB, 854 F.2d 1063 (7th Cir. 1988) (holding that employer's statement that it had to reduce wages to remain competitive did not obligate employer to permit union examination of its books and records).

ter—although it does not address abuses which flow from any standard such as this, i.e. the willingness of employers to articulate reasoning other than their need to adhere to a position so that they will not have to open up their books. Such sham bargaining and outright game playing can only be eliminated through periodic disclosure, such as the Organisation for Economic Co-Operation and Development has established, which are written into law. This would, of course, necessitate an amendment to the National Labor Relations Act itself. But it may be that an amendment is the best response here as well as in the Section 8(a)(2) context.

F. *Decision Making*

The next step beyond information sharing is an involvement in some sense in employer decision making. The Worker Adjustment and Retraining Act of 1988[25] obliges employers to provide 60 day notice where either a closure of the operation or a substantial lay-off is to be instituted.[26] The statute is an important one in the sense that it provides employees an opportunity not previously available to find other work opportunities and to relocate, if necessary, and to avail themselves of retraining opportunities at a time which is propitious from the perpspective of obtaining employment opportunities. Moreover, under a Maine statute which the Supreme Court has found to be constitutional,[27] severance pay may be provided as well.

But the 1988 law does not provide for bargaining before the decision is made. There one must look to the National Labor Relations Act itself. Again, the most important aspect of that statute relates to disclosure obligations because, if made on a periodic basis, they can put workers and unions in a position to adjust their demands, accept concessions and formulate proposals of their own based upon the real facts of economic life—and to do it early enough in a non-crisis environment when there may still be time to save jobs. This is not generally the case when bargaining takes place relating to the decision, let alone the effects of it.

Although the duty to bargain about decisions to close, to lay-off substantial numbers of employees, to relocate operations and to enter into sales agreements which may affect the employee's job security is theoretically addressed by the National Labor Relations Act itself, the Supreme Court's *First National Maintenance* decision, which

25. Worker Adjustment and Retraining Notification Act, Pub. L. No. 100-379, 102 Stat. 890 (1988).

26. Worker Adjustment and Retraining Notification Act, Pub. L. No. 100-379, § 3(a), 102 Stat. 890, 891 (1988).

27. *See* Fort Halifax Packing Co., Inc. v. Coyne, 482 U.S. 1 (1987).

holds that complete and partial plant closures are not mandatory subjects under the Act and therefore not issues over which employers are obliged to bargain with the union to the point of impasse, has seriously circumscribed the meaningful dialogue which might otherwise take place. Outside the plant closure arena, the Board and circuit courts of appeals seem to have arrived at a *modus vivendi* which makes the obligation to bargain turn upon the extent to which labor costs are a controlling factor in the employer's decision.[28] My own judgement is that this in itself is an unsatisfactory approach given the potential for litigation on this issue and the fact that, because of the law previously described, information about labor cost matters may not be forthcoming—and indeed, ironically, is less likely to be forthcoming because of the fact that this very same information is going to be the subject of litigation before the Board. And the parties will view verification in negotiations as the equivalent of discovery in litigation.

This has led some to conclude that institutions such as those which have found acceptance and success in western Europe, i.e., workers and trade union representatives on the board of directors, may be an appropriate response. The objective is to obtain access to information which relates to such things as future investments, plant building, etc. which can have a bearing upon job security. Here, I focus upon minority representation or parity on the board such as that which exists in Germany and Sweden and other northern European countries.[29]

While employee ownership of corporations is increasing along with ESOP's and the debate about them, real employee control seems to be most likely to emerge in the most dire economic circumstances. This is true even of union initiatives in the airlines industry and companies such as Pan Am and Eastern and others where unions are interested in control through the support of investors who will adopt a conciliatory posture towards the labor movement. It is, after all, the adversity that faces these employers and the consequent desperate situation in which employees find themselves, which has prompted the unions to take this kind of interest in corporate fate.

The dilemma is the same one confronted in connection with our earlier discussion of Section 8(a)(2), i.e., just as a union which might have supervisors as members might fall under the domination of the

28. *But see* Arrow Automotive Indus. v. NLRB, 128 L.R.R.M. (BNA) 3137 (4th Cir. 1988).

29. *See* Gould, *Workers in Management: Northern Europe's Labor Laboratory*, 223 NATION 210-12 (1976).

company, so also there is a conflict of interest for union leaders who must simultaneously wear two hats and bargain with the company across the table. Part of the answer here may be provision of board seats for either union representatives who are not involved with the company itself or employees supported by the union who are not part of the union hierarchy at least as it relates to the company in question.

Unions and employers have taken a number of approaches to this matter. The Teamsters, for instance, have supported individuals who have no formal association with the labor organization for members on the board. The United Auto Workers, on the other hand, in their relationship with the Chrysler Corporation have insisted that the UAW president himself sit on the board. Chrysler, initially insisting that Douglas Fraser was selected as an individual, resisted the appointment of his successor but ultimately acquiesced in the union demand for his appointment.

Here, in addition to problems under the Act relating to company unionism, clearly a union may not insist to the point of impasse on appointment of such individuals inasmuch as the Court in *First National Maintenance* has made it clear that labor is not to be regarded as a partner with management under the Act and that appointment to the board of directors is properly characterized as "management prerogative" under the duty to bargain cases under the NRLA.

III. Conclusion

Practices have and will continue to change in this area. The law must reflect the social realities which are emerging. Industrial democracy will be translated into change at all levels of the employment relationship, knowing no boundaries throughout the corporate structure which would screen it off from the very top of the hierarchical ladder.

Name Index

www.ingramcontent.com/pod-product-compliance
Lightning Source LLC
LaVergne TN
LVHW102106300926
849161LV00014B/3061